KT-496-340

CRICKET ANNUAL 2019

72nd edition

EDITED BY IAN MARSHALL

All statistics by the Editor unless otherwise stated

FOREWORD

The summer of 2019 should be one all cricket fans can look forward to, with both the men's and women's Ashes and the ICC World Cup to entertain us. England go into all three tournaments with confidence, and victories in any of them would boost the profile of the game throughout the nation. But, despite all of this, along with the renewed energy shown by many of our counties to attract fans, the rising profile and support for the Kia Super League, and the excellent crowds to watch Joe Root and Eoin Morgan's sides, cricket goes into the 2019 season at something of a crossroads. And there is one major reason for this.

On 21 February, the ECB announced the playing conditions for their new competition, The Hundred, which will be played over a five-week period in the height of the summer, starting in 2020. As such, they have decided the new format is to be the centrepiece of the season. By doing this, they diminish the three formats that already exist, while supporters of the 18 counties will either see their teams deprived of their best players, or they will have to decide if they want to switch long-held allegiances to a new franchise entity.

To say that The Hundred has not been universally welcomed by cricket fans is an understatement, not that you would know it from the press release, which stated that a county vote 17-1 in favour of the new competition showed 'overwhelming support'. But to many cricket fans, it appeared little more than a version of the game invented by a marketing 'genius' who didn't much like or understand cricket. One of its aims, apparently, was to simplify the game for those who found T20 too complex to follow. But how bowling ten balls from one end at a time, with either one or two bowlers used, is simpler than one bowler bowling six deliveries will never be clear to me. For the ECB's chief executive Tom Harrison, it has 'optimised short-form cricket'. And we all like a bit of optimisation.

The ECB has tried to justify its decision by pointing out that a few games will be aired on terrestrial television, and that this should attract a new audience to cricket. Could the ECB simply not have tried harder to find a way to bring their current formats to terrestrial viewers? The fact is that we already have three compelling formats of cricket, and it is difficult to see why, if you don't currently like it, 100 balls a side will appeal when 120 balls doesn't.

After all, a good game of red-ball cricket can be like a great novel or box set, keeping you glued to the end, with a series of twists and turns along the way. Examples of that would include the tied Championship fixture when Somerset needed 78 for victory last summer, but Lancashire took the last two wickets with the scores level; or Sri Lanka's stunning one-wicket win over South Africa in Durban in February, when Kusal Perera's brilliant unbeaten 153 helped his side home with a world-record last-wicket partnership of 78 to win a match. By comparison, the 50-over game is like a film or a mini-series, with scope for colour and context, but with fewer subplots. Twenty20 is like *Death in Paradise* – enjoyable and fun to watch, but rarely lingering in the mind. Where does that leave The Hundred? Insert your own example of shallow TV dross.

But for now, let us hope England have a successful summer, as there is no doubt that winning the World Cup and the Ashes would do much more to inspire the next generation of cricketers and bring new fans to the game than The Hundred will ever do. A key part of both men's teams is Jos Buttler, this year's cover star, whose recall to the Test side was a typically bold decision by Ed Smith, the chief selector. Buttler has shown himself to be one of the most innovative and exciting batsmen in the world, and his form could prove crucial to England's success in both competitions.

Ian Marshall
Eastbourne, 18 March 2018

GUIDE TO USING PLAYFAIR

The basic layout of *Playfair* has remained the same for this edition. The Annual is divided into five sections, as follows: Test match cricket, county cricket, international limited-overs cricket (including the ICC World Cup and Twenty20), other cricket (IPL, Big Bash, Kia Super League, Ireland and women's international cricket), and fixtures for the coming season. Each section, where applicable, begins with a preview of forthcoming events, followed by events during the previous year, then come the player records, and finally the records sections.

Within the players' register, there has been some debate with the county scorers over those who are defined as 'Released/Retired', pointing out that some players are drafted in for a game or two, and may re-appear in the current season, despite not having a contract as the book goes to press. What I try to do is to ensure that everyone who appeared in last season's games is included somewhere – this way, at least, if they do play in 2019 their details are available to readers. Players' Second XI Championship debuts and their England Under-19 Test appearances are given for those under the age of 25.

In the county limited-overs records in the Register, those records denoted by '50ov' cover any limited-overs game of 50 or more overs – in the early days, each team could have as many as 65 overs per innings. The '40ov' section refers to games of 40 or 45 overs per innings.

Records are provided for two formats of the women's game – limited-overs and T20 – and there is an England women's register, plus major women's fixtures. Women's Test match records can be found in *Playfair 2018*, there having been no Tests in the last year.

ACKNOWLEDGEMENTS AND THANKS

As I say every year, this book could not have been compiled without the assistance of many people giving so generously of their time and expertise, so I must thank the following for all they have done to help ensure this edition of *Playfair Cricket Annual* could be written:

At the counties, I would like to thank the following for their help over the last year: Derbyshire –Tom Skinner and John Brown; Durham – Luke Bidwell and William Dobson; Essex – George Haberman and Tony Choat; Glamorgan – Andrew Hignell; Gloucestershire – Lizzie Allen and Adrian Bull; Hampshire – Tim Tremlett and Kevin Baker; Kent – Liam Knight and Lorne Hart; Lancashire – Diana Lloyd and Chris Rimmer; Leicestershire – Dan Nice and Paul Rogers; Middlesex – Steven Fletcher and Don Shelley; Northamptonshire – Tony Kingston; Nottinghamshire – Helen Palmer and Roger Marshall; Somerset – Spencer Bishop and Gerald Stickley; Surrey – Steve Howes and Phil Makepeace; Sussex – Colin Bowley and Mike Charman; Warwickshire – Keith Cook and Mel Smith; Worcestershire – Carrie Lloyd and Sue Drinkwater; Yorkshire – Janet Bairstow and John Potter.

Thanks to Alan Fordham for the Principal and Second XI Fixtures, and Philip August for the Minor Counties. Philip Bailey once again provided the first-class and List A career records, and he continues to be a huge help in compiling the book, with an eagle eye for detail.

At Headline, my thanks yet again go to Jonathan Taylor for his support and encouragement; Louise Rothwell ensures the book is always printed in record time (and may have to set a new one this year – thank you!); Robert Chilver did a brilliant job with the *Playfair* website last summer and ensured it was kept as up-to-date as possible. John Skermer is a vital part of the team, doing a typically excellent and speedy job checking the proofs. At Letterpart, the *Playfair* typesetter since 1994, Chris Leggett and Caroline Leggett ensured the book was laid out superbly, and that we somehow managed to squeeze a quart into a pint pot.

But, as always, my biggest thanks go to my family for their patience and support. With my office out of action, this book was pretty much written on the dining room table, which meant that daughters Kiri and Sophia had to find alternative places to entertain themselves. My wife Sugra was extremely understanding, and at least this year the deadline didn't coincide with Mothers' Day, so we may be able to have a family day out then, along with my own parents, too. Thank you all.

ENGLAND v AUSTRALIA

SERIES RECORDS

1876-77 to 2017-18

HIGHEST INNINGS TOTALS

England	in England	903-7d		The Oval	1938
	in Australia	644		Sydney	2010-11
Australia	in England	729-6d		Lord's	1930
	in Australia	662-9d		Perth	2017-18

LOWEST INNINGS TOTALS

England	in England	52		The Oval	1948
	in Australia	45		Sydney	1886-87
Australia	in England	36		Birmingham	1902
	in Australia	42		Sydney	1887-88

HIGHEST MATCH AGGREGATE 1753 for 40 wickets Adelaide 1920-21
LOWEST MATCH AGGREGATE 291 for 40 wickets Lord's 1888

HIGHEST INDIVIDUAL INNINGS

England	in England	364	L.Hutton	The Oval	1938
	in Australia	287	R.E.Foster	Sydney	1903-04
Australia	in England	334	D.G.Bradman	Leeds	1930
	in Australia	307	R.M.Cowper	Melbourne	1965-66

HIGHEST AGGREGATE OF RUNS IN A SERIES

England	in England	732	(av 81.33)	D.I.Gower (6 Tests)	1985
	in Australia	905	(av 113.12)	W.R.Hammond	1928-29
Australia	in England	974	(av 139.14)	D.G.Bradman	1930
	in Australia	810	(av 90.00)	D.G.Bradman	1936-37

RECORD WICKET PARTNERSHIPS – ENGLAND

1st	323	J.B.Hobbs (178)/W.Rhodes (179)	Melbourne	1911-12
2nd	382	L.Hutton (364)/M.Leyland (187)	The Oval	1938
3rd	262	W.R.Hammond (177)/ D.R.Jardine (98)	Adelaide	1928-29
4th	310	P.D.Collingwood (206)/K.P.Pietersen (158)	Adelaide	2006-07
5th	237	D.J.Malan (140)/J.M.Bairstow (119)	Perth	2017-18
6th	215	L.Hutton (364)/J.Hardstaff jr (169*)	The Oval	1938
	215	G.Boycott (107)/A.P.E.Knott (135)	Nottingham	1977
7th	143	F.E.Woolley (133*)/J.Vine (36)	Sydney	1911-12
8th	124	E.H.Hendren (169)/H.Larwood (70)	Brisbane	1928-29
9th	151	W.H.Scotton (90)/W.W.Read (117)	The Oval	1884
10th	130	R.E.Foster (287)/W.Rhodes (40*)	Sydney	1903-04

RECORD WICKET PARTNERSHIPS – AUSTRALIA

1st	329	G.R.Marsh (138)/M.A.Taylor (219)	Nottingham	1989
2nd	451	W.H.Ponsford (266)/D.G.Bradman (244)	The Oval	1934
3rd	276	D.G.Bradman (187)/A.L.Hassett (128)	Brisbane	1946-47
4th	388	W.H.Ponsford (181)/D.G.Bradman (304)	Leeds	1934
5th	405	S.G.Barnes (234)/D.G.Bradman (234)	Sydney	1946-47
6th	346	J.H.W.Fingleton (136)/D.G.Bradman (270)	Melbourne	1936-37
7th	165	C.Hill (188)/H.Trumble (46)	Melbourne	1897-98
8th	243	R.J.Hartigan (116)/C.Hill (160)	Adelaide	1907-08
9th	154	S.E.Gregory (201)/J.M.Blackham (74)	Sydney	1894-95
10th	163	P.J.Hughes (81*)/A.C.Agar (98)	Nottingham	2013

BEST INNINGS BOWLING ANALYSIS

England	in England	10- 53	J.C.Laker	Manchester	1956
	in Australia	8- 35	G.A.Lohmann	Sydney	1886-87
Australia	in England	8- 31	F.Laver	Manchester	1909
	in Australia	9-121	A.A.Mailey	Melbourne	1920-21

BEST MATCH BOWLING ANALYSIS

England	in England	19- 90	J.C.Laker	Manchester	1956
	in Australia	15-124	W.Rhodes	Melbourne	1903-04
Australia	in England	16-137	R.A.L.Massie	Lord's	1972
	in Australia	13- 77	M.A.Noble	Melbourne	1901-02

HIGHEST AGGREGATE OF WICKETS IN A SERIES

England	in England	46	(av 9.60)	J.C.Laker	1956
	in Australia	38	(av 23.18)	M.W.Tate	1924-25
Australia	in England	42	(av 21.26)	T.M.Alderman (6 Tests)	1981
	in Australia	41	(av 12.85)	R.M.Hogg (6 Tests)	1978-79

RESULTS SUMMARY
ENGLAND v AUSTRALIA – IN ENGLAND

| | Tests | Series | | | The Oval | | | Manchester | | | Lord's | | | Nottingham | | | Leeds | | | Birmingham | | | Sheffield | | | Cardiff | | |
		E	A	D	E	A	D	E	A	D	E	A	D	E	A	D	E	A	D	E	A	D	E	A	D	E	A	D
1880	1	1	–	–	1	–	–	–	–	–	–	–	–	–	–	–	–	–	–	–	–	–	–	–	–	–	–	–
1882	1	–	1	–	–	1	–	–	–	–	–	–	–	–	–	–	–	–	–	–	–	–	–	–	–	–	–	–
1884	3	1	–	2	–	–	1	–	1	–	1	–	1	–	–	–	–	–	–	–	–	–	–	–	–	–	–	–
1886	3	3	–	–	1	–	–	1	–	–	1	–	–	–	–	–	–	–	–	–	–	–	–	–	–	–	–	–
1888	3	2	1	–	1	–	–	1	–	–	–	1	–	–	–	–	–	–	–	–	–	–	–	–	–	–	–	–
1890	2	2	–	–	1	–	–	1	–	–	–	–	–	–	–	–	–	–	–	–	–	–	–	–	–	–	–	–
1893	3	1	–	2	1	–	–	–	–	1	–	1	–	–	–	–	–	–	–	–	–	–	–	–	–	–	–	–
1896	3	2	1	–	1	–	–	–	1	–	1	–	–	–	–	–	–	–	–	–	–	–	–	–	–	–	–	–
1899	5	–	1	4	–	1	–	1	–	1	–	1	–	–	1	–	–	–	1	–	–	–	–	–	–	–	–	–
1902	5	1	2	2	1	–	–	–	1	–	–	1	–	–	–	1	–	–	1	–	1	–	–	–	–	–	–	–
1905	5	2	–	3	–	1	1	1	–	–	–	1	1	–	–	1	–	–	1	–	–	–	–	–	–	–	–	–
1909	5	1	2	2	–	–	1	–	–	1	1	–	–	–	1	–	–	1	–	–	1	–	–	–	–	–	–	–
1912	3	1	–	2	1	–	–	–	–	1	–	–	1	–	–	–	–	–	–	–	–	–	–	–	–	–	–	–
1921	5	–	3	2	–	–	1	–	1	–	–	1	–	–	1	–	–	–	1	–	–	–	–	–	–	–	–	–
1926	5	1	–	4	1	–	–	–	–	1	–	–	1	–	–	1	–	–	1	–	–	–	–	–	–	–	–	–
1930	5	1	2	2	–	1	–	1	–	–	1	–	–	–	–	1	–	1	–	–	–	–	–	–	–	–	–	–
1934	5	1	2	2	1	–	–	–	–	1	–	1	–	–	1	–	–	–	1	–	–	–	–	–	–	–	–	–
1938	4	1	1	2	1	–	–	–	–	1	–	–	1	–	–	1	–	1	–	–	–	–	–	–	–	–	–	–
1948	5	–	4	1	–	1	–	–	1	–	–	1	–	–	1	–	–	1	–	–	–	–	–	–	–	–	–	–
1953	5	1	–	4	1	–	–	–	–	1	–	–	1	–	–	1	–	–	1	–	–	–	–	–	–	–	–	–
1956	5	2	1	2	–	–	1	1	–	–	–	1	–	–	1	–	–	1	–	1	–	–	–	–	–	–	–	–
1961	5	1	2	2	1	–	–	–	1	–	–	1	–	–	–	1	–	–	1	–	–	–	–	–	–	–	–	–
1964	5	–	1	4	–	–	1	–	1	–	–	1	–	–	–	1	–	–	1	–	–	–	–	–	–	–	–	–
1968	5	1	1	3	1	–	–	–	1	–	–	1	–	–	–	1	–	–	1	–	–	–	–	–	–	–	–	–
1972	5	2	2	1	1	–	–	–	1	–	1	–	–	–	–	1	–	1	–	–	–	–	–	–	–	–	–	–
1975	4	–	1	3	–	–	1	–	–	1	–	1	–	–	–	1	–	–	1	1	–	–	–	–	–	–	–	–
1977	5	3	–	2	1	–	–	–	1	–	1	–	–	1	–	–	1	–	–	–	–	–	–	–	–	–	–	–
1980	1	–	–	1	–	–	–	–	–	–	–	–	1	–	–	–	–	–	–	–	–	–	–	–	–	–	–	–
1981	6	3	1	2	1	–	–	1	–	–	–	1	–	–	–	1	1	–	–	1	–	–	–	–	–	–	–	–
1985	6	3	1	2	1	–	–	1	–	–	–	1	–	1	–	–	–	–	1	1	–	–	–	–	–	–	–	–
1989	6	–	4	2	–	1	–	–	1	–	–	1	–	–	1	–	–	1	–	1	–	–	–	–	–	–	–	–
1993	6	1	4	1	1	–	–	–	1	–	–	1	–	–	1	–	–	1	–	1	–	–	–	–	–	–	–	–
1997	6	2	3	1	1	–	–	–	1	–	1	–	–	–	1	–	–	1	–	1	–	–	–	–	–	–	–	–
2001	5	1	4	–	–	1	–	–	1	–	–	1	–	–	1	–	1	–	–	–	–	–	–	–	–	–	–	–
2005	5	2	1	2	–	–	1	–	–	1	1	–	–	–	1	–	1	–	–	–	–	–	–	–	–	–	–	–
2009	5	2	1	2	1	–	–	–	–	1	–	1	–	–	1	–	–	1	–	–	1	Chester-le-St	–	1
2013	5	3	–	2	–	1	–	1	–	–	1	–	–	–	–	1	–	1	–	1	–	–	–	–	–	–	–	–
2015	5	3	2	–	–	1	–	1	–	–	–	1	–	1	–	–	1	–	–	–	–	–	–	–	–	–	–	–
	166	51	49	66	16	7	14	7	7	15	7	7	14	6	7	9	7	9	8	6	3	5	1	1	–	1	–	1

ENGLAND v AUSTRALIA – IN AUSTRALIA

	Tests	Series			Melbourne			Sydney			Adelaide			Brisbane			Perth		
		E	A	D	E	A	D	E	A	D	E	A	D	E	A	D	E	A	D
1876-77	2	1	1	–	1	1	–	–	–	–	–	–	–	–	–	–	–	–	–
1878-79	1	–	1	–	–	1	–	–	–	–	–	–	–	–	–	–	–	–	–
1881-82	4	–	2	2	–	–	2	–	2	–	–	–	–	–	–	–	–	–	–
1882-83	4	2	2	–	1	1	–	1	1	–	–	–	–	–	–	–	–	–	–
1884-85	5	3	2	–	2	–	–	–	2	–	1	–	–	–	–	–	–	–	–
1886-87	2	2	–	–	–	–	–	2	–	–	–	–	–	–	–	–	–	–	–
1887-88	1	1	–	–	–	–	–	1	–	–	–	–	–	–	–	–	–	–	–
1891-92	3	1	2	–	–	1	–	–	1	–	1	–	–	–	–	–	–	–	–
1894-95	5	3	2	–	2	–	–	1	1	–	–	1	–	–	–	–	–	–	–
1897-98	5	1	4	–	–	2	–	1	1	–	–	1	–	–	–	–	–	–	–
1901-02	5	1	4	–	–	2	–	1	1	–	–	1	–	–	–	–	–	–	–
1903-04	5	3	2	–	1	1	–	2	–	–	–	1	–	–	–	–	–	–	–
1907-08	5	1	4	–	1	1	–	–	2	–	–	1	–	–	–	–	–	–	–
1911-12	5	4	1	–	2	–	–	1	1	–	1	–	–	–	–	–	–	–	–
1920-21	5	–	5	–	–	2	–	–	2	–	–	1	–	–	–	–	–	–	–
1924-25	5	1	4	–	1	1	–	–	2	–	–	1	–	–	–	–	–	–	–
1928-29	5	4	1	–	1	1	–	1	–	–	1	–	–	1	–	–	–	–	–
1932-33	5	4	1	–	–	1	–	2	–	–	1	–	–	1	–	–	–	–	–
1936-37	5	2	3	–	–	2	–	1	–	–	–	1	–	1	–	–	–	–	–
1946-47	5	–	3	2	–	–	1	–	2	–	–	–	1	–	1	–	–	–	–
1950-51	5	1	4	–	1	1	–	–	1	–	–	1	–	–	1	–	–	–	–
1954-55	5	3	1	1	1	–	–	1	–	1	1	–	–	–	1	–	–	–	–
1958-59	5	–	4	1	–	2	–	–	–	1	–	1	–	–	1	–	–	–	–
1962-63	5	1	1	3	1	–	–	–	1	1	–	–	1	–	–	1	–	–	–
1965-66	5	1	1	3	–	–	2	1	–	–	–	1	–	–	–	1	–	–	–
1970-71	6	–	2	4	–	–	1	2	–	–	–	–	1	–	–	1	–	–	1
1974-75	6	1	4	1	1	–	1	–	1	–	–	1	–	–	1	–	–	1	–
1976-77	1	–	1	–	–	1	–	–	–	–	–	–	–	–	–	–	–	–	–
1978-79	6	5	1	–	–	1	–	2	–	–	1	–	–	1	–	–	1	–	–
1979-80	3	–	3	–	–	1	–	–	1	–	–	–	–	–	–	–	–	1	–
1982-83	5	1	2	2	1	–	–	–	–	1	–	1	–	–	1	–	–	–	1
1986-87	5	2	1	2	1	–	–	–	1	–	–	–	1	1	–	–	–	–	1
1987-88	1	–	–	1	–	–	–	–	–	1	–	–	–	–	–	–	–	–	–
1990-91	5	–	3	2	–	1	–	–	–	1	–	–	1	–	1	–	–	1	–
1994-95	5	1	3	1	–	1	–	–	–	1	1	–	–	–	1	–	–	1	–
1998-99	5	1	3	1	1	–	–	–	1	–	–	1	–	–	–	1	–	1	–
2002-03	5	1	4	–	–	1	–	1	–	–	–	1	–	–	1	–	–	1	–
2006-07	5	–	5	–	–	1	–	–	1	–	–	1	–	–	1	–	–	1	–
2010-11	5	3	1	1	1	–	–	1	–	–	1	–	–	–	–	1	–	1	–
2013-14	5	–	5	–	–	1	–	–	1	–	–	1	–	–	1	–	–	1	–
2017-18	5	–	4	1	–	–	1	–	1	–	–	1	–	–	1	–	–	1	–
	180	57	95	28	20	28	8	22	27	7	9	18	5	5	12	5	1	10	3
Totals	**346**	**108**	**144**	**94**															

Matches abandoned without a ball bowled (Manchester 1890 and 1938, Melbourne 1970-71) are excluded from these tables.

2000 RUNS

	Tests	I	NO	HS	Runs	Avge	100	50
D.G.Bradman (A)	37	63	7	334	5028	89.78	19	12
J.B.Hobbs (E)	41	71	4	187	3636	54.26	12	15
A.R.Border (A)	47	82	19	200*	3548	56.31	8	21
D.I.Gower (E)	42	77	4	215	3269	44.78	9	12
S.R.Waugh (A)	46	73	18	177*	3200	58.18	10	14
G.Boycott (E)	38	71	9	191	2945	47.50	7	14
W.R.Hammond (E)	33	58	3	251	2852	51.85	9	7
H.Sutcliffe (E)	27	46	5	194	2741	66.85	8	16
C.Hill (A)	41	76	1	188	2660	35.46	4	16
J.H.Edrich (E)	32	57	3	175	2644	48.96	7	13
G.A.Gooch (E)	42	79	0	196	2632	33.31	4	16
G.S.Chappell (A)	35	65	8	144	2619	45.94	9	12
M.A.Taylor (A)	33	61	2	219	2496	42.30	6	15
A.N.Cook (E)	35	64	2	244*	2493	40.20	5	11
R.T.Ponting (A)	35	58	2	196	2476	44.21	8	9
M.C.Cowdrey (E)	43	75	4	113	2433	34.26	5	11
L.Hutton (E)	27	49	6	364	2428	56.46	5	14
R.N.Harvey (A)	37	68	5	167	2416	38.34	6	12
V.T.Trumper (A)	40	74	5	185*	2263	32.79	6	9
D.C.Boon (A)	31	57	8	184*	2237	45.65	7	8
W.M.Lawry (A)	29	51	5	166	2233	48.54	7	13
M.E.Waugh (A)	29	51	7	140	2204	50.09	6	11
S.E.Gregory (A)	52	92	7	201	2193	25.80	4	8
W.W.Armstrong (A)	42	71	9	158	2172	35.03	4	6
K.P.Pietersen (E)	27	50	2	227	2158	44.95	4	13
I.M.Chappell (A)	30	56	4	192	2138	41.11	4	16
K.F.Barrington (E)	23	39	6	256	2111	63.96	5	13
M.J.Clarke (A)	30	53	6	187	2109	44.87	7	7
A.R.Morris (A)	24	43	2	206	2080	50.73	8	8
S.P.D.Smith (A)	23	41	5	239	2026	56.27	8	6

D.G.Bradman holds the unique record of scoring 2000 runs in both countries in this series (2674 runs in England and 2354 in Australia); J.B.Hobbs is the only other batsman to score 2000 runs in either country (2493 runs in Australia).

100 WICKETS

	Tests	Balls	Runs	Wkts	Avge	Best	5wI	10wM
S.K.Warne (A)	36	10757	4535	195	23.25	8- 71	11	4
D.K.Lillee (A)	29	8516	3507	167	21.00	7- 89	11	4
G.D.McGrath (A)	30	7280	3286	157	20.92	8- 38	10	–
I.T.Botham (E)	36	8479	4093	148	27.65	6- 78	9	2
H.Trumble (A)	31	7895	2945	141	20.88	8- 65	9	3
R.G.D.Willis (E)	35	7294	3346	128	26.14	8- 43	7	–
M.A.Noble (A)	39	6845	2860	115	24.86	7- 17	9	2
R.R.Lindwall (A)	29	6728	2559	114	22.44	7- 63	6	–
W.Rhodes (E)	41	5791	2616	109	24.00	8- 68	6	1
S.F.Barnes (E)	20	5749	2288	106	21.58	7- 60	12	1
C.V.Grimmett (A)	22	9224	3439	106	32.44	6- 37	11	2
D.L.Underwood (E)	29	8000	2770	105	26.38	7- 50	4	2
A.V.Bedser (E)	21	7065	2859	104	27.49	7- 44	7	2
J.M.Anderson (E)	31	7027	3594	104	34.55	6- 47	5	1
G.Giffen (A)	31	6457	2791	103	27.09	7-117	7	1
W.J.O'Reilly (A)	19	7864	2587	102	25.36	7- 54	8	3
R.Peel (E)	20	5216	1715	101	16.98	7- 31	5	1
C.T.B.Turner (A)	17	5195	1670	101	16.53	7- 43	11	2
T.M.Alderman (A)	17	4717	2117	100	21.17	6- 47	11	1
J.R.Thomson (A)	21	4951	2418	100	24.18	6- 46	5	–

100 WICKET-KEEPING DISMISSALS

	Tests	Ct	St	Total
R.W.Marsh (A)	42	141	7	148
I.A.Healy (A)	33	123	12	135
A.P.E.Knott (E)	34	97	8	105

R.W.Marsh (141 catches) and W.A.S.Oldfield (A), (31 stumpings) hold the respective individual records in Anglo-Australian Tests.

TOURING TEAMS REGISTER 2019

Neither Ireland nor Australia had selected their 2019 touring teams at the time of going to press. The following players, who had represented Australia in Test matches since 1 December 2017, were still available for selection; for details of the Ireland players, see the register on pp 325-327.

AUSTRALIA

Full Names	Birthdate	Birthplace	Team	Type	F-C Debut
BANCROFT, Cameron Timothy	19.11.92	Perth	W Australia	RHB/RM	2013-14
BIRD, Jackson Munro	11.12.86	Sydney	Tasmania	RHB/RFM	2011-12
BURNS, Joseph Anthony	06.09.89	Brisbane	Queensland	RHB/RM	2010-11
CUMMINS, Patrick James	08.05.93	Sydney	NSW	RHB/RF	2010-11
FINCH, Aaron James	17.11.86	Colac, Vic	Victoria	RHB/SLA	2007-08
HANDSCOMB, Peter Stephen Patrick	26.04.91	Melbourne	Victoria	RHB/OB	2011-12
HARRIS, Marcus Sinclair	21.07.92	Perth	Victoria	LHB/OB	2010-11
HAZLEWOOD, Josh Reginald	08.01.91	Tamworth, NSW	NSW	LHB/RFM	2008-09
HEAD, Travis Michael	29.12.93	Adelaide	S Australia	LHB/OB	2011-12
HOLLAND, Jonathan Mark	29.05.87	Sandringham, Vic	Victoria	RHB/SLA	2008-09
KHAWAJA, Usman Tariq	18.12.86	Islamabad, Pak	Queensland	LHB/RM	2007-08
LABUSCHAGNE, Marnus	22.06.94	Klerksdorp, SA	Queensland	RHB/LB	2014-15
LYON, Nathan Michael	20.11.87	Young, NSW	NSW	RHB/OB	2010-11
MARSH, Mitchell Ross	20.10.91	Perth	W Australia	RHB/RMF	2009-10
MARSH, Shaun Edward	09.07.83	Narrogin, WA	W Australia	LHB/SLA	2000-01
PAINE, Timothy David	08.12.84	Hobart	Tasmania	RHB/WK	2005-06
PATTERSON, Kurtis Robert	05.05.93	Hurstville, NSW	NSW	LHB/OB	2011-12
RENSHAW, Matthew Thomas	28.03.96	Middlesbro', Eng	Queensland	LHB/OB	2014-15
RICHARDSON, Jhye Avon	20.09.96	Murdoch, WA	W Australia	RHB/RF	2015-16
SAYERS, Chadd James	31.08.87	Henley Beach	S Australia	RHB/RM	2010-11
SIDDLE, Peter Matthew	25.11.84	Traralgon, Vic	Victoria	RHB/RFM	2005-06
SMITH, Steven Peter Devereux	02.06.89	Sydney	NSW	RHB/LBG	2007-08
STARC, Mitchell Aaron	30.01.90	Sydney	NSW	LHB/LF	2008-09
WARNER, David Andrew	27.10.86	Paddington, NSW	NSW	LHB/LB	2008-09

STATISTICAL HIGHLIGHTS IN 2018 TESTS

Including Tests from No. 2287 (Australia v England, 5th Test) and No. 2291 (South Africa v India, 1st Test) to No. 2334 (Australia v India, 3rd Test), No. 2337 (New Zealand v Sri Lanka, 2nd Test) and No. 2338 (South Africa v Pakistan, 1st Test).

† = National record

TEAM HIGHLIGHTS
HIGHEST INNINGS TOTALS

713-9d	Sri Lanka v Bangladesh	Chittagong
649-7d	Australia v England	Sydney
649-9d	India v West Indies	Rajkot

HIGHEST FOURTH INNINGS TOTAL

362-8	Australia (set 462) v Pakistan	Dubai (DSC)

LOWEST INNINGS TOTALS

43†	Bangladesh v West Indies	North Sound
58	England v New Zealand	Auckland
73	South Africa v Sri Lanka	Galle
90	New Zealand v Pakistan	Dubai (DSC)
93	West Indies v Sri Lanka	Bridgetown

HIGHEST MATCH AGGREGATE

1533-24	Bangladesh (513 & 307-5) v Sri Lanka (713-9d)	Chittagong

BATSMEN'S MATCH (Qualification: 1200 runs, average 60 per wicket)

63.87 (1533-24)	Bangladesh (513 & 307-5) v Sri Lanka (713-9d)	Chittagong

LARGE MARGINS OF VICTORY

Inns & 272 runs†	India (649-9d) beat West Indies (181 & 196)	Rajkot
Inns & 262 runs	India (474) beat Afghanistan (109 & 103)	Bengaluru
492 runs†	South Africa (488 & 344-6d) beat Australia (221 & 119)	Johannesburg
423 runs†	New Zealand (178 & 585-4d) beat Sri Lanka (104 & 236)	Christchurch
373 runs†	Pakistan (282 & 400-9d) beat Australia (145 & 164)	Abu Dhabi

NARROW MARGINS OF VICTORY

4 runs	New Zealand (153 & 249) beat Pakistan (227 & 171)	Abu Dhabi

ALL ELEVEN SCORING DOUBLE FIGURES

Bangladesh (508, lowest score 12*) v West Indies	Mirpur

BATTING HIGHLIGHTS
DOUBLE HUNDREDS

T.W.M.Latham	264*	New Zealand v Sri Lanka	Wellington
Mushfiqur Rahim	219*	Bangladesh v Zimbabwe	Dhaka

HUNDRED IN EACH INNINGS OF A MATCH

Mominul Haque 176	105	Bangladesh v Sri Lanka	Chittagong

FASTEST HUNDRED

S.Dhawan (107)	87 balls India v Afghanistan	Bengaluru

MOST SIXES IN AN INNINGS

9   S.O.Hetmyer (93)   West Indies v Bangladesh   Dhaka

100 RUNS OR MORE IN BOUNDARIES IN AN INNINGS

Runs	6s	4s			
100	2	22	B.K.G.Mendis	Sri Lanka v Bangladesh	Chittagong

HUNDRED ON TEST DEBUT

B.T.Foakes	(107)	England v Sri Lanka	Galle
K.J.O'Brien	(118)	Ireland v Pakistan	Dublin
P.P.Shaw	(134)	India v West Indies	Rajkot

CARRYING BAT THROUGH COMPLETED INNINGS

D.Elgar	(86*)	South Africa (177) v India	Johannesburg
D.Elgar	(141*)	South Africa (311) v Australia	Cape Town

Equalling D.L.Haynes' record of carrying his bat three times in a Test career.

F.D.M.Karunaratne	(158*)	Sri Lanka (287) v South Africa	Galle
T.W.M.Latham	(264*)	New Zealand (578) v Sri Lanka	Wellington

A record high score for someone carrying their bat in Tests.

LONG INNINGS (Qualification: 600 mins and/or 400 balls)

Mins	*Balls*			
	421	Haris Sohail (147)	Pakistan v New Zealand	Dubai (DSC)
694	489	T.W.M.Latham (264*)	New Zealand v Sri Lanka	Wellington
	421	Mushfiqur Rahim (219*)	Bangladesh v Zimbabwe	Dhaka

NOTABLE PARTNERSHIPS

Qualifications: 1st-4th wkts: 250 runs; 5th-6th: 225; 7th: 200; 8th: 175; 9th: 150; 10th: 100.

Second Wicket
308   B.K.G.Mendis/D.M.de Silva   Sri Lanka v Bangladesh   Chittagong

Third Wicket
259   A.N.Cook/J.E.Root   England v India   The Oval

Fourth Wicket
274   B.K.G.Mendis/A.D.Mathews   Sri Lanka v New Zealand   Wellington
266†   Mominul Haque/Mushfiqur Rahim   Bangladesh v Zimbabwe   Dhaka

BOWLING HIGHLIGHTS

EIGHT WICKETS IN AN INNINGS

S.T.Gabriel	8-62	West Indies v Sri Lanka	Gros Islet
K.A.Maharaj	9-129	South Africa v Sri Lanka	Colombo (SSC)

Second best analysis on record for South Africa.

Yasir Shah	8-41	Pakistan v New Zealand	Dubai (DSC)

TEN WICKETS IN A MATCH

S.T.Gabriel	13-121	West Indies v Sri Lanka	Gros Islet
J.O.Holder	11-103	West Indies v Bangladesh	Kingston
K.A.Maharaj	12-283	South Africa v Sri Lanka	Colombo (SSC)
Mehedi Hasan†	12-117	Bangladesh v West Indies	Mirpur
Mohammad Abbas	10-95	Pakistan v Australia	Abu Dhabi
D.Olivier	11-96	South Africa v Pakistan	Centurion
M.D.K.Perera	10-78	Sri Lanka v South Africa	Galle
K.Rabada	11-150	South Africa v Australia	Port Elizabeth

Taijul Islam	11-170	Bangladesh v Zimbabwe	Sylhet
U.T.Yadav	10-133	India v West Indies	Hyderabad
Yasir Shah	14-184	Pakistan v New Zealand	Dubai (DSC)

FIVE WICKETS IN AN INNINGS ON DEBUT

Nayeem Hasan	5-61	Bangladesh v West Indies	Chittagong
L.T.Ngidi	6-39	South Africa v India	Centurion
A.Y.Patel	5-59	New Zealand v Pakistan	Abu Dhabi
M.K.P.A.D.Perera	5-24	Sri Lanka v Bangladesh	Mirpur

BOWLING UNCHANGED THROUGHOUT AN INNINGS

T.A.Boult (10.4-3-32-6)/T.G.Southee (10-3-25-4)   New Zealand v England   Auckland

60 OVERS IN AN INNINGS

Taijul Islam   67.3-13-219-4 Bangladesh v Sri Lanka   Chittagong

200 RUNS CONCEDED IN AN INNINGS

| Taijul Islam | 67.3-13-219-4 | Bangladesh v Sri Lanka | Chittagong |
| D.Bishoo | 54-3-217-4 | West Indies v India | Rajkot |

WICKET-KEEPING HIGHLIGHTS

SIX WICKET-KEEPING DISMISSALS IN AN INNINGS

R.R.Pant   6ct   India v Australia   Adelaide

NINE OR MORE WICKET-KEEPING DISMISSALS IN A MATCH

R.R.Pant	11ct	India v Australia	Adelaide
	Equalling the world record.		
W.P.Saha	10ct	India v South Africa	Cape Town

NO BYES CONCEDED IN AN INNINGS OF 550

578   D.P.D.N.Dickwella Sri Lanka v New Zealand   Wellington

FIELDING HIGHLIGHTS

FOUR OR MORE CATCHES IN AN INNINGS IN THE FIELD

S.P.D.Smith	5ct	Australia v South Africa	Cape Town
A.J.Finch	4ct	Australia v India	Adelaide
Imam-ul-Haq	4ct	Pakistan v Australia	Dubai (DCS)
	All four catches off the bowling of Bilal Asif.		
K.K.Jennings	4ct	England v Sri Lanka	Colombo (SSC)
B.K.G.Mendis	4ct	Sri Lanka v West Indies	Bridgetown
K.L.Rahul	4ct	India v England	Nottingham

SIX OR MORE CATCHES IN A MATCH IN THE FIELD

K.L.Rahul	7ct	India v England	Nottingham
K.K.Jennings	6ct	England v Sri Lanka	Colombo (SSC)
S.P.D.Smith	6ct	Australia v South Africa	Cape Town

LEADING TEST AGGREGATES IN 2018

1000 RUNS IN 2018

	M	I	NO	HS	Runs	Avge	100	50
V.Kohli (I)	13	24	–	153	**1322**	55.08	5	5
B.K.G.Mendis (SL)	12	23	1	196	**1023**	46.50	3	4

RECORD CALENDAR YEAR RUNS AGGREGATE

	M	I	NO	HS	Runs	Avge	100	50
M.Yousuf (P) (2006)	11	19	1	202	**1788**	99.33	9	3

RECORD CALENDAR YEAR RUNS AVERAGE

	M	I	NO	HS	Runs	Avge	100	50
G.St A.Sobers (WI) (1958)	7	12	3	365*	**1193**	132.55	5	3

1000 RUNS IN DEBUT CALENDAR YEAR

	M	I	NO	HS	Runs	Avge	100	50
M.A.Taylor (A) (1989)	11	20	1	219	**1219**	64.15	4	5
A.C.Voges (A) (2015)	12	18	6	269*	**1028**	85.66	4	3
A.N.Cook (E) (2006)	13	24	2	127	**1013**	46.04	4	3

50 WICKETS IN 2018

	M	O	R	W	Avge	Best	5wI	10wM
K.Rabada (SA)	10	331.1	1044	**52**	20.07	6-54	2	1
M.D.K.Perera (SL)	11	470.0	1466	**50**	29.32	6-32	3	1

RECORD CALENDAR YEAR WICKETS AGGREGATE

	M	O	R	W	Avge	Best	5wI	10wM
M.Muralitharan (SL) (2006)	11	588.4	1521	**90**	16.90	8-70	9	5
S.K.Warne (A) (2005)	14	691.4	2043	**90**	22.70	6-46	6	2

MOST WICKET-KEEPING DISMISSALS IN 2018

	M	Dis	Ct	St
Q.de Kock (SA)	10	47	45	2

RECORD CALENDAR YEAR DISMISSALS AGGREGATE

	M	Dis	Ct	St
J.M.Bairstow (E) (2016)	17	70	66	4

20 CATCHES BY FIELDERS IN 2018

	M	Ct
B.K.G.Mendis (SL)	12	21

RECORD CALENDAR YEAR FIELDER'S AGGREGATE

	M	Ct
G.C.Smith (SA) (2008)	15	30

TEST MATCH SCORES
SOUTH AFRICA v AUSTRALIA (1st Test)

At Kingsmead, Durban, on 1, 2, 3, 4, 5 March 2018.
Toss: Australia. Result: **AUSTRALIA** won by 118 runs.
Debuts: None.

AUSTRALIA

C.T.Bancroft	c de Kock b Philander	5	st de Kock b Maharaj		53
D.A.Warner	c de Villiers b Philander	51	c sub (P.W.A.Mulder) b Rabada		28
U.T.Khawaja	c de Kock b Rabada	14	c de Kock b Maharaj		6
*S.P.D.Smith	c de Villiers b Maharaj	56	lbw b Elgar		38
S.E.Marsh	c de Villiers b Maharaj	40	c de Villiers b Morkel		33
M.R.Marsh	c Morkel b Philander	96	c Amla b Rabada		6
†T.D.Paine	c de Kock b Rabada	25	c de Villiers b Maharaj		14
P.J.Cummins	b Maharaj	3	b Maharaj		26
M.A.Starc	b Maharaj	35	c Elgar b Morkel		7
N.M.Lyon	c de Bruyn b Maharaj	12	c Amla b Morkel		2
J.R.Hazlewood	not out	2	not out		9
Extras	(B 4, LB 8)	12	(LB 5)		5
Total	(110.4 overs; 486 mins)	351	(74.4 overs; 338 mins)		227

SOUTH AFRICA

D.Elgar	c and b Lyon	7	(2) c Paine b Starc		9
A.K.Markram	c Bancroft b Cummins	32	(1) c Paine b M.R.Marsh		143
H.M.Amla	c Bancroft b Lyon	0	lbw b Hazlewood		8
A.B.de Villiers	not out	71	run out		6
*F.du Plessis	c Paine b Starc	15	b Cummins		4
T.B.de Bruyn	c Paine b Starc	6	c Paine b Hazlewood		36
†Q.de Kock	b Lyon	20	lbw b Hazlewood		83
V.D.Philander	c Paine b Starc	8	c Paine b Starc		6
K.A.Maharaj	b Hazlewood	0	b Starc		0
K.Rabada	lbw b Starc	3	b Starc		0
M.Morkel	b Starc	0	not out		3
Extras			(B 2, LB 3, NB 1)		6
Total	(51.4 overs; 239 mins)	162	(92.4 overs; 408 mins)		298

SOUTH AFRICA	O	M	R	W		O	M	R	W	FALL OF WICKETS			
											A	SA	A	SA
Morkel	22	3	75	0		15	4	47	3				
Philander	27	12	59	3		14	4	35	0	*Wkt*	*1st*	*1st*	*2nd*	*2nd*
Maharaj	33.4	5	123	5		29.4	4	102	4	1st	15	27	56	29
Rabada	25	7	74	2		13	5	28	2	2nd	39	27	71	39
Markram	1	0	2	0						3rd	95	55	108	39
De Bruyn	2	0	6	0						4th	151	92	146	49
Elgar						(5)	3	1	10	1	5th	177	108	156	136
										6th	237	150	175	283
AUSTRALIA										7th	251	158	185	290
Starc	10.4	3	34	5		18	2	75	4	8th	300	159	203	290
Hazlewood	13	5	31	1		15.4	4	61	3	9th	341	162	209	290
Lyon	16	3	50	3		32	7	86	0	10th	351	162	227	298
Cummins	12	2	47	1		15	3	47	1					
M.R.Marsh						7	2	21	1					
Smith						5	3	3	0					

Umpires: H.D.P.K.Dharmasena (*Sri Lanka*) (52) and S.Ravi (*India*) (25).
Referee: J.J.Crowe (*New Zealand*) (86).   **Test No. 2296/95 (SA422/A809)**

SOUTH AFRICA v AUSTRALIA (2nd Test)

At St George's Park, Port Elizabeth, on 9, 10 11, 12 March 2018.
Toss: Australia. Result: **SOUTH AFRICA** won by six wickets.
Debuts: None.

AUSTRALIA

C.T.Bancroft	c de Kock b Philander	38	b Ngidi		24
D.A.Warner	b Ngidi	63	b Rabada		13
U.T.Khawaja	c de Kock b Philander	4	lbw b Rabada		75
*S.P.D.Smith	lbw b Rabada	25	c de Kock b Maharaj		11
S.E.Marsh	lbw b Rabada	24	c de Kock b Rabada		1
†T.D.Paine	b Ngidi	36	(7) not out		28
M.R.Marsh	c de Kock b Rabada	4	(6) b Rabada		45
P.J.Cummins	c de Kock b Rabada	0	c de Bruyn b Rabada		5
M.A.Starc	b Rabada	8	c de Kock b Rabada		1
N.M.Lyon	b Ngidi	17	c de Kock b Ngidi		5
J.R.Hazlewood	not out	10	c Ngidi b Maharaj		17
Extras	(LB 14)	14	(B 2, LB 10, W 2)		14
Total	**(71.3 overs; 325 mins)**	**243**	**(79 overs; 362 mins)**		**239**

SOUTH AFRICA

D.Elgar	c Paine b Hazlewood	57	(2) c and b Lyon		5
A.K.Markram	lbw b Cummins	11	(1) c Smith b Hazlewood		21
K.Rabada	b Cummins	29			
H.M.Amla	b Starc	56	(3) c Paine b Cummins		27
A.B.de Villiers	not out	126	(4) c Bancroft b Lyon		28
*F.du Plessis	lbw b M.R.Marsh	9	(5) not out		2
T.B.de Bruyn	lbw b M.R.Marsh	1	(6) not out		15
†Q.de Kock	b Lyon	9			
V.D.Philander	c Bancroft b Cummins	36			
K.A.Maharaj	b Hazlewood	30			
L.T.Ngidi	run out	5			
Extras	(B 9, LB 2, W 2)	13	(B 4)		4
Total	**(118.4 overs; 558 mins)**	**382**	**(4 wkts; 22.5 overs; 98 mins)**		**102**

SOUTH AFRICA	O	M	R	W	O	M	R	W	FALL OF WICKETS				
Philander	18	7	25	2	18	5	56	0		A	SA	A	SA
Rabada	21	2	96	5	22	9	54	6	*Wkt*	*1st*	*1st*	*2nd*	*2nd*
Ngidi	13.3	0	51	3	(4) 13	5	24	2	1st	98	22	27	22
Maharaj	18	1	51	0	(3) 23	2	90	2	2nd	104	67	62	32
Elgar	1	0	6	0					3rd	117	155	77	81
Markram					(5) 3	1	3	0	4th	161	155	86	81
									5th	166	159	173	
AUSTRALIA									6th	170	183	186	
Starc	33.4	5	110	1	3	0	15	0	7th	170	227	202	
Hazlewood	30	5	98	2	6	0	26	1	8th	182	311	204	
Cummins	24	6	79	3	(4) 4.5	0	13	1	9th	212	369	211	
Lyon	22	5	58	1	(3) 9	0	44	2	10th	243	382	239	
M.R.Marsh	9	1	26	2									

Umpires: H.D.P.K.Dharmasena (*Sri Lanka*) (53), C.B.Gaffaney (*New Zealand*) (19) and
S.Ravi (*India*) (26).
Referee: J.J.Crowe (*New Zealand*) (87).   **Test No. 2297/96 (SA423/A810)**
S.Ravi replaced C.B.Gaffaney after the first day.

SOUTH AFRICA v AUSTRALIA (3rd Test)

At Newlands, Cape Town, on 22, 23, 24, 25 March 2018.
Toss: South Africa. Result: **SOUTH AFRICA** won by 322 runs.
Debuts: None.   ‡ (P.S.P.Handscomb)

SOUTH AFRICA

D.Elgar	not out	141	(2)	c Smith b Cummins	14
A.K.Markram	c Smith b Hazlewood	0	(1)	c Cummins b Starc	84
H.M.Amla	c Cummins b Hazlewood	31		c Bancroft b Cummins	31
A.B.de Villiers	c Warner b Cummins	64		c S.E.Marsh b Hazlewood	63
*F.du Plessis	c Smith b Cummins	5		lbw b Lyon	20
T.Bavuma	c Smith b Cummins	1		c sub‡ b Hazlewood	5
†Q.de Kock	c Paine b Cummins	3		c Paine b Cummins	65
V.D.Philander	c Paine b M.R.Marsh	8		not out	52
K.A.Maharaj	c Bancroft b Starc	3	(10)	c Cummins b Lyon	5
K.Rabada	c Smith b Lyon	22	(9)	st Paine b Lyon	20
M.Morkel	c Smith b Lyon	4		c Khawaja b Hazlewood	6
Extras	(B 13, LB 11, NB 3, W 2)	29		(B 4, LB 1, NB 1, W 2)	8
Total	**(97.5 overs; 434 mins)**	**311**		**(112.2 overs; 492 mins)**	**373**

AUSTRALIA

C.T.Bancroft	lbw b Philander	77		run out	26
D.A.Warner	b Rabada	30		c de Villiers b Rabada	32
U.T.Khawaja	c Rabada b Morkel	5		c de Villiers b Maharaj	1
*S.P.D.Smith	c Elgar b Morkel	5		c Elgar b Morkel	7
S.E.Marsh	c de Kock b Morkel	26		c Markram b Maharaj	0
M.R.Marsh	c de Kock b Philander	5		c de Villiers b Morkel	16
†T.D.Paine	not out	34		not out	9
P.J.Cummins	c de Villiers b Rabada	4		c Elgar b Morkel	0
M.A.Starc	c de Villiers b Rabada	2		c Markram b Morkel	7
N.M.Lyon	c Elgar b Morkel	47		run out	0
J.R.Hazlewood	c Amla b Rabada	10		c Philander b Morkel	5
Extras	(B 1, LB 5, NB 4)	10		(B 4)	4
Total	**(69.5 overs; 328 mins)**	**255**		**(39.4 overs; 187 mins)**	**107**

AUSTRALIA	O	M	R	W		O	M	R	W		FALL OF WICKETS				
												SA	A	SA	A
Starc	21	3	81	2		9	5	98	1		Wkt	1st	1st	2nd	2nd
Hazlewood	23	4	59	2		25.2	5	69	3		1st	6	43	28	57
Lyon	19.5	6	43	2	(4)	31	2	102	3		2nd	92	61	104	59
Cummins	26	6	78	4	(3)	27	5	67	3		3rd	220	72	151	59
M.R.Marsh	7	2	26	1	(6)	5	0	26	0		4th	234	150	196	59
Smith	1	1	0	0	(5)	1	0	6	0		5th	236	150	201	75
											6th	242	156	269	86
SOUTH AFRICA											7th	254	173	324	86
Philander	15	5	26	2	(2)	6	2	17	0		8th	257	175	354	94
Rabada	20.5	1	91	4	(1)	12	6	31	1		9th	307	241	362	94
Morkel	21	7	87	4		9.4	3	23	5		10th	311	255	373	107
Maharaj	12	3	35	0		12	2	32	2						
Bavuma	1	0	10	0											

Umpires: R.K.Illingworth (*England*) (32) and N.J.Llong (*England*) (50).
Referee: A.J.Pycroft (*Zimbabwe*) (58).   Test No. 2298/97 (SA424/A811)

SOUTH AFRICA v AUSTRALIA (4th Test)

At New Wanderers Stadium, Johannesburg, on 30, 31 March, 1, 2, 3 April 2018.
Toss: South Africa. Result: **SOUTH AFRICA** won by 492 runs.
Debut: Australia – C.J.Sayers.

SOUTH AFRICA

D.Elgar	c Sayers b Lyon	19	(2) c S.E.Marsh b Lyon		81
A.K.Markram	c M.R.Marsh b Cummins	152	(1) c Handscomb b Cummins		37
H.M.Amla	c Handscomb b Cummins	27	c M.R.Marsh b Lyon		16
A.B.de Villiers	c Paine b Sayers	69	c Paine b Cummins		6
*F.du Plessis	lbw b Cummins	0	c Handscomb b Cummins		120
T.Bavuma	not out	95	not out		35
K.Rabada	c Renshaw b Sayers	0			
†Q.de Kock	c M.R.Marsh b Lyon	39	(7) lbw b Cummins		4
V.D.Philander	c Khawaja b Lyon	12	(8) not out		33
K.A.Maharaj	c Paine b Cummins	45			
M.Morkel	c Handscomb b Cummins	0			
Extras	(B 13, LB 12, W 5)	30	(B 4, LB 8)		12
Total	**(136.5 overs; 599 mins)**	**488**	**(6 wkts dec; 105 overs; 452 mins)**		**344**

AUSTRALIA

M.T.Renshaw	c de Kock b Philander	8	lbw b Morkel	5
J.A.Burns	c du Plessis b Rabada	4	lbw b Morkel	42
U.T.Khawaja	c de Kock b Philander	53	lbw b Maharaj	7
P.S.P.Handscomb	b Philander	0	b Philander	24
S.E.Marsh	c de Villiers b Maharaj	16	c Bavuma b Philander	7
M.R.Marsh	b Morkel	4	c de Kock b Philander	0
†*T.D.Paine	c Elgar b Rabada	62	c de Kock b Philander	7
P.J.Cummins	lbw b Maharaj	50	b Philander	1
N.M.Lyon	c Elgar b Rabada	8	run out	9
C.J.Sayers	c Amla b Maharaj	0	c Elgar b Philander	0
J.R.Hazlewood	not out	1	not out	9
Extras	(B 3, LB 9, NB 3)	15	(LB 1, NB 7)	8
Total	**(70 overs; 321 mins)**	**221**	**(46.4 overs; 210 mins)**	**119**

AUSTRALIA	O	M	R	W		O	M	R	W
Hazlewood	26	3	86	0		21	6	41	0
Sayers	35	9	78	2		14	2	68	0
Cummins	28.5	5	83	5	(4)	18	5	58	4
Lyon	40	3	182	3	(3)	41	13	116	2
M.R.Marsh	6	1	30	0		8	0	40	0
Renshaw	1	0	4	0		3	0	9	0

SOUTH AFRICA	O	M	R	W		O	M	R	W
Philander	18	8	30	3	(2)	13	5	21	6
Rabada	19	7	53	3	(1)	8	3	16	0
Morkel	12.2	3	34	1	(4)	10.4	5	28	2
Maharaj	20	3	92	3	(3)	13	2	47	1
Markram	0.4	0	0	0		2	0	6	0

		FALL OF WICKETS			
			SA	A	SA	A
		Wkt	1st	1st	2nd	2nd
		1st	53	10	54	21
		2nd	142	34	79	34
		3rd	247	38	94	68
		4th	247	90	264	88
		5th	299	96	266	88
		6th	299	96	273	95
		7th	384	195	–	99
		8th	412	206	–	100
		9th	488	207	–	100
		10th	488	221	–	119

Umpires: I.J.Gould (*England*) (65) and N.J.Llong (*England*) (51).
Referee: A.J.Pycroft (*Zimbabwe*) (59).   **Test No. 2299/98 (SA425/A812)**

NEW ZEALAND v ENGLAND (1st Test)

At Eden Park, Auckland, on 22, 23, 24, 25, 26 March 2018 (day/night).
Toss: New Zealand. Result: **NEW ZEALAND** won by an innings and 49 runs.
Debuts: None.

ENGLAND

A.N.Cook	c Latham b Boult	5	c Watling b Boult	2
M.D.Stoneman	c Watling b Southee	11	c Boult b Wagner	55
*J.E.Root	b Boult	0	c Watling b Boult	51
D.J.Malan	c Watling b Boult	2	c Latham b Southee	23
B.A.Stokes	b Boult	0	c Southee b Wagner	66
†J.M.Bairstow	c and b Southee	0	c Williamson b Astle	26
M.M.Ali	b Southee	0	lbw b Boult	28
C.R.Woakes	b Boult	5	c Nicholls b Wagner	52
C.Overton	not out	33	lbw b Astle	3
S.C.J.Broad	c Williamson b Southee	0	not out	1
J.M.Anderson	c Nicholls b Boult	1	c Boult b Astle	1
Extras	(LB 1)	1	(B 8, LB 2, NB 1, W 1)	12
Total	**(20.4 overs; 94 mins)**	**58**	**(126.1 overs; 519 mins)**	**320**

NEW ZEALAND

J.A.Raval	c Bairstow b Anderson	3
T.W.M.Latham	c Woakes b Broad	26
*K.S.Williamson	lbw b Anderson	102
L.R.P.L.Taylor	c Woakes b Anderson	20
H.M.Nicholls	not out	145
†B.J.Watling	c Bairstow b Broad	31
C.de Grandhomme	c Bairstow b Overton	29
T.D.Astle	b Broad	18
T.G.Southee	c and b Root	25
N.Wagner	not out	9
T.A.Boult		
Extras	(B 4, LB 9, W 6)	19
Total	**(8 wkts dec; 141 overs; 615 mins)**	**427**

NEW ZEALAND	O	M	R	W		O	M	R	W
Boult	10.4	3	32	6		27	9	67	3
Southee	10	3	25	4		26	4	86	1
De Grandhomme						24	10	40	0
Wagner						32	11	77	3
Astle						16.1	5	39	3
Williamson						1	0	1	0

ENGLAND	O	M	R	W
Anderson	29	10	87	3
Broad	34	9	78	3
Overton	25	7	70	1
Woakes	33	9	107	0
Ali	17	1	59	0
Root	6	0	13	1

FALL OF WICKETS			
	E	NZ	E
Wkt	1st	1st	2nd
1st	6	8	6
2nd	6	92	94
3rd	16	123	132
4th	18	206	142
5th	18	260	181
6th	18	309	217
7th	23	341	300
8th	23	413	304
9th	27	–	319
10th	58	–	320

Umpires: B.N.J.Oxenford (*Australia*) (47) and P.R.Reiffel (*Australia*) (36).
Referee: Sir R.B.Richardson (*West Indies*) (15).   Test No. 2300/102 (NZ425/E996)

NEW ZEALAND v ENGLAND (2nd Test)

At Hagley Oval, Christchurch, on 30, 31 March, 1, 2, 3 April 2018.
Toss: New Zealand. Result: **MATCH DRAWN**.
Debut: England – M.J.Leach.

ENGLAND

A.N.Cook	b Boult	2	c Watling b Boult		14
M.D.Stoneman	c Latham b Southee	35	c Watling b Southee		60
J.M.Vince	lbw b Southee	18	c Taylor b Wagner		76
*J.E.Root	b Southee	37	c Watling b Wagner		54
D.J.Malan	lbw b Boult	0	c Nicholls b de Grandhomme		53
B.A.Stokes	c Watling b Boult	25	c Raval b de Grandhomme		12
†J.M.Bairstow	c Taylor b Boult	101	c Nicholls b Wagner		36
S.C.J.Broad	c Sodhi b Southee	5	c Sodhi b de Grandhomme		12
M.A.Wood	b Southee	52	b de Grandhomme		9
M.J.Leach	c Watling b Southee	16	not out		14
J.M.Anderson	not out	0			
Extras	(B 9, LB 5, NB 1, W 1)	16	(B 4, LB 3, NB 3, W 2)		12
Total	**(96.5 overs; 412 mins)**	**307**	**(9 wkts dec; 106.4 overs; 452 mins)**		**352**

NEW ZEALAND

J.A.Raval	c Bairstow b Anderson	5	(2) c Stoneman b Broad		17
T.W.M.Latham	c Bairstow b Broad	0	(1) c Vince b Leach		83
*K.S.Williamson	c Bairstow b Anderson	22	c Bairstow b Broad		0
L.R.P.L.Taylor	c Cook b Broad	2	c Cook b Leach		13
H.M.Nicholls	lbw b Broad	0	c Cook b Anderson		13
†B.J.Watling	b Anderson	85	c Anderson b Wood		19
C.de Grandhomme	c Bairstow b Broad	72	c Leach b Wood		45
T.G.Southee	b Anderson	50	(10) not out		0
I.S.Sodhi	c Bairstow b Broad	1	(8) not out		56
N.Wagner	not out	24	(9) c Vince b Root		7
T.A.Boult	c Malan b Broad	16			
Extras	(LB 1)	1	(LB 2, NB 1)		3
Total	**(93.3 overs; 421 mins)**	**278**	**(8 wkts; 124.4 overs; 481 mins)**		**256**

NEW ZEALAND	O	M	R	W	O	M	R	W
Boult	28.5	5	87	4	28	5	89	2
Southee	26	7	62	6	19	4	65	1
De Grandhomme	17	4	44	0	26	2	94	4
Wagner	20	5	69	0	22.4	5	51	2
Sodhi	5	0	31	0	11	0	46	0

ENGLAND	O	M	R	W	O	M	R	W
Anderson	24	5	76	4	26	8	37	1
Broad	22.3	5	54	6	24	6	72	2
Wood	21	3	69	0	22	10	45	2
Leach	19	3	52	0	32	15	61	2
Root	1	0	9	0	12.4	5	28	1
Stokes	6	2	17	0	4	3	2	0
Malan					4	1	9	0

FALL OF WICKETS

	E	NZ	E	NZ
Wkt	1st	1st	2nd	2nd
1st	6	0	24	42
2nd	38	14	147	42
3rd	93	17	165	66
4th	94	17	262	91
5th	94	36	262	135
6th	151	178	282	162
7th	164	226	300	219
8th	259	231	312	256
9th	307	239	352	–
10th	307	278	–	–

Umpires: M.Erasmus (*South Africa*) (49) and B.N.J.Oxenford (*Australia*) (48).
Referee: Sir R.B.Richardson (*West Indies*) (16). **Test No. 2301/103 (NZ426/E997)**

IRELAND v PAKISTAN (Only Test)

At The Village, Malahide, Dublin, on 11, 12, 13, 14, 15 May 2018.
Toss: Ireland. Result: **PAKISTAN** won by five wickets.
Debuts: Ireland – All bar W.B.Rankin; Pakistan – Imam-ul-Haq, Faheem Ashraf.

PAKISTAN					
Azhar Ali	c Porterfield b Rankin	4		c Stirling b Murtagh	2
Imam-ul-Haq	lbw b Murtagh	7		not out	74
Haris Sohail	c Porterfield b Thompson	31		c Joyce b Rankin	7
Asad Shafiq	c Balbirnie b Rankin	62		b Murtagh	1
Babar Azam	c Stirling b Murtagh	14		run out	59
†*Sarfraz Ahmed	c Stirling b Thompson	20		lbw b Thompson	8
Shadab Khan	lbw b Murtagh	55		not out	4
Faheem Ashraf	c N.J.O'Brien b Thompson	83			
Mohammad Amir	c N.J.O'Brien b Murtagh	13			
Mohammad Abbas	not out	4			
Rahat Ali	not out	0			
Extras	(B 1, LB 10, NB 4, W 2)	17		(NB 5)	5
Total	**(9 wkts dec; 96 overs; 411 mins)**	**310**		**(5 wkts; 45 overs; 199 mins)**	**160**

IRELAND					
E.C.Joyce	lbw b Abbas	4		run out	43
*W.T.S.Porterfield	b Amir	1		c Ahmed b Amir	32
A.Balbirnie	lbw b Abbas	0		lbw b Abbas	0
†N.J.O'Brien	lbw b Abbas	0		b Amir	18
P.R.Stirling	c Azam b Ashraf	17		lbw b Abbas	11
K.J.O'Brien	c Imam b Amir	40		c Sohail b Abbas	118
S.R.Thompson	b Khan	3	(8)	b Khan	53
T.E.Kane	c Azam b Khan	0	(9)	b Abbas	14
G.C.Wilson	not out	33	(7)	c Sohail b Amir	12
W.B.Rankin	c Ahmed b Abbas	17		b Abbas	6
T.J.Murtagh	c Imam b Khan	5		not out	5
Extras	(B 8, LB 1, W 1)	10		(B 1, LB 20, NB 2, W 4)	27
Total	**(47.2 overs; 202 mins)**	**130**		**(129.3 overs; 579 mins)**	**339**

IRELAND	O	M	R	W		O	M	R	W
Murtagh	25	5	45	4		16	3	55	2
Rankin	21	3	75	2		12	1	57	1
Kane	20	2	86	0	(4)	6	1	17	0
Thompson	22	4	62	3	(3)	11	4	31	1
K.J.O'Brien	6	1	20	0					
Stirling	2	0	11	0					
PAKISTAN									
Mohammad Amir	10	5	9	2		29.2	9	63	3
Mohammad Abbas	11	4	44	4		28.3	10	66	5
Rahat Ali	7	0	18	0		23	3	75	0
Faheem Ashraf	5	2	18	1		18	3	51	0
Shadab Khan	13.2	3	31	3		30.4	7	63	1
Haris Sohail	1	0	1	0					

FALL OF WICKETS	P	Ire	Ire	P
Wkt	*1st*	*1st*	*2nd*	*2nd*
1st	13	5	69	2
2nd	13	5	69	13
3rd	71	5	94	14
4th	104	7	95	140
5th	153	36	127	152
6th	159	61	157	–
7th	276	61	271	–
8th	304	73	321	–
9th	306	107	332	–
10th	–	130	339	–

Umpires: R.K.Illingworth (*England*) (33) and N.J.Llong (*England*) (52).
Referee: B.C.Broad (*England*) (94). **Test No. 2302/1 (Ire1/P413)**

ENGLAND v PAKISTAN (1st Test)

At Lord's, London, on 24, 25, 26, 27 May 2018.
Toss: England. Result: **PAKISTAN** won by nine wickets.
Debut: England – D.M.Bess.

ENGLAND

Batsman	First innings		Second innings	
A.N.Cook	b Amir	70	lbw b Abbas	1
M.D.Stoneman	b Abbas	4	b Khan	9
*J.E.Root	c Ahmed b Hasan	4	lbw b Abbas	68
D.J.Malan	c Ahmed b Hasan	6	c Ahmed b Amir	12
†J.M.Bairstow	b Ashraf	27	b Amir	0
B.A.Stokes	lbw b Abbas	38	c sub (Fakhar Zaman) b Khan	9
J.C.Buttler	c Shafiq b Hasan	14	lbw b Abbas	67
D.M.Bess	c Shafiq b Abbas	5	b Amir	57
M.A.Wood	c Amir b Hasan	7	c Ahmed b Amir	4
S.C.J.Broad	lbw b Abbas	0	c Ahmed b Abbas	0
J.M.Anderson	not out	0	not out	0
Extras	(B 1, LB 6, NB 1, W 1)	9	(B 4, LB 9, W 2)	15
Total	**(58.2 overs)**	**184**	**(82.1 overs)**	**242**

PAKISTAN

Batsman	First innings		Second innings	
Azhar Ali	lbw b Anderson	50	b Anderson	4
Imam-ul-Haq	lbw b Broad	4	not out	18
Haris Sohail	c Bairstow b Wood	39	not out	39
Asad Shafiq	c Malan b Stokes	59		
Babar Azam	retired hurt	68		
†*Sarfraz Ahmed	c Wood b Stokes	9		
Shadab Khan	c Bairstow b Stokes	52		
Faheem Ashraf	b Anderson	37		
Mohammad Amir	not out	24		
Hasan Ali	c Buttler b Anderson	0		
Mohammad Abbas	c Bairstow b Wood	5		
Extras	(LB 14, NB 1, W 1)	16	(B 3, LB 2)	5
Total	**(114.3 overs)**	**363**	**(1 wkt; 12.4 overs)**	**66**

PAKISTAN	O	M	R	W		O	M	R	W
Mohammad Amir	14	3	41	1		18.1	3	36	4
Mohammad Abbas	14	7	23	4		17	3	41	4
Hasan Ali	15.2	2	51	4	(4)	19	3	58	0
Faheem Ashraf	9	2	28	1	(3)	9	2	31	0
Shadab Khan	6	0	34	0		19	2	63	2

ENGLAND	O	M	R	W		O	M	R	W
Anderson	26	6	82	3		3	0	12	1
Broad	25	9	61	1		3	1	13	0
Wood	24.3	6	74	2	(4)	3	1	7	0
Stokes	22	5	73	3					
Bess	17	0	59	0	(3)	3.4	0	29	0

FALL OF WICKETS

	E	P	E	P
Wkt	1st	1st	2nd	2nd
1st	12	12	1	12
2nd	33	87	31	-
3rd	43	119	91	-
4th	100	203	91	-
5th	149	227	104	-
6th	168	318	110	-
7th	168	332	236	-
8th	180	337	241	-
9th	180	363	242	-
10th	184	-	242	-

Umpires: R.J.Tucker (*Australia*) (60) and P.R.Reiffel (*Australia*) (37).
Referee: J.J.Crowe (*New Zealand*) (88).   Test No. 2303/82 (E998/P414)
Babar Azam retired hurt at 246-5.

ENGLAND v PAKISTAN (2nd Test)

At Headingley, Leeds, on 1, 2, 3 June 2018.
Toss: Pakistan. Result: **ENGLAND** won by an innings and 55 runs.
Debuts: England – S.M.Curran; Pakistan – Usman Salahuddin.

PAKISTAN

Azhar Ali	lbw b Broad	2	b Anderson		11
Imam-ul-Haq	c Root b Broad	0	lbw b Bess		34
Haris Sohail	c Malan b Woakes	28	c Bess b Anderson		8
Asad Shafiq	c Cook b Woakes	27	c Bairstow b Broad		5
Usman Salahuddin	lbw b Broad	4	c Root b Bess		33
†*Sarfraz Ahmed	b Anderson	14	lbw b Woakes		8
Shadab Khan	c Jennings b Curran	56	c Cook b Curran		4
Faheem Ashraf	lbw b Anderson	0	c Malan b Bess		3
Mohammad Amir	c Bairstow b Anderson	13	not out		7
Hasan Ali	c and b Woakes	24	c Cook b Broad		9
Mohammad Abbas	not out	1	c Root b Broad		1
Extras	(LB 5)	5	(B 5, LB 5, NB 1)		11
Total	**(48.1 overs)**	**174**	**(46 overs)**		**134**

ENGLAND

A.N.Cook	c Ahmed b Hasan	46
K.K.Jennings	c Ahmed b Ashraf	29
*J.E.Root	c Ahmed b Amir	45
D.M.Bess	c Shafiq b Khan	49
D.J.Malan	c Sohail b Amir	28
†J.M.Bairstow	c Ahmed b Ashraf	21
J.C.Buttler	not out	80
C.R.Woakes	c Ahmed b Abbas	17
S.M.Curran	c Shafiq b Abbas	20
S.C.J.Broad	c Abbas b Ashraf	2
J.M.Anderson	c Sohail b Hasan	5
Extras	(B 8, LB 13)	21
Total	**(106.2 overs)**	**363**

ENGLAND	O	M	R	W		O	M	R	W
Anderson	15	6	43	3		10	2	35	2
Broad	15	6	38	3		12	2	28	3
Woakes	11	1	55	1	(4)	6	0	18	1
Curran	7.1	0	33	1	(3)	7	2	10	1
Bess						11	1	33	3

PAKISTAN	O	M	R	W
Mohammad Amir	23	5	72	2
Mohammad Abbas	26	8	78	2
Hasan Ali	20.2	4	82	2
Faheem Ashraf	20	4	60	3
Shadab Khan	17	2	50	1

FALL OF WICKETS

	P	E	P
Wkt	1st	1st	2nd
1st	0	53	20
2nd	17	104	30
3rd	49	138	42
4th	62	200	84
5th	78	212	97
6th	78	260	102
7th	79	285	111
8th	113	319	115
9th	156	344	124
10th	174	363	134

Umpires: B.N.J.Oxenford (*Australia*) (49) and R.J.Tucker (*Australia*) (61).
Referee: J.J.Crowe (*New Zealand*) (89).   **Test No. 2304/83 (E999/P415)**

WEST INDIES v SRI LANKA (1st Test)

At Queen's Park Oval, Port of Spain, Trinidad, on 6, 7, 8, 9, 10 June 2018.
Toss: West Indies. Result: **WEST INDIES** won by 226 runs.
Debuts: None.

‡(J.D.F.Vandersay)

WEST INDIES

K.C.Brathwaite	c Dickwella b Lakmal	3	c Dickwella b Kumara	16
D.S.Smith	run out	7	b Lakmal	20
K.O.A.Powell	b Kumara	38	c sub‡ b M.D.K.Perera	88
S.D.Hope	c Dickwella b Kumara	44	c Mendis b Kumara	1
R.L.Chase	c Mathews b Herath	38	b Herath	12
†S.O.Dowrich	not out	125	lbw b Kumara	13
*J.O.Holder	c Dickwella b Kumara	40	lbw b Herath	39
D.Bishoo	c Silva b Lakmal	40	not out	16
K.A.J.Roach	c Chandimal b Kumara	39	not out	11
M.L.Cummins	not out	0		
S.T.Gabriel				
Extras	(B 14, LB 20, NB 4, W 2)	40	(B 4, LB 2, NB 1)	7
Total	**(8 wkts dec; 154 overs)**	**414**	**(7 wkts dec; 72 overs)**	**223**

SRI LANKA

B.K.G.Mendis	c Holder b Gabriel	4	c Dowrich b Gabriel	102
M.D.K.J.Perera	c Chase b Roach	0	c Smith b Gabriel	12
*L.D.Chandimal	c Chase b Gabriel	44	c Brathwaite b Chase	27
A.D.Mathews	c Chase b Holder	11	c Dowrich b Holder	31
A.R.S.Silva	b Roach	5	c and b Bishoo	14
†D.P.D.N.Dickwella	run out	31	(7) lbw b Chase	19
M.D.K.Perera	c Hope b Bishoo	20	(8) not out	3
H.M.R.K.B.Herath	c sub (S.O.Hetmyer) b Cummins	5	(9) c Hope b Bishoo	0
R.A.S.Lakmal	b Bishoo b Cummins	15	(10) c Dowrich b Chase	1
P.L.S.Gamage	not out	0	(6) lbw b Bishoo	3
C.B.R.L.S.Kumara	c Dowrich b Cummins	8	c Dowrich b Chase	0
Extras	(B 8, LB 16, NB 6, W 12)	42	(B 3, LB 4, NB 7)	14
Total	**(55.4 overs)**	**185**	**(83.2 overs)**	**226**

SRI LANKA	O	M	R	W		O	M	R	W
Lakmal	29	11	55	2		12	2	32	1
Gamage	26	6	67	0		15	3	43	0
M.D.K.Perera	35	5	84	0	(5)	12	1	50	1
Kumara	31	4	95	4		9	0	40	3
Herath	32	9	67	1	(3)	24	5	52	2
Mendis	1	0	12	0					

WEST INDIES	O	M	R	W		O	M	R	W
Roach	10	3	34	2		13	3	57	0
Gabriel	13	0	48	2		15	2	52	2
Cummins	12.4	4	39	3	(4)	12	4	23	0
Holder	7	1	15	1	(3)	14	6	24	1
Bravo	13	2	25	1					
Bishoo					(5)	19	2	48	3
Chase					(6)	8.2	1	15	4

FALL OF WICKETS

	WI	SL	WI	SL
Wkt	1st	1st	2nd	2nd
1st	4	2	36	21
2nd	40	16	55	123
3rd	80	30	75	175
4th	134	43	119	189
5th	147	121	149	195
6th	237	140	191	218
7th	339	148	203	222
8th	414	156	–	225
9th	–	175	–	226
10th	–	185	–	226

Umpires: Alim Dar (*Pakistan*) (118) and R.A.Kettleborough (*England*) (51).
Referee: J.Srinath (*India*) (38).   **Test No. 2305/18 (WI531/SL270)**
L.D.Chandimal retired hurt at 49-1 and resumed at 189-4.

WEST INDIES v SRI LANKA (2nd Test)

At Darren Sammy National Cricket Stadium, Gros Islet, St Lucia, on 14, 15, 16, 17, 18 June 2018.
Toss: Sri Lanka. Result: **MATCH DRAWN**.
Debuts: Sri Lanka – C.A.K.Rajitha, M.L.Udawatte.

SRI LANKA

M.D.K.J.Perera	c Holder b Roach	32		c Dowrich b Gabriel	20
M.L.Udawatte	c Holder b Gabriel	0		c Bishoo b Roach	19
D.M.de Silva	b Gabriel	12	(4)	c Smith b Gabriel	3
B.K.G.Mendis	c Dowrich b Holder	45	(5)	b Gabriel	87
*L.D.Chandimal	not out	119	(6)	c Dowrich b Roach	39
A.R.S.Silva	c Holder b Gabriel	6	(7)	c Dowrich b Gabriel	48
†D.P.D.N.Dickwella	c Hope b Gabriel	16	(8)	c Powell b Gabriel	62
M.K.P.A.D.Perera	c Dowrich b Roach	2	(9)	b Gabriel	23
R.A.S.Lakmal	b Gabriel	10	(10)	lbw b Gabriel	7
C.A.K.Rajitha	c Dowrich b Roach	4	(3)	lbw b Gabriel	0
C.B.R.L.S.Kumara	c Hope b Roach	0		not out	0
Extras	(B 1, LB 2, NB 2, W 2)	7		(B 12, LB 8, NB 11, W 3)	34
Total	(79 overs)	253		(91.4 overs)	342

WEST INDIES

K.C.Brathwaite	c Dickwella b Rajitha	22	not out	59
D.S.Smith	lbw b M.K.P.A.D.Perera	61	c de Silva b Rajitha	1
K.O.A.Powell	c Mendis b Kumara	27	c Udawatte b Rajitha	2
S.D.Hope	c de Silva b Lakmal	19	b Lakmal	39
R.L.Chase	c Lakmal b Kumara	41	b Lakmal	13
†S.O.Dowrich	c Dickwella b Lakmal	55	c de Silva b M.K.P.A.D.Perera	8
*J.O.Holder	c Dickwella b Rajitha	15	not out	15
D.Bishoo	c Mendis b Rajitha	2		
K.A.J.Roach	lbw b Kumara	13		
M.L.Cummins	not out	8		
S.T.Gabriel	c de Silva b Kumara	3		
Extras	(B 11, LB 8, NB 1, W 9, Pen 5)	34	(LB 10)	10
Total	(100.3 overs)	300	(5 wkts; 60.3 overs)	147

WEST INDIES	O	M	R	W		O	M	R	W
Roach	18	8	49	4		21	3	78	2
Gabriel	16	4	59	5		20.4	6	62	8
Cummins	19	5	69	0	(4)	13	1	44	0
Holder	14	2	56	1	(3)	15	5	38	0
Bishoo	11	3	15	0		11	0	58	0
Chase	1	0	2	0		10	1	38	0
Brathwaite						1	0	4	0

FALL OF WICKETS				
	SL	WI	SL	WI
Wkt	1st	1st	2nd	2nd
1st	0	59	32	6
2nd	15	115	34	8
3rd	59	149	44	55
4th	126	163	48	64
5th	148	241	165	117
6th	179	254	199	–
7th	190	261	298	–
8th	206	279	307	–
9th	237	292	334	–
10th	253	300	342	–

SRI LANKA	O	M	R	W		O	M	R	W
Lakmal	24	6	50	2		17.3	3	48	2
M.K.P.A.D.Perera	25	7	81	1	(4)	19	7	33	1
Rajitha	22	6	49	3	(2)	13	3	23	2
Kumara	26.3	4	86	4	(3)	10	3	28	0
De Silva	3	0	10	0		1	0	5	0

Umpires: Alim Dar (*Pakistan*) (119) and I.J.Gould (*England*) (66).
Referee: J.Srinath (*India*) (39).   **Test No. 2306/19 (WI532/SL271)**
S.D.Hope retired hurt at 25-2 and resumed at 64-4.

WEST INDIES v SRI LANKA (3rd Test)

At Kensington Oval, Bridgetown, Barbados, on 23, 24, 25, 26 June 2018 (day/night).
Toss: West Indies. Result: **SRI LANKA** won by four wickets.
Debuts: None.

WEST INDIES

K.C.Brathwaite	c Gunathilleke b Lakmal	2	c Udawatte b Lakmal		2
D.S.Smith	c de Silva b Lakmal	2	b Lakmal		0
K.O.A.Powell	c Mendis b Kumara	4	c Dickwella b Kumara		7
S.D.Hope	c Mendis b Rajitha	11	b Kumara		0
R.L.Chase	b Rajitha	14	c M.D.K.J.Perera b Lakmal		5
†S.O.Dowrich	lbw b Kumara	71	c Lakmal b Rajitha		16
*J.O.Holder	c M.D.K.Perera b Rajitha	74	c Mendis b Rajitha		15
D.Bishoo	c Mendis b Kumara	0	b Rajitha		0
K.A.J.Roach	not out	11	not out		23
M.L.Cummins	c Mendis b M.D.K.Perera	2	c de Silva b M.D.K.Perera		14
S.T.Gabriel	c Dickwella b Kumara	2	run out		6
Extras	(B 4, LB 6, W 1)	11	(LB 4, W 1)		5
Total	**(69.3 overs; 327 mins)**	**204**	**(31.2 overs; 144 mins)**		**93**

SRI LANKA

M.D.K.J.Perera	c Dowrich b Roach	0	(8)	not out	28
M.L.Udawatte	lbw b Roach	4		lbw b Roach	0
M.D.Gunathilleke	lbw b Holder	29	(1)	c Bishoo b Holder	21
B.K.G.Mendis	b Gabriel	22		lbw b Holder	25
D.M.de Silva	lbw b Gabriel	8	(3)	b Holder	17
A.R.S.Silva	c Dowrich b Gabriel	11	(5)	c Smith b Holder	1
†D.P.D.N.Dickwella	c Smith b Holder	42	(6)	b Holder	6
M.D.K.Perera	not out	11	(7)	not out	23
*R.A.S.Lakmal	c sub (K.M.A.Paul) b Holder	0			
C.A.K.Rajitha	b Holder	0			
C.B.R.L.S.Kumara	run out	0			
Extras	(B 9, LB 14, NB 3, W 12)	27	(B 8, LB 15)		23
Total	**(59 overs; 296 mins)**	**154**	**(6 wkts; 40.2 overs; 202 mins)**		**144**

SRI LANKA	O	M	R	W		O	M	R	W
Lakmal	19	5	52	2		11.3	3	25	3
Kumara	23.3	5	58	4		8.2	1	31	2
Rajitha	17	1	68	3		8	1	20	3
M.D.K.Perera	10	3	16	1		3.3	0	13	1

WEST INDIES	O	M	R	W		O	M	R	W
Roach	12	5	30	2		10	1	33	1
Gabriel	15	2	52	3		9	1	26	0
Cummins	15	6	29	0	(4)	6	1	17	0
Holder	16	8	19	4	(3)	14.2	4	41	5
Bishoo	1	0	1	0		1	0	4	0

FALL OF WICKETS

	WI	SL	WI	SL
Wkt	1st	1st	2nd	2nd
1st	3	0	1	9
2nd	8	16	8	30
3rd	8	75	9	48
4th	24	81	14	50
5th	53	85	14	74
6th	168	118	41	81
7th	183	147	41	–
8th	189	147	56	–
9th	201	150	82	–
10th	204	154	93	–

Umpires: I.J.Gould (*England*) (67) and R.A.Kettleborough (*England*) (52).
Referee: J.Srinath (*India*) (40).　　**Test No. 2307/20 (WI533/SL272)**

INDIA v AFGHANISTAN (Only Test)

At M.Chinnaswamy Stadium, Bengaluru, on 14, 15 June 2018.
Toss: India. Result: **INDIA** won by an innings and 262 runs.
Debuts: Afghanistan – All.

INDIA

M.Vijay	lbw b Momand	105
S.Dhawan	c Nabi b Ahmadzai	107
K.L.Rahul	b Ahmadzai	54
C.A.Pujara	c Nabi b Zadran	35
*A.M.Rahane	lbw b Khan	10
†K.D.Karthik	run out	4
H.H.Pandya	c Zazai b Momand	71
R.Ashwin	c Zazai b Ahmadzai	18
R.A.Jadeja	c Shah b Nabi	20
I.Sharma	lbw b Khan	8
U.T.Yadav	not out	20
Extras	(B 1, LB 12, NB 1, W 2)	16
Total	**(104.5 overs; 472 mins)**	**474**

AFGHANISTAN

Mohammad Shahazad	run out	14		c Karthik b Yadav	13
Javed Ahmadi	b Sharma	1		c Dhawan b Yadav	3
Rahmat Shah	lbw b Yadav	14		c Rahane b Sharma	4
†Afsar Zazai	b Sharma	6	(7)	b Jadeja	1
Hashmatullah Shahidi	lbw b Ashwin	11		not out	36
*Asghar Stanikzai	b Ashwin	11		c Dhawan b Jadeja	25
Mohammad Nabi	c Sharma b Ashwin	24	(4)	lbw b Yadav	0
Rashid Khan	c Yadav b Jadeja	7		b Jadeja	12
Yamin Ahmadzai	c Jadeja b Ashwin	0		b Sharma	1
Mujeeb Zadran	st Karthik b Jadeja	15		c Yadav b Jadeja	3
Wafadar Momand	not out	6		b Ashwin	0
Extras		–		(B 4, LB 1)	5
Total	**(27.5 overs; 125 mins)**	**109**		**(38.4 overs; 165 mins)**	**103**

AFGHANISTAN	O	M	R	W		O	M	R	W
Yamin Ahmadzai	19	7	51	3					
Wafadar Momand	21	5	100	2					
Mohammad Nabi	13	0	65	1					
Rashid Khan	34.5	2	154	2					
Mujeeb Zadran	15	1	75	1					
Asghar Stanikzai	2	0	16	0					

INDIA	O	M	R	W		O	M	R	W
Yadav	6	1	18	1	(2)	7	1	26	3
Sharma	5	0	28	2	(1)	7	2	17	2
Pandya	5	0	18	0		4	2	6	0
Ashwin	8	1	27	4		11.4	3	32	1
Jadeja	3.5	1	18	2		9	3	17	4

	FALL OF WICKETS		
	I	Af	Af
Wkt	1st	1st	2nd
1st	168	15	19
2nd	280	21	22
3rd	284	35	22
4th	318	35	24
5th	328	50	61
6th	334	59	62
7th	369	78	82
8th	436	87	85
9th	440	88	98
10th	474	109	103

Umpires: C.B.Gaffaney (*New Zealand*) (20) and P.R.Reiffel (*Australia*) (38).
Referee: A.J.Pycroft (*Zimbabwe*) (60).   Test No. 2308/1 (I522/Af1)

WEST INDIES v BANGLADESH (1st Test)

At Sir Vivian Richards Stadium, North Sound, Antigua, on 4, 5, 6 July 2018.
Toss: West Indies. Result: **WEST INDIES** won by an innings and 219 runs.
Debut: Bangladesh – Abu Jayed.

BANGLADESH

Tamim Iqbal	c Dowrich b Roach	4	c Hope b Gabriel		13
Liton Das	c Chase b Cummins	25	c Brathwaite b Holder		2
Mominul Haque	c Hope b Roach	1	b Gabriel		0
Mushfiqur Rahim	lbw b Roach	0	b Gabriel		8
*Shakib Al Hasan	c Holder b Roach	0	c Holder b Gabriel		12
Mahmudullah	c Dowrich b Roach	0	c Chase b Holder		15
†Nurul Hasan	c Holder b Cummins	4	(8) c and b Cummins		64
Mehedi Hasan	c Smith b Cummins	1	(7) c Dowrich b Holder		2
Kamrul Islam	c Dowrich b Holder	0	b Gabriel		7
Rubel Hossain	not out	6	b Cummins		16
Abu Jayed	b Holder	2	not out		0
Extras		–	(B 1, NB 1, W 3)		5
Total	**(18.4 overs)**	**43**	**(40.2 overs)**		**144**

WEST INDIES

K.C.Brathwaite	c Mehedi b Shakib	121
D.S.Smith	c Nurul b Abu	58
K.O.A.Powell	c Liton b Mahmudullah	48
D.Bishoo	b Kamrul	19
S.D.Hope	c Tamim b Abu	67
R.L.Chase	lbw b Mehedi	2
†S.O.Dowrich	c Liton b Shakib	4
*J.O.Holder	c Liton b Mehedi	33
K.A.J.Roach	lbw b Mehedi	33
M.L.Cummins	not out	1
S.T.Gabriel	c Shakib b Abu	5
Extras	(B 3, LB 8, NB 1, W 3)	15
Total	**(137.3 overs)**	**406**

WEST INDIES	O	M	R	W		O	M	R	W
Roach	5	1	8	5					
Gabriel	5	0	14	0		12	3	77	5
Holder	4.4	0	10	2	(1)	15	3	30	3
Cummins	4	2	11	3	(3)	7.2	2	16	2
Bishoo					(4)	5	1	16	0
Chase					(5)	1	0	4	0

BANGLADESH	O	M	R	W
Abu Jayed	26.3	7	84	3
Rubel Hossain	17	3	44	0
Kamrul Islam	20	3	69	1
Shakib Al Hasan	27	2	71	2
Mehedi Hasan	34	6	101	3
Mahmudullah	11	1	18	1
Mominul Haque	2	0	8	1

FALL OF WICKETS			
	B	WI	B
Wkt	1st	1st	2nd
1st	10	113	14
2nd	16	194	14
3rd	18	246	16
4th	18	272	36
5th	18	281	43
6th	34	288	50
7th	34	338	63
8th	35	394	88
9th	35	400	143
10th	43	406	144

Umpires: R.K.Illingworth (*England*) (34) and R.A.Kettleborough (*England*) (53).
Referee: B.C.Broad (*England*) (95).   **Test No. 2309/13 (WI534/B107)**

WEST INDIES v BANGLADESH (2nd Test)

At Sabina Park, Kingston, Jamaica, on 12, 13, 14 July 2018.
Toss: Bangladesh. Result: **WEST INDIES** won by 166 runs.
Debut: West Indies – K.M.A.Paul.

WEST INDIES

K.C.Brathwaite	c Taijul b Mehedi	110		b Shakib	8
D.S.Smith	c Mominul b Mehedi	2		st Nurul b Shakib	16
K.O.A.Powell	lbw b Mehedi	29	(4)	lbw b Shakib	18
S.D.Hope	c Nurul b Taijul	29	(5)	lbw b Taijul	4
S.O.Hetmyer	c Nurul b Abu	86	(6)	lbw b Abu	18
R.L.Chase	lbw b Abu	20	(7)	b Mehedi	32
†S.O.Dowrich	c Mehedi b Taijul	6	(8)	not out	12
*J.O.Holder	not out	33	(2)	st Nurul b Mehedi	1
K.M.A.Paul	c Mominul b Mehedi	0	(3)	st Nurul b Shakib	13
M.L.Cummins	lbw b Mehedi	0		b Shakib	1
S.T.Gabriel	b Abu	12		b Shakib	0
Extras	(B 20, LB 7)	27		(B 1, LB 2, NB 2, W 1)	6
Total	**(112 overs)**	**354**		**(45 overs)**	**129**

BANGLADESH

Tamim Iqbal	b Paul	47		lbw b Holder	0
Liton Das	lbw b Gabriel	12		c Hope b Paul	33
Mominul Haque	c Hope b Gabriel	0		lbw b Chase	15
*Shakib Al Hasan	b Holder	32		b Holder	54
Mahmudullah	lbw b Holder	0		c Hope b Chase	4
Mushfiqur Rahim	c Hope b Holder	24		b Holder	31
†Nurul Hasan	lbw b Paul	0		lbw b Holder	0
Mehedi Hasan	lbw b Cummins	3		c Smith b Gabriel	10
Taijul Islam	b Holder	18		not out	13
Kamrul Islam	not out	0		lbw b Holder	0
Abu Jayed	b Holder	0		b Holder	0
Extras	(LB 5, NB 8)	13		(B 4, LB 2, NB 2)	8
Total	**(46.1 overs)**	**149**		**(42 overs)**	**168**

BANGLADESH	O	M	R	W		O	M	R	W
Abu Jayed	18	7	38	3		8	1	21	1
Shakib Al Hasan	22	3	60	0	(4)	17	5	33	6
Mehedi Hasan	29	9	93	5	(2)	11	2	45	2
Taijul Islam	25	4	82	2	(5)	7	0	24	1
Kamrul Islam	10	1	34	0	(3)	2	0	3	0
Mahmudullah	8	1	20	0					

WEST INDIES	O	M	R	W		O	M	R	W
Gabriel	10	3	19	2	(2)	9	2	29	1
Paul	9	2	25	2	(3)	7	0	34	1
Cummins	9	1	34	1	(4)	5	1	20	0
Holder	10.1	1	44	5	(1)	13	3	59	6
Chase	8	0	22	0		8	4	20	2

FALL OF WICKETS

	WI	B	WI	B
Wkt	1st	1st	2nd	2nd
1st	9	20	19	2
2nd	59	20	28	40
3rd	138	79	53	52
4th	247	79	60	67
5th	297	117	64	121
6th	302	117	97	121
7th	318	128	122	138
8th	318	135	124	162
9th	319	149	129	168
10th	354	149	129	168

Umpires: R.K.Illingworth (*England*) (35) and S.Ravi (*India*) (27).
Referee: B.C.Broad (*England*) (96).   **Test No. 2310/14 (WI535/B108)**

SRI LANKA v SOUTH AFRICA (1st Test)

At Galle International Stadium, on 12, 13, 14 July 2018.
Toss: Sri Lanka. Result: **SRI LANKA** won by 278 runs.
Debuts: None.

SRI LANKA

M.D.Gunathilleke	c de Kock b Rabada	26		c Rabada b Maharaj	17
F.D.M.Karunaratne	not out	158		c Amla b Rabada	60
D.M.de Silva	b Shamsi	11		b Maharaj	9
B.K.G.Mendis	c Rabada b Steyn	24		lbw b Maharaj	0
A.D.Mathews	c de Kock b Rabada	1		b Maharaj	35
A.R.S.Silva	c Markram b Rabada	0		run out	13
†D.P.D.N.Dickwella	c Amla b Shamsi	18		c de Kock b Rabada	9
M.D.K.Perera	c de Kock b Philander	1		lbw b Rabada	0
H.M.R.K.B.Herath	run out	1	(10)	lbw b Shamsi	0
*R.A.S.Lakmal	c de Kock b Rabada	10	(9)	not out	33
P.A.D.L.R.Sandakan	st de Kock b Shamsi	25		c Bavuma b Steyn	6
Extras	(B 7, LB 1, NB 2, W 2)	12		(B 2, LB 4)	6
Total	**(78.4 overs)**	**287**		**(57.4 overs)**	**190**

SOUTH AFRICA

D.Elgar	c Mathews b Perera	8	(2)	st Dickwella b Perera	4
A.K.Markram	c Mathews b Herath	0	(1)	st Dickwella b Herath	19
K.A.Maharaj	lbw b Herath	3	(8)	c Sandakan b Perera	9
H.M.Amla	c Mendis b Perera	15	(3)	c de Silva b Perera	0
T.Bavuma	b Sandakan	17	(4)	c de Silva b Perera	2
*F.du Plessis	b Lakmal	49	(5)	c Mathews b Herath	1
†Q.de Kock	b Perera	3	(6)	lbw b Perera	10
V.D.Philander	lbw b Perera	18	(7)	not out	22
K.Rabada	b Lakmal	2		b Perera	0
D.W.Steyn	c Mathews b Lakmal	8		c and b Herath	2
T.Shamsi	not out	0		lbw b Sandakan	2
Extras	(B 2, NB 1)	3		(B 2)	2
Total	**(54.3 overs)**	**126**		**(28.5 overs)**	**73**

SOUTH AFRICA	O	M	R	W		O	M	R	W	FALL OF WICKETS				
Philander	8	1	28	1	(5)	3	0	10	0		SL	SA	SL	SA
Steyn	13	0	54	1		11.4	1	35	1	Wkt	1st	1st	2nd	2nd
Rabada	14	1	50	4	(1)	12	0	44	3	1st	44	1	51	12
Maharaj	17	3	49	0	(3)	20	5	58	4	2nd	70	9	64	16
Shamsi	25.4	2	91	3	(4)	11	0	37	1	3rd	115	13	64	24
Elgar	1	0	7	0						4th	119	40	92	25
										5th	119	48	117	32
SRI LANKA										6th	161	51	132	36
Herath	19	5	39	2		14	4	38	3	7th	164	115	134	58
Perera	23	8	46	4		14	4	32	6	8th	176	115	156	58
Sandakan	8	1	18	1		0.5	0	1	1	9th	224	123	163	67
Lakmal	4.3	0	21	3						10th	287	126	190	73

Umpires: R.R.Reiffel (*Australia*) (39) and R.J.Tucker (*Australia*) (62).
Referee: Sir R.B.Richardson (*West Indies*) (17). **Test No. 2311/26 (SL273/SA426)**

SRI LANKA v SOUTH AFRICA (2nd Test)

At Sinhalese Sports Club, Colombo, on 20, 21, 22, 23 July 2018.
Toss: Sri Lanka. Result: **SRI LANKA** won by 199 runs.
Debuts: None.

SRI LANKA

M.D.Gunathilleke	c Rabada b Maharaj	57	c Elgar b Maharaj	61
F.D.M.Karunaratne	c de Kock b Maharaj	53	c de Kock b Ngidi	85
D.M.de Silva	lbw b Maharaj	60	lbw b Maharaj	0
B.K.G.Mendis	c Rabada b Maharaj	21	run out	18
A.D.Mathews	c du Plessis b Maharaj	10	c du Plessis b Maharaj	71
A.R.S.Silva	b Rabada	22	not out	32
†D.P.D.N.Dickwella	c du Plessis b Maharaj	5	not out	7
M.D.K.Perera	c Ngidi b Maharaj	17		
M.K.P.A.D.Perera	not out	43		
*R.A.S.Lakmal	c Markram b Maharaj	0		
H.M.R.K.B.Herath	c Elgar b Maharaj	35		
Extras	(B 4, LB 2, NB 1, W 8)	15	(NB 1)	1
Total	**(104.1 overs; 458 mins)**	**338**	**(5 wkts dec; 81 overs; 327 mins)**	**275**

SOUTH AFRICA

A.K.Markram	lbw b Herath	7	(2) lbw b Herath	14
D.Elgar	c de Silva b M.K.P.A.D.Perera	0	(1) lbw b M.D.K.Perera	37
T.B.de Bruyn	c Dickwella b M.K.P.A.D.Perera	3	b Herath	101
H.M.Amla	c Mendis b M.D.K.Perera	19	b Herath	6
*F.du Plessis	c Dickwella b M.D.K.Perera	48	c Mathews b M.K.P.A.D.Perera	7
T.Bavuma	c Mendis b M.D.K.Perera	1	(7) c Dickwella b Herath	63
†Q.de Kock	lbw b M.K.P.A.D.Perera	32	(8) lbw b Herath	8
K.A.Maharaj	c Karunaratne b M.K.P.A.D.Perera	2	(6) lbw b M.K.P.A.D.Perera	0
K.Rabada	c Mathews b M.D.K.Perera	1	c Mathews b M.D.K.Perera	18
D.W.Steyn	lbw b M.K.P.A.D.Perera	0	c Gunathilleke b Herath	6
L.T.Ngidi	not out	0	not out	4
Extras	(NB 1)	1	(B 16, LB 5, NB 4, W 1)	26
Total	**(34.5 overs; 139 mins)**	**124**	**(86.5 overs; 324 mins)**	**290**

SOUTH AFRICA	O	M	R	W		O	M	R	W	FALL OF WICKETS				
											SL	SA	SL	SA
Steyn	17	3	60	0	(5)	11	2	30	0	*Wkt*	*1st*	*1st*	*2nd*	*2nd*
Rabada	20	3	55	1		8	0	42	0	1st	116	4	91	23
Ngidi	14.2	1	54	0	(6)	9	5	9	1	2nd	117	8	102	80
Maharaj	41.1	10	129	9	(1)	40	4	154	3	3rd	153	15	136	100
Markram	8.4	1	24	0	(3)	7	1	18	0	4th	169	70	199	113
Elgar	3	1	10	0	(7)	1	0	2	0	5th	223	85	263	113
De Bruyn					(4)	5	0	20	0	6th	238	114	–	236
										7th	247	119	–	246
SRI LANKA										8th	264	124	–	280
M.D.K.Perera	12.5	1	40	4	(2)	30	4	90	2	9th	264	124	–	280
M.K.P.A.D.Perera	13	2	52	5	(3)	19	2	67	2	10th	338	124	–	290
Herath	9	1	32	1	(1)	32.5	9	98	6					
Lakmal						2	0	8	0					
De Silva						2	0	5	0					
Gunathilleke						1	0	1	0					

Umpires: N.J.Llong (*England*) (53) and R.J.Tucker (*Australia*) (63).
Referee: Sir R.B.Richardson (*West Indies*) (18).   **Test No. 2312/27 (SL274/SA427)**

ENGLAND v INDIA (1st Test)

At Edgbaston, Birmingham, on 1, 2, 3, 4 August 2018.
Toss: England. Result: **ENGLAND** won by 31 runs.
Debuts: None.

ENGLAND

A.N.Cook	b Ashwin	13	b Ashwin	0
K.K.Jennings	b Shami	42	c Rahul b Ashwin	8
*J.E.Root	run out	80	c Rahul b Ashwin	14
D.J.Malan	lbw b Shami	8	c Rahane b Sharma	20
†J.M.Bairstow	b Yadav	70	c Dhawan b Sharma	28
B.A.Stokes	c and b Ashwin	21	c Kohli b Sharma	6
J.C.Buttler	lbw b Ashwin	0	c Karthik b Sharma	1
S.M.Curran	c Karthik b Shami	24	c Karthik b Yadav	63
A.U.Rashid	lbw b Sharma	13	b Yadav	16
S.C.J.Broad	lbw b Ashwin	1	c Dhawan b Sharma	11
J.M.Anderson	not out	2	not out	0
Extras	(B 9, LB 4)	13	(B 10, LB 2, NB 1)	13
Total	**(89.4 overs)**	**287**	**(53 overs)**	**180**

INDIA

M.Vijay	lbw b Curran	20	lbw b Broad	6
S.Dhawan	c Malan b Curran	26	c Bairstow b Broad	13
K.L.Rahul	b Curran	4	c Bairstow b Stokes	13
*V.Kohli	c Broad b Rashid	149	lbw b Stokes	51
A.M.Rahane	c Jennings b Stokes	15	c Bairstow b Curran	2
†K.D.Karthik	b Stokes	0	(7) c Malan b Anderson	20
H.H.Pandya	lbw b Curran	22	(8) c Cook b Stokes	31
R.Ashwin	b Anderson	10	(6) c Bairstow b Anderson	13
Mohammed Shami	c Malan b Anderson	2	c Bairstow b Stokes	0
I.Sharma	lbw b Rashid	5	lbw b Rashid	11
U.T.Yadav	not out	1	not out	0
Extras	(B 4, LB 11, NB 4, W 1)	20	(B 1, LB 1)	2
Total	**(76 overs)**	**274**	**(54.2 overs)**	**162**

INDIA	O	M	R	W		O	M	R	W	FALL OF WICKETS				
Yadav	17	2	56	1	(4)	7	1	20	2		E	I	E	I
Sharma	17	1	46	1	(3)	13	0	51	5	*Wkt*	*1st*	*1st*	*2nd*	*2nd*
Ashwin	26	7	62	4	(2)	21	4	59	3	1st	26	50	9	19
Mohammed Shami	19.4	2	64	3	(1)	12	2	38	0	2nd	98	54	18	22
Pandya	10	1	46	0						3rd	112	59	39	46
										4th	216	100	70	63
ENGLAND										5th	223	100	85	78
Anderson	22	7	41	2		16	2	50	2	6th	224	148	86	112
Broad	10	2	40	0		14	2	43	2	7th	243	169	87	141
Curran	17	1	74	4	(4)	6	0	18	1	8th	278	182	135	141
Rashid	8	0	31	2	(5)	4	1	9	1	9th	283	217	176	154
Stokes	19	4	73	4	(3)	14.2	2	40	4	10th	287	274	180	162

Umpires: Alim Dar (*Pakistan*) (120) and C.B.Gaffaney (*New Zealand*) (21).
Referee: J.J.Crowe (*New Zealand*) (90).
Test No. 2313/118 (E1000/I523)

ENGLAND v INDIA (2nd Test)

At Lord's, London, on 9 (*no play*), 10, 11, 12 August 2018.
Toss: England. Result: **ENGLAND** won by an innings and 159 runs.
Debut: England – O.J.D.Pope.

INDIA

M.Vijay	b Anderson	0	c Bairstow b Anderson		0
K.L.Rahul	c Bairstow b Anderson	8	lbw b Anderson		10
C.A.Pujara	run out	1	b Broad		17
*V.Kohli	c Buttler b Woakes	23	(5) c Pope b Broad		17
A.M.Rahane	c Cook b Anderson	18	(4) c Jennings b Broad		13
H.H.Pandya	c Buttler b Woakes	11	lbw b Woakes		26
†K.D.Karthik	b Curran	1	lbw b Broad		0
R.Ashwin	lbw b Broad	29	not out		33
Kuldeep Yadav	lbw b Anderson	0	b Anderson		0
Mohammed Shami	not out	10	lbw b Anderson		0
I.Sharma	lbw b Anderson	0	c Pope b Woakes		2
Extras	(LB 5, NB 1)	6	(B 6, LB 6)		12
Total	**(35.2 overs)**	**107**	**(47 overs)**		**130**

ENGLAND

A.N.Cook	c Karthik b Sharma	21
K.K.Jennings	lbw b Shami	11
*J.E.Root	lbw b Shami	19
O.J.D.Pope	lbw b Pandya	28
†J.M.Bairstow	c Karthik b Pandya	93
J.C.Buttler	lbw b Shami	24
C.R.Woakes	not out	137
S.M.Curran	c Shami b Pandya	40
A.U.Rashid		
S.C.J.Broad		
J.M.Anderson		
Extras	(B 11, LB 10, NB 1, W 1)	23
Total	**(7 wkts dec; 88.1 overs)**	**396**

ENGLAND	O	M	R	W		O	M	R	W	FALL OF WICKETS			
											I	E	I
Anderson	13.2	5	20	5		12	5	23	4		*1st*	*1st*	*2nd*
Broad	10	2	37	1		16	6	44	4	*Wkt*			
Woakes	6	2	19	2		4	2	24	2	1st	0	28	0
Curran	6	0	26	1		9	1	27	0	2nd	10	32	13
										3rd	15	77	35
INDIA										4th	49	89	50
Sharma	22	4	101	1						5th	61	131	61
Mohammed Shami	23	4	96	3						6th	62	320	61
Kuldeep Yadav	9	1	44	0						7th	84	396	116
Pandya	17.1	0	66	3						8th	96	–	121
Ashwin	17	1	68	0						9th	96	–	125
										10th	107	–	130

Umpires: Alim Dar (*Pakistan*) (121) and M.Erasmus (*South Africa*) (50).
Referee: J.J.Crowe (*New Zealand*) (91).   Test No. 2314/119 (E1001/I524)

ENGLAND v INDIA (3rd Test)

At Trent Bridge, Nottingham, on 18, 19, 20, 21, 22 August 2018.
Toss: England. Result: **INDIA** won by 203 runs.
Debut: India – R.R.Pant.

INDIA

S.Dhawan	c Buttler b Woakes	35	st Bairstow b Rashid		44
K.L.Rahul	lbw b Woakes	23	b Stokes		36
C.A.Pujara	c Rashid b Woakes	14	c Cook b Stokes		72
*V.Kohli	c Stokes b Rashid	97	lbw b Woakes		103
A.M.Rahane	c Cook b Broad	81	b Rashid		29
H.H.Pandya	c Buttler b Anderson	18	not out	(7)	52
†R.R.Pant	b Broad	24	c Cook b Anderson	(6)	1
R.Ashwin	b Broad	14	not out	(9)	1
I.Sharma	not out	1			
Mohammed Shami	c Broad b Anderson	3	c Cook b Rashid	(8)	3
J.J.Bumrah	b Anderson	0			
Extras	(B 12, LB 6, W 1)	19	(B 1, LB 9, W 1)		11
Total	(94.5 overs)	329	(7 wkts dec; 110 overs)		352

ENGLAND

A.N.Cook	c Pant b Sharma	29	c Rahul b Sharma		17
K.K.Jennings	c Pant b Bumrah	20	c Pant b Rahul		13
*J.E.Root	c Rahul b Pandya	16	c Rahul b Bumrah		13
O.J.D.Pope	c Pant b Sharma	10	c Kohli b Shami		16
†J.M.Bairstow	c Rahul b Pandya	15	b Bumrah	(7)	0
B.A.Stokes	c Rahul b Shami	62	c Rahul b Pandya	(5)	62
J.C.Buttler	c sub (S.N.Thakur) b Bumrah	39	lbw b Bumrah	(6)	106
C.R.Woakes	c Pant b Pandya	8	c Pant b Bumrah		4
A.U.Rashid	c Pant b Pandya	5	not out		33
S.C.J.Broad	lbw b Pandya	0	c Rahul b Bumrah		20
J.M.Anderson	not out	0	c Rahane b Ashwin		11
Extras	(B 4, LB 1, NB 2, W 1)	8	(B 2, LB 16, NB 4)		22
Total	(38.2 overs)	161	(104.5 overs)		317

ENGLAND	O	M	R	W		O	M	R	W	FALL OF WICKETS				
Anderson	25.5	8	64	3		22	7	55	1		I	E	I	E
Broad	25	8	72	3		16	3	60	0	*Wkt*	*1st*	*1st*	*2nd*	*2nd*
Stokes	15	1	54	0	(4)	20	3	68	2	1st	60	54	60	27
Woakes	20	2	75	3	(3)	22	4	49	1	2nd	65	54	111	32
Rashid	9	0	46	1		27	2	101	3	3rd	82	75	224	62
Root						3	0	9	0	4th	241	86	281	62
										5th	279	108	282	231
INDIA										6th	307	110	329	231
Mohammed Shami	10	2	56	1	(4)	19	3	78	1	7th	323	118	349	241
Bumrah	12.2	2	37	2	(1)	29	8	85	5	8th	326	128	–	241
Ashwin	1	0	3	0		22.5	8	44	1	9th	329	128	–	291
Sharma	9	2	32	2	(2)	20	4	70	2	10th	329	161	–	317
Pandya	6	1	28	5		14	5	22	1					

Umpires: M.Erasmus (*South Africa*) (51) and C.B.Gaffaney (*New Zealand*) (22).
Referee: J.J.Crowe (*New Zealand*) (92).   Test No. 2315/120 (E1002/I525)

ENGLAND v INDIA (4th Test)

At The Rose Bowl, Southampton, on 30, 31 August, 1, 2 September 2018.
Toss: England. Result: **ENGLAND** won by 60 runs.
Debuts: None.

ENGLAND

A.N.Cook	c Kohli b Pandya	17	c Rahul b Bumrah		12
K.K.Jennings	lbw b Bumrah	0	lbw b Shami		36
*J.E.Root	c b Sharma	4	(4) run out		48
J.M.Bairstow	c Pant b Bumrah	6	(5) b Shami		0
B.A.Stokes	lbw b Shami	23	(6) c Rahane b Ashwin		30
†J.C.Buttler	c Kohli b Shami	21	(7) lbw b Sharma		69
M.M.Ali	c Bumrah b Ashwin	40	(3) c Rahul b Sharma		9
S.M.Curran	b Ashwin	78	run out		46
A.U.Rashid	lbw b Sharma	6	c Pant b Shami		11
S.C.J.Broad	lbw b Bumrah	17	c Pant b Shami		0
J.M.Anderson	not out	0	not out		1
Extras	(B 23, LB 9, NB 2)	34	(B 7, LB 2)		9
Total	**(76.4 overs)**	**246**	**(96.1 overs)**		**271**

INDIA

S.Dhawan	c Buttler b Broad	23	c Stokes b Anderson		17
K.L.Rahul	lbw b Broad	19	b Broad		0
C.A.Pujara	not out	132	lbw b Anderson		5
*V.Kohli	c Cook b Curran	46	c Cook b Ali		58
A.M.Rahane	lbw b Stokes	11	lbw b Ali		51
†R.R.Pant	lbw b Ali	0	(7) c Cook b Ali		18
H.H.Pandya	c Root b Ali	4	(6) c Root b Stokes		0
R.Ashwin	b Ali	1	lbw b Curran		25
Mohammed Shami	b Ali	0	(10) c Anderson b Ali		8
I.Sharma	c Cook b Ali	14	(9) lbw b Stokes		0
J.J.Bumrah	c Cook b Broad	6	not out		0
Extras	(B 9, LB 1, NB 3, W 4)	17	(LB 1, W 1)		2
Total	**(84.5 overs)**	**273**	**(69.4 overs)**		**184**

INDIA	O	M	R	W		O	M	R	W
Bumrah	20	5	46	3	(2)	19	3	51	1
Sharma	16	6	26	2	(3)	15	4	36	2
Pandya	8	0	51	1	(5)	9	0	34	0
Mohammed Shami	18	2	51	2		16	0	57	4
Ashwin	14.4	3	40	2	(1)	37.1	7	84	1
ENGLAND									
Anderson	18	2	50	0		11	2	33	2
Broad	18.5	5	63	3		10	2	23	1
Curran	16	4	41	0	(5)	3.4	2	1	1
Jennings	2	0	4	0					
Rashid	7	0	19	0	(6)	7	3	21	0
Ali	16	1	63	5	(3)	26	3	71	4
Stokes	7	1	23	1	(4)	12	3	34	2

FALL OF WICKETS

	E	I	E	I
Wkt	1st	1st	2nd	2nd
1st	1	37	24	4
2nd	15	50	33	17
3rd	28	142	92	123
4th	36	161	92	123
5th	69	181	122	127
6th	86	189	178	150
7th	167	195	233	153
8th	177	195	260	154
9th	240	227	260	163
10th	246	273	271	184

Umpires: H.D.P.K.Dharmasena (*Sri Lanka*) (54) and B.N.J.Oxenford (*Australia*) (50).
Referee: A.J.Pycroft (*Zimbabwe*) (61).   **Test No. 2316/121 (E1003/I526)**

ENGLAND v INDIA (5th Test)

At The Oval, London, on 7, 8, 9, 10, 11 September 2018.
Toss: England. Result: **ENGLAND** won by 118 runs.
Debut: India – G.H.Vihari.

ENGLAND

A.N.Cook	b Bumrah	71	c Pant b Vihari		147
K.K.Jennings	c Rahul b Jadeja	23	b Shami		10
M.M.Ali	c Pant b Sharma	50	b Jadeja		24
*J.E.Root	lbw b Bumrah	0	c sub (H.H.Pandya) b Vihari		125
†J.M.Bairstow	c Pant b Sharma	0	b Shami		18
B.A.Stokes	lbw b Jadeja	11	c Rahul b Jadeja		37
J.C.Buttler	c Rahane b Jadeja	89	c Shami b Jadeja		0
S.M.Curran	c Pant b Sharma	0	c Pant b Vihari		21
A.U.Rashid	lbw b Bumrah	15	not out		20
S.C.J.Broad	c Rahul b Jadeja	38			
J.M.Anderson	not out	0			
Extras	(B 26, LB 9)	35	(B 14, LB 4, W 2, Pen 5)		25
Total	**(122 overs)**	**332**	**(8 wkts dec; 112.3 overs)**		**423**

INDIA

K.L.Rahul	b Curran	37	b Rashid		149
S.Dhawan	lbw b Broad	3	lbw b Anderson		1
C.A.Pujara	c Bairstow b Anderson	37	lbw b Anderson		0
*V.Kohli	c Root b Stokes	49	c Bairstow b Broad		0
A.M.Rahane	c Cook b Anderson	0	c Jennings b Ali		37
G.H.Vihari	c Bairstow b Ali	56	c Bairstow b Stokes		0
†R.R.Pant	c Cook b Stokes	5	c Ali b Rashid		114
R.A.Jadeja	not out	86	c Bairstow b Curran		13
I.Sharma	c Bairstow b Ali	4	c Bairstow b Curran		5
Mohammed Shami	c Broad b Rashid	1	b Anderson		0
J.J.Bumrah	run out	0	not out		0
Extras	(B 4, LB 10)	14	(B 10, LB 16)		26
Total	**(95 overs)**	**292**	**(94.3 overs)**		**345**

INDIA	O	M	R	W		O	M	R	W		FALL OF WICKETS				
												E	I	E	I
Bumrah	30	9	83	3		23	4	61	0		Wkt	1st	1st	2nd	2nd
Sharma	31	12	62	3		8	3	13	0		1st	60	6	27	1
Vihari	1	0	1	0	(5)	9.3	1	37	3		2nd	133	70	62	1
Mohammed Shami	30	7	72	0	(3)	25	3	110	2		3rd	133	101	321	2
Jadeja	30	0	79	4	(4)	47	3	179	3		4th	134	103	321	120
											5th	171	154	355	121
ENGLAND											6th	177	160	356	325
Anderson	21	7	54	2		22.3	11	45	3		7th	181	237	397	328
Broad	20	6	50	1		12	1	43	1		8th	214	249	423	336
Stokes	16	2	56	2	(5)	13	1	60	1		9th	312	260	–	345
Curran	11	1	49	1		9	2	23	2		10th	332	292	–	345
Ali	17	3	50	1	(3)	17	2	68	1						
Rashid	10	2	19	1		15	2	63	2						
Root						6	1	17	0						

Umpires: H.D.P.K.Dharmasena (*Sri Lanka*) (55) and J.S.Wilson (*West Indies*) (11).
Referee: A.J.Pycroft (*Zimbabwe*) (62).　　　　Test No. 2317/122 (E1004/1527)

INDIA v WEST INDIES (1st Test)

At Saurashtra CA Stadium, Rajkot, on 4, 5, 6 October 2018.
Toss: India. Result: **INDIA** won by an innings and 272 runs.
Debuts: India – P.P.Shaw; West Indies – S.H.Lewis.

INDIA

P.P.Shaw	c and b Bishoo	134
K.L.Rahul	lbw b Gabriel	0
C.A.Pujara	c Dowrich b Lewis	86
*V.Kohli	c Bishoo b Lewis	139
A.M.Rahane	c Dowrich b Chase	41
†R.R.Pant	c Paul b Bishoo	92
R.A.Jadeja	not out	100
R.Ashwin	c Dowrich b Bishoo	7
Kuldeep Yadav	lbw b Bishoo	12
U.T.Yadav	c Lewis b Brathwaite	22
Mohammed Shami	not out	2
Extras	(B 9, LB 1, NB 4)	14
Total	**(9 wkts dec; 149.5 overs)**	**649**

WEST INDIES

*K.C.Brathwaite	b Shami	2	c Shaw b Ashwin	10
K.O.A.Powell	lbw b Shami	1	c Shaw b Kuldeep	83
S.D.Hope	b Ashwin	10	lbw b Kuldeep	17
S.O.Hetmyer	run out	10	c Rahul b Kuldeep	11
S.W.Ambris	c Rahane b Jadeja	12	st Pant b Kuldeep	0
R.L.Chase	b Ashwin	53	c Ashwin b Kuldeep	20
†S.O.Dowrich	b Kuldeep	10	not out	16
K.M.A.Paul	c Pujara b Yadav	47	c Yadav b Jadeja	15
D.Bishoo	not out	17	c Pant b Ashwin	9
S.H.Lewis	b Ashwin	0	lbw b Jadeja	4
S.T.Gabriel	st Pant b Ashwin	1	c Kuldeep b Jadeja	4
Extras	(B 16, LB 2)	18	(B 5, LB 1, NB 1)	7
Total	**(48 overs; 200mins)**	**181**	**(50.5 overs; 173 mins)**	**196**

WEST INDIES	O	M	R	W		O	M	R	W
Gabriel	21	1	84	1					
Paul	15	1	61	0					
Lewis	20	0	93	2					
Bishoo	54	3	217	4					
Chase	26	1	137	1					
Brathwaite	13.5	1	47	1					
INDIA									
Mohammed Shami	9	2	22	2		3	0	11	0
Yadav	11	3	20	1	(3)	3	0	16	0
Ashwin	11	2	37	4	(2)	18	2	71	2
Jadeja	7	1	22	1	(5)	12.5	1	35	3
Kuldeep Yadav	11	1	62	1	(4)	14	2	57	5

FALL OF WICKETS			
	I	WI	WI
Wkt	1st	1st	2nd
1st	3	2	32
2nd	209	7	79
3rd	232	21	97
4th	337	32	138
5th	470	49	138
6th	534	74	151
7th	545	147	172
8th	571	159	185
9th	626	159	192
10th	–	181	196

Umpires: I.J.Gould (*England*) (68) and N.J.Llong (*England*) (54).
Referee: B.C.Broad (*England*) (97).   **Test No. 2318/95 (I528/WI536)**

INDIA v WEST INDIES (2nd Test)

At Rajiv Gandhi International Stadium, Hyderabad, on 12, 13, 14 October 2018.
Toss: West Indies. Result: **INDIA** won by ten wickets.
Debut: India – S.N.Thakur.

WEST INDIES

K.C.Brathwaite	lbw b Kuldeep	14	c Pant b Yadav		0
K.O.A.Powell	c Jadeja b Ashwin	22	c Rahane b Ashwin		0
S.D.Hope	lbw b Yadav	36	c Rahane b Jadeja		28
S.O.Hetmyer	lbw b Kuldeep	12	c Pujara b Kuldeep		17
S.W.Ambris	c Jadeja b Kuldeep	18	lbw b Jadeja		38
R.L.Chase	b Yadav	106	b Yadav		6
†S.O.Dowrich	lbw b Yadav	30	b Yadav		0
*J.O.Holder	c Pant b Yadav	52	c Pant b Jadeja		19
D.Bishoo	b Yadav	2	not out		10
J.A.Warrican	not out	8	b Ashwin		7
S.T.Gabriel	c Pant b Yadav	0	b Yadav		1
Extras	(B 4, LB 7)	11	(LB 1)		1
Total	(101.4 overs; 388 mins)	311	(46.1 overs; 197 mins)		127

INDIA

K.L.Rahul	b Holder	4	(2) not out		33
P.P.Shaw	c Hetmyer b Warrican	70	(1) not out		33
C.A.Pujara	c sub (J.N.Hamilton) b Gabriel	10			
*V.Kohli	lbw b Holder	45			
A.M.Rahane	c Hope b Holder	80			
†R.R.Pant	c Hetmyer b Gabriel	92			
R.A.Jadeja	lbw b Holder	0			
R.Ashwin	b Gabriel	35			
Kuldeep Yadav	b Holder	6			
U.T.Yadav	c sub (J.N.Hamilton) b Warrican	2			
S.N.Thakur	not out	4			
Extras	(B 12, LB 2, NB 5)	19	(B 6, LB 2, NB 1)		9
Total	(106.4 overs; 487 mins)	367	(0 wkts; 16.1 overs; 65 mins)		75

INDIA	O	M	R	W		O	M	R	W		FALL OF WICKETS			
Yadav	26.4	3	88	6		12.1	3	45	4			WI	I	WI	I
Thakur	1.4	0	9	0							Wkt	1st	1st	2nd	2nd
Ashwin	24.2	7	49	1	(2)	10	4	24	2		1st	32	61	0	–
Kuldeep Yadav	29	2	85	3	(3)	13	1	45	1		2nd	52	98	6	–
Jadeja	20	2	69	0	(4)	11	5	12	3		3rd	86	102	45	–
											4th	92	162	45	–
WEST INDIES											5th	113	314	68	–
Gabriel	20.4	1	107	3							6th	182	314	70	–
Holder	23	5	56	5	(1)	4	0	17	0		7th	286	322	108	–
Warrican	31	7	84	2	(2)	4	0	17	0		8th	296	334	109	–
Chase	9	1	22	0		4	0	14	0		9th	311	339	126	–
Bishoo	21	4	78	0	(3)	4.1	0	19	0		10th	311	367	127	–
Brathwaite	2	0	6	0											

Umpires: I.J.Gould (*England*) (69) and B.N.J.Oxenford (*Australia*) (51).
Referee: B.C.Broad (*England*) (98). **Test No. 2319/96 (I529/WI537)**

PAKISTAN v AUSTRALIA (1st Test)

At Dubai Sports City, on 7, 8, 9, 10, 11 October 2018.
Toss: Pakistan. Result: **MATCH DRAWN**.
Debuts: Pakistan – Bilal Asif; Australia – A.J.Finch, T.M.Head, M.Labuschagne.

PAKISTAN

Batsman	1st innings		2nd innings	
Imam-ul-Haq	c Paine b Lyon	76	c and b Holland	48
Mohammad Hafeez	lbw b Siddle	126	c Labuschagne b Holland	17
Azhar Ali	c Starc b Holland	18	(4) lbw b Holland	4
Haris Sohail	c Paine b Lyon	110	(5) lbw b Labuschagne	39
Mohammad Abbas	b Siddle	1		
Asad Shafiq	c Paine b Labuschagne	80	c M.R.Marsh b Lyon	41
Babar Azam	run out	4	not out	28
†*Sarfraz Ahmed	run out	15		
Bilal Asif	b Siddle	12	(3) c Head b Lyon	0
Wahab Riaz	not out	7		
Yasir Shah	c Paine b Starc	3		
Extras	(B 6, LB 21, NB 3)	30	(B 2, LB 2)	4
Total	(164.2 overs)	482	(6 wkts dec; 57.5 overs)	181

AUSTRALIA

Batsman	1st innings		2nd innings	
U.T.Khawaja	c Imam b Asif	85	(2) lbw b Shah	141
A.J.Finch	c Shafiq b Abbas	62	(1) lbw b Abbas	49
S.E.Marsh	c Shafiq b Asif	7	c Ahmed b Abbas	0
M.R.Marsh	lbw b Abbas	12	lbw b Abbas	0
T.M.Head	c Sohail b Asif	0	lbw b Hafeez	72
M.Labuschagne	c Imam b Asif	0	lbw b Shah	13
†*T.D.Paine	c Imam b Asif	7	not out	61
M.A.Starc	c Ahmed b Abbas	0	c Azam b Shah	1
P.M.Siddle	b Abbas	0	lbw b Shah	0
N.M.Lyon	c Imam b Asif	6	not out	5
J.M.Holland	not out	0		
Extras	(B 6, LB 7)	13	(B 13, LB 4, NB 3)	20
Total	(83.3 overs)	202	(8 wkts; 139.5 overs)	362

AUSTRALIA	O	M	R	W		O	M	R	W
Starc	36.2	11	90	1		6	1	18	0
Siddle	29	11	58	3	(3)	2	1	3	0
Lyon	52	12	114	2	(2)	25.5	6	58	2
Holland	29	1	126	1		20	3	83	3
Labuschagne	8	0	29	1	(6)	3	0	9	1
M.R.Marsh	10	0	38	0					
Head					(5)	6	0	6	0

PAKISTAN	O	M	R	W		O	M	R	W
Mohammad Abbas	19	9	29	4		27	7	56	3
Wahab Riaz	11	2	39	0	(4)	16	3	42	0
Yasir Shah	28	6	80	0		43.5	9	114	4
Mohammad Hafeez	3	1	2	0	(2)	6	0	29	1
Bilal Asif	21.3	7	36	6		37	8	87	0
Azhar Ali	1	0	3	0					
Haris Sohail					(6)	9	1	16	0
Asad Shafiq					(7)	1	0	1	0

FALL OF WICKETS

	P	A	P	A
Wkt	1st	1st	2nd	2nd
1st	205	142	37	87
2nd	222	160	38	87
3rd	244	167	45	87
4th	260	171	110	219
5th	410	171	110	252
6th	418	183	181	331
7th	456	183	–	333
8th	470	191	–	333
9th	473	202	–	
10th	482	202	–	

Umpires: R.K.Illingworth (*England*) (36) and R.A.Kettleborough (*England*) (54).
Referee: R.S.Madugalle (*Sri Lanka*) (182).   **Test No. 2320/63 (P416/A813)**

PAKISTAN v AUSTRALIA (2nd Test)

At Sheikh Zayed Stadium, Abu Dhabi, on 16, 17, 18, 19 October 2018.
Toss: Pakistan. Result: **PAKISTAN** won by 373 runs.
Debuts: Pakistan – Fakhar Zaman, Mir Hamza.   ‡ (Mohammad Rizwan)

PAKISTAN

Fakhar Zaman	lbw b Labuschagne	94	c and b Lyon	66
Mohammad Hafeez	c Labuschagne b Starc	4	c Head b Starc	6
Azhar Ali	c and b Lyon	15	run out	64
Haris Sohail	c Head b Lyon	0	st Paine b Lyon	17
Asad Shafiq	c Labuschagne b Lyon	0	c sub (A.C.Agar) b Labuschagne	44
Babar Azam	b Lyon	0	lbw b M.R.Marsh	99
†*Sarfraz Ahmed	c Siddle b Labuschagne	94	lbw b Labuschagne	81
Bilal Asif	c Paine b Labuschagne	12	c Head b Lyon	15
Yasir Shah	b M.R.Marsh	28	lbw b Lyon	4
Mohammad Abbas	b Starc	10	not out	0
Mir Hamza	not out	4	not out	0
Extras	(B 11, LB 6, NB 4)	21	(LB 2, NB 2)	4
Total	**(81 overs)**	**282**	**(9 wkts dec; 120 overs)**	**400**

AUSTRALIA

U.T.Khawaja	c Ahmed b Abbas	3	absent hurt	
A.J.Finch	c Zaman b Asif	39	(1) lbw b Abbas	31
P.M.Siddle	lbw b Abbas	4	(8) lbw b Shah	3
S.E.Marsh	c Sohail b Abbas	3	(2) b Hamza	4
T.M.Head	c Shafiq b Abbas	14	(3) c sub‡ b Abbas	36
M.R.Marsh	c Shafiq b Shah	13	(4) lbw b Abbas	5
M.Labuschagne	run out	25	(5) c sub‡ b Abbas	43
†*T.D.Paine	lbw b Asif	3	(6) b Abbas	0
M.A.Starc	lbw b Abbas	34	(7) lbw b Shah	28
N.M.Lyon	b Asif	2	(9) not out	6
J.M.Holland	not out	3	(10) c Sohail b Shah	3
Extras	(LB 3)	3	(LB 5)	5
Total	**(50.4 overs)**	**145**	**(49.4 overs)**	**164**

AUSTRALIA	O	M	R	W		O	M	R	W
Starc	12	3	37	2		7	0	32	1
Siddle	10	3	39	0		23	4	68	0
M.R.Marsh	7	2	21	1	(6)	13	3	39	1
Lyon	27	5	78	4	(3)	43	8	135	4
Holland	13	3	45	0	(4)	16	3	46	0
Labuschagne	12	2	45	3	(5)	16	1	74	2
Head						2	0	4	0

PAKISTAN	O	M	R	W	O	M	R	W
Mohammad Abbas	12.4	4	33	5	17	2	62	5
Mir Hamza	9	2	27	0	6	0	40	1
Yasir Shah	19	3	59	1	21.4	5	45	3
Bilal Asif	10	3	23	3	5	2	12	0

FALL OF WICKETS

Wkt	P 1st	A 1st	P 2nd	A 2nd
1st	5	16	15	10
2nd	57	20	106	71
3rd	57	36	154	77
4th	57	56	160	78
5th	57	75	235	78
6th	204	85	368	145
7th	226	91	390	151
8th	247	128	394	155
9th	264	132	400	164
10th	282	145	—	—

Umpires: R.K.Illingworth (*England*) (37) and S.Ravi (*India*) (28).
Referee: R.S.Madugalle (*Sri Lanka*) (183).   Test No. 2321/64 (P417/A814)

BANGLADESH v ZIMBABWE (1st Test)

At Sylhet International Cricket Stadium, on 3, 4, 5, 6 November 2018.
Toss: Zimbabwe. Result: **ZIMBABWE** won by 151 runs.
Debuts: Bangladesh – Ariful Haque, Nazmul Islam; Zimbabwe – W.P.Masakadza,
B.A.Mavuta.   ‡(C.R.Ervine)

ZIMBABWE

*H.Masakadza	lbw b Abu	52	lbw b Mehedi		48
B.B.Chari	b Taijul	13	b Mehedi		4
B.R.M.Taylor	c Nazmul Hossain b Taijul	6	c Imrul b Taijul		24
S.C.Williams	c Mehedi b Mahmudullah	88	b Taijul		20
Sikandar Raza	b Nazmul Islam	19	b Taijul		25
P.J.Moor	not out	63	c Liton b Taijul		0
†R.W.Chakabva	c Nazmul Hossain b Taijul	28	c Mahmudullah b Nazmul Islam		20
W.P.Masakadza	c Mushfiqur b Taijul	4	lbw b Mehedi		17
B.A.Mavuta	lbw b Nazmul Islam	3	c Ariful b Nazmul Islam		6
K.M.Jarvis	c Mehedi b Taijul	4	not out		1
T.L.Chatara	c Liton b Taijul	0	lbw b Taijul		8
Extras	(B 1, LB 1)	2	(B 4, LB 4)		8
Total	**(117.3 overs)**	**282**	**(65.4 overs)**		**181**

BANGLADESH

Liton Das	c Chakabva b Jarvis	9	lbw b Sikandar Raza		23
Imrul Kayes	b Chatara	5	b Sikandar Raza		43
Mominul Haque	c H.Masakadza b Sikandar Raza	11	b Jarvis		9
Nazmul Hossain	c Chakabva b Chatara	5	(5) c Sikandar Raza b Mavuta		13
*Mahmudullah	b Chatara	0	(4) c sub‡ b Sikandar Raza		16
†Mushfiqur Rahim	c Chakabva b Jarvis	31	c W.P.Masakadza b Mavuta		13
Ariful Haque	not out	41	c Chakabva b W.P.Masakadza		38
Mehedi Hasan	c and b Williams	21	c Chakabva b Mavuta		7
Taijul Islam	c Chakabva b Sikandar Raza	8	c Taylor b W.P.Masakadza		0
Nazmul Islam	c Chari b Sikandar Raza	4	lbw b Mavuta		0
Abu Jayed	run out	0	not out		0
Extras	(B 7, LB 1)	8	(B 5, LB 2)		7
Total	**(51 overs)**	**143**	**(63.1 overs)**		**169**

BANGLADESH	O	M	R	W		O	M	R	W
Abu Jayed	21	3	68	1	(3)	7	1	25	0
Taijul Islam	39.3	7	108	6	(1)	28.4	8	62	5
Ariful Haque	4	1	7	0					
Mehedi Hasan	27	8	45	0		19	7	48	3
Nazmul Islam	23	6	49	2	(2)	6	1	27	2
Mahmudullah	3	0	3	1	(4)	1	1	7	0
Mominul Haque					(6)	1	0	4	0

ZIMBABWE	O	M	R	W		O	M	R	W
Jarvis	11	2	28	2		14	5	29	1
Chatara	10	4	19	3		9	2	25	0
Mavuta	6	0	27	0	(5)	10	2	21	4
Sikandar Raza	12	2	35	3	(3)	17	1	41	3
W.P.Masakadza	8	2	21	0	(6)	5.1	0	33	2
Williams	4	0	5	1	(4)	8	2	13	0

FALL OF WICKETS

	Z	B	Z	B
Wkt	1st	1st	2nd	2nd
1st	35	8	19	56
2nd	47	14	47	67
3rd	85	19	101	83
4th	129	19	121	102
5th	201	49	121	111
6th	261	78	130	132
7th	268	108	165	150
8th	273	131	172	151
9th	282	143	173	155
10th	282	143	181	169

Umpires: R.A.Kettleborough (*England*) (55) and R.J.Tucker (*Australia*) (64).
Referee: R.S.Madugalle (*Sri Lanka*) (184).   **Test No. 2322/15 (B109/Z106)**

BANGLADESH v ZIMBABWE (2nd Test)

At Shere Bangla National Stadium, Mirpur, Dhaka, on 11, 12, 13, 14, 15 November 2018.
Toss: Bangladesh. Result: **BANGLADESH** won by 218 runs.
Debuts: Bangladesh – Mithun Ali, Khaled Ahmed.

BANGLADESH

Batsman	1st innings		2nd innings	
Liton Das	c Mavuta b Jarvis	9	b Jarvis	6
Imrul Kayes	c Chakabva b Jarvis	0	c Mavuta b Jarvis	3
Mominul Haque	c Chari b Chatara	161	c Chakabva b Tiripano	1
Mithun Ali	c Taylor b Tiripano	0	c Chakabva b Sikandar Raza	67
†Mushfiqur Rahim	not out	219	c Mavuta b Tiripano	7
Taijul Islam	c Chakabva b Jarvis	4		
*Mahmudullah	c Chakabva b Jarvis	36	(6) not out	101
Ariful Haque	c Chari b Jarvis	4	(7) b Williams	5
Mehedi Hasan	not out	68	(8) not out	27
Mustafizur Rahman				
Khaled Ahmed				
Extras	(B 9, LB 8, NB 3, W 1)	21	(B 5, LB 1, W 1)	7
Total	**(7 wkts dec; 160 overs)**	**522**	**(6 wkts dec; 54 overs)**	**224**

ZIMBABWE

Batsman	1st innings		2nd innings	
*H.Masakadza	c Mehedi b Taijul	14	c Mominul b Mehedi	25
B.B.Chari	c Mominul b Mehedi	53	lbw b Taijul	43
D.T.Tiripano	c Mehedi b Taijul	8	(8) c Liton b Mehedi	0
B.R.M.Taylor	c Taijul b Mehedi	110	(3) not out	106
S.C.Williams	b Taijul	11	(4) b Mustafizur	13
Sikandar Raza	b Taijul	0	(5) c and b Taijul	12
P.J.Moor	lbw b Ariful	83	(6) c Imrul b Mehedi	13
†R.W.Chakabva	c Mominul b Taijul	10	(7) run out	2
B.A.Mavuta	c Ariful b Mehedi	0	c Taijul b Mehedi	0
K.M.Jarvis	not out	9	c Khaled b Mehedi	1
T.L.Chatara	absent hurt		absent hurt	
Extras	(B 5, LB 1)	6	(B 1, LB 3, W 5)	9
Total	**(105.3 overs)**	**304**	**(83.1 overs)**	**224**

ZIMBABWE	O	M	R	W		O	M	R	W
Jarvis	28	6	71	5		11	2	27	2
Chatara	22.2	12	34	1					
Tiripano	24.4	6	65	1	(2)	11	1	31	2
Sikandar Raza	22	1	111	0		7	0	39	1
Williams	30	4	80	0	(3)	16	2	69	1
Mavuta	31	3	137	0	(5)	9	0	52	0
Masakadza	2	0	7	0					
BANGLADESH									
Mustafizur Rahman	21	8	58	0		10	2	19	1
Khaled Ahmed	18	7	48	0	(3)	12	4	45	0
Taijul Islam	40.3	10	107	5	(2)	37	5	93	2
Mehedi Hasan	20	3	61	3		18.1	5	38	5
Mahmudullah	2	0	14	0	(6)	1	0	1	0
Ariful Haque	4	2	10	1	(5)	3	1	7	0
Mominul Haque						2	0	17	0

FALL OF WICKETS

	B	Z	B	Z
Wkt	1st	1st	2nd	2nd
1st	13	20	9	68
2nd	16	40	10	70
3rd	26	96	10	99
4th	292	129	25	120
5th	299	131	143	186
6th	372	270	151	199
7th	378	290	–	201
8th	–	290	–	213
9th	–	304	–	224
10th	–	–	–	–

Umpires: H.D.P.K.Dharmasena (*Sri Lanka*) (56) and R.A.Kettleborough (*England*) (56).
Referee: R.S.Madugalle (*Sri Lanka*) (185). Test No. 2323/16 (B110/Z107)

SRI LANKA v ENGLAND (1st Test)

At Galle International Stadium, on 6, 7, 8, 9 November 2018.
Toss: England. Result: **ENGLAND** won by 211 runs.
Debuts: England – R.J.Burns, B.T.Foakes.

ENGLAND

R.J.Burns	c Dickwella b Lakmal	9	run out		23
K.K.Jennings	b M.D.K.Perera	46	not out		146
M.M.Ali	b Lakmal	0	c Herath b M.D.K.Perera		3
*J.E.Root	b Herath	35	c Dickwella b Herath		3
B.A.Stokes	b M.D.K.Perera	7	b M.D.K.Perera		62
J.C.Buttler	c Dickwella b M.D.K.Perera	38	c Silva b Herath		35
†B.T.Foakes	c de Silva b Lakmal	107	c Mendis b M.K.P.A.D.Perera		37
S.M.Curran	c Chandimal b M.K.P.A.D.Perera	48	not out		
A.U.Rashid	c de Silva b M.D.K.Perera	35			
M.J.Leach	c Dickwella b M.D.K.Perera	15			
J.M.Anderson	not out	0			
Extras	(B 1, LB 1)	2	(B 4, LB 7, NB 2)		13
Total	**(97 overs)**	**342**	**(6 wkts dec; 93 overs)**		**322**

SRI LANKA

F.D.M.Karunaratne	Foakes b Anderson	4	c and b Ali		26
J.K.Silva	lbw b Curran	1	lbw b Leach		30
D.M.de Silva	b Ali	14	c Root b Stokes		21
B.K.G.Mendis	c Stokes b Leach	19	c Ali b Leach		45
A.D.Mathews	c Jennings b Ali	52	c Buttler b Ali		53
*L.D.Chandimal	st Foakes b Rashid	33	b Leach		1
†D.P.D.N.Dickwella	c Buttler b Ali	28	c Stokes b Ali		16
M.D.K.Perera	c Buttler b Leach	21	c Stokes b Rashid		30
M.K.P.A.D.Perera	c Foakes b Ali	0	c Stokes b Ali		8
R.A.S.Lakmal	c Anderson b Rashid	15	not out		14
H.M.R.K.B.Herath	not out	14	run out		5
Extras	(LB 2)	2	(LB 1)		1
Total	**(68 overs)**	**203**	**(85.1 overs)**		**250**

SRI LANKA	O	M	R	W		O	M	R	W
Lakmal	18	5	73	3	(2)	9	2	30	0
M.D.K.Perera	31	6	75	5	(1)	30	3	94	2
M.K.P.A.D.Perera	20	2	96	1	(4)	18.5	2	87	1
Herath	25	4	78	1	(3)	23	1	59	2
De Silva	3	0	18	0		12.1	2	41	0

ENGLAND	O	M	R	W		O	M	R	W
Anderson	10	0	26	1	(2)	12	2	27	0
Curran	6	1	16	1	(1)	5	1	15	0
Leach	18	2	41	2	(5)	21	1	60	3
Ali	21	4	66	4	(3)	20	2	71	4
Rashid	9	1	30	2	(4)	18.1	0	59	1
Stokes	4	0	22	0		8	2	16	1
Root						1	0	1	0

FALL OF WICKETS

	E	SL	E	SL
Wkt	1st	1st	2nd	2nd
1st	10	4	60	51
2nd	10	10	67	59
3rd	72	34	74	98
4th	98	40	181	144
5th	103	115	258	154
6th	164	136	319	190
7th	252	171	–	197
8th	306	173	–	229
9th	330	175	–	239
10th	342	203	–	250

Umpires: M.Erasmus (*South Africa*) (52) and C.B.Gaffaney (*New Zealand*) (23).
Referee: A.J.Pycroft (*Zimbabwe*) (63). **Test No. 2324/32 (SL275/E1005)**

SRI LANKA v ENGLAND (2nd Test)

At Pallekele International Cricket Stadium, Kandy, on 14, 15, 16, 17, 18 November 2018.
Toss: England. Result: **ENGLAND** won by 57 runs.
Debuts: None.

ENGLAND

Batsman	Dismissal 1	R		Dismissal 2	R
R.J.Burns	c de Silva b M.K.P.A.D.Perera	43	(2)	lbw b Pushpakumara	59
K.K.Jennings	c Dickwella b Lakmal	1	(3)	c de Silva b M.K.P.A.D.Perera	26
B.A.Stokes	lbw b M.D.K.Perera	14	(5)	lbw b M.D.K.Perera	0
*J.E.Root	b Pushpakumara	14		lbw b M.K.P.A.D.Perera	124
J.C.Buttler	c Karunaratne b Pushpakumara	63	(6)	b M.K.P.A.D.Perera	34
M.M.Ali	lbw b Pushpakumara	10	(7)	lbw b M.K.P.A.D.Perera	10
†B.T.Foakes	c de Silva b M.D.K.Perera	19	(8)	not out	65
S.M.Curran	c Karunaratne b M.D.K.Perera	64	(9)	b M.K.P.A.D.Perera	0
A.U.Rashid	lbw b M.D.K.Perera	31	(10)	lbw b M.K.P.A.D.Perera	2
M.J.Leach	b M.K.P.A.D.Perera	7	(1)	lbw b M.K.P.A.D.Perera	1
J.M.Anderson	not out	7		b M.D.K.Perera	12
Extras	(B 4, LB 3, Pen 5)	12		(B 4, LB 9)	13
Total	**(75.4 overs)**	**290**		**(80.4 overs)**	**346**

SRI LANKA

Batsman	Dismissal 1	R		Dismissal 2	R
F.D.M.Karunaratne	run out	63		c Foakes b Rashid	57
J.K.Silva	b Leach	6		st Foakes b Leach	4
P.M.Pushpakumara	c Burns b Ali	4	(11)	c and b Leach	1
D.M.de Silva	c Foakes b Rashid	59	(3)	c Jennings b Leach	1
B.K.G.Mendis	c Stokes b Leach	1	(4)	lbw b Leach	1
A.D.Mathews	c Foakes b Rashid	20	(5)	lbw b Ali	88
A.R.S.Silva	c Ali b Rashid	85	(6)	c Root b Ali	37
†D.P.D.N.Dickwella	lbw b Root	25	(7)	c Stokes b Ali	35
M.D.K.Perera	lbw b Ali	15	(8)	lbw b Leach	2
M.K.P.A.D.Perera	lbw b Ali	31	(9)	not out	8
*R.A.S.Lakmal	not out	15	(10)	b Ali	0
Extras	(B 6, LB 6)	12		(B 5, LB 4)	9
Total	**(103 overs)**	**336**		**(74 overs)**	**243**

SRI LANKA	O	M	R	W		O	M	R	W
Lakmal	12	1	44	1	(5)	4	0	14	0
M.D.K.Perera	24.4	5	61	4	(1)	20.4	2	96	3
Pushpakumara	23	4	89	2	(2)	27	1	101	1
De Silva	2	0	4	0			0	7	0
M.K.P.A.D.Perera	14	1	80	2	(3)	25	0	115	6

ENGLAND	O	M	R	W		O	M	R	W
Anderson	14	2	40	0		5	2	12	0
Curran	4	0	19	0					
Leach	29	5	70	2	(2)	28	2	83	5
Ali	25	1	85	2	(3)	19	2	72	4
Rashid	22	2	75	3	(4)	17	1	52	1
Root	8	0	26	1	(5)		0	15	0
Stokes	1	0	9	0					

FALL OF WICKETS

	E‡	SL	E	SL
Wkt	1st	1st	2nd	2nd
1st	12	22	4	14
2nd	49	31	77	16
3rd	70	127	108	26
4th	94	136	109	103
5th	139	146	183	176
6th	170	165	219	221
7th	176	211	301	226
8th	221	252	301	240
9th	230	308	305	240
10th	290	336	346	243

Umpires: M.Erasmus (*South Africa*) (53) and S.Ravi (*India*) (29).
Referee: A.J.Pycroft (*Zimbabwe*) (64). **Test No. 2325/33 (SL276/E1006)**
‡Penalty runs added in throughout, so actual fall of wickets was 7-1, etc.

SRI LANKA v ENGLAND (3rd Test)

At Sinhalese Sports Club, Colombo, on 23, 24, 25, 26 November 2018.
Toss: England. Result: **ENGLAND** won by 42 runs.
Debuts: None.

ENGLAND

Batsman	First innings		Second innings	
R.J.Burns	b Perera	14	lbw b Perera	7
K.K.Jennings	c Silva b Pushpakumara	13	lbw b Perera	1
J.M.Bairstow	b Sandakan	110	c sub (J.K.Silva) b Perera	15
*J.E.Root	c Gunathilleke b Sandakan	46	c and b Pushpakumara	0
B.A.Stokes	c de Silva b Sandakan	57	c Pushpakumara b Perera	42
J.C.Buttler	c and b Sandakan	16	st Dickwella b Sandakan	64
M.M.Ali	c Mathews b Perera	33	c de Silva b Sandakan	22
†B.T.Foakes	c Dickwella b Pushpakumara	13	not out	36
A.U.Rashid	not out	21	c Dickwella b Pushpakumara	24
S.C.J.Broad	b Sandakan	0	c Mendis b Pushpakumara	1
M.J.Leach	c Mathews b Perera	2	c Dickwella b Perera	0
Extras	(B 7, LB 3, NB 1)	11	(B 3, LB 4, NB 3, W 1)	11
Total	**(92.5 overs)**	**336**	**(69.5 overs)**	**230**

SRI LANKA

Batsman	First innings		Second innings	
M.D.Gunathilleke	c Jennings b Leach	18	c Stokes b Ali	6
F.D.M.Karunaratne	c Jennings b Rashid	83	b Ali	23
D.M.de Silva	c Jennings b Rashid	73	lbw b Leach	0
B.K.G.Mendis	c Stokes b Rashid	27	run out	86
A.D.Mathews	c Foakes b Stokes	5	c Broad b Stokes	5
A.R.S.Silva	c Jennings b Rashid	5	(7) lbw b Ali	65
†D.P.D.N.Dickwella	c Foakes b Stokes	5	(8) c Jennings b Leach	19
M.D.K.Perera	c Foakes b Stokes	0	(9) c Jennings b Ali	5
*R.A.S.Lakmal	not out	3	(10) lbw b Leach	11
P.A.D.L.R.Sandakan	run out	2	(6) c Stokes b Leach	7
P.M.Pushpakumara	lbw b Rashid	13	not out	42
Extras	(LB 7, W 1)	8	(B 8, NB 2, W 5)	15
Total	**(65.5 overs)**	**240**	**(86.4 overs)**	**284**

SRI LANKA	O	M	R	W		O	M	R	W
Lakmal	11	2	33	0	(4)	3	1	7	0
Perera	32.5	1	113	3	(1)	29.5	3	88	5
Pushpakumara	20	3	64	2	(2)	12	2	28	2
Sandakan	22	0	95	5	(5)	16	1	76	2
De Silva	5	0	16	0	(3)	9	1	24	0
Gunathilleke	2	0	5	0					
ENGLAND									
Broad	9	2	36	0		5	0	14	0
Leach	18	2	59	1	(3)	28.4	4	72	4
Ali	13	2	55	0	(2)	26	3	92	4
Rashid	13.5	2	49	5	(5)	19	1	73	0
Root	2	0	4	0					
Stokes	10	1	30	3	(4)	8	1	25	1

FALL OF WICKETS

	E	SL	E	SL
Wkt	1st	1st	2nd	2nd
1st	22	31	3	15
2nd	36	173	20	24
3rd	136	187	35	34
4th	235	200	39	52
5th	254	205	128	82
6th	265	222	168	184
7th	294	222	171	214
8th	328	222	215	225
9th	329	224	217	226
10th	336	240	230	284

Umpires: C.B.Gaffaney (*New Zealand*) (24) and S.Ravi (*India*) (30).
Referee: A.J.Pycroft (*Zimbabwe*) (65). Test No. 2326/34 (SL277/E1007)

PAKISTAN v NEW ZEALAND (1st Test)

At Sheikh Zayed Stadium, Abu Dhabi, on 16, 17, 18, 19 November 2018.
Toss: New Zealand. Result: **NEW ZEALAND** won by 4 runs.
Debut: New Zealand – A.Y.Patel.

NEW ZEALAND

J.A.Raval	c Ahmed b Abbas	7	c Ahmed b Hasan		46
T.W.M.Latham	c Hafeez b Shah	13	b Hasan		0
*K.S.Williamson	c Ahmed b Hasan	63	b Shah		37
L.R.P.L.Taylor	c Ahmed b Shah	2	lbw b Hasan		19
H.M.Nicholls	c Ahmed b Abbas	28	c Ahmed b Shah		55
†B.J.Watling	lbw b Sohail	10	lbw b Shah		59
C.de Grandhomme	lbw b Hasan	0	lbw b Shah		3
I.S.Sodhi	lbw b Sohail	4	b Hasan		18
N.Wagner	c Shafiq b Asif	12	b Shah		0
A.Y.Patel	lbw b Shah	6	not out		6
T.A.Boult	not out	4	c Hafeez b Hasan		0
Extras	(LB 4)	4	(B 4, NB 1, W 1)		6
Total	**(66.3 overs)**	**153**	**(100.4 overs)**		**249**

PAKISTAN

Imam-ul-Haq	c Williamson b de Grandhomme	6	lbw b Patel		27
Mohammad Hafeez	c Williamson b Boult	20	c de Grandhomme b Sodhi		10
Azhar Ali	c Watling b Boult	22	lbw b Patel		65
Haris Sohail	c Latham b Sodhi	38	c and b Sodhi		4
Asad Shafiq	b Boult	43	c Watling b Wagner		45
Babar Azam	c Watling b Boult	62	run out		13
†*Sarfraz Ahmed	c Wagner b Patel	2	c Watling b Patel		3
Bilal Asif	st Watling b Patel	11	b Patel		0
Yasir Shah	c Watling b Wagner	9	c Taylor b Wagner		0
Hasan Ali	c Taylor b de Grandhomme	4	c sub (T.G.Southee) b Patel		0
Mohammad Abbas	not out	0	not out		0
Extras	(B 4, LB 4, NB 1, W 1)	10	(B 4)		4
Total	**(83.2 overs)**	**227**	**(58.4 overs)**		**171**

PAKISTAN	O	M	R	W	O	M	R	W	FALL OF WICKETS				
Mohammad Abbas	12	7	13	2	22	10	31	0		NZ	P	NZ	P
Hasan Ali	16	6	38	2	17.4	3	45	5	*Wkt*	*1st*	*1st*	*2nd*	*2nd*
Bilal Asif	13	1	33	1	(5) 14	3	43	0	1st	20	27	0	40
Yasir Shah	16.3	2	54	3	(3) 37	6	110	5	2nd	35	27	86	44
Haris Sohail	8	2	11	2	(4) 7	1	12	0	3rd	39	91	105	48
Mohammad Hafeez	1	1	0	0	3	1	4	0	4th	111	91	108	130
									5th	123	174	220	147
NEW ZEALAND									6th	123	177	224	154
Boult	18.2	6	54	4	7	0	29	0	7th	128	195	227	154
De Grandhomme	13	6	30	2	3	0	15	0	8th	133	220	227	155
Patel	24	4	64	2	23.4	4	59	5	9th	149	227	294	164
Wagner	18	5	30	1	(5) 13	4	27	2	10th	153	227	249	171
Sodhi	10	0	41	1	(4) 12	0	37	2					

Umpires: I.J.Gould (*England*) (70) and B.N.J.Oxenford (*Australia*) (52).
Referee: J.Srinath (*India*) (41).

Test No. 2327/56 (P418/NZ427)

PAKISTAN v NEW ZEALAND (2nd Test)

At Dubai Sports City Stadium, on 24, 25, 26, 27 November 2018.
Toss: Pakistan. Result: **PAKISTAN** won by an innings and 16 runs.
Debuts: None.

PAKISTAN

Imam-ul-Haq	c Latham b de Grandhomme	9
Mohammad Hafeez	c Latham b de Grandhomme	9
Azhar Ali	run out	81
Haris Sohail	c Watling b Boult	147
Asad Shafiq	c Wagner b Patel	12
Babar Azam	not out	127
†*Sarfraz Ahmed	not out	30
Bilal Asif		
Yasir Shah		
Hasan Ali		
Mohammad Abbas		
Extras	(B 2, NB 1)	3
Total	**(5 wkts dec; 167 overs)**	**418**

NEW ZEALAND

J.A.Raval	b Shah	31	st Ahmed b Shah	2
T.W.M.Latham	c Imam b Shah	22	c Ahmed b Hasan	50
*K.S.Williamson	not out	28	c Ahmed b Shah	30
L.R.P.L.Taylor	b Shah	0	c Shah b Asif	82
H.M.Nicholls	b Shah	0	b Hasan	77
†B.J.Watling	run out	1	lbw b Shah	27
C.de Grandhomme	lbw b Hasan	0	b Hasan	14
I.S.Sodhi	c Ahmed b Shah	0	b Shah	4
N.Wagner	lbw b Shah	0	c Hasan b Shah	10
A.Y.Patel	lbw b Shah	4	not out	5
T.A.Boult	st Ahmed b Shah	0	c Ahmed b Shah	0
Extras	(LB 3, NB 1)	4	(B 9, LB 2)	11
Total	**(35.3 overs)**	**90**	**(112.5 overs)**	**312**

NEW ZEALAND	O	M	R	W		O	M	R	W
Boult	34	7	106	1					
De Grandhomme	30	11	44	2					
Wagner	37	12	63	0					
Patel	39	5	120	1					
Sodhi	22	1	63	0					
Williamson	5	0	20	0					

PAKISTAN	O	M	R	W		O	M	R	W
Mohammad Abbas	9	4	18	0		15	7	29	0
Hasan Ali	10	5	25	1		19	7	46	3
Mohammad Hafeez	2	1	1	0	(4)	3	1	6	0
Yasir Shah	12.3	1	41	8	(3)	44.5	9	143	6
Bilal Asif	2	1	2	0		27	5	61	1
Haris Sohail						4	0	16	0

FALL OF WICKETS			
	P	NZ	NZ
Wkt	1st	1st	2nd
1st	18	50	10
2nd	25	61	66
3rd	151	61	146
4th	174	61	198
5th	360	63	255
6th	–	69	270
7th	–	72	285
8th	–	72	301
9th	–	90	311
10th	–	90	312

Umpires: B.N.J.Oxenford (*Australia*) (53) and P.R.Reiffel (*Australia*) (40).
Referee: J.Srinath (*India*) (42).   **Test No. 2328/57 (P419/NZ428)**

PAKISTAN v NEW ZEALAND (3rd Test)

At Sheikh Zayed Stadium, Abu Dhabi, on 3, 4, 5, 6, 7 December 2018.
Toss: New Zealand. Result: **NEW ZEALAND** won by 123 runs.
Debuts: Pakistan – Shaheen Shah Afridi; New Zealand – W.E.R.Somerville.

NEW ZEALAND

J.A.Raval	lbw b Shah	45		lbw b Afridi	0
T.W.M.Latham	lbw b Afridi	4		c Sohail b Shah	10
*K.S.Williamson	c Shafiq b Hasan	89		lbw b Hasan	139
L.R.P.L.Taylor	b Shah	0	(5)	c Asif b Afridi	22
H.M.Nicholls	b Shah	1	(6)	not out	126
†B.J.Watling	not out	77	(8)	b Shah	0
C.de Grandhomme	c Shafiq b Asif	20		c Asif b Shah	26
T.G.Southee	c Azam b Asif	2	(9)	not out	15
W.E.R.Somerville	b Asif	12	(4)	lbw b Shah	4
A.Y.Patel	c Shafiq b Asif	6			
T.A.Boult	b Asif	1			
Extras	(B 11, LB 6)	17		(B 9, LB 1, NB 1)	11
Total	**(116.1 overs)**	**274**		**(7 wkts dec; 113 overs)**	**353**

PAKISTAN

Imam-ul-Haq	c Southee b Boult	9		c Nicholls b Patel	22
Mohammad Hafeez	c Southee b Boult	0		b Southee	8
Azhar Ali	c Patel b Somerville	134		c Watling b de Grandhomme	5
Haris Sohail	c Watling b Southee	34		c Taylor b Somerville	9
Asad Shafiq	lbw b Patel	104		c Watling b Somerville	0
Babar Azam	b Somerville	14		c Southee b Patel	51
†*Sarfraz Ahmed	c Raval b Somerville	25		b Somerville	28
Bilal Asif	c Taylor b Patel	11		c Watling b Southee	12
Yasir Shah	run out	1		c Patel b Southee	4
Hasan Ali	b Somerville	0		c Williamson b Patel	4
Shaheen Shah Afridi	not out	0		not out	2
Extras	(B 6, LB 9, NB 1)	16		(B 4, LB 6, NB 1)	11
Total	**(135 overs)**	**348**		**(56.1 overs)**	**156**

PAKISTAN	O	M	R	W	O	M	R	W
Hasan Ali	20	6	58	1	16	5	62	1
Shaheen Shah Afridi	23	6	52	1	20	5	85	2
Yasir Shah	41	11	75	3	39	8	129	4
Bilal Asif	30.1	4	65	5	36	6	62	0
Haris Sohail	2	0	7	0				
Azhar Ali					(5)	1	0	0
Mohammad Hafeez					(6)	1	0	0

NEW ZEALAND	O	M	R	W	O	M	R	W
Southee	25	5	56	1	12	3	42	3
Boult	26	7	66	2	6	4	7	0
De Grandhomme	13	2	36	0	4	1	3	1
Patel	35	5	100	2	14.1	4	42	3
Somerville	36	8	75	4	20	2	52	3

FALL OF WICKETS

	NZ	P	NZ	P
Wkt	1st	1st	2nd	2nd
1st	24	0	1	19
2nd	70	17	24	32
3rd	70	85	37	43
4th	72	286	60	43
5th	176	304	272	55
6th	203	312	334	98
7th	209	333	334	131
8th	254	346	–	137
9th	272	347	–	150
10th	274	348	–	156

Umpires: I.J.Gould (*England*) (71) and P.R.Reiffel (*Australia*) (41).
Referee: J.Srinath (*India*) (43).

Test No. 2329/58 (P420/NZ429)

BANGLADESH v WEST INDIES (1st Test)

At Zahur Ahmed Chowdhury Stadium, Chittagong, on 22, 23, 24 November 2018.
Toss: Bangladesh. Result: **BANGLADESH** won by 64 runs.
Debut: Bangladesh – Nayeem Hasan.

BANGLADESH

Batsman	1st innings			2nd innings	
Imrul Kayes	c Ambris b Warrican	44		b Warrican	2
Soumya Sarkar	c Dowrich b Roach	0		c Brathwaite b Chase	11
Mominul Haque	c Dowrich b Gabriel	120		lbw b Chase	12
Mithun Ali	c Dowrich b Bishoo	20		b Bishoo	17
*Shakib Al Hasan	b Gabriel	34		c Gabriel b Warrican	1
†Mushfiqur Rahim	lbw b Gabriel	4		b Gabriel	19
Mahmudullah	b Gabriel	3	(8)	c Hope b Bishoo	31
Mehedi Hasan	b Warrican	22	(7)	c Dowrich b Bishoo	18
Nayeem Hasan	c Hope b Warrican	26		c Hope b Bishoo	5
Taijul Islam	not out	39		c Warrican b Chase	1
Mustafizur Rahman	lbw b Warrican	0		not out	2
Extras	(B 3, LB 5, NB 4)	12		(B 2, LB 1, NB 3)	6
Total	**(92.4 overs; 416 mins)**	**324**		**(35.5 overs; 161 mins)**	**125**

WEST INDIES

Batsman	1st innings			2nd innings	
*K.C.Brathwaite	c Soumya b Shakib	13		lbw b Taijul	8
K.O.A.Powell	lbw b Taijul	14		st Mushfiqur b Shakib	0
S.D.Hope	b Shakib	1		c Mushfiqur b Shakib	3
S.W.Ambris	lbw b Nayeem	19		c Mushfiqur b Taijul	43
R.L.Chase	c Imrul b Nayeem	31		lbw b Taijul	0
S.O.Hetmyer	c Mushfiqur b Mehedi	63		c Nayeem b Mehedi	27
†S.O.Dowrich	not out	63		lbw b Taijul	5
D.Bishoo	lbw b Nayeem	7		b Taijul	2
K.A.J.Roach	lbw b Nayeem	2		lbw b Taijul	1
J.A.Warrican	b Nayeem	12		c Shakib b Mehedi	41
S.T.Gabriel	c Mahmudullah b Shakib	5		not out	0
Extras	(B 6, LB 2, NB 2, Pen 5)	15		(B 9)	9
Total	**(64 overs; 258 mins)**	**246**		**(35.2 overs; 144 mins)**	**139**

WEST INDIES	O	M	R	W		O	M	R	W
Roach	17	2	63	1		1	0	11	0
Gabriel	20	3	70	4	(5)	3	0	24	1
Chase	11	0	42	0		6.5	1	18	3
Warrican	21.4	6	62	4	(2)	16	2	43	2
Bishoo	15	0	60	1	(4)	9	0	26	4
Brathwaite	8	1	19	0					

BANGLADESH	O	M	R	W		O	M	R	W
Mustafizur Rahman	2	1	4	0	(5)	2	0	11	0
Mehedi Hasan	15	0	67	1	(4)	8	1	27	2
Taijul Islam	20	3	51	1		11.2	2	33	6
Shakib Al Hasan	11	1	43	3	(1)	7	0	30	2
Nayeem Hasan	14	2	61	5	(2)	7	1	29	0
Mahmudullah									

FALL OF WICKETS

Wkt	1st B	1st WI	2nd B	2nd WI
1st	1	29	13	5
2nd	105	30	13	11
3rd	153	31	32	11
4th	222	77	35	11
5th	226	88	53	44
6th	230	180	69	51
7th	235	199	106	69
8th	259	205	123	75
9th	324	225	123	138
10th	324	246	125	139

Umpires: Alim Dar (*Pakistan*) (122) and R.K.Illingworth (*England*) (38).
Referee: D.C.Boon (*Australia*) (50).   Test No. 2330/15 (B111/WI538)

BANGLADESH v WEST INDIES (2nd Test)

At Shere Bangla National Stadium, Mirpur, Dhaka, on 30 November, 1, 2 December 2018.
Toss: Bangladesh. Result: **BANGLADESH** won by an innings and 164 runs.
Debut: Bangladesh – Shadman Islam.

BANGLADESH

Shadman Islam	lbw b Bishoo	76
Soumya Sarkar	c Hope b Chase	19
Mominul Haque	c Chase b Roach	29
Mithun Ali	b Bishoo	29
*Shakib Al Hasan	c Hope b Roach	80
†Mushfiqur Rahim	b Lewis	14
Mahmudullah	b Warrican	136
Liton Das	b Brathwaite	54
Mehedi Hasan	c Dowrich b Warrican	18
Taijul Islam	c Dowrich b Brathwaite	26
Nayeem Hasan	not out	12
Extras	(B 2, LB 8, NB 4, W 1)	15
Total	**(154 overs)**	**508**

WEST INDIES

*K.C.Brathwaite	b Shakib	0	lbw b Shakib		1
K.O.A.Powell	b Mehedi	4	st Mushfiqur b Mehedi		6
S.D.Hope	b Mehedi	10	c Shakib b Mehedi		25
S.W.Ambris	b Shakib	7	lbw b Taijul		4
R.L.Chase	b Mehedi	0	c Mominul b Taijul		3
S.O.Hetmyer	c and b Mehedi	39	c Mithun b Mehedi		93
†S.O.Dowrich	lbw b Mehedi	37	c Soumya b Nayeem		3
D.Bishoo	c Shadman b Mehedi	1	c Soumya b Mehedi		12
K.A.J.Roach	c Liton b Mehedi	1	not out		37
J.A.Warrican	not out	5	c and b Mehedi		0
S.H.Lewis	lbw b Shakib	0	lbw b Taijul		20
Extras	(B 4, LB 3)	7	(B 6, LB 3)		9
Total	**(36.4 overs)**	**111**	**(59.2 overs)**		**213**

WEST INDIES	O	M	R	W		O	M	R	W
Roach	25	4	61	2					
Lewis	20	2	69	1					
Chase	28	0	111	1					
Warrican	38	5	91	2					
Bishoo	28	1	109	2					
Brathwaite	15	0	57	2					

BANGLADESH	O	M	R	W		O	M	R	W
Shakib Al Hasan	15.4	4	27	3		14	3	65	1
Mehedi Hasan	16	1	58	7		20	2	59	5
Nayeem Hasan	3	0	9	0	(5)	14	2	34	1
Taijul Islam	1	0	10	0	(3)	10.2	1	40	3
Mahmudullah	1	1	0	0	(4)	1	0	6	0

FALL OF WICKETS			
	B	WI	WI
Wkt	1st	1st	2nd
1st	42	0	2
2nd	87	6	14
3rd	151	17	23
4th	161	20	29
5th	190	29	85
6th	301	86	96
7th	393	88	143
8th	416	92	166
9th	472	110	171
10th	508	111	213

Umpires: Alim Dar (*Pakistan*) (123) and R.S.A.Palliyaguruge (*Sri Lanka*) (1).
Referee: A.J.Pycroft (*Zimbabwe*) (66).   **Test No. 2331/16 (B112/WI539)**

AUSTRALIA v INDIA (1st Test)

At Adelaide Oval, on 6, 7, 8, 9, 10 December 2018.
Toss: India. Result: **INDIA** won by 31 runs.
Debut: Australia – M.S.Harris.

INDIA

K.L.Rahul	c Finch b Hazlewood	2	c Paine b Hazlewood		44
M.Vijay	c Paine b Starc	11	c Handscomb b Starc		18
C.A.Pujara	run out	123	c Finch b Lyon		71
*V.Kohli	c Khawaja b Cummins	3	c Finch b Lyon		34
A.M.Rahane	c Handscomb b Hazlewood	13	c Starc b Lyon		70
R.G.Sharma	c Harris b Lyon	37	c Handscomb b Lyon		1
†R.R.Pant	c Paine b Lyon	25	c Finch b Lyon		28
R.Ashwin	c Handscomb b Cummins	25	c Harris b Starc		5
I.Sharma	b Starc	4	c Finch b Starc		0
Mohammed Shami	c Paine b Hazlewood	6	c Harris b Lyon		0
J.J.Bumrah	not out	0	not out		0
Extras	(LB 1)	1	(B 21, LB 13, W 2)		36
Total	**(88 overs; 388 mins)**	**250**	**(106.5 overs; 465 mins)**		**307**

AUSTRALIA

A.J.Finch	b I.Sharma	0	c Pant b Ashwin		11
M.S.Harris	c Vijay b Ashwin	26	c Pant b Shami		26
U.T.Khawaja	c Pant b Ashwin	28	c R.G.Sharma b Ashwin		8
S.E.Marsh	b Ashwin	2	c Pant b Shami		60
P.S.P.Handscomb	c Pant b Bumrah	34	c Pujara b Shami		14
T.M.Head	c Pant b Shami	72	c Rahane b I.Sharma		14
†*T.D.Paine	c Pant b I.Sharma	5	c Pant b Bumrah		41
P.J.Cummins	lbw b Bumrah	10	c Kohli b Bumrah		28
M.A.Starc	c Pant b Bumrah	15	c Pant b Shami		28
N.M.Lyon	not out	24	not out		38
J.R.Hazlewood	c Pant b Shami	0	c Rahul b Ashwin		13
Extras	(B 6, LB 10, NB 2, W 1)	19	(B 1, LB 6, NB 3)		10
Total	**(98.4 overs; 419 mins)**	**235**	**(119.5 overs; 504 mins)**		**291**

AUSTRALIA	O	M	R	W		O	M	R	W
Starc	19	4	63	2		21.5	7	40	3
Hazlewood	20	3	52	3		23	13	43	1
Cummins	19	3	49	2		18	4	55	0
Lyon	28	2	83	2		42	7	122	6
Head	2	1	2	0		2	0	13	0

INDIA	O	M	R	W		O	M	R	W
I.Sharma	20	6	47	2		19	4	48	1
Bumrah	24	9	47	3		24	8	68	3
Mohammed Shami	16.4	6	58	2	(4)	20	4	65	3
Ashwin	34	9	57	3	(3)	52.5	13	92	3
Vijay	4	1	10	0		4	0	11	0

FALL OF WICKETS

	I	A	I	A
Wkt	1st	1st	2nd	2nd
1st	3	0	63	28
2nd	15	45	76	44
3rd	19	59	147	60
4th	41	87	234	84
5th	86	120	248	115
6th	127	127	282	156
7th	189	177	303	187
8th	210	204	303	228
9th	250	235	303	259
10th	250	235	307	291

Umpires: H.D.P.K.Dharmasena (*Sri Lanka*) (57) and N.J.Llong (*England*) (55).
Referee: R.S.Madugalle (*Sri Lanka*) (186).   **Test No. 2332/95 (A815/1530)**

49

AUSTRALIA v INDIA (2nd Test)

At Perth Stadium, on 14, 15, 16, 17, 18 December 2018.
Toss: Australia. Result: **AUSTRALIA** won by 146 runs.
Debuts: None.

AUSTRALIA

M.S.Harris	c Rahane b Vihari	70	b Bumrah		20
A.J.Finch	lbw b Bumrah	50	c Pant b Shami		25
U.T.Khawaja	c Pant b Yadav	5	c Pant b Shami		72
S.E.Marsh	c Rahane b Vihari	45	c Pant b Shami		5
P.S.P.Handscomb	c Kohli b Shami	7	lbw b Shami		13
T.M.Head	c Shami b Sharma	58	c Sharma b Shami		19
†*T.D.Paine	lbw b Bumrah	38	c Kohli b Shami		37
P.J.Cummins	b Yadav	19	b Bumrah		1
M.A.Starc	c Pant b Sharma	6	b Bumrah		14
N.M.Lyon	not out	9	c Vihari b Shami		5
J.R.Hazlewood	c Pant b Sharma	0	not out		17
Extras	(B 4, LB 7, NB 1, W 7)	19	(B 8, LB 3, W 4)		15
Total	**(108.3 overs; 488 mins)**	**326**	**(93.2 overs; 417 mins)**		**243**

INDIA

K.L.Rahul	b Hazlewood	2	b Starc		0
M.Vijay	b Starc	0	b Lyon		20
C.A.Pujara	c Paine b Starc	24	c Paine b Hazlewood		4
*V.Kohli	c Handscomb b Cummins	123	c Khawaja b Lyon		17
A.M.Rahane	c Paine b Lyon	51	c Head b Hazlewood		30
G.H.Vihari	c Paine b Hazlewood	20	c Harris b Starc		28
†R.R.Pant	c Starc b Lyon	36	c Handscomb b Lyon		30
Mohammed Shami	c Paine b Lyon	0	(10) not out		0
I.Sharma	c and b Lyon	4	c Paine b Cummins		0
U.T.Yadav	not out	4	(8) c and b Starc		2
J.J.Bumrah	c Khawaja b Lyon	4	c and b Cummins		0
Extras	(B 4, LB 7, NB 2, W 5)	18	(B 6, W 3)		9
Total	**(105.5 overs; 452 mins)**	**283**	**(56 overs; 246 mins)**		**140**

INDIA	O	M	R	W		O	M	R	W		FALL OF WICKETS				
												A	I	A	I
Sharma	20.3	7	41	4		16	1	45	1		Wkt	1st	1st	2nd	2nd
Bumrah	26	8	53	2		25.2	10	39	3		1st	112	6	59	0
Yadav	23	3	78	2	(4)	14	0	61	0		2nd	130	8	64	13
Mohammed Shami	24	3	80	0	(3)	24	8	56	6		3rd	134	82	85	48
Vihari	14	1	53	2		14	4	31	0		4th	148	173	120	55
Vijay	1	0	10	0							5th	232	223	192	98
											6th	251	251	192	119
AUSTRALIA											7th	310	252	198	137
Starc	24	4	79	2		17	3	46	3		8th	310	254	198	139
Hazlewood	21	8	66	2		11	3	24	2		9th	326	279	207	140
Cummins	26	4	60	1		9	0	25	2		10th	326	283	243	140
Lyon	34.5	7	67	5		19	3	39	3						

Umpires: H.D.P.K.Dharmasena (*Sri Lanka*) (58) and C.B.Gaffaney (*New Zealand*) (25).
Referee: R.S.Madugalle (*Sri Lanka*) (187).   **Test No. 2333/96 (A816/I531)**

AUSTRALIA v INDIA (3rd Test)

At Melbourne Cricket Ground, on 26, 27, 28, 29, 30 December 2018.
Toss: India. Result: **INDIA** won by 137 runs.
Debut: India – M.A.Agarwal.

INDIA

G.H.Vihari	c Finch b Cummins	8	c Khawaja b Cummins	13
M.A.Agarwal	c Paine b Cummins	76	b Cummins	42
C.A.Pujara	b Cummins	106	c Harris b Cummins	0
*V.Kohli	c Finch b Starc	82	c Harris b Cummins	0
A.M.Rahane	lbw b Lyon	34	c Paine b Cummins	1
R.G.Sharma	not out	63	c S.E.Marsh b Hazlewood	5
†R.R.Pant	c Khawaja b Starc	39	c Paine b Hazlewood	33
R.A.Jadeja	c Paine b Hazlewood	4	c Khawaja b Cummins	5
Mohammed Shami			not out	0
I.Sharma				
J.J.Bumrah				
Extras	(B 15, LB 14, NB 1, W 1)	31	(B 5, LB 1, W 1)	7
Total	**(7 wkts dec; 169.4 overs)**	**443**	**(8 wkts dec; 37.3 overs)**	**106**

AUSTRALIA

M.S.Harris	c I.Sharma b Bumrah	22	c Agarwal b Jadeja	13
A.J.Finch	c Agarwal b I.Sharma	8	c Kohli b Bumrah	3
U.T.Khawaja	c Agarwal b Jadeja	21	lbw b Shami	33
S.E.Marsh	lbw b Bumrah	19	lbw b Bumrah	44
T.M.Head	b Bumrah	20	b I.Sharma	34
M.R.Marsh	c Rahane b Jadeja	9	c Kohli b Jadeja	10
†*T.D.Paine	c Pant b Bumrah	22	c Pant b Jadeja	26
P.J.Cummins	b Shami	17	c Pujara b Bumrah	63
M.A.Starc	not out	7	b Shami	18
N.M.Lyon	lbw b Bumrah	0	c Pant b I.Sharma	7
J.R.Hazlewood	b Bumrah	0	not out	0
Extras	(B 4, NB 1, W 1)	6	(B 2, LB 6, W 2)	10
Total	**(66.5 overs)**	**151**	**(89.3 overs)**	**261**

AUSTRALIA	O	M	R	W	O	M	R	W	FALL OF WICKETS
Starc	28	7	87	2	3	1	11	0	
Hazlewood	31.4	10	86	1	10.3	3	22	2	
Lyon	48	7	110	1	13	1	40	0	
Cummins	34	10	72	3	11	3	27	6	
M.R.Marsh	26	4	51	0					
Finch	2	0	8	0					

		I	A	I	A
	Wkt	1st	1st	2nd	2nd
	1st	40	24	28	6
	2nd	123	36	28	33
	3rd	293	53	28	63
	4th	299	89	32	114
	5th	361	92	44	135
	6th	437	102	83	157
	7th	443	138	100	176
	8th	–	147	106	215
	9th	–	151	–	261
	10th	–	151	–	261

INDIA	O	M	R	W	O	M	R	W
I.Sharma	13	2	41	1	14.3	1	40	2
Bumrah	15.5	4	33	6	19	3	53	3
Jadeja	25	8	45	2	32	6	82	3
Mohammed Shami	10	2	27	1	21	2	71	2
Vihari	3	2	1	0	3	1	7	0

Umpires: M.Erasmus (*South Africa*) (54) and I.J.Gould (*England*) (72).
Referee: A.J.Pycroft (*Zimbabwe*) (67). **Test No. 2334/97 (A817/I532)**

AUSTRALIA v INDIA (4th Test)

At Sydney Cricket Ground, on 3, 4, 5, 6, 7 (*no play*) January 2019.
Toss: India. Result: **MATCH DRAWN**.
Debuts: None.

INDIA

M.A.Agarwal	c Starc b Lyon	77
K.L.Rahul	c Marsh b Hazlewood	9
C.A.Pujara	c and b Lyon	193
*V.Kohli	c Paine b Hazlewood	23
A.M.Rahane	c Paine b Starc	18
G.H.Vihari	c Labuschagne b Lyon	42
†R.R.Pant	not out	159
R.A.Jadeja	b Lyon	81
Kuldeep Yadav		
Mohammed Shami		
J.J.Bumrah		
Extras	(B 2, LB 13, W 5)	20
Total	**(7 wkts dec; 167.2 overs; 722 mins)**	**622**

AUSTRALIA

M.S.Harris	b Jadeja	79	(2) not out		2
U.T.Khawaja	c Pujara b Kuldeep	27	(1) not out		4
M.Labuschagne	c Rahane b Shami	38			
S.E.Marsh	c Rahane b Jadeja	8			
T.M.Head	c and b Kuldeep	20			
P.S.P.Handscomb	b Bumrah	37			
†*T.D.Paine	b Kuldeep	5			
P.J.Cummins	b Shami	25			
M.A.Starc	not out	29			
N.M.Lyon	lbw b Kuldeep	0			
J.R.Hazlewood	lbw b Kuldeep	21			
Extras	(B 4, LB 2, W 5)	11			
Total	**(104.5 overs; 414 mins)**	**300**	**(0 wkts; 4 overs; 17 mins)**		**6**

AUSTRALIA	O	M	R	W	O	M	R	W
Starc	26	0	123	1				
Hazlewood	35	11	105	2				
Cummins	28	5	101	0				
Lyon	57.2	8	178	4				
Labuschagne	16	0	76	0				
Head	4	0	20	0				
Khawaja	1	0	4	0				
INDIA								
Mohammed Shami	19	2	58	2	2	1	4	0
Bumrah	21	5	62	1	2	1	2	0
Jadeja	32	11	73	2				
Kuldeep Yadav	31.5	6	99	5				
Vihari	1	0	2	0				

FALL OF WICKETS

	I	A	A
Wkt	1st	1st	2nd
1st	10	72	–
2nd	126	128	–
3rd	180	144	–
4th	228	152	–
5th	329	192	–
6th	418	198	–
7th	622	236	–
8th	–	257	–
9th	–	258	–
10th	–	300	–

Umpires: I.J.Gould (*England*) (73) and R.A.Kettleborough (*England*) (57).
Referee: A.J.Pycroft (*Zimbabwe*) (68).   **Test No. 2335/98 (A818/1533)**

NEW ZEALAND v SRI LANKA (1st Test)

At Basin Reserve, Wellington, on 15, 16, 17, 18, 19 December 2018.
Toss: New Zealand. Result: **MATCH DRAWN**.
Debuts: None.

SRI LANKA

M.D.Gunathilleke	lbw b Southee	1	lbw b Boult		3
F.D.M.Karunaratne	c Watling b Wagner	79	c Boult b Southee		10
D.M.de Silva	c Watling b Southee	1	b Southee		0
B.K.G.Mendis	c Patel b Southee	2	not out		141
A.D.Mathews	c Watling b Southee	83	not out		120
*L.D.Chandimal	c Patel b Southee	6			
†D.P.D.N.Dickwella	not out	80			
M.D.K.Perera	c Watling b de Grandhomme	16			
R.A.S.Lakmal	c Nicholls b Wagner	3			
C.A.K.Rajitha	c Watling b Boult	2			
C.B.R.L.S.Kumara	c de Grandhomme b Southee	0			
Extras	(LB 7, NB 2)	9	(LB 2, NB 3, W 8)		13
Total	(90 overs; 401 mins)	282	(3 wkts; 115 overs; 479 mins)		287

NEW ZEALAND

J.A.Raval	c Dickwella b Kumara	43
T.W.M.Latham	not out	264
*K.S.Williamson	c Rajitha b de Silva	91
L.R.P.L.Taylor	c Karunaratne b Kumara	50
H.M.Nicholls	c Rajitha b Perera	50
†B.J.Watling	c Dickwella b Kumara	0
C.de Grandhomme	c Rajitha b de Silva	49
T.G.Southee	run out	6
N.Wagner	c de Silva b Lakmal	0
A.Y.Patel	b Perera	6
T.A.Boult	c Dickwella b Kumara	11
Extras	(LB 5, NB 2, W 1)	8
Total	(157.3 overs; 694 mins)	578

NEW ZEALAND	O	M	R	W		O	M	R	W
Boult	27	6	83	1	(2)	25	4	62	1
Southee	27	7	68	6	(1)	25	8	52	2
De Grandhomme	13	2	35	1	(4)	13	4	24	0
Wagner	20	2	75	2	(3)	23	4	100	0
Patel	3	0	14	0		28	10	46	0
Raval						1	0	1	0

SRI LANKA	O	M	R	W
Lakmal	31	6	88	1
Rajitha	34	5	144	0
Mathews	4	3	1	0
Perera	40	1	156	2
Kumara	31.3	2	127	4
De Silva	15	0	54	2
Gunathilleke	2	1	3	0

FALL OF WICKETS

	SL	NZ	SL
Wkt	1st	1st	2nd
1st	5	59	5
2nd	7	221	10
3rd	9	312	13
4th	142	426	–
5th	167	426	–
6th	187	499	–
7th	223	520	–
8th	240	520	–
9th	275	549	–
10th	282	578	–

Umpires: M.A.Gough (*England*) (7) and R.J.Tucker (*Australia*) (65).
Referee: Sir R.B.Richardson (*West Indies*) (19).   **Test No. 2336/33 (NZ430/SL278)**

NEW ZEALAND v SRI LANKA (2nd Test)

At Hagley Oval, Christchurch, on 26, 27, 28, 29, 30 December 2018.
Toss: Sri Lanka. Result: **NEW ZEALAND** won by 423 runs.
Debuts: None.

NEW ZEALAND

Batsman	1st innings		2nd innings	
J.A.Raval	c Chandimal b Lakmal	6	c Mendis b Perera	74
T.W.M.Latham	c Mendis b Lakmal	10	c Dickwella b Chameera	176
*K.S.Williamson	c Dickwella b Lakmal	2	*c Mendis b Kumara	48
L.R.P.L.Taylor	run out	27	lbw b Kumara	40
H.M.Nicholls	b Lakmal	1	not out	162
†B.J.Watling	c Perera b Kumara	46		
C.de Grandhomme	c Chameera b Kumara	1	(6) not out	71
T.G.Southee	c Gunathilleke b Perera	68		
N.Wagner	c Mendis b Lakmal	0		
A.Y.Patel	c Lakmal b Kumara	2		
T.A.Boult	not out	1		
Extras	(B 6, LB 7, NB 1)	14	(B 5, LB 3, NB 3, W 3)	14
Total	**(50 overs; 247 mins)**	**178**	**(4 wkts dec; 153 overs; 640 mins)**	**585**

SRI LANKA

Batsman	1st innings		2nd innings	
M.D.Gunathilleke	c Raval b Southee	8	c Watling b Southee	4
F.D.M.Karunaratne	c Williamson b Southee	7	c Watling b Boult	0
*L.D.Chandimal	c Watling b Southee	6	c Nicholls b Wagner	56
B.K.G.Mendis	c Watling b de Grandhomme	15	c sub (M.J.Henry) b Wagner	67
A.D.Mathews	not out	33	retired hurt	22
A.R.S.Silva	c Southee b Boult	21	c Watling b Wagner	18
†D.P.D.N.Dickwella	c Southee b Boult	4	b Southee	19
M.D.K.Perera	lbw b Boult	0	c Williamson b Wagner	22
R.A.S.Lakmal	lbw b Boult	0	b Boult	18
P.V.D.Chameera	lbw b Boult	0	lbw b Boult	3
C.B.R.L.S.Kumara	lbw b Boult	0	not out	0
Extras	(B 5, LB 5)	10	(B 4, LB 2, W 1)	7
Total	**(41 overs; 186 mins)**	**104**	**(106.2 overs; 468 mins)**	**236**

SRI LANKA	O	M	R	W	O	M	R	W
Lakmal	19	5	54	5	30	6	96	0
Kumara	14	4	49	3	32	6	134	2
Mathews	4	1	6	0				
Chameera	8	1	43	0	(3) 30	5	147	1
Perera	5	1	13	1	(4) 41	3	149	1
Gunathilleke					(5) 16	2	45	0
Karunaratne					(6) 4	2	6	0

NEW ZEALAND	O	M	R	W	O	M	R	W
Boult	15	8	30	6	28.2	11	77	3
Southee	15	5	35	3	27	13	61	2
De Grandhomme	6	0	19	1	10	1	23	0
Wagner	5	0	10	0	29	10	48	4
Patel					12	9	21	0

FALL OF WICKETS

Wkt	NZ 1st	SL 1st	NZ 2nd	SL 2nd
1st	16	10	121	1
2nd	17	20	189	9
3rd	22	21	247	126
4th	36	51	461	158
5th	57	94	–	181
6th	64	100	–	208
7th	172	100	–	233
8th	175	100	–	233
9th	177	104	–	236
10th	178	104	–	–

Umpires: M.A.Gough (*England*) (8) and R.K.Illingworth (*England*) (39).
Referee: Sir R.B.Richardson (*West Indies*) (20). **Test No. 2337/34 (NZ431/SL279)**
A.D.Mathews retired hurt at 155-3.

SOUTH AFRICA v PAKISTAN (1st Test)

At SuperSport Park, Centurion, on 26, 27, 28 December 2018.
Toss: Pakistan. Result: **SOUTH AFRICA** won by six wickets.
Debuts: None.

PAKISTAN

Imam-ul-Haq	lbw b Rabada	0	b Olivier		57
Fakhar Zaman	c Elgar b Steyn	12	c Rabada b Olivier		12
Shan Masood	b Olivier	19	c Maharaj b Steyn		65
Azhar Ali	c de Bruyn b Olivier	36	c Rabada b Olivier		0
Asad Shafiq	lbw b Olivier	7	c de Kock b Steyn		6
Babar Azam	c du Plessis b Rabada	71	b Rabada		6
†*Sarfraz Ahmed	b Olivier	0	c du Plessis b Rabada		0
Mohammad Amir	b Olivier	1	b Rabada		12
Yasir Shah	lbw b Rabada	4	c de Kock b Olivier		0
Hasan Ali	not out	21	not out		11
Shaheen Shah Afridi	c de Kock b Olivier	0	c Markram b Olivier		4
Extras	(B 7, LB 2, W 1)	10	(B 6, LB 10, W 1)		17
Total	**(47 overs; 223 mins)**	**181**	**(56 overs; 265 mins)**		**190**

SOUTH AFRICA

A.K.Markram	lbw b Hasan	12	(2) lbw b Hasan		0
D.Elgar	c Azhar b Afridi	22	(1) c Ahmed b Masood		50
H.M.Amla	c Azam b Amir	8	not out		63
T.B.de Bruyn	c Ahmed b Amir	29	st Ahmed b Shah		10
*F.du Plessis	c Azam b Afridi	0	c Hasan b Afridi		0
T.Bavuma	c Ahmed b Afridi	53	not out		13
D.W.Steyn	c Ahmed b Amir	23			
†Q.de Kock	c Zaman b Amir	45			
K.A.Maharaj	lbw b Hasan	4			
K.Rabada	c Shafiq b Afridi	19			
D.Olivier	not out	0			
Extras	(LB 3, NB 3, W 2)	8	(B 4, LB 5, W 6)		15
Total	**(60 overs; 284 mins)**	**223**	**(4 wkts; 50.4 overs; 230 mins)**		**151**

SOUTH AFRICA	O	M	R	W	O	M	R	W
Steyn	13	1	66	1	15	4	34	2
Rabada	17	4	59	3	15	4	47	3
Olivier	14	3	37	6	15	3	59	5
Maharaj	3	1	10	0	11	2	34	0
PAKISTAN								
Mohammad Amir	20	6	62	4	12	5	24	0
Hasan Ali	18	4	70	2	13	6	39	1
Shaheen Shah Afridi	18	1	64	4	15	1	53	1
Yasir Shah	4	0	24	0	7.4	1	20	1
Shan Masood					3	1	6	1

FALL OF WICKETS

	P	SA	P	SA
Wkt	1st	1st	2nd	2nd
1st	1	19	44	0
2nd	17	43	101	119
3rd	54	43	103	137
4th	62	43	134	137
5th	86	112	142	–
6th	86	146	142	–
7th	96	170	158	–
8th	111	189	159	–
9th	178	220	185	–
10th	181	223	190	–

Umpires: B.N.J.Oxenford (*Australia*) (54) and S.Ravi (*India*) (31).
Referee: D.C.Boon (*Australia*) (51).   **Test No. 2338/24 (SA428/P421)**

SOUTH AFRICA v PAKISTAN (2nd Test)

At Newlands, Cape Town, on 3, 4, 5, 6 January 2019.
Toss: South Africa. Result: **SOUTH AFRICA** won by nine wickets.
Debuts: None.

PAKISTAN

Batsman	1st innings		2nd innings	
Imam-ul-Haq	lbw b Philander	8	c Elgar b Steyn	6
Fakhar Zaman	c Bavuma b Steyn	1	(6) c and b Rabada	7
Shan Masood	c de Kock b Rabada	44	(2) c de Kock b Steyn	61
Azhar Ali	c Amla b Olivier	2	(3) lbw b Rabada	6
Asad Shafiq	c Elgar b Rabada	20	(4) c de Kock b Philander	88
Babar Azam	c du Plessis b Olivier	2	(5) c Amla b Rabada	72
†*Sarfraz Ahmed	c de Kock b Olivier	56	lbw b Olivier	6
Mohammad Amir	not out	22	c de Kock b Steyn	0
Yasir Shah	c du Plessis b Olivier	5	c sub (M.Z.Hamza) b Steyn	5
Mohammad Abbas	c de Kock b Steyn	0	not out	10
Shaheen Shah Afridi	c de Kock b Steyn	3	c Philander b Rabada	14
Extras	(B 8, LB 2, NB 1, W 3)	14	(B 9, LB 4, NB 4, W 2)	19
Total	(51.1 overs; 254 mins)	**177**	(70.4 overs; 339 mins)	**294**

SOUTH AFRICA

Batsman	1st innings		2nd innings	
A.K.Markram	b Masood	78		
D.Elgar	c Ahmed b Amir	20	(1) not out	24
H.M.Amla	b Abbas	24	retired hurt	2
T.B.de Bruyn	c Azam b Afridi	13	(2) c Ahmed b Abbas	4
*F.du Plessis	c Ahmed b Afridi	103	(4) not out	3
T.Bavuma	c Ahmed b Afridi	75		
†Q.de Kock	c Shafiq b Amir	59		
V.D.Philander	b Amir	16		
K.Rabada	b Amir	11		
D.W.Steyn	c Zaman b Afridi	13		
D.Olivier	not out	10		
Extras	(B 5, LB 1, NB 3)	9	(B 4, NB 1, W 5)	10
Total	(124.1 overs; 563 mins)	**431**	(1 wkt; 9.5 overs; 48 mins)	**43**

SOUTH AFRICA	O	M	R	W		O	M	R	W
Steyn	15.1	3	48	3	(2)	19	2	85	4
Philander	11	3	36	1	(1)	19	6	51	1
Rabada	10	2	35	2	(4)	16.4	2	61	4
Olivier	15	3	48	4	(3)	16	3	84	0

PAKISTAN	O	M	R	W		O	M	R	W
Mohammad Amir	33	9	88	4		5	2	17	0
Mohammad Abbas	34	8	100	1		4	0	14	1
Shaheen Shah Afridi	27.1	3	123	4					
Yasir Shah	21	1	79	0					
Shan Masood	5	1	19	1					
Asad Shafiq	4	0	16	0					
Azhar Ali					(3)	0.5	0	8	0

FALL OF WICKETS

	P	SA	P	SA
Wkt	1st	1st	2nd	2nd
1st	9	56	10	4
2nd	13	123	27	
3rd	19	126	159	
4th	51	149	194	
5th	54	305	201	
6th	114	356	220	
7th	156	394	221	
8th	162	407	247	
9th	163	408	270	
10th	177	431	294	

Umpires: B.N.J.Oxenford (*Australia*) (55) and J.S.Wilson (*West Indies*) (12).
Referee: D.C.Boon (*Australia*) (52). **Test No. 2339/25 (SA429/P422)**
H.M.Amla retired hurt at 23-1.

SOUTH AFRICA v PAKISTAN (3rd Test)

At New Wanderers Stadium, Johannesburg, on 11, 12, 13, 14 January 2019.
Toss: South Africa. Result: **SOUTH AFRICA** won by 107 runs.
Debut: South Africa – M.Z.Hamza.

SOUTH AFRICA

A.K.Markram	c Ahmed b Ashraf	90	(2) c Ahmed b Abbas		21
*D.Elgar	c Ahmed b Abbas	5	(1) c Ahmed b Amir		5
H.M.Amla	c Shafiq b Khan	41	c Ahmed b Hasan		71
T.B.de Bruyn	lbw b Abbas	49	c Shafiq b Ashraf		7
M.Z.Hamza	c Ahmed b Amir	41	lbw b Ashraf		0
T.Bavuma	c Ahmed b Amir	8	c Ahmed b Khan		23
†Q.de Kock	c Abbas b Ashraf	18	c Hasan b Khan		129
V.D.Philander	lbw b Hasan	1	lbw b Amir		14
K.Rabada	c Ahmed b Hasan	0	c Khan b Ashraf		21
D.W.Steyn	not out	2	not out		0
D.Olivier	c Abbas b Ashraf	0	c Ahmed b Khan		1
Extras	(LB 2, NB 4, W 1)	7	(B 2, LB 6, NB 2, W 1)		11
Total	**(77.4 overs; 339 mins)**	**262**	**(80.3 overs; 393 mins)**		**303**

PAKISTAN

Imam-ul-Haq	c Elgar b Philander	43	c de Kock b Steyn		35
Shan Masood	c de Kock b Philander	2	c de Kock b Steyn		37
Azhar Ali	c de Kock b Philander	0	c de Kock b Olivier		15
Mohammad Abbas	c de Bruyn b Olivier	11	(11) run out		9
Asad Shafiq	c de Kock b Olivier	0	(4) c Elgar b Philander		65
Babar Azam	c Rabada b Amla	49	(5) c de Kock b Olivier		21
†*Sarfraz Ahmed	c Amla b Rabada	50	(6) b Olivier		0
Shadab Khan	c de Bruyn b Rabada	5	(7) not out		47
Faheem Ashraf	c Hamza b Olivier	0	(8) c Markram b Rabada		15
Mohammad Amir	c Hamza b Olivier	10	(9) c Markram b Rabada		4
Hasan Ali	not out	0	(10) c and b Rabada		22
Extras	(B 5, LB 10)	15	(LB 2, NB 1)		3
Total	**(49.4 overs; 226 mins)**	**185**	**(65.4 overs; 304 mins)**		**273**

PAKISTAN	O	M	R	W	O	M	R	W
Mohammad Amir	15.4	2	36	2	20	2	56	2
Mohammad Abbas	18	6	44	2	18	3	73	1
Hasan Ali	17	3	75	2	17	1	83	1
Faheem Ashraf	15	2	57	3	14	3	42	3
Shadab Khan	10	2	39	1	11.3	0	41	3
Asad Shafiq	2	0	9	0				

SOUTH AFRICA	O	M	R	W		O	M	R	W
Steyn	12	4	35	0		20	2	80	2
Philander	13	4	43	3		14	4	41	1
Rabada	11.4	0	41	2	(4)	16	2	75	3
Olivier	13	2	51	5	(3)	15	2	74	3
Elgar						0.4	0	1	0

FALL OF WICKETS

	SA	P	SA	P
Wkt	1st	1st	2nd	2nd
1st	6	6	24	67
2nd	132	6	29	74
3rd	154	53	45	104
4th	229	53	45	162
5th	238	91	93	162
6th	244	169	195	179
7th	249	169	223	204
8th	257	169	302	208
9th	262	185	302	242
10th	262	185	303	273

Umpires: S.Ravi (*India*) (32) and J.S.Wilson (*West Indies*) (13).
Referee: D.C.Boon (*Australia*) (53).   Test No. 2340/26 (SA430/P423)

WEST INDIES v ENGLAND (1st Test)

At Kensington Oval, Bridgetown, Barbados, on 23, 24, 25, 26 January 2019.
Toss: West Indies. Result: **WEST INDIES** won by 381 runs.
Debut: West Indies – J.D.Campbell.

WEST INDIES

K.C.Brathwaite	c Root b Stokes	40		lbw b Ali	24
J.D.Campbell	lbw b Ali	44		c Jennings b Stokes	33
S.D.Hope	c Foakes b Anderson	57		c Jennings b Stokes	3
D.M.Bravo	lbw b Stokes	2		c Stokes b Ali	1
R.L.Chase	c Root b Anderson	54		c Stokes b Ali	0
S.O.Hetmyer	c Foakes b Stokes	81		c Buttler b Curran	31
†S.O.Dowrich	c Buttler b Anderson	0		not out	116
*J.O.Holder	c and b Anderson	5		not out	202
K.A.J.Roach	c Root b Stokes	0			
A.S.Joseph	c Buttler b Anderson	0			
S.T.Gabriel	not out	0			
Extras	(LB 5, NB 1)	6		(B 1, LB 1, NB 3)	5
Total	**(101.3 overs)**	**289**		**(6 wkts dec; 103.1 overs)**	**415**

ENGLAND

R.J.Burns	b Roach	2		b Chase	84
K.K.Jennings	c Hope b Holder	17		c Holder b Joseph	14
J.M.Bairstow	b Roach	12		c Hope b Gabriel	30
*J.E.Root	lbw b Holder	4		c Bravo b Chase	22
B.A.Stokes	lbw b Roach	0		lbw b Chase	34
J.C.Buttler	c Dowrich b Roach	4		c Campbell b Chase	26
M.M.Ali	c Joseph b Roach	0		c Holder b Chase	0
†B.T.Foakes	c Dowrich b Joseph	2		c Hetmyer b Chase	5
S.M.Curran	c Hope b Gabriel	14		st Hope b Chase	17
A.U.Rashid	c Holder b Joseph	12		c Brathwaite b Chase	1
J.M.Anderson	not out	0		not out	4
Extras	(B 4, LB 6)	10		(B 4, NB 2, W 3)	9
Total	**(30.2 overs)**	**77**		**(80.4 overs)**	**246**

ENGLAND	O	M	R	W		O	M	R	W
Anderson	30	13	46	5		18	4	58	0
Curran	12	3	54	0		17	1	69	1
Stokes	25.3	2	59	4	(4)	25	3	81	2
Ali	12	1	59	1	(3)	20	3	78	3
Rashid	17	1	56	0		9	0	61	0
Root	5	0	10	0		10	0	37	0
Jennings						4.1	0	29	0

WEST INDIES	O	M	R	W		O	M	R	W
Roach	11	7	17	5		14	3	58	0
Gabriel	7	2	15	1		16.5	2	55	1
Holder	8	3	15	2		12	6	24	0
Joseph	4.2	1	20	2	(5)	12	4	35	1
Chase					(4)	21.4	2	60	8
Campbell						4.1	0	10	0

FALL OF WICKETS				
	WI	E	WI	E
Wkt	1st	1st	2nd	2nd
1st	53	23	52	85
2nd	126	35	60	134
3rd	128	44	61	143
4th	174	44	61	167
5th	240	48	61	215
6th	250	48	120	217
7th	261	49	–	218
8th	264	61	–	228
9th	289	73	–	234
10th	289	77	–	246

Umpires: C.B.Gaffaney (*New Zealand*) (26) and R.J.Tucker (*Australia*) (66).
Referee: J.J.Crowe (*New Zealand*) (93).   **Test No. 2341/155 (WI540/E1008)**

WEST INDIES v ENGLAND (2nd Test)

At Sir Vivian Richards Stadium, North Sound, Antigua, on 31 January, 1, 2 February 2019.
Toss: West Indies. Result: **WEST INDIES** won by ten wickets.
Debut: England – J.L.Denly.

ENGLAND

R.J.Burns	c Holder b Roach	4	c Campbell b Holder		16
J.L.Denly	c Dowrich b Joseph	6	b Joseph		17
J.M.Bairstow	lbw b Roach	52	b Holder		14
*J.E.Root	c Hope b Joseph	7	c Dowrich b Joseph		7
J.C.Buttler	c Campbell b Holder	1	lbw b Holder		24
B.A.Stokes	c Dowrich b Gabriel	14	b Roach		11
M.M.Ali	c Gabriel b Roach	60	b Roach		4
†B.T.Foakes	b Gabriel	35	lbw b Roach		13
S.M.Curran	c sub (S.S.J.Brooks) b Roach	6	not out		13
S.C.J.Broad	not out	0	lbw b Roach		0
J.M.Anderson	b Gabriel	1	c Joseph b Holder		0
Extras	(W 1)	1	(LB 3, W 10)		13
Total	(61 overs)	187	(42.1 overs)		132

WEST INDIES

K.C.Brathwaite	c sub (K.K.Jennings) b Ali	49	not out	5
J.D.Campbell	c Buttler b Stokes	47	not out	11
S.D.Hope	c Bairstow b Broad	44		
D.M.Bravo	st Bairstow b Ali	50		
R.L.Chase	b Broad	4		
S.O.Hetmyer	c Anderson b Ali	21		
†S.O.Dowrich	c Buttler b Broad	31		
*J.O.Holder	c Bairstow b Anderson	22		
K.A.J.Roach	c Stokes b Anderson	6		
A.S.Joseph	c Burns b Stokes	7		
S.T.Gabriel	not out	1		
Extras	(B 8, LB 13, NB 2, W 1)	24	(LB 1)	1
Total	(131 overs)	306	(0 wkts; 2.1 overs)	17

WEST INDIES	O	M	R	W	O	M	R	W	FALL OF WICKETS				
Roach	15	5	30	4	13	2	52	4		E	WI	E	WI
Gabriel	15	5	45	3	10	3	22	0	Wkt	1st	1st	2nd	2nd
Joseph	10	3	38	2	(4) 7	4	12	2	1st	4	70	35	–
Holder	13	5	43	1	(3) 12.1	2	43	4	2nd	16	133	49	–
Chase	8	1	31	0					3rd	34	151	56	–
									4th	55	155	59	–
ENGLAND									5th	78	186	88	–
Anderson	29	5	73	2	1.1	0	10	0	6th	93	236	96	–
Broad	36	16	53	3	1	0	6	0	7th	178	281	118	–
Stokes	27	8	58	2					8th	186	289	118	–
Curran	13	0	38	0					9th	186	298	125	–
Ali	25	4	62	3					10th	187	306	132	–
Denly	1	0	1	0									

Umpires: H.D.P.K.Dharmasena (*Sri Lanka*) (59) and C.B.Gaffaney (*New Zealand*) (27).
Referee: J.J.Crowe (*New Zealand*) (94). **Test No. 2342/156 (WI541/E1009)**

WEST INDIES v ENGLAND (3rd Test)

At Darren Sammy National Cricket Stadium, Gros Islet, St Lucia, on 9, 10, 11, 12 February 2019.
Toss: West Indies. Result: **ENGLAND** won by 232 runs.
Debuts: None.

ENGLAND

R.J.Burns	lbw b Paul	29	c Joseph b Paul		10
K.K.Jennings	c Bravo b Paul	8	b Joseph		23
J.L.Denly	lbw b Gabriel	20	c Dowrich b Gabriel		69
*J.E.Root	c Dowrich b Joseph	15	c Hetmyer b Gabriel		122
J.C.Buttler	b Gabriel	67	b Roach		56
B.A.Stokes	c Dowrich b Roach	79	not out		48
†J.M.Bairstow	b Roach	2			
M.M.Ali	c Bravo b Joseph	13			
M.A.Wood	c Joseph b Roach	6			
S.C.J.Broad	not out	0			
J.M.Anderson	c Paul b Roach	0			
Extras	(B 5, LB 11, NB 6, W 16)	38	(B 13, LB 9, NB 3, W 8)		33
Total	(101.5 overs)	277	(5 wkts dec; 105.2 overs)		361

WEST INDIES

*K.C.Brathwaite	c Anderson b Ali	12	c Stokes b Anderson		8
J.D.Campbell	lbw b Ali	41	c Ali b Anderson		0
S.D.Hope	c Burns b Wood	1	c Broad b Wood		14
D.M.Bravo	c Root b Wood	6	c Root b Anderson		0
R.L.Chase	c Burns b Wood	0	not out		102
S.O.Hetmyer	c Root b Wood	8	run out		19
†S.O.Dowrich	lbw b Broad	38	c Stokes b Ali		19
K.M.A.Paul	st Bairstow b Ali	9	(11) c and b Stokes		4
K.A.J.Roach	not out	16	(8) c Wood b Ali		29
A.S.Joseph	c Broad b Ali	2	(9) c Anderson b Ali		34
S.T.Gabriel	b Wood	4	(10) c Bairstow b Stokes		3
Extras	(LB 4, NB 3, W 10)	17	(B 1, LB 5, NB 2, W 4)		12
Total	(47.2 overs)	154	(69.5 overs)		252

WEST INDIES	O	M	R	W	O	M	R	W
Roach	25.5	11	48	4	18	6	45	1
Gabriel	24	6	49	2	23.2	1	95	2
Joseph	17	2	61	2	(4) 16	2	72	1
Paul	21	7	58	2	(3) 5	1	11	1
Chase	10	0	40	0	31	1	92	0
Brathwaite	4	0	5	0	12	2	24	0

ENGLAND	O	M	R	W	O	M	R	W
Anderson	9	3	31	0	11	2	27	3
Broad	15	4	42	1	14	6	22	0
Ali	15	4	36	4	(5) 21	1	99	3
Wood	8.2	2	41	5	12	1	52	1
Stokes					(3) 8.5	2	30	2
Denly					3	0	16	0

FALL OF WICKETS				
	E	WI	E	WI
Wkt	1st	1st	2nd	2nd
1st	30	57	19	5
2nd	69	57	73	10
3rd	69	59	147	10
4th	107	59	254	31
5th	232	74	361	76
6th	256	79	–	110
7th	270	104	–	156
8th	275	145	–	212
9th	277	148	–	236
10th	277	154	–	252

Umpires: H.D.P.K.Dharmasena (*Sri Lanka*) (60) and R.J.Tucker (*Australia*) (67).
Referee: J.J.Crowe (*New Zealand*) (95).   **Test No. 2343/157 (WI542/E1010)**

AUSTRALIA v SRI LANKA (1st Test)

At Woolloongabba, Brisbane, on 24, 25, 26 January 2019 (day/night).
Toss: Sri Lanka. Result: **AUSTRALIA** won by an innings and 40 runs.
Debuts: Australia – K.R.Patterson, J.A.Richardson.

SRI LANKA

F.D.M.Karunaratne	c Paine b Lyon	24	c Paine b Cummins		3
H.D.R.L.Thirimanne	c Labuschagne b Cummins	12	c Paine b Cummins		32
*L.D.Chandimal	c Burns b Richardson	5	c Patterson b Cummins		0
B.K.G.Mendis	b Richardson	14	c Burns b Cummins		1
A.R.S.Silva	c Paine b Cummins	9	c Burns b Cummins		3
D.M.de Silva	c Paine b Richardson	5	b Richardson		14
†D.P.D.N.Dickwella	c Patterson b Cummins	64	c Harris b Richardson		24
M.D.K.Perera	c Labuschagne b Starc	1	c Patterson b Cummins		8
R.A.S.Lakmal	c Labuschagne b Starc	7	st Paine b Lyon		24
P.V.D.Chameera	c Patterson b Cummins	0	not out		5
C.B.R.L.S.Kumara	not out	0	absent hurt		
Extras	(NB 2, W 1)	3	(B 9, LB 15, NB 1)		25
Total	**(56.4 overs)**	**144**	**(50.5 overs)**		**139**

AUSTRALIA

M.S.Harris	c Thirimanne b Kumara	44
J.A.Burns	c Mendis b Lakmal	15
U.T.Khawaja	c Perera b Kumara	11
N.M.Lyon	c Mendis b Lakmal	1
M.Labuschagne	c Thirimanne b de Silva	81
T.M.Head	lbw b Lakmal	84
K.R.Patterson	lbw b Lakmal	30
†*T.D.Paine	c Mendis b Lakmal	0
P.J.Cummins	c Dickwella b Chameera	0
M.A.Starc	not out	26
J.A.Richardson	c Karunaratne b Perera	1
Extras	(B 6, LB 17, NB 5, W 2)	30
Total	**(106.2 overs)**	**323**

AUSTRALIA	O	M	R	W	O	M	R	W		FALL OF WICKETS		
Starc	12	2	41	2	14	0	56	0		SL	A	SL
Richardson	14	5	26	3	13	5	19	2	Wkt	1st	1st	2nd
Cummins	14.4	3	39	4	(4) 15	8	23	6	1st	26	37	15
Lyon	16	3	38	1	(3) 8.5	3	17	1	2nd	31	72	17
									3rd	54	76	19
SRI LANKA									4th	58	82	35
Lakmal	27	9	75	5					5th	66	248	69
Kumara	15	5	37	1					6th	91	272	79
Chameera	21	3	68	1					7th	102	272	109
Perera	32.2	9	84	2					8th	106	278	110
De Silva	8	3	22	1					9th	144	304	139
Karunaratne	10	0	14	0					10th	144	323	–

Umpires: M.Erasmus (*South Africa*) (55) and R.K.Illingworth (*England*) (40).
Referee: J.Srinath (*India*) (44).   **Test No. 2344/30 (A819/SL280)**
M.D.K.Perera retired hurt at 93-6 and resumed at 102-7.

AUSTRALIA v SRI LANKA (2nd Test)

At Manuka Oval, Canberra, on 1, 2, 3, 4 February 2019.
Toss: Australia. Result: **AUSTRALIA** won by 366 runs.
Debut: Sri Lanka – C.Karunaratne.

AUSTRALIA

M.S.Harris	c C.Karunaratne b Fernando	11	c Mendis b Rajitha		14
J.A.Burns	b Rajitha	180	c Mendis b Fernando		9
U.T.Khawaja	c Mendis b Fernando	0	not out		101
M.Labuschagne	c Dickwella b C.Karunaratne	6	c Dickwella b Rajitha		4
T.M.Head	lbw b Fernando	161	not out		59
K.R.Patterson	not out	114			
†*T.D.Paine	not out	45			
P.J.Cummins					
M.A.Starc					
J.A.Richardson					
N.M.Lyon					
Extras	(LB 3, NB 10, W 4)	17	(NB 6, W 3)		9
Total	**(5 wkts dec; 132 overs)**	**534**	**(3 wkts dec; 47 overs)**		**196**

SRI LANKA

F.D.M.Karunaratne	c Patterson b Starc	59	b Starc		8
H.D.R.L.Thirimanne	c Khawaja b Lyon	41	c and b Cummins		30
*L.D.Chandimal	c Paine b Starc	15	c Labuschagne b Starc		4
B.K.G.Mendis	b Cummins	6	(5) c Patterson b Labuschagne		42
M.D.K.J.Perera	retired hurt	29	(6) c Paine b Starc		0
D.M.de Silva	hit wkt b Starc	25	(7) c Head b Richardson		6
†D.P.D.N.Dickwella	lbw b Labuschagne	25	(4) b Starc		27
C.Karunaratne	c Starc b Lyon	0	c Paine b Cummins		22
M.D.K.Perera	c Paine b Starc	10	c Paine b Cummins		4
C.A.K.Rajitha	not out	0	not out		2
M.V.T.Fernando	b Starc	0	b Starc		0
Extras	(B 1, LB 4)	5	(B 1, LB 1, W 2)		4
Total	**(68.3 overs)**	**215**	**(51 overs)**		**149**

SRI LANKA	O	M	R	W		O	M	R	W
Rajitha	28	5	103	1	(2)	13	2	64	2
Fernando	30	3	126	3	(1)	11	1	43	1
C.Karunaratne	22	0	130	1	(4)	4	1	18	0
M.D.K.Perera	32	4	112	0	(3)	15	3	52	0
De Silva	20	2	60	0		4	0	19	0

AUSTRALIA	O	M	R	W		O	M	R	W
Starc	13.3	2	54	5		18	2	46	5
Richardson	15	4	49	0		9	1	29	1
Cummins	14	3	32	1	(4)	8	2	15	3
Lyon	24	6	70	2	(3)	13	1	51	0
Labuschagne	2	1	5	1					

FALL OF WICKETS

	A	SL	A	SL
Wkt	1st	1st	2nd	2nd
1st	11	90	16	18
2nd	15	101	25	28
3rd	28	120	37	58
4th	336	180	–	83
5th	404	181	–	83
6th	–	182	–	97
7th	–	215	–	143
8th	–	215	–	143
9th	–	215	–	148
10th	–	–	–	149

Umpires: M.A.Gough (*England*) (9) and R.K.Illingworth (*England*) (41).
Referee: J.Srinath (*India*) (45).   **Test No. 2345/31 (A820/SL281)**
M.D.K.J.Perera retired hurt at 157-3.

SOUTH AFRICA v SRI LANKA (1st Test)

At Kingsmead, Durban, on 13, 14, 15, 16 February 2019.
Toss: Sri Lanka. Result: **SRI LANKA** won by one wicket.
Debuts: Sri Lanka – L.Ambuldeniya, B.O.P.Fernando.

SOUTH AFRICA

Batsman	1st innings		2nd innings	
A.K.Markram	b M.V.T.Fernando	11	(2) c Mendis b Rajitha	28
D.Elgar	c Dickwella b M.V.T.Fernando	0	(1) c and b Ambuldeniya	35
H.M.Amla	c Mendis b Lakmal	3	c Thirimanne b M.V.T.Fernando	16
T.Bavuma	run out	47	lbw b Ambuldeniya	3
*F.du Plessis	c Dickwella b Rajitha	35	lbw b M.V.T.Fernando	90
†Q.de Kock	c M.V.T.Fernando b Rajitha	80	lbw b Ambuldeniya	55
V.D.Philander	c and b Rajitha	4	b Ambuldeniya	18
K.A.Maharaj	c Dickwella b M.V.T.Fernando	29	b M.V.T.Fernando	4
K.Rabada	c B.O.P.Fernando b M.V.T.Fernando	3	c Dickwella b Ambuldeniya	0
D.W.Steyn	b Ambuldeniya	15	b M.V.T.Fernando	1
D.Olivier	not out	0	not out	2
Extras	(LB 6, NB 2)	8	(LB 2, NB 3, W 2)	7
Total	**(59.4 overs; 295 mins)**	**235**	**(79.1 overs; 359 mins)**	**259**

SRI LANKA

Batsman	1st innings		2nd innings	
*F.D.M.Karunaratne	lbw b Philander	30	lbw b Philander	20
H.D.R.L.Thirimanne	c de Kock b Steyn	0	c du Plessis b Rabada	21
B.O.P.Fernando	lbw b Steyn	19	c du Plessis b Steyn	37
B.K.G.Mendis	c du Plessis b Philander	12	c de Kock b Olivier	0
M.D.K.J.Perera	c sub (M.Z.Hamza) b Steyn	51	not out	153
†D.P.D.N.Dickwella	c Steyn b Olivier	8	c and b Steyn	0
D.M.de Silva	c Olivier b Rabada	23	lbw b Maharaj	48
R.A.Lakmal	c Markram b Steyn	4	c du Plessis b Maharaj	0
L.Ambuldeniya	c Steyn b Rabada	24	c Markram b Olivier	4
C.A.K.Rajitha	run out	12	lbw b Maharaj	1
M.V.T.Fernando	not out	1	not out	6
Extras	(B 3, LB 3, W 1)	7	(LB 13, W 1)	14
Total	**(59.2 overs; 283 mins)**	**191**	**(9 wkts; 85.3 overs; 394 mins)**	**304**

SRI LANKA	O	M	R	W	O	M	R	W
Lakmal	14	3	29	1	20	5	52	0
M.V.T.Fernando	17	1	62	4	17.1	2	71	4
Rajitha	14.4	0	68	3	13	1	54	1
Karunaratne	3	0	9	0				
Ambuldeniya	10	1	51	1	(4) 26	3	66	5
B.O.P.Fernando	1	0	10	0	1	0	6	0
D.M.de Silva					(5) 2	0	8	0

SOUTH AFRICA	O	M	R	W	O	M	R	W
Steyn	20	7	48	4	18	1	71	2
Philander	10	2	32	2	8	3	13	1
Rabada	12.2	2	48	2	(4) 22.3	3	97	1
Olivier	13	2	36	1	(5) 16	3	35	2
Maharaj	3	0	16	0	(3) 20	1	71	3
Elgar	1	0	5	0				
Markram					(6) 1	0	4	0

FALL OF WICKETS				
	SA	SL	SA	SL
Wkt	1st	1st	2nd	2nd
1st	0	19	36	42
2nd	9	51	70	42
3rd	17	53	77	52
4th	89	76	95	110
5th	110	99	191	110
6th	131	133	251	206
7th	178	142	255	206
8th	186	152	256	215
9th	219	184	256	226
10th	235	191	259	

Umpires: Alim Dar (*Pakistan*) (124) and R.A.Kettleborough (*England*) (58).
Referee: Sir R.B.Richardson (*West Indies*) (21). Test No. 2346/28 (SA431/SL282)

SOUTH AFRICA v SRI LANKA (2nd Test)

At St George's Park, Port Eliizabeth, on 21, 22, 23 February 2019.
Toss: South Africa. Result: **SRI LANKA** won by eight wickets.
Debut: South Africa – P.W.A.Mulder.

SOUTH AFRICA

D.Elgar	b M.V.T.Fernando	6	(2) c Dickwella b M.V.T.Fernando		2
A.K.Markram	lbw b Rajitha	60	(1) c B.O.P.Fernando b Rajitha		18
H.M.Amla	b M.V.T.Fernando	0	c Mendis b de Silva		32
T.Bavuma	run out	0	c Dickwella b Rajitha		6
*F.du Plessis	b Karunaratne	25	not out		50
†Q.de Kock	b de Silva	86	c and b Lakmal		1
P.W.A.Mulder	lbw b Rajitha	9	c Mendis b de Silva		5
K.A.Maharaj	c Dickwella b Rajitha	0	lbw b Lakmal		6
K.Rabada	c Dickwella b de Silva	22	c Mendis b Lakmal		0
D.W.Steyn	not out	5	c Thirimanne b de Silva		0
D.Olivier	c Dickwella b M.V.T.Fernando	0	lbw b Lakmal		6
Extras	(B 1, LB 6, NB 4)	11	(LB 1, NB 1)		2
Total	**(61.2 overs; 286 mins)**	**222**	**(44.3 overs; 210 mins)**		**128**

SRI LANKA

*F.D.M.Karunaratne	c de Kock b Rabada	17	c de Kock b Olivier	19
H.D.R.L.Thirimanne	c and b Olivier	29	c de Kock b Rabada	10
B.O.P.Fernando	b Olivier	0	not out	75
B.K.G.Mendis	c de Kock b Olivier	16	not out	84
C.A.K.Rajitha	b Rabada	1		
M.D.K.J.Perera	c de Kock b Rabada	20		
D.M.de Silva	c de Kock b Mulder	19		
†D.P.D.N.Dickwella	c Elgar b Rabada	42		
R.A.Lakmal	lbw b Maharaj	7		
M.V.T.Fernando	not out	0		
L.Ambuldeniya	absent hurt			
Extras	(LB 1, NB 2)	3	(B 4, LB 5)	9
Total	**(37.4 overs; 181 mins)**	**154**	**(2 wkts; 45.4 overs; 193 mins)**	**197**

SRI LANKA	O	M	R	W	O	M	R	W	FALL OF WICKETS				
										SA	SL	SA	SL
Lakmal	13	2	33	0	16.3	3	39	4		1st	1st	2nd	2nd
M.V.T.Fernando	18.2	2	62	3	10	1	32	1	Wkt				
Rajitha	15	2	67	3	7	1	20	2	1st	15	25	10	32
Ambuldeniya	5.3	0	26	0					2nd	15	34	31	34
Karunaratne	4.3	1	12	1					3rd	15	59	51	–
De Silva	5	0	15	2	(4) 11	1	36	3	4th	73	64	90	–
									5th	130	66	91	–
SOUTH AFRICA									6th	145	97	100	–
Steyn	10	2	39	0	8	0	38	0	7th	157	128	113	–
Rabada	12.4	3	38	4	15	2	53	1	8th	216	154	115	–
Olivier	10	1	61	3	12	2	46	1	9th	221	154	116	–
Mulder	3	2	6	1	4	1	6	0	10th	222	–	128	–
Maharaj	2	0	9	1	6.4	0	45	0					

Umpires: Alim Dar (*Pakistan*) (125) and I.J.Gould (*England*) (74).
Referee: Sir R.B.Richardson (*West Indies*) (22).   Test No. 2347/29 (SA432/SL283)

INTERNATIONAL UMPIRES AND REFEREES 2019

ELITE PANEL OF UMPIRES 2019

The Elite Panel of ICC Umpires and Referees was introduced in April 2002 to raise standards and guarantee impartial adjudication. Two umpires from this panel stand in Test matches while one officiates with a home umpire from the Supplementary International Panel in limited-overs internationals.

Full Names	Birthdate	Birthplace	Tests	Debut	LOI	Debut
ALIM Sarwar DAR	06.06.68	Jhang, Pakistan	125	2003-04	197	1999-00
DHARMASENA, H.D.P.Kumar	24.04.71	Colombo, Sri Lanka	60	2010-11	90	2008-09
ERASMUS, Marais	27.02.64	George, South Africa	55	2009-10	82	2007-08
GAFFANEY, Christopher Blair	30.11.75	Dunedin, New Zealand	27	2014	60	2010
GOULD, Ian James	19.08.57	Taplow, England	74	2008-09	135	2006
ILLINGWORTH, Richard Keith	23.08.63	Bradford, England	41	2012-13	59	2010
KETTLEBOROUGH, Richard Allan	15.03.73	Sheffield, England	58	2010-11	76	2009
LLONG, Nigel James	11.02.69	Ashford, England	56	2007-08	123	2006
OXENFORD, Bruce Nicholas James	05.03.60	Southport, Australia	55	2010-11	90	2007-08
RAVI, Sundaram	22.04.66	Bangalore, India	32	2013-14	41	2011-12
REIFFEL, Paul Ronald	19.04.66	Box Hill, Australia	42	2012	60	2008-09
TUCKER, Rodney James	28.08.64	Sydney, Australia	67	2009-10	78	2008-09

ELITE PANEL OF REFEREES 2019

Full Names	Birthdate	Birthplace	Tests	Debut	LOI	Debut
BOON, David Clarence	29.12.60	Launceston, Australia	54	2011	123	2011
BROAD, Brian Christopher	29.09.57	Bristol, England	98	2003-04	303	2003-04
CROWE, Jeffrey John	14.09.58	Auckland, New Zealand	95	2004-05	276	2003-04
MADUGALLE, Ranjan Senerath	22.04.59	Kandy, Sri Lanka	187	1993-94	344	1993-94
PYCROFT, Andrew John	06.06.56	Harare, Zimbabwe	68	2009	170	2009
RICHARDSON, Sir Richard Benjamin	12.01.62	Five Islands, Antigua	22	2016	39	2016
SRINATH, Javagal	31.08.69	Mysore, India	45	2006	218	2006-07

INTERNATIONAL UMPIRES PANEL 2019

Nominated by their respective cricket boards, members from this panel officiate in home LOIs and supplement the Elite panel for Test matches. The number of Test matches/LOI in which they have stood is shown in brackets.

Afghanistan	Ahmed Shah Pakteen (-/11)	Ahmed Shah Durrani (-/3)	Bismallah Jan Shinwari (-/3)
Australia	S.D.Fry (7/49)	P.Wilson (-/23)	S.J.Nogajski (-/5)
			G.A.Abood (-/1)
Bangladesh	Tanvir Ahmed (-/-)	Sharfuddoula (-/41)	Masudur Rahman (-/6)
			Gazi Sohel (-/-)
England	R.J.Bailey (-/22)	M.A.Gough (9/49)	R.T.Robinson (-/15)
			A.G.Wharf (-/2)
India	C.Shamshuddin (-/38)	A.K.Chaudhary (-/18)	C.K.Nandan (-/6)
			N.N.Menon (-/20)
Ireland	M.Hawthorne (-/27)	R.Black (-/6)	A.J.Neill (-/5)
			P.A.Reynolds (-/1)
New Zealand	W.J.Knights (-/15)	C.M.Brown (-/15)	S.B.Haig (-/5)
Pakistan	Shozab Raza (-/22)	Ahsan Raza (-/31)	Asif Yaqoob (-/-)
			Rashid Riaz (-/-)
South Africa	A.T.Holdstock (-/16)	S.George (-/39)	B.P.Jele (-/10)
			Allahudien Paleker (-/1)
Sri Lanka	R.E.J.Martinesz (8/46)	R.S.A.Palliyaguruge (1/71)	R.R.Wimalasiri (-/11)
			L.E.Hannibal (-/2)
West Indies	G.O.Brathwaite (-/394)	J.S.Wilson (13/56)	L.S.Reifer (-/3)
			N.Duguid (-/6)
Zimbabwe	R.B.Tiffin (44/154)	T.J.Matibiri (-/23)	L.Rusere (-/9)
			I.Chabi (-/-)

Test Match and LOI statistics to 8 March 2019.

TEST MATCH CAREER RECORDS

These records, complete to 27 February 2019, contain all players registered for county cricket in 2018 at the time of going to press, plus those who have played Test cricket since 16 November 2017 (Test No. 2280).

ENGLAND – BATTING AND FIELDING

	M	I	NO	HS	Runs	Avge	100	50	Ct/St
M.M.Ali	58	100	8	155*	2769	30.09	5	14	32
T.R.Ambrose	11	16	1	102	447	29.80	1	3	31
J.M.Anderson	148	207	86	81	1174	9.70	–	1	91
J.M.Bairstow	63	109	6	167*	3806	36.95	6	20	160/11
J.T.Ball	4	8	–	31	67	8.37	–	–	1
G.S.Ballance	23	42	2	156	1498	37.45	4	7	22
G.J.Batty	9	12	2	38	149	14.90	–	–	3
I.R.Bell	118	205	24	235	7727	42.69	22	46	100
D.M.Bess	2	3	–	57	111	37.00	–	1	1
R.S.Bopara	13	19	1	143	575	31.94	3	–	6
S.G.Borthwick	1	2	–	4	5	2.50	–	–	2
T.T.Bresnan	23	26	4	91	575	26.13	–	3	8
S.C.J.Broad	126	183	24	169	3064	19.27	1	12	42
R.J.Burns	6	12	–	84	300	25.00	–	2	4
J.C.Buttler	31	54	6	106	1722	35.87	1	14	68
R.Clarke	2	3	–	55	96	32.00	–	1	1
A.N.Cook	161	291	16	294	12472	45.35	33	57	175
M.S.Crane	1	2	–	4	6	3.00	–	–	–
S.M.Curran	9	16	2	78	454	32.42	–	3	–
T.K.Curran	2	3	1	39	66	33.00	–	–	–
L.A.Dawson	3	6	2	66*	84	21.00	–	1	2
J.L.Denly	2	4	–	69	112	28.00	–	1	–
B.M.Duckett	4	7	–	56	110	15.71	–	1	1
S.T.Finn	36	47	22	56	279	11.16	–	1	8
B.T.Foakes	5	10	2	107	332	41.50	1	1	10/2
A.D.Hales	11	21	–	94	573	27.28	–	5	8
H.Hameed	3	6	1	82	219	43.80	–	2	4
K.K.Jennings	17	32	1	146*	781	25.19	2	1	17
C.J.Jordan	8	11	1	35	180	18.00	–	–	14
M.J.Leach	4	7	1	16	55	9.16	–	–	2
A.Lyth	7	13	–	107	265	20.38	1	–	8
D.J.Malan	15	26	–	140	724	27.84	1	6	11
E.J.G.Morgan	16	24	1	130	700	30.43	2	3	11
G.Onions	9	10	7	17*	30	10.00	–	–	–
C.Overton	3	6	2	41*	98	24.50	–	–	1
S.R.Patel	6	9	–	42	151	16.77	–	3	3
L.E.Plunkett	13	20	5	55*	238	15.86	–	1	3
O.J.D.Pope	2	3	–	28	54	18.00	–	–	2
A.U.Rashid	19	33	5	61	540	19.28	–	2	4
S.D.Robson	7	11	–	127	336	30.54	1	1	5
T.S.Roland-Jones	4	6	2	25	82	20.50	–	–	–
J.E.Root	80	147	12	254	6685	49.51	16	41	91
B.A.Stokes	52	95	2	258	3152	33.89	6	17	55
M.D.Stoneman	11	20	1	60	526	27.68	–	5	1
M.E.Trescothick	76	143	10	219	5825	43.79	14	29	95
J.M.Vince	13	22	–	83	548	24.90	–	3	8
T.Westley	5	9	1	59	193	24.12	–	1	1
C.R.Woakes	26	43	10	137*	1012	30.66	1	4	12
M.A.Wood	13	23	5	52	297	16.50	–	1	5

TESTS ENGLAND – BOWLING

	O	M	R	W	Avge	Best	5wI	10wM
M.M.Ali	1782.2	260	6438	177	36.37	6- 53	5	1
J.M.Anderson	5389.1	1365	15490	575	26.93	7- 42	27	3
J.T.Ball	102	23	343	3	114.33	1- 47	–	–
G.S.Ballance	2	1	5	0	–	–	–	–
G.J.Batty	285.4	38	914	15	60.93	3- 55	–	–
I.R.Bell	18	3	76	1	76.00	1- 33	–	–
D.M.Bess	31.4	1	121	3	40.33	3- 33	–	–
R.S.Bopara	72.2	10	290	1	290.00	1- 39	–	–
S.G.Borthwick	13	0	82	4	20.50	3- 33	–	–
T.T.Bresnan	779	185	2357	72	32.73	5- 48	1	–
S.C.J.Broad	4289.3	1004	12698	437	29.05	8- 15	16	2
R.Clarke	29	11	60	4	15.00	2- 7	–	–
A.N.Cook	3	0	7	1	7.00	1- 6	–	–
M.S.Crane	48	3	193	1	193.00	1-193	–	–
S.M.Curran	148.5	19	513	15	34.20	4- 74	–	–
T.K.Curran	66	14	200	2	100.00	1- 65	–	–
L.A.Dawson	87.4	12	298	7	42.57	4-101	–	–
J.L.Denly	4	0	17	0	–	–	–	–
S.T.Finn	1068.4	190	3800	125	30.40	6- 79	5	–
A.D.Hales	3	1	2	0	–	–	–	–
K.K.Jennings	12.1	1	55	0	–	–	–	–
C.J.Jordan	255	74	752	21	35.80	4- 18	–	–
M.J.Leach	193.4	34	498	20	24.90	5- 83	1	–
A.Lyth	1	1	0	0	–	–	–	–
D.J.Malan	26	4	70	0	–	–	–	–
G.Onions	267.4	69	957	32	29.90	5- 38	1	–
C.Overton	84	11	296	7	42.28	3-105	–	–
S.R.Patel	143	23	421	7	60.14	2- 27	–	–
L.E.Plunkett	443.1	71	1536	41	37.46	5- 64	1	–
A.U.Rashid	636	50	2390	60	39.83	5- 49	2	–
T.S.Roland-Jones	89.2	23	334	17	19.64	5- 57	1	–
J.E.Root	328	70	986	20	49.30	2- 9	–	–
B.A.Stokes	1221.2	221	4054	127	31.92	6- 22	4	–
M.E.Trescothick	50	6	155	1	155.00	1- 34	–	–
J.M.Vince	4	1	13	0	–	–	–	–
T.Westley	4	0	12	0	–	–	–	–
C.R.Woakes	766.4	170	2372	72	32.94	6- 70	2	1
M.A.Wood	401.2	95	1345	36	37.36	5- 41	1	–

AUSTRALIA – BATTING AND FIELDING

	M	I	NO	HS	Runs	Avge	100	50	Ct/St
A.C.Agar	4	7	1	98	195	32.50	–	1	–
C.T.Bancroft	8	14	1	82*	402	30.92	–	3	11
G.J.Bailey	5	8	1	53	183	26.14	–	1	10
J.M.Bird	9	9	6	19*	43	14.33	–	–	2
J.A.Burns	16	28	–	180	1123	40.10	4	4	18
H.W.R.Cartwright	2	2	–	37	55	27.50	–	–	–
P.J.Cummins	20	30	4	63	528	20.30	–	2	9
J.P.Faulkner	1	2	–	23	45	22.50	–	–	–
C.J.Ferguson	1	2	–	3	4	2.00	–	–	–
A.J.Finch	5	10	–	62	278	27.80	–	2	7
P.S.P.Handscomb	16	29	5	110	934	38.91	2	4	28
M.S.Harris	6	11	1	79	327	32.70	–	2	7
J.R.Hazlewood	44	55	24	39	388	12.51	–	–	15
T.M.Head	8	14	1	161	663	51.00	1	5	6
J.M.Holland	4	7	5	3	6	3.00	–	–	1
U.T.Khawaja	41	71	6	174	2765	42.53	8	14	32
M.Labuschagne	5	8	–	81	210	26.25	–	1	8

	M	I	NO	HS	Runs	Avge	100	50	Ct/St
N.M.Lyon	86	111	34	47	923	11.98	–	–	41
M.R.Marsh	31	53	5	181	1219	25.39	2	3	15
S.E.Marsh	38	68	2	182	2265	34.31	6	10	23
G.J.Maxwell	7	14	1	104	339	26.07	1	–	5
T.D.Paine	21	35	7	92	984	35.14	–	5	87/5
K.R.Patterson	2	2	1	114*	144	144.00	1	–	6
M.T.Renshaw	11	20	1	184	636	33.47	1	3	8
J.A.Richardson	2	1	–	1	1	1.00	–	–	–
C.J.Sayers	1	2	–	0	0	0.00	–	–	1
P.M.Siddle	64	90	14	51	1080	14.21	–	2	17
S.P.D.Smith	64	117	16	239	6199	61.37	23	24	96
M.A.Starc	51	78	15	99	1377	21.85	–	9	25
D.A.Warner	74	137	5	253	6363	48.20	21	29	54

AUSTRALIA – BOWLING

	O	M	R	W	Avge	Best	5wI	10wM
A.C.Agar	145.4	31	410	9	45.55	3- 46	–	–
J.M.Bird	322.2	80	1042	34	30.64	5- 59	1	–
H.W.R.Cartwright	9	1	31	0	–	–	–	–
P.J.Cummins	733.3	160	2070	94	22.02	6- 23	4	1
J.P.Faulkner	27.4	4	98	6	16.33	4- 51	–	–
A.J.Finch	2	0	8	0	–	–	–	–
J.R.Hazlewood	1595.5	407	4452	164	27.14	6- 67	6	–
T.M.Head	11	1	45	0	–	–	–	–
J.M.Holland	160	23	574	9	63.77	3- 83	–	–
U.T.Khawaja	2	0	5	0	–	–	–	–
M.Labuschagne	60	5	244	9	27.11	3- 45	–	–
N.M.Lyon	3650.5	684	11059	343	32.24	8- 50	14	2
M.R.Marsh	446.1	78	1537	35	43.91	4- 61	–	–
G.J.Maxwell	77	4	341	8	42.62	4-127	–	–
M.T.Renshaw	4	0	13	0	–	–	–	–
J.A.Richardson	51	15	123	6	20.50	3- 26	–	–
C.J.Sayers	49	11	146	2	73.00	2- 78	–	–
P.M.Siddle	2220.5	594	6482	214	30.28	6- 54	8	–
S.P.D.Smith	223.1	24	933	17	54.88	3- 18	–	–
M.A.Starc	1755.2	344	5951	211	28.20	6- 50	11	2
D.A.Warner	57	1	269	4	67.25	2- 45	–	–

SOUTH AFRICA – BATTING AND FIELDING

	M	I	NO	HS	Runs	Avge	100	50	Ct/St
K.J.Abbott	11	14	–	17	95	6.78	–	–	4
H.M.Amla	124	215	16	311*	9282	46.64	28	41	108
T.Bavuma	36	59	7	102*	1716	33.00	1	13	1
T.B.de Bruyn	9	18	1	101	346	20.35	1	–	10
Q.de Kock	40	66	5	129*	2398	39.31	4	17	166/9
M.de Lange	2	2	–	9	9	4.50	–	–	1
A.B.de Villiers	114	191	18	278*	8765	50.66	22	46	222/5
F.du Plessis	58	98	14	137	3608	42.95	9	19	53
D.Elgar	56	96	8	199	3412	38.77	11	13	59
M.Z. Hamza	1	2	–	41	41	20.50	–	–	2
S.R.Harmer	5	6	1	13	58	11.60	–	–	1
H.G.Kuhn	4	8	–	34	113	14.12	–	–	1
K.A.Maharaj	25	38	6	45	446	13.93	–	–	6
A.K.Markram	17	31	–	152	1358	43.80	4	6	15
M.Morkel	86	104	23	40	944	11.65	–	–	25
P.W.A.Mulder	1	2	–	9	14	7.00	–	–	–
L.T.Ngidi	4	7	3	5	15	3.75	–	–	2
D.Olivier	10	12	5	10*	26	3.71	–	–	2

	M	I	NO	HS	Runs	Avge	100	50	Ct/St
W.D.Parnell	6	4	–	23	67	16.75	–	–	3
A.L.Phehlukwayo	4	4	2	9	19	9.50	–	–	2
V.D.Philander	58	82	18	74	1538	24.03	–	8	17
K.Rabada	37	52	9	34	507	11.79	–	–	21
T.Shamsi	2	4	3	18*	20	20.00	–	–	–
D.W.Steyn	93	119	27	76	1251	13.59	–	2	26
S.van Zyl	12	17	2	101*	395	26.33	1	–	6
D.J.Vilas	6	9	–	26	94	10.44	–	–	13

SOUTH AFRICA – BOWLING

	O	M	R	W	Avge	Best	5wI	10wM
K.J.Abbott	346.5	95	886	39	22.71	7- 29	3	–
H.M.Amla	9	0	37	0	–	–	–	–
T.Bavuma	16	1	61	1	61.00	1- 29	–	–
T.B.de Bruyn	17	1	74	0	–	–	–	–
M.de Lange	74.4	10	277	9	30.77	7- 81	1	–
A.B.de Villiers	34	6	104	2	52.00	2- 49	–	–
F.du Plessis	13	0	69	0	–	–	–	–
D.Elgar	164.3	12	623	14	44.50	4- 22	–	–
S.R.Harmer	191.2	34	588	20	29.40	4- 61	–	–
K.A.Maharaj	838	154	2674	94	28.44	9-129	5	1
A.K.Markram	25.2	3	70	0	–	–	–	–
M.Morkel	2749.4	605	8550	309	27.66	6- 23	8	–
P.W.A.Mulder	7	3	12	1	12.00	1- 6	–	–
L.T.Ngidi	103.1	28	293	15	19.53	6- 39	1	–
D.Olivier	240	43	924	48	19.25	6- 37	3	1
W.D.Parnell	92.4	11	414	15	27.60	4- 51	–	–
A.L.Phehlukwayo	41.4	9	147	11	13.36	3- 13	–	–
V.D.Philander	1736.4	458	4632	214	21.64	6- 21	13	2
K.Rabada	1138.2	234	3833	176	21.77	7-112	9	4
T.Shamsi	80.3	10	278	6	46.33	3- 91	–	–
D.W.Steyn	3101.2	660	10077	439	22.95	7- 51	26	5
S.van Zyl	67.1	15	168	6	24.66	3- 20	–	–

WEST INDIES – BATTING AND FIELDING

	M	I	NO	HS	Runs	Avge	100	50	Ct/St
S.W.Ambris	6	12	1	43	166	15.09	–	–	2
D.Bishoo	36	61	15	45	707	15.36	–	–	20
K.C.Brathwaite	56	106	7	212	3449	34.83	8	17	26
D.M.Bravo	52	94	4	218	3459	38.43	8	17	50
J.D.Campbell	3	6	1	47	176	35.20	–	–	3
R.L.Chase	29	53	4	137*	1621	33.08	5	7	13
M.L.Cummins	13	20	6	24*	95	6.78	–	–	2
S.O.Dowrich	30	55	8	125*	1402	29.82	3	8	74/5
F.H.Edwards	55	88	28	30	394	6.56	–	–	16
S.T.Gabriel	43	62	21	20*	198	4.82	–	–	16
S.O.Hetmyer	13	25	–	93	754	30.16	–	5	6
J.O.Holder	37	64	11	202*	1783	33.64	3	8	29
S.D.Hope	29	54	2	147	1459	28.05	2	5	36/1
A.S.Joseph	9	15	–	34	84	5.60	–	–	6
S.H.Lewis	2	4	–	20	24	6.00	–	–	1
K.M.A.Paul	3	6	–	47	96	16.00	–	–	2
K.O.A.Powell	40	76	1	134	2011	26.81	3	6	29
R.Rampaul	18	31	8	40*	335	14.56	–	–	3
R.A.Reifer	1	2	1	29	52	52.00	–	–	–
K.A.J.Roach	53	85	17	41	827	12.16	–	–	16
D.S.Smith	43	76	2	147	1760	23.78	1	8	36
J.E.Taylor	46	73	7	106	856	12.96	1	1	8
J.A.Warrican	7	13	8	41	138	27.60	–	–	2

TESTS

WEST INDIES – BOWLING

	O	M	R	W	Avge	Best	5wI	10wM
D.Bishoo	1344.3	174	4350	117	37.17	8-49	4	1
K.C.Brathwaite	307.3	26	993	17	58.41	6-29	1	–
D.M.Bravo	1	0	2	0	–	–	–	–
J.D.Campbell	4.1	0	10	0	–	–	–	–
R.L.Chase	647.2	68	2223	50	44.46	8-60	2	–
M.L.Cummins	309.2	58	1015	37	37.59	6-48	1	–
F.H.Edwards	1600.2	183	6249	165	37.87	7-87	12	–
S.T.Gabriel	1139.4	201	3849	129	29.83	8-62	5	1
J.O.Holder	984	253	2576	93	27.69	6-59	5	1
A.S.Joseph	254.1	60	821	25	32.84	3-53	–	–
S.H.Lewis	40	2	162	3	54.00	2-93	–	–
K.M.A.Paul	57	11	189	6	31.50	2-25	–	–
K.O.A.Powell	1	1	0	0	–	–	–	–
R.Rampaul	573.2	111	1705	49	34.75	4-48	–	–
R.A.Reifer	30	9	88	2	44.00	1-36	–	–
K.A.J.Roach	1573	341	5000	184	27.17	6-48	9	1
D.S.Smith	1	0	3	0	–	–	–	–
J.E.Taylor	1292.5	258	4480	130	34.46	6-47	4	–
J.A.Warrican	232.4	28	806	21	38.38	4-62	–	–

NEW ZEALAND – BATTING AND FIELDING

	M	I	NO	HS	Runs	Avge	100	50	Ct/St
T.D.Astle	3	4	–	35	56	14.00	–	–	2
T.A.Blundell	2	3	1	107*	136	68.00	1	–	2
T.A.Boult	59	76	37	52*	562	14.41	–	1	30
C.de Grandhomme	15	24	2	105	721	32.77	1	4	10
M.J.Guptill	47	89	1	189	2586	29.38	3	17	50
M.J.Henry	9	14	3	66	216	19.63	–	1	5
T.W.M.Latham	41	74	3	264*	2953	41.59	8	15	41
H.M.Nicholls	23	36	5	162*	1350	43.54	4	8	17
A.Y.Patel	5	7	2	6*	35	7.00	–	–	4
J.S.Patel	24	38	8	47	381	12.70	–	–	13
J.A.Raval	16	27	1	88	902	34.69	–	7	16
M.J.Santner	17	21	–	73	535	25.47	–	2	7
I.S.Sodhi	17	25	4	63	448	21.33	–	3	11
W.E.R.Somerville	1	2	–	12	16	8.00	–	–	–
T.G.Southee	63	95	9	77*	1550	18.02	–	5	43
L.R.P.L.Taylor	90	161	19	290	6523	45.93	17	30	131
N.Wagner	40	53	13	37	464	11.60	–	–	10
B.J.Watling	59	95	14	142*	3057	37.74	6	16	200/7
K.S.Williamson	70	125	11	242*	5865	51.44	19	29	63

NEW ZEALAND – BOWLING

	O	M	R	W	Avge	Best	5wI	10wM
T.D.Astle	51.1	11	148	4	37.00	3- 39	–	–
T.A.Boult	2197.1	501	6501	233	27.90	6- 30	7	1
C.de Grandhomme	374.5	95	929	31	29.96	6- 41	1	–
M.J.Guptill	71.2	8	298	8	37.25	3- 11	–	–
M.J.Henry	359.1	65	1163	25	46.52	4- 93	–	–
A.Y.Patel	178.5	41	466	13	35.84	5- 59	1	–
J.S.Patel	972.1	202	3078	65	47.35	5-110	1	–
J.A.Raval	1	0	1	0	–	–	–	–
M.J.Santner	450.2	96	1260	34	37.05	3- 60	–	–
I.S.Sodhi	531	73	1992	41	48.58	4- 60	–	–
W.E.R.Somerville	56	10	127	7	18.114	4- 75	–	–
T.G.Southee	2353.2	536	7095	237	29.93	7- 64	8	1
L.R.P.L.Taylor	16	3	48	2	24.00	2- 4	–	–

NEW ZEALAND – BOWLING (continued)

	O	M	R	W	Avge	Best	5wI	10wM
N.Wagner	1460.3	306	4564	158	28.08	7-39	5	–
K.S.Williamson	344.3	47	1150	29	39.65	4-44	–	–

INDIA – BATTING AND FIELDING

	M	I	NO	HS	Runs	Avge	100	50	Ct/St
M.A.Agarwal	2	3	–	77	195	65.00	–	2	3
R.Ashwin	65	93	12	124	2361	29.14	4	11	23
J.J.Bumrah	10	15	6	6	14	1.55	–	–	3
S.Dhawan	34	58	1	190	2315	40.61	7	5	28
R.A.Jadeja	41	60	14	100*	1485	32.28	1	10	31
K.D.Karthik	26	42	1	129	1025	25.00	1	7	57/6
V.Kohli	77	131	8	243	6613	53.76	25	20	72
Kuldeep Yadav	6	6	–	26	51	8.50	–	–	3
B.Kumar	21	29	4	63*	552	22.08	–	3	8
Mohammed Shami	40	56	17	51*	433	11.10	–	1	9
H.H.Pandya	11	18	1	108	532	31.29	1	4	7
R.R.Pant	9	15	1	159*	696	49.71	2	2	40/2
P.A.Patel	25	38	8	71	934	31.13	–	6	62/10
C.A.Pujara	68	114	8	206*	5426	51.18	18	20	45
A.M.Rahane	56	95	9	188	3488	40.55	9	17	73
K.L.Rahul	34	56	2	199	1905	35.27	5	11	43
W.P.Saha	32	46	8	117	1164	30.63	3	5	75/10
I.Sharma	90	124	43	31*	627	7.74	–	–	19
R.G.Sharma	27	47	7	177	1585	39.62	3	10	25
P.P.Shaw	2	3	1	134	237	118.50	1	1	2
S.N.Thakur	1	1	1	4*	4	–	–	–	–
G.H.Vihari	4	7	–	56	167	23.85	–	1	1
M.Vijay	61	105	1	167	3982	38.28	12	15	49
U.T.Yadav	41	47	21	30	283	10.88	–	–	14

INDIA – BOWLING

	O	M	R	W	Avge	Best	5wI	10wM
R.Ashwin	3062	629	8700	342	25.43	7-59	26	7
J.J.Bumrah	402.4	95	1073	49	21.89	6-33	3	–
S.Dhawan	9	2	18	0	–	–	–	–
R.A.Jadeja	1913.2	487	4548	192	23.68	7-48	9	1
V.Kohli	27.1	2	76	0	–	–	–	–
Kuldeep Yadav	164.5	22	579	24	24.12	5-57	2	–
B.Kumar	558	141	1644	63	26.09	6-82	4	–
Mohammed Shami	1260.2	219	4254	144	29.54	6-56	4	–
H.H.Pandya	156.1	19	528	17	31.05	5-28	1	–
C.A.Pujara	1	0	2	0	–	–	–	–
I.Sharma	2866	561	9155	267	34.28	7-74	8	1
R.G.Sharma	55.4	3	202	2	101.00	1-26	–	–
S.N.Thakur	1.4	0	9	0	–	–	–	–
G.H.Vihari	45.3	9	132	5	26.40	3-37	–	–
M.Vijay	64	6	198	1	198.00	1-12	–	–
U.T.Yadav	1109.5	186	3983	119	33.47	6-88	2	1

PAKISTAN – BATTING AND FIELDING

	M	I	NO	HS	Runs	Avge	100	50	Ct/St
Asad Shafiq	69	117	6	137	4323	38.94	12	23	67
Azhar Ali	73	139	8	302*	5669	43.27	15	31	61
Babar Azam	21	40	5	127*	1235	35.28	1	11	16
Bilal Asif	5	8	–	15	73	9.12	–	–	2
Faheem Ashraf	4	6	–	83	138	23.00	–	1	2
Fakhar Zaman	3	6	–	94	192	32.00	–	2	3
Haris Sohail	10	19	1	147	726	40.33	2	2	8

TESTS   PAKISTAN – BATTING AND FIELDING (continued)

	M	I	NO	HS	Runs	Avge	100	50	Ct/St
Hasan Ali	9	15	5	29	155	15.50	–	–	4
Imam-ul-Haq	10	19	2	76	483	28.41	–	3	7
Mir Hamza	1	2	2	4*	4	–	–	–	–
Mohammad Abbas	14	21	11	11	63	6.30	–	–	4
Mohammad Amir	36	67	11	48	751	13.41	–	–	5
Mohammad Hafeez	55	105	8	224	3652	37.64	10	12	45
Rahat Ali	21	31	13	35*	136	7.55	–	–	9
Sarfraz Ahmed	49	86	13	112	2657	36.39	3	18	146/21
Shadab Khan	5	9	2	56	240	34.28	–	3	1
Shaheen Shah Afridi	3	6	2	14	23	5.75	–	–	–
Shan Masood	15	30	–	125	793	26.43	1	5	10
Usman Salahuddin	1	2	–	33	37	18.50	–	–	–
Wahab Riaz	27	41	5	39	306	8.50	–	–	5
Yasir Shah	35	52	6	38*	508	11.04	–	–	19

PAKISTAN – BOWLING

	O	M	R	W	Avge	Best	5wI	10wM
Asad Shafiq	44.4	1	152	2	76.00	1- 7	–	–
Azhar Ali	141.2	8	602	8	75.25	2- 35	–	–
Bilal Asif	195.4	40	424	16	26.50	6- 36	2	–
Faheem Ashraf	90	18	287	11	26.09	3- 42	–	–
Haris Sohail	64	9	156	7	22.28	3- 1	–	–
Hasan Ali	289.3	72	896	31	28.90	5- 45	1	–
Mir Hamza	15	2	67	1	67.00	1- 40	–	–
Mohammad Abbas	506	146	1245	66	18.86	5- 33	4	1
Mohammad Amir	1269.5	292	3627	119	30.47	6- 44	4	–
Mohammad Hafeez	677.5	118	1808	53	34.11	4- 16	–	–
Rahat Ali	704.3	127	2264	58	39.03	6-127	2	–
Shadab Khan	147.3	19	466	12	38.83	3- 31	–	–
Shaheen Shah Afridi	103.1	16	377	12	31.41	4- 64	–	–
Shan Masood	12	3	44	2	22.00	1- 6	–	–
Wahab Riaz	836.2	118	2884	83	34.50	5- 63	2	–
Yasir Shah	1882.1	305	5832	203	28.72	8- 41	16	3

SRI LANKA – BATTING AND FIELDING

	M	I	NO	HS	Runs	Avge	100	50	Ct/St
L.Ambuldeniya	2	2	–	24	28	14.00	–	–	1
P.V.D.Chameera	8	15	2	19	69	5.30	–	–	4
L.D.Chandimal	53	97	7	164	3768	41.86	11	17	76/10
D.M.de Silva	25	48	2	173	1495	32.50	4	5	25
D.P.D.N.Dickwella	31	58	4	83	1626	30.11	–	11	78/17
B.O.P.Fernando	2	4	1	75*	131	43.66	–	1	2
M.V.T.Fernando	5	9	5	6*	11	2.75	–	–	1
P.L.S.Gamage	5	8	4	3	6	1.50	–	–	–
M.D.Gunathilleke	8	16	–	61	299	18.68	–	2	6
H.M.R.K.B.Herath	93	144	28	80*	1699	14.64	–	3	24
C.Karanaratne	1	2	–	22	22	11.00	–	–	1
F.D.M.Karunaratne	60	117	4	196	4074	36.05	8	22	47
C.B.R.L.S.Kumara	15	22	9	10	44	3.38	–	–	3
R.A.S.Lakmal	57	90	23	42	740	11.04	–	–	16
A.D.Mathews	80	144	20	160	5554	44.79	9	33	65
B.K.G.Mendis	38	75	3	196	2639	36.65	6	9	61
M.D.K.Perera	38	68	7	95	1126	18.45	–	6	19
M.D.K.J.Perera	16	29	3	153*	910	35.00	2	4	17/8
M.K.P.A.D.Perera	5	9	2	43*	135	19.28	–	–	1
P.M.Pushpakumara	4	8	2	42*	102	17.00	–	–	2
C.A.K.Rajitha	6	9	2	12	22	3.14	–	–	4
W.S.R.Samarawickrama	4	8	–	38	125	15.62	–	–	4

	M	I	NO	HS	Runs	Avge	100	50	Ct/St
P.A.D.L.R.Sandakan	11	17	6	25	117	10.63	–	–	6
M.D.Shanaka	3	6	1	17	29	5.80	–	–	1
A.R.S.Silva	12	23	3	109	702	35.10	1	5	2
J.K.Silva	39	74	–	139	2099	28.36	3	12	34/1
H.D.R.L.Thirimanne	33	64	6	155*	1328	22.89	1	5	19
M.L.Udawatte	2	4	–	19	23	5.75	–	–	2

SRI LANKA – BOWLING

	O	M	R	W	Avge	Best	5wI	10wM
L.Ambuldeniya	41.3	4	143	6	23.83	5- 66	–	–
P.V.D.Chameera	231.5	19	984	24	41.00	5- 47	1	–
D.M.de Silva	229.1	18	804	15	53.60	3- 36	–	–
B.O.P.Fernando	2	0	16	0	–	–	–	–
M.V.T.Fernando	131.3	13	499	19	26.26	4- 62	–	–
P.L.S.Gamage	185.2	39	573	10	57.30	2- 38	–	–
M.D.Gunathilleke	33	3	111	1	111.00	1- 16	–	–
H.M.R.K.B.Herath	4332.1	814	12157	433	28.07	9-127	34	9
C.Karunaratne	26	1	148	1	148.00	1-130	–	–
F.D.M.Karunaratne	38.3	4	138	2	69.00	1- 12	–	–
C.B.R.L.S.Kumara	464.5	55	1822	50	36.44	6-122	1	–
R.A.S.Lakmal	1721.3	330	5402	137	39.43	5- 54	3	–
A.D.Mathews	646	158	1745	33	52.87	4- 44	–	–
B.K.G.Mendis	13	1	55	1	55.00	1- 10	–	–
M.D.K.Perera	1618.4	225	5196	153	33.96	6- 32	8	2
M.K.P.A.D.Perera	168.5	26	655	27	24.35	6-115	3	–
P.M.Pushpakumara	143.2	14	520	14	37.14	3- 28	–	–
C.A.K.Rajitha	184.4	27	680	23	29.56	3- 20	–	–
P.A.D.L.R.Sandakan	343.5	37	1276	37	34.48	5- 95	2	–
M.D.Shanaka	73.1	12	261	9	29.00	3- 46	–	–
H.D.R.L.Thirimanne	14	1	51	0	–	–	–	–

M.K.P.A.D.Perera is also known as A.Dananjaya.

ZIMBABWE – BATTING AND FIELDING

	M	I	NO	HS	Runs	Avge	100	50	Ct/St
R.P.Burl	1	2	–	16	16	8.00	–	–	1
R.W.Chakabva	14	28	2	101	678	26.07	1	4	25/3
B.B.Chari	7	14	–	80	254	18.14	–	2	8
T.L.Chatara	9	16	2	22	90	6.42	–	–	–
C.J.Chibhabha	3	6	–	60	124	20.66	–	1	–
A.G.Cremer	19	38	5	102*	540	16.36	1	–	12
C.R.Ervine	15	30	2	160	941	33.60	2	3	15
K.M.Jarvis	12	22	10	25*	126	10.50	–	–	3
H.Masakadza	38	76	2	158	2223	30.04	5	8	29
W.P.Masakadza	1	2	–	17	21	10.50	–	–	1
B.A.Mavuta	2	4	–	6	9	2.25	–	–	3
P.J.Moor	8	16	1	83	533	35.53	–	5	9/1
C.B.Mpofu	15	28	10	33	105	5.83	–	–	4
B.Muzarabani	1	2	1	10	14	14.00	–	–	–
Sikandar Raza	12	24	–	127	818	34.08	1	6	22
B.R.M.Taylor	28	56	4	171	1840	35.38	6	8	27
D.T.Tiripano	7	14	3	49*	227	20.63	–	–	2
S.C.Williams	10	20	–	119	553	27.65	1	2	9

TESTS

ZIMBABWE – BOWLING

	O	M	R	W	Avge	Best	5wI	10wM
B.B.Chari	3	0	12	0	–	–	–	–
T.L.Chatara	282.3	88	663	24	27.62	5- 61	1	–
C.J.Chibhabha	41	4	162	1	162.00	1- 44	–	–
A.G.Cremer	702.2	71	2604	57	45.68	5-125	1	–
K.M.Jarvis	381.3	67	1270	46	27.60	5- 54	3	–
T.Kamungozi	26	6	58	1	58.00	1- 51	–	–
H.Masakadza	194	49	489	16	30.56	3- 24	–	–
W.P.Masakadza	13.1	2	54	2	27.00	2- 33	–	–
B.A.Mavuta	56	3	237	4	59.25	4- 21	–	–
C.B.Mpofu	414.5	86	1392	29	48.00	4- 92	–	–
B.Muzarabani	13	2	48	0	–	–	–	–
Sikandar Raza	283.5	32	989	20	49.45	5- 99	1	–
B.R.M.Taylor	7	0	38	0	–	–	–	–
D.T.Tiripano	207.4	40	606	13	46.61	3- 91	–	–
S.C.Williams	247.1	30	772	17	45.41	3- 20	–	–

BANGLADESH – BATTING AND FIELDING

	M	I	NO	HS	Runs	Avge	100	50	Ct/St
Abdur Razzak	13	22	6	43	248	15.50	–	–	4
Abu Jayed	3	6	2	2	2	0.50	–	–	–
Ariful Haque	2	4	1	41*	88	29.33	–	–	2
Imrul Kayes	37	72	2	150	1776	25.37	3	4	35
Kamrul Islam	7	14	5	25*	51	5.66	–	–	–
Khaled Ahmed	1	–	–	–	–	–	–	–	1
Liton Das	13	22	–	94	558	25.36	–	4	22/2
Mahmudullah	43	81	5	136	2407	31.67	3	15	36/1
Mehedi Hasan	18	34	6	68*	543	19.39	–	2	17
Mithun Ali	3	5	–	67	133	26.60	–	1	1
Mominul Haque	33	61	4	181	2513	44.08	8	12	25
Mosaddek Hossain	2	4	1	75	104	34.66	–	1	2
Mushfiqur Rahim	66	123	9	200	4006	35.14	6	19	102/15
Mustafizur Rahman	12	17	6	10*	40	3.63	–	–	1
Nayeem Hasan	2	3	1	26	43	21.50	–	–	1
Nazmul Hossain	2	4	–	18	48	12.00	–	–	2
Nazmul Islam	1	2	–	4	4	2.00	–	–	–
Nurul Hasan	3	6	–	64	115	19.16	–	–	5/3
Rubel Hossain	26	45	19	45*	259	9.96	–	–	11
Sabbir Rahman	11	22	2	66	481	24.05	–	4	3
Sanjamul Islam	1	1	–	24	24	24.00	–	–	–
Shadman Islam	1	1	–	76	76	76.00	–	1	1
Shakib Al Hasan	55	103	7	217	3807	39.65	5	24	22
Soumya Sarkar	12	22	–	86	588	26.72	–	4	15
Taijul Islam	23	38	6	39*	334	10.43	–	–	12
Tamim Iqbal	56	108	1	206	4049	37.84	8	25	14

BANGLADESH – BOWLING

	O	M	R	W	Avge	Best	5wI	10wM
Abdur Razzak	502.3	69	1673	28	59.75	4-63	–	–
Abu Jayed	80.3	19	236	8	29.50	3-38	–	–
Ariful Haque	11	4	24	1	24.00	1-10	–	–
Imrul Kayes	4	0	12	0	–	–	–	–
Kamrul Islam	125	13	504	8	63.00	3-87	–	–
Khaled Ahmed	30	11	93	0	–	–	–	–
Mahmudullah	556.3	56	1907	41	46.51	5-51	1	–
Mehedi Hasan	768.1	97	2502	84	29.78	7-58	7	2
Mominul Haque	72.1	2	281	4	70.25	3-27	–	–
Mosaddek Hossain	10	0	45	0	–	–	–	–
Mustafizur Rahman	293.3	61	911	27	33.74	4-37	–	–

TESTS   **BANGLADESH – BOWLING (continued)**

	O	M	R	W	Avge	Best	5wI	10wM
Nayeem Hasan	38	5	133	6	22.16	5- 61	1	–
Nazmul Hossain	0.4	0	13	0	–	–	–	–
Nazmul Islam	29	7	76	4	19.00	2- 27	–	–
Rubel Hossain	678	70	2651	33	80.33	5-166	1	–
Sabbir Rahman	24	1	98	0	–	–	–	–
Sanjamul Islam	45	2	153	1	153.00	1-153	–	–
Shakib Al Hasan	2129	389	6415	205	31.29	7- 36	18	2
Soumya Sarkar	42.4	1	159	1	159.00	1- 45	–	–
Taijul Islam	938.4	142	2974	97	30.65	8- 39	7	1
Tamim Iqbal	5	0	20	0	–	–	–	–

IRELAND – BATTING AND FIELDING

	M	I	NO	HS	Runs	Avge	100	50	Ct/St
A.Balbirnie	1	2	–	0	0	0.00	–	–	1
E.C.Joyce	1	2	–	43	47	23.50	–	–	–
T.E.Kane	1	2	–	14	14	7.00	–	–	–
T.J.Murtagh	1	2	1	5*	10	10.00	–	–	–
K.J.O'Brien	1	2	–	118	158	79.00	1	–	–
N.J.O'Brien	1	2	–	18	18	9.00	–	–	2
W.T.S.Porterfield	1	2	–	32	33	16.50	–	–	2
W.B.Rankin †	1	2	–	17	23	11.50	–	–	–
P.R.Stirling	1	2	–	17	28	14.00	–	–	3
S.R.Thompson	1	2	–	53	56	28.00	–	1	–
G.C.Wilson	1	2	1	33*	45	45.00	–	–	–

IRELAND – BOWLING

	O	M	R	W	Avge	Best	5wI	10wM
T.E.Kane	26	3	103	0	–	–	–	–
T.J.Murtagh	41	8	100	6	16.66	4-45	–	–
K.J.O'Brien	6	1	20	0	–	–	–	–
W.B.Rankin	33	4	132	3	44.00	2-75	–	–
P.R.Stirling	2	0	11	0	–	–	–	–
S.R.Thompson	33	8	93	4	23.25	4-93	–	–

† W.B.Rankin made one Test appearance for England, v A in Jan 2014, scoring 13 and 0, with bowling figures of 0-34 and 1-47.

AFGHANISTAN – BATTING AND FIELDING

	M	I	NO	HS	Runs	Avge	100	50	Ct/St
Afsar Zazai	1	2	–	6	7	3.50	–	–	2
Asghar Stanikzai	1	2	–	25	36	18.00	–	–	–
Hashmatullah Shahidi	1	2	1	36*	47	47.00	–	–	–
Javed Ahmadi	1	2	–	3	4	2.00	–	–	–
Mohammad Nabi	1	2	–	24	24	12.00	–	–	2
Mohammad Shahzad	1	2	–	14	27	13.50	–	–	–
Mujeeb Zadran	1	2	–	15	18	9.00	–	–	–
Rahmat Shah	1	2	–	14	18	9.00	–	–	1
Rashid Khan	1	2	–	12	19	9.50	–	–	–
Wafadar Momand	1	2	1	6*	6	6.00	–	–	–
Yamin Ahmadzai	1	2	1	1	1	0.50	–	–	–

AFGHANISTAN – BOWLING

	O	M	R	W	Avge	Best	5wI	10wM
Asghar Stanikzai	2	0	16	0	–	–	–	–
Mohammad Nabi	13	0	65	1	65.00	1- 65	–	–
Mujeeb Zadran	15	1	75	1	75.00	1- 75	–	–
Rashid Khan	34.5	2	154	2	77.00	2-154	–	–
Wafadar Momand	21	5	100	2	50.00	2-100	–	–
Yamin Ahmadzai	19	7	51	3	17.00	3- 51	–	–

INTERNATIONAL TEST MATCH RESULTS

Complete to 27 February 2019.

Opponents		Tests	Won by										Tied	Drawn
			E	A	SA	WI	NZ	I	P	SL	Z	B		
England	Australia	346	108	144	–	–	–	–	–	–	–	–	–	94
	South Africa	149	61	–	33	–	–	–	–	–	–	–	–	55
	West Indies	157	49	–	–	57	–	–	–	–	–	–	–	51
	New Zealand	103	48	–	–	–	10	–	–	–	–	–	–	45
	India	122	47	–	–	–	–	26	–	–	–	–	–	49
	Pakistan	83	25	–	–	–	–	–	21	–	–	–	–	37
	Sri Lanka	34	15	–	–	–	–	–	–	8	–	–	–	11
	Zimbabwe	6	3	–	–	–	–	–	–	–	0	–	–	3
	Bangladesh	10	9	–	–	–	–	–	–	–	–	1	–	0
Australia	South Africa	98	–	52	26	–	–	–	–	–	–	–	–	20
	West Indies	116	–	58	–	32	–	–	–	–	–	–	1	25
	New Zealand	57	–	31	–	–	8	–	–	–	–	–	–	18
	India	98	–	42	–	–	–	28	–	–	–	–	1	27
	Pakistan	64	–	31	–	–	–	–	15	–	–	–	–	18
	Sri Lanka	31	–	19	–	–	–	–	–	4	–	–	–	8
	Zimbabwe	3	–	3	–	–	–	–	–	–	0	–	–	0
	Bangladesh	6	–	5	–	–	–	–	–	–	–	1	–	0
South Africa	West Indies	28	–	–	18	3	–	–	–	–	–	–	–	7
	New Zealand	45	–	–	25	–	4	–	–	–	–	–	–	16
	India	36	–	–	15	–	–	11	–	–	–	–	–	10
	Pakistan	26	–	–	15	–	–	–	4	–	–	–	–	7
	Sri Lanka	29	–	–	14	–	–	–	–	9	–	–	–	6
	Zimbabwe	9	–	–	8	–	–	–	–	–	0	–	–	1
	Bangladesh	12	–	–	10	–	–	–	–	–	–	0	–	2
West Indies	New Zealand	47	–	–	–	13	15	–	–	–	–	–	–	19
	India	96	–	–	–	30	–	20	–	–	–	–	–	46
	Pakistan	52	–	–	–	17	–	–	20	–	–	–	–	15
	Sri Lanka	20	–	–	–	4	–	–	–	9	–	–	–	7
	Zimbabwe	10	–	–	–	7	–	–	–	–	0	–	–	3
	Bangladesh	16	–	–	–	10	–	–	–	–	–	4	–	2
New Zealand	India	57	–	–	–	–	10	21	–	–	–	–	–	26
	Pakistan	58	–	–	–	–	12	–	25	–	–	–	–	21
	Sri Lanka	34	–	–	–	–	15	–	–	8	–	–	–	11
	Zimbabwe	17	–	–	–	–	11	–	–	–	0	–	–	6
	Bangladesh	13	–	–	–	–	10	–	–	–	–	0	–	3
India	Pakistan	59	–	–	–	–	–	9	12	–	–	–	–	38
	Sri Lanka	44	–	–	–	–	–	20	–	7	–	–	–	17
	Zimbabwe	11	–	–	–	–	–	7	–	–	2	–	–	2
	Bangladesh	9	–	–	–	–	–	7	–	–	–	0	–	2
	Afghanistan	1	–	–	–	–	–	1	–	–	–	–	–	0
Pakistan	Sri Lanka	53	–	–	–	–	–	–	19	16	–	–	–	18
	Zimbabwe	17	–	–	–	–	–	–	10	–	3	–	–	4
	Bangladesh	10	–	–	–	–	–	–	9	–	–	0	–	1
	Ireland	1	–	–	–	–	–	–	1	–	–	–	–	0
Sri Lanka	Zimbabwe	18	–	–	–	–	–	–	–	13	0	–	–	5
	Bangladesh	20	–	–	–	–	–	–	–	16	–	1	–	3
Zimbabwe	Bangladesh	16	–	–	–	–	–	–	–	–	7	6	–	3
		2347	365	385	164	173	95	150	136	90	12	13	2	762

76

	Tests	Won	Lost	Drawn	Tied	Toss Won
England	1010	365	300	345	–	492
Australia	820†	386†	222	210	2	408†
South Africa	432	164	144	124	–	209
West Indies	542	173	193	175	1	282
New Zealand	431	95	171	165	–	215
India	533	150	165	217	1	269
Pakistan	423	136	128	159	–	200
Sri Lanka	283	90	107	86	–	153
Zimbabwe	107	12	68	27	–	60
Bangladesh	112	13	83	16	–	59
Ireland	1	–	1	–	–	1
Afghanistan	1	–	1	–	–	–

† total includes Australia's victory against the ICC World XI.

INTERNATIONAL TEST CRICKET RECORDS

(To 27 February 2019)

TEAM RECORDS

HIGHEST INNINGS TOTALS

952-6d	Sri Lanka v India	Colombo (RPS)	1997-98
903-7d	England v Australia	The Oval	1938
849	England v West Indies	Kingston	1929-30
790-3d	West Indies v Pakistan	Kingston	1957-58
765-6d	Pakistan v Sri Lanka	Karachi	2008-09
760-7d	Sri Lanka v India	Ahmedabad	2009-10
759-7d	India v England	Chennai	2016-17
758-8d	Australia v West Indies	Kingston	1954-55
756-5d	Sri Lanka v South Africa	Colombo (SSC)	2006
751-5d	West Indies v England	St John's	2003-04
749-9d	West Indies v England	Bridgetown	2008-09
747	West Indies v South Africa	St John's	2004-05
735-6d	Australia v Zimbabwe	Perth	2003-04
730-6d	Sri Lanka v Bangladesh	Dhaka	2013-14
729-6d	Australia v England	Lord's	1930
726-9d	India v Sri Lanka	Mumbai	2009-10
713-3d	Sri Lanka v Zimbabwe	Bulawayo	2003-04
713-9d	Sri Lanka v Bangladesh	Chittagong	2017-18
710-7d	England v India	Birmingham	2011
708	Pakistan v England	The Oval	1987
707	India v Sri Lanka	Colombo (SSC)	2010
705-7d	India v Australia	Sydney	2003-04
701	Australia v England	The Oval	1934
699-5	Pakistan v India	Lahore	1989-90
695	Australia v England	The Oval	1930
692-8d	West Indies v England	The Oval	1995
690	New Zealand v Pakistan	Sharjah	2014-15
687-8d	West Indies v England	The Oval	1976
687-6d	India v Bangladesh	Hyderabad	2016-17
682-6d	South Africa v England	Lord's	2003
681-8d	West Indies v England	Port-of-Spain	1953-54
680-8d	New Zealand v India	Wellington	2013-14

679-7d	Pakistan v India	Lahore	2005-06
676-7	India v Sri Lanka	Kanpur	1986-87
675-5d	India v Pakistan	Multan	2003-04
674	Australia v India	Adelaide	1947-48
674-6	Pakistan v India	Faisalabad	1984-85
674-6d	Australia v England	Cardiff	2009
671-4	New Zealand v Sri Lanka	Wellington	1990-91
668	Australia v West Indies	Bridgetown	1954-55
664	India v England	The Oval	2007
662-9d	Australia v England	Perth	2017-18
660-5d	West Indies v New Zealand	Wellington	1994-95
659-8d	Australia v England	Sydney	1946-47
659-4d	Australia v India	Sydney	2011-12
658-8d	England v Australia	Nottingham	1938
658-9d	South Africa v West Indies	Durban	2003-04
657-8d	Pakistan v West Indies	Bridgetown	1957-58
657-7d	India v Australia	Calcutta	2000-01
656-8d	Australia v England	Manchester	1964
654-5	England v South Africa	Durban	1938-39
653-4d	England v India	Lord's	1990
653-4d	Australia v England	Leeds	1993
652-8d	West Indies v England	Lord's	1973
652	Pakistan v India	Faisalabad	1982-83
652-7d	England v India	Madras	1984-85
652-7d	Australia v South Africa	Johannesburg	2001-02
651	South Africa v Australia	Cape Town	2008-09
650-6d	Australia v West Indies	Bridgetown	1964-65

The highest for Zimbabwe is 563-9d (v WI, Harare, 2001), and for Bangladesh 638 (v SL, Galle, 2012-13).

LOWEST INNINGS TOTALS

† One batsman absent

26	New Zealand v England	Auckland	1954-55
30	South Africa v England	Port Elizabeth	1895-96
30	South Africa v England	Birmingham	1924
35	South Africa v England	Cape Town	1898-99
36	Australia v England	Birmingham	1902
36	South Africa v Australia	Melbourne	1931-32
42	Australia v England	Sydney	1887-88
42	New Zealand v Australia	Wellington	1945-46
42†	India v England	Lord's	1974
43	South Africa v England	Cape Town	1888-89
43	Bangladesh v West Indies	North Sound	2018
44	Australia v England	The Oval	1896
45	England v Australia	Sydney	1886-87
45	South Africa v Australia	Melbourne	1931-32
45	New Zealand v South Africa	Cape Town	2012-13
46	England v West Indies	Port-of-Spain	1993-94
47	South Africa v England	Cape Town	1888-89
47	New Zealand v England	Lord's	1958
47	West Indies v England	Kingston	2003-04
47	Australia v South Africa	Cape Town	2011-12
49	Pakistan v South Africa	Johannesburg	2012-13

The lowest for Sri Lanka is 71 (v P, Kandy, 1994-95) and for Zimbabwe 51 (v NZ, Napier, 2011-12).

BATTING RECORDS
5000 RUNS IN TESTS

Runs			M	I	NO	HS	Avge	100	50
15921	S.R.Tendulkar	I	200	329	33	248*	53.78	51	68
13378	R.T.Ponting	A	168	287	29	257	51.85	41	62
13289	J.H.Kallis	SA/ICC	166	280	40	224	55.37	45	58
13288	R.S.Dravid	I/ICC	164	286	32	270	52.31	36	63
12472	A.N.Cook	E	161	291	16	294	45.35	33	57
12400	K.C.Sangakkara	SL	134	233	17	319	57.40	38	52
11953	B.C.Lara	WI/ICC	131	232	6	400*	52.88	34	48
11867	S.Chanderpaul	WI	164	280	49	203*	51.37	30	66
11814	D.P.M.D.Jayawardena	SL	149	252	15	374	49.84	34	50
11174	A.R.Border	A	156	265	44	205	50.56	27	63
10927	S.R.Waugh	A	168	260	46	200	51.06	32	50
10122	S.M.Gavaskar	I	125	214	16	236*	51.12	34	45
10099	Younus Khan	P	118	213	19	313	52.05	34	33
9282	H.M.Amla	SA	124	215	16	311*	46.64	28	41
9265	G.C.Smith	SA/ICC	117	205	13	277	48.25	27	38
8900	G.A.Gooch	E	118	215	6	333	42.58	20	46
8832	Javed Miandad	P	124	189	21	280*	52.57	23	43
8830	Inzamam-ul-Haq	P/ICC	120	200	22	329	49.60	25	46
8781	V.V.S.Laxman	I	134	225	34	281	45.97	17	56
8765	A.B.de Villiers	SA	114	191	18	278*	50.66	22	46
8643	M.J.Clarke	A	115	198	22	329*	49.10	28	27
8625	M.L.Hayden	A	103	184	14	380	50.73	30	29
8586	V.Sehwag	I/ICC	104	180	6	319	49.34	23	32
8540	I.V.A.Richards	WI	121	182	12	291	50.23	24	45
8463	A.J.Stewart	E	133	235	21	190	39.54	15	45
8231	D.I.Gower	E	117	204	18	215	44.25	18	39
8181	K.P.Pietersen	E	104	181	8	227	47.28	23	35
8114	G.Boycott	E	108	193	23	246*	47.72	22	42
8032	G.St A.Sobers	WI	93	160	21	365*	57.78	26	30
8029	M.E.Waugh	A	128	209	17	153*	41.81	20	47
7728	M.A.Atherton	E	115	212	7	185*	37.70	16	46
7727	I.R.Bell	E	118	205	24	235	42.69	22	46
7696	J.L.Langer	A	105	182	12	250	45.27	23	30
7624	M.C.Cowdrey	E	114	188	15	182	44.06	22	38
7558	C.G.Greenidge	WI	108	185	16	226	44.72	19	34
7530	Mohammad Yousuf	P	90	156	12	223	52.29	24	33
7525	M.A.Taylor	A	104	186	13	334*	43.49	19	40
7515	C.H.Lloyd	WI	110	175	14	242*	46.67	19	39
7487	D.L.Haynes	WI	116	202	25	184	42.29	18	39
7422	D.C.Boon	A	107	190	20	200	43.65	21	32
7289	G.Kirsten	SA	101	176	15	275	45.27	21	34
7249	W.R.Hammond	E	85	140	16	336*	58.45	22	24
7214	C.H.Gayle	WI	103	182	11	333	42.18	15	37
7212	S.C.Ganguly	I	113	188	17	239	42.17	16	35
7172	S.P.Fleming	NZ	111	189	10	274*	40.06	9	46
7110	G.S.Chappell	A	87	151	19	247*	53.86	24	31
7037	A.J.Strauss	E	100	178	6	177	40.91	21	27
6996	D.G.Bradman	A	52	80	10	334	99.94	29	13
6973	S.T.Jayasuriya	SL	110	188	14	340	40.07	14	31
6971	L.Hutton	E	79	138	15	364	56.67	19	33
6868	D.B.Vengsarkar	I	116	185	22	166	42.13	17	35
6806	K.F.Barrington	E	82	131	15	256	58.67	20	35
6744	G.P.Thorpe	E	100	179	28	200*	44.66	16	39

			M	I	NO	HS	Avge	100	50
6685	J.E.Root	E	80	147	12	254	49.51	16	41
6613	V.Kohli	I	77	131	8	243	53.76	25	20
6523	L.R.P.L.Taylor	NZ	90	161	19	290	45.93	17	30
6453	B.B.McCullum	NZ	101	176	9	302	38.64	12	31
6363	D.A.Warner	A	74	137	5	253	48.20	21	29
6361	P.A.de Silva	SL	93	159	11	267	42.97	20	22
6235	M.E.K.Hussey	A	79	137	16	195	51.52	19	29
6227	R.B.Kanhai	WI	79	137	6	256	47.53	15	28
6215⁻	M.Azharuddin	I	99	147	9	199	45.03	22	21
6199	S.P.D.Smith	A	64	117	16	239	61.37	23	24
6167	H.H.Gibbs	SA	90	154	7	228	41.95	14	26
6149	R.N.Harvey	A	79	137	10	205	48.41	21	24
6080	G.R.Viswanath	I	91	155	10	222	41.93	14	35
5949	R.B.Richardson	WI	86	146	12	194	44.39	16	27
5865	K.S.Williamson	NZ	70	125	11	242*	51.44	19	29
5842	R.R.Sarwan	WI	87	154	8	291	40.01	15	31
5825	M.E.Trescothick	E	76	143	10	219	43.79	14	29
5807	D.C.S.Compton	E	78	131	15	278	50.06	17	28
5768	Salim Malik	P	103	154	22	237	43.69	15	29
5764	N.Hussain	E	96	171	16	207	37.19	14	33
5762	C.L.Hooper	WI	102	173	15	233	36.46	13	27
5719	M.P.Vaughan	E	82	147	9	197	41.44	18	18
5669	Azhar Ali	P	73	139	8	302*	43.27	15	31
5570	A.C.Gilchrist	A	96	137	20	204*	47.60	17	26
5554	A.D.Mathews	SL	80	144	20	160	44.79	9	33
5515	M.V.Boucher	SA/ICC	147	206	24	125	30.30	5	35
5502	M.S.Atapattu	SL	90	156	15	249	39.02	16	17
5492	T.M.Dilshan	SL	87	145	11	193	40.98	16	23
5462	T.T.Samaraweera	SL	81	132	20	231	48.76	14	30
5444	M.D.Crowe	NZ	77	131	11	299	45.36	17	18
5426	C.A.Pujara	I	68	114	8	206*	51.18	18	20
5410	J.B.Hobbs	E	61	102	7	211	56.94	15	28
5357	K.D.Walters	A	74	125	14	250	48.26	15	33
5345	I.M.Chappell	A	75	136	10	196	42.42	14	26
5334	J.G.Wright	NZ	82	148	7	185	37.82	12	23
5312	M.J.Slater	A	74	131	7	219	42.84	14	21
5248	Kapil Dev	I	131	184	15	163	31.05	8	27
5234	W.M.Lawry	A	67	123	12	210	47.15	13	27
5222	Misbah-ul-Haq	P	75	132	20	161*	46.62	10	39
5200	I.T.Botham	E	102	161	6	208	33.54	14	22
5138	J.H.Edrich	E	77	127	9	310*	43.54	12	24
5105	A.Ranatunga	SL	93	155	12	135*	35.69	4	38
5062	Zaheer Abbas	P	78	124	11	274	44.79	12	20

The most for Zimbabwe is 4794 by A.Flower (112 innings), and for Bangladesh 4049 by Tamim Iqbal (108 innings).

750 RUNS IN A SERIES

Runs			*Series*	M	I	NO	HS	Avge	100	50
974	D.G.Bradman	A v E	1930	5	7	–	334	139.14	4	–
905	W.R.Hammond	E v A	1928-29	5	9	1	251	113.12	4	–
839	M.A.Taylor	A v E	1989	6	11	1	219	83.90	2	5
834	R.N.Harvey	A v SA	1952-53	5	9	–	205	92.66	4	3
829	I.V.A.Richards	WI v E	1976	4	7	–	291	118.42	3	2
827	C.L.Walcott	WI v A	1954-55	5	10	–	155	82.70	5	2
824	G.St A.Sobers	WI v P	1957-58	5	8	2	365*	137.33	3	3

Runs			Series	M	I	NO	HS	Avge	100	50
810	D.G.Bradman	A v E	1936-37	5	9	–	270	90.00	3	1
806	D.G.Bradman	A v SA	1931-32	5	5	1	299*	201.50	4	–
798	B.C.Lara	WI v E	1993-94	5	8	–	375	99.75	2	2
779	E.de C.Weekes	WI v I	1948-49	5	7	–	194	111.28	4	2
774	S.M.Gavaskar	I v WI	1970-71	4	8	3	220	154.80	4	3
769	S.P.D.Smith	A v I	2014-15	4	8	2	192	128.16	4	2
766	A.N.Cook	E v A	2010-11	5	7	1	235*	127.66	3	2
765	B.C.Lara	WI v E	1995	6	10	1	179	85.00	3	3
761	Mudassar Nazar	P v I	1982-83	5	8	2	231	126.83	4	1
758	D.G.Bradman	A v E	1934	5	8	–	304	94.75	2	1
753	D.C.S.Compton	E v SA	1947	5	8	–	208	94.12	4	2
752	G.A.Gooch	E v I	1990	3	6	–	333	125.33	3	2

HIGHEST INDIVIDUAL INNINGS

400*	B.C.Lara	WI v E	St John's	2003-04
380	M.L.Hayden	A v Z	Perth	2003-04
375	B.C.Lara	WI v E	St John's	1993-94
374	D.P.M.D.Jayawardena	SL v SA	Colombo (SSC)	2006
365*	G.St A.Sobers	WI v P	Kingston	1957-58
364	L.Hutton	E v A	The Oval	1938
340	S.T.Jayasuriya	SL v I	Colombo (RPS)	1997-98
337	Hanif Mohammed	P v WI	Bridgetown	1957-58
336*	W.R.Hammond	E v NZ	Auckland	1932-33
334*	M.A.Taylor	A v P	Peshawar	1998-99
334	D.G.Bradman	A v E	Leeds	1930
333	G.A.Gooch	E v I	Lord's	1990
333	C.H.Gayle	WI v SL	Galle	2010-11
329*	M.J.Clarke	A v I	Sydney	2011-12
329	Inzamam-ul-Haq	P v NZ	Lahore	2001-02
325	A.Sandham	E v WI	Kingston	1929-30
319	V.Sehwag	I v SA	Chennai	2007-08
319	K.C.Sangakkara	SL v B	Chittagong	2013-14
317	C.H.Gayle	WI v SA	St John's	2004-05
313	Younus Khan	P v SL	Karachi	2008-09
311*	H.M.Amla	SA v E	The Oval	2012
311	R.B.Simpson	A v E	Manchester	1964
310*	J.H.Edrich	E v NZ	Leeds	1965
309	V.Sehwag	I v P	Multan	2003-04
307	R.M.Cowper	A v E	Melbourne	1965-66
304	D.G.Bradman	A v E	Leeds	1934
303*	K.K.Nair	I v E	Chennai	2016-17
302*	Azhar Ali	P v WI	Dubai (DSC)	2016-17
302	L.G.Rowe	WI v E	Bridgetown	1973-74
302	B.B.McCullum	NZ v I	Wellington	2013-14
299*	D.G.Bradman	A v SA	Adelaide	1931-32
299	M.D.Crowe	NZ v SL	Wellington	1990-91
294	A.N.Cook	E v I	Birmingham	2011
293	V.Sehwag	I v SL	Mumbai	2009-10
291	I.V.A.Richards	WI v E	The Oval	1976
291	R.R.Sarwan	WI v E	Bridgetown	2008-09
290	L.R.P.L.Taylor	NZ v A	Perth	2015-16
287	R.E.Foster	E v A	Sydney	1903-04
287	K.C.Sangakkara	SL v SA	Colombo (SSC)	2006
285*	P.B.H.May	E v WI	Birmingham	1957
281	V.V.S.Laxman	I v A	Calcutta	2000-01

280*	Javed Miandad	P v I	Hyderabad	1982-83
278*	A.B.de Villiers	SA v P	Abu Dhabi	2010-11
278	D.C.S.Compton	E v P	Nottingham	1954
277	B.C.Lara	WI v A	Sydney	1992-93
277	G.C.Smith	SA v E	Birmingham	2003
275*	D.J.Cullinan	SA v NZ	Auckland	1998-99
275	G.Kirsten	SA v E	Durban	1999-00
275	D.P.M.D.Jayawardena	SL v I	Ahmedabad	2009-10
274*	S.P.Fleming	NZ v SL	Colombo (SSC)	2002-03
274	R.G.Pollock	SA v A	Durban	1969-70
274	Zaheer Abbas	P v E	Birmingham	1971
271	Javed Miandad	P v NZ	Auckland	1988-89
270*	G.A.Headley	WI v E	Kingston	1934-35
270	D.G.Bradman	A v E	Melbourne	1936-37
270	R.S.Dravid	I v P	Rawalpindi	2003-04
270	K.C.Sangakkara	SL v Z	Bulawayo	2004
269*	A.C.Voges	A v WI	Hobart	2015-16
268	G.N.Yallop	A v P	Melbourne	1983-84
267*	B.A.Young	NZ v SL	Dunedin	1996-97
267	P.A.de Silva	SL v NZ	Wellington	1990-91
267	Younus Khan	P v I	Bangalore	2004-05
266	W.H.Ponsford	A v E	The Oval	1934
266	D.L.Houghton	Z v SL	Bulawayo	1994-95
264*	T.W.M.Latham	NZ v SL	Wellington	2018-19
263	A.N.Cook	E v P	Abu Dhabi	2015-16
262*	D.L.Amiss	E v WI	Kingston	1973-74
262	S.P.Fleming	NZ v SA	Cape Town	2005-06
261*	R.R.Sarwan	WI v B	Kingston	2004
261	F.M.M.Worrell	WI v E	Nottingham	1950
260	C.C.Hunte	WI v P	Kingston	1957-58
260	Javed Miandad	P v E	The Oval	1987
260	M.N.Samuels	WI v B	Khulna	2012-13
259*	M.J.Clarke	A v SA	Brisbane	2012-13
259	G.M.Turner	NZ v WI	Georgetown	1971-72
259	G.C.Smith	SA v E	Lord's	2003
258	T.W.Graveney	E v WI	Nottingham	1957
258	S.M.Nurse	WI v NZ	Christchurch	1968-69
258	B.A.Stokes	E v SA	Cape Town	2015-16
257*	Wasim Akram	P v Z	Sheikhupura	1996-97
257	R.T.Ponting	A v I	Melbourne	2003-04
256	R.B.Kanhai	WI v I	Calcutta	1958-59
256	K.F.Barrington	E v A	Manchester	1964
255*	D.J.McGlew	SA v NZ	Wellington	1952-53
254	D.G.Bradman	A v E	Lord's	1930
254	V.Sehwag	I v P	Lahore	2005-06
254	J.E.Root	E v P	Manchester	2016
253*	H.M.Amla	SA v I	Nagpur	2009-10
253	S.T.Jayasuriya	SL v P	Faisalabad	2004-05
253	D.A.Warner	A v NZ	Perth	2015-16
251	W.R.Hammond	E v A	Sydney	1928-29
250	K.D.Walters	A v NZ	Christchurch	1976-77
250	S.F.A.F.Bacchus	WI v I	Kanpur	1978-79
250	J.L.Langer	A v E	Melbourne	2002-03

The highest for Bangladesh is 219* by Mushfiqur Rahim (v Z, Dhaka, 2018-19).

20 HUNDREDS

Opponents

Player	200	Inn	E	A	SA	WI	NZ	I	P	SL	Z	B
51 S.R.Tendulkar I	6	329	7	11	7	3	4	–	2	9	3	5
45 J.H.Kallis SA	2	280	8	5	–	8	6	7	6	1	3	1
41 R.T.Ponting A	6	287	8	–	8	7	2	8	5	1	1	1
38 K.C.Sangakkara SL	11	233	3	1	3	3	4	5	10	–	2	7
36 R.S.Dravid I	5	286	7	2	2	5	6	–	5	3	3	3
34 Younus Khan P	6	213	4	4	4	3	2	5	–	8	1	3
34 S.M.Gavaskar I	4	214	4	8	–	13	2	–	5	2	–	–
34 B.C.Lara WI	9	232	7	9	4	–	1	2	4	5	1	1
34 D.P.M.D.Jayawardena SL	7	252	8	2	6	1	3	6	2	–	1	5
33 A.N.Cook E	5	291	–	5	2	6	3	7	5	3	–	2
32 S.R.Waugh A	1	260	10	–	2	7	2	2	3	3	1	2
30 M.L.Hayden † A	2	184	5	–	6	5	1	6	1	3	2	–
30 S.Chanderpaul WI	2	280	5	5	5	–	2	7	1	–	1	4
29 D.G.Bradman A	12	80	19	–	4	2	–	4	–	–	–	–
28 M.J.Clarke A	4	198	7	–	5	1	4	7	1	3	–	–
28 H.M.Amla SA	4	215	6	5	–	1	4	5	2	2	–	3
27 G.C.Smith SA	5	205	7	3	–	7	2	–	4	–	1	3
27 A.R.Border A	2	265	8	–	–	3	5	4	6	1	–	–
26 G.St A.Sobers WI	2	160	10	4	–	–	1	8	3	–	–	–
25 V.Kohli I	6	131	5	7	2	2	3	–	–	5	–	1
25 Inzamam-ul-Haq P			5	1	–	4	3	3	–	5	2	2
24 G.S.Chappell A	4	151	9	–	–	5	3	1	6	–	–	–
24 Mohammad Yousuf P	4	156	6	1	–	7	1	4	–	1	2	2
24 I.V.A.Richards WI	3	182	8	5	–	–	1	8	2	–	–	–
23 S.P.D.Smith A	2	117	8	–	1	2	2	7	2	1	–	–
23 V.Sehwag I	6	180	2	3	5	2	2	–	4	5	–	–
23 K.P.Pietersen E	3	181	–	4	3	3	2	6	2	3	–	–
23 J.L.Langer A	3	182	5	–	2	3	3	4	4	2	–	–
23 Javed Miandad P	6	189	2	6	–	2	7	5	–	1	–	–
22 W.R.Hammond E	7	140	–	9	6	1	4	2	–	–	–	–
22 M.Azharuddin I	–	147	6	2	4	–	2	–	3	5	–	–
22 M.C.Cowdrey E	–	188	–	5	3	6	2	3	3	–	–	–
22 A.B.de Villiers SA	2	191	2	6	–	6	–	3	4	1	–	–
22 G.Boycott E	1	193	–	7	1	5	2	4	3	–	–	–
22 I.R.Bell E	1	205	–	4	2	2	1	4	4	2	–	3
21 D.A.Warner A	1	137	3	–	4	1	4	4	3	2	–	–
21 R.N.Harvey A	2	137	6	–	8	3	–	4	–	–	–	–
21 G.Kirsten SA	3	176	5	2	–	3	2	3	2	1	1	2
21 A.J.Strauss E	–	178	–	4	3	6	3	3	2	–	1	–
21 D.C.Boon A	1	190	7	–	–	3	3	6	1	1	–	–
20 K.F.Barrington E	1	131	–	5	3	2	3	3	4	–	–	–
20 P.A.de Silva SL	2	159	2	1	–	2	2	5	8	–	1	1
20 M.E.Waugh A	–	209	6	–	4	4	1	3	–	1	1	–
20 G.A.Gooch E	2	215	–	4	5	4	5	1	1	–	–	–

† Includes century scored for Australia v ICC in 2005-06.

The most for New Zealand is 19 by K.S.Williamson (125 innings), for Zimbabwe 12 by A.Flower (112), and for Bangladesh 8 by Mominul Haque (61) and Tamim Iqbal (108).

The most double hundreds by batsmen not included above are 6 by M.S.Atapattu (16 hundreds for Sri Lanka), 4 by L.Hutton (19 for England), 4 by C.G.Greenidge (19 for West Indies), 4 by Zaheer Abbas (12 for Pakistan), and 4 by B.B.McCullum (12 for New Zealand).

HIGHEST PARTNERSHIP FOR EACH WICKET

1st	415	N.D.McKenzie/G.C.Smith	SA v B	Chittagong	2007-08
2nd	576	S.T.Jayasuriya/R.S.Mahanama	SL v I	Colombo (RPS)	1997-98
3rd	624	K.C.Sangakkara/D.P.M.D.Jayawardena	SL v SA	Colombo (SSC)	2006
4th	449	A.C.Voges/S.E.Marsh	A v WI	Hobart	2015-16
5th	405	S.G.Barnes/D.G.Bradman	A v E	Sydney	1946-47
6th	399	B.A.Stokes/J.M.Bairstow	E v SA	Cape Town	2015-16
7th	347	D.St E.Atkinson/C.C.Depeiza	WI v A	Bridgetown	1954-55
8th	332	I.J.L.Trott/S.C.J.Broad	E v P	Lord's	2010
9th	195	M.V.Boucher/P.L.Symcox	SA v P	Johannesburg	1997-98
10th	198	J.E.Root/J.M.Anderson	E v I	Nottingham	2014

BOWLING RECORDS
200 WICKETS IN TESTS

Wkts			M	Balls	Runs	Avge	5 wI	10 wM
800	M.Muralitharan	SL/ICC	133	44039	18180	22.72	67	22
708	S.K.Warne	A	145	40705	17995	25.41	37	10
619	A.Kumble	I	132	40850	18355	29.65	35	8
575	J.M.Anderson	E	148	32335	15490	26.93	27	3
563	G.D.McGrath	A	124	29248	12186	21.64	29	3
519	C.A.Walsh	WI	132	30019	12688	24.44	22	3
439	D.W.Steyn	SA	93	18608	10077	22.95	26	5
437	S.C.J.Broad	E	126	25737	12698	29.05	16	2
434	Kapil Dev	I	131	27740	12867	29.64	23	2
433	H.M.R.K.B.Herath	SL	93	25993	12157	28.07	34	9
431	R.J.Hadlee	NZ	86	21918	9612	22.30	36	9
421	S.M.Pollock	SA	108	24453	9733	23.11	16	1
417	Harbhajan Singh	I	103	28580	13537	32.46	25	5
414	Wasim Akram	P	104	22627	9779	23.62	25	5
405	C.E.L.Ambrose	WI	98	22104	8500	20.98	22	3
390	M.Ntini	SA	101	20834	11242	28.82	18	4
383	I.T.Botham	E	102	21815	10878	28.40	27	4
376	M.D.Marshall	WI	81	17584	7876	20.94	22	4
373	Waqar Younis	P	87	16224	8788	23.56	22	5
362	Imran Khan	P	88	19458	8258	22.81	23	6
362	D.L.Vettori	NZ/ICC	113	28814	12441	34.36	20	3
355	D.K.Lillee	A	70	18467	8493	23.92	23	7
355	W.P.J.U.C.Vaas	SL	111	23438	10501	29.58	12	2
343	N.M.Lyon	A	86	21905	11059	32.24	14	2
342	R.Ashwin	I	65	18372	8700	25.43	26	7
330	A.A.Donald	SA	72	15519	7344	22.25	20	3
325	R.G.D.Willis	E	90	17357	8190	25.20	16	—
313	M.G.Johnson	A	73	16001	8891	28.40	12	3
311	Z.Khan	I	92	18785	10247	32.94	11	1
310	B.Lee	A	76	16531	9554	30.81	10	—
309	M.Morkel	SA	86	16498	8550	27.66	8	—
309	L.R.Gibbs	WI	79	27115	8989	29.09	18	2
307	F.S.Trueman	E	67	15178	6625	21.57	17	3
297	D.L.Underwood	E	86	21862	7674	25.83	17	6
292	J.H.Kallis	SA/ICC	166	20232	9535	32.65	5	—
291	C.J.McDermott	A	71	16586	8332	28.63	14	2
267	I.Sharma	I	90	17196	9155	34.28	8	1
266	B.S.Bedi	I	67	21364	7637	28.71	14	1
261	Danish Kaneria	P	61	17697	9082	34.79	15	2
259	J.Garner	WI	58	13169	5433	20.97	7	—
259	J.N.Gillespie	A	71	14234	6770	26.13	8	—
255	G.P.Swann	E	60	15349	7642	29.96	17	3
252	J.B.Statham	E	70	16056	6261	24.84	9	1
249	M.A.Holding	WI	60	12680	5898	23.68	13	2

Wkts			M	Balls	Runs	Avge	5 wI	10 wM
248	R.Benaud	A	63	19108	6704	27.03	16	1
248	M.J.Hoggard	E	67	13909	7564	30.50	7	1
246	G.D.McKenzie	A	60	17681	7328	29.78	16	3
242	B.S.Chandrasekhar	I	58	15963	7199	29.74	16	2
237	T.G.Southee	NZ	63	14120	7095	29.93	8	1
236	A.V.Bedser	E	51	15918	5876	24.89	15	5
236	J.Srinath	I	67	15104	7196	30.49	10	1
236	Abdul Qadir	P	67	17126	7742	32.80	15	5
235	G.St A.Sobers	WI	93	21599	7999	34.03	6	–
234	A.R.Caddick	E	62	13558	6999	29.91	13	1
233	T.A.Boult	NZ	59	13183	6501	27.90	7	1
233	C.S.Martin	NZ	71	14026	7878	33.81	10	1
229	D.Gough	E	58	11821	6503	28.39	9	–
228	R.R.Lindwall	A	61	13650	5251	23.03	12	–
226	S.J.Harmison	E/ICC	63	13375	7192	31.82	8	1
226	A.Flintoff	E/ICC	79	14951	7410	32.78	3	–
218	C.L.Cairns	NZ	62	11698	6410	29.40	13	1
216	C.V.Grimmett	A	37	14513	5231	24.21	21	7
216	H.H.Streak	Z	65	13559	6079	28.14	7	–
214	V.D.Philander	SA	58	10420	4632	21.64	13	2
214	P.M.Siddle	A	64	13325	6482	30.28	8	–
212	M.G.Hughes	A	53	12285	6017	28.38	7	1
211	M.A.Starc	A	51	10532	5951	28.20	11	2
208	S.C.G.MacGill	A	44	11237	6038	29.02	12	2
208	Saqlain Mushtaq	P	49	14070	6206	29.83	13	3
205	Shakib Al Hasan	B	55	12774	6415	31.29	18	2
203	Yasir Shah	P	35	11293	5832	28.72	16	3
202	A.M.E.Roberts	WI	47	11136	5174	25.61	11	2
202	J.A.Snow	E	49	12021	5387	26.66	8	1
200	J.R.Thomson	A	51	10535	5601	28.00	8	–

35 OR MORE WICKETS IN A SERIES

Wkts		Series		M	Balls	Runs	Avge	5 wI	10 wM
49	S.F.Barnes	E v SA	1913-14	4	1356	536	10.93	7	3
46	J.C.Laker	E v A	1956	5	1703	442	9.60	4	2
44	C.V.Grimmett	A v SA	1935-36	5	2077	642	14.59	5	3
42	T.M.Alderman	A v E	1981	6	1950	893	21.26	4	–
41	R.M.Hogg	A v E	1978-79	6	1740	527	12.85	5	2
41	T.M.Alderman	A v E	1989	6	1616	712	17.36	6	1
40	Imran Khan	P v I	1982-83	6	1339	558	13.95	4	2
40	S.K.Warne	A v E	2005	5	1517	797	19.92	3	2
39	A.V.Bedser	E v A	1953	5	1591	682	17.48	5	1
39	D.K.Lillee	A v E	1981	6	1870	870	22.30	2	1
38	M.W.Tate	E v A	1924-25	5	2528	881	23.18	5	1
37	W.J.Whitty	A v SA	1910-11	5	1395	632	17.08	2	–
37	H.J.Tayfield	SA v E	1956-57	5	2280	636	17.18	4	1
37	M.G.Johnson	A v E	2013-14	5	1132	517	13.97	3	–
36	A.E.E.Vogler	SA v E	1909-10	5	1349	783	21.75	4	1
36	A.A.Mailey	A v E	1920-21	5	1465	946	26.27	4	2
36	G.D.McGrath	A v E	1997	6	1499	701	19.47	2	–
35	G.A.Lohmann	E v SA	1895-96	3	520	203	5.80	4	2
35	B.S.Chandrasekhar	I v E	1972-73	5	1747	662	18.91	4	–
35	M.D.Marshall	WI v E	1988	5	1219	443	12.65	3	1

The most for New Zealand is 33 by R.J.Hadlee (3 Tests v A, 1985-86), for Sri Lanka 30 by M.Muralitharan (3 Tests v Z, 2001-02), for Zimbabwe 22 by H.H.Streak (3 Tests v P, 1994-95), and for Bangladesh 19 by Mehedi Hasan (2 Tests v E, 2016-17).

15 OR MORE WICKETS IN A TEST († On debut)

19- 90	J.C.Laker	E v A	Manchester	1956
17-159	S.F.Barnes	E v SA	Johannesburg	1913-14
16-136†	N.D.Hirwani	I v WI	Madras	1987-88
16-137†	R.A.L.Massie	A v E	Lord's	1972
16-220	M.Muralitharan	SL v E	The Oval	1998
15- 28	J.Briggs	E v SA	Cape Town	1888-89
15- 45	G.A.Lohmann	E v SA	Port Elizabeth	1895-96
15- 99	C.Blythe	E v SA	Leeds	1907
15-104	H.Verity	E v A	Lord's	1934
15-123	R.J.Hadlee	NZ v A	Brisbane	1985-86
15-124	W.Rhodes	E v A	Melbourne	1903-04
15-217	Harbhajan Singh	I v A	Madras	2000-01

The best analysis for South Africa is 13-132 by M.Ntini (v WI, Port-of-Spain, 2004-05), for West Indies 14-149 by M.A.Holding (v E, The Oval, 1976), for Pakistan 14-116 by Imran Khan (v SL, Lahore, 1981-82), for Zimbabwe 11-257 by A.G.Huckle (v NZ, Bulawayo, 1997-98), and for Bangladesh 12-117 by Mehedi Hasan (v WI, Dhaka, 2018-19).

NINE OR MORE WICKETS IN AN INNINGS

10- 53	J.C.Laker	E v A	Manchester	1956
10- 74	A.Kumble	I v P	Delhi	1998-99
9- 28	G.A.Lohmann	E v SA	Johannesburg	1895-96
9- 37	J.C.Laker	E v A	Manchester	1956
9- 51	M.Muralitharan	SL v Z	Kandy	2001-02
9- 52	R.J.Hadlee	NZ v A	Brisbane	1985-86
9- 56	Abdul Qadir	P v E	Lahore	1987-88
9- 57	D.E.Malcolm	E v SA	The Oval	1994
9- 65	M.Muralitharan	SL v E	The Oval	1998
9- 69	J.M.Patel	I v A	Kanpur	1959-60
9- 83	Kapil Dev	I v WI	Ahmedabad	1983-84
9- 86	Sarfraz Nawaz	P v A	Melbourne	1978-79
9- 95	J.M.Noreiga	WI v I	Port-of-Spain	1970-71
9-102	S.P.Gupte	I v WI	Kanpur	1958-59
9-103	S.F.Barnes	E v SA	Johannesburg	1913-14
9-113	H.J.Tayfield	SA v E	Johannesburg	1956-57
9-121	A.A.Mailey	A v E	Melbourne	1920-21
9-127	H.M.R.K.B.Herath	SL v P	Colombo (SSC)	2014
9-129	K.A.Maharaj	SA v SL	Colombo (SSC)	2018

The best analysis for Zimbabwe is 8-109 by P.A.Strang (v NZ, Bulawayo, 2000-01), and for Bangladesh 8-39 by Taijul Islam (v Z, Dhaka, 2014-15).

HAT-TRICKS

F.R.Spofforth	Australia v England	Melbourne	1878-79
W.Bates[7]	England v Australia	Melbourne	1882-83
J.Briggs	England v Australia	Sydney	1891-92
G.A.Lohmann	England v South Africa	Port Elizabeth	1895-96
J.T.Hearne	England v Australia	Leeds	1899
H.Trumble	Australia v England	Melbourne	1901-02
H.Trumble	Australia v England	Melbourne	1903-04
T.J.Matthews (2)[2]	Australia v South Africa	Manchester	1912
M.J.C.Allom[1]	England v New Zealand	Christchurch	1929-30
T.W.J.Goddard	England v South Africa	Johannesburg	1938-39
P.J.Loader	England v West Indies	Leeds	1957
L.F.Kline	Australia v South Africa	Cape Town	1957-58
W.W.Hall	West Indies v Pakistan	Lahore	1958-59

G.M.Griffin[7]	South Africa v England	Lord's	1960
L.R.Gibbs	West Indies v Australia	Adelaide	1960-61
P.J.Petherick[1/7]	New Zealand v Pakistan	Lahore	1976-77
C.A.Walsh[5]	West Indies v Australia	Brisbane	1988-89
M.G.Hughes[3/7]	Australia v West Indies	Perth	1988-89
D.W.Fleming[1]	Australia v Pakistan	Rawalpindi	1994-95
S.K.Warne	Australia v England	Melbourne	1994-95
D.G.Cork	England v West Indies	Manchester	1995
D.Gough[7]	England v Australia	Sydney	1998-99
Wasim Akram[4]	Pakistan v Sri Lanka	Lahore	1998-99
Wasim Akram[4]	Pakistan v Sri Lanka	Dhaka	1998-99
D.N.T.Zoysa[5]	Sri Lanka v Zimbabwe	Harare	1999-00
Abdul Razzaq	Pakistan v Sri Lanka	Galle	2000-01
G.D.McGrath	Australia v West Indies	Perth	2000-01
Harbhajan Singh[7]	India v Australia	Calcutta	2000-01
Mohammad Sami[7]	Pakistan v Sri Lanka	Lahore	2001-02
J.J.C.Lawson[7]	West Indies v Australia	Bridgetown	2002-03
Alok Kapali[7]	Bangladesh v Pakistan	Peshawar	2003
A.M.Blignaut	Zimbabwe v Bangladesh	Harare	2003-04
M.J.Hoggard	England v West Indies	Bridgetown	2003-04
J.E.C.Franklin	New Zealand v Bangladesh	Dhaka	2004-05
I.K.Pathan[6/7]	India v Pakistan	Karachi	2005-06
R.J.Sidebottom[7]	England v New Zealand	Hamilton	2007-08
P.M.Siddle	Australia v England	Brisbane	2010-11
S.C.J.Broad	England v India	Nottingham	2011
Sohag Gazi	Bangladesh v New Zealand	Chittagong	2013-14
S.C.J.Broad[4]	England v Sri Lanka	Leeds	2014
H.M.R.K.B.Herath	Sri Lanka v Australia	Galle	2016
M.M.Ali	England v South Africa	The Oval	2017

[1] On debut. [2] Hat-trick in each innings. [3] Involving both innings. [4] In successive Tests. [5] His first 3 balls (second over of the match). [6] The fourth, fifth and sixth balls of the match. [7] On losing side.

WICKET-KEEPING RECORDS

150 DISMISSALS IN TESTS†

Total			Tests	Ct	St
555	M.V.Boucher	South Africa/ICC	147	532	23
416	A.C.Gilchrist	Australia	96	379	37
395	I.A.Healy	Australia	119	366	29
355	R.W.Marsh	Australia	96	343	12
294	M.S.Dhoni	India	90	256	38
270	B.J.Haddin	Australia	66	262	8
270†	P.J.L.Dujon	West Indies	81	265	5
269	A.P.E.Knott	England	95	250	19
256	M.J.Prior	England	79	243	13
241†	A.J.Stewart	England	133	227	14
228	Wasim Bari	Pakistan	81	201	27
219	R.D.Jacobs	West Indies	65	207	12
219	T.G.Evans	England	91	173	46
217	D.Ramdin	West Indies	74	205	12
206	Kamran Akmal	Pakistan	53	184	22
201†	A.C.Parore	New Zealand	78	194	7
198	S.M.H.Kirmani	India	88	160	38
197	B.J.Watling	New Zealand	59	190	7
189	D.L.Murray	West Indies	62	181	8

Total			Tests	Ct	St
187	A.T.W.Grout	Australia	51	163	24
179†	B.B.McCullum	New Zealand	101	168	11
176	I.D.S.Smith	New Zealand	63	168	8
175	Q.de Kock	South Africa	40	166	9
174	R.W.Taylor	England	57	167	7
167	Sarfraz Ahmed	Pakistan	49	146	21
165	R.C.Russell	England	54	153	12
161†	J.M.Bairstow	England	63	150	11
156	H.A.P.W.Jayawardena	Sri Lanka	58	124	32
152	D.J.Richardson	South Africa	42	150	2
151†	K.C.Sangakkara	Sri Lanka	134	131	20
151†	A.Flower	Zimbabwe	63	142	9

The most for Bangladesh is 112 (97 ct, 15 st) by Mushfiqur Rahim in 66 Tests.

† *Excluding catches taken in the field*

25 OR MORE DISMISSALS IN A SERIES

29	B.J.Haddin	Australia v England	2013
28	R.W.Marsh	Australia v England	1982-83
27 (inc 2st)	R.C.Russell	England v South Africa	1995-96
27 (inc 2st)	I.A.Healy	Australia v England (6 Tests)	1997
26 (inc 3st)	J.H.B.Waite	South Africa v New Zealand	1961-62
26	R.W.Marsh	Australia v West Indies (6 Tests)	1975-76
26 (inc 5st)	I.A.Healy	Australia v England (6 Tests)	1993
26 (inc 1st)	M.V.Boucher	South Africa v England	1998
26 (inc 2st)	A.C.Gilchrist	Australia v England	2001
26 (inc 2st)	A.C.Gilchrist	Australia v England	2006-07
26 (inc 1st)	T.D.Paine	Australia v England	2017-18
25 (inc 1st)	I.A.Healy	Australia v England	1994-95
25 (inc 2st)	A.C.Gilchrist	Australia v England	2002-03
25	A.C.Gilchrist	Australia v India	2007-08

TEN OR MORE DISMISSALS IN A TEST

11	R.C.Russell	England v South Africa	Johannesburg	1995-96
11	A.B.de Villiers	South Africa v Pakistan	Johannesburg	2012-13
11	R.R.Pant	India v Australia	Adelaide	2018-19
10	R.W.Taylor	England v India	Bombay	1979-80
10	A.C.Gilchrist	Australia v New Zealand	Hamilton	1999-00
10	W.P.Saha	India v South Africa	Cape Town	2017-18
10	Sarfraz Ahmed	Pakistan v South Africa	Johannesburg	2018-19

SEVEN DISMISSALS IN AN INNINGS

7	Wasim Bari	Pakistan v New Zealand	Auckland	1978-79
7	R.W.Taylor	England v India	Bombay	1979-80
7	I.D.S.Smith	New Zealand v Sri Lanka	Hamilton	1990-91
7	R.D.Jacobs	West Indies v Australia	Melbourne	2000-01

FIVE STUMPINGS IN AN INNINGS

5	K.S.More	India v West Indies	Madras	1987-88

FIELDING RECORDS
100 CATCHES IN TESTS

Total			Tests	Total			Tests
210	R.S.Dravid	India/ICC	164	122	I.V.A.Richards	West Indies	121
205	D.P.M.D.Jayawardena	Sri Lanka	149	121†	A.B.de Villiers	South Africa	114
200	J.H.Kallis	South Africa/ICC	166	121	A.J.Strauss	England	100
196	R.T.Ponting	Australia	168	120	I.T.Botham	England	102
181	M.E.Waugh	Australia	128	120	M.C.Cowdrey	England	114
175	A.N.Cook	England	161	115	C.L.Hooper	West Indies	102
171	S.P.Fleming	New Zealand	111	115	S.R.Tendulkar	India	200
169	G.C.Smith	South Africa/ICC	117	112	S.R.Waugh	Australia	168
164	B.C.Lara	West Indies/ICC	131	110	R.B.Simpson	Australia	62
157	M.A.Taylor	Australia	104	110	W.R.Hammond	England	85
156	A.R.Border	Australia	156	109	G.St A.Sobers	West Indies	93
139	Younus Khan	Pakistan	118	108	H.M.Amla	South Africa	124
135	V.V.S.Laxman	India	134	108	S.M.Gavaskar	India	125
134	M.J.Clarke	Australia	115	105	I.M.Chappell	Australia	75
131	L.R.P.L.Taylor	New Zealand	90	105	M.Azharuddin	India	99
128	M.L.Hayden	Australia	103	105	G.P.Thorpe	England	100
125	S.K.Warne	Australia	145	103	G.A.Gooch	England	118
122	G.S.Chappell	Australia	87	100	I.R.Bell	England	118

The most for Zimbabwe is 60 by A.D.R.Campbell (60) and for Bangladesh 36 by Mahmudullah (43).
† *Excluding catches taken when wicket-keeping.*

15 CATCHES IN A SERIES

15	J.M.Gregory	Australia v England	1920-21

SEVEN OR MORE CATCHES IN A TEST

8	A.M.Rahane	India v Sri Lanka	Galle	2015
7	G.S.Chappell	Australia v England	Perth	1974-75
7	Yajurvindra Singh	India v England	Bangalore	1976-77
7	H.P.Tillekeratne	Sri Lanka v New Zealand	Colombo (SSC)	1992-93
7	S.P.Fleming	New Zealand v Zimbabwe	Harare	1997-98
7	M.L.Hayden	Australia v Sri Lanka	Galle	2003-04
7	K.L.Rahul	India v England	Nottingham	2018

FIVE CATCHES IN AN INNINGS

5	V.Y.Richardson	Australia v South Africa	Durban	1935-36
5	Yajurvindra Singh	India v England	Bangalore	1976-77
5	M.Azharuddin	India v Pakistan	Karachi	1989-90
5	K.Srikkanth	India v Australia	Perth	1991-92
5	S.P.Fleming	New Zealand v Zimbabwe	Harare	1997-98
5	G.C.Smith	South Africa v Australia	Perth	2012-13
5	D.J.G.Sammy	West Indies v India	Mumbai	2013-14
5	D.M.Bravo	West Indies v Bangladesh	Kingstown	2014
5	A.M.Rahane	India v Sri Lanka	Galle	2015
5	J.Blackwood	West Indies v Sri Lanka	Colombo (PSS)	2015-16
5	S.P.D.Smith	Australia v South Africa	Cape Town	2017-18

APPEARANCE RECORDS
100 TEST MATCH APPEARANCES

			Opponents									
			E	A	SA	WI	NZ	I	P	SL	Z	B
200	S.R.Tendulkar	India	32	39	25	21	24	–	18	25	9	7
168†	R.T.Ponting	Australia	35	–	26	24	17	29	15	14	3	4

			E	A	SA	WI	NZ	I	P	SL	Z	B
168	S.R.Waugh	Australia	46	–	16	32	23	18	20	8	3	2
166†	J.H.Kallis	South Africa/ICC	31	28	–	24	18	18	19	15	6	6
164	S.Chanderpaul	West Indies	35	20	24	–	21	25	14	7	8	10
164†	R.S.Dravid	India/ICC	21	32	21	23	15	–	15	20	9	7
161	A.N.Cook	England	–	35	19	20	15	30	20	16	–	6
156	A.R.Border	Australia	47	–	6	31	23	20	22	7	–	–
149	D.P.M.D.Jayawardena	Sri Lanka	23	16	18	11	13	18	29	–	8	13
148	J.M.Anderson	England	–	31	24	20	14	27	15	13	2	2
147†	M.V.Boucher	South Africa/ICC	25	20	–	24	17	14	15	17	6	8
145†	S.K.Warne	Australia	36	–	24	19	20	14	15	13	1	2
134	V.V.S.Laxman	India	17	29	19	22	10	–	15	13	6	3
134	K.C.Sangakkara	Sri Lanka	22	11	17	12	12	17	23	–	5	15
133†	M.Muralitharan	Sri Lanka/ICC	16	12	15	12	14	22	16	–	14	11
133	A.J.Stewart	England	–	33	23	24	16	9	13	9	6	–
132	A.Kumble	India	19	20	21	17	11	–	15	18	7	4
132	C.A.Walsh	West Indies	36	38	10	–	10	15	15	18	3	2
131	Kapil Dev	India	27	20	4	25	10	–	29	14	2	–
131†	B.C.Lara	West Indies/ICC	30	30	18	–	11	17	12	8	2	2
128	M.E.Waugh	Australia	29	–	18	28	14	14	15	9	1	–
126	S.C.J.Broad	England	–	27	18	17	14	20	16	11	–	3
125	S.M.Gavaskar	India	38	20	–	27	9	–	24	7	–	–
124	H.M.Amla	South Africa	21	21	–	9	14	21	14	14	2	8
124	Javed Miandad	Pakistan	22	24	–	17	18	28	–	12	3	–
124†	G.D.McGrath	Australia	30	–	17	23	14	11	17	8	1	2
121	I.V.A.Richards	West Indies	36	34	–	–	7	28	16	–	–	–
120†	Inzamam-ul-Haq	Pakistan/ICC	19	13	13	15	12	10	–	20	11	6
119	I.A.Healy	Australia	33	–	12	28	11	9	14	11	1	–
118	I.R.Bell	England	–	33	11	12	13	20	13	10	–	6
118	G.A.Gooch	England	–	42	3	26	15	19	10	3	–	–
118	Younus Khan	Pakistan	17	11	14	15	11	9	–	29	5	7
117	D.I.Gower	England	–	42	–	19	13	24	17	2	–	–
117†	G.C.Smith	South Africa/ICC	21	21	–	14	13	15	16	7	2	8
116	D.L.Haynes	West Indies	36	33	1	–	10	19	16	1	–	–
116	D.B.Vengsarkar	India	26	24	–	25	11	–	22	8	–	–
115	M.A.Atherton	England	–	33	18	27	11	7	11	4	4	–
115†	M.J.Clarke	Australia	35	–	14	12	11	22	10	8	–	2
114	M.C.Cowdrey	England	–	43	14	21	18	8	10	–	–	–
114	A.B.de Villiers	South Africa	20	24	–	13	10	20	12	7	4	4
113	S.C.Ganguly	India	12	24	17	12	8	–	12	14	9	5
113†	D.L.Vettori	New Zealand/ICC	17	18	14	10	–	15	9	11	9	9
111	S.P.Fleming	New Zealand	19	14	15	11	–	13	9	13	11	6
111	W.P.J.U.C.Vaas	Sri Lanka	15	12	11	9	10	14	18	–	15	7
110	S.T.Jayasuriya	Sri Lanka	14	13	15	10	13	10	17	–	13	5
110	C.H.Lloyd	West Indies	34	29	–	–	8	28	11	–	–	–
108	G.Boycott	England	–	38	7	29	15	13	6	–	–	–
108	C.G.Greenidge	West Indies	29	32	–	–	10	23	14	–	–	–
108	S.M.Pollock	South Africa	23	13	–	16	11	12	12	13	5	3
107	D.C.Boon	Australia	31	–	6	22	17	11	11	9	–	–
105†	J.L.Langer	Australia	21	–	11	18	14	14	13	8	3	2
104	K.P.Pietersen	England	–	27	10˙	14	8	16	14	11	–	4
104†	V.Sehwag	India/ICC	17	23	15	10	12	–	9	11	3	4
104	M.A.Taylor	Australia	33	–	11	20	11	9	12	8	–	–
104	Wasim Akram	Pakistan	18	13	4	17	9	12	–	19	10	2
103	C.H.Gayle	West Indies	20	8	16	–	12	14	8	10	8	7
103	Harbhajan Singh	India	14	18	11	11	13	–	9	16	7	4
103†	M.L.Hayden	Australia	20	–	19	15	11	18	6	7	2	4

				Opponents								
				E	A	SA	WI	NZ	I	P	SL	Z	B
103	Salim Malik	Pakistan		19	15	1	7	18	22	–	15	6	–
102	I.T.Botham	England		–	36	–	20	15	14	14	3	–	–
102	C.L.Hooper	West Indies		24	25	10	–	2	19	14	6	2	–
101	G.Kirsten	South Africa		22	18	–	13	13	10	11	9	3	2
101	B.B.McCullum	New Zealand		16	16	13	13	–	10	8	12	4	9
101	M.Ntini	South Africa		18	15	–	15	11	10	9	12	3	8
100	A.J.Strauss	England		–	20	16	18	9	12	13	8	–	4
100	G.P.Thorpe	England		–	16	16	27	13	5	8	9	2	4

† Includes appearance in the Australia v ICC 'Test' in 2005-06. The most for Zimbabwe is 67 by G.W.Flower, and for Bangladesh 66 by Mushfiqur Rahim.

100 CONSECUTIVE TEST APPEARANCES

159	A.N.Cook	England	May 2006 to September 2018
153	A.R.Border	Australia	March 1979 to March 1994
107	M.E.Waugh	Australia	June 1993 to October 2002
106	S.M.Gavaskar	India	January 1975 to February 1987
101	B.B.McCullum	New Zealand	March 2004 to February 2016

50 TESTS AS CAPTAIN

			Won	Lost	Drawn	Tied
109	G.C.Smith	South Africa	53	29	27	–
93	A.R.Border	Australia	32	22	38	1
80	S.P.Fleming	New Zealand	28	27	25	–
77	R.T.Ponting	Australia	48	16	13	–
74	C.H.Lloyd	West Indies	36	12	26	–
60	M.S.Dhoni	India	27	18	15	–
59	A.N.Cook	England	24	22	13	–
57	S.R.Waugh	Australia	41	9	7	–
56	Misbah-ul-Haq	Pakistan	26	19	11	–
56	A.Ranatunga	Sri Lanka	12	19	25	–
54	M.A.Atherton	England	13	21	20	–
53	W.J.Cronje	South Africa	27	11	15	–
51	M.P.Vaughan	England	26	11	14	–
50	I.V.A.Richards	West Indies	27	8	15	–
50	M.A.Taylor	Australia	26	13	11	–
50	A.J.Strauss	England	24	11	15	–

The most for Zimbabwe is 21 by A.D.R.Campbell and H.H.Streak, and for Bangladesh 34 by Mushfiqur Rahim.

60 TEST UMPIRING APPEARANCES

128	S.A.Bucknor	(West Indies)	28.04.1989 to 22.03.2009
125	Alim Dar	(Pakistan)	21.10.2003 to 23.02.2019
108	R.E.Koertzen	(South Africa)	26.12.1992 to 24.07.2010
95	D.J.Harper	(Australia)	28.11.1998 to 23.06.2011
92	D.R.Shepherd	(England)	01.08.1985 to 07.06.2005
84	B.F.Bowden	(New Zealand)	11.03.2000 to 03.05.2015
78	D.B.Hair	(Australia)	25.01.1992 to 08.06.2008
74	I.J.Gould	(England)	19.11.2008 to 23.02.2019
74	S.J.A.Taufel	(Australia)	26.12.2000 to 20.08.2012
73	S.Venkataraghavan	(India)	29.01.1993 to 20.01.2004
67	R.J.Tucker	(Australia)	15.02.2010 to 12.02.2019
66	H.D.Bird	(England)	05.07.1973 to 24.06.1996
60	H.D.P.K.Dharmasena	(Sri Lanka)	04.11.2010 to 12.02.2019

THE FIRST-CLASS COUNTIES
REGISTER, RECORDS AND 2018 AVERAGES

All statistics are to 15 March 2019.

ABBREVIATIONS – General

*	not out/unbroken partnership	IT20	International Twenty20
b	born	l-o	limited-overs
BB	Best innings bowling analysis	LOI	Limited-Overs Internationals
Cap	Awarded 1st XI County Cap	Tests	International Test Matches
f-c	first-class	F-c Tours	Overseas tours involving first-class
HS	Highest Score		appearances

Awards

PCA 2018   Professional Cricketers' Association Player of 2018
Wisden 2017   One of *Wisden Cricketers' Almanack*'s Five Cricketers of 2017
YC 2018   Cricket Writers' Club Young Cricketer of 2018

ECB Competitions

CB40	Clydesdale Bank 40 (2010-12)
CC	Specsavers County Championship
CGT	Cheltenham & Gloucester Trophy (2001-06)
FPT	Friends Provident Trophy (2007-09)
NL	National League (1999-2005)
P40	NatWest PRO 40 League (2006-09)
RLC	Royal London One-Day Cup (2014-18)
T20	Twenty20 Competition
Y40	Yorkshire Bank 40 (2013)

Education

Ac	Academy
BHS	Boys' High School
C	College
CS	Comprehensive School
GS	Grammar School
HS	High School
I	Institute
S	School
SFC	Sixth Form College
SS	Secondary School
TC	Technical College
U	University
UWIC	University of Wales Institute, Cardiff

Playing Categories

LBG	Bowls right-arm leg-breaks and googlies
LF	Bowls left-arm fast
LFM	Bowls left-arm fast-medium
LHB	Bats left-handed
LM	Bowls left-arm medium pace
LMF	Bowls left-arm medium fast
OB	Bowls right-arm off-breaks
RF	Bowls right-arm fast
RFM	Bowls right-arm fast-medium
RHB	Bats right-handed
RM	Bowls right-arm medium pace
RMF	Bowls right-arm medium-fast
SLA	Bowls left-arm leg-breaks
SLC	Bowls left-arm 'Chinamen'
WK	Wicket-keeper

Teams (see also p 230)

AS	Adelaide Strikers
BH	Brisbane Heat
BMT	Bulawayo Metropolitan Tuskers
CC&C	Combined Campuses & Colleges
CD	Central Districts
CSK	Chennai Super Kings
DC	Deccan Chargers
DD	Delhi Daredevils
EL	England Lions
EP	Eastern Province

GL	Gujarat Lions
GW	Griqualand West
HB	Habib Bank Limited
HH	Hobart Hurricanes
KKR	Kolkata Knight Riders
KRL	Khan Research Laboratories
KXIP	Kings XI Punjab
KY	Kurunegala Youth
KZN	KwaZulu-Natal Inland
ME	Mashonaland Eagles
MI	Mumbai Indians
MR	Melbourne Renegades
MS	Melbourne Stars
MSC	Mohammedan Sporting Club
MT	Matabeleland Tuskers
MWR	Mid West Rhinos
NBP	National Bank of Pakistan
ND	Northern Districts
NSW	New South Wales
NT	Northern Transvaal
NW	North West
(O)FS	(Orange) Free State
PIA	Pakistan International Airlines
PDSC	Prime Doleshwar Sporting Club
PS	Perth Scorchers
PT	Pakistan Television
PTC	Pakistan Telecommunication Company
PW	Pune Warriors
Q	Queensland
RCB	Royal Challengers Bangalore
RPS	Rising Pune Supergiant
RR	Rajasthan Royals
RS	Rising Stars
SA	South Australia
SH	Sunrisers Hyderabad
SJD	Sheikh Jamal Dhanmondi
SLPA	Sri Lanka Ports Authority
SNGPL	Sui Northern Gas Pipelines Limited
SR	Southern Rocks
SS	Sydney Sixers
SSGC	Sui Southern Gas Corporation
ST	Sydney Thunder
Tas	Tasmania
T&T	Trinidad & Tobago
TU	Tamil Union
UB	United Bank Limited
Vic	Victoria
WA	Western Australia
WAPDA	Water & Power Development Authority
WP	Western Province

DERBYSHIRE

Formation of Present Club: 4 November 1870
Inaugural First-Class Match: 1871
Colours: Chocolate, Amber and Pale Blue
Badge: Rose and Crown
County Champions: (1) 1936
NatWest Trophy Winners: (1) 1981
Benson and Hedges Cup Winners: (1) 1993
Sunday League Winners: (1) 1990
Twenty20 Cup Winners: (0) best – Quarter-Finalist 2005, 2017

Chief Executive: Ryan Duckett, Derbyshire County Cricket Club, The Pattonair County Ground, Nottingham Road, Derby, DE21 6DA • Tel: 01332 388101 • Email: info@derbyshireccc.com • Web: www. derbyshireccc.com • Twitter: @DerbyshireCCC (49,407 followers)

Head of Cricket: David Houghton. **Assistant Coach**: Steve Kirby. **T20 Head Coach**: Dominic Cork. **Captain**: B.A.Godleman. **Vice-Captain**: tba. **Overseas Players**: K.W.Richardson (T20 only) and L.V.van Beek. **2019 Testimonial**: None. **Head Groundsman**: Neil Godrich. **Scorer**: John Brown. ‡ New registration. NQ Not qualified for England.

CONNERS, Samuel (George Spencer Ac), b Nottingham 13 Feb 1999. 6'0". RHB, RM. Squad No 59. Derbyshire 2nd XI debut 2016. England U19 2018. Awaiting 1st XI debut.

CRITCHLEY, Matthew James John (St Michael's HS, Chorley), b Preston, Lancs 13 Aug 1996. 6'2". RHB, LB. Squad No 20. Debut (Derbyshire) 2015. Derbyshire 2nd XI debut 2014. HS 137* v Northants (Derby) 2015. BB 6-106 (10-194 match) v Northants (Chesterfield) 2018. LO HS 64 North v South (Bridgetown) 2017-18. LO BB 4-48 v Northants (Derby) 2015 (RLC). T20 HS 72*. T20 BB 3-32.

DAL, Anuj Kailash (Durban HS; Nottingham HS), b Newcastle-upon-Tyne, Northumb 8 Jul 1996. 5'9". RHB, RM. Squad No 65. Debut (Derbyshire) 2018. Nottinghamshire 2nd XI 2013-17. HS 25 v Sussex (Hove) 2018. BB –. T20 HS 35.

GLEADALL, Alfie Frank (Westfield Sports C, Sheffield), b Chesterfield 28 May 2000. 5'10". RHB, RMF. Squad No 17. Debut (Derbyshire) 2018. Derbyshire 2nd XI debut 2017. England U19 2018. HS 27* and BB 1-20 v Durham (Chester-le-St) 2018 – only f-c game. LO HS –. LO BB –.

GODLEMAN, Billy Ashley (Islington Green S), b Islington, London 11 Feb 1989. 6'3". LHB, LB. Squad No 1. Middlesex 2005-09. Essex 2010-12. Derbyshire debut 2013; cap 2015; captain 2016 to date. 1000 runs (1): 1069 (2015). HS 204 v Worcs (Derby) 2016. BB –. LO HS 137 v Warwks (Birmingham) 2018 (RLC). T20 HS 77.

HAMIDULLAH QADRI (Derby Moor S; Chellaston Ac), b Kandahar, Afghanistan 5 Dec 2000. 5'9". RHB, OB. Squad No 75. Debut (Derbyshire) 2017, taking 5-60 v Glamorgan (Cardiff), the youngest to take 5 wkts on CC debut, and the first born this century to play f-c cricket in England. England U19 2018-19. HS 15* v Kent (Derby) 2018. BB 5-60 (*see above*). LO HS 4 v Notts (Nottingham) 2018 (RLC). LO BB 1-31 v Northants (Northampton) 2018 (RLC). T20 BB –.

HOSEIN, Harvey Richard (Denstone C), b Chesterfield 12 Aug 1996. 5'10". RHB, WK. Squad No 16. Debut (Derbyshire) 2014, taking seven catches in an innings and UK record-equalling 11 in match v Surrey (The Oval). Derbyshire 2nd XI debut 2010, aged 13y 287d. HS 108 v Worcs (Worcester) 2016. LO HS 40 v Notts (Mkt Warsop) 2016 (RLC). T20 HS 0*.

HUGHES, Alex Lloyd (Ounsdale HS, Wolverhampton), b Wordsley, Staffs 29 Sep 1991. 5'10". RHB, RM. Squad No 18. Debut (Derbyshire) 2013; cap 2017. HS 142 v Glos (Bristol) 2017. BB 4-46 v Glamorgan (Derby) 2014. LO HS 96* v Leics (Leicester) 2016 (RLC). LO BB 3-31 v Leics (Derby) 2015 (RLC). T20 HS 43*. T20 BB 4-42.

LACE, Thomas Cresswell (Millfield S), b Hammersmith, Middx 27 May 1998. 5'8". RHB, WK. Squad No 27. Debut (Derbyshire) 2018. Middlesex 2nd XI debut 2015. On loan from Middlesex for 2019. HS 43 v Kent (Derby) 2018.

McKIERNAN, Matthew Harry ('**Mattie**') (Lowton HS; St John Rigby C, Wigan), b Billinge, Lancs 14 Jun 1994. 6'0". RHB, LB. Squad No 21. Lancashire 2nd XI 2013-17. Leicestershire 2nd XI 2016-17. Hampshire 2nd XI 2018. Warwickshire 2nd XI 2018. Cumberland 2016-17. Awaiting Derbyshire f-c and l-o debut. T20 HS 1*. T20 BB –.

MADSEN, Wayne Lee (Kearsney C, Durban; U of South Africa), b Durban, South Africa 2 Jan 1984. Nephew of M.B.Madsen (Natal 1967-68 to 1978-79), T.R.Madsen (Natal 1976-77 to 1989-90) and H.R.Fotheringham (Natal, Transvaal 1971-72 to 1989-90), cousin of G.S.Fotheringham (KwaZulu-Natal 2008-09 to 2009-10). 5'11". RHB, OB. Squad No 77. KwaZulu-Natal 2003-04 to 2007-08. Dolphins 2006-07 to 2007-08. Derbyshire debut 2009, scoring 170 v Glos (Cheltenham); cap 2011; captain 2012-15; testimonial 2017. Qualified for England by residence in February 2015. 1000 runs (5); most – 1292 (2016). HS 231* v Northants (Northampton) 2012. BB 3-45 KZN v EP (Pt Elizabeth) 2007-08. De BB 2-9 v Sussex (Hove) 2013. LO HS 138 v Hants (Derby) 2014 (RLC). LO BB 3-27 v Durham (Derby) 2013 (Y40). T20 HS 86*. T20 BB 2-20.

PALLADINO, Antonio Paul (Cardinal Pole SS; Anglia Polytechnic U), b Tower Hamlets, London 29 Jun 1983. 6'0". RHB, RMF. Squad No 28. Cambridge UCCE 2003-05. Essex 2003-10. Namibia 2009-10. Derbyshire debut 2011; cap 2012; testimonial 2018. HS 106 v Australia A (Derby) 2012. CC HS 68 v Warwks (Birmingham) 2013. 50 wkts (3); most – 56 (2012). BB 7-53 v Kent (Derby) 2012. Hat-trick v Leics (Leicester) 2012. LO HS 31 Namibia v Boland (Windhoek) 2009-10. LO BB 5-49 v Lancs (Derby) 2014 (RLC). T20 HS 14*. T20 BB 4-21.

NQ**RAMPAUL, Ravi**, b Preysal, Trinidad 15 Oct 1984. 6'1". LHB, RFM. Squad No 41. Trinidad & Tobago 2001-02 to date. Surrey 2016-17. Derbyshire debut 2018. IPL: RCB 2013-14. **Tests** (WI): 18 (2009-10 to 2012-13); HS 40* v A (Adelaide) 2009-10; BB 4-48 v P (Providence) 2011. **LOI** (WI): 92 (2003-04 to 2015-16); HS 86* v I (Visakhapatnam) 2011-12; BB 5-49 v B (Khulna) 2012-13. **IT20** (WI): 23 (2007 to 2015-16); HS 8 v Ire (Providence) 2010; BB 3-16 v A (Colombo, RPS) 2012-13. F-c Tours (WI): E 2007, 2012; A 2009-10; SA 2003-04 (WI A); I 2011-12; B 2011-12, 2012-13. HS 64* WI A v SL A (Basseterre) 2006-07. CC HS 18* v Durham (Derby) 2018. BB 7-51 T&T v Barbados (Pointe-a-Pierre) 2006-07. CC BB 5-85 Sy v Somerset (Oval) 2016. De BB 3-53 v Northants (Northampton) 2018. LO HS 86* (*see LOI*). LO BB 5-48 v Yorks (Derby) 2018 (RLC). T20 HS 23*. T20 BB 5-9.

94

REECE, Luis Michael (St Michael's HS, Chorley; Leeds Met U), b Taunton, Somerset 4 Aug 1990. 6'1". LHB, LM. Squad No 10. Leeds/Bradford MCCU 2012-13. Lancashire 2013-15, no f-c appearances in 2016. Derbyshire debut 2017. MCC 2014. Unicorns 2011-12. HS 168 v Northants (Derby) 2017, sharing De record 1st wkt partnership of 333 with B.A.Godleman. BB 7-20 v Glos (Derby) 2018. LO HS 92 v Durham (Derby) 2018 (RLC). LO BB 4-35 Unicorns v Glos (Exmouth) 2011 (CB40). T20 HS 97*. T20 BB 3-33.

‡NQ**RICHARDSON, Kane** William, b Eudunda, S Australia 12 Feb 1991. RHB, RMF. S Australia 2010-11 to date. IPL: PW 2013. RR 2014. RCB 2016. Big Bash: AS 2011-12 to 2016-17. MR 2017-18 to date. Joins Derbyshire in 2019 for T20 only. **LOI** (A): 18 (2012-13 to 2018); HS 19 v NZ (Auckland) 2015-16; BB 5-68 v I (Canberra) 2015-16. **IT20** (A): 9 (2014-15 to 2018); HS 9 v I (Adelaide) 2015-16; BB 3-33 v E (Melbourne) 2017-18. HS 49 SA v Tas (Adelaide) 2013-14. BB 5-69 SA v WA (Adelaide, GS) 2016-17. LO HS 36 SA v Tas (Sydney, HO) 2016-17. LO BB 6-48 SA v Q (Adelaide) 2012-13. T20 HS 45. T20 BB 4-22.

NQ**SMIT, Daryn** (Northwood S; U of SA), b Durban, South Africa 28 Jan 1984. 5'11". RHB, LB, occ WK. Squad No 11. KwaZulu Natal 2004-05 to 2016-17. Dolphins 2005-06 to 2016-17. Derbyshire debut 2017; qualifies as a non-overseas player. 1000 runs (0+1): 1081 (2015-16). HS 156* KZN v NW (Durban) 2015-16. De BB 45* v Durham (Derby) 2017. BB 7-27 KZN v SW Districts (Durban) 2013-14. De BB –. LO HS 109 Dolphins v Warriors (East London) 2011-12. LO BB 4-39 KZN v GW (Kimberley) 2013-14. T20 HS 57. T20 BB 3-19.

TAYLOR, James Philip Arthur (Trentham HS), b Stoke-on-Trent, Staffs 19 Jan 2001. Younger brother of T.A.I.Taylor (*see LEICESTERSHIRE*). 6'2". RHB, RM. Squad No 32. Debut (Derbyshire) 2017. Derbyshire 2nd XI debut 2016. HS 0* and BB 1-14 v West Indians (Derby) 2017 – only 1st XI game.

‡NQ**VAN BEEK, Logan** Verjus, b Christchurch, New Zealand 7 Sep 1990. Grandson of S.C.Guillen (Trinidad, Canterbury, West Indies and New Zealand 1947-48 to 1960-61). 6'1". RHB, RMF. Squad No 37. Canterbury 2009-10 to 2016-17. Netherlands 2017. Wellington 2017-18 to date. **IT20** (Neth): 8 (2013-14 to 2015-16); HS 4* v B (Dharamsala) 2015-16; BB 3-9 v E (Chattogram) 2013-14. F-c Tour (NZA): UAE 2018-19 (v P A). HS 111* Cant v Otago (Christchurch) 2015-16. BB 6-46 Well v Auckland (Auckland) 2017-18. LO HS 64* Neth v Z (Amstelveen) 2017. LO BB 6-18 Neth v UAE (Voorburg) 2017. T20 HS 24*. T20 BB 3-9.

RELEASED/RETIRED

(Having made a County 1st XI appearance in 2018)

BRODRICK, Calum Ashley James (John Taylor HS, Barton-under-Needwood), b Burton-upon-Trent, Staffs 24 Jan 1998. 5'11". LHB, RM. Derbyshire 2017-18. Derbyshire 2nd XI debut 2014. HS 52 v West Indians (Derby) 2017. CC HS 19 v Durham (Chester-le-St) 2018. LO HS 11 v Lancs (Derby) 2018 (RLC). T20 HS 14.

DAVIS, W.S. – *see LEICESTERSHIRE*.

NOFERGUSON, Lachlan Hammond ('**Lockie**'), b Auckland, New Zealand 13 Jun 1991. RHB, RF. Auckland 2012-13 to date. Derbyshire 2018. IPL: RPS 2017. **LOI** (NZ): 27 (2016-17 to 2018-19); HS 19 v E (Mt Maunganui) 2017-18; BB 5-45 v P (Dubai, DSC) 2018-19. **IT20** (NZ): 5 (2016-17 to 2018-19); HS 1 v P (Dubai, DSC) 2018-19; BB 3-21 v B (Auckland) 2018-19. F-c Tour (NZA): 1 2017-18. HS 41 Auckland v Canterbury (Rangiora) 2016-17. De HS 16 v Kent (Derby) 2018 and 16 v Middx (Lord's) 2018. BB 7-34 (12-78 match) Auckland v Otago (Auckland) 2017-18. De BB 4-56 v Glos (Derby) 2018. LO HS 24 Auckland v Otago (Auckland) 2016-17. LO BB 6-27 Auckland v ND (Auckland) 2016-17. T20 HS 8*. T20 BB 4-26.

NOMacLEOD, Calum Scott (Hillpark S, Glasgow), b Glasgow, Scotland 15 Nov 1988. 6'0". RHB, RMF. Scotland 2007 to date. Warwickshire 2008-09. Durham 2014-16. Derbyshire 2018 (T20 only). **LOI** (Scot): 57 (2008 to 2018); HS 175 v Canada (Christchurch) 2013-14; BB 2-26 v Kenya (Aberdeen) 2013. **IT20** (Scot): 37 (2009 to 2018-19); HS 60 v Hong Kong (Abu Dhabi) 2016-17; BB 2-17 v Kenya (Aberdeen) 2013. F-c Tours (Scot): UAE 2011-12, 2012-13; Namibia 2011-12. HS 84 Du v Lancs (Manchester) 2014. BB 4-66 Scot v Canada (Aberdeen) 2009. LO HS 175 (*see LOI*). LO BB 3-37 Scot v UAE (Queenstown) 2013-14. T20 HS 104*. T20 BB 2-17.

NONICHOLLS, Henry Michael (St Andrew's C), b Christchurch, New Zealand 15 Nov 1991. LHB, OB. Canterbury 2011-12 to date. Big Bash: ST 2015-16. Derbyshire 2018 (T20 only). **Tests** (NZ): 24 (2015-15 to 2018-19); HS 162* v SL (Christchurch) 2018-19. **LOI** (NZ): 41 (2015-16 to 2018-19); HS 124* v SL (Nelson) 2018-19. **IT20** (NZ): 5 (2015-16 to 2018-19); HS 7 v B (Kolkata) 2015-16. F-c Tours (NZ): SA 2016; I 2016-17, 2017-18 (NZA); Z 2016; UAE 2018-19 (v P). HS 162* (*see Tests*). BB –. LO HS 178 Cant v Wellington (Wellington) 2014-15. LO BB –. T20 HS 67*.

OLIVIER, D. – *see YORKSHIRE*.

NOSHARIF, Safayaan Mohammad (Buckhaven HS), b Huddersfield, Yorks 24 May 1991. RHB, RMF. Scotland 2011-12 to date. Derbyshire 2018 (l-o and T20 only). Northamptonshire 2nd XI 2016-17. **LOI** (Scot): 36 (2011 to 2018); HS 34 v Ire (Harare) 2017-18; BB 5-33 v Z (Bulawayo) 2017-18. **IT20** (Scot): 32 (2011-12 to 2018-19); HS 26 v Netherlands (Edinburgh) 2015; BB 4-24 v UAE (Dubai, ICCA) 2015-16. HS 60 Scot v Ire (Dublin, CA) 2013. BB 4-94 Scot v PNG (Port Moresby) 2017-18. LO HS 34 (*see LOI*). LO BB 5-33 (*see LOI*). T20 HS 26. T20 BB 4-24.

SLATER, B.T. – *see NOTTINGHAMSHIRE*.

NOVILJOEN, GC ('**Hardus**') b Witbank, South Africa 6 Mar 1989. 6'5". RHB, RF. Easterns 2008-09 to 2011-12. Titans 2009-10 to 2011-12. Lions 2012-13 to 2017-18. Kent 2016. Derbyshire 2017-18. **Tests** (SA): 1 (2015-16); HS 20* and BB 1-79 v E (Johannesburg) 2015-16. F-c Tours (SA A): A 2014, 2016; I 2015; Z 2016. HS 72 Lions v Titans (Centurion) 2015-16. CC HS 63 K v Northants (Beckenham) 2016. De HS 60* v Middx (Derby) 2018. 50 wkts (0+1): 68 (2010-11). BB 8-90 (15-170 match – best match figs for De since 1952) v Sussex (Hove) 2017. LO HS 54* Easterns v Boland (Paarl) 2011-12. LO BB 6-19 Lions v Titans (Centurion) 2012-13. T20 HS 41*. T20 BB 5-16.

NQWAHAB RIAZ, b Lahore, Pakistan 28 Jun 1985. RHB, LF. Lahore 2001-02 to 2006-07. Karachi Port Trust 2003-04. Hyderabad 2003-04 to 2004-05. National Bank 2007-08 to 2014-15. Kent 2011. Lahore Shalimar 2012-13. WAPDA 2017-18 to date. Surrey 2015 (T20 only). Essex 2016 (T20 only). Derbyshire 2018 (T20 only). **Tests** (P): 27 (2010 to 2018-19); HS 39 v E (Manchester) 2016; BB 5-63 v E (Oval) 2010. **LOI** (P): 79 (2007-08 to 2017); HS 54* v Z (Brisbane) 2014-15; BB 5-46 v I (Mohali) 2010-11. **IT20** (P): 27 (2007-08 to 2016-17); HS 30* v NZ (Auckland) 2010-11; BB 3-18 v E (Manchester) 2016. F-c Tours (P): E 2010, 2016; A 2009 (P A), 2016-17; WI 2011; NZ 2010-11, 2016-17; SL 2009 (P A), 2014, 2015; B 2014-15. HS 84 NBP v WAPDA (Lahore) 2011-12. CC HS 34 K v Surrey (Canterbury) 2011. 50 wkts (0+2); most – 68 (2007-08). BB 9-59 (12-120 match) Lahore S v Lahore Ravi (Lahore) 2012-13. CC BB 4-94 K v Leics (Leicester) 2011. LO HS 77 NBP v PT (Rawalpindi) 2013-14. LO BB 5-24 NBP v SNGPL (Sargodha) 2008-09. T20 HS 53. T20 BB 5-17.

WHEELDON, Daniel Maurice (Wilsthorpe Community S), b Nottingham 14 Mar 1989. RHB, RFM. Derbyshire 2018. Unicorns (l-o) 2011-12. HS 33* and BB 1-12 v Northants (Chesterfield) 2018. LO HS 14 Uni v Lancs (Colwyn Bay) 2011 (CB40). LO BB 3-31 Uni v Glos (Bristol) 2011 (CB40).

NQWILSON, Gary Craig (Methodist C, Belfast; Manchester Met U), b Dundonald, N Ireland 5 Feb 1986. 5'10". RHB, WK. Ireland 2005 to date. Surrey 2010-16; cap 2014. Derbyshire 2017-18; T20 captain 2018. **Tests** (Ire): 1 (2018); HS 33* v P (Dublin) 2018. **LOI** (Ire): 99 (2007 to 2018); HS 113 v Netherlands (Dublin) 2010. **IT20** (Ire): 61 (2008 to 2018); HS 65* v Scotland (Dubai, DSC) 2016-17. HS 160* Sy v Leics (Oval) 2014. De HS 97 v Kent (Canterbury) 2017 and 97 v Leics (Derby) 2017. BB –. LO HS 113 (*see LOI*). T20 HS 80.

C.M.MacDonell and M.D.Sonczak left the staff without making a County 1st XI appearance in 2018.

DERBYSHIRE 2018

RESULTS SUMMARY

	Place	Won	Lost	Drew	NR
Specsavers County Champ (2nd Division)	7th	4	7	3	
All First-Class Matches		4	7	3	
Royal London One-Day Cup (North Group)	5th	4	4		
Vitality Blast (North Group)	7th	5	7		2

SPECSAVERS COUNTY CHAMPIONSHIP AVERAGES
BATTING AND FIELDING

Cap		M	I	NO	HS	Runs	Avge	100	50	Ct/St
	B.T.Slater	9	17	1	99	676	42.25	–	6	3
2011	W.L.Madsen	14	27	–	144	1016	37.62	2	7	25
	L.M.Reece	6	11	1	157*	349	34.90	1	1	2
2017	A.L.Hughes	14	27	1	103	737	28.34	1	5	9
	M.J.J.Critchley	14	26	1	105	705	28.20	1	4	9
	G.C.Wilson	8	14	1	66	357	27.46	–	2	16
	T.C.Lace	4	8	–	43	219	27.37	–	–	1
	H.R.Hosein	8	16	2	66*	376	26.85	–	3	12/1
2015	B.A.Godleman	14	27	2	122	658	26.32	2	3	8
	D.Smit	4	8	2	45*	129	21.50	–	–	11
	G.C.Viljoen	12	22	2	60*	386	19.30	–	1	1
2012	A.P.Palladino	12	23	6	32	317	18.64	–	–	1
	A.K.Dal	4	7	–	25	107	15.28	–	–	2
	S.M.Ervine	2	4	–	26	51	12.75	–	–	2
	D.Olivier	7	11	2	40*	78	8.66	–	–	–
	R.Rampaul	8	11	5	18*	51	8.50	–	–	2
	L.H.Ferguson	5	10	2	16	51	6.37	–	–	4
	Hamidullah Qadri	4	8	2	15*	33	5.50	–	–	2

Also batted: M.K.Andersson (1 match) 11, 0 (2 ct); C.A.J.Brodrick (1) 0, 19 (2 ct);
W.S.Davis (1) 6; M.H.A.Footitt (1) 0, 0* (1 ct); A.F.Gleadall (1) 27*, 2; D.M.Wheeldon (1)
33*, 2.

BOWLING

	O	M	R	W	Avge	Best	5wI	10wM
L.M.Reece	64.1	13	186	11	16.90	7- 20	1	–
A.P.Palladino	369	94	1006	51	19.72	6- 29	3	1
A.L.Hughes	87	19	255	10	25.50	4- 57	–	–
D.Olivier	251.3	47	852	31	27.48	5- 20	2	1
G.C.Viljoen	356.1	55	1225	38	32.23	4- 51	–	–
L.H.Ferguson	164.3	22	618	18	34.33	4- 56	–	–
M.J.J.Critchley	285.5	14	1218	32	38.06	6-106	1	1
R.Rampaul	183.3	35	651	13	50.07	3- 53	–	–

Also bowled:
Hamidullah Qadri 78.1 7 319 8 39.87 3- 66
M.K.Andersson 14-3-43-4; A.K.Dal 1-0-1-0; W.S.Davis 11-3-39-2; S.M.Ervine
18-0-65-0; M.H.A.Footitt 15-2-57-1; A.F.Gleadall 13.3-1-59-1; W.L.Madsen 42.4-9-152-4;
D.M.Wheeldon 13-2-48-1.

Derbyshire played no first-class fixtures outside the County Championship in 2018. The
First-Class Averages (pp 230–245) give the records of Derbyshire players in all first-class
county matches, with the exception of M.K.Andersson, S.M.Ervine, M.H.A.Footitt and
B.T.Slater, whose first-class figures for Derbyshire are as above.

DERBYSHIRE RECORDS

FIRST-CLASS CRICKET

Highest Total	For 801-8d		v	Somerset	Taunton	2007
	V 677-7d		by	Yorkshire	Leeds	2013
Lowest Total	For 16		v	Notts	Nottingham	1879
	V 23		by	Hampshire	Burton upon T	1958
Highest Innings	For 274	G.A.Davidson	v	Lancashire	Manchester	1896
	V 343*	P.A.Perrin	for	Essex	Chesterfield	1904

Highest Partnership for each Wicket

1st	333	L.M.Reece/B.A.Godleman	v	Northants	Derby	2017
2nd	417	K.J.Barnett/T.A.Tweats	v	Yorkshire	Derby	1997
3rd	316*	A.S.Rollins/K.J.Barnett	v	Leics	Leicester	1997
4th	328	P.Vaulkhard/D.Smith	v	Notts	Nottingham	1946
5th	302*†	J.E.Morris/D.G.Cork	v	Glos	Cheltenham	1993
6th	212	G.M.Lee/T.S.Worthington	v	Essex	Chesterfield	1932
7th	258	M.P.Dowman/D.G.Cork	v	Durham	Derby	2000
8th	198	K.M.Krikken/D.G.Cork	v	Lancashire	Manchester	1996
9th	283	A.Warren/J.Chapman	v	Warwicks	Blackwell	1910
10th	132	A.Hill/M.Jean-Jacques	v	Yorkshire	Sheffield	1986

† 346 runs were added for this wicket in two separate partnerships

Best Bowling	For 10- 40	W.Bestwick	v	Glamorgan	Cardiff	1921
(Innings)	V 10- 45	R.L.Johnson	for	Middlesex	Derby	1994
Best Bowling	For 17-103	W.Mycroft	v	Hampshire	Southampton	1876
(Match)	V 16-101	G.Giffen	for	Australians	Derby	1886

Most Runs – Season	2165	D.B.Carr	(av 48.11)	1959
Most Runs – Career	23854	K.J.Barnett	(av 41.12)	1979-98
Most 100s – Season	8	P.N.Kirsten		1982
Most 100s – Career	53	K.J.Barnett		1979-98
Most Wkts – Season	168	T.B.Mitchell	(av 19.55)	1935
Most Wkts – Career	1670	H.L.Jackson	(av 17.11)	1947-63
Most Career W-K Dismissals	1304	R.W.Taylor	(1157 ct; 147 st)	1961-84
Most Career Catches in the Field	563	D.C.Morgan		1950-69

LIMITED-OVERS CRICKET

Highest Total	50ov	366-4	v	Comb Univs	Oxford	1991
	40ov	321-5	v	Essex	Leek	2013
	T20	222-5	v	Yorkshire	Leeds	2010
		222-5	v	Notts	Nottingham	2017
Lowest Total	50ov	73	v	Lancashire	Derby	1993
	40ov	60	v	Kent	Canterbury	2008
	T20	72	v	Leics	Derby	2013
Highest Innings	50ov	173*	M.J.Di Venuto	v	Derbys CB	Derby	2000
	40ov	141*	C.J.Adams	v	Kent	Chesterfield	1992
	T20	111	W.J.Durston	v	Notts	Nottingham	2010
Best Bowling	50ov	8-21	M.A.Holding	v	Sussex	Hove	1988
	40ov	6- 7	M.Hendrick	v	Notts	Nottingham	1972
	T20	5-27	T.Lungley	v	Leics	Leicester	2009

DURHAM

Formation of Present Club: 23 May 1882
Inaugural First-Class Match: 1992
Colours: Navy Blue, Yellow and Maroon
Badge: Coat of Arms of the County of Durham
County Champions: (3) 2008, 2009, 2013
Friends Provident Trophy Winners: (1) 2007
Royal London One-Day Cup Winners: (1) 2014
Twenty20 Cup Winners: (0); best – Finalist 2016

Chief Executive: Tim Bostock, Emirates Riverside, Chester-le-Street, Co Durham DH3 3QR • Tel: 0191 387 1717 • Email: marketing@durhamccc.co.uk • Web: www.durhamccc.co.uk • Twitter: @DurhamCricket (62,191 followers)

Director of Cricket: Marcus North. **Lead High Performance Coach**: James Franklin. **Bowling Coach**: Neil Killeen. **Assistant Coach**: Alan Walker. **Captain**: tba. **Overseas Players**: C.T.Bancroft and D.J.M.Short (T20 only). **2019 Testimonial**: C.Rushworth. **Head Groundsman**: Vic Demain. **Scorer**: William Dobson. ‡ New registration. NQ Not qualified for England.

Durham initially awarded caps immediately after their players joined the staff but revised this policy in 1998, capping players on merit, past 'awards' having been nullified. Durham abolished both their capping and 'awards' systems after the 2005 season.

‡NOBANCROFT, Cameron Timothy (Aquinas C, Perth), b Attadale, Perth, Australia 19 Nov 1992. 6'0". RHB, RM, occ WK. W Australia 2013-14 to date. Gloucestershire 2016-17; cap 2016. Big Bash: PS 2014-15 to date. **Tests** (A): 8 (2017-18); HS 82* v E (Brisbane) 2017-18. **IT20** (A): 1 (2015-16); HS 0* v I (Sydney) 2015-16. F-c Tours (A): SA 2017-18; I 2015 (Aus A). HS 228* WA v SA (Perth) 2017-18. CC HS 206* Gs v Kent (Bristol) 2017. LO HS 176 WA v SA (Sydney, HO) 2015-16. T20 HS 87*.

BURNHAM, Jack Tony Arthur (Deerness Valley CS, Durham), b Durham 18 Jan 1997. 6'1". RHB, RM. Squad No 8. Debut (Durham) 2015. Durham 2nd XI debut 2014. Northumberland 2013. Suspended during the 2018 season. HS 135 v Surrey (Oval) 2016. LO HS 26 v Northants (Northampton) 2016 (RLC). T20 HS 53*.

CARSE, Brydon Alexander (Pearson HS, Pt Elizabeth), b Port Elizabeth, South Africa 31 Jul 1995. Son of J.A.Carse (Rhodesia, W Province, E Province, Northants, Border, Griqualand W 1977-78 to 1992-93). 6'1½". RHB, RF. Squad No 99. Debut (Durham) 2016. No 1st XI appearances in 2018. Durham 2nd XI debut 2015. HS 61* v Sussex (Chester-le-St) 2017. BB 3-38 v Lancs (Chester-le-St) 2016. T20 HS 3. T20 BB 1-11.

CLARK, Graham (St Benedict's Catholic HS, Whitehaven), b Whitehaven, Cumbria 16 Mar 1993. Younger brother of J.Clark (*see SURREY*). 6'1". RHB, LB. Squad No 7. Debut (Durham) 2015. HS 109 v Glamorgan (Chester-le-St) 2017. BB 1-10 v Sussex (Arundel) 2018. LO HS 114 v Worcs (Worcester) 2017 (RLC). LO BB 3-18 v Leics (Leicester) 2018 (RLC). T20 HS 91*. T20 BB –.

COUGHLIN, Josh (St Robert of Newminster Catholic CS, Washington), b Sunderland 29 Sep 1997. Younger brother of P.Coughlin (*see NOTTINGHAMSHIRE*); nephew of T.Harland (Durham 1974-78). 6'4". LHB, RM. Squad No 29. Debut (Durham) 2016. Durham 2nd XI debut 2015. England U19 2016. HS 19 and BB 2-31 v Derbys (Chester-le-St) 2018.

HARDING, George Harvey Idris (Brine Leas HS, Nantwich; Myerscough C), b Poole, Dorset 12 Oct 1996. 6'6". RHB, SLA. Squad No 39. Debut (Durham) 2017. Durham 2nd XI debut 2015. Northumberland 2016. HS 7 v Glos (Cheltenham) 2018. BB 4-111 v Glamorgan (Swansea) 2017. LO HS 18* v Lancs (Chester-le-St) 2017 (RLC). LO BB 2-52 v Worcs (Worcester) 2017 (RLC).

HARTE, Gareth Jason (King Edward VII S), b Johannesburg, South Africa 15 Mar 1993. 5'9". RHB, RM. Squad No 93. Debut (Durham) 2018. HS 114 v Derbys (Chester-le-St) 2018. BB 2-26 v Leics (Leicester) 2018. LO HS 48 v Worcs (Gosforth) 2018 (RLC). LO BB 2-35 v Notts (Chester-le-St) 2018 (RLC). T20 HS 11.

ᴺᴼ**JONES, Michael** Alexander (Ormskirk S; Myerscough C), b Ormskirk, Lancs 5 Jan 1998. 6'2". RHB, OB. Debut (Durham) 2018. Durham 2nd XI debut 2017. Derbyshire 2nd XI 2017. Leicestershire 2nd XI 2017. **LOI** (Scot): 5 (2017-18); HS 87 v Ire (Dubai, ICCA) 2017-18. HS 10 v Derbys (Chester-le-St) 2018 – only 1st XI game for Durham. LO HS 87 (*see LOI*).

LEES, Alexander Zak (Holy Trinity SS, Halifax), b Halifax, Yorks 14 Apr 1993. 6'3". LHB, LB. Squad No 19. Yorkshire 2010-18; cap 2014; captain (l-o) 2016. Durham debut 2018. MCC 2017. YC 2014. 1000 runs (2); most – 1199 (2016). HS 275* Y v Derbys (Chesterfield) 2013. Du HS 69 v Glamorgan (Cardiff) 2018. BB 2-51 Y v Middx (Lord's) 2016. LO HS 102 Y v Northants (Northampton) 2014 (RLC). T20 HS 67*.

ᴺᴼ**MAIN, Gavin** Thomas, b Lanark, Scotland 28 Feb 1995. 6'2". RHB, RMF. Squad No 20. Debut (Durham) 2014. Durham 2nd XI debut 2013. **IT20** (Scot): 4 (2015 to 2015-16); HS – ; BB 1-13 v Hong Kong (Nagpur) 2015-16. HS 13 v Northants (Chester-le-St) 2017. BB 3-72 v Notts (Nottingham) 2014. LO BB 2-35 Scot v Nepal (Alloway) 2015. T20 BB 1-13.

POTTS, Matthew ('Matty') James (St Robert of Newminster Catholic S), b Sunderland 29 Oct 1998. 6'0". RHB, RM. Squad No 35. Debut (Durham) 2017. Durham 2nd XI debut 2016. England U19 2017. HS 53* v Derbys (Chester-le-St) 2017. BB 3-48 v Glamorgan (Chester-le-St) 2017. LO HS 30 and LO BB 3-69 v Yorks (Chester-le-St) 2018 (RLC).

ᴺᴼ**POYNTER, Stuart** William (Teddington S), b Hammersmith, London 18 Oct 1990. Younger brother of A.D.Poynter (Middlesex and Ireland 2005-11). 5'9". RHB, WK. Squad No 90. Middlesex 2010. Ireland 2011 to date. Warwickshire 2013. Durham debut 2016. **Tests** (Ire): 1 (2018-19); HS 1 v Afg (Dehradun) 2018-19. **LOI** (Ire): 20 (2014 to 2018-19); HS 36 v SL (Dublin) 2016. **IT20** (Ire): 25 (2015 to 2018-19); HS 39 v Scotland (Dubai, DSC) 2016-17. F-c Tour (Ire): Z 2015-16. HS 170 v Derbys (Derby) 2018, sharing Du record 6th wkt partnership of 278 with M.J.Richardson. LO HS 109 Ire v Sri Lanka A (Belfast) 2014. T20 HS 61*.

PRINGLE, Ryan David (Durham SFC), b Sunderland 17 Apr 1992. 6'0". RHB, OB. Squad No 17. Debut (Durham) 2014. Northumberland 2011-12. HS 99 v Hants (Chester-le-St) 2015. BB 7-107 (10-260 match) v Hants (Southampton) 2016. LO HS 125 v Derbys (Derby) 2016 (RLC). LO BB 2-39 v Northants (Northampton) 2016 (RLC) and 2-39 v Notts (Chester-le-St) 2018 (RLC). T20 HS 35. T20 BB 3-30.

RAINE, Benjamin Alexander (St Aidan's RC SS, Sunderland) b Sunderland, 14 Sep 1991. 6'0". LHB, RMF. Squad No 44. Debut (Durham) 2011. Leicestershire 2013-18; cap 2018. HS 72 Le v Lancs (Manchester) 2018. 50 wkts (1): 61 (2015). BB 6-66 Le v Notts (Leicester) 2017. LO HS 83 Le v Worcs (Worcester) 2018 (RLC). LO BB 3-31 Le v Northants (Northampton) 2018 (RLC). T20 HS 113 v Warwks (Birmingham) 2018 – Le record. T20 BB 3-7.

RICHARDSON, Michael John (Rondebosch HS; Stonyhurst C, Nottingham U), b Pt Elizabeth, South Africa 4 Oct 1986. Son of D.J.Richardson (South Africa, EP and NT 1977-78 to 1997-98), grandson of J.H.Richardson (NE Transvaal and Transvaal B 1952-53 to 1960-61), nephew of R.P.Richardson (WP 1984-85 to 1988-89). 5'10". RHB, WK. Squad No 10. Debut (Durham) 2010. Colombo CC 2014-15. 1000 runs (1): 1007 (2015). HS 148 v Yorks (Chester-le-St) 2014. LO HS 111 v Warwks (Chester-le-St) 2017 (RLC). T20 HS 53.

^{NQ}**RIMMINGTON, Nathan** John (Wellington C), b Redcliffe, Queensland, Australia 11 Nov 1982. 5'10". RHB, RFM. Squad No 11. Queensland 2005-06 to date. W Australia 2011-12 to 2016-17. Hampshire 2014. Durham debut 2018. Derbyshire (T20 only) 2015. IPL: KXIP 2011. Big Bash: PS 2011-12 to 2012-13. MR 2012-13 to 2016-17. HS 102* WA v NSW (Sydney) 2011-12. CC HS 65* H v Essex (Colchester) 2014. Du HS 61 v Warwks (Chester-le-St) 2018. BB 5-27 WA v Q (Perth) 2014-15. CC BB 3-39 v Kent (Chester-le-St) 2018. LO HS 55 WA v Tas (Sydney) 2014-15. LO BB 4-34 WA v SA (Perth) 2016-17 T20 HS 26. T20 BB 5-27.

RUSHWORTH, Christopher (Castle View CS, Sunderland), b Sunderland 11 Jul 1986. Cousin of P.Mustard (Durham, Mountaineers, Auckland, Lancashire and Gloucestershire 2002-17). 6'2". RHB, RMF. Squad No 22. Debut (Durham) 2010; testimonial 2019. MCC 2013, 2015. Northumberland 2004-05. PCA 2015. HS 57 v Kent (Canterbury) 2017. 50 wkts (4); most – 88 (2015). BB 9-52 (15-95 match – Du record) v Northants (Chester-le-St) 2014. Hat-trick v Hants (Southampton) 2015. LO HS 38* v Derbys (Chester-le-St) 2015 (RLC). LO BB 5-31 v Notts (Chester-le-St) 2010 (CB40). T20 HS 5. T20 BB 3-14.

SALISBURY, Matthew Edward Thomas (Shenfield HS; Anglia Ruskin U), b Chelmsford, Essex 18 Apr 1993. 6'0½". RHB, RMF. Squad No 32. Cambridge MCCU 2012-13. Essex 2014-15. Hampshire 2017. Durham debut 2018. Suffolk 2016. HS 37 v Warwks (Birmingham) 2018. BB 6-37 v Middx (Chester-le-St) 2018. LO HS 5* Ex v Leics (Chelmsford) 2014 (RLC). LO BB 4-55 Ex v Lancs (Chelmsford) 2014 (RLC). T20 HS 1*. T20 BB 2-19.

‡^{NQ}**SHORT, D'Arcy** John Matthew, b Katherine, N Territory, Australia 9 Aug 1990. LHB, SLC. W Australia 2016-17 to date. IPL: RR 2018. Big Bash: HH 2016-17 to date. Joins Durham in 2019 for T20 only. **LOI** (A): 4 (2018 to 2018-19); HS 47* v E (Manchester) 2018; BB –. **IT20** (A): 20 (2017-18 to 2018-19); HS 76 v NZ (Auckland) 2017-18 and 76 v P (Harare) 2018; BB 1-13 v P (Abu Dhabi) 2018-19. HS 66 WA v SA (Adelaide, GS) 2017-18. BB 3-78 WA v Vic (Melbourne) 2017-18. LO HS 257 (inc world record 23 sixes) WA v Q (Sydney, HO) 2018-19 – 3rd highest l-o score on record. LO BB 3-53 WA v Vic (Perth) 2017-18. T20 HS 122*. T20 BB 2-17.

SMITH, William Rew (Bedford S; Collingwood C, Durham U), b Luton, Beds 28 Sep 1982. 5'9". RHB, OB. Squad No 2. Nottinghamshire 2002-06. Durham UCCE 2003-05; captain 2004-05. British U 2004-05. Durham debut 2007; captain 2009-10 (part). Hampshire 2014-17; cap 2015. Bedfordshire 1999-2002. 1000 runs (1): 1187 (2014). HS 210 H v Lancs (Southampton) 2016. Du HS 201* v Surrey (Guildford) 2008. BB 3-34 DU v Leics (Leicester) 2005. CC BB 2-27 H v Kent (Southampton) 2014. Du BB 2-30 v Durham MCCU (Chester-le-St) 2013. LO HS 120* v Surrey (Chester-le-St) 2013 (Y40). LO BB 2-19 Du v Derbys (Derby) 2013 (Y40). T20 HS 55. T20 BB 3-15.

STEEL, Cameron Tate (Scotch C, Perth, Australia; Millfield S; Durham U), b San Francisco, USA 13 Sep 1995. 5'10". RHB, LB. Squad No 14. Durham MCCU 2014-16. Durham debut 2017. Middlesex 2nd XI 2013-16. Somerset 2nd XI 2013. Durham 2nd XI debut 2016. HS 224 v Leics (Leicester) 2017. BB 2-7 v Glamorgan (Cardiff) 2018. LO HS 77 v Notts (Nottingham) 2017 (RLC). LO BB –. T20 HS 37. T20 BB 2-60.

STOKES, Benjamin Andrew (Cockermouth S), b Christchurch, Canterbury, New Zealand 4 Jun 1991. 6'1". LHB, RFM. Squad No 38. Debut (Durham) 2010. IPL: RPS 2017. RR 2018. Big Bash: MR 2014-15. YC 2013. *Wisden* 2015. **ECB Test & LO Central Contract 2018-19. Tests**: 52 (2013-14 to 2018-19); HS 258 v SA (Cape Town) 2015-16, setting E record fastest double century in 163 balls; BB 6-22 v WI (Lord's) 2017. **LOI**: 79 (2011 to 2018-19); HS 102* v A (Birmingham) 2017; BB 5-61 v A (Southampton) 2013. **IT20**: 23 (2011 to 2018-19); HS 38 v I (Nagpur) 2016-17; BB 3-26 v NZ (Delhi) 2015-16. F-c Tours: A 2013-14; SA 2015-16; WI 2010-11 (EL), 2014-15, 2018-19; NZ 2017-18; I 2016-17; SL 2018-19; B 2016-17; UAE 2015-16 (v P). HS 258 (*see Tests*). Du HS 185 v Lancs (Chester-le-St) 2011, sharing Du record 4th wkt partnership of 331 with D.M.Benkenstein. BB 7-67 (10-121 match) v Sussex (Chester-le-St) 2014. LO HS 164 v Notts (Chester-le-St) 2014 (RLC) – Du record. LO BB 5-61 (*see LOI*). T20 HS 103*. T20 BB 4-16.

TREVASKIS, Liam (Q Elizabeth GS, Penrith), b Carlisle, Cumberland 18 Apr 1999. 5'8". LHB, SLA. Squad No 80. Debut (Durham) 2017. Durham 2nd XI debut 2015. HS 9 and BB 1-69 v Worcs (Worcester) 2017 – only f-c game. T20 HS 26. T20 BB 4-16.

WEIGHELL, William James (Stokesley S), b Middlesbrough, Yorks 28 Jan 1994. 6'4". LHB, RMF. Squad No 28. Debut (Durham) 2015. Northumberland 2012-15. HS 84 v Kent (Chester-le-St) 2018. BB 7-32 v Leics (Chester-le-St) 2018. LO HS 23 v Lancs (Manchester) 2018 (RLC). LO BB 5-57 v Warwks (Birmingham) 2017 (RLC). T20 HS 28. T20 BB 3-28.

WHITEHEAD, Benjamin Guy (Hetton S), b Sunderland 28 Apr 1997. 6'0". RHB, LBG. Squad No 97. Awaiting f-c debut. Durham 2nd XI debut 2014. Northumberland 2015-16. T20 HS 2*. T20 BB 2-23.

WOOD, Mark Andrew (Ashington HS; Newcastle C), b Ashington 11 Jan 1990. 5'11". RHB, RF. Squad No 33. Debut (Durham) 2011. IPL: CSK 2018. Northumberland 2008-10. **ECB L-O Central Contract 2018-19. Tests**: 13 (2015 to 2018-19); HS 52 v NZ (Christchurch) 2017-18; BB 5-41 v WI (Gros Islet) 2018-19. **LOI**: 40 (2015 to 2018-19); HS 13 v A (Manchester) 2015; BB 4-33 v A (Birmingham) 2017. **IT20**: 4 (2015 to 2017-18); HS 5* v A (Hobart) 2017-18 and 5* v NZ (Wellington) 2017-18; BB 3-26 v NZ (Manchester) 2015. F-c Tours (EL): SA 2014-15; WI 2018-19; NZ 2017-18; SL 2013-14; UAE 2015-16 (v P). HS 72* v Kent (Chester-le-St) 2017. BB 6-46 v Derbys (Derby) 2018. LO HS 24 EL v Pakistan A (Abu Dhabi) 2018-19. LO BB 4-33 (*see LOI*). T20 HS 27*. T20 BB 4-25.

RELEASED/RETIRED

(Having made a County 1st XI appearance in 2018)

COLLINGWOOD, Paul David (Blackfyne CS; Derwentside C), b Shotley Bridge 26 May 1976. 5'11". RHB, RM. Durham 1996-2018, debut v Northants (Chester-le-St) taking wicket of D.J.Capel with his first ball before scoring 91 and 16; cap 1998; benefit 2007; captain 2012 (*part*) to 2018; testimonial 2017. MCC 2018. IPL: DD 2009-10. MBE 2005. *Wisden* 2007. **Tests**: 68 (2003-04 to 2010-11); 1000 runs (1): 1121 (2006); HS 206 v A (Adelaide) 2006-07; BB 3-23 v NZ (Wellington) 2007-08. **LOI**: 197 (2001 to 2010-11, 25 as captain); 1000 runs (1): 1064 (2007); HS 120* v A (Melbourne) 2006-07; BB 6-31 v B (Nottingham) 2005 – record analysis for E, and first to score a hundred (112*) and take six wickets in same LOI. **IT20**: 36, inc 1 for a World XI in 2017 (2005 to 2010-11, 30 as captain); HS 79 v WI (Oval) 2007; BB 4-22 v SL (Southampton) 2006. F-c Tours: A 2006-07, 2010-11; SA 2009-10; WI 2003-04, 2008-09; NZ 2007-08; I 2005-06, 2008-09; P 2005-06; SL 2003-04, 2007-08; B 2009-10. 1000 runs (3); most – 1120 (2005). HS 206 (*see Tests*). Du HS 190 v SL (Chester-le-St) 2002 and 190 v Derbys (Derby) 2005, sharing Du record 4th wkt partnership of 250 with D.M.Benkenstein. BB 5-52 v Somerset (Stockton) 2005. LO HS 132 v Northants (Northampton) 2015 (RLC). LO BB 6-31 (*see LOI*). T20 HS 108* v Worcs (Worcester) 2017 – Du record. T20 BB 5-6 v Northants (Chester-le-St) 2011 – Du record.

DAVIES, Ryan Christopher (Sandwich TS), b Thanet, Kent 5 Nov 1996. 5'9". RHB, WK. Kent 2015. Somerset 2016. Durham 2018. Kent 2nd XI 2013-15. England U19 2014-15 to 2015. HS 86 Sm v Lancs (Manchester) 2016, sharing Sm record 8th wkt partnership of 236 with P.D.Trego. Du HS 20 v Warwks (Chester-le-St) 2018. LO HS 61* v Leics (Leicester) 2018 (RLC). T20 HS 27.

NQIMRAN TAHIR, Mohammad (Government Pakistan Angels HS and MAO College, Lahore), b Lahore, Pakistan 4 Jun 1979. 5'11". RHB, LB. Lahore City 1996-97 to 1997-98. WAPDA 1998-99. REDCO 1999-00. Lahore Whites 2000-01. SNGPL 2001-02 to 2003-04. Sialkot 2002-03. Middlesex 2003. Lahore Blues 2004-05. PIA 2004-05 to 2006-07. Lahore Ravi 2005-06. Yorkshire (1 match) 2007. Titans 2007-08 to 2009-10. Hampshire 2008-14; cap 2009. Easterns 2008-09 to 2009-10. Warwickshire 2010; cap 2010. Dolphins 2010-11 to 2016-17. Lions 2012-13 to 2013-14. Nottinghamshire 2015-16; cap 2015. Derbyshire 2017. Durham 2018 (T20 only). IPL: DD 2014-16. RPS 2017. CSK 2018. Staffordshire 2004-05. Qualified for SA on 1 Apr 2009. **Tests** (SA): 20 (2011-12 to 2015-16); HS 29* v SL (Centurion) 2011-12; BB 5-32 v P (Dubai) 2013-14. **LOI** (SA): 96 (2010-11 to 2018-19); HS 29 v WI (Bridgetown) 2016; LO BB 7-45 v WI (Basseterre) 2016. **IT20** (SA): 37 (2013 to 2018-19); HS 9* v Netherlands (Chittagong) 2013-14; BB 5-23 v Z (East London) 2018-19. F-c Tours (SA): E 2012; A 2012-13; NZ 2011-12; I 2015-16; SL 2004-05 (Pak A), 2014; UAE 2013-14 (v P). HS 77* H v Somerset (Southampton) 2009. 50 wkts (2+2); most – 74 (2004-05). BB 8-42 (12-133 match) Dolphins v Knights (Kimberley) 2015-16. UK BB 7-66 (12-189 match) H v Lancs (Manchester) 2008. LO HS 41* Staffs v Lancs (Stone) 2004 (CGT). LO BB 7-45 (see LOI). T20 HS 23. T20 BB 5-23.

NQLATHAM, Thomas William Maxwell, b Christchurch, New Zealand 2 Apr 1992. Son of R.T.Latham (Canterbury and New Zealand 1980-81 to 1994-95). 5'9". RHB, RM, WK. Canterbury 2010-11 to date. Kent 2016. Durham 2017-18; l-o captain 2018. **Tests** (NZ): 42 (2013-14 to 2018-19); HS 264* v SL (Wellington) 2018-19. **LOI** (NZ): 85 (2011-12 to 2018-19); HS 137 v B (Christchurch) 2016-17. **IT20** (NZ): 13 (2012 to 2017-18); HS 39 v I (Delhi) 2017-18. F-c Tours (NZ): E 2013, 2014 (NZ A), 2015 (A 2015-16; SA 2016; WI 2014; I 2013-14 (NZ A), 2016-17; SL 2013-14 (NZ A); Z 2016; UAE 2014-15 (v P), 2018-19 (v P). HS 264* (see Tests). Du HS 147 v Glos (Cheltenham) 2018. BB 1-7 NZ v Cricket Australia (Sydney) 2015-16. LO HS 137 (see LOI). T20 HS 110.

NQMcCARTHY, Barry John (St Michael's C, Dublin; Dublin U), b Dublin, Ireland 13 Sep 1992. 5'11". RHB, RMF. Durham 2015-18. **LOI** (Ire): 24 (2016 to 2018-19); HS 16* v NZ (Dublin) 2017; BB 5-46 v Afg (Sharjah) 2017-18. **IT20** (Ire): 6 (2016-17 to 2018); HS 11* v Netherlands (Rotterdam) 2018; BB 4-33 v Afg (Greater Noida) 2016-17. HS 51* v Hants (Chester-le-St) 2016. BB 6-63 v Kent (Canterbury) 2017. LO HS 43 v Leics (Leicester) 2018 (RLC). LO BB 5-46 (see LOI). T20 HS 11*. T20 BB 4-31.

NQMARKRAM, Aiden Kyle, b Pretoria, South Africa 4 Oct 1994. RHB, OB. Northerns 2014-15 to 2016-17. Titans 2016-17 to date. Durham 2018. **Tests** (SA): 17 (2017-18 to 2018-19); HS 152 v A (Johannesburg) 2017-18; BB –. **LOI** (SA): 16 (2017-18 to 2018-19); HS 66 v B (East London) 2017-18; BB 2-18 v B (East London) 2017-18. F-c Tours (SA): E 2017 (SAA); SL 2018. 1000 runs (0+1): 1439 (2017-18). HS 182 Northerns v WP (Cape Town) 2015-16. Du HS 94 and BB 1-1 v Leics (Chester-le-St) 2018. LO HS 183 Titans v Lions (Johannesburg) 2016-17. LO BB 4-45 SAA v EL (Northampton) 2018. T20 HS 82. T20 BB 3-21.

NQPATEL, Akshar Rajeshbhai, b Anand, Gujarat, India 20 Jan 1994. LHB, SLA. Gujarat 2012-13 to date. Durham 2018. IPL: KXIP 2014 to date. **LOI**: 38 (2014 to 2017-18); HS 38 v NZ (Ranchi) 2016-17; BB 3-34 v SL (Dambulla) 2017. **IT20** (I): 11 (2015 to 2017-18); HS 20* v Z (Harare) 2016; BB 3-17 v Z (Harare) 2015. HS 110* Gujarat v Baroda (Jaipur) 2016-17. Du HS 95* v Glamorgan (Cardiff) 2018. BB 7-54 v Warwks (Birmingham) 2018. LO HS 93 Gujarat v Karnataka (Kolkata) 2013-14. LO BB 6-43 Gujarat v Tamil Nadu (Alur) 2015-16. T20 HS 48. T20 BB 4-21.

DURHAM 2018

RESULTS SUMMARY

	Place	Won	Lost	Drew	NR	Aband
Specsavers County Champ (2nd Division)	8th	4	7	2		1
All First-Class Matches		4	7	2		1
Royal London One-Day Cup (North Group)	9th	2	6			
Vitality Blast (North Group)	QF	9	5		1	

SPECSAVERS COUNTY CHAMPIONSHIP AVERAGES

BATTING AND FIELDING

Cap		M	I	NO	HS	Runs	Avge	100	50	Ct/St
	T.W.M.Latham	4	8	–	147	366	45.75	1	2	8
	W.J.Weighell	3	5	–	84	185	37.00	–	1	1
	C.T.Steel	12	22	–	160	638	29.00	1	4	9
	G.J.Harte	8	15	–	114	382	25.46	2	–	4
	S.W.Poynter	11	20	1	170	475	25.00	1	1.	34/1
	A.K.Markram	3	5	–	94	124	24.80	–	1	4
	A.R.Patel	4	7	1	95*	147	24.50	–	1	1
	A.Z.Lees	6	11	–	69	256	23.27	–	1	3
	M.A.Wood	4	7	2	61*	115	23.00	–	1	1
	N.J.Rimmington	7	13	1	61	255	21.25	–	1	1
	W.R.Smith	9	17	–	90	357	21.00	–	2	5
	M.J.Richardson	10	18	–	115	377	20.94	1	1	3
	G.Clark	12	22	–	64	460	20.90	–	2	9
1998	P.D.Collingwood	11	20	–	47	299	14.95	–	–	12
	B.J.McCarthy	6	11	1	43	111	11.10	–	–	2
	J.Coughlin	2	4	–	19	42	10.50	–	–	1
	M.E.T.Salisbury	10	19	5	37	141	10.07	–	–	1
	C.Rushworth	12	22	12	11*	72	7.20	–	–	2
	R.C.Davies	3	6	–	20	27	4.50	–	–	7

Also batted (1 match each): M.W.Dixon 8*; G.H.I.Harding 0, 7; M.A.Jones 10, 3; M.J.Potts 15*, 36; R.D.Pringle 34, 3 (1 ct); B.A.Stokes 3, 9 (2 ct).

BOWLING

	O	M	R	W	Avge	Best	5wI	10wM
A.R.Patel	99.4	33	235	18	13.05	7-54	1	–
M.A.Wood	109.1	24	293	17	17.23	6-46	2	–
C.Rushworth	386.4	83	1201	60	20.01	8-51	3	1
W.J.Weighell	108.3	23	304	15	20.26	7-32	1	–
M.E.T.Salisbury	293.1	54	1090	44	24.77	6-37	1	–
B.J.McCarthy	130.3	21	460	14	32.85	4-58	–	–
N.J.Rimmington	167.4	34	606	11	55.09	3-39	–	–
Also bowled:								
B.A.Stokes	43	11	118	8	14.75	5-52	1	–
P.D.Collingwood	49	15	116	6	19.33	2-25	–	–
C.T.Steel	46.2	4	202	9	22.44	2- 7	–	–

G.Clark 13.5-0-51-2; J.Coughlin 35-3-139-3; M.W.Dixon 28.2-6-108-2; G.H.I.Harding 30-4-106-0; G.J.Harte 45.1-7-148-3; A.K.Markram 1.4-1-1-1; M.J.Potts 5-0-37-1; R.D.Pringle 28-2-74-3; W.R.Smith 66.1-6-204-4.

Durham played no first-class fixtures outside the County Championship in 2018. The First-Class Averages (pp 230–245) give the records of Durham players in all first-class county matches, with the exception of A.Z.Lees, B.A.Stokes and M.A.Wood, whose first-class figures for Durham are as above.

DURHAM RECORDS

FIRST-CLASS CRICKET

Highest Total	For 648-5d		v	Notts	Chester-le-St[2]	2009
	V 810-4d		by	Warwicks	Birmingham	1994
Lowest Total	For 61		v	Leics	Leicester	2018
	V 18		by	Durham MCCU	Chester-le-St[2]	2012
Highest Innings	For 273	M.L.Love	v	Hampshire	Chester-le-St[2]	2003
	V 501*	B.C.Lara	for	Warwicks	Birmingham	1994

Highest Partnership for each Wicket

1st	334*	S.Hutton/M.A.Roseberry	v	Oxford U	Oxford	1996
2nd	274	M.D.Stoneman/S.G.Borthwick	v	Middlesex	Chester-le-St[2]	2014
3rd	212	M.J.Di Venuto/D.M.Benkenstein	v	Essex	Chester-le-St[2]	2010
4th	331	B.A.Stokes/D.M.Benkenstein	v	Lancashire	Chester-le-St[2]	2011
5th	247	G.J.Muchall/I.D.Blackwell	v	Worcs	Worcester	2011
6th	278	M.J.Richardson/S.W.Poynter	v	Derbyshire	Derby	2018
7th	315	D.M.Benkenstein/O.D.Gibson	v	Yorkshire	Leeds	2006
8th	147	P.Mustard/L.E.Plunkett	v	Yorkshire	Leeds	2009
9th	150	P.Mustard/P.Coughlin	v	Lancashire	Chester-le-St[2]	2011
10th	103	M.M.Betts/D.M.Cox	v	Sussex	Hove	1996

Best Bowling	For 10- 47	O.D.Gibson	v	Hampshire	Chester-le-St[2]	2007
(Innings)	V 9- 34	J.A.R.Harris	for	Middlesex	Lord's	2015
Best Bowling	For 15- 95	C.Rushworth	v	Northants	Chester-le-St[2]	2014
(Match)	V 13-103	J.A.R.Harris	for	Middlesex	Lord's	2015

Most Runs – Season	1654	M.J.Di Venuto	(av 78.76)	2009
Most Runs – Career	12030	P.D.Collingwood	(av 33.98)	1996-2018
Most 100s – Season	7	K.K.Jennings		2016
Most 100s – Career	25	P.D.Collingwood		1996-2018
Most Wkts – Season	80	O.D.Gibson	(av 20.75)	2007
Most Wkts – Career	527	G.Onions	(av 25.58)	2004-17
Most Career W-K Dismissals	638	P.Mustard	(619 ct; 19 st)	2002-16
Most Career Catches in the Field	246	P.D.Collingwood		1996-2018

LIMITED-OVERS CRICKET

Highest Total	50ov	353-8		v	Notts	Chester-le-St[2]	2014
	40ov	325-9		v	Surrey	The Oval	2011
	T20	225-2		v	Leics	Chester-le-St[2]	2010
Lowest Total	50ov	82		v	Worcs	Chester-le-St[1]	1968
	40ov	72		v	Warwicks	Birmingham	2002
	T20	78		v	Lancashire	Chester-le-St[2]	2009
Highest Innings	50ov	164	B.A.Stokes	v	Notts	Chester-le-St[2]	2014
	40ov	150*	B.A.Stokes	v	Warwicks	Birmingham	2011
	T20	108*	P.D.Collingwood	v	Worcs	Worcester	2017
Best Bowling	50ov	7-32	S.P.Davis	v	Lancashire	Chester-le-St[1]	1983
	40ov	6-31	N.Killeen	v	Derbyshire	Derby	2000
	T20	5- 6	P.D.Collingwood	v	Northants	Chester-le-St[2]	2011

[1] Chester-le-Street CC (Ropery Lane) [2] Emirates Riverside

ESSEX

Formation of Present Club: 14 January 1876
Inaugural First-Class Match: 1894
Colours: Blue, Gold and Red
Badge: Three Seaxes above Scroll bearing 'Essex'
County Champions: (7) 1979, 1983, 1984, 1986, 1991, 1992, 2017
NatWest/Friends Prov Trophy Winners: (3) 1985, 1997, 2008
Benson and Hedges Cup Winners: (2) 1979, 1998
Pro 40/National League (Div 1) Winners: (2) 2005, 2006
Sunday League Winners: (3) 1981, 1984, 1985
Twenty20 Cup Winners: (0); best – Semi-Finalist 2006, 2008, 2010

Chief Executive: Derek Bowden, The Cloudfm County Ground, New Writtle Street, Chelmsford CM2 0PG • Tel: 01245 252420 • Email: administration@essexcricket.org.uk • Web: www.essexcricket.org.uk • Twitter: @EssexCricket (82,461 followers)

Head Coach: Anthony McGrath. **Assistant Head Coach**: Andre Nel. **Captain**: R.N.ten Doeschate. **Vice-Captain**: T.Westley. **Overseas Players**: Mohammad Amir (T20 only), P.M.Siddle and A.Zampa (T20 only). **2019 Testimonial**: None. **Head Groundsman**: Stuart Kerrison. **Scorer**: Tony Choat. ‡ New registration. ᴺᑫ Not qualified for England.

BEARD, Aaron Paul (Boswells S, Chelmsford), b Chelmsford 15 Oct 1997. LHB, RFM. Squad No 14. Debut (Essex) 2016. England U19 2016 to 2016-17. No 1st XI appearances in 2018. HS 58* v Durham MCCU (Chelmsford) 2017. CC HS 4* (twice). BB 4-62 v Sri Lankans (Chelmsford) 2016. CC BB 3-47 v Lancs (Chelmsford) 2017.

BOPARA, Ravinder Singh (Brampton Manor S; Barking Abbey Sports C), b Newham, London 4 May 1985. 5'8". RHB, RM. Squad No 25. Debut (Essex) 2002; cap 2005; benefit 2015; captain (l-o only) 2016. Auckland 2009-10. Dolphins 2010-11. IPL: KXIP 2009 to 2009-10. SH 2015. Big Bash: SS 2013-14. MCC 2006, 2008. YC 2008. **Tests**: 13 (2007-08 to 2012); HS 143 v WI (Lord's) 2009; BB 1-39 v SL (Galle) 2007-08. **LOI**: 120 (2006-07 to 2014-15); HS 101* v Ire (Dublin) 2013; BB 4-38 v SA (Birmingham) 2010. **IT20**: 38 (2008 to 2014); HS 65* v A (Hobart) 2013-14; BB 4-10 v WI (Oval) 2011. F-c Tours: WI 2008-09, 2010-11 (EL); SL 2007-08, 2011-12. 1000 runs (1): 1256 (2008). HS 229 v Northants (Chelmsford) 2007. BB 5-49 v Derbys (Chelmsford) 2016. LO HS 201* v Leics (Leicester) 2008 (FPT) – Ex record. LO BB 5-63 Dolphins v Warriors (Pietermaritzburg) 2010-11. T20 HS 105*. T20 BB 6-16.

BROWNE, Nicholas Lawrence Joseph (Trinity Catholic HS, Woodford Green), b Leytonstone 24 Mar 1991. 6'3½". LHB, LB. Squad No 10. Debut (Essex) 2013; cap 2015. MCC 2016. 1000 runs (3); most – 1262 (2016). HS 255 v Derbys (Chelmsford) 2016. BB –. LO HS 99 v Glamorgan (Chelmsford) 2016 (RLC). T20 HS 38.

CHOPRA, Varun (Ilford County HS), b Barking, Essex 21 Jun 1987. 6'1". RHB, LB. Squad No 6. Debut (Essex) 2006, scoring 106 v Glos (Chelmsford) on CC debut; cap 2018. Warwickshire 2010-16; cap 2012; captain 2015. Tamil Union 2011-12. F-c Tour (EL): SL 2013-14. 1000 runs (3); most – 1203 (2011). HS 233* TU v Sinhalese (Colombo, PSS) 2011-12. CC HS 228 Wa v Worcs (Worcester) 2011 (in 2nd CC game of season, having scored 210 v Somerset in 1st). Ex HS 155 v Glos (Bristol) 2008. BB –. LO HS 160 v Somerset (Chelmsford) 2018 (RLC). T20 HS 116.

COLES, Matthew Thomas (Maplesden Noakes S; Mid-Kent C), b Maidstone, Kent 26 May 1990. 6'3". LHB, RFM. Squad No 1. Kent 2009-17; cap 2012. Hampshire 2013-14. Essex debut 2018. HS 103* K v Yorks (Leeds) 2012. Ex HS 10* v Worcs (Chelmsford) 2018. 50 wkts (2); most – 67 (2015). BB 6-51 K v Northants (Northampton) 2012. Ex BB 5-123 v Surrey (Oval) 2018. LO HS 100 K v Surrey (Oval) 2015 (RLC). LO BB 6-32 K v Yorks (Leeds) 2012 (CB40). T20 HS 54. T20 BB 4-27.

COOK, Sir Alastair Nathan (Bedford S), b Gloucester 25 Dec 1984. 6'3". LHB, OB. Squad No 26. Debut (Essex) 2003; cap 2005; benefit 2014. MCC 2004-07, 2015. YC 2005. *Wisden* 2011. Knighted in 2019 New Year's honours list. **Tests**: 161 (2005-06 to 2018, 59 as captain); 1000 runs (5); most – 1364 (2015); HS 294 v I (Birmingham) 2011. Scored 60 and 104* v I (Nagpur) 2005-06 on debut, and 71 and 147 in final Test v I (Oval) 2018. Second, after M.A.Taylor, to score 1000 runs in the calendar year of his debut. Finished career after appearing in world record 159 consecutive Tests. BB 1-6 v I (Nottingham) 2014. **LOI**: 92 (2006 to 2014-15, 69 as captain); 1000 runs (1); most – 137 v P (Abu Dhabi) 2011-12. **IT20**: 4 (2007 to 2009-10); HS 26 v SA (Centurion) 2009-10. F-c Tours (C=Captain): A 2006-07, 2010-11, 2013-14C, 2017-18; SA 2009-10, 2015-16C; WI 2005-06 (Eng A), 2008-09, 2014-15C; NZ 2007-08, 2012-13C, 2017-18; I 2005-06, 2008-09, 2012-13C, 2016-17C; SL 2004-05 (Eng A), 2007-08, 2011-12; B 2009-10C, 2016-17C; UAE 2011-12 (v P), 2015-16C (v P). 1000 runs (7+1); most – 1466 (2005). HS 294 (*see Tests*). CC HS 195 v Northants (Northampton) 2005. BB 3-13 v Northants (Chelmsford) 2005. LO HS 137 (*see LOI*). BB –. T20 HS 100*.

COOK, Samuel James (Great Baddow HS & SFC; Loughborough U), b Chelmsford 4 Aug 1997. RHB, RFM. Squad No 16. Loughborough MCCU 2016-17. Essex debut 2017. Essex 2nd XI debut 2014. HS 14 v Hants (Chelmsford) 2018. BB 5-18 v Hants (Southampton) 2017. LO HS 1* v Surrey (Chelmsford) 2018 (RLC). LO BB 1-21 v Kent (Chelmsford) 2018 (RLC). T20 HS 0*. T20 BB 1-27.

‡**NQDELPORT, Cameron** Scott (Kloof Senior S, Durban; Westville BHS), b Durban, South Africa 12 May 1989. 5'10". LHB, RM. Squad No 89. KwaZulu-Natal 2008-09 to 2016-17. Dolphins 2008-09 to 2011-12. Leicestershire 2017 (white ball 2016-18). Big Bash: ST 2014-15. HS 163 KZN v Northerns (Centurion) 2010-11. CC HS 20 Le v Glamorgan (Leicester) 2017. BB 2-10 KZN v Northern Cape (Chatsworth) 2016-17. LO HS 169* Dolphins v Knights (Bloemfontein) 2014-15. LO BB 4-42 Dolphins v Titans (Durban) 2011-12. T20 HS 117*. T20 BB 4-17.

NQHARMER, Simon Ross, b Pretoria, South Africa 10 Feb 1993. RHB, OB. Squad No 11. Eastern Province 2009-10 to 2011-12. Warriors 2010-11 to date. Essex debut 2017 (Kolpak signing); cap 2018. **Tests** (SA): 5 (2014-15 to 2015-16); HS 13 v I (Nagpur) 2015-16; BB 4-61 v I (Mohali) 2015-16. F-c Tours (SA): A 2014 (SA A); I 2015-16; B 2015; Ire 2012 (SA A). HS 102* v Surrey (Oval) 2018. 50 wkts (2+1); most – 74 (2017). BB 9-95 (14-172 match) v Middx (Chelmsford) 2017. LO HS 44* v Surrey (Oval) 2017. LO BB 4-42 Warriors v Lions (Potchefstroom) 2011-12. T20 HS 43. T20 BB 3-22.

KHUSHI, Feroze Isa Nazir (Kelmscott S, Walthamstow; Leyton SFC), b Whipps Cross 23 Jun 1999. RHB, OB. Squad No 23. Essex 2nd XI debut 2015. Awaiting 1st XI debut.

LAWRENCE, Daniel William (Trinity Catholic HS, Woodford Green), b Whipps Cross 12 Jul 1997. 6'2". RHB, LB. Squad No 28. Debut (Essex) 2015; cap 2017. Essex 2nd XI debut 2013, aged 15y 321d. England U19 2015. 1000 runs (1): 1070 (2016). HS 161 v Surrey (Oval) 2015. BB 2-63 v MCC (Bridgetown) 2017-18. CC BB 1-5 v Kent (Chelmsford) 2016. LO HS 115 v Kent (Chelmsford) 2018 (RLC). LO BB 3-35 v Middx (Lord's) 2016 (RLC). T20 HS 86. T20 BB 3-21.

NQMOHAMMAD AMIR, b Gujar Khan, Punjab, Pakistan 13 Apr 1992. LHB, LF. Squad No 5. Federal Areas 2008-09. National Bank 2008-09 to 2009-10. SSGC 2015-16 to date. Essex debut 2017. **Tests** (P): 36 (2009 to 2018-19); HS 48 v A (Brisbane) 2016-17; BB 6-44 v WI (Kingston) 2017. **LOI** (P): 49 (2009 to 2018-19); HS 73* v NZ (Abu Dhabi) 2009-10; BB 4-28 v SL (Colombo, RPS) 2009. **IT20** (P): 42 (2009 to 2018-19); HS 21* v A (Birmingham) 2010; BB 4-13 v SL (Lahore) 2017-18. F-c Tours (P): E 2010, 2016, 2018; A 2009-10, 2016-17; SA 2018-19; WI 2017; NZ 2009-10, 2016-17; WI 2017; SL 2009; Ire 2018. HS 66 SSGC v Lahore Blues (Lahore) 2015-16. Ex HS 22* v Somerset (Chelmsford) 2017. 50 wkts (0+1): 56 (2008-09). BB 7-61 (10-97 match) NBP v Lahore Shalimar (Lahore) 2008-09. Ex BB 5-18 (10-72 match) v Yorks (Scarborough) 2017. LO HS 73* (*see LOI*). LO BB 5-36 Sindh v Islamabad (Faisalabad) 2016. T20 HS 21*. T20 BB 4-13.

NIJJAR, Aron Stuart Singh (Ilford County HS), b Goodmayes 24 Sep 1994. LHB, SLA. Squad No 24. Debut (Essex) 2015. Essex 2nd XI debut 2013. Suffolk 2016. BB 2-33 v Northants (Chelmsford) 2015. BB 2-33 v Lancs (Chelmsford) 2015. LO HS 21 v Yorks (Chelmsford) 2015 (RLC). LO BB 1-39 v Sussex (Hove) 2015 (RLC). T20 HS 1-30.

PATEL, Rishi Ketan (Brentwood S), b Chigwell 26 Jul 1998. RHB, LB. Squad No 12. Essex 2nd XI debut 2015. Awaiting 1st XI debut.

PEPPER, Michael-Kyle Steven (The Perse S), b Harlow 25 Jun 1998. Younger brother of C.A.Pepper (Cambridgeshire 2013-16). RHB, WK. Squad No 19. Debut (Essex) 2018. Essex 2nd XI debut 2017. Cambridgeshire 2014-16. HS 22 v Somerset (Chelmsford) 2018. T20 HS 27.

PLOM, Jack Henry (Gable Hall S; S Essex C), b Basildon 27 Aug 1999. LHB, RFM. Squad No 77. Debut (Essex) 2018 – did not bat or bowl. Essex 2nd XI debut 2016.

PORTER, James Alexander (Oak Park HS, Newbury Park; Epping Forest C), b Leytonstone 25 May 1993. 5'11½". RHB, RFM. Squad No 44. Debut (Essex) 2014, taking a wkt with his 5th ball; cap 2015. *Wisden* 2017. F-c Tours (EL): WI 2017-18; I 2018-19; UAE 2018-19 (v P A). HS 34 v Glamorgan (Cardiff) 2015. 50 wkts (4); most – 85 (2017). BB 7-41 (11-98 match) v Worcs (Chelmsford) 2018. LO HS 6 South v North (Cave Hill) 2017-18 and 6 EL v P A (Dubai, ICCA) 2018-19. LO BB 4-29 v Glamorgan (Chelmsford) 2018 (RLC). T20 HS 1*. T20 BB 4-20.

NQQUINN, Matthew Richard, b Auckland, New Zealand 28 Feb 1993. RHB, RMF. Squad No 94. Auckland 2012-13 to 2015-16. Essex debut 2016. UK passport. HS 50 Auckland v Canterbury (Auckland) 2013-14. Ex HS 16 v Notts (Chelmsford) 2018. BB 7-76 (11-163 match) v Glos (Cheltenham) 2016. LO HS 36 Auckland v CD (Auckland) 2013-14. LO BB 4-71 v Sussex (Hove) 2016 (RLC). T20 HS 8*. T20 BB 4-20.

NQSIDDLE, Peter Matthew, b Traralgon, Victoria, Australia 25 Nov 1984. 6'1½". RHB, RFM. Squad No 64. Victoria 2005-06 to date. Nottinghamshire 2014; cap 2014. Lancashire 2015. Essex debut 2018. Big Bash: MR 2013-14 to 2014-15. AS 2017-18 to date. **Tests** (A): 64 (2008-09 to 2018-19); HS 51 v I (Delhi) 2012-13; BB 6-54 v E (Brisbane) 2010-11. **LOI** (A): 20 (2008-09 to 2018-19); HS 10* v I (Melbourne) 2011-12; BB 3-55 v E (Centurion) 2009-10. **IT20** (A): 2 (2008-09 to 2010-11); HS 1* and BB 2-24 v NZ (Sydney) 2008-09. F-c Tours (A): E 2009, 2013, 2015; SA 2008-09, 2011-12, 2013-14; WI 2011-12; NZ 2015-16; I 2008-09 (Aus A), 2008-09, 2012-13; SL 2011; Z 2011 (Aus A); UAE 2014-15 (v P), 2018-19 (v P). HS 103* Aus A v Scotland (Edinburgh) 2013. CC HS 89 La v Northants (Northampton) 2015. Ex HS 33* v Lancs (Chelmsford) 2018. 50 wkts (0+1): 54 (2011-12). BB 8-54 Vic v S Aus (Adelaide) 2014-15. CC BB 5-37 v Worcs (Worcester) 2018. LO HS 62 Vic v Q (N Sydney) 2017-18. LO BB 4-27 Vic v Tas (Hobart) 2008-09. T20 HS 9*. T20 BB 4-29.

NQ**SNATER, Shane** (St John's C, Harare), b Harare, Zimbabwe 24 Mar 1996. RHB, RM. Squad No 29. Netherlands 2016 to date. Awaiting Essex f-c debut. Essex 2nd XI debut 2017. **LOI** (Neth): 2 (2018); HS 12 and BB 1-41 v Nepal (Amstelveen) 2018. **IT20** (Neth): 6 (2018 to 2018-19); HS 6 v Scotland (Amstelveen) 2018; BB 2-25 v Ire (Rotterdam) 2018. HS 50* and BB 5-88 Neth v Namibia (Dubai, ICCA) 2017-18. LO HS 23* Neth v Nepal (Kwekwe) 2017-18. LO BB 5-60 v Somerset (Chelmsford) 2018 (RLC). T20 HS 6. T20 BB 2-25.

NQ**Ten DOESCHATE, Ryan** Neil (Fairbairn C; Cape Town U), b Port Elizabeth, South Africa 30 Jun 1980. 5'10½". RHB, RMF. Squad No 27. Debut (Essex) 2003; cap 2006; captain (l-o) 2014-15; captain 2016 to date. EU passport – Dutch ancestry. Netherlands 2005 to 2009-10. Otago 2012-13. IPL: KKR 2011-15. Big Bash: AS 2014-15. **LOI** (Ne): 33 (2006 to 2010-11); HS 119 v E (Nagpur) 2010-11; BB 4-31 v Canada (Nairobi) 2006-07. **IT20** (Ne): 13 (2008 to 2018-19); HS 56 v Kenya (Belfast) 2008; BB 3-23 v Scotland (Belfast) 2008. F-c Tours (Ne): SA 2006-07, 2007-08; K 2005-06, 2009-10; Ireland 2005. 1000 runs (1): 1226 (2016). HS 259* and BB 6-20 Neth v Canada (Pretoria) 2006. Ex HS 173* v Somerset (Chelmsford) 2018. Ex BB 6-57 v New Zealanders (Chelmsford) 2008. CC BB 5-13 v Hants (Chelmsford) 2010. LO HS 180 v Scotland (Chelmsford) 2013 (Y40) – Ex 40-over record, inc 15 sixes. LO BB 5-50 v Glos (Bristol) 2007 (FPT). T20 HS 121*. T20 BB 4-24.

WALTER, Paul Ian (Billericay S), b Basildon 28 May 1994. LHB, LMF. Squad No 22. Debut (Essex) 2016. Essex 2nd XI debut 2015. HS 68* v West Indians (Chelmsford) 2017. CC HS 47 and BB 3-44 v Derbys (Derby) 2016. LO HS 19 South v North (Bridgetown) 2017-18. LO BB 4-37 v Middx (Chelmsford) 2017 (RLC). T20 HS 40. T20 BB 3-24.

WESTLEY, Thomas (Linton Village C; Hills Road SFC), b Cambridge 13 March 1989. 6'2". RHB, OB. Squad No 21. Debut (Essex) 2007; cap 2013. MCC 2007, 2009, 2016. Durham MCCU 2010-11. Cambridgeshire 2005. **Tests**: 5 (2017); HS 59 v SA (Oval) 2017. F-c Tour (EL): SL 2016-17. 1000 runs (1): 1435 (2016). HS 254 v Worcs (Chelmsford) 2016. BB 4-55 DU v Durham (Durham) 2010. CC BB 4-75 v Surrey (Colchester) 2015. LO HS 134 v Middx (Radlett) 2018 (RLC). LO BB 4-60 v Northants (Northampton) 2014 (RLC). T20 HS 109*. T20 BB 2-27.

WHEATER, Adam Jack Aubrey (Millfield S), b Whipps Cross 13 Feb 1990. 5'6". RHB, WK. Squad No 31. Debut (Essex) 2008. Cambridge MCCU 2010. Matabeleland Tuskers 2010-11 to 2012-13. Badureliya Sports Club 2011-12. Northern Districts 2012-13. Hampshire 2013-16; cap 2016. HS 204* H v Warwks (Birmingham) 2016. Ex HS 164 v Northants (Chelmsford) 2011, sharing Ex record 6th wkt partnership of 253 with J.S.Foster. BB 1-86 v Leics (Leicester) 2012 – in contrived circumstances. LO HS 135 v Essex (Chelmsford) 2014 (RLC). T20 HS 78.

NQ**ZAMPA, Adam**, b Shellharbour, NSW, Australia 31 Mar 1992. RHB, LB. Squad No 88. New South Wales 2012-13. S Australia 2013-14 to date. Essex debut 2018 (T20 only). IPL: RPS 2016-17. Big Bash: ST 2012-13. AS 2013-14 to 2014-15. MS 2015-16 to date. **LOI** (A): 39 (2015-16 to 2018-19); HS 22 v SA (Adelaide) 2018-19; BB 3-16 v WI (Providence) 2016. **IT20** (A): 22 (2015-16 to 2018-19); HS 9 v P (Dubai, DSC) 2018-19; BB 3-16 v SL (Colombo, RPS) 2016. HS 74 SA v WA (Adelaide) 2014-15. BB 6-62 (10-119 match) SA v Q (Adelaide) 2016-17. LO HS 66 SA v Q (N Sydney) 2013-14. LO BB 4-18 SA v WA (Brisbane) 2014-15. T20 HS 17*. T20 BB 6-19.

RELEASED/RETIRED

(Having made a County 1st XI appearance in 2018)

Syed **ASHAR** Ahmed **ZAIDI**, b Karachi, Pakistan 13 Jul 1981. LHB, SLA. UK citizen. Islamabad 1999-00 to 2009-10. PTC 2003-04 to 2005-06. Rawalpindi 2003-04 to 2004-05. KRL 2006-07. Federal Areas 2007-08. Sussex 2013-15. Essex 2016-17. HS 202 Islamabad v Sialkot (Sialkot) 2009-10. CC HS 106 Sx v Warwks (Birmingham) 2015. Ex HS 37 v Glos (Cheltenham) 2016. BB 4-50 Islamabad v Hyderabad (Islamabad) 2009-10. CC BB 4-57 Sx v Yorks (Hove) 2013. Ex BB 3-17 v Somerset (Taunton) 2017. LO HS 141 Rupganj v Old DOHS (Mirpur) 2014-15. LO BB 4-39 Gazi Tank v PDSC (Mirpur) 2013-14. T20 HS 59*. T20 BB 4-11.

^{NQ}**DIXON, Matt**hew William (Servite C, Perth), b Subiaco, W Australia 12 Jun 1992. RHB, RF. W Australia 2010-11 to 2015-16. Essex 2016-17. Durham 2018 (on loan). UK passport. HS 22 WA v Q (Perth) 2011-12. Ex HS 14 and BB 5-124 v Kent (Canterbury) 2016. LO HS 12 Cricket Australia XI v WA (Sydney) 2015-16. LO BB 3-40 CA v Tas (Sydney) 2015-16. T20 HS 1. T20 BB 3-32.

FOSTER, James Savin (Forest S, Snaresbrook; Collingwood C, Durham U), b Whipps Cross 15 Apr 1980. 6'0". RHB, WK. British U 2000-01. Essex 2000-18; cap 2001; captain 2010 (*part*); benefit 2011. Durham UCCE 2001. MCC 2004, 2008-10. **Tests**: 7 (2001-02 to 2002-03); HS 48 v I (Bangalore) 2001-02. **LOI**: 11 (2001-02); HS 13 v I (Bombay) 2001-02. **IT20**: 5 (2009); HS 14* v P (Oval) 2009. F-c Tours: A 2002-03; WI 2000-01 (Eng A); NZ 2001-02; I 2001-02, 2007-08 (Eng A). 1000 runs (1): 1037 (2004). HS 212 v Leics (Chelmsford) 2004. BB 1-122 v Northants (Northampton) 2008 – in contrived circumstances. LO HS 83* v Durham, inc 5 sixes in 5 balls off S.G.Borthwick (Chester-le-St) 2009 (P40). T20 HS 65*.

^{NQ}**VIJAY, Murali**, b Madras, India 1 Apr 1984. RHB, OB. Tamil Nadu 2006-07 to date. Central Districts 2008-09. Essex 2018. IPL: CSK 2009-18. DD 2014. KXIP 2015-16. **Tests** (I): 61 (2008-09 to 2018-19); HS 167 v A (Hyderabad) 2012-13; BB 1-12 v E (Lord's) 2014. **LOI** (I): 17 (2009-10 to 2015); HS 72 v Z (Harare) 2015; BB 1-19 v Z (Harare) 2015 – different matches. **IT20** (I): 9 (2010 to 2015); HS 48 v Afg (Gros Islet) 2010. F-c Tours (I): E 2014, 2018; A 2014-15, 2018-19; SA 2010-11, 2013 (IA), 2013-14, 2017-18; WI 2011, 2016; NZ 2008-09 (IA), 2013-14; SL 2010, 2015; B 2009-10, 2015. 1000 runs (0+1): 1024 (2012-13). HS 266 Rest of India v Rajasthan (Bangalore) 2012-13. CC HS 100 v Notts (Nottingham) 2018 – on debut. BB 3-46 India Green v India Red (Lucknow) 2017. LO HS 155 India B v India A (Rajkot) 2012-13. LO BB 3-13 TN v Karnataka (Visakhapatnam) 2008-09. T20 HS 127. T20 BB –.

^{NQ}**WAGNER, Neil**, b Pretoria, South Africa 13 Mar 1986. LHB, LMF. Northerns 2005-06 to 2007-08. Titans 2006-07 to 2007-08. Otago 2008-09 to 2017-18. Northamptonshire 2014. Lancashire 2016. Essex 2017-18. Northern Districts 2018-19. **Tests** (NZ): 42 (2012 to 2018-19); HS 47 v B (Hamilton) 2018-19. BB 7-39 v WI (Wellington) 2017-18. F-c Tours (NZ): E 2013, 2015; SA 2012-13, 2016; WI 2012, 2014; I 2016-17; Z 2007 (SA Acad), 2016; B 2013-14; UAE 2018-19 (v P). HS 70 Otago v Wellington (Queenstown) 2009-10. Ex HS 50 v Surrey (Chelmsford) 2017. 50 wkts (0+2); most – 51 (2010-11, 2012-13). BB 7-39 (*see Tests*). Ex BB 6-48 v Somerset (Taunton) 2017. LO HS 42 Otago v CD (Dunedin) 2014-15. LO BB 5-34 Otago v Wellington (Wellington) 2008-09. T20 HS 16*. T20 BB 4-33.

C.J.Taylor left the staff without making a County 1st XI appearance in 2018.

ESSEX 2018

RESULTS SUMMARY

	Place	Won	Lost	Tied	Drew	NR	Aband
Specsavers County Champ (1st Division)	3rd	7	4		2		1
All First-Class Matches		7	4		3		1
Royal London One-Day Cup (South Group)	QF	5	4				
Vitality Blast (South Group)	7th	2	8	1		3	

SPECSAVERS COUNTY CHAMPIONSHIP AVERAGES

BATTING AND FIELDING

Cap		M	I	NO	HS	Runs	Avge	100	50	Ct/St
	M.Vijay	3	5	–	100	323	64.60	1	3	1
2005	R.S.Bopara	13	22	4	133*	751	41.72	2	4	8
2006	R.N.ten Doeschate	12	20	2	173*	680	37.77	1	4	13
2005	A.N.Cook	6	11	–	96	412	37.45	–	4	6
	A.J.A.Wheater	8	13	3	68*	340	34.00	–	3	23/1
2013	T.Westley	13	23	1	134	687	31.22	2	2	2
2018	S.R.Harmer	13	20	3	102*	460	27.05	1	1	13
	N.Wagner	3	4	1	37	80	26.66	–	–	3
	M.R.Quinn	3	5	4	16	26	26.00	–	–	–
2015	N.L.J.Browne	10	17	–	86	414	24.35	–	3	8
2001	J.S.Foster	4	7	–	69	165	23.57	–	1	13/1
2017	D.W.Lawrence	12	21	1	124	468	23.40	1	1	10
	P.M.Siddle	7	11	2	33*	158	17.55	–	–	–
2018	V.Chopra	7	13	–	61	201	15.46	–	1	7
	S.J.Cook	10	11	7	14	56	14.00	–	–	1
	M.S.Pepper	2	4	–	22	53	13.25	–	–	–
	M.T.Coles	4	5	1	10*	37	9.25	–	–	1
2015	J.A.Porter	13	17	3	31	88	6.28	–	–	2

Also batted: P.I.Walter (1 match) 7, 14.

BOWLING

	O	M	R	W	Avge	Best	5wI	10wM
P.M.Siddle	234.4	47	607	37	16.40	5- 37	3	–
S.R.Harmer	526.2	136	1394	57	24.45	6- 87	3	–
J.A.Porter	432.3	81	1429	58	24.63	7- 41	3	1
S.J.Cook	219.3	60	684	27	25.33	5- 28	1	–
M.R.Quinn	101	19	306	12	25.50	3- 23	–	–
M.T.Coles	124	27	393	13	30.23	5-123	1	–

Also bowled:

R.S.Bopara	80.2	9	304	9	33.77	3- 30	–	–
N.Wagner	109	9	421	9	46.77	3-122	–	–

N.L.J.Browne 1-0-4-0; D.W.Lawrence 3-0-15-0; P.I.Walter 11-1-39-2; T.Westley 26-9-65-3.

The First-Class Averages (pp 230–245) give the records of Essex players in all first-class county matches (Essex's other opponents being Cambridge MCCU), with the exception of A.N.Cook and M.Vijay, whose first-class figures for Essex are as above, and:
J.A.Porter 14-17-3-31-88-6.28-0-0-2ct. 432.3-81-1429-58-24.63-7/41-3-1.

ESSEX RECORDS

FIRST-CLASS CRICKET

Highest Total	For 761-6d		v Leics	Chelmsford	1990
	V 803-4d		by Kent	Brentwood	1934
Lowest Total	For 20		v Lancashire	Chelmsford	2013
	V 14		by Surrey	Chelmsford	1983
Highest Innings	For 343*	P.A.Perrin	v Derbyshire	Chesterfield	1904
	V 332	W.H.Ashdown	for Kent	Brentwood	1934

Highest Partnership for each Wicket

1st	373	N.L.J.Browne/A.N.Cook	v Middlesex	Chelmsford	2017
2nd	403	G.A.Gooch/P.J.Prichard	v Leics	Chelmsford	1990
3rd	347*	M.E.Waugh/N.Hussain	v Lancashire	Ilford	1992
4th	314	Salim Malik/N.Hussain	v Surrey	The Oval	1991
5th	339	J.C.Mickleburgh/J.S.Foster	v Durham	Chester-le-St[2]	2010
6th	253	A.J.A.Wheater/J.S.Foster	v Northants	Chelmsford	2011
7th	261	J.W.H.T.Douglas/J.Freeman	v Lancashire	Leyton	1914
8th	263	D.R.Wilcox/R.M.Taylor	v Warwicks	Southend	1946
9th	251	J.W.H.T.Douglas/S.N.Hare	v Derbyshire	Leyton	1921
10th	218	F.H.Vigar/T.P.B.Smith	v Derbyshire	Chesterfield	1947

Best Bowling	For 10- 32	H.Pickett	v Leics	Leyton	1895
(Innings)	V 10- 40	E.G.Dennett	for Glos	Bristol	1906
Best Bowling	For 17-119	W.Mead	v Hampshire	Southampton[1]	1895
(Match)	V 17- 56	C.W.L.Parker	for Glos	Gloucester	1925

Most Runs – Season	2559	G.A.Gooch	(av 67.34)	1984
Most Runs – Career	30701	G.A.Gooch	(av 51.77)	1973-97
Most 100s – Season	9	J.O'Connor		1929, 1934
	9	D.J.Insole		1955
Most 100s – Career	94	G.A.Gooch		1973-97
Most Wkts – Season	172	T.P.B Smith	(av 27.13)	1947
Most Wkts – Career	1610	T.P.B.Smith	(av 26.68)	1929-51
Most Career W-K Dismissals	1231	B.Taylor	(1040 ct; 191 st)	1949-73
Most Career Catches in the Field	519	K.W.R.Fletcher		1962-88

LIMITED-OVERS CRICKET

Highest Total	50ov	391-5		v Surrey	The Oval	2008
	40ov	368-7		v Scotland	Chelmsford	2013
	T20	242-3		v Sussex	Chelmsford	2008
Lowest Total	50ov	57		v Lancashire	Lord's	1996
	40ov	69		v Derbyshire	Chesterfield	1974
	T20	74		v Middlesex	Chelmsford	2013
Highest Innings	50ov	201*	R.S.Bopara	v Leics	Leicester	2008
	40ov	180	R.N.ten Doeschate	v Scotland	Chelmsford	2013
	T20	152*	G.R.Napier	v Sussex	Chelmsford	2008
Best Bowling	50ov	5- 8	J.K.Lever	v Middlesex	Westcliff	1972
		5- 8	G.A.Gooch	v Cheshire	Chester	1995
	40ov	8-26	K.D.Boyce	v Lancashire	Manchester	1971
	T20	6-16	T.G.Southee	v Glamorgan	Chelmsford	2011

GLAMORGAN

Formation of Present Club: 6 July 1888
Inaugural First-Class Match: 1921
Colours: Blue and Gold
Badge: Gold Daffodil
County Champions: (3) 1948, 1969, 1997
Pro 40/National League (Div 1) Winners: (2) 2002, 2004
Sunday League Winners: (1) 1993
Twenty20 Cup Winners: (0); best – Semi-Finalist 2004, 2017

GLAMORGAN

Chief Executive: Hugh Morris, Sophia Gardens, Cardiff, CF11 9XR • Tel: 02920 409380 • email: info@glamorgancricket.co.uk • Web: www.glamorgancricket.com • Twitter: @GlamCricket (55,376 followers)

Director of Cricket: Mark Wallace. **Interim Head Coach:** Matthew Maynard. **2nd XI Coach:** Steve Watkin. **Player Development Manager:** Richard Almond. **Captain:** C.B.Cooke (f-c and l-o) and C.A.Ingram (T20). **Overseas Player:** S.E.Marsh (tbc). **2019 Testimonial:** G.G.Wagg. **Head Groundsman:** Robin Saxton. **Scorer:** Andrew K.Hignell. ‡ New registration. ᴺᵠ Not qualified for England.

BROWN, Connor Rhys (Y Pant CS; Cardiff U), b Caerphilly 28 Apr 1997. RHB, OB. Squad No 28. Cardiff MCCU 2017. Glamorgan debut 2017. Glamorgan 2nd XI debut 2014. Wales MC 2014-15. HS 35 v Glos (Cardiff) 2017. BB –. LO HS 98 v Surrey (Oval) 2018 (RLC).

BULL, Kieran Andrew (Q Elizabeth HS, Haverfordwest; Cardiff Met U), b Haverfordwest 5 Apr 1995. 6'2". RHB, OB. Squad No 11. Debut (Glamorgan) 2014. Cardiff MCCU 2015. Wales MC 2012-13. HS 31 v Glos (Swansea) 2015. BB 4-62 v Kent (Canterbury) 2014. LO HS –. LO BB 1-40 v Middx (Lord's) 2015 (RLC).

CAREY, Lukas John (Pontarddulais CS; Gower SFC), b Carmarthen 17 Jul 1997. 6'0". RHB, RFM. Squad No 17. Debut (Glamorgan) 2016. Glamorgan 2nd XI debut 2014. Wales MC 2016. HS 54 v Worcs (Worcester) 2017. BB 4-85 v Northants (Northampton) 2017. LO HS 12 v Hants (Swansea) 2018 (RLC). LO BB 2-57 v Somerset (Taunton) 2018 (RLC). T20 BB 1-19.

CARLSON, Kiran Shah (Whitchurch HS; Cardiff U), b Cardiff 16 May 1998. 5'8". RHB, OB. Squad No 5. Glamorgan 2nd XI debut 2015. Wales MC 2014. Debut (Glamorgan) 2016. HS 191 v Glos (Cardiff) 2017. BB 5-28 v Northants (Northampton) 2016 – on debut. Youngest ever to score a century & take five wkts in an innings in a f-c career, aged 18y 119d. LO HS 63 v Somerset (Cardiff) 2017 (RLC). LO BB 1-30 v Middx (Radlett) 2017 (RLC). T20 HS 58. T20 BB –.

COOKE, Christopher Barry (Bishops S, Cape Town; U of Cape Town), b Johannesburg, South Africa 30 May 1986. 5'11". RHB, WK. Squad No 46. W Province 2009-10. Glamorgan debut 2013; cap 2016; captain 2019. HS 171 v Kent (Canterbury) 2014. LO HS 137* v Somerset (Taunton) 2012 (CB40). T20 HS 65*.

CULLEN, Thomas Nicholas (Aquinas C, Stockport; Cardiff Met U), b Perth, Australia 4 Jan 1992. RHB, WK. Squad No 54. Cardiff MCCU 2015-17. Glamorgan debut 2017. HS 42 v Sussex (Colwyn Bay) 2017.

^{NQ}**De LANGE, Marchant**, b Tzaneen, South Africa 13 Oct 1990. RHB, RF. Squad No 90. Easterns 2010-11 to 2015-16. Titans 2010-11 to 2015-16. Knights 2016-17 to date. Free State 2016-17. Glamorgan debut 2017. IPL: KKR 2012. MI 2014-15. Not overseas due to wife's UK passport. **Tests** (SA): 2 (2011-12); HS 9 and BB 7-81 v SL (Durban) 2011-12 – on debut. **LOI** (SA): 4 (2011-12 to 2015-16); HS – ; BB 4-46 v NZ (Auckland) 2011-12. **IT20** (SA): 6 (2011-12 to 2015-16); HS – ; BB 2-26 v WI (Durban) 2014-15. F-c Tours (SA): A 2014 (SA A); NZ 2011-12. HS 90 v Leics (Leicester) 2018. BB 7-23 Knights v Titans (Centurion) 2016-17. Gm BB 5-62 v Glos (Bristol) 2018. LO HS 53 Knights v Lions (Kimberley) 2017-18. LO BB 5-49 v Hants (Southampton) 2017 (RLC). T20 HS 27*. T20 BB 4-23.

‡**HEMPHREY, Charles** Richard (Harvey GS, Folkestone), b Doncaster, Yorks 31 Aug 1990. RHB, OB. Squad No 22. Queensland 2014-15 to date. Derbyshire 2nd XI 2010. HS 118 Q v SA (Brisbane) 2014-15. BB 2-56 Q v SA (Adelaide) 2015-16. LO HS 58 Q v Tas (Townsville) 2018-19. LO BB 1-18 Q v Cricket Australia (Sydney, DO) 2015-16.

HOGAN, Michael Garry, b Newcastle, New South Wales, Australia 31 May 1981. British passport. 6'5''. RHB, RFM. Squad No 31. W Australia 2009-10 to 2015-16. Glamorgan debut/cap 2013; captain 2018. Big Bash: HH 2011-12 to 2012-13. HS 57 v Lancs (Colwyn Bay) 2015. 50 wkts (3); most – 67 (2013). BB 7-92 v Glos (Bristol) 2013. LO HS 27 WA v Vic (Melbourne) 2011-12. LO BB 5-44 WA v Vic (Melbourne) 2010-11. T20 HS 17*. T20 BB 5-17.

^{NQ}**INGRAM, Colin** Alexander, b Port Elizabeth, South Africa 3 Jul 1985. LHB, LB. Squad No 41. Free State 2004-05 to 2005-06. Eastern Province 2005-06 to 2008-09. Warriors 2006-07 to 2016-17. Somerset 2014. Glamorgan debut 2015 (Kolpak signing); cap 2017; captain (T20) 2018 to date. IPL: DD 2011. Big Bash: AS 2017-18 to date. **LOI** (SA): 31 (2010-11 to 2013-14); HS 124 v Z (Bloemfontein) 2010-11 – on debut; BB –. **IT20** (SA): 9 (2010-11 to 2011-12); HS 78 v I (Johannesburg) 2011-12. HS 190 EP v KZN (Port Elizabeth) 2008-09. Gm HS 155* v Notts (Cardiff) 2017. BB 4-16 EP v Boland (Port Elizabeth) 2005-06. Gm BB 3-90 v Essex (Chelmsford) 2015. LO HS 142 v Essex (Cardiff) 2017 (RLC). LO BB 4-39 v Middx (Radlett) 2017 (RLC). T20 HS 127*. T20 BB 4-32.

LAWLOR, Jeremy Lloyd (Monmouth S; Cardiff Met U), b Cardiff 4 Nov 1995. Son of P.J.Lawlor (Glamorgan 1981). 6'0''. RHB, RM. Squad No 6. Cardiff MCCU 2015-17. Glamorgan debut 2015. Glamorgan 2nd XI debut 2012. Wales MC 2013. HS 81 CfU v Hants (Southampton) 2016. Gm HS 21 v Leics (Cardiff) 2018. LO BB 3-59 v Sussex (Hove) 2018.

LLOYD, David Liam (Darland HS; Shrewsbury S), b St Asaph, Denbighs 15 May 1992. 5'9''. RHB, RM. Squad No 73. Debut (Glamorgan) 2012. Wales MC 2010-11. HS 119 v Glos (Bristol) 2018. BB 3-36 v Northants (Swansea) 2016. LO HS 92 v Middx (Cardiff) 2018 (RLC). LO BB 5-53 v Kent (Swansea) 2017 (RLC). T20 HS 97*. T20 BB 2-13.

McILROY, Jamie Peter (Builth Wells HS), b Hereford 19 Jun 1994. RHB, LFM. Squad No 35. Glamorgan 2nd XI debut 2017. MCC YC 2018. Worcestershire 2nd XI 2018. Gloucestershire 2nd XI 2018. Herefordshire 2014 to date. Awaiting 1st XI debut.

^{NQ}**MARSH, Shaun** Edward, b Narrogin, WA, Australia 9 Jul 1983. Son of G.R.Marsh (WA and Australia 1977-78 to 1993-94) and elder brother of M.R.Marsh (WA and Australia 2009-10 to date). 6'0''. LHB, SLA. Squad No 43. Western Australia 2000-01 to date. Yorkshire 2017. Glamorgan debut 2018. IPL: KXIP 2007-08 to 2017. Big Bash: PS 2011-12 to date. **Tests** (A): 38 (2011 to 2018-19); HS 182 v WI (Hobart) 2015-16. **LOI** (A): 65 (2008 to 2018-19); HS 151 v Scotland (Edinburgh) 2013. **IT20** (A): 15 (2008 to 2015-16); HS 47* v SL (Melbourne) 2012-13. F-c Tours (A): E 2015; SA 2011-12, 2013 (Aus A), 2013-14, 2017-18; WI 2015; I 2016-17; SL 2011, 2016; UAE 2018-19 (v P). HS 182 (*see Tests*). CC HS 125* Y v Surrey (Oval) 2017. Gm HS 111 v Glos (Bristol) 2018. BB 2-20 WA v NSW (Sydney) 2003-04. LO HS 186 WA v Cricket Australia (Sydney) 2015-16. LO BB 1-14 WA v Vic (Perth) 2002-03. T20 HS 115. T20 BB –.

MESCHEDE, Craig Anthony Joseph (King's C, Taunton), b Johannesburg, South Africa 21 Nov 1991. 6'1". RHB, RMF. Squad No 44. Somerset 2011-14. Glamorgan debut 2016. HS 107 v Northants (Cardiff) 2015. BB 5-84 v Essex (Chelmsford) 2016. LO HS 45 v Hants (Swansea) 2016 (RLC). LO BB 4-5 Sm v Leics (Taunton) 2013 (Y40). T20 HS 77*. T20 BB 3-9.

MORGAN, Alan Owen (Ysgol Gyfun yr Strade, Llanelli; Cardiff U), b Swansea 14 Apr 1994. 5'11". RHB, SLA. Squad No 29. Cardiff MCCU 2014. Glamorgan debut 2016. Wales MC 2012-16. HS 103* v Worcs (Worcester) 2016. BB 2-37 v Northants (Northampton) 2016. LO HS 29 and LO BB 2-49 v Pakistan A (Newport) 2016.

MURPHY, Jack Roger (Greenhill S, Tenby; Cardiff Met U), b Haverfordwest 15 Jul 1995. 6'7". LHB, LFM. Squad No 7. Cardiff MCCU 2015. Glamorgan debut 2017. Glamorgan 2nd XI debut 2011. Wales MC 2011-13. HS 80 v Kent (Canterbury) 2018. BB 2-90 CfU v Glamorgan (Cardiff) 2015. Gm BB 1-41 v Derbys (Swansea) 2018. LO HS 10 v Somerset (Taunton) 2018 (RLC). LO BB –.

‡ROOT, William ('Billy') Thomas (Worksop C; Leeds Beckett U), b Sheffield, Yorks 5 Aug 1992. Younger brother of J.E.Root (*see YORKSHIRE*). LHB, OB. Squad No 66. Leeds/ Bradford MCCU 2015-16. Nottinghamshire 2015-18. Suffolk 2014. HS 133 LBU v Sussex (Hove) 2016. CC HS 132 and BB 3-29 Nt v Sussex (Hove) 2017. LO HS 107* Nt v Warwks (Birmingham) 2017 (RLC). LO BB 1-27 Nt v Northants (Welbeck) 2018 (RLC). T20 HS 40. T20 BB –.

SALTER, Andrew Graham (Milford Haven SFC; Cardiff Met U), b Haverfordwest 1 Jun 1993. 5'9". RHB, OB. Squad No 21. Cardiff MCCU 2012-14. Glamorgan debut 2013. Wales MC 2010-11. HS 88 v Glos (Cardiff) 2017. BB 4-80 v Warwks (Birmingham) 2018. LO HS 51 v Pakistan A (Newport) 2016. LO BB 2-41 v Notts (Nottingham) 2012 (CB40) and 2-41 v Notts (Lord's) 2013 (Y40). T20 HS 37*. T20 BB 3-34.

SELMAN, Nicholas James (Matthew Flinders Anglican C, Buderim), b Brisbane, Australia 18 Oct 1995. 6'4". RHB, RM. Squad No 9. Debut (Glamorgan) 2016. Kent 2nd XI debut 2014. Gloucestershire 2nd XI 2015. HS 142* v Glos (Cardiff) 2017. BB –. LO HS 92 v Kent (Canterbury) 2018 (RLC). T20 HS 66.

SISODIYA, Prem (Clifton C; Cardiff Met U), b Cardiff 21 Sep 1998. RHB, SLA. Squad No 32. Debut (Glamorgan) 2018. Wales MC 2017. HS 38 and BB 3-54 v Derbys (Swansea) 2018.

NOSMITH, Ruaidhrí Alexander James (Llandaff Cathedral S; Shrewsbury S; Bristol U), b Glasgow, Scotland 5 Aug 1994. 6'1". RHB, RM. Squad No 20. Debut (Glamorgan) 2013. Scotland 2017. Glamorgan 2nd XI debut 2011. Wales MC 2010-16. **LOI** (Scot: 2 (2016); HS 10 and BB 1-34 v Afg (Edinburgh) 2016. **IT20** (Scot: 2 (2018-19); HS 9* v Netherlands (Al Amerat) 2018-19; BB –. HS 57* v Glos (Bristol) 2014. BB 5-87 v Durham (Cardiff) 2018. LO HS 14 v Hants (Swansea) 201 (RLC). LO BB 4-7 v Oman (Al Amerat) 2018-19. T20 HS 22*. T20 BB 4-6.

SZYMANSKI, Kazimierz Bolelsaw (King's C, Taunton), b Torquay, Devon 5 Sep 1999. RHB, RM. Squad No 49. Glamorgan 2nd XI debut 2017. Awaiting 1st XI debut.

TAYLOR, Callum Zinzan (The Southport S), b Newport, Monmouths 19 Jun 1998. RHB, OB. Squad No 42. Glamorgan 2nd XI debut 2017. Wales MC 2017. Awaiting 1st XI debut.

^{NQ}**van der GUGTEN, Timm**, b Hornsby, Sydney, Australia 25 Feb 1991. 6'1½". RHB, RFM. Squad No 64. New South Wales 2011-12. Netherlands 2012 to date. Glamorgan debut 2016; cap 2018. Big Bash: HH 2014-15. **LOI** (Neth): 4 (2011-12 to 2013); HS 2 (twice); BB 5-24 v Canada (King City, NW) 2013. **IT20** (Neth): 29 (2011-12 to 2018-19); HS 13 v Scotland (Amstelveen) 2018; BB 3-18 v B (The Hague) 2012. HS 60* v Glos (Cardiff) 2018. 50 wkts (1): 56 (2016). BB 7-42 v Kent (Cardiff) 2018. LO HS 36 Neth v Nepal (Amstelveen) 2016; LO BB 5-24 (*see LOI*). T20 HS 21*. T20 BB 5-21.

WAGG, Graham Grant (Ashlawn S, Rugby), b Rugby, Warwks 28 Apr 1983. 6'0". RHB, LM. Squad No 8. Warwickshire 2002-04. Derbyshire 2006-10; cap 2007. Glamorgan debut 2011; cap 2013; testimonial 2019. F-c Tour (Eng A): I 2003-04. HS 200 v Surrey (Guildford) 2015. 50 wkts (2); most – 59 (2008). BB 6-29 v Surrey (Oval) 2014. LO HS 62* v Essex (Cardiff) 2015 (RLC). LO BB 4-35 De v Durham (Derby) 2008 (FPT). T20 HS 62. T20 BB 5-14 v Worcs (Worcester) 2013 – Gm record.

WALKER, Roman Isaac (Ysgol Bryn Alyn), b Wrexham 6 Aug 2000. RHB, RFM. Squad No 37. Glamorgan 2nd XI debut 2016. Wales MC 2018. Awaiting 1st XI debut.

RELEASED/RETIRED

(Having made a County 1st XI appearance in 2018)

BURNS, J.A. – *see LANCASHIRE*.

^{NQ}**COOK, Stephen** Craig, b Johannesburg, South Africa 29 Nov 1982. Son of S.J.Cook (Transvaal, Somerset & South Africa, 1972-73 to 1994-95). RHB, RM. Gauteng 2000-01 to date. Lions 2004-05 to date. North West 2015-16. Durham 2017. Glamorgan 2018. **Tests** (SA): 11 (2015-16 to 2016-17); HS 117 v SL (Pt Elizabeth) 2016-17. F-c Tours (SA A)(C=Captain): A 2016C, 2016-17 (SA); NZ 2016-17 (SA); SL 2010; Z 2016C. 1000 runs (0+4); most – 1642 (2009-10). HS 390 Lions v Warriors (East London) 2009-10 – record score in SA. CC HS 89* Du v Glamorgan (Chester-le-St) 2017. Gm HS 36 v Leics (Cardiff) 2018. BB 3-42 Lions v Dolphins (Durban) 2008-09. LO HS 127* Lions v Cobras (Johannesburg) 2015-16. LO BB 1-2 Lions v Titans (Johannesburg) 2008-09. T20 HS 66.

DONALD, A.H.T. – *see HAMPSHIRE*.

^{NQ}**KHAWAJA, Usman** Tariq (Westfield Sports HS; U of NSW), b Islamabad, Pakistan 18 Dec 1986. 5'9". LHB, RM. NSW 2007-08 to 2011-12. Derbyshire 2011-12. Queensland 2012-13 to date. Lancashire 2014. Glamorgan 2018. IPL: RPS 2016. Big Bash: ST 2011-12 to date. **Tests** (A): 41 (2010-11 to 2018-19); HS 174 v NZ (Brisbane) 2015-16. **LOI** (A): 24 (2012-13 to 2018-19); HS 104 v I (Ranchi) 2018-19. **IT20** (A): 9 (2015-16 to 2016); HS 58 v B (Bangalore) 2015-16. F-c Tours (A): E 2013; SA 2011-12, 2017-18; NZ 2015-16; I 2012-13, 2015 (Aus A); SL 2011, 2016; Z 2011 (Aus A); B 2017; UAE 2018-19 (v P). 1000 runs (0+1): 1013 (2016-17). HS 214 and BB 1-21 NSW v SA (Adelaide) 2010-11. CC HS 135 De v Kent (Canterbury) 2011. Gm HS 126 v Derbys (Swansea) 2018. LO HS 166 Q v Tas (Sydney) 2014-15. T20 HS 109*.

GLAMORGAN 2018

RESULTS SUMMARY

	Place	Won	Lost	Drew	NR
Specsavers County Champ (2nd Division)	9th	2	10	2	
All First-Class Matches		2	10	2	
Royal London One-Day Cup (South Group)	9th	1	7		
Vitality Blast (South Group)	6th	7	6		1

SPECSAVERS COUNTY CHAMPIONSHIP AVERAGES
BATTING AND FIELDING

Cap		M	I	NO	HS	Runs	Avge	100	50	Ct/St
	U.T.Khawaja	4	8	–	126	420	52.50	3	–	2
	M.de Lange	3	5	1	90	142	35.50	–	2	1
	D.L.Lloyd	10	18	2	119	474	29.62	1	1	3
	S.E.Marsh	4	7	–	111	203	29.00	1	1	1
	J.R.Murphy	12	23	2	80	533	25.38	–	2	4
2016	C.B.Cooke	14	26	1	69	606	24.24	–	4	41/1
	K.S.Carlson	13	25	1	152	567	23.62	1	1	5
	C.A.J.Meschede	4	8	1	55	151	21.57	–	2	1
	R.A.J.Smith	7	14	2	52*	246	20.50	–	1	1
	N.J.Selman	12	23	–	42	403	17.52	–	–	21
	T.van der Gugten	10	18	5	60*	217	16.69	–	2	2
	K.A.Bull	4	8	3	30	76	15.20	–	–	2
	S.C.Cook	4	8	–	36	120	15.00	–	–	3
	A.O.Morgan	3	6	–	36	89	14.83	–	–	1
	A.G.Salter	10	17	3	72*	204	14.57	–	1	8
	P.Sisodiya	2	4	1	38	41	13.66	–	–	1
2013	G.G.Wagg	4	8	–	33	102	12.75	–	–	–
2013	M.G.Hogan	13	21	8	28	152	11.69	–	–	7
	A.H.T.Donald	4	7	1	27	67	11.16	–	–	2
	J.L.Lawlor	3	6	–	21	49	8.16	–	–	3
	C.R.Brown	6	12	–	33	95	7.91	–	–	3
	L.J.Carey	6	8	–	28	58	7.25	–	–	2
	T.N.Cullen	2	4	–	20	29	7.25	–	–	2

BOWLING

	O	M	R	W	Avge	Best	5wI	10wM
T.van der Gugten	287	69	936	43	21.76	7- 42	2	–
M.G.Hogan	393.3	101	1014	45	22.53	5- 49	2	–
M.de Lange	114.4	22	383	16	23.93	5- 62	1	–
K.A.Bull	85.4	14	278	11	25.27	3- 36	–	–
R.A.J.Smith	155.3	24	593	20	29.65	5- 87	1	–
A.G.Salter	245	45	759	18	42.16	4- 80	–	–
L.J.Carey	172	36	592	13	45.53	4-105	–	–
Also bowled:								
P.Sisodiya	63.2	12	151	7	21.57	3- 54	–	–
G.G.Wagg	82.4	13	258	8	32.25	3- 25	–	–
C.A.J.Meschede	76	8	327	9	36.33	2- 30	–	–
D.L.Lloyd	105.3	19	343	9	38.11	2- 31	–	–

K.S.Carlson 1-0-5-0; J.L.Lawlor 29.1-3-110-4; A.O.Morgan 12.1-2-46-0; J.R.Murphy 16.3-2-73-1; N.J.Selman 1-0-6-0.

Glamorgan played no first-class fixtures outside the County Championship in 2018. The First-Class Averages (pp 230–245) give the records of Glamorgan players in all first-class county matches.

GLAMORGAN RECORDS

FIRST-CLASS CRICKET

Highest Total	For 718-3d		v	Sussex	Colwyn Bay	2000
	V 712		by	Northants	Northampton	1998
Lowest Total	For 22		v	Lancashire	Liverpool	1924
	V 33		by	Leics	Ebbw Vale	1965
Highest Innings	For 309*	S.P.James	v	Sussex	Colwyn Bay	2000
	V 322*	M.B.Loye	for	Northants	Northampton	1998

Highest Partnership for each Wicket

1st	374	M.T.G.Elliott/S.P.James	v	Sussex	Colwyn Bay	2000
2nd	252	M.P.Maynard/D.L.Hemp	v	Northants	Cardiff	2002
3rd	313	D.E.Davies/W.E.Jones	v	Essex	Brentwood	1948
4th	425*	A.Dale/I.V.A.Richards	v	Middlesex	Cardiff	1993
5th	264	M.Robinson/S.W.Montgomery	v	Hampshire	Bournemouth	1949
6th	240	J.Allenby/M.A.Wallace	v	Surrey	The Oval	2009
7th	211	P.A.Cottey/O.D.Gibson	v	Leics	Swansea	1996
8th	202	D.Davies/J.J.Hills	v	Sussex	Eastbourne	1928
9th	203*	J.J.Hills/J.C.Clay	v	Worcs	Swansea	1929
10th	143	T.Davies/S.A.B.Daniels	v	Glos	Swansea	1982

Best Bowling	For 10- 51	J.Mercer	v	Worcs	Worcester	1936
(Innings)	V 10- 18	G.Geary	for	Leics	Pontypridd	1929
Best Bowling	For 17-212	J.C.Clay	v	Worcs	Swansea	1937
(Match)	V 16- 96	G.Geary	for	Leics	Pontypridd	1929

Most Runs – Season	2276	H.Morris	(av 55.51)		1990
Most Runs – Career	34056	A.Jones	(av 33.03)		1957-83
Most 100s – Season	10	H.Morris			1990
Most 100s – Career	54	M.P.Maynard			1985-2005
Most Wkts – Season	176	J.C.Clay	(av 17.34)		1937
Most Wkts – Career	2174	D.J.Shepherd	(av 20.95)		1950-72
Most Career W-K Dismissals	933	E.W.Jones	(840 ct; 93 st)		1961-83
Most Career Catches in the Field	656	P.M.Walker			1956-72

LIMITED-OVERS CRICKET

Highest Total	50ov	429	v	Surrey	The Oval	2002
	40ov	328-4	v	Lancashire	Colwyn Bay	2011
	T20	240-3	v	Surrey	The Oval	2015
Lowest Total	50ov	68	v	Lancashire	Manchester	1973
	40ov	42	v	Derbyshire	Swansea	1979
	T20	88	v	Sussex	Cardiff	2018
Highest Innings	50ov	169* J.A.Rudolph	v	Sussex	Hove	2014
	40ov	155* J.H.Kallis	v	Surrey	Pontypridd	1999
	T20	116* I.J.Thomas	v	Somerset	Taunton	2004
Best Bowling	50ov	6-20 S.D.Thomas	v	Comb Univs	Cardiff	1995
	40ov	7-16 S.D.Thomas	v	Surrey	Swansea	1998
	T20	5-14 G.G.Wagg	v	Worcs	Worcester	2013

GLOUCESTERSHIRE

Formation of Present Club: 1871
Inaugural First-Class Match: 1870
Colours: Blue, Gold, Brown, Silver, Green and Red
Badge: Coat of Arms of the City and County of Bristol
County Champions (since 1890): (0); best – 2nd 1930, 1931, 1947, 1959, 1969, 1986
Gillette/NatWest/C&G Trophy Winners: (5) 1973, 1999, 2000, 2003, 2004
Benson and Hedges Cup Winners: (3) 1977, 1999, 2000
Pro 40/National League (Div 1) Winners: (1) 2000
Royal London One-Day Cup Winners: (1) 2015
Twenty20 Cup Winners: (0); best – Finalist 2007

Chief Executive: Will Brown, Bristol County Ground, Nevil Road, Bristol BS7 9EJ • Tel: 0117 910 8000 • Email: info@gloscricket.co.uk • Web: www.gloscricket.co.uk • Twitter: @Gloscricket (48,774 followers)

Head Coach: Richard Dawson. **Asst Head Coach**: Ian Harvey. **Captains**: C.D.J.Dent (f-c & l-o) and M.Klinger (T20). **Vice-Captain**: J.M.R.Taylor. **Overseas Players**: .M.Klinger and D.J.Worrall. **2019 Testimonial**: I.A.Cockbain. **Head Groundsman**: Sean Williams. **Scorer**: Adrian Bull. ‡ New registration. NQ Not qualified for England.

Gloucestershire revised their capping policy in 2004 and now award players with their County Caps when they make their first-class debut.

BRACEY, James Robert (Filton CS), b Bristol 3 May 1997. Younger brother of S.N.Bracey (Cardiff MCCU 2014-15). 6'1". LHB, WK. Squad No 25. Debut (Gloucestershire) 2016; cap 2016. Loughborough MCCU 2017-18. Gloucestershire 2nd XI debut 2015. HS 156 v Glamorgan (Cardiff) 2017.

CHARLESWORTH, Ben Geoffrey (St Edward's S), b Oxford 19 Nov 2000. Son of G.M.Charlesworth (Griqualand W and Oxford U 1989-90 to 1993). 6'2½". LHB, RM/OB. Debut (Gloucestershire) 2018; cap 2018. Gloucestershire 2nd XI debut 2016. Oxfordshire 2016. England U19 2018 to 2018-19. HS 77* and BB 3-25 v Middx (Bristol) 2018.

COCKBAIN, Ian Andrew (Maghull HS), b Bootle, Liverpool 17 Feb 1987. Son of I.Cockbain (Lancs and Minor Cos 1979-94). 6'0". RHB, RM. Squad No 28. Debut (Gloucestershire) 2011; cap 2011; testimonial 2019. MCC YC 2008-10. HS 151* v Surrey (Bristol) 2014. BB 1-23 v Durham MCCU (Bristol) 2016. LO HS 108* v Middx (Lord's) 2017 (RLC). T20 HS 123.

CURRILL, Oliver Charles (Chipping Campden Academy), b Banbury, Oxon 27 Feb 1997. 6'4". RHB, RMF. Debut (Gloucestershire) 2017; cap 2017. Gloucestershire 2nd XI debut 2015. No 1st XI appearances in 2018. BB –.

DENT, Christopher David James (Backwell CS; Alton C), b Bristol 20 Jan 1991. 5'9". LHB, WK, occ SLA. Squad No 15. Debut (Gloucestershire) 2010; cap 2010; captain 2018 to date. 1000 runs (3); most – 1336 (2016). HS 268 v Glamorgan (Bristol) 2015. BB 2-21 v Sussex (Hove) 2016. LO HS 151* v Glamorgan (Cardiff) 2013 (Y40). LO BB 4-43 v Leics (Bristol) 2012 (CB40). T20 HS 63*. T20 BB 1-4.

DRISSELL, George Samuel (Bedminster Down SS; Filton C), b Bristol 20 Jan 1999. 6'1½". RHB, OB. Debut (Gloucestershire) 2017; cap 2017. Gloucestershire 2nd XI debut 2016. HS 19 v Warwks (Birmingham) 2018. BB 2-38 v Sussex (Cheltenham) 2018. LO HS 0 and LO BB – v Middx (Bristol) 2018 (RLC).

HAMMOND, Miles Arthur Halhead (St Edward's S, Oxford), b Cheltenham 11 Jan 1996. 5'11". LHB, OB. Squad No 88. Debut (Gloucestershire) 2013; cap 2013. England U19 2012-13. Gloucestershire 2nd XI debut 2011, aged 14y 120d. HS 123* v Middx (Bristol) 2018. BB 1-96 v Glamorgan (Bristol) 2013. LO HS 0. LO BB 2-18 v Northants (Northampton) 2015 (RLC). T20 HS 51. T20 BB –.

HANKINS, George Thomas (Millfield S), b Bath, Somerset 4 Jan 1997. 6'1½". RHB, OB. Squad No 21. Debut (Gloucestershire) 2016; cap 2016. Gloucestershire 2nd XI debut 2014. England U19 2016. HS 116 v Northants (Northampton) 2016. BB –. LO HS 92 v Kent (Beckenham) 2018 (RLC). T20 HS 14.

HIGGINS, Ryan Francis (Bradfield C), b Harare, Zimbabwe 6 Jan 1995. 5'10". RHB, RM. Squad No 29. Middlesex 2017. Gloucestershire debut/cap 2018. Middlesex 2nd XI debut 2012. HS 105 v Durham (Cheltenham) 2018. BB 5-21 v Sussex (Hove) 2018. LO HS 81* v Surrey (Oval) 2018 (RLC). LO BB 4-50 ECB XI v India A (Leeds) 2018. T20 HS 68*. T20 BB 5-13.

HOWELL, Benny Alexander Cameron (The Oratory S), b Bordeaux, France 5 Oct 1988. Son of J.B.Howell (Warwickshire 2nd XI 1978). 5'11". RHB, RM. Squad No 13. Hampshire 2011. Gloucestershire debut/cap 2012. Berkshire 2007. HS 163 v Glamorgan (Cardiff) 2017. BB 5-57 v Leics (Leicester) 2013. LO HS 122 v Surrey (Croydon) 2011 (CB40). LO BB 3-37 v Yorks (Leeds) 2015 (RLC). T20 HS 57. T20 BB 4-26.

NO**KLINGER, Michael** (Scopus Memorial C, Kew), b Kew, Melbourne, Australia 4 Jul 1980. 5'10½". RHB. Squad No 2. Victoria 1999-00 to 2007-08. S Australia 2008-09 to 2013-14. Worcestershire 2012; cap 2012. Gloucestershire debut/cap 2013; captain 2013-15; T20 captain 2016 to date. W Australia 2014-15 to 2016-17. Big Bash: AS 2011-12 to 2013-14. PS 2014-15 to date. **IT20** (A): 3 (2016-17); HS 62 v SL (Adelaide) 2016-17. 1000 runs (1+2); most – 1203 (2008-09). HS 255 SA v WA (Adelaide) 2008-09. Gs HS 163 v Hants (Bristol) 2013. LO HS 166* v Hants (Bristol) 2016 (RLC). T20 HS 126* v Essex (Bristol) 2015 – Gs record.

LIDDLE, Christopher John (Nunthorpe CS; Teesside Tertiary C), b Middlesbrough, Yorks 1 Feb 1984. 6'5". RHB, LFM. Squad No 23. Leicestershire 2005-06. Sussex 2007-15. Gloucestershire debut/cap 2017. HS 53 Sx v Worcs (Hove) 2007. Gs HS 21 v Durham (Bristol) 2017. BB 3-42 Le v Somerset (Leicester) 2006. Gs BB 2-23 v Cardiff MCCU (Bristol) 2018. LO HS 18 Sx v Warwks (Rugby) 2015 (RLC). LO BB 5-18 Sx v Netherlands (Amstelveen) 2011 (CB40). T20 HS 16. T20 BB 5-17.

PAYNE, David Alan (Lytchett Minster S), b Poole, Dorset, 15 Feb 1991. 6'2". RHB, LMF. Squad No 14. Debut (Gloucestershire) 2011; cap 2011. Dorset 2009. HS 67* v Glamorgan (Cardiff) 2016. BB 6-26 v Leics (Bristol) 2011. LO HS 23 v Kent (Canterbury) 2016 (RLC). LO BB 7-29 v Essex (Chelmsford) 2010 (CB40), inc 4 wkts in 4 balls and 6 wkts in 9 balls – Gs record. T20 HS 10. T20 BB 5-24 v Middx (Richmond) 2015 – Gs record.

NO**RODERICK, Gareth** Hugh (Maritzburg C), b Durban, South Africa 29 Aug 1991. 6'0". RHB, WK. Squad No 27. UK passport. KZN 2010-11 to 2011-12. Gloucestershire debut/cap 2013; captain 2016-17. HS 171 v Leics (Bristol) 2014. LO HS 104 v Leics (Leicester) 2015 (RLC). T20 HS 32.

SMITH, Thomas Michael John (Seaford Head Community C; Sussex Downs C), b Eastbourne, Sussex 29 Aug 1987. 5'9". RHB, SLA. Squad No 6. Sussex 2007-09. Surrey 2009 (l-o only). Middlesex 2010-13. Gloucestershire debut/cap 2013. HS 80 v Surrey (Bristol) 2014. BB 4-35 v Kent (Canterbury) 2014. LO HS 65 Sy v Leics (Leicester) 2009 (P40). LO BB 4-26 v Sussex (Cheltenham) 2016 (RLC). T20 HS 36*. T20 BB 5-24.

TAVARÉ, William Andrew (Bristol GS; Loughborough U), b Bristol 1 Jan 1990. Nephew of C.J.Tavaré (Kent, Somerset & England 1974-93). 6'0". RHB, RM. Squad No 4. Loughborough MCCU 2010-12. Gloucestershire debut/cap 2014. No 1st XI appearances in 2018. 1000 runs (1): 1014 (2014). HS 139 v Hants (Bristol) 2014 – on CC debut. BB –. LO HS 77 v Hants (Bristol) 2014 (RLC) – on l-o debut.

TAYLOR, Jack Martin Robert (Chipping Norton S), b Banbury, Oxfordshire 12 Nov 1991. Elder brother of M.D.Taylor (*see below*). 5'11". RHB, OB. Squad No 10. Debut (Gloucestershire) 2010; cap 2010. Oxfordshire 2009-11. HS 156 v Northants (Cheltenham) 2015. BB 4-16 Glamorgan (Bristol) 2016. LO HS 68 v Somerset (Bristol) 2017 (RLC). LO BB 4-38 v Hants (Bristol) 2014 (RLC). T20 HS 80. T20 BB 4-16.

TAYLOR, Matthew David (Chipping Norton S), b Banbury, Oxfordshire 8 Jul 1994. Younger brother of J.M.R.Taylor (*see above*). 6'0". RHB, LMF. Squad No 36. Debut (Gloucestershire) 2013; cap 2013. Gloucestershire 2nd XI debut 2011. Oxfordshire 2011-12. HS 48 v Glamorgan (Bristol) 2018. BB 5-15 v Cardiff MCCU (Bristol) 2018. CC BB 5-75 v Hants (Bristol) 2014. LO HS 16 v Kent (Canterbury) 2016 (RLC). LO BB 3-48 v Somerset (Bristol) 2017 (RLC). T20 HS 9*. T20 BB 3-16.

NQ**van BUUREN, Graeme** Lourens, b Pretoria, South Africa 22 Aug 1990. 5'6". RHB, SLA. Squad No 12. Northerns 2009-10 to 2015-16. Titans 2012-13 to 2014-15. Gloucestershire debut/cap 2016. HS 235 Northerns v EP (Centurion) 2014-15. Gs HS 172* v Worcs (Worcester) 2016. BB 4-12 Northerns v SW Districts (Oudtshoorn) 2012-13. Gs BB 4-18 v Durham MCCU (Bristol) 2017. CC BB 3-15 v Glamorgan (Bristol) 2016. LO HS 119* Northerns v EP (Pt Elizabeth, Grey HS) 2013-14. LO BB 5-35 Northerns v SW Districts (Pretoria) 2011-12. T20 HS 64. T20 BB 5-8.

‡NQ**WHITTINGHAM, Stuart** Gordon (Christ's Hospital, Horsham; Loughborough U), b Derby 10 Feb 1994. 6'0". RHB, RFM. Squad No 19. Loughborough MCCU 2015. Sussex 2016-18. MCC Universities 2013. **LOI** (Scot): 4 (2017-18); HS 3* and BB 3-58 v Ire (Dubai, ICCA) 2017-18. **IT20** (Scot): 3 (2018); HS – ; BB 2-33 v Ire (Deventer) 2018. HS 22 Sx v Notts (Hove) 2017. BB 5-70 Scot v Ire (Dubai, DSC) 2017-18. CC BB 5-80 Sx v Derbys (Hove) 2017. LO HS 3* (*see LOI*). LO BB 3-35 Scot v Nepal (Bulaway) 2017-18. T20 HS –. T20 BB 2-33.

NQ**WORRALL, Daniel** James (Kardina International C; U of Melbourne), b Melbourne, Australia 10 Jul 1991. RHB, RFM. Squad No 41. S Australia 2012-13 to date. Gloucestershire debut/cap 2018. Big Bash: MS 2013-14 to date. **LOI** (A): 3 (2016-17); HS 6* v SA (Centurion) 2016-17; BB 1-43 v SA (Benoni) 2016-17. HS 50 v Glamorgan (Bristol) 2018. BB 7-64 (10-148 match) SA v WA (Adelaide) 2018-19. LO HS 16 SA v Tas (N Sydney) 2017-18. LO BB 5-62 SA v Vic (Hobart) 2017-18. T20 HS 16. T20 BB 4-23.

RELEASED/RETIRED

(Having made a County 1st XI appearance in 2018)

LINTOTT, Jacob ('Jake') Benedict (Queen's C, Taunton), b Taunton, Somerset 22 Apr 1993. RHB, SLA. Awaiting f-c debut. Hampshire 2017 (T20 only). Dorset 2011-15. Wiltshire 2016-17. T20 HS 8. T20 BB 2-26.

MILES, C.N. – *see WARWICKSHIRE.*

[NQ]**NOEMA-BARNETT, Kieran**, b Dunedin, New Zealand 4 Jun 1987. 6'1". LHB, RM. Central Districts 2008-09 to date. Gloucestershire 2015-18; cap 2015. HS 108 CD v Otago (Alexandra) 2018-19. Gs HS 84 v Worcs (Bristol) 2016. BB 4-20 CD v Otago (Dunedin) 2010-11. Gs BB 4-31 v Worcs (Cheltenham) 2017. LO HS 74 CD v ND (New Plymouth) 2016-17. LO BB 3-42 CD v Auckland (Auckland) 2013-14. T20 HS 57*. T20 BB 3-18.

NORWELL, L.C. – *see WARWICKSHIRE.*

[NQ]**TYE, Andrew** James (Padbury Senior HS, WA), b Perth, Australia 12 Dec 1986. 6'4". RHB, RMF. W Australia 2014-15 to date. Gloucestershire 2016-18 (T20 only). IPL: GL 2017. KXIP 2018. Big Bash: ST 2013-14. PS 2014-15 to date. **LOI** (A): 7 (2017-18 to 2018); HS 19 v E (Oval) 2018; BB 5-46 v E (Perth) 2017-18. **IT20** (A): 26 (2015-16 to 2018-19); HS 20 v E (Birmingham) 2018; BB 4-23 v NZ (Sydney) 2017-18. HS 10 WA v Tas (Hobart) 2014-15. BB 3-47 WA v Q (Brisbane) 2014-15. LO HS 28* WA v NSW (Sydney) 2013-14. LO BB 6-46 WA v Q (Sydney, HO) 2018-19. T20 HS 42. T20 BB 5-17.

COUNTY CAPS AWARDED IN 2018

Derbyshire	–
Durham	–
Essex	V.Chopra, S.R.Harmer
Glamorgan	T.van der Gugten
Gloucestershire	B.G.Charlesworth, R.F.Higgins, D.J.Worrall
Hampshire	F.H.Edwards, C.P.Wood
Kent	M.J.Henry, H.G.Kuhn
Lancashire	T.E.Bailey, J.C.Buttler, K.K.Jennings, G.Onions, D.J.Vilas
Leicestershire	Mohammad Abbas, B.A.Raine
Middlesex	S.S.Eskinazi
Northamptonshire	J.J.Cobb, B.W.Sanderson
Nottinghamshire	K.C.Brathwaite, L.R.P.L.Taylor
Somerset	T.B.Abell, R.E.van der Merwe
Surrey	S.G.Borthwick, S.M.Curran, M.Morkel, O.J.D.Pope, M.D.Stoneman
Sussex	I.Sharma
Warwickshire	S.R.Hain
Worcestershire (colours)	M.J.Guptill, T.M.Head, A.G.Milton, W.D.Parnell, D.Y.Pennington, B.J.Twohig, O.E.Westbury, L.Wood
Yorkshire	B.O.Coad

Durham abolished their capping system after 2005. Gloucestershire award caps on first-class debut. Worcestershire award club colours on Championship debut. Glamorgan's capping system is now based on a player's number of appearances and not on his performances.

GLOUCESTERSHIRE 2018

RESULTS SUMMARY

	Place	Won	Lost	Drew	NR
Specsavers County Champ (2nd Division)	5th	5	4	5	
All First-Class Matches		5	4	6	
Royal London One-Day Cup (South Group)	7th	2	3		3
Vitality Blast (South Group)	QF	8	5		2

SPECSAVERS COUNTY CHAMPIONSHIP AVERAGES

BATTING AND FIELDING

Cap†		M	I	NO	HS	Runs	Avge	100	50	Ct/St
2015	K.Noema-Barnett	8	14	5	73*	323	35.88	–	2	10
2010	C.D.J.Dent	14	28	3	214*	851	34.04	1	4	11
2013	M.A.H.Hammond	8	16	2	123*	476	34.00	2	2	6
2016	J.R.Bracey	14	27	3	125*	785	32.70	2	2	14
2012	B.A.C.Howell	13	24	1	67	604	26.26	–	4	9
2018	B.G.Charlesworth	6	9	1	77*	194	24.25	–	2	2
2013	G.H.Roderick	12	22	1	67	500	23.80	–	4	48
2018	D.J.Worrall	4	5	1	50	94	23.50	–	1	2
2018	R.F.Higgins	14	24	2	105	482	21.90	1	2	6
2010	J.M.R.Taylor	10	18	–	112	384	21.33	1	–	4
2016	G.L.van Buuren	7	14	1	83	275	21.15	–	2	2
2011	D.A.Payne	7	11	6	31	86	17.20	–	–	1
2011	C.N.Miles	13	20	5	38*	201	13.40	–	–	3
2013	M.D.Taylor	14	19	3	48	177	11.06	–	–	4
2017	G.S.Drissell	5	9	–	19	76	8.44	–	–	–
2017	C.J.Liddle	2	4	2	6*	11	5.50	–	–	–

Also batted (1 match each): I.A.Cockbain (cap 2011) 0 (1 ct); G.T.Hankins (cap 2016) 3, 10 (1 ct); L.C.Norwell (cap 2011) 2, 1.

BOWLING

	O	M	R	W	Avge	Best	5wI	10wM
R.F.Higgins	353.5	99	882	48	18.37	5-21	2	–
C.N.Miles	328.1	61	1180	56	21.07	5-50	2	–
D.J.Worrall	119.1	33	348	16	21.75	4-45	–	–
M.D.Taylor	344	61	1171	46	25.45	5-81	1	–
D.A.Payne	204.2	42	573	22	26.04	4-25	–	–

Also bowled:
K.Noema-Barnett 78 13 260 7 37.14 2-34 – –
B.G.Charlesworth 21.1-7-47-4; C.D.J.Dent 4-3-2-0; G.S.Drissell 83-10-272-4; M.A.H.Hammond 3-0-14-0; B.A.C.Howell 28.5-5-122-4; C.J.Liddle 31-5-99-2; L.C.Norwell 9-3-20-0; G.L.van Buuren 72-8-246-4.

The First-Class Averages (pp 230–245) give the records of Gloucestershire players in all first-class county matches (Gloucestershire's other opponents being Cardiff MCCU), with the exception of J.R.Bracey, whose first-class figures for Gloucestershire are as above.

† Gloucestershire revised their capping policy in 2004 and now award players with their County Caps when they make their first-class debut.

GLOUCESTERSHIRE RECORDS

FIRST-CLASS CRICKET

Highest Total	For	695-9d		v	Middlesex	Gloucester	2004
	V	774-7d		by	Australians	Bristol	1948
Lowest Total	For	17		v	Australians	Cheltenham .	1896
	V	12		by	Northants	Gloucester	1907
Highest Innings	For	341	C.M.Spearman	v	Middlesex	Gloucester	2004
	V	319	C.J.L.Rogers	for	Northants	Northampton	2006

Highest Partnership for each Wicket

1st	395	D.M.Young/R.B.Nicholls	v	Oxford U	Oxford	1962
2nd	256	C.T.M.Pugh/T.W.Graveney	v	Derbyshire	Chesterfield	1960
3rd	392	G.H.Roderick/A.P.R.Gidman	v	Leics	Bristol	2014
4th	321	W.R.Hammond/W.L.Neale	v	Leics	Gloucester	1937
5th	261	W.G.Grace/W.O.Moberley	v	Yorkshire	Cheltenham	1876
6th	320	G.L.Jessop/J.H.Board	v	Sussex	Hove	1903
7th	248	W.G.Grace/E.L.Thomas	v	Sussex	Hove	1896
8th	239	W.R.Hammond/A.E.Wilson	v	Lancashire	Bristol	1938
9th	193	W.G.Grace/S.A.P.Kitcat	v	Sussex	Bristol	1896
10th	137	C.N.Miles/L.C.Norwell	v	Worcs	Cheltenham	2014

Best Bowling	For	10-40	E.G.Dennett	v	Essex	Bristol	1906
(Innings)	V	10-66	A.A.Mailey	for	Australians	Cheltenham	1921
		10-66	K.Smales	for	Notts	Stroud	1956
Best Bowling	For	17-56	C.W.L.Parker	v	Essex	Gloucester	1925
(Match)	V	15-87	A.J.Conway	for	Worcs	Moreton-in-M	1914

Most Runs – Season	2860	W.R.Hammond	(av 69.75)	1933
Most Runs – Career	33664	W.R.Hammond	(av 57.05)	1920-51
Most 100s – Season	13	W.R.Hammond		1938
Most 100s – Career	113	W.R.Hammond		1920-51
Most Wkts – Season	222	T.W.J.Goddard	(av 16.80)	1937
	222	T.W.J.Goddard	(av 16.37)	1947
Most Wkts – Career	3170	C.W.L.Parker	(av 19.43)	1903-35
Most Career W-K Dismissals	1054	R.C.Russell	(950 ct; 104 st)	1981-2004
Most Career Catches in the Field	719	C.A.Milton		1948-74

LIMITED-OVERS CRICKET

Highest Total	50ov	401-7		v	Bucks	Wing	2003
	40ov	344-6		v	Northants	Cheltenham	2001
	T20	254-3		v	Middlesex	Uxbridge	2011
Lowest Total	50ov	82		v	Notts	Bristol	1987
	40ov	49		v	Middlesex	Bristol	1978
	T20	68		v	Hampshire	Bristol	2010
Highest Innings	50ov	177	A.J.Wright	v	Scotland	Bristol	1997
	40ov	153	C.M.Spearman	v	Warwicks	Gloucester	2003
	T20	126*	M.Klinger	v	Essex	Bristol	2015
Best Bowling	50ov	6-13	M.J.Proctor	v	Hampshire	Southampton[1]	1977
	40ov	7-29	D.A.Payne	v	Essex	Chelmsford	2010
	T20	5-24	D.A.Payne	v	Middlesex	Richmond	2015

HAMPSHIRE

Formation of Present Club: 12 August 1863
Inaugural First-Class Match: 1864
Colours: Blue, Gold and White
Badge: Tudor Rose and Crown
County Champions: (2) 1961, 1973
NatWest/C&G/FP Trophy Winners: (3) 1991, 2005, 2009
Benson and Hedges Cup Winners: (2) 1988, 1992
Sunday League Winners: (3) 1975, 1978, 1986
Clydesdale Bank Winners: (1) 2012
Royal London One-Day Cup Winners: (1) 2018
Twenty20 Cup Winners: (2) 2010, 2012

HAMPSHIRE
CRICKET

Chairman: David Mann, The Ageas Bowl, Botley Road, West End, Southampton SO30 3XH • Tel: 023 8047 2002 • Email: enquiries@ageasbowl.com • Web: www.ageasbowl.com • Twitter: @hantscricket (65,029 followers)

CEO: David Mann. **Cricket Operations Manager**: Tim Tremlett. **Director of Cricket**: Giles White. **1st XI Manager**: Adrian Birrell. **Assistant Coach**: Alfonso Thomas. **Batting Coach**: Tony Middleton. **Captain**: J.M.Vince. **Overseas Player**: F.D.M.Karunaratne. **2019 Testimonial**: None. **Head Groundsman**: Nigel Gray. **Scorer**: Kevin Baker. ‡ New registration. ^NQ Not qualified for England.

^NQ**ABBOTT**, Kyle John (Kearnsey C, KZN), b Empangeni, South Africa 18 Jun 1987. 6'3½". RHB, RFM. Squad No 11. KwaZulu-Natal 2008-09 to 2009-10. Dolphins 2008-09 to 2014-15. Hampshire debut 2014; cap 2017 (Kolpak signing). Worcestershire 2016. IPL: KXIP 2016. **Tests** (SA): 11 (2012-13 to 2016-17); HS 17 v A (Adelaide) 2016-17; BB 7-29 v P (Centurion) 2012-13. **LOI** (SA): 28 (2012-13 to 2016-17); HS 23 v Z (Bulawayo) 2014; BB 4-21 v Ire (Canberra) 2014-15. **IT20** (SA): 21 (2012-13 to 2015-16); HS 9* v NZ (Centurion) 2015; BB 3-20 v B (Dhaka) 2015. F-c Tours (SA): A 2016-17; I 2015-16. HS 97* v Lancs (Manchester) 2017. 50 wkts (2+1): 65 (2012-13). BB 8-45 (12-96 match) Dolphins v Cobras (Cape Town) 2012-13. H BB 7-41 v Yorks (Leeds) 2017. Hat-trick v Worcs (Worcester) 2018. LO HS 56 v Surrey (Oval) 2017 (RLC). LO BB 4-21 (*see LOI*). T20 HS 30. T20 BB 5-14.

ALSOP, Thomas Philip (Lavington S), b High Wycombe, Bucks 26 Nov 1995. Younger brother of O.J.Alsop (Wiltshire 2010-12). 5'11". LHB, WK, occ SLA. Squad No 9. Debut (Hampshire) 2014. England Lions 2016-17. MCC 2017. Hampshire 2nd XI debut 2013. England U19 2014 to 2015. HS 117 v Surrey (The Oval) 2016. LO HS 116 v Surrey (Southampton) 2016 (RLC). T20 HS 85.

‡**BARKER**, Keith Hubert Douglas (Moorhead HS; Fulwood C, Preston), b Manchester 21 Oct 1986. Son of K.H.Barker (British Guiana 1960-61 to 1963-64). Played football for Blackburn Rovers and Rochdale. 6'3". LHB, LMF. Squad No 10. Warwickshire 2009-18; cap 2013. HS 125 Wa v Surrey (Guildford) 2013. 50 wkts (3); most – 62 (2016). BB 6-40 Wa v Somerset (Taunton) 2012. LO HS 56 Wa v Scotland (Birmingham) 2011 (CB40). LO BB 4-33 Wa v Scotland (Birmingham) 2010 (CB40). T20 HS 46. T20 BB 4-19.

BERG, Gareth Kyle (South African College S), b Cape Town, South Africa 18 Jan 1981. 6'0". RHB, RMF. Squad No 13. England qualified through residency. Middlesex 2008-14; cap 2010. Hampshire debut 2015; cap 2016. Italy 2011-12 to 2013-14 (T20 only). HS 130* M v Leics (Leicester) 2011, sharing M record 9th wkt partnership of 172 with T.J.Murtagh. H HS 99* v Yorks (Southampton) 2017. BB 6-56 v Yorks (Southampton) 2016. LO HS 75 M v Glamorgan (Lord's) 2013 (Y40). LO BB 4-24 M v Worcs (Worcester) 2011 (CB40). T20 HS 90. T20 BB 4-20.

CAME, Harry Robert Charles (Bradfield C), b Basingstoke 27 Aug 1998. Son of P.R.C.Came (Hampshire 2nd XI 1986-87); grandson of K.C.Came (Free Foresters 1957); great-grandson of R.W.V.Robins (Middlesex, Cambridge U & England 1925-58). 5'9". RHB, OB. Squad No 4. Hampshire 2nd XI debut 2017. Kent 2nd XI 2017-18. Awaiting 1st XI debut.

CRANE, Mason Sydney (Lancing C), b Shoreham-by-Sea, Sussex 18 Feb 1997. 5'7". RHB, LB. Squad No 32. Debut (Hampshire) 2015. NSW 2016-17. MCC 2017. Hampshire 2nd XI debut 2013. **Test**: 1 (2017-18); HS 4 and BB 1-193 v A (Sydney) 2017-18 **IT20**: 2 (2017); HS – ; BB 1-39 v SA (Cardiff) 2017. F-c Tours: A 2017-18; WI 2017-18 (EL). HS 29 v Somerset (Taunton) 2017. BB 5-35 v Warwks (Southampton) 2015. LO HS 21* v Sussex (Hove) 2018 (RLC). LO BB 4-30 v Middx (Southampton) 2015 (RLC). T20 HS 3*. T20 BB 3-15.

DAWSON, Liam Andrew (John Bentley S, Calne), b Swindon, Wilts 1 Mar 1990. 5'8". RHB, SLA. Squad No 8. Debut (Hampshire) 2007; cap 2013. Mountaineers 2011-12. Essex 2015 (on loan). Wiltshire 2006-07. **Tests**: 3 (2016-17 to 2017); HS 66* v I (Chennai) 2016-17; BB 2-34 v SA (Lord's) 2017. **LOI**: 3 (2016 to 2018-19); HS 10 and BB 2-70 v P (Cardiff) 2016. **IT20**: 6 (2016 to 2017-18); HS 10 v NZ (Hamilton) 2017-18; BB 3-27 v SL (Southampton) 2016. F-c Tour: I 2016-17. HS 169 v Somerset (Southampton) 2011. BB 7-51 Mountaineers v ME (Mutare) 2011-12 (also scored 100* in same match). H BB 5-29 v Leics (Southampton) 2012. LO HS 113* SJD v Kalabagan (Savar) 2014-15. LO BB 6-47 v Sussex (Southampton) 2015 (RLC). T20 HS 82. T20 BB 5-17.

‡**DONALD, Aneurin** Henry Thomas (Pontarddulais CS), b Swansea, Glamorgan 20 Dec 1996. 6'2". RHB, OB. Squad No 12. Glamorgan 2014-18. Glamorgan 2nd XI 2012-18. Wales MC 2012. 1000 runs (1): 1088 (2016). HS 234 Gm v Derbys (Colwyn Bay) 2016, in 123 balls, equalling world record for fastest 200, inc 15 sixes, going from 0-127* between lunch and tea, and 127-234 after tea. LO HS 53 Gm v Sussex (Cardiff) 2016 (RLC). T20 HS 76.

^{NQ}**EDWARDS, Fidel** Henderson (St James's SS), b Gays, St Peter, Barbados 6 Feb 1982. 5'11". RHB, RFM. Squad No 82. Half-brother of P.T.Collins (Barbados, Surrey, Middlesex & West Indies 1996-97 to 2011-12). Barbados 2001-02 to 2013-14. Hampshire debut 2015 (Kolpak signing); cap 2018. MCC 2018. IPL: DC 2009 to 2009-10. Big Bash: ST 2011-12. **Tests** (WI): 55 (2003 to 2012-13); HS 30 v I (Roseau) 2011; BB 7-87 v NZ (Napier) 2008-09. **LOI** (WI): 50 (2003-04 to 2009); HS 13 v NZ (Wellington) 2008-09; BB 6-22 v Z (Harare) 2003-04 – on debut. **IT20** (WI): 20 (2007-08 to 2012-13); HS 7* v E (Oval) 2011; BB 3-23 v A (Bridgetown) 2011-12. F-c Tours (WI): E 2004, 2007, 2009, 2012; A 2005-06; SA 2003-04, 2007-08; NZ 2005-06, 2008-09; I 2011-12, 2013-14 (WI A); P 2006-07; Z 2003-04; B 2011-12, 2012-13. HS 40 Bar v Jamaica (Bridgetown) 2007-08. H HS 20 v Surrey (Southampton) 2017. 50 wkts (1): 54 (2018). BB 7-87 (see Tests). H BB 6-50 v Notts (Southampton) 2018. LO HS 21* Bar v Jamaica (Providence) 2007-08. LO BB 6-22 (see LOI). T20 HS 11*. T20 BB 5-22.

‡**FULLER, James** Kerr (Otago U, NZ), b Cape Town, South Africa 24 Jan 1990. UK passport. 6'3". RHB, RFM. Squad No 26. Otago 2009-10 to 2012-13. Gloucestershire 2011-15; cap 2011. Middlesex 2016-18. HS 93 M v Somerset (Taunton) 2016. BB 6-24 (10-79 match) Otago v Wellington (Dunedin) 2012-13. CC BB 6-47 Gs v Surrey (Oval) 2014. Hat-trick v Worcs (Cheltenham) 2013. LO HS 45 Gs v Surrey (Bristol) 2015 (RLC). LO BB 6-35 M v Netherlands (Amstelveen) 2012 (CB40). T20 HS 46*. T20 BB 6-28 v Hants (Southampton) 2018 – M record.

^{NQ}**HOLLAND, Ian** Gabriel (Ringwood Secondary C, Melbourne), b Stevens Point, Wisconsin, USA 3 Oct 1990. 6'0". RHB, RMF. Squad No 22. Victoria 2015-16. Hampshire debut 2017. HS 58* v Surrey (Oval) 2017. BB 4-16 v Somerset (Southampton) 2017. LO HS 11* v Glamorgan (Southampton) 2017 (RLC). LO BB 2-57 v Kent (Canterbury) 2017 (RLC). T20 BB 1-33.

‡[NQ]**KARUNARATNE, Frank Dimuth** Madushanka (St Joseph's C), b Colombo, Sri Lanka 28 Apr 1988. 6'0''. LHB, RM. Sinhalese Sports Club 2008-09 to date. Basnahira North 2009-10. Dambulla District 2017-18. **Tests** (SL): 60 (2012-13 to 2018-19, 2 as captain); HS 196 v P (Dubai, DSC) 2017-18; BB 1-12 v SA (Port Elizabeth) 2018-19. **LOI** (SL): 17 (2011 to 2016-17); HS 60 v Scotland (Edinburgh) 2011; BB –. F-c Tours (SL): E 2011 (SL A), 2014, 2016; A 2012-13, 2018-19; SA 2012 (SL A), 2016-17, 2018-19 (capt); WI 2013 (SL A); NZ 2014-15 2015-16, 2018-19; I 2017-18; Z 2016-17; B 2013-14, 2017-18; UAE 2013-14 (v P), 2017-18 (v P). 1000 runs (0+1): 1186 (2009-10). HS 212 SL A v EL (Dambulla) 2016-17. BB 1-6 SL A v WI A (Pallekelle) 2016-17. LO HS 132 Sinhalese v KY (Kurunegala) 2017-18. LO BB 2-13 Sinhalese v Saracens (Colombo, SSC) 2009-10. T20 HS 80.

McMANUS, Lewis David (Clayesmore S, Bournemouth), b Poole, Dorset 9 Oct 1994. 5'10''. RHB, WK. Squad No 18. Debut (Hampshire) 2015. Hampshire 2nd XI debut 2011. Dorset 2011-13. HS 132* v Surrey (Southampton) 2016. LO HS 47 v Barbados (Bridgetown) 2017-18. T20 HS 59.

NORTHEAST, Sam Alexander (Harrow S), b Ashford, Kent 16 Oct 1989. 5'11''. RHB, LB. Squad No 17. Kent 2007-17; cap 2012; captain 2016-17. Hampshire debut 2018. MCC 2013, 2018. 1000 runs (3); most – 1402 (2016). HS 191 K v Derbys (Canterbury) 2016. H HS 129 v Surrey (Oval) 2018. BB 1-60 K v Glos (Cheltenham) 2014. LO HS 132 K v Somerset (Taunton) 2014 (RLC). T20 HS 114.

ORGAN, Felix Spencer (Canford S), b Sydney, Australia 2 Jun 1999. 5'9''. RHB, OB. Debut (Hampshire) 2017. Hampshire 2nd XI debut 2015. No 1st XI appearances in 2018. HS 16 v Middx (Uxbridge) 2017. LO HS 0. LO BB 1-6 v CC&C (Lucas Street) 2017-18.

[NQ]**ROSSOUW, Rilee** Roscoe, b Bloemfontein, South Africa, 9 Oct 1989. 6'1''. LHB, OB. Squad No 30. Free State 2007-08 to 2012-13. Eagles 2008-09 to 2009-10. Knights 2010-11 to 2016-17. Hampshire debut 2018 (Kolpak signing). IPL: RCB 2014-15. **LOI** (SA): 36 (2014 to 2016-17); HS 132 v WI (Centurion) 2014-15; BB 1-17 v Z (Harare) 2014. **IT20** (SA): 15 (2014-15 to 2015-16); HS 78 v A (Adelaide) 2014-15. F-c Tours (SA A): A 2014; SL 2010; B 2010. 1000 runs (0+1): 1261 (2009-10). HS 319 Eagles v Titans (Centurion) 2009-10, sharing in 3rd highest 2nd wkt partnership in all f-c cricket of 480 with D.Elgar. H HS 120* v Lancs (Manchester) 2018. BB 1-1 Knights v Cobras (Cape Town) 2013-14. LO HS 156 v Somerset (Taunton) 2017 (RLC). LO BB 1-17 (*see LOI*). T20 HS 100*. T20 BB 1-8.

SCRIVEN, Thomas Antony Rhys (Magdalen Coll S), b Oxford 18 Nov 1998. 6'0½''. RHB, RMF. Awaiting f-c debut. Hampshire 2nd XI debut 2016. T20 BB –.

SOAMES, Oliver Courteney (Cheltenham C; Loughborough U), b Kingston upon Thames, Surrey, 27 Oct 1995. 5'8''. RHB, RM/OB. Squad No 27. Loughborough MCCU 2018. Hampshire debut 2018. Hampshire 2nd XI debut 2017. HS 29 v Lancs (Southampton) 2018.

STEVENSON, Ryan Anthony (King Edward VI Community C), b Torquay, Devon 2 Apr 1992. 6'2''. RHB, RMF. Squad No 47. Debut (Hampshire) 2015. Devon 2015. HS 30 v Durham (Chester-le-St) 2015. BB 1-15 v Notts (Nottingham) 2015. LO HS 0. LO BB 1-28 v Essex (Southampton) 2016 (RLC). T20 HS 4*. T20 BB 2-28.

TAYLOR, Bradley Jacob (Eggar's S, Alton), b Winchester 14 Mar 1997. 5'11''. RHB, OB. Squad No 93. Debut (Hampshire) 2013. Hampshire 2nd XI debut 2013. England U19 2014 to 2014-15. HS 36 v Cardiff MCCU (Southampton) 2016. CC HS 20 and BB 4-64 v Lancs (Southport) 2013. LO HS 69 v CC&C (Bridgetown) 2017-18. LO BB 4-26 v CC&C (Lucas Street) 2017-18. T20 HS 9*. T20 BB 2-20.

VINCE, James Michael (Warminster S), b Cuckfield, Sussex 14 Mar 1991. 6'2". RHB, RM. Squad No 14. Debut (Hampshire) 2009; cap 2013; captain 2016 to date. Wiltshire 2007-08. Big Bash: ST 2016-17 to 2017-18. SS 2018-19. **Tests**: 13 (2016 to 2017-18); HS 83 v A (Brisbane) 2017-18; BB –. **LOI**: 6 (2015 to 2018); HS 51 v SL (Cardiff) 2016. **IT20**: 7 (2015-16 to 2017-18); HS 46 v P (Sharjah) 2015-16. F-c Tours: A 2017-18; SA 2014-15 (EL); NZ 2017-18; SL 2013-14 (EL). 1000 runs (2); most – 1525 (2014). HS 240 v Essex (Southampton) 2014. BB 5-41 v Loughborough MCCU (Southampton) 2013. CC BB 2-2 v Lancs (Southport) 2013. LO 178 v Glamorgan (Southampton) 2017 (RLC) – H record. LO BB 1-18 EL v Australia A (Sydney) 2012-13. T20 HS 107*. T20 BB 1-5.

WEATHERLEY, Joe James (King Edward VI S, Southampton), b Winchester 19 Jan 1997. 6'1". RHB, OB. Squad No 5. Debut (Hampshire) 2016. Kent 2017 (on loan). Hampshire 2nd XI debut 2014. England U19 2014-15. HS 126* v Lancs (Manchester) 2018. BB 1-2 v Notts (Southampton) 2018. LO HS 105* v Kent (Southampton) 2018 (RLC). LO BB 4-25 v T&T (Cave Hill) 2017-18. T20 HS 43. T20 BB –.

NQ**WHEAL, Brad**ley Thomas James (Clifton C), b Durban, South Africa 28 Aug 1996. 5'9". RHB, RMF. Squad No 58. Debut (Hampshire) 2015. **LOI** (Scot): 11 (2015-16 to 2017-18); HS 14 v Ire (Harare) 2017-18; BB 3-34 v WI (Harare) 2017-18. **IT20** (Scot): 5 (2015-16 to 2016-17); HS 2* and BB 3-20 v Hong Kong (Mong Kok) 2015-16. HS 25* v Somerset (Taunton) 2018. BB 6-51 v Notts (Nottingham) 2016. LO HS 18* v CC&C (Bridgetown) 2017-18. LO BB 4-38 v Kent (Southampton) 2016 (RLC). T20 HS 16. T20 BB 3-20.

WOOD, Christopher Philip (Alton C), b Basingstoke 27 June 1990. 6'2". RHB, LM. Squad No 25. Debut (Hampshire) 2010; cap 2018. HS 105* v Leics (Leicester) 2012. BB 5-39 v Kent (Canterbury) 2014. LO HS 41 v Essex (Southampton) 2013 (Y40). LO BB 5-22 v Glamorgan (Cardiff) 2012 (CB40). T20 HS 27. T20 BB 5-32.

RELEASED/RETIRED

(Having made a County 1st XI appearance in 2018)

ADAMS, James Henry Kenneth (Sherborne S; University C, London; Loughborough U), b Winchester 23 Sep 1980. 6'2". LHB, LM. British U 2002-04. Hampshire 2002-18; cap 2006; captain 2012-15; benefit 2015. Loughborough UCCE 2003-04 – scoring 107 v Somerset (Taunton) on debut. MCC 2013. Dorset 1998. F-c Tour (EL): WI 2010-11. 1000 runs (5); most – 1351 (2009). HS 262* v Notts (Nottingham) 2006. BB 2-16 v Durham (Chester-le-St) 2004. LO HS 131 v Warwks (Birmingham) 2010 (CB40). LO BB 1-34 v Essex (Chelmsford) 2007 (FPT). T20 HS 101*. T20 BB –.

NQ**AMLA, Hashim** Mahomed, b Durban, South Africa 31 Mar 1983. Younger brother of A.M.Amla (Natal B, KZN, Dolphins 1997-98 to 2012-13). RHB, RM/OB. KZN 1999-00 to 2003-04. Dolphins 2004-05 to 2011-12. Essex 2009. Nottinghamshire 2010; cap 2010. Surrey 2013-14. Derbyshire 2015. Cape Cobras 2015-16 to date. Hampshire 2018. IPL: KXIP 2016-17. *Wisden* 2012. **Tests** (SA): 124 (2004-05 to 2018-19, 14 as captain); 1000 runs (3); most – 1249 (2010); HS 311* v E (Oval) 2012; BB –. **LOI** (SA): 174 (2007-08 to 2018-19, 9 as captain); 1000 runs (2); most – 1062 (2015); HS 159 v Ire (Canberra) 2014-15. **IT20** (SA): 44 (2008-09 to 2018, 2 as captain); HS 97* v A (Cape Town) 2015-16. F-c Tours (SA) (C=Captain): E 2008, 2012, 2017; A 2008-09, 2012-13, 2016-17; WI 2010; NZ 2011-12, 2016-17; I 2004-05, 2007-08 (SA A), 2007-08, 2009-10, 2015-16C; P 2007-08; SL 2005-06 (SA A), 2006, 2014C, 2018; Z 2004 (SA A), 2007 (SA A), 2014C; B 2007-08, 2015C; UAE 2010-11, 2013-14 (v P). 1000 runs (0+2); most – 1126 (2005-06). HS 311* (*see Tests*). CC HS 181 Ex v Glamorgan (Chelmsford) 2009 – on debut. H HS 112 v Notts (Nottingham) 2018. BB 1-10 SA A v India A (Kimberley) 2001-02. LO HS 159 (*see LOI*). T20 HS 104*.

DICKINSON, Calvin Miles (St Edward's S, Oxford; Oxford Brookes U), b Durban, South Africa 3 Nov 1996. RHB, WK. UK passport. Oxford MCCU 2016. Hampshire 2017. Worcestershire 2nd XI 2015. Essex 2nd XI 2016. HS 99 v SA A (Southampton) 2017. LO HS 21 v T&T (Lucas Street) 2017-18. T20 HS 51.

ERVINE, Sean Michael (Lomagundi C, Chinhoyi), b Harare, Zimbabwe 6 Dec 1982. Elder brother of C.R.Ervine (Midlands, SR, MT, Bulawayo Metropolitan Tuskers & Zimbabwe 2003-04 to date); son of R.M.Ervine (Rhodesia 1977-78); grandson of M.A.Den (Rhodesia 1935-36); nephew of N.B.Ervine (Rhodesia 1977-78) and G.M.Den (Rhodesia and Eastern Province 1963-64 to 1969-70). 6'2". LHB, RMF. CFX Academy 2000-01 to 2001. Midlands 2001-02 to 2003-04. Hampshire 2005-18; cap 2005; qualified for England in 2013 season; benefit 2016. W Australia 2006-07 to 2007-08. Southern Rocks 2009-10. Matabeleland Tuskers 2011-12 to 2012-13. Derbyshire 2018 (on loan). **Tests** (Z): 5 (2003 to 2003-04); HS 86 v B (Harare) 2003-04; BB 4-146 v A (Perth) 2003-04. **LOI** (Z): 42 (2001-02 to 2003-04); HS 100 v I (Adelaide) 2003-04; BB 3-29 v P (Sharjah) 2001-02. F-c Tours (Z): E 2003; A 2003-04. 1000 runs (1): 1090 (2016). HS 237* v Somerset (Southampton) 2010. BB 6-82 Midlands v Mashonaland (Kwekwe) 2002-03. H BB 5-60 v Glamorgan (Cardiff) 2005. LO HS 167* v Ireland (Southampton) 2009 (FPT). LO BB 5-50 v Glamorgan (Cardiff) 2005 (CGT). T20 HS 82. T20 BB 4-12.

NQMUNRO, Colin, b Durban, South Africa 11 Mar 1987. LHB, RM. Auckland 2006-07 to date. Worcestershire 2015. Hampshire 2018 (T20 only). IPL: KKR 2016. DD 2018. Big Bash: SS 2016-17. **Tests** (NZ): 1 (2012-13); HS 15 and BB 2-40 v SA (Port Elizabeth) 2012-13. **LOI** (NZ): 51 (2012-13 to 2018-19); HS 87 v B (Christchurch) 2016-17 and 87 v SL (Mt Manganui) 2018-19; BB 2-10 v P (Dunedin) 2017-18. **IT20** (NZ): 52 (2012-13 to 2018-19); HS 109* v I (Rajkot) 2017-18; BB 1-12 v P (Wellington) 2017-18. F-c Tours (NZ): SA 2012-13; SL 2013-14. HS 281 Auckland v CD (Napier) 2014-15, inc world record 23 sixes. CC HS 34 Wo v Hants (Southampton) 2015. BB 4-36 Auckland v CD (Auckland) 2010-11. LO HS 174* Auckland v Canterbury (Auckland) 2017-18. LO BB 3-45 Auckland v Otago (Oamaru) 2010-11. T20 HS 109*. T20 BB 4-15.

MUJEEB ZADRAN – *see MIDDLESEX*.

NQSTEYN, Dale Willem, b Phalaborwa, South Africa 27 Jun 1983. RHB, RF. Northerns 2003-04 to 2005-06. Titans 2004-05 to 2009-10. Essex 2005. Warwickshire 2007; cap 2007. Hampshire 2018. Glamorgan 2016 (T20 only). IPL: RCB 2007-08 to 2009-10. DC 2011-12. SH 2013-15. GL 2016. *Wisden* 2012. **Tests** (SA): 93 (2004-05 to 2018-19); HS 76 v A (Melbourne) 2008-09; 50 wkts (3); most – 74 (2008); BB 7-51 v I (Nagpur) 2009-10. **LOI** (SA): 122 (+2 for Africa XI) (2005 to 2018-19); HS 60 v Z (Bloemfontein) 2018-19; BB 6-39 v P (Port Elizabeth) 2013-14. **IT20** (SA): 42 (2007-08 to 2015-16); HS 5 v E (Bridgetown) 2010 and 5 v Netherlands (Chittagong) 2013-14; BB 4-9 v WI (Port Elizabeth) 2007-08. F-c Tours (SA): E 2008, 2012; A 2008-09, 2012-13, 2016-17; WI 2010; NZ 2011-12; I 2007-08 (SA A), 2009-10, 2015-16; P 2007-08; SL 2005-06 (SA A), 2006, 2014, 2018; Z 2014; B 2007-08, 2015; UAE 2010-11 (v P), 2013-14 (v P). HS 82 Ex v Durham (Chester-le-St) 2005. H HS 25 v Worcs (Worcester) 2018. 50 wkts (0+2); most – 69 (2005-06). BB 8-41 (14-110 match) Titans v Eagles (Bloemfontein) 2007-08. CC BB 5-49 Wa v Worcs (Worcester) 2007. LO HS 60 (*see LOI*). LO BB 6-39 (*see LOI*). T20 HS 27*. T20 BB 4-9.

TOPLEY, Reece James William (Royal Hospital S, Ipswich), b Ipswich, Suffolk 21 February 1994. Son of T.D.Topley (Surrey, Essex, GW 1985-94) and nephew of P.A.Topley (Kent 1972-75). 6'7". RHB, LMF. Essex 2011-15; cap 2013. Hampshire 2016-17. **LOI**: 10 (2015 to 2015-16); HS 6 v A (Manchester) 2015; BB 4-50 v SA (Port Elizabeth) 2015-16. **IT20**: 6 (2015 to 2015-16); HS 1* v SA (Johannesburg) 2015-16; BB 3-24 v P (Dubai, DSC) 2015-16. F-c Tour (EL): SL 2013-14. HS 16 and H BB 1-56 v Yorks (Southampton) 2017. BB 6-29 (11-85 match) Ex v Worcs (Chelmsford) 2013. LO HS 19 Ex v Somerset (Taunton) 2011 (CB40). LO BB 4-16 EL v WI A (Northampton) 2018. T20 HS 5*. T20 BB 4-26.

A.H.J.A.Hart and C.B.Sole left the staff without making a County 1st XI appearance in 2018.

HAMPSHIRE 2018

RESULTS SUMMARY

	Place	Won	Lost	Drew	Tied	NR
Specsavers County Champ (1st Division)	5th	4	5	5		
All First-Class Matches		4	5	6		
Royal London One-Day Cup (South Group)	**Winners** 7	2				1
Vitality Blast (South Group)	8th	2	9		1	2

SPECSAVERS COUNTY CHAMPIONSHIP AVERAGES
BATTING AND FIELDING

Cap		M	I	NO	HS	Runs	Avge	100	50	Ct/St
	H.M.Amla	5	9	–	112	492	54.66	2	3	2
2013	J.M.Vince	14	25	1	201*	962	40.08	3	2	5
	R.R.Rossouw	9	17	3	120*	489	34.92	1	1	8
	T.P.Alsop	8	14	1	99	397	30.53	–	4	22
2016	G.K.Berg	9	14	2	84*	335	27.91	–	2	4
2013	L.A.Dawson	10	17	2	72	385	25.66	–	1	6
2017	K.J.Abbott	14	22	5	60*	436	25.64	–	2	–
	S.A.Northeast	10	18	–	129	451	25.05	1	1	5
2006	J.H.K.Adams	14	25	1	147	582	24.25	1	1	15
	J.J.Weatherley	12	21	1	126*	459	22.95	1	2	5
	L.D.McManus	7	12	1	66	211	19.18	–	1	9
2018	C.P.Wood	3	5	1	26	56	14.00	–	–	2
	I.G.Holland	7	11	1	31	135	13.50	–	–	3
	D.W.Steyn	5	7	1	25	65	10.83	–	–	1
	B.T.J.Wheal	5	7	1	25*	63	10.50	–	–	7
	O.C.Soames	4	7	–	29	69	9.85	–	–	–
2018	F.H.Edwards	14	20	9	14	75	6.81	–	–	3

Also batted: S.M.Ervine (1 match – cap 2005) 8, 10; O.P.Rayner (2) 0, 0 (2 ct); B.J.Taylor (1) 5, 16.

BOWLING

	O	M	R	W	Avge	Best	5wI	10wM
D.W.Steyn	142.3	30	382	20	19.10	5- 66	1	–
K.J.Abbott	348.3	70	1182	51	23.17	6- 39	4	1
I.G.Holland	151	42	389	15	25.93	3- 48	–	–
F.H.Edwards	362.2	55	1443	54	26.72	6- 50	2	–
L.A.Dawson	205.2	36	627	20	31.35	4- 30	–	–
B.T.J.Wheal	114.5	17	462	11	42.00	2- 46	–	–
G.K.Berg	200.1	41	654	15	43.60	5-130	1	–
Also bowled:								
O.P.Rayner	72	17	196	5	39.20	4- 54	–	–
C.P.Wood	72	13	268	6	44.66	2- 56	–	–

J.H.K.Adams 1-0-3-0; T.P.Alsop 3-0-12-1; B.J.Taylor 16-4-50-2; J.M.Vince 5-1-17-0;
J.J.Weatherley 14-1-65-2.

The First-Class Averages (pp 230–245) give the records of Hampshire players in all first-class county matches (Hampshire's other opponents being Cardiff MCCU), with the exception of O.P.Rayner and O.C.Soames, whose first-class figures for Hampshire are as above, and:
S.M.Ervine 2-3-1-65*-83-41.50-0-1-0ct. Did not bowl.

HAMPSHIRE RECORDS

FIRST-CLASS CRICKET

Highest Total	For 714-5d		v	Notts	Southampton[2]	2005
	V 742		by	Surrey	The Oval	1909
Lowest Total	For 15		v	Warwicks	Birmingham	1922
	V 23		by	Yorkshire	Middlesbrough	1965
Highest Innings	For 316	R.H.Moore	v	Warwicks	Bournemouth	1937
	V 303*	G.A.Hick	for	Worcs	Southampton[1]	1997

Highest Partnership for each Wicket

1st	347	V.P.Terry/C.L.Smith	v	Warwicks	Birmingham	1987
2nd	373	J.H.K.Adams/M.A.Carberry	v	Somerset	Taunton	2011
3rd	523	M.A.Carberry/N.D.McKenzie	v	Yorkshire	Southampton[2]	2011
4th	367	J.H.K.Adams/S.M.Ervine	v	Warwicks	Southampton[2]	2017
5th	235	G.Hill/D.F.Walker	v	Sussex	Portsmouth	1937
6th	411	R.M.Poore/E.G.Wynyard	v	Somerset	Taunton	1899
7th	325	G.Brown/C.H.Abercrombie	v	Essex	Leyton	1913
8th	257	N.Pothas/A.J.Bichel	v	Glos	Cheltenham	2005
9th	230	D.A.Livingstone/A.T.Castell	v	Surrey	Southampton[1]	1962
10th	192	H.A.W.Bowell/W.H.Livsey	v	Worcs	Bournemouth	1921

Best Bowling	For	9- 25	R.M.H.Cottam	v	Lancashire	Manchester	1965
(Innings)	V	10- 46	W.Hickton	for	Lancashire	Manchester	1870
Best Bowling	For	16- 88	J.A.Newman	v	Somerset	Weston-s-Mare	1927
(Match)	V	17-103	W.Mycroft	for	Derbyshire	Southampton	1876

Most Runs – Season	2854	C.P.Mead	(av 79.27)	1928
Most Runs – Career	48892	C.P.Mead	(av 48.84)	1905-36
Most 100s – Season	12	C.P.Mead		1928
Most 100s – Career	138	C.P.Mead		1905-36
Most Wkts – Season	190	A.S.Kennedy	(av 15.61)	1922
Most Wkts – Career	2669	D.Shackleton	(av 18.23)	1948-69
Most Career W-K Dismissals	700	R.J.Parks	(630 ct; 70 st)	1980-92
Most Career Catches in the Field	629	C.P.Mead		1905-36

LIMITED-OVERS CRICKET

Highest Total	50ov	371-4		v	Glamorgan	Southampton[1]	1975
	40ov	353-8		v	Middlesex	Lord's	2005
	T20	249-8		v	Derbyshire	Derby	2017
Lowest Total	50ov	50		v	Yorkshire	Leeds	1991
	40ov	43		v	Essex	Basingstoke	1972
	T20	85		v	Sussex	Southampton[2]	2008
Highest Innings	50ov	178	J.M.Vince	v	Glamorgan	Southampton[2]	2017
	40ov	172	C.G.Greenidge	v	Surrey	Southampton[1]	1987
	T20	124*	M.J.Lumb	v	Essex	Southampton[2]	2009
Best Bowling	50ov	7-30	P.J.Sainsbury	v	Norfolk	Southampton[1]	1965
	40ov	6-20	T.E.Jesty	v	Glamorgan	Cardiff	1975
	T20	5-14	A.D.Mascarenhas	v	Sussex	Hove	2004

[1] County Ground (Northlands Road) [2] Ageas Bowl

KENT

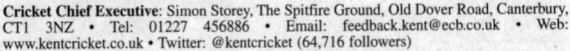

Formation of Present Club: 1 March 1859
Substantial Reorganisation: 6 December 1870
Inaugural First-Class Match: 1864
Colours: Maroon and White
Badge: White Horse on a Red Ground
County Champions: (6) 1906, 1909, 1910, 1913, 1970, 1978
Joint Champions: (1) 1977
Gillette Cup Winners: (2) 1967, 1974
Benson and Hedges Cup Winners: (3) 1973, 1976, 1978
Pro 40/National League (Div 1) Winners: (1) 2001
Sunday League Winners: (4) 1972, 1973, 1976, 1995
Twenty20 Cup Winners: (1) 2007

Cricket Chief Executive: Simon Storey, The Spitfire Ground, Old Dover Road, Canterbury, CT1 3NZ • Tel: 01227 456886 • Email: feedback.kent@ecb.co.uk • Web: www.kentcricket.co.uk • Twitter: @kentcricket (64,276 followers)

Director of Cricket: Paul Downton. **Head Coach**: Matt Walker. **Assistant Coach**: Allan Donald. **Captain**: S.W.Billings. **Vice-Captain**: J.L.Denly. **Overseas Players**: A.F.Milne, Mohammad Nabi (both T20 only) and M.T.Renshaw. **2019 Testimonial**: J.L.Denly. **Head Groundsman**: Adrian Llong. **Scorer**: Lorne Hart. ‡ New registration. NQ Not qualified for England.

BELL-DRUMMOND, Daniel James (Millfield S), b Lewisham, London 4 Aug 1993. 5'10". RHB, RMF. Squad No 23. Debut (Kent) 2011; cap 2015. MCC 2014, 2018. 1000 runs (1): 1058 (2014). HS 206* v Loughborough MCCU (Canterbury) 2016. CC HS 153 v Hants (Southampton) 2014. BB 1-1 v Glos (Bristol) 2018. LO HS 171* EL v SL A (Canterbury) 2016. LO BB –. T20 HS 112*.

BILLINGS, Samuel William (Haileybury S; Loughborough U), b Pembury 15 Jun 1991. 5'11". RHB, WK. Squad No 7. Loughborough MCCU 2011, scoring 131 v Northants (Loughborough) on f-c debut. Kent debut 2011; cap 2015; captain 2018 to date. MCC 2015. IPL: DD 2016-17. CSK 2018. Big Bash: SS 2016-17 to 2017-18. **LOI**: 15 (2015 to 2018); HS 62 v SA (Chittagong) 2016-17. **IT20**: 21 (2015 to 2018-19); HS 87 v WI (Basseterre) 2018-19 – world record IT20 score by a No 6 batsman. F-c Tours (EL): I 2018-19; UAE 2018-19 (v P). HS 171 v Glos (Bristol) 2016. LO HS 175 EL v P A (Canterbury) 2016. T20 HS 95*.

BLAKE, Alexander James (Hayes SS; Leeds Met U), b Farnborough 25 Jan 1989. 6'1". LHB, RMF. Squad No 10. Debut (Kent) 2008; cap 2017. Leeds/Bradford UCCE 2009-11 (not f-c). HS 105* v Yorks (Leeds) 2010. BB 2-9 v Pakistanis (Canterbury) 2010. CC BB 1-60 v Hants (Southampton) 2010. LO HS 116 v Somerset (Taunton) 2017 (RLC). LO BB 2-13 v Yorks (Leeds) 2011 (CB40). T20 HS 71*.

CLAYDON, Mitchell Eric (Westfield Sports HS, Sydney), b Fairfield, NSW, Australia 25 Nov 1982. 6'4". LHB, RMF. Squad No 8. Yorkshire 2005-06. Durham 2007-13. Canterbury 2010-11. Kent debut 2013; cap 2016. HS 77 v Leics (Leicester) 2014. 50 wkts (2); most – 59 (2014). BB 6-104 Du v Somerset (Taunton) 2011. K BB 5-42 v Worcs (Canterbury) 2016. LO HS 19 Du v Glos (Bristol) 2009 (FPT) and 19 v Middx (Canterbury) 2017 (RLC). LO BB 5-31 v Guyana (North Sound) 2017-18. T20 HS 19. T20 BB 5-26.

COX, Jordan Matthew (Felsted S), b Margate 21 Oct 2000. 5'8". RHB, WK. Squad No 22. Kent 2nd XI debut 2017. England U19 2018-19. Awaiting 1st XI debut.

CRAWLEY, Zak (Tonbridge S), b Bromley 3 Feb 1998. 6'6". RHB, RM. Squad No 16. Debut (Kent) 2017. Kent 2nd XI debut 2013, aged 15y 199d. HS 168 v Glamorgan (Canterbury) 2018. LO HS 99* v Leeward Is (North Sound) 2017-18. T20 HS 3.

DENLY, Joseph Liam (Chaucer TC), b Canterbury 16 Mar 1986. 6'0". RHB, LB. Squad No 6. Kent debut 2004; cap 2008. Middlesex 2012-14; cap 2012; testimonial 2019. MCC 2013. PCA 2018. **Tests**: 2 (2018-19); HS 69 v WI (Gros Islet) 2018-19; BB –. **LOI**: 9 (2009 to 2009-10); HS 67 v Ire (Belfast) 2009 – on debut. **IT20**: 9 (2009 to 2018-19); HS 30 v WI (Gros Islet) 2018-19; BB 4-19 v SL (Colombo, RPS) 2018-19. F-c Tours: WI 2018-19; NZ 2008-09 (Eng A); I 2007-08 (Eng A). 1000 runs (4); most – 1267 (2017). HS 227 v Worcs (Worcester) 2017. BB 4-36 v Derbys (Derby) 2018. LO HS 150* v Glamorgan (Canterbury) 2018 (RLC) – K record. LO BB 4-35 v Jamaica (North Sound) 2017-18. T20 HS 127 v Essex (Chelmsford) 2017 – K record. T20 BB 4-19.

DICKSON, Sean Robert, b Johannesburg, South Africa 2 Sep 1991. 5'10". RHB, RM. Squad No 58. Northerns 2013-14 to 2014-15. Kent debut 2015. UK passport holder and now England qualified. HS 318 v Northants (Beckenham) 2017, 2nd highest score in K history, sharing K record 2nd wkt partnership of 382 with J.L.Denly. BB 1-15 Northerns v GW (Centurion) 2014-15. K BB –. LO HS 99 v Middx (Lord's) 2016 (RLC). T20 HS 53. T20 BB 1-9.

HAGGETT, Calum John (Millfield S), b Taunton, Somerset 30 Oct 1990. 6'3". LHB, RMF. Squad No 25. Debut (Kent) 2013. HS 80 v Surrey (Oval) 2015. HS 4-15 v Derbys (Derby) 2016. LO HS 45 v Leeward Is (Coolidge) 2016-17. LO BB 4-59 v Windward Is (Coolidge) 2016-17. T20 HS 20. T20 BB 2-12.

IMRAN QAYYUM (Villiers HS, Southall; Greenford SFC; City U), b Ealing, Middx 23 May 1993. 6'0". RHB, SLA. Squad No 11. Debut (Kent) 2016. HS 39 v Leics (Canterbury) 2017. BB 3-158 v Northants (Northampton) 2016. LO HS 18 v Leeward Is (Coolidge) 2016-17. LO BB 4-33 v USA (North Sound) 2017-18. T20 HS 21*. T20 BB 3-40.

‡**NOKLAASSEN, Fred**erick Jack, b Haywards Heath, Sussex 13 Nov 1992. 6'4". RHB, LMF. Squad No 18. Awaiting f-c debut. **LOI** (Neth): 2 (2018); HS 13 v Nepal (Amstelveen) 2018; BB 3-30 v Nepal (Amstelveen 2018 – separate matches. **IT20** (Neth): 8 (2018 to 2018-19); HS 9 and BB 3-31 v Ire (Al Amerat) 2018-19. LO HS 13 (*see LOI*). LO BB 3-30 (*see LOI*). T20 HS 9. T20 BB 3-31.

NOKUHN, Heino Gunther, b Piet Relief, Mpumalanga, South Africa 1 Apr 1984. RHB, WK. Squad No 4. Northerns 2004-05 to 2015-16. Titans 2005-06 to date. Kent debut2018 (Kolpak signing); cap 2018. **Tests** (SA): 4 (2017); HS 34 v E (Nottingham) 2017. **IT20** (SA): 7 (2009-10 to 2016-17); HS 29 v SL (Johannesburg) 2016-17. F-c Tours (SAA): E 2017 (SA); A 2014; SL 2010; Z 2016; B 2010; Ire 2012. 1000 runs (+1): 1159 (2015-16). HS 244* Titans v Lions (Benoni) 2014-15. Scored 200* SAA v Hants (Southampton) 2017 on UK debut. K HS 96* v Leics (Leicester) 2018. LO HS 141* SAA v Bangladesh A (Benoni) 2011. T20 HS 83*.

NOMILNE, Adam Fraser, b Palmerston North, New Zealand 13 Apr 1992. RHB, RF. Squad No 20. Central Districts 2009-10 to date. Kent debut 2017. IPL: RCB 2016-17. **LOI** (NZ): 40 (2012-13 to 2017-18); HS 36 v A (Wellington) 2015-16; BB 3-49 v P (Auckland) 2015-16. **IT20** (NZ): 21 (2010-11 to 2018-19); HS 10* v SA (Centurion) 2015; BB 4-37 v P (Auckland) 2015-16. F-c Tour (NZ A): SL 2013-14. HS 97 and BB 5-47 CD v Otago (Napier) 2012-13. K HS 51 v Notts (Nottingham) 2017. K BB 4-68 v Durham (Chester-le-St) 2017. LO HS 45 NZ A v SL A (Lincoln) 2015-16. LO BB 5-61 NZ A v SL A (Pallekele) 2013-14. T20 HS 18*. T20 BB 5-11 v Somerset (Taunton) 2017 – K record.

‡**MILNES, Matt**hew Edward (West Bridgford CS; Durham U), b Nottingham 29 Jul 1994. RHB, RMF. Squad No 29. Durham MCCU 2014. Nottinghamshire 2018. Durham 2nd XI 2014-15. MCC Univs 2015. Nottinghamshire 2nd XI 2016-18. HS 43 Nt v Yorks (Nottingham) 2018. BB 4-44 Nt v Essex (Chelmsford) 2018.

‡^{NQ}**MOHAMMAD NABI** Eisakhil, b Peshawar, Pakistan 7 Mar 1985. RHB, OB. MCC 2007-11. Pakistan Customs 2007-08 to 2009-10. Leicestershire 2014. Nottinghamshire 2018. IPL: SH 2017-18. Big Bash: MR 2017-18 to date. **Tests** (Afg): 2 (2018 to 2018-19); HS 24 v Ire (Bengaluru) 2018; BB 3-36 v Ire (Dehradun) 2018-19. **LOI** (Afg): 111 (2009 to 2018-19); HS 116 v Z (Bulawayo) 2015-16; BB 4-30 v Ire (Greater Noida) 2016-17. **IT20** (Afg): 68 (2009-10 to 2018-19); HS 89 v Ire (Greater Noida) 2016-17; BB 4-10 v Ire (Dubai, DSC) 2016-17. HS 117 Afg v UAE (Sharjah) 2011-12. BB 6-33 Afg v Namibia (Windhoek) 2013. LO HS 146 MSC v PDSC (Bogra) 2013-14. LO BB 5-12 Afg v Namibia (Windhoek) 2013. T20 HS 89. T20 BB 4-10.

PODMORE, Harry William (Twyford HS), b Hammersmith, London 23 Jul 1994. 6'3". RHB, RMF. Squad No 1. Glamorgan 2016-17 (on loan). Middlesex 2016 to 2016-17. Derbyshire 2017 (on loan). Kent debut 2018. Middlesex 2nd XI 2011-17. MCC YC 2013. Durham 2nd XI 2017. HS 66* De v Sussex (Hove) 2017. K HS 53 v Glos (Bristol) 2018. BB 6-36 v Middx (Canterbury) 2018. LO HS 6* v Worcs (Worcester) 2018 (RLC). LO BB 4-57 v Notts (Nottingham) 2018 (RLC). T20 HS 9. T20 BB 3-13.

‡^{NQ}**RENSHAW, Matt**hew Thomas, b Middlesbrough, Yorks 28 Mar 1996. 6'0". LHB, OB. Squad No 77. Queensland 2014-15 to date. Somerset 2018. Big Bash: BH 2017-18 to date. MCC YC 2014. **Tests** (A): 11 (2016-17 to 2017-18); HS 184 v P (Sydney) 2016-17; BB –. F-c Tours (A): SA 2017-18; I 2016-17, 2018-19 (Aus A); B 2017; UAE 2018-19 (v P). HS 184 (*see Tests*). CC HS 112 Sm v Yorks (Taunton) 2018. BB 1-12 Q v Vic (Melbourne) 2017-18. LO HS 88 Q v Cricket Aus (Brisbane, AB) 2016-17. LO BB –. T20 HS 90*.

RILEY, Adam Edward Nicholas (Beths GS, Bexley; Loughborough U), b Sidcup 23 Mar 1992. 6'2". RHB, OB. Squad No 33. Debut (Kent) 2011. Loughborough MCCU 2012-14. MCC 2015. F-c Tour (EL): SA 2014-15. HS 34 v Derbys (Canterbury) 2015. 50 wkts (1): 57 (2014). BB 7-150 v Hants (Southampton) 2013. LO HS 21* v Leeward Is (Coolidge) 2016-17. LO BB 4-40 v Leeward Is (Coolidge) 2017-18. T20 HS 5*. T20 BB 4-22.

ROBINSON, Oliver Graham (Hurtsmere S, Greenwich), b Sidcup 1 Dec 1998. 5'8". RHB, WK, occ RM. Squad No 21. Debut (Kent) 2018. Kent 2nd XI debut 2015. England U19 2017 to 2018. HS 26 v Leics (Leicester) 2018. LO HS –.

ROUSE, Adam Paul (Perrins Community Sports C; Peter Symonds C, Winchester), b Harare, Zimbabwe 30 Jun 1992. 5'10". RHB, WK. Squad No 12. Hampshire 2013. Gloucestershire 2014; cap 2014. Kent debut 2016. Surrey 2018 (on loan). HS 95* v Derbys (Canterbury) 2017. LO HS 75* v Jamaica (North Sound) 2017-18. T20 HS 35*.

STEVENS, Darren Ian (Hinckley C), b Leicester 30 Apr 1976. 5'11". RHB, RM. Squad No 3. Leicestershire 1997-2004; cap 2002. Kent debut/cap 2005; benefit 2016. MCC 2002. F-c Tour (ECB Acad): SL 2002-03. 1000 runs (3); most – 1304 (2013). HS 208 v Glamorgan (Canterbury) 2005 and 208 v Middx (Uxbridge) 2009. 50 wkts (3); most – 63 (2017). BB 8-75 v Leics (Canterbury) 2017. LO HS 147 v Glamorgan (Swansea) 2018 (RLC). LO BB 6-25 v Surrey (Beckenham) 2018 (RLC). T20 HS 90. T20 BB 4-14.

^{NQ}**STEWART, Grant** (All Saints C, Maitland; U of Newcastle), b Kalgoorlie, W Australia 19 Feb 1994. 6'2". RHB, RMF. Squad No 9. UK qualified due to Italian mother. Debut (Kent) 2017. HS 103 and BB 6-22 v Middx (Canterbury) 2018. LO HS 44 v USA (North Sound) 2017-18. LO BB 3-17 v Guyana (Coolidge) 2017-18. T20 HS 5*. T20 BB 1-40.

THOMAS, Ivan Alfred Astley (John Roan S, Blackheath; Leeds U), b Greenwich, London 25 Sep 1991. 6'4". RHB, RMF. Squad No 5. Leeds/Bradford MCCU 2012-14. Kent debut 2012. HS 13 v Australians (Canterbury) 2015. CC HS 7* v Glos (Bristol) 2015. BB 5-91 v Leics (Leicester) 2018. LO HS 6 v Guyana (North Sound) 2017-18. LO BB 4-30 v Jamaica (North Sound) 2017-18. T20 HS 3*. T20 BB 2-42.

RELEASED/RETIRED

(Having made a County 1st XI appearance in 2018)

NQ**BRATHWAITE, Carlos** Ricardo, b Christ Church, Barbados 18 Jul 1988. RHB, RFM. CC&C 2010-11. Barbados 2011-12 to 2015-16. Kent 2018 (T20 only). IPL: DD 2016-17. SH 2018. Big Bash: ST 2016-17. SS 2017-18. Tests (WI): 3 (2015-16 to 2016); HS 69 v A (Sydney) 2015-16; BB 1-30 v A (Melbourne) 2015-16. **LOI** (WI): 33 (2011-12 to 2018-19); HS 50 v E (St George's) 2018-19; BB 5-27 v PNG (Harare) 2017-18. **IT20** (WI): 38 (2011-12 to 2018-19); HS 37* v P (Port of Spain) 2016-17; BB 3-20 v E (Chester-le-St) 2017. F-c Tours (WI): A 2015-16; SL 2014-15 (WI A). HS 109 Bar v T&T (Bridgetown) 2013-14. BB 7-90 CC&C v T&T (St Augustine) 2010-11 – on debut. LO HS 113 WI v SL Board Pres (Colombo, CC) 2015-16. LO BB 5-27 (*see LOI*). T20 HS 64*. T20 BB 4-15.

GIDMAN, William Robert Simon (Wycliffe C; Berkshire C of Agriculture), b High Wycombe, Bucks 14 Feb 1985. Younger brother of A.P.R.Gidman (Gloucestershire, Worcestershire 2002-15). 6'2". LHB, RM. Durham 2007. Gloucestershire 2011-14; cap 2011, becoming first player for Gs to score 1000 runs and take 50 wkts in debut season. Nottinghamshire 2015. Kent 2016-18. 1000 runs (1): 1006 (2011). HS 143 and BB 6-15 (10-43 match) Gs v Leics (Bristol) 2013 – only the fifth Gs player to score a century and take ten wkts in a match. K HS 99* v Sussex (Hove) 2016. 50 wkts (2); most – 55 (2013). K BB 5-47 v Pakistanis (Canterbury) 2018. LO HS 94 v Windward Is (Coolidge) 2016-17. LO BB 4-20 v Guyana (Coolidge) 2017-18. T20 HS 40*. T20 BB 2-23.

NQ**HENRY, Matthew** James, b Christchurch, New Zealand 14 Dec 1991. RHB, RFM. Canterbury 2010-11 to date. Worcestershire 2016. Kent 2018; cap 2018. Derbyshire 2017 (T20 only). IPL: KXIP 2017. **Tests** (NZ): 10 (2015 to 2018-19); HS 66 v A (Christchurch) 2015-16; BB 4-93 v E (Lord's) 2015 and 4-93 v SA (Hamilton) 2016-17. **LOI** (NZ): 43 (2013-14 to 2018-19); HS 48* v P (Wellington) 2015-16; BB 5-30 v P (Abu Dhabi) 2014-15. **IT20** (NZ): 6 (2014-15 to 2016-17); HS 10 v P (Auckland) 2015-16; BB 3-44 v SL (Mt Maunganui) 2015-16. F-c Tours (NZ): E 2014 (NZ A), 2015; A 2015-16; I 2016-17, 2017-18 (NZA); SL 2013-14 (NZ A). HS 81 v Derbys (Derby) 2018. 50 wkts (1): 75 (2018). BB 7-42 (11-114 match) v Northants (Canterbury) 2018. LO HS 48* (*see LOI*). LO BB 6-45 Canterbury v Auckland (Auckland) 2012-13. T20 HS 42. T20 BB 4-43.

HUNN, Matthew David (St Joseph's C, Ipswich), b Colchester, Essex 22 Mar 1994. 6'4". RHB, RMF. Kent 2013-18. Suffolk 2011-13. Kent HS 32* v Glos (Canterbury) 2016. BB 5-99 v Australians (Canterbury) 2015. CC BB 4-47 v Essex (Tunbridge W) 2015. LO HS 5* v Lancs (Canterbury) 2015 (RLC). LO BB 2-31 v Sussex (Canterbury) 2015 (RLC). T20 HS –. T20 BB 3-30.

NQ**STOINIS, Marcus** Peter (Hale S, Wembley Downs, Perth; U of WA), b Perth, W Australia 16 Aug 1989. RHB, RMF. W Australia 2008-09 to date. Victoria 2012-13 to 2016-17. Kent 2018 (T20 only). IPL: KXIP 2016-18. Big Bash: PS 2012-13. MS 2013-14 to date. **LOI** (A): 28 (2015 to 2018-19); HS 146* v NZ (Auckland) 2016-17; BB 3-34 v SA (Perth) 2018-19. **IT20** (A): 19 (2015 to 2018-19); HS 33* and BB 2-27 v I (Brisbane) 2018-19. F-c Tour (Aus A): I 2015. HS 170 Vic v Tas (Melbourne) 2013-14. BB 4-73 WA v Vic (Perth) 2018-19. LO HS 146* (*see LOI*). LO BB 4-43 Vic v SA (Sydney, BO) 2015-16. T20 HS 99. T20 BB 4-15.

J.C.Tredwell left the staff without making a County 1st XI appearance in 2018.

KENT 2018

RESULTS SUMMARY

	Place	Won	Lost	Drew	NR
Specsavers County Champ (2nd Division)	2nd	10	3	1	
All First-Class Matches		10	3	3	
Royal London One-Day Cup (South Group)	Finalist	7	4		
Vitality Blast (South Group)	QF	8	3		4

SPECSAVERS COUNTY CHAMPIONSHIP AVERAGES
BATTING AND FIELDING

Cap		M	I	NO	HS	Runs	Avge	100	50	Ct/St
2008	J.L.Denly	14	24	–	119	828	34.50	3	3	3
2018	H.G.Kuhn	14	26	3	96*	780	33.91	–	6	21
	Z.Crawley	14	24	–	168	755	31.45	1	4	11
2015	S.W.Billings	8	14	2	85	370	30.83	–	2	20/2
	S.R.Dickson	14	26	1	134*	710	28.40	3	1	25
	G.Stewart	10	17	1	103	414	25.87	1	2	3
2018	M.J.Henry	11	17	3	81	303	21.64	–	2	2
2015	D.J.Bell-Drummond	13	24	2	61	436	19.81	–	1	3
2005	D.I.Stevens	11	18	2	89	310	19.37	–	2	2
	H.W.Podmore	14	22	7	53	285	19.00	–	1	2
	A.E.N.Riley	4	6	3	23	56	18.66	–	–	6
	A.P.Rouse	7	11	–	55	187	17.00	–	1	24
	O.G.Robinson	3	4	–	26	59	14.75	–	–	1
	C.J.Haggett	2	4	–	31	53	13.25	–	–	
	W.R.S.Gidman	3	4	–	19	27	6.75	–	–	2
	I.A.A.Thomas	11	14	8	4*	17	2.83	–	–	6

Also batted: M.E.Claydon (1 match – cap 2016) 5, 0.

BOWLING

	O	M	R	W	Avge	Best	5wI	10wM
M.J.Henry	382.4	83	1161	75	15.48	7-42	5	3
J.L.Denly	160.1	28	426	23	18.52	4-36	–	–
D.I.Stevens	295.4	76	799	42	19.02	6-26	2	–
G.Stewart	164.5	26	505	22	22.95	6-22	1	–
H.W.Podmore	339.2	80	1002	43	23.30	6-36	1	–
I.A.A.Thomas	183	31	630	24	26.25	5-91	1	–

Also bowled:
A.E.N.Riley	134.2	33	334	9	37.11	4-68	–	–

D.J.Bell-Drummond 7-3-8-2; M.E.Claydon 11.4-0-27-2; W.R.S.Gidman 18.4-2-56-2; C.J.Haggett 18-7-44-4.

The First-Class Averages (pp 230–245) give the records of Kent players in all first-class county matches (Kent's other opponents being Oxford MCCU and the Pakistanis), with the exception of:
A.P.Rouse 9-12-1-55-199-18.09-0-1-26ct. Did not bowl.
S.W.Billings 7-9-2-70*-287-41.00-0-1-12ct.

KENT RECORDS

FIRST-CLASS CRICKET

Highest Total	For 803-4d		v	Essex	Brentwood	1934
	V 676		by	Australians	Canterbury	1921
Lowest Total	For 18		v	Sussex	Gravesend	1867
	V 16		by	Warwicks	Tonbridge	1913
Highest Innings	For 332	W.H.Ashdown	v	Essex	Brentwood	1934
	V 344	W.G.Grace	for	MCC	Canterbury	1876

Highest Partnership for each Wicket

1st	300	N.R.Taylor/M.R.Benson	v	Derbyshire	Canterbury	1991
2nd	382	S.R.Dickson/J.L.Denly	v	Northants	Beckenham	2017
3rd	323	R.W.T.Key/M.van Jaarsveld	v	Surrey	Tunbridge Wells	2005
4th	368	P.A.de Silva/G.R.Cowdrey	v	Derbyshire	Maidstone	1995
5th	277	F.E.Woolley/L.E.G.Ames	v	N Zealanders	Canterbury	1931
6th	315	P.A.de Silva/M.A.Ealham	v	Notts	Nottingham	1995
7th	248	A.P.Day/E.Humphreys	v	Somerset	Taunton	1908
8th	222	S.A.Northeast/J.C.Tredwell	v	Essex	Chelmsford	2016
9th	171	M.A.Ealham/P.A.Strang	v	Notts	Nottingham	1997
10th	235	F.E.Woolley/A.Fielder	v	Worcs	Stourbridge	1909

Best Bowling	For 10- 30	C.Blythe	v	Northants	Northampton	1907
(Innings)	V 10- 48	C.H.G.Bland	for	Sussex	Tonbridge	1899
Best Bowling	For 17- 48	C.Blythe	v	Northants	Northampton	1907
(Match)	V 17-106	T.W.J.Goddard	for	Glos	Bristol	1939

Most Runs – Season	2894	F.E.Woolley	(av 59.06)	1928
Most Runs – Career	47868	F.E.Woolley	(av 41.77)	1906-38
Most 100s – Season	10	F.E.Woolley		1928, 1934
Most 100s – Career	122	F.E.Woolley		1906-38
Most Wkts – Season	262	A.P.Freeman	(av 14.74)	1933
Most Wkts – Career	3340	A.P.Freeman	(av 17.64)	1914-36
Most Career W-K Dismissals	1253	F.H.Huish	(901 ct; 352 st)	1895-1914
Most Career Catches in the Field	773	F.E.Woolley		1906-38

LIMITED-OVERS CRICKET

Highest Total	50ov	384-6		v	Berkshire	Finchampstead	1994
		384-8		v	Surrey	Beckenham	2018
	40ov	337-7		v	Sussex	Canterbury	2013
	T20	231-7		v	Surrey	The Oval	2015
		231-5		v	Somerset	Canterbury	2018
Lowest Total	50ov	60		v	Somerset	Taunton	1979
	40ov	83		v	Middlesex	Lord's	1984
	T20	72		v	Hampshire	Southampton[2]	2011
Highest Innings	50ov	150*	J.L.Denly	v	Glamorgan	Canterbury	2018
	40ov	146	A.Symonds	v	Lancashire	Tunbridge Wells	2004
	T20	127	J.L.Denly	v	Essex	Chelmsford	2017
Best Bowling	50ov	8-31	D.L.Underwood	v	Scotland	Edinburgh	1987
	40ov	6- 9	R.A.Woolmer	v	Derbyshire	Chesterfield	1979
	T20	5-11	A.F.Milne	v	Somerset	Taunton	2017

LANCASHIRE

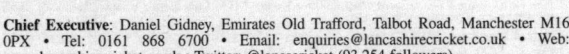

Formation of Present Club: 12 January 1864
Inaugural First-Class Match: 1865
Colours: Red, Green and Blue
Badge: Red Rose
County Champions (since 1890): (8) 1897, 1904, 1926, 1927, 1928, 1930, 1934, 2011
Joint Champions: (1) 1950
Gillette/NatWest Trophy Winners: (7) 1970, 1971, 1972, 1975, 1990, 1996, 1998
Benson and Hedges Cup Winners: (4) 1984, 1990, 1995, 1996
Pro 40/National League (Div 1) Winners: (1) 1999.
Sunday League Winners: (4) 1969, 1970, 1989, 1998
Twenty20 Cup Winners: (1) 2015

Chief Executive: Daniel Gidney, Emirates Old Trafford, Talbot Road, Manchester M16 0PX • Tel: 0161 868 6700 • Email: enquiries@lancashirecricket.co.uk • Web: www.lancashirecricket.co.uk • Twitter: @lancscricket (93,254 followers)

Director of Cricket: Paul Allott. **Head Coach**: Glen Chapple. **Assistant Coach/Development Director**: Mark Chilton. **Captain**: D.J.Vilas. **Overseas Players**: J.A.Burns, J.P.Faulkner (T20 only) and G.J.Maxwell. **2019 Testimonial**: S.J.Croft. **Head Groundsman**: Matthew Merchant. **Scorer**: Chris Rimmer. ‡ New registration. NQ Not qualified for England.

ANDERSON, James Michael (St Theodore RC HS and SFC, Burnley), b Burnley 30 Jul 1982. 6'2". LHB, RFM. Squad No 9. Debut (Lancashire) 2002; cap 2003; benefit 2012. Auckland 2007-08. YC 2003. *Wisden* 2008. OBE 2015. **ECB Test Central Contract 2018-19. Tests**: 148 (2003 to 2018-19); HS 81 v I (Nottingham) 2014, sharing a world Test record 10th wkt partnership of 198 with J.E.Root; 50 wkts (3); most – 57 (2010); BB 7-42 v WI (Lord's) 2017. **LOI**: 194 (2002-03 to 2014-15); HS 28 v NZ (Southampton) 2013; BB 5-23 v SA (Port Elizabeth) 2009-10. Hat-trick v P (Oval) 2003 – 1st for E in 373 LOI. **IT20**: 19 (2006-07 to 2009-10); HS 1* v A (Sydney) 2006-07; BB 3-23 v Netherlands (Lord's) 2009. F-c Tours: A 2006-07, 2010-11, 2013-14, 2017-18; SA 2004-05, 2009-10, 2015-16; WI 2003-04, 2005-06 (Eng A) (part), 2008-09, 2014-15, 2018-19; NZ 2007-08, 2012-13, 2017-18; I 2005-06 (part), 2008-09, 2012-13, 2016-17; SL 2003-04, 2007-08, 2011-12, 2018-19; UAE 2011-12 (v P), 2015-16 (v P). HS 81 (see *Tests*). La HS 42 v Surrey (Manchester) 2015. 50 wkts (4); most – 60 (2005, 2017). BB 7-42 (see *Tests*). La BB 7-77 v Essex (Chelmsford) 2015. Hat-trick v Essex (Manchester) 2003. LO HS 28 (see *LOI*). LO BB 5-23 (see *LOI*). T20 HS 16. T20 BB 3-23.

BAILEY, Thomas Ernest (Our Lady's Catholic HS, Preston), b Preston 21 Apr 1991. 6'4". RHB, RMF. Squad No 8. Debut (Lancashire) 2012; cap 2018. F-c Tour (EL): I 2018-19. HS 66 v Surrey (Manchester) 2018. 50 wkts (1): 65 (2018). BB 5-12 v Leics (Leicester) 2015. LO HS 33 v Yorks (Manchester) 2018 (RLC). LO BB 3-31 v Middx (Blackpool) 2015 (RLC). T20 HS 10. T20 BB 2-24.

BALDERSON, George Philip (Cheadle Hulme HS), b Manchester 11 Oct 2000. 5'11". LHB, RM. Lancashire 2nd XI debut 2018. England U19 2018-19. Awaiting 1st XI debut.

BOHANNON, Joshua James (Harper Green HS), b Bolton 9 Apr 1997. 5'8". RHB, RMF. Squad No 20. Debut (Lancashire) 2018. Lancashire 2nd XI debut 2014. HS 78* v Worcs (Southport) 2018. BB 3-46 v Hants (Southampton) 2018. LO HS 25 v Derbys (Derby) 2018 (RLC). LO BB –. T20 HS 23.

‡**NQBURNS, Joseph** Antony, b Herston, Brisbane, Australia 6 Sep 1989. RHB, RM. Queensland 2010-11 to date. Leicestershire 2013. Middlesex 2015. Glamorgan 2018 (T20 only). Big Bash: BH 2012-13 to date. **Tests** (A): 16 (2014-15 to 2018-19); HS 180 v SL (Canberra) 2018-19. **LOI** (A): 6 (2015); HS 69 v Ire (Belfast) 2015. F-c Tours (A): E 2012 (Aus A); SA 2017-18; NZ 2015-16; I 2015 (Aus A); SL 2016. HS 202* Q v SA (Cairns) 2017-18. CC HS 87 M v Worcs (Uxbridge) 2015. BB 1-0 Q v Tas (Brisbane) 2016-17. LO HS 154 Aus A v IA (Chennai) 2015. LO BB 1-20 Q v WA (Sydney, HO) 2018-19. T20 HS 81*. T20 BB 1-8.

BUTTLER, Joseph Charles (King's C, Taunton), b Taunton, Somerset 8 Sep 1990. 6'0". RHB, WK. Squad No 6. Somerset 2009-13; cap 2013. Lancashire debut 2014; cap 2018. IPL: MI 2016-17. RR 2018. Big Bash: MR 2013-14, ST 2017-18 to date. **ECB Test & L-O Central Contract 2018-19. Tests**: 31 (2014 to 2018-19); HS 106 v I (Nottingham) 2018. **LOI**: 127 (2011-12 to 2018-19); HS 150 v WI (St George's) 2018-19. **IT20**: 66 (2011 to 2018-19); HS 73* v SL (Southampton) 2016. HS 144 Sm v Hants (Southampton) 2010. La HS 100* v Durham (Chester-le-St) 2014. BB –. LO HS 150 (*see LOI*). T20 HS 95*.

CROFT, Steven John (Highfield HS, Blackpool; Myerscough C), b Blackpool 11 Oct 1984. 5'10". RHB, OB. Squad No 15. Debut (Lancashire) 2005; cap 2010; captain 2017; testimonial 2018. Auckland 2008-09. HS 156 v Northants (Manchester) 2014. BB 6-41 v Worcs (Manchester) 2012. LO HS 127 v Warwks (Birmingham) 2017 (RLC). LO BB 4-24 v Scotland (Manchester) 2008 (FPT). T20 HS 94*. T20 BB 3-6.

DAVIES, Alexander Luke (Queen Elizabeth GS, Blackburn), b Darwen 23 Aug 1994. 5'7". RHB, WK. Squad No 17. Debut (Lancashire) 2012; cap 2017. Lancashire 2nd XI debut 2011. F-c Tour (EL): WI 2017-18. 1000 runs (1): 1046 (2017). HS 140* v Essex (Chelmsford) 2017. LO HS 147 v Durham (Manchester) 2018 (RLC). T20 HS 94*.

NQFAULKNER, James Peter, b Launceston, Tasmania, Australia 29 Apr 1990. Son of P.I.Faulkner (Tasmania 1982-83 to 1989-90). 6'1". RHB, LMF. Squad No 44. Tasmania 2008-09 to date. Lancashire debut 2016. IPL: PW 2011. KXIP 2012. RR 2013-15. GL 2016-17 Big Bash: MS 2011-12 to 2017-18. HH 2018-19. **Tests** (A): 1 (2013); HS 23 and BB 4-51 (Oval) 2013. **LOI** (A): 69 (2012-13 to 2017-18); HS 116 v I (Bangalore) 2013-14; BB 4-32 v P (Brisbane) 2016-17. **IT20** (A): 24 (2011-12 to 2016-17); HS 41* v SA (Adelaide) 2014-15; BB 5-27 v P (Mohali) 2015-16. F-c Tour (A): E 2013. HS 121 v Surrey (Oval) 2015. BB 5-5 Tas v SA (Hobart) 2010-11. La BB 5-39 v Essex (Manchester) 2015. LO HS 116 (*see LOI*). LO BB 4-20 Tas v Vic (Melbourne) 2010-11. T20 HS 73. T20 BB 5-16.

GLEESON, Richard James (Baines HS), b Blackpool, Lancs 2 Dec 1987. 6'3". RHB, RFM. Squad No 34. Northamptonshire 2015-18. Lancashire debut 2018. MCC 2018. Cumberland 2010-15. F-c Tour (EL): WI 2017-18. HS 31 Nh v Glos (Bristol) 2016. La HS 9* v Yorks (Leeds) 2018. BB 6-79 Nh v Kent (Canterbury) 2018. La BB 3-34 v Hants (Southampton) 2018. Hat-trick MCC v Essex (Bridgetown) 2017-18. LO HS 13 EL v West Indies A (Coolidge) 2017-18. LO BB 5-47 v Worcs (Worcester) 2016 (RLC). T20 HS 7*. T20 BB 3-12.

GUEST, Brooke David (Kent Street Senior HS, Perth, WA; Murdoch U, Perth), b Whitworth Park, Manchester 14 May 1997. 5'11''. RHB, WK. Squad No 29. Debut (Lancashire) 2018. Lancashire 2nd XI debut 2016. HS 8 v Hants (Southampton) 2018 – only 1st XI appearance.

HAMEED, Haseeb (Bolton S), b Bolton 17 Jan 1997. 6'2''. RHB, LB. Squad No 23. Debut (Lancashire) 2015; cap 2016. Lancashire 2nd XI debut 2013. England U19 2014-15 to 2015. **Tests**: 3 (2016-17); HS 82 v I (Rajkot) 2016-17 – on debut. F-c Tours: WI 2017-18 (EL); I 2016-17; SL 2016-17 (EL). 1000 runs (1): 1198 (2016). HS 122 v Notts (Nottingham) 2016. BB –. LO HS 88 v Leics (Manchester) 2017 (RLC).

HARTLEY, Tom (Merchant Taylors S), b 3 May 1998. RHB, SLA. Lancashire 2nd XI debut 2018. Awaiting 1st XI debut.

HURT, Liam Jack (Balshaw's CE HS, Leyland), b Preston 15 Mar 1994. 6'4''. RHB, RMF. Squad No 22. Awaiting f-c debut. LO HS 15 and LO BB 2-59 Le v Durham (Leicester) 2015 (RLC) – only 1st XI appearance.

JENNINGS, Keaton Kent (King Edward VII S, Johannesburg), b Johannesburg, South Africa 19 Jun 1992. Son of R.V.Jennings (Transvaal 1973-74 to 1992-93), brother of D.Jennings (Gauteng and Easterns 1999 to 2003-04), nephew of K.E.Jennings (Northern Transvaal 1981-82 to 1982-83). 6'4''. LHB, RM. Squad No 1. Gauteng 2011-12. Durham 2012-17; captain 2017 (1-o only). Lancashire debut/cap 2018. **Tests**: 17 (2016-17 to 2018-19); HS 146* v SL (Galle) 2018-19; scored 112 v I (Mumbai) on debut; BB –. F-c Tours (C=Captain): WI 2017-18 (EL)C, 2018-19; I 2016-17; SL 2016-17 (EL), 2018-19. 1000 runs (1): 1602 (2016), inc seven hundreds (Du record). HS 221* Du v Yorks (Chester-le-St) 2016. La HS 177 v Worcs (Worcester) 2018. BB 3-37 Du v Sussex (Chester-le-St) 2017. La BB –. LO HS 139 Du v Warwks (Birmingham) 2017 (RLC). LO BB 2-19 v Worcs (Worcester) 2018 (RLC). T20 HS 88. T20 BB 4-37.

JONES, Robert Peter (Bridgewater HS), b Warrington, Cheshire 3 Nov 1995. 5'10''. RHB, LB. Squad No 12. Debut (Lancashire) 2016. Lancashire 2nd XI debut 2013. Cheshire 2014. England U19 2014. HS 106* v Middx (Manchester) 2016. BB 1-18 v Worcs (Worcester) 2018. LO HS 17 v Derbys (Derby) 2018 (RLC). T20 HS –.

LAMB, Daniel John (St Michael's HS, Chorley; Cardinal Newman C, Preston), b Preston 7 Sep 1995. 6'0''. RHB, RM. Squad No 26. Debut (Lancashire) 2018. Lancashire 2nd XI debut 2013. HS 20* v Somerset (Taunton) 2018. BB – . LO HS 4* and LO BB 2-51 v Durham (Chester-le-St) 2017 (RLC). T20 HS 24. T20 BB 3-30.

LAVELLE, George Isaac Davies (Merchant Taylors S), b 24 Mar 2000. 5.8''. LHB. WK. Lancashire 2nd XI debut 2017. England U19 2018. Awaiting 1st XI debut.

LESTER, Toby James (Rossall S; Loughborough U), b Blackpool 5 Apr 1993. 6'4''. LHB, LMF. Squad No 5. Loughborough MCCU 2012-14. Lancashire debut 2015. MCC Univs 2012-14. HS 8 (twice) v Worcs (Southport) 2018. BB 3-50 v Essex (Manchester) 2015. T20 HS 7*. T20 BB 4-25.

LIVINGSTONE, Liam Stephen (Chetwynde S, Barrow-in-Furness), b Barrow-in-Furness, Cumberland 4 Aug 1993. 6'1''. RHB, LB. Squad No 7. Debut (Lancashire) 2016; cap 2017; captain 2018. **IT20**: 2 (2017); HS 16 v SA (Taunton) 2017. F-c Tours (EL): WI 2017-18; SL 2016-17. HS 224 v Warwks (Manchester) 2017. BB 6-52 v Surrey (Manchester) 2017. LO HS 129 EL v SA A (Northampton) 2017. LO BB 3-51 v Yorks (Manchester) 2016 (RLC). T20 HS 100. T20 BB 4-17.

MAHMOOD, Saqib (Matthew Moss HS, Rochdale), b Birmingham, Warwks 25 Feb 1997. 6'3''. RHB, RFM. Squad No 25. Debut (Lancashire) 2016. England U19 2014. F-c Tour (EL): WI 2017-18. HS 9 EL v WI A (North Sound) 2017-18. La HS 4* v Yorks (Leeds) 2017. BB 4-50 v Surrey (Manchester) 2017. LO HS 27* North v South (Dubai, DCS) 2016-17. LO BB 5-60 North v South (Bridgetown) 2017-18. T20 HS –. T20 BB 4-14.

‡NQ**MAXWELL, Glenn** James, b Kew, Melbourne, Australia 14 Oct 1988. 5'9''. RHB, OB. Squad No 32. Victoria 2010-11 to date. Hampshire 2014. Yorkshire 2015. IPL: DD 2012 and 2018. MI 2013. KXIP 2014-17. Big Bash: MR 2011-12. MS 2012-13 to date. **Tests** (A): 7 (2012-13 to 2017); HS 104 v I (Ranchi) 2016-17; BB 4-127 v I (Hyderabad) 2012-13. **LOI** (A): 95 (2012 to 2018-19); HS 102 v SL (Sydney) 2014-15; BB 4-46 v E (Perth) 2014-15. **IT20** (A): 59 (2012 to 2018-19); HS 145* v SL (Pallekele) 2016; BB 3-10 v E (Hobart) 2014-15. F-c Tours (A): I 2012-13, 2016-17; SA/Z 2013 (Aus A); B 2017; UAE 2014-15 (v P). HS 278 Vic v NSW (Sydney, NO) 2017-18. CC HS 140 Y v Durham (Scarborough) 2015. BB 4-42 Vic v SA (Melbourne) 2012-13. CC BB 3-55 Y v Middx (Leeds) 2015. LO HS 146 H v Lancs (Manchester) 2014 (RLC). LO BB 4-46 (*see LOI*). T20 HS 145*. T20 BB 3-10.

MORLEY, Jack P., b Rochdale 25 Jun 1991. LHB, SLA. Lancashire 2nd XI debut 2018. England U19 2018-19. Awaiting 1st XI debut.

ONIONS, Graham (St Thomas More RC S, Blaydon), b Gateshead, Tyne & Wear 9 Sep 1982. 6'1''. RHB, RFM. Squad No 99. Durham 2004-17; benefit 2015. Dolphins 2013-14. Lancashire debut/cap 2018. MCC 2007-08, 2015-16. *Wisden* 2009. **Tests**: 9 (2009 to 2012); HS 17* v A (Lord's) 2009; BB 5-38 v WI (Lord's) 2009 – on debut. **LOI**: 4 (2009 to 2009-10); HS 1 v A (Centurion) 2009-10; BB 2-58 v SL (Johannesburg) 2009-10. F-c Tours: SA 2009-10; NZ 2012-13; I 2007-08 (EL), 2012-13; SL 2013-14; B 2006-07 (Eng A); UAE 2011-12 (*part*). HS 65 Du v Notts (Chester-le-St) 2016. La HS 41 v Essex (Manchester) 2018. 50 wkts (8); most – 73 (2013). BB 9-67 Du v Notts (Nottingham) 2012. La BB 6-55 v Notts (Nottingham) 2018. LO HS 30* v Worcs (Worcester) 2018 (RLC). LO BB 4-45 Du v Lancs (Chester-le-St) 2013 (Y40). T20 HS 31. T20 BB 3-15.

PARKINSON, Matthew William (Bolton S), b Bolton 24 Oct 1996. Twin brother of C.F.Parkinson (*see LEICESTERSHIRE*). 6'0''. RHB, LB. Squad No 28. Debut (Lancashire) 2016. Staffordshire 2014. England U19 2015. HS 13 v Middx (Lord's) 2017. BB 5-49 v Warwks (Manchester) 2016 – on debut. LO HS 15* EL v WI A (Coolidge) 2017-18. LO BB 5-68 v Notts (Manchester) 2018. T20 HS 7*. T20 BB 4-23.

PARRY, Stephen David (Audenshaw HS), b Manchester 12 Jan 1986. 6'0''. RHB, SLA. Squad No 4. Debut (Lancashire) 2007, taking 5-23 v Durham U (Durham); cap 2015. Cumberland 2005-06. Big Bash: BH 2014-15. **LOI**: 2 (2013-14); HS – ; BB 3-32 v WI (North Sound) 2013-14. **IT20**: 5 (2013-14 to 2015-16); HS 1 v Netherlands (Chittagong) 2013-14; BB 2-33 v P (Dubai, DSC) 2015-16. HS 44 v Somerset (Manchester) 2017. CC BB 5-45 v Middx (Southport) 2017. BB 5-23 (*see above*). LO HS 31 v Essex (Chelmsford) 2009 (FPT). LO BB 5-17 v Surrey (Manchester) 2013 (Y40). T20 HS 15*. T20 BB 5-13 v Worcs (Manchester) 2016 – La record.

NQ**VILAS, Dane** James, b Johannesburg, South Africa 10 Jun 1985. 6'2''. RHB, WK. Squad No 33. Gauteng 2006-07 to 2009-10. Lions 2008-09 to 2009-10. W Province 2010-11. Cape Cobras 2011-12 to 2016-17. Lancashire debut 2017; cap 2018; captain 2019. Dolphins 2017-18 to date. **Tests** (SA): 6 (2015 to 2015-16); HS 26 v E (Johannesburg) 2015-16. **IT20** (SA): 1 (2011-12); HS –. F-c Tours (SA): A 2016 (SA A), I 2015 (SA A), 2015-16; Z 2016 (SA A), B 2015. HS 244 v Hants (Manchester) 2017. LO HS 120 Gauteng v Namibia (Windhoek) 2009-10 and 120 WP v Namibia (Windhoek) 2010-11. T20 HS 71*

(Having made a County 1st XI appearance in 2018)

BROWN, Karl Robert (Hesketh Fletcher HS, Atherton), b Bolton 17 May 1988. 5'10". RHB, RMF. Lancashire 2006-18; cap 2015. Moors Sports Club 2011-12. HS 132 v Glamorgan (Manchester) 2015. BB 2-30 v Notts (Nottingham) 2009. LO HS 129 v Yorks (Manchester) 2014 (RLC). T20 HS 69.

NQCHANDERPAUL, Shivnarine (Cove and John SS, Unity Village), b Unity Village, Demerara, Guyana 16 Aug 1974. 5'8". LHB, LB. Guyana 1991-92 to date. Durham 2007-09. Lancashire 2010-18; cap 2010. Warwickshire 2011. Derbyshire 2013-14; cap 2014. IPL: RCB 2007-08. *Wisden* 2007. **Tests** (WI): 164 (1993-94 to 2015, 14 as captain); 1000 runs (1): 1065 (2002); HS 203* v SA (Georgetown) 2004-05; BB 1-2 v A (Adelaide) 1996-97. **LOI** (WI): 268 (1994-95 to 2010-11, 16 as captain); HS 150 v SA (E London) 1998-99; BB 3-18 v I (Sharjah) 1997-98. **IT20** (WI): 22 (2005-06 to 2010); HS 41 v E (Oval) 2007. F-c Tours (WI) (C=Captain): E 1995, 2000, 2004, 2007, 2009, 2012; A 1995-96, 1996-97, 2000-01, 2005-06C, 2009-10; SA 1998-99, 2003-04, 2007-08, 2014-15; NZ 1994-95, 1999-00, 2005-06C, 2008-09, 2013-14; I 1994-95, 2002-03, 2011-12, 2013-14; P 1997-98, 2001-02 (Sharjah), 2006-07; SL 2005C, 2010-11; Z 2001, 2003-04; B 1999-00, 2002-03, 2011-12, 2012-13; K 2001. 1000 runs (1+1); most – 1107 (2004-05). HS 303* Guyana v Jamaica (Kingston) 1995-96. CC HS 201* Du v Worcs (Worcester) 2009. La HS 182 v Surrey (Oval) 2017. BB 4-48 Guyana v Leeward Is (Basseterre) 1992-93. LO HS 150 (*see LOI*). LO BB 4-22 Guyana v Trinidad (Hampton Court) 1995-96. T20 HS 87*.

CLARK, J. – *see SURREY.*

LILLEY, A.M. – *see LEICESTERSHIRE.*

NQMENNIE, Joe Matthew, b Coffs Harbour, NSW, Australia 24 Dec 1988. 6'3". RHB, RMF. South Australia 2011-12 to date. Lancashire 2018. Big Bash: PS 2012-13 to 2013-14. HH 2014-15 to 2015-16. SS 2015-16. MR 2017-18 to date. **Tests** (A): 1 (2016-17); HS 10 and BB 1-85 v SA (Hobart) 2016-17. **LOI** (A): 2 (2016-17); HS 1 v SA (Johannesburg) 2016-17; HS 81* Sc v PNG (Port Moresby) 2012-13. La HS 68* v Surrey (Manchester) 2018. 50 wkts (0+1): 51 (2015-16). BB 7-96 SA v WA (Perth) 2011-12. La BB 4-43 v Worcs (Worcester) 2018. LO HS 43* SA v Cricket Australia (Brisbane, AB) 2017-18. LO BB 5-36 SA v Q (Brisbane, AB) 2017-18. T20 HS 5. T20 BB 3-20.

NQWATT, Mark Robert James, b Edinburgh, Scotland 29 Jul 1996. LHB, SLA. Scotland 2016 to date. Lancashire 2018 (T20 only). **LOI** (Scot): 18 (2016 to 2018); HS 31* v Ire (Harare) 2017-18; BB 3-21 v PNG (Dubai, DSC) 2017-18. **IT20** (Scot): 26 (2015 to 2018-19); HS 11* v Hong Kong (Mong Kok) 2015-16; BB 5-27 v Netherlands (Dubai, ICCA) 2015-16. HS 81* Sc v PNG (Port Moresby) 2017-18. BB 3-60 Sc v Ire (Dubai, DSC) 2017-18. LO HS 36 Sc v Oman (Al Amerat) 2018-19. LO BB 3-21 (*see LOI*). T20 HS 11*. T20 BB 5-27.

NQZAHIR KHAN, b Afghanistan 20 Dec 1998. LHB, SLC. Afghanistan 2015-16 to date. Mis Ainak Region 2017-18. Lancashire 2018 (T20 only). **LOI** (Afg): 1 (2018-19); HS – ; BB 2-55 v Ire (Dehradun) 2018-19. **IT20** (Afg): 1 (2018-19); HS 1* Afg v PNG (Sharjah) 2015-16. BB 5-31 Afg v Namibia (Greater Noida) 2016. LO HS 1 and LO BB 6-36 Band-e-Amir v Speen Ghar (Khost) 2017. T20 HS 4. T20 BB 5-19.

S.C.Kerrigan left the staff without making a County 1st XI appearance in 2018.

LANCASHIRE 2018

RESULTS SUMMARY

	Place	Won	Lost	Tied	Drew	NR
Specsavers County Champ (1st Division)	7th	3	7	1	3	
All First-Class Matches		3	7	1	4	
Royal London One-Day Cup (North Group)	6th	3	4			1
Vitality Blast (North Group)	SF	9	6			1

SPECSAVERS COUNTY CHAMPIONSHIP AVERAGES
BATTING AND FIELDING

Cap		M	I	NO	HS	Runs	Avge	100	50	Ct/St
2018	K.K.Jennings	10	16	1	177	709	47.26	3	1	9
2018	D.J.Vilas	14	23	2	235*	792	37.71	3	1	50/4
	J.Clark	10	16	–	82	538	33.62	–	5	2
	J.M.Mennie	7	11	4	68*	232	33.14	–	2	1
	J.J.Bohannon	5	9	1	78*	255	31.87	–	2	2
2017	A.L.Davies	14	24	–	115	732	30.50	1	5	19/1
2017	L.S.Livingstone	10	16	2	48*	336	24.00	–	–	15
2010	S.J.Croft	8	13	–	62	276	21.23	–	2	10
2010	S.Chanderpaul	8	13	–	65	257	19.76	–	2	–
	R.P.Jones	5	8	–	68	137	17.12	–	1	6
2015	K.R.Brown	2	4	–	43	67	16.75	–	–	1
2018	T.E.Bailey	14	22	2	66	308	15.40	–	1	5
	D.J.Lamb	4	6	2	20*	57	14.25	–	–	1
	K.A.Maharaj	3	5	–	38	66	13.20	–	–	2
2016	H.Hameed	10	17	–	31	165	9.70	–	–	6
2018	G.Onions	12	19	4	41	135	9.00	–	–	1
	M.W.Parkinson	6	11	5	9*	35	5.83	–	–	1
2003	J.M.Anderson	3	4	–	8	14	3.50	–	–	1
	S.D.Parry	3	4	–	6	7	1.75	–	–	–

Also batted: J.C.Buttler (1 match – cap 2018) 3, 59 (2 ct); R.J.Gleeson (2) 9*, 0*, 0*; B.D.Guest (1) 8, 0; T.J.Lester (1) 8, 8; A.M.Lilley (1) 28; S.Mahmood (1) 0.

BOWLING

	O	M	R	W	Avge	Best	5wI	10wM
K.A.Maharaj	103.4	23	283	17	16.64	7- 37	1	1
R.J.Gleeson	57	15	196	10	19.60	3- 34	–	–
T.E.Bailey	439.4	106	1258	64	19.65	5- 53	1	–
J.M.Mennie	192.5	44	601	28	21.46	4- 43	–	–
G.Onions	379.3	72	1241	57	21.77	6- 55	2	–
J.Clark	198.3	22	688	24	28.66	5- 58	1	–
M.W.Parkinson	155.1	23	481	16	30.06	5-101	1	–
Also bowled:								
J.J.Bohannon	27	3	103	5	20.60	3- 46	–	–
L.S.Livingstone	86.5	18	214	7	30.57	3- 27	–	–
J.M.Anderson	100	29	280	9	31.11	4- 26	–	–

S.J.Croft 7-2-11-0; K.K.Jennings 14-0-92-0; R.P.Jones 6-0-19-1; D.J.Lamb 28-1-146-0; T.J.Lester 27.1-2-78-3; A.M.Lilley 28.3-6-89-2; S.Mahmood 21-4-57-2; S.D.Parry 97-14-274-3.

The First-Class Averages (pp 230–245) give the records of their players in all first-class county matches (Lancashire's other opponents being Loughborough MCCU), with the exception of J.M.Anderson, J.C.Buttler and R.J.Gleeson, whose first-class figures for Lancashire are as above, and:
K.K.Jennings 11-17-1-177-753-47.06-3-1-10ct. 19-0-109-0.

LANCASHIRE RECORDS

FIRST-CLASS CRICKET

Highest Total	For 863		v	Surrey	The Oval	1990
	V 707-9d		by	Surrey	The Oval	1990
Lowest Total	For 25		v	Derbyshire	Manchester	1871
	V 20		by	Essex	Chelmsford	2013
Highest Innings	For 424	A.C.MacLaren	v	Somerset	Taunton	1895
	V 315*	T.W.Hayward	for	Surrey	The Oval	1898

Highest Partnership for each Wicket

1st	368	A.C.MacLaren/R.H.Spooner	v	Glos	Liverpool	1903
2nd	371	F.B.Watson/G.E.Tyldesley	v	Surrey	Manchester	1928
3rd	501	A.N.Petersen/A.G.Prince	v	Glamorgan	Colwyn Bay	2015
4th	358	S.P.Titchard/G.D.Lloyd	v	Essex	Chelmsford	1996
5th	360	S.G.Law/C.L.Hooper	v	Warwicks	Birmingham	2003
6th	278	J.Iddon/H.R.W.Butterworth	v	Sussex	Manchester	1932
7th	248	G.D.Lloyd/I.D.Austin	v	Yorkshire	Leeds	1997
8th	158	J.Lyon/R.M.Ratcliffe	v	Warwicks	Manchester	1979
9th	142	L.O.S.Poidevin/A.Kermode	v	Sussex	Eastbourne	1907
10th	173	J.Briggs/R.Pilling	v	Surrey	Liverpool	1885

Best Bowling	For	10-46	W.Hickton	v	Hampshire	Manchester	1870
(Innings)	V	10-40	G.O.B.Allen	for	Middlesex	Lord's	1929
Best Bowling	For	17-91	H.Dean	v	Yorkshire	Liverpool	1913
(Match)	V	16-65	G.Giffen	for	Australians	Manchester	1886

Most Runs – Season	2633	J.T.Tyldesley	(av 56.02)		1901
Most Runs – Career	34222	G.E.Tyldesley	(av 45.20)		1909-36
Most 100s – Season	11	C.Hallows			1928
Most 100s – Career	90	G.E.Tyldesley			1909-36
Most Wkts – Season	198	E.A.McDonald	(av 18.55)		1925
Most Wkts – Career	1816	J.B.Statham	(av 15.12)		1950-68
Most Career W-K Dismissals	925	G.Duckworth	(635 ct; 290 st)		1923-38
Most Career Catches in the Field	556	K.J.Grieves			1949-64

LIMITED-OVERS CRICKET

Highest Total	50ov	381-3		v	Herts	Radlett	1999
	40ov	324-4		v	Worcs	Worcester	2012
	T20	231-4		v	Yorkshire	Manchester	2015
Lowest Total	50ov	59		v	Worcs	Worcester	1963
	40ov	68		v	Yorkshire	Leeds	2000
		68		v	Surrey	The Oval	2002
	T20	91		v	Derbyshire	Manchester	2003
Highest Innings	50ov	162*	A.R.Crook	v	Bucks	Wormsley	2005
	40ov	143	A.Flintoff	v	Essex	Chelmsford	1999
	T20	103*	A.N.Petersen	v	Leics	Leicester	2016
Best Bowling	50ov	6-10	C.E.H.Croft	v	Scotland	Manchester	1982
	40ov	6-25	G.Chapple	v	Yorkshire	Leeds	1998
	T20	5-13	S.D.Parry	v	Worcs	Manchester	2016

LEICESTERSHIRE

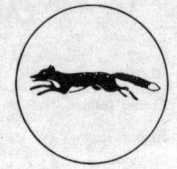

Formation of Present Club: 25 March 1879
Inaugural First-Class Match: 1894
Colours: Dark Green and Scarlet
Badge: Gold Running Fox on Green Ground
County Champions: (3) 1975, 1996, 1998
Benson and Hedges Cup Winners: (3) 1972, 1975, 1985
Sunday League Champions: (2) 1974, 1977
Twenty20 Cup Winners: (3) 2004, 2006, 2011

Chief Executive: Karen Rothery, Fischer County Ground, Grace Road, Leicester LE2 8EB • Tel: 0116 283 2128 • Email: enquiries@leicestershireccc.co.uk • Web: www.leicestershireccc.co.uk • Twitter: @leicsccc (49,011 followers)

Head Coach: Paul Nixon. **Assistant Coach:** John Sadler. **Captain:** P.J.Horton. **Overseas Players:** C.N.Ackermann and Mohammad Abbas. **2019 Testimonial:** None. **Head Groundsman:** Andy Ward. **Scorer:** Paul Rogers. ‡ New registration. NQ Not qualified for England.

NQ**ACKERMANN, Colin** Niel (Grey HS, Port Elizabeth; U of SA), b George, South Africa 4 Apr 1991. RHB, OB. Squad No 48. Eastern Province 2010-11 to 2015-16. Warriors 2013-14 to date. Leicestershire debut 2017. 1000 runs (0+1): 1200 (2013-14). HS 196* v Middx (Leicester) 2018. BB 3-45 v Northants (Northampton) 2017. LO HS 92 Warriors v Cobras (Port Elizabeth) 2015-16. LO BB 4-48 Warriors v Dolphins (Durban) 2017-18. T20 HS 79*. T20 BB 3-21.

ALI, Aadil Masud (Lancaster S, Leicester; Q Elizabeth C), b Leicester 29 Dec 1994. 5'11". RHB, OB. Squad No 14. Debut (Leicestershire) 2015. Leicestershire 2nd XI debut 2013. HS 80 v Glos (Leicester) 2015. BB 1-10 v Worcs (Worcester) 2017. LO HS 88 v Worcs (Leicester) 2017 (RLC). LO BB 1-31 v Notts (Mkt Warsop) 2017 (RLC). T20 HS 35*. T20 BB 2-22.

BUTCHART, Donald Norton (Oakham S), b Harare, Zimbabwe 18 Dec 1998. Son of I.P.Butchart (Zimbabwe & Mashonaland 1980-81 to 1994-95). RHB, RM. Awaiting f-c debut. Leicestershire 2nd XI debut 2018. LO HS 12 v India A (Leicester) 2012.

NQ**COSGROVE, Mark** James, b Elizabeth, Adelaide, S Australia 14 Jun 1984. 5'9". LHB, RM. Squad No 55. S Australia 2002-03 to 2015-16. Glamorgan 2006-10; cap 2006. Tasmania 2010-11 to 2013-14. Leicestershire debut/cap 2015; captain 2015-17. Big Bash: HH 2011-12. ST 2012-13 to 2014-15. SS 2013-14. **LOI** (A): 3 (2005-06 to 2006-07); HS 74 v B (Fatullah) 2005-06 – on debut; BB 1-1 v WI (Kuala Lumpur) 2006-07. 1000 runs (4); most – 1279 (2016). HS 233 Gm v Derbys (Derby) 2006. Le HS 188 v Derbys (Derby) 2017. BB 3-3 SA v Tas (Adelaide) 2006-07. CC BB Gm 3-30 v Derbys (Derby) 2009. Le BB 2-14 v Worcs (Worcester) 2016. LO HS 121 SA v WA (Perth) 2005-06. LO BB 2-21 SA v Q (Brisbane) 2005-06. T20 HS 89. T20 BB 2-11.

‡**DAVIS, Will**iam Samuel (Stafford GS), b 6 Mar 1996. 6'1". RHB, RFM. Squad No 44. Derbyshire 2015-18. Derbyshire 2nd XI debut 2013. HS 25 De v Sussex (Hove) 2016. BB 7-146 De v Glamorgan (Colwyn Bay) 2016. LO HS –.

DEARDEN, Harry Edward (Tottington HS), b Bury, Lancs 7 May 1997. LHB, OB. Squad No 5. Debut (Leicestershire) 2016. Lancashire 2nd XI 2014-15. Cheshire 2016. HS 87 v Glamorgan (Leicester) 2017. BB 1-0 v Kent (Leicester) 2017. LO HS 31 v India A (Leicester) 2018.

DEXTER, Neil John (Northwood HS, Durban; Varsity C; U of South Africa), b Johannesburg, South Africa 21 Aug 1984. 6'0''. RHB, RMF. Squad No 17. Kent 2005-08. Essex 2008. Middlesex 2009-15; cap 2010; captain 2010 (*part*) to 2013. Leicestershire debut 2016. Qualified for England in 2010. HS 163* M v Northants (Northampton) 2014. Le HS 136 v Glos (Leicester) 2016. BB 6-63 M v Lancs (Lord's) 2014. Le BB 5-52 v Sussex (Leicester) 2016. LO HS 135* K v Glamorgan (Cardiff) 2006 (CGT). LO BB 4-22 v Lancs (Leicester) 2016 (RLC). T20 HS 73. T20 BB 4-21.

EVANS, Samuel Thomas (Lancaster S, Leicester; Wyggeston & QE I C; Leicester U), b Leicester 20 Dec 1997. RHB, OB. Squad No 21. Loughborough MCCU 2017-18. Leicestershire debut 2017. Leicestershire 2nd XI debut 2015. HS 114 LU v Northants (Northampton) 2017. Le HS 29 v Northants (Leicester) 2017 and 29 v Derbys (Derby) 2018. LO HS 20 v India A (Leicester) 2018.

FUNNELL, James Harry (Uppingham S), b Leicester 31 May 1999. LHB, RM. Leicestershire 2nd XI debut 2018. Awaiting f-c debut. LO HS 1* and LO BB 1-67 v India A (Leicester) 2018 – only 1st XI appearance.

GRIFFITHS, Gavin Timothy (St Mary's C, Crosby), b Ormskirk, Lancs 19 Nov 1993. 6'2''. RHB, RMF. Squad No 93. Debut (Leicestershire) 2017. Lancashire 2014-15 (l-o only). Hampshire 2016 (T20 only). HS 40 v Middx (Leicester) 2018. BB 6-49 (10-83 match) v Durham (Chester-le-St) 2018. LO HS 15* v Notts (Leicester) 2018 (RLC). LO BB 4-30 v Northants (Northampton) 2018 (RLC). T20 HS 11. T20 BB 3-28.

HILL, Lewis John (Hastings HS, Hinckley; John Cleveland C), b Leicester 5 Oct 1990. 5'7½''. RHB, WK, occ RM. Squad No 23. Debut (Leicestershire) 2015. Unicorns 2012-13. HS 126 v Surrey (Oval) 2015. LO HS 86 v Durham (Leicester) 2015 (RLC). T20 HS 31*.

HORTON, Paul James (St Margaret's HS, Liverpool), b Sydney, Australia 20 Sep 1982. 5'10''. RHB, RM. Squad No 2. UK resident since 1997. Lancashire 2003-15; cap 2007. Matabeleland Tuskers 2010-11 to 2011-12. Leicestershire debut 2016; captain 2018 (*part*) to date. 1000 runs (3); most – 1116 (2007). HS 209 MT v SR (Masvingo) 2010-11. CC HS 173 La v Somerset (Taunton) 2009. Le HS 117* v Worcs (Worcester) 2016. BB 2-6 v Sussex (Leicester) 2016. LO HS 111* La v Derbys (Manchester) 2009 (FPT). LO BB 1-7 v Lancs (Leicester) 2016 (RLC). T20 HS 71*.

JAVID, Ateeq (Aston Manor S), b Birmingham 15 Oct 1991. 5'8''. RHB, OB. Squad No 99. Warwickshire 2009-17. Leicestershire debut 2018. HS 133 Wa v Somerset (Birmingham) 2013. Le HS 58 v Durham (Leicester) 2018. BB 1-1 Wa v Lancs (Manchester) 2014. Le BB 1-30 v Sussex (Leicester) 2018. LO HS 43 Wa v Kent (Canterbury) 2013 (Y40). LO BB 4-42 Wa v Yorks (Leeds) 2016 (RLC). T20 HS 51*. T20 BB 4-17.

^{NQ}**KLEIN, Dieter** (Hoerskool, Lichtenburg), b Lichtenburg, South Africa 31 Oct 1988. 5'10''. RHB, LMF. Squad No 77. North West 2007-08 to 2015-16. Lions 2012-13 to 2013-14. Leicestershire debut 2016. HS 94 v Glamorgan (Cardiff) 2018. BB 8-72 NW v Northerns (Potchefstroom) 2014-15. Le BB 6-80 v Northants (Northampton) 2017. LO HS 26 v Durham (Gosforth) 2017 (RLC). LO BB 5-35 NW v Northerns (Pretoria) 2012-13. T20 HS 16. T20 BB 3-27.

‡**LILLEY, Arron** Mark (Mossley Hollins HS; Ashton SFC), b Tameside, Lancs 1 Apr 1991. 6'1''. RHB, OB. Squad No 7. Lancashire 2013-18. HS 63 and BB 5-23 La v Derbys (Southport) 2015. LO HS 16 La v Notts (Manchester) 2018 (RLC). LO BB 4-30 La v Derbys (Manchester) 2013 (Y40). T20 HS 47. T20 BB 3-31.

MIKE, Benjamin Wentworth Munro (Loughborough GS), b Nottingham 24 Aug 1998. Son of G.W.Mike (Nottinghamshire 1989-96). RHB, RM. Squad No 8. Debut (Leicestershire) 2018. Leicestershire 2nd XI debut 2017. HS 39 v Warwks (Leicester) 2018. BB 5-37 (9-94 match) v Sussex (Hove) 2018 – on debut. LO HS 10 v India A (Leicester) 2018. LO BB –.

^{NQ}**MOHAMMAD ABBAS**, b Sialkot, Pakistan 10 Mar 1990. RHB, RMF. Squad No 26. Sialkot 2008-09 to 2012-13. KRL 2015-16 to 2016-17. SNGPL 2017-18 to date. Leicestershire debut/cap 2018. **Tests** (P): 14 (2017 to 2018-19); HS 11 v SA (Johannesburg) 2018-19; BB 5-33 v A (Abu Dhabi) 2018-19. F-c Tours (P): E 2018; SA 2018-19; WI 2017; Ire 2018. HS 40 and BB 8-46 (14-93 match) KRL v Karachi Whites (Karachi) 2016-17. Le HS 32* v Sussex (Hove) 2018. 50 wkts (1+2); most 71 (2016-17). Le BB 6-48 v Kent (Leicester) 2018. LO HS 15* KRL v HB (Karachi) 2016-17. LO BB 4-31 KRL v SNGPL (Karachi) 2016-17. T20 HS 15*. T20 BB 3-22.

PARKINSON, Callum Francis (Bolton S), b Bolton, Lancs 24 Oct 1996. Twin brother of M.W.Parkinson (see *LANCASHIRE*). RHB, SLA. Squad No 10. Derbyshire 2016. Leicestershire debut 2017. Staffordshire 2015-16. HS 75 v Kent (Canterbury) 2017. BB 8-148 (10-185 match) v Worcs (Worcester) 2017. LO HS 52* v Notts (Leicester) 2018 (RLC). LO BB 1-34 v Derbys (Derby) 2018 (RLC). T20 HS 27*. T20 BB 4-20.

SWINDELLS, Harry John (Brockington C; Lutterworth S), b Leicester 21 Feb 1999. 5'7". RHB, WK. Squad No 28. Awaiting f-c debut. Leicestershire 2nd XI debut 2015. England U19 2017. LO HS 28 v India A (Leicester) 2018. T20 HS 15.

TAYLOR, Thomas Alex Ian (Trentham HS, Stoke-on-Trent), b Stoke-on-Trent, Staffs 21 Dec 1994. Elder brother of J.P.A.Taylor (see *DERBYSHIRE*). 6'2". RHB, RMF. Squad No 16. Derbyshire 2014-17. Leicestershire debut 2018. HS 80 De v Kent (Derby) 2016. Le HS 26 and Le BB 4-15 v Glamorgan (Cardiff) 2018. De BB 6-61 De v Lancs (Derby) 2015. LO HS –. LO BB 3-48 De v Worcs (Worcester) 2014 (RLC).

‡**WRIGHT, Christopher** Julian Clement (Eggars S, Alton; Anglia Ruskin U), b Chipping Norton, Oxon 14 Jul 1985. 6'3". RHB, RFM. Squad No 31. Cambridge UCCE 2004-05. Middlesex 2004-07. Tamil Union 2005-06. Essex 2008-11. Warwickshire 2011-18; cap 2013. HS 77 Ex v Cambridge MCCU (Cambridge) 2011. CC HS 72 Wa v Derbys (Birmingham) 2018. 50 wkts (1): 67 (2012). BB 6-22 Ex v Leics (Leicester) 2008. LO HS 42 Ex v Glos (Cheltenham) 2011 (CB40). LO BB 4-20 Ex v Unicorns (Chelmsford) 2011 (CB40). T20 HS 6*. T20 BB 4-24.

RELEASED/RETIRED

(Having made a County 1st XI appearance in 2018)

^{NQ}**AARON, Varun** Raymond (Loyola S, Jamshedpur; Jain C, Bangalore), b Jamshedpur, Bihar 29 Oct 1989. RHB, RFM. Jharkhand 2008-09 to date. Durham 2014. Leicestershire 2018. IPL: DD 2011-12. RCB 2014-16. KWIP 2017. **Tests** (I): 9 (2011-12 to 2015-16); HS 9 and BB 3-97 v E (Manchester) 2014. **LOI** (I): 9 (2011-12 to 2014-15); HS 6* v WI (Cuttack) 2011-12; BB 3-24 v E (Mumbai) 2014. F-c Tours (I): E 2014; A 2014-15, 2016 (I A); SL 2015; B 2015. HS 72 Jharkhand v Goa (Porvorim) 2010-11. CC HS 13 Du v Northants (Chester-le-St) 2014. Le HS 8 v Durham (Chester-le-St) 2018. BB 6-32 Jharkhand v Haryana (Lahli) 2018-19. CC BB 4-65 v Glamorgan (Leicester) 2018. LO HS 34 Jharkhand v Gujarat (Indore) 2010-11. LO BB 5-47 East Zone v West Zone (Jaipur) 2010-11. T20 HS 17*. T20 BB 3-16.

ARSHAD, Usman (Beckfoot GS, Bingley), b Bradford, Yorks 9 Jan 1993. 5'11". RHB, RMF. Durham 2013-16. Leicestershire 2018. Northumberland 2011-18. HS 84 Du v Yorks (Chester-le-St) 2016. Le HS 9 v Warwks (Leicester) 2018. BB 4-78 Du v Northants (Northampton) 2014. LO HS 25 Du v Surrey (Chester-le-St) 2015 (RLC). LO BB 3-50 Du v Warwks (Gosforth) 2016 (RLC). T20 HS 43. T20 BB 3-18.

CARBERRY, Michael Alexander (St John Rigby Catholic C), b Croydon, Surrey 29 Sep 1980. 6'0". LHB, RM. Surrey 2001-02. Kent 2003-05. Hampshire 2006-17; cap 2006. Leicestershire 2017-18; captain 2018 (*part*). MCC 2008, 2015. Big Bash: PS 2014-15. **Tests:** 6 (2009-10 to 2013-14); HS 60 v A (Adelaide) 2013-14. **LOI:** 6 (2013 to 2014); HS 63 v A (Cardiff) 2013. **IT20:** 1 (2014); HS 7 v SL (Oval) 2014. F-c Tours: A 2013-14; B 2006-07 (Eng A), 2009-10. 1000 runs (4); most – 1275 (2015). HS 300* H v Yorks (Southampton) 2011, sharing in UK 3rd highest and UK record 3rd wkt partnership of 523 with N.D.McKenzie. Le HS 73 v Durham (Chester-le-St) 2018. BB 2-85 H v Durham (Chester-le-St) 2006. LO HS 150* H v Lancs (Southampton) 2013 (Y40). LO BB 3-37 H v Derbys (Derby) 2013 (Y40). T20 HS 100*. T20 BB 1-16.

CHAPPELL, Z.J. – *see NOTTINGHAMSHIRE.*

DELPORT, C.S. – *see ESSEX.*

ECKERSLEY, Edmund John Holden ('Ned') (St Benedict's GS, Ealing), b Oxford 9 Aug 1989. 6'0". RHB, WK, occ OB. Leicestershire 2011-18; cap 2013. Mountaineers 2011-12. MCC 2013. 1000 runs (1): 1302 (2013). HS 158 v Derbys (Derby) 2017. BB 2-29 v Lancs (Manchester) 2013. LO HS 108 v Yorks (Leicester) 2013 (Y40). T20 HS 43.

JONES, Richard Alan (Grange HS and King Edward VI C, Stourbridge; Loughborough U), b Wordsley, Stourbridge, Worcs 6 Nov 1986. 6'2". RHB, RMF. Squad No 25. Worcestershire 2007-13; cap 2007. Matabeleland Tuskers 2011-12. Warwickshire 2014-15. Leicestershire 2014-18. HS 62 MT v SR (Bulawayo) 2011-12. UK HS 53* Wo v Durham (Worcester) 2009. Le HS 33 v Worcs (Worcester) 2016. BB 7-115 Wo v Sussex (Hove) 2010. Le BB 2-41 v Glos (Cheltenham) 2016. LO HS 26 Wa v Notts (Nottingham) 2016 (RLC). LO BB 2-40 v Durham (Leicester) 2018 (RLC). T20 HS 9. T20 BB 5-34.

MOHAMMAD NABI – *see KENT.*

RAINE, B.A. – *see DURHAM.*

WELLS, Thomas Joshua (Gartree HS; Beauchamp C, Leicester), b Grantham, Lincs 15 Mar 1993. Father, John Wells, played rugby for Leicester. 6'2". RHB, RMF. Leicestershire 2013-17. HS 87* v Sri Lankans (Leicester) 2016. CC HS 82 v Hants (Leicester) 2013. BB 4-46 v Loughborough MCCU (Leicester) 2017. CC BB 3-68 v Lancs (Leicester) 2015. LO HS 69 v Notts (Leicester) 2018 (RLC). LO BB 3-44 v Warwks (Leicester) 2017 (RLC). T20 HS 64*. T20 BB 1-5.

M.L.Pettini and R.J.Sayer left the staff without making a County 1st XI appearance in 2018.

LEICESTERSHIRE 2018

RESULTS SUMMARY

	Place	Won	Lost	Drew	NR
Specsavers County Champ (2nd Division)	6th	5	7	2	
All First-Class Matches		5	7	2	
Royal London One-Day Cup (North Group)	8th	2	6		
Vitality Blast (North Group)	8th	5	8		1

SPECSAVERS COUNTY CHAMPIONSHIP AVERAGES

BATTING AND FIELDING

Cap		M	I	NO	HS	Runs	Avge	100	50	Ct/St
	Z.J.Chappell	4	5	2	40	145	48.33	–	–	1
	C.N.Ackermann	14	24	2	196*	876	39.81	2	3	10
	N.J.Dexter	12	20	3	87	585	34.41	–	3	9
	D.Klein	5	9	3	94	202	33.66	–	1	2
	M.A.Carberry	4	6	–	73	193	32.16	–	1	1
	P.J.Horton	12	22	1	88	594	28.28	–	5	3
	G.T.Griffiths	12	18	8	40	225	22.50	–	–	2
	H.E.Dearden	10	18	2	74	357	22.31	–	2	6
2018	B.A.Raine	11	17	–	65	371	21.82	–	1	5
	L.J.Hill	9	15	2	85	241	18.53	–	1	29
2015	M.J.Cosgrove	14	24	–	75	440	18.33	–	3	6
2013	E.J.H.Eckersley	7	12	–	74	220	18.33	–	2	26
	A.Javid	6	10	–	58	157	15.70	–	1	2
	C.F.Parkinson	12	19	1	48	252	14.00	–	–	1
	B.W.M.Mike	4	7	–	39	96	13.71	–	–	2
	S.T.Evans	3	5	–	29	50	10.00	–	–	1
2018	Mohammad Abbas	10	15	6	32*	84	9.33	–	–	1
	V.R.Aaron	3	5	1	8	14	3.50	–	–	–

Also batted (1 match each): U.Arshad 9, 0; R.A.Jones 0 (1 ct); D.W.Sayer 6, 21 (2 ct); T.A.I.Taylor 5, 26.

BOWLING

	O	M	R	W	Avge	Best	5wI	10wM
Z.J.Chappell	76	13	255	16	15.93	6-44	1	–
Mohammad Abbas	345.1	101	886	50	17.72	6-48	5	1
B.W.M.Mike	87.2	10	385	19	20.26	5-37	1	–
B.A.Raine	395.1	90	1146	51	22.47	4-44	–	–
G.T.Griffiths	269	67	882	36	24.50	6-49	1	1
N.J.Dexter	169	40	494	18	27.44	3-17	–	–
C.F.Parkinson	239	42	824	10	82.40	3-50	–	–

Also bowled:

C.N.Ackermann	43.3	5	137	9	15.22	2-26	–	–
T.A.I.Taylor	34	11	92	6	15.33	4-15	–	–
V.R.Aaron	86	11	359	9	39.88	4-65	–	–
D.Klein	94	17	400	5	80.00	2-23	–	–

U.Arshad 16-2-81-0; M.A.Carberry 2-0-7-0; M.J.Cosgrove 3-0-8-0; A.Javid 26.2-3-78-2; R.A.Jones 13-1-44-1; D.W.Sayer 5-1-28-0.

Leicestershire played no first-class fixtures outside the County Championship in 2018. The First-Class Averages (pp 230–245) give the records of Leicestershire players in all first-class county matches, with the exception of Mohammad Abbas and S.T.Evans, whose first-class figures for Leicestershire are as above.

LEICESTERSHIRE RECORDS

FIRST-CLASS CRICKET

Highest Total	For	701-4d		v	Worcs	Worcester	1906
	V	761-6d		by	Essex	Chelmsford	1990
Lowest Total	For	25		v	Kent	Leicester	1912
	V	24		by	Glamorgan	Leicester	1971
		24		by	Oxford U	Oxford	1985
Highest Innings	For	309*	H.D.Ackerman	v	Glamorgan	Cardiff	2006
	V	355*	K.P.Pietersen	for	Surrey	The Oval	2015

Highest Partnership for each Wicket

1st	390	B.Dudleston/J.F.Steele	v	Derbyshire	Leicester	1979
2nd	289*	J.C.Balderstone/D.I.Gower	v	Essex	Leicester	1981
3rd	436*	D.L.Maddy/B.J.Hodge	v	L'boro UCCE	Leicester	2003
4th	360*	J.W.A.Taylor/A.B.McDonald	v	Middlesex	Leicester	2010
5th	330	J.W.A.Taylor/S.J.Thakor	v	L'boro MCCU	Leicester	2011
6th	284	P.V.Simmons/P.A.Nixon	v	Durham	Chester-le-St	1996
7th	219*	J.D.R.Benson/P.Whitticase	v	Hampshire	Bournemouth	1991
8th	195	J.W.A.Taylor/J.K.H.Naik	v	Derbyshire	Leicester	2009
9th	160	R.T.Crawford/W.W.Odell	v	Worcs	Leicester	1902
10th	228	R.Illingworth/K.Higgs	v	Northants	Leicester	1977

Best Bowling	For	10- 18	G.Geary	v	Glamorgan	Pontypridd	1929
(Innings)	V	10- 32	H.Pickett	for	Essex	Leyton	1895
Best Bowling	For	16- 96	G.Geary	v	Glamorgan	Pontypridd	1929
(Match)	V	16-102	C.Blythe	for	Kent	Leicester	1909

Most Runs – Season	2446	L.G.Berry	(av 52.04)	1937
Most Runs – Career	30143	L.G.Berry	(av 30.32)	1924-51
Most 100s – Season	7	L.G.Berry		1937
	7	W.Watson		1959
	7	B.F.Davison		1982
Most 100s – Career	45	L.G.Berry		1924-51
Most Wkts – Season	170	J.E.Walsh	(av 18.96)	1948
Most Wkts – Career	2131	W.E.Astill	(av 23.18)	1906-39
Most Career W-K Dismissals	905	R.W.Tolchard	(794 ct; 111 st)	1965-83
Most Career Catches in the Field	426	M.R.Hallam		1950-70

LIMITED-OVERS CRICKET

Highest Total	50ov	406-5		v	Berkshire	Leicester	1996
	40ov	344-4		v	Durham	Chester-le-St[2]	1996
	T20	229-5		v	Warwicks	Birmingham	2018
Lowest Total	50ov	56		v	Northants	Leicester	1964
		56		v	Minor Cos	Wellington	1982
	40ov	36		v	Sussex	Leicester	1973
	T20	90		v	Notts	Nottingham	2014
Highest Innings	50ov	201	V.J.Wells	v	Berkshire	Leicester	1996
	40ov	154*	B.J.Hodge	v	Sussex	Horsham	2004
	T20	113	B.A.Raine	v	Warwicks	Birmingham	2018
Best Bowling	50ov	6-16	C.M.Willoughby	v	Somerset	Leicester	2005
	40ov	6-17	K.Higgs	v	Glamorgan	Leicester	1973
	T20	5-11	C.J.McKay	v	Worcs	Worcester	2017

MIDDLESEX

Formation of Present Club: 2 February 1864
Inaugural First-Class Match: 1864
Colours: Blue
Badge: Three Seaxes
County Champions (since 1890): (11) 1903, 1920, 1921, 1947, 1976, 1980, 1982, 1985, 1990, 1993, 2016
Joint Champions: (2) 1949, 1977
Gillette/NatWest Trophy Winners: (4) 1977, 1980, 1984, 1988
Benson and Hedges Cup Winners: (2) 1983, 1986
Sunday League Winners: (1) 1992
Twenty20 Cup Winners: (1) 2008

Chief Executive: Richard Goatley, Lord's Cricket Ground, London NW8 8QN • Tel: 020 7289 1300 • Email: enquiries@middlesexccc.com • Web: www.middlesexccc.com • Twitter: @Middlesex_CCC (59,823 followers)

Managing Director of Cricket: Angus Fraser MBE. **Head Coach**: Stuart Law. **Assistant Coach**: Nic Pothas. **Captain**: D.J.Malan. **Overseas Players**: A.B.de Villiers (T20 only) and Mujeeb Zadran (T20 only). **2019 Beneficiary**: D.J.Malan. **Head Groundsman**: Karl McDermott. **Scorer**: Don Shelley. ‡ New registration. NQ Not qualified for England.

ANDERSSON, Martin Kristoffer (Reading Blue Coat S), b Reading, Berks 6 Sep 1996. 6'1". RHB, RM. Squad No 24. Debut (Leeds/Bradford MCCU) 2017. Derbyshire 2018 (on loan). Middlesex debut 2018. Middlesex 2nd XI debut 2013. Berkshire 2015-16. HS 34 and M BB 2-15 v Durham (Chester-le-St) 2018. BB 4-25 De v Glamorgan (Derby) 2018. T20 HS 1. T20 BB –.

BAMBER, Ethan Read (Mill Hill S), b Westminster 17 Dec 1998. RHB, RMF. Squad No 54. Debut (Middlesex) 2018. Middlesex 2nd XI debut 2015. Berkshire 2017. HS 27* and BB 4-81 v Glos (Bristol) 2018.

BARBER, Thomas Edward (Bournemouth GS), b Poole, Dorset 31 May 1994. 6'3". RHB, LFM. Squad No 25. Debut (Middlesex) 2018. Hampshire 2014 (1-o only). Dorset 2016. HS 3 and BB – v Sussex (Hove) 2018. LO HS 1 South v North (Cave Hill) 2017-18. LO BB 3-62 v Australians (Lord's) 2017-18. T20 HS 2. T20 BB 4-28.

DAVIES, Jack Leo Benjamin (Wellington C), b Reading, Berks 30 Mar 2000. Son of A.G.Davies (Cambridge U 1982-89). 5'10". LHB, WK. Squad No 23. Middlesex 2nd XI debut 2017. Berkshire 2017-18. England U19 2018. Awaiting 1st XI debut.

‡**NQDe VILLIERS**, Abraham Benjamin ('AB'), b Pretoria, South Africa 17 Feb 1984. RHB, RM, WK. Squad No 11. Northerns 2003-04. Titans 2004-05 to 2017-18. Joins Middlesex in 2019 for T20 only. IPL: DD 2007-08 to 2009-10. RCB 2011 to date. **Tests** (SA): 114 (2004-05 to 2017-18, 3 as captain); 1000 runs (2); most – 1061 (2008); HS 278* v P (Abu Dhabi) 2010-11; BB 2-49 v WI (St John's) 2005. **LOI** (SA): 223 (+ 5 for Africa; 2004-05 to 2017-18, 103 as captain); 1000 runs (3); most – 1209 (2007); HS 176 v B (Paarl) 2017-18; BB 2-15 v UAE (Wellington) 2014-15. **IT20** (SA): 78 (2005-06 to 2017-18, 18 as captain); HS 79* v Scotland (Oval) 2009. F-c Tours (SA): E 2008, 2012; A 2005-06, 2008-09, 2012-13; WI 2005, 2010; NZ 2011-12; I 2008, 2009-10, 2015-16; P 2007-08; SL 2006, 2014; Z 2014; B 2007-08; UAE 2010-11 (v P), 2013-14 (v P). 1000 runs (0+1): 1122 (2004-05). HS 278* (*see Tests*). BB 2-49 (*see Tests*). LO HS 176 (*see LOI*). LO BB 2-15 (*see LOI*). T20 HS 133*.

NQESKINAZI, Stephen Sean (Christ Church GS, Claremont; U of WA), b Johannesburg, South Africa 28 Mar 1994. 6'2". RHB, WK. Squad No 28. Debut (Middlesex) 2015; cap 2018. UK passport. HS 179 v Warwks (Birmingham) 2017. LO HS 49 v Glamorgan (Cardiff) 2018 (RLC). T20 HS 57*.

FINN, Steven Thomas (Parmiter's S, Garston), b Watford, Herts 4 Apr 1989. 6'7½". RHB, RFM. Squad No 9. Debut (Middlesex) 2005; cap 2009. Otago 2011-12. YC 2010. **Tests**: 36 (2009-10 to 2016-17); HS 56 v NZ (Dunedin) 2012-13; BB 6-79 v A (Birmingham) 2015. **LOI**: 69 (2010-11 to 2017); HS 35 v A (Brisbane) 2010-11; BB 5-33 v I (Brisbane) 2014-15. **IT20**: 21 (2011 to 2015); HS 8* v I (Colombo, RPS) 2012-13; BB 3-16 v NZ (Pallekele) 2012-13. F-c Tours: A 2010-11, 2013-14; SA 2015-16; NZ 2012-13; I 2012-13; SL 2011-12; B 2009-10, 2016-17; UAE 2011-12 (v P). HS 56 (*see Tests*). M HS 41* v Oxford MCCU (Oxford) 2015. CC HS 37* v Warwks (Birmingham) 2014. 50 wkts (2); most – 64 (2010). BB 9-37 (14-106 match) v Worcs (Worcester) 2010. LO HS 42* v Glamorgan (Cardiff) 2014 (RLC). LO BB (*see LOI*) and 5-33 v Derbys (Lord's) 2011 (CB40). T20 HS 8*. T20 BB 4-24.

GUBBINS, Nicholas Richard Trail (Radley C; Leeds U), b Richmond, Surrey 31 Dec 1993. 6'0½". LHB, LB. Squad No 18. Leeds/Bradford MCCU 2013-15. Middlesex debut 2014; cap 2016. F-c Tour (EL): WI 2017-18; SL 2016-17; UAE 2016-17 (v Afg), 2018-19 (v P A). 1000 runs (1): 1409 (2016). HS 201* v Lancs (Lord's) 2016. BB – . LO HS 141 v Sussex (Hove) 2015 (RLC). T20 HS 46.

HARRIS, James Alexander Russell (Pontardulais CS; Gorseinon C), b Morriston, Swansea, Glamorgan 16 May 1990. 6'0". RHB, RMF. Squad No 5. Glamorgan 2007-14, making debut aged 16y 351d – youngest Gm player to take an f-c wicket; cap 2010. Middlesex debut 2013; cap 2015. Kent 2017 (on loan). MCC 2016. Wales MC 2005-08. F-c Tours (EL): WI 2010-11; SL 2013-14. HS 87* Gm v Notts (Swansea) 2007. M HS 79* v Northants (Northampton) 2018. 50 wkts (3); most – 73 (2015). BB 9-34 (13-103 match) v Durham (Lord's) 2015 – record innings and match analysis v Durham. Took 12-118 in match for Gm v Glos (Bristol) 2007 – youngest (17y 3d) to take 10 wickets in any CC match. LO HS 32 v Hants (Southampton) 2015 (RLC). LO BB 4-38 v Glamorgan (Lord's) 2015 (RLC). T20 HS 18. T20 BB 4-23.

HELM, Thomas George (Misbourne S, Gt Missenden), b Stoke Mandeville Hospital, Bucks 7 May 1994. 6'4". RHB, RMF. Squad No 7. Debut (Middlesex) 2013. Glamorgan 2014 (on loan). Buckinghamshire 2011. F-c Tour (EL): SL 2016-17. HS 52 v Derbys (Derby) 2018. BB 5-59 v Warwks (Birmingham) 2017. LO HS 30 v Surrey (Lord's) 2018 (RLC). LO BB 5-33 EL v SL A (Colombo, CCC) 2016-17. T20 HS 28*. T20 BB 5-11.

HOLDEN, Max David Edward (Sawston Village C; Hills Road SFC, Cambridge), b Cambridge 18 Dec 1997. 5'11". LHB, OB. Squad No 4. Northamptonshire 2017 (on loan). Middlesex debut 2017. Middlesex 2nd XI debut 2013. England U19 2014-15 to 2016-17. F-c Tour (EL): I 2018-19. HS 153 and BB 2-59 Nh v Kent (Beckenham) 2017. M HS 119* v Derbys (Lord's) 2018. M BB 1-15 v Leics (Leicester) 2018. LO HS 71 and LO BB 1-29 v Australians (Lord's) 2018. T20 HS 84. T20 BB – .

MALAN, Dawid Johannes (Paarl HS), b Roehampton, Surrey 3 Sep 1987. Son of D.J.Malan (WP B and Transvaal B 1978-79 to 1981-82), elder brother of C.C.Malan (Loughborough MCCU 2009-10). 6'0". LHB, LB. Squad No 29. Boland 2005-06. Middlesex debut 2008, scoring 132* v Northants (Uxbridge); cap 2010; T20 captain 2016 to date; captain 2018 to date. MCC 2010-11, 2013. **Tests**: 15 (2017 to 2018); HS 140 v A (Perth) 2017-18; BB – . **IT20**: 5 (2017 to 2017-18); HS 78 v SA (Cardiff) 2017; BB 1-27 v NZ (Hamilton) 2017-18. F-c Tours: A 2017-18; NZ 2017-18. 1000 runs (2); most – 1137 runs (2014). HS 182* v Notts (Nottingham) 2015. BB 5-61 v Lancs (Liverpool) 2012. LO HS 185* EL v SL A (Northampton) 2016. LO BB 4-25 PDSC v Partex (Savar) 2014-15. T20 HS 115*. T20 BB 2-10.

MORGAN, Eoin Joseph Gerard (Catholic University S), b Dublin, Ireland 10 Sep 1986. 6'0". LHB, RM. Squad No 16. UK passport. Ireland 2004 to 2007-08. Middlesex debut 2006; cap 2008; l-o captain 2014-15. IPL: RCB 2009-10. KKR 2011-13. SH 2015-16. KXIP 2017. Big Bash: ST 2013-14 to 2016-17. *Wisden* 2010. **ECB L-O Central Contract 2018-19. Tests**: 16 (2010 to 2011-12); HS 130 v P (Nottingham) 2010. **LOI** (E/Ire): 217 (23 for Ire 2006 to 2008-09; 194 for E 2009 to 2018-19, 95 as captain); HS 124* v Ireland (Dublin) 2013. **IT20**: 79 (2009 to 2018-19, 36 as captain); HS 85* v SA (Johannesburg) 2009-10. F-c Tours (Ire): A 2010-11 (E); NZ 2008-09 (Eng A); Namibia 2005-06; UAE 2006-07, 2007-08, 2011-12 (v P). 1000 runs (1): 1085 (2008). HS 209* Ire v UAE (Abu Dhabi) 2006-07. M HS 191 v Notts (Nottingham) 2014. BB 2-24 v Notts (Lord's) 2007. LO HS 161 v Kent (Canterbury) 2009 (FPT). LO BB –. T20 HS 85*.

‡[NQ]**MUJEEB ZADRAN** (also known as Mujeeb Ur Rahman), b Khost, Afghanistan 28 Mar 2001. RHB, OB. Squad No 88. Hampshire 2018 (T20 only). Joins Middlesex for T20 only. IPL: KXIP 2018. Big Bash: BH 2018-19. **Tests** (Afg): 1 (2018); HS 15 and BB 1-75 v I (Bengalaru) 2018. **LOI** (Afg): 27 (2017-18 to 2018-19); HS 15 v Z (Sharjah) 2017-18; BB 5-50 v Z (Sharjah) 2017-18 – separate matches. **IT20** (Afg): 9 (2017-18 to 2018-19); HS 0*; BB 3-17 v Ire (Bready) 2018. F-c Tour (Afg): I 2018. HS 15 (*see Tests*). BB 1-75 (*see Tests*). LO HS 15 (*see LOI*). LO BB 5-50 (*see LOI*). T20 HS 27. T20 BB 4-16.

[NQ]**MURTAGH, Timothy** James (John Fisher S; St Mary's C), b Lambeth, London 2 Aug 1981. Elder brother of C.P.Murtagh (Loughborough UCCE and Surrey 2005-09), nephew of A.J.Murtagh (Hampshire and EP 1973-77). 6'0". LHB, RFM. Squad No 34. British U 2000-03. Surrey 2001-06. Middlesex debut 2007; cap 2008; benefit 2015. Ireland 2012-13 to date. MCC 2010. **Tests** (Ire): 2 (2018 to 2018-19); HS 54* v Afg (Dehradun) 2018-19; BB 4-45 v P (Dublin) 2018. **LOI** (Ire): 49 (2012 to 2018-19); HS 23* v Scotland (Belfast) 2013; BB 4-30 v Afg (Belfast) 2018. **IT20** (Ire): 14 (2012 to 2015-16); HS 12* v UAE (Abu Dhabi) 2015-16; BB 3-23 v PNG (Townsville) 2015. HS 74* Sy v Middx (Oval) 2004 and 74* Sy v Warwks (Croydon) 2005. M HS 55 v Leics (Leicester) 2011, sharing M record 9th wkt partnership of 172 with G.K.Berg. 50 wkts (7); most – 85 (2011). BB 7-82 v Derbys (Derby) 2009. LO HS 35* v Surrey (Lord's) 2008 (FPT). LO BB 4-14 Sy v Derbys (Derby) 2005 (NL). T20 HS 40*. T20 BB 6-24 Sy v Middx (Lord's) 2005 – Sy record and 5th best UK figs.

RAYNER, Oliver Philip (St Bede's S, Upper Dicker), b Fallingbostel, W Germany, 1 Nov 1985. 6'5". RHB, OB. Squad No 2. Sussex 2006-11, scoring 101 v Sri Lankans (Hove) – first hundred on debut for Sussex since 1920. Middlesex debut 2011; cap 2015. Hampshire 2018 (on loan). MCC 2014. F-c Tours (EL): SL 2013-14, 2016-17; UAE 2016-17 (v Afg). HS 143* v Notts (Nottingham) 2012. 50 wkts (1): 51 (2016). BB 8-46 (15-118 match) v Surrey (Oval) 2013. LO HS 61 Sx v Lancs (Hove) 2006 (P40). LO BB 4-35 v Notts (Lord's) 2015 (RLC). T20 HS 41*. T20 BB 5-18.

ROBSON, Sam David (Marcellin C, Randwick), b Paddington, Sydney, Australia 1 Jul 1989. Elder brother of A.J.Robson (Leicestershire and Sussex 2013-17). 6'0". RHB, LB. Squad No 12. Qualified for England in April 2013. Debut (Middlesex) 2009; cap 2013. **Tests**: 7 (2014); HS 127 v SL (Leeds) 2014. **LOI** (EL): SA 2014-15; SL 2013-14. 1000 runs (2); most – 1180 (2013). HS 231* v Warwks (Lord's) 2013. BB 1-4 EL v SL A (Dambulla) 2013-14. M BB –. LO HS 88 v Notts (Lord's) 2015 (RLC). T20 HS 28*.

ROLAND-JONES, Tobias Skelton ('Toby') (Hampton S; Leeds U), b Ashford 29 Jan 1988. 6'4". RHB, RFM. Squad No 21. Debut (Middlesex) 2010; cap 2012. MCC 2011. *Wisden* 2016. Leeds/Bradford UCCE 2009 (not f-c). **Tests**: 4 (2017); HS 25 and BB 5-57 v SA (Oval) 2017. **LOI**: 1 (2017); HS 37* and BB 1-34 v SA (Lord's) 2017. F-c Tours (EL): WI 2017-18; SL 2016-17; UAE 2016-17 (v Afg). HS 103* v Yorks (Lord's) 2015. 50 wkts (2); most – 64 (2012). BB 6-50 (12-105 match) v Northants (Northampton) 2014. Hat-tricks (2): v Derbys (Lord's) 2013, and v Yorks (Lord's) 2016 – at end of match to secure the Championship. LO HS 65 v Glos (Lord's) 2017 (RLC). LO BB 4-10 v Hants (Southampton) 2017 (RLC). T20 HS 30. T20 BB 4-25.

SCOTT, George Frederick Buchan (Beechwood Park S; St Albans S; Leeds U), b Hemel Hempstead, Herts 6 Nov 1995. Younger brother of J.E.B.Scott (Hertfordshire 2013 to date) and elder brother of C.F.B.Scott (Middlesex 2nd XI 2015 to date). 6'2". RHB, RM. Squad No 17. Leeds/Bradford MCCU 2015-16. Middlesex debut 2018. Middlesex 2nd XI debut 2013. Hertfordshire 2011-14. HS 16* LBU v Sussex (Hove) 2016. M HS 13 v Kent (Canterbury) 2018. BB 2-67 LBU v Sussex (Hove) 2015. M BB – . LO HS 4 v Notts (Lord's) 2015 (RLC). LO BB –. T20 HS 38*. T20 BB 1-14.

SIMPSON, John Andrew (St Gabriel's RC HS), b Bury, Lancs 13 Jul 1988. 5'10". LHB, WK. Squad No 20. Debut (Middlesex) 2009; cap 2011. MCC 2018. Cumberland 2007. HS 143 v Surrey (Lord's) 2011. LO HS 82* v Sussex (Lord's) 2017 (RLC). T20 HS 84*.

NQ**SOWTER, Nathan** Adam (Hill Sport HS, NSW), b Penrith, NSW, Australia 12 Oct 1992. 5'10". RHB, LB. Squad No 72. Debut (Middlesex) 2017. HS 37 and BB 1-23 v Warwks (Lord's) 2017. LO HS 29 v Surrey (Lord's) 2018 (RLC). LO BB 3-43 v Sussex (Hove) 2018 (RLC). T20 HS 12. T20 BB 4-23.

NQ**STIRLING, Paul** Robert (Belfast HS), b Belfast, N Ireland 3 Sep 1990. Father Brian Stirling was an international rugby referee. 5'10". RHB, OB. Squad No 39. Ireland 2007-08 to date. Middlesex debut 2013; cap 2016. **Tests** (Ire): 2 (2018 to 2018-19); HS 26 v Afg (Dehradun) 2018-19; BB –. **LOI** (Ire): 104 (2008 to 2018-19); HS 177 v Canada (Toronto) 2010; BB 6-55 v Afg (Greater Noida) 2016-17 – Ire record figures. **IT20** (Ire): 58 (2009 to 2018-19); HS 91 v Afg (Dehradun) 2018-19; BB 3-21 v B (Belfast) 2012. F-c Tours (Ire): WI 2009-10; Kenya 2011-12; Z 2015-16; UAE 2013-14. HS 146 Ire v UAE (Dublin) 2015. M HS 111 v Yorks (Leeds) 2017. BB 2-27 Ire v Namibia (Windhoek) 2015-16. M BB 2-31 v Oxford MCCU (Oxford) 2015. CC BB 2-43 v Surrey (Lord's) 2013. LO HS 177 (see LOI). LO BB 6-55 (see LOI). T20 HS 109. T20 BB 4-10.

WHITE, Robert George (Harrow S; Loughborough U), b 15 Sep 1995. 5'9". RHB, WK, occ RM. Squad No 14. Loughborough MCCU 2015-17. Middlesex debut 2018. Middlesex 2nd XI debut 2013. HS 69 LU v Northants (Northampton) 2017. M HS 35 v Northants (Northampton) 2018. LO HS 12 v Australians (Lord's) 2018. T20 HS 11*.

RELEASED/RETIRED
(Having made a County 1st XI appearance in 2018)

AGAR, A.C. – see WARWICKSHIRE.

NQ**BRAVO, Dwayne** John, b Santa Cruz, Trinidad 7 Oct 1983. Older half-brother of D.M.Bravo (Trinidad & Tobago, Nottinghamshire and WI 2006-07 to date). RHB, RMF. Trinidad & Tobago 2001-02 to 2012-13. Kent 2006. Surrey 2016 (T20 only). Middlesex 2018 (T20 only). IPL: MI 2007-08 to 2009-10. CSK 2011 to date. GL 2016. Big Bash: SS 2011-12. MR 2013-14 to 2017-18. MS 2018-19. **Tests** (WI): 40 (2004 to 2010-11, 1 as captain): HS 113 v A (Hobart) 2005-06; BB 6-55 v E (Manchester) 2004. **LOI** (WI): 164 (2004 to 2014-15, 37 as captain); HS 112* v E (Ahmedabad) 2006-07; BB 6-43 v Z (St George's) 2012-13. **IT20** (WI): 66 (2005-06 to 2016-17, 6 as captain); HS 66* v I (Lord's) 2009; BB 4-28 v SL (Colombo, RPS) 2015-16. F-c Tours (WI): E 2002 (WI A), 2004, 2007; A 2005-06, 2009-10; SA 2007-08; NZ 2005-06; P 2006-07; SL 2010-11. HS 197 T&T v West Indies B (Couva) 2003-04. CC HS 76 K v Lancs (Canterbury) 2006. BB 6-11 T&T v Windward Is (St George's) 2002-03. CC BB 6-12 K v Notts (Nottingham) 2006. LO HS 112* (see LOI). LO BB 6-43 (see LOI). T20 HS 70*. T20 BB 5-23.

NQ**CARTWRIGHT, Hilton** William Raymond, b Harare, Zimbabwe 14 Feb 1992. RHB, RM. W Australia 2012-13 to date. Big Bash: PS 2012-13 to date. **Tests** (A): 2 (2016-17 to 2017); HS 37 v P (Sydney) 2016-17; BB –. **LOI** (A): 2 (2017-18); HS 1 (twice). F-c Tours (A): NZ 2015-16 (Cricket Aus); B 2017. HS 170* WA v NSW (Perth) 2016-17. M HS 80 v Leics (Leicester) 2018. BB 4-33 v Glos (Lord's) 2018. LO HS 99 Cricket Aus v Q (Sydney, DO) 2015-16. LO BB 3-26 Aus Nat Perf XI v Aus A (Townsville) 2016. T20 HS 68*. T20 BB 2-41.

RELEASED/RETIRED continued on p 168

MIDDLESEX 2018

RESULTS SUMMARY

		Place	Won	Lost	Tied	Drew
Specsavers County Champ (2nd Division)		4th	7	4		3
All First-Class Matches			7	4		4
Royal London One-Day Cup (South Group)		6th	4	4		
Vitality Blast (South Group)		9th	2	11	1	

SPECSAVERS COUNTY CHAMPIONSHIP AVERAGES

BATTING AND FIELDING

Cap		M	I	NO	HS	Runs	Avge	100	50	Ct/St
2018	S.S.Eskinazi	12	22	1	97	740	35.23	–	5	16
2016	N.R.T.Gubbins	9	17	–	107	585	34.41	1	2	2
2015	J.A.R.Harris	12	22	8	79*	454	32.42	–	3	6
	M.D.E.Holden	13	24	3	119*	632	30.09	1	3	4
2010	D.J.Malan	12	22	1	119	613	29.19	1	4	12
2013	S.D.Robson	13	24	1	134	633	27.52	1	2	7
	T.G.Helm	4	6	2	52	102	25.50	–	1	2
2011	J.A.Simpson	8	14	–	39	309	22.07	–	–	23/3
2012	T.S.Roland-Jones	2	4	–	46	79	19.75	–	–	–
	J.K.Fuller	8	16	3	71	242	18.61	–	1	3
2016	P.R.Stirling	6	11	–	52	199	18.09	–	1	4
	M.K.Andersson	3	6	2	34	72	18.00	–	–	–
	H.W.R.Cartwright	7	12	–	80	204	17.00	–	1	7
2008	T.J.Murtagh	11	19	4	40	200	13.33	–	–	3
2015	O.P.Rayner	9	15	2	28	172	13.23	–	–	14
2008	E.J.G.Morgan	6	11	–	76	121	11.00	–	1	4
	E.R.Bamber	6	10	3	27*	76	10.85	–	–	2
2009	S.T.Finn	4	6	–	27	50	8.33	–	–	–
	R.H.Patel	2	4	–	20	33	8.25	–	–	1
	R.G.White	5	10	–	35	71	7.10	–	–	14

Also batted: T.E.Barber (2 matches) 0*, 3, 0; G.F.B.Scott (1) 3, 13.

BOWLING

	O	M	R	W	Avge	Best	5wI	10wM
T.J.Murtagh	359.5	95	888	58	15.31	5-38	2	–
E.R.Bamber	203.5	37	567	28	20.25	4-81	–	–
J.A.R.Harris	384.5	67	1253	61	20.54	7-83	3	–
H.W.R.Cartwright	122.2	16	410	19	21.57	4-33	–	–
J.K.Fuller	227.2	25	845	28	30.17	4-49	–	–
Also bowled:								
M.K.Andersson	56	2	198	8	24.75	2-15	–	–
R.H.Patel	48.2	9	177	6	29.50	3-58	–	–
T.G.Helm	74.5	12	236	7	33.71	3-46	–	–
S.T.Finn	108	9	395	9	43.88	2-34	–	–
O.P.Rayner	146.5	35	334	7	47.71	2-23	–	–

T.E.Barber 34-4-131-0; M.D.E.Holden 40-3-145-1; D.J.Malan 48-3-145-3; S.D.Robson 4-0-27-0; T.S.Roland-Jones 21-0-98-2; G.F.B.Scott 12-3-23-0; P.R.Stirling 24-3-81-2.

The First-Class Averages (pp 230–245) give the records of Middlesex players in all first-class county matches (Middlesex's other opponents being Durham MCCU), with the exception of M.K.Andersson, N.R.T.Gubbins and D.J.Malan, whose first-class figures for Middlesex are as above, and:
O.P.Rayner 10-15-2-28-172-13.23-0-0-14ct. 146.5-35-334-7-47.71-2/23-0-0.

MIDDLESEX RECORDS

FIRST-CLASS CRICKET

Highest Total	For 642-3d		v	Hampshire	Southampton[1]	1923
	V 850-7d		by	Somerset	Taunton	2007
Lowest Total	For 20		v	MCC	Lord's	1864
	V 31		by	Glos	Bristol	1924
Highest Innings	For 331*	J.D.B.Robertson	v	Worcs	Worcester	1949
	V 341	C.M.Spearman	for	Glos	Gloucester	2004

Highest Partnership for each Wicket

1st	372	M.W.Gatting/J.L.Langer	v	Essex	Southgate	1998
2nd	380	F.A.Tarrant/J.W.Hearne	v	Lancashire	Lord's	1914
3rd	424*	W.J.Edrich/D.C.S.Compton	v	Somerset	Lord's	1948
4th	325	J.W.Hearne/E.H.Hendren	v	Hampshire	Lord's	1919
5th	338	R.S.Lucas/T.C.O'Brien	v	Sussex	Hove	1895
6th	270	J.D.Carr/P.N.Weekes	v	Glos	Lord's	1994
7th	271*	E.H.Hendren/F.T.Mann	v	Notts	Nottingham	1925
8th	182*	M.H.C.Doll/H.R.Murrell	v	Notts	Lord's	1913
9th	172	G.K.Berg/T.J.Murtagh	v	Leics	Leicester	2011
10th	230	R.W.Nicholls/W.Roche	v	Kent	Lord's	1899

Best Bowling	For 10- 40	G.O.B.Allen	v	Lancashire	Lord's	1929
(Innings)	V 9- 38	R.C.R-Glasgow†	for	Somerset	Lord's	1924
Best Bowling	For 16-114	G.Burton	v	Yorkshire	Sheffield	1888
(Match)	16-114	J.T.Hearne	v	Lancashire	Manchester	1898
	V 16-100	J.E.B.B.P.Q.C.Dwyer	for	Sussex	Hove	1906

Most Runs – Season	2669	E.H.Hendren	(av 83.41)	1923
Most Runs – Career	40302	E.H.Hendren	(av 48.81)	1907-37
Most 100s – Season	13	D.C.S.Compton		1947
Most 100s – Career	119	E.H.Hendren		1907-37
Most Wkts – Season	158	F.J.Titmus	(av 14.63)	1955
Most Wkts – Career	2361	F.J.Titmus	(av 21.27)	1949-82
Most Career W-K Dismissals	1223	J.T.Murray	(1024 ct; 199 st)	1952-75
Most Career Catches in the Field	561	E.H.Hendren		1907-37

LIMITED-OVERS CRICKET

Highest Total	50ov	367-6	v	Sussex	Hove	2015
	40ov	350-6	v	Lancashire	Lord's	2012
	T20	221-2	v	Sussex	Hove	2015
		221-5	v	Surrey	The Oval	2018
Lowest Total	50ov	41	v	Essex	Westcliff	1972
	40ov	23	v	Yorkshire	Leeds	1974
	T20	92	v	Surrey	Lords	2013
Highest Innings	50ov	163 A.J.Strauss	v	Surrey	The Oval	2008
	40ov	147* M.R.Ramprakash	v	Worcs	Lord's	1990
	T20	129 D.T.Christian	v	Kent	Canterbury	2014
Best Bowling	50ov	7-12 W.W.Daniel	v	Minor Cos E	Ipswich	1978
	40ov	6- 6 R.W.Hooker	v	Surrey	Lord's	1969
	T20	6-28 J.K.Fuller	v	Hampshire	Southampton[2]	2018

† R.C.Robertson-Glasgow

NORTHAMPTONSHIRE

Formation of Present Club: 31 July 1878
Inaugural First-Class Match: 1905
Colours: Maroon
Badge: Tudor Rose
County Champions: (0); best – 2nd 1912, 1957, 1965, 1976
Gillette/NatWest/C&G/FP Trophy Winners: (2) 1976, 1992
Benson and Hedges Cup Winners: (1) 1980
Twenty20 Cup Winners: (2) 2013, 2016

est. 1878
NORTHAMPTONSHIRE
COUNTY CRICKET CLUB

Chief Executive: Ray Payne, County Ground, Abington Avenue, Northampton, NN1 4PR • Tel: 01604 514455 • Email: post@nccc.co.uk • Web: www.northantscricket.com • Twitter: @NorthantsCCC (51,452 followers)

Head Coach: David Ripley. **Assistant Coach/Bowling Lead**: Phil Rowe. **Batting Lead**: David Sales. **Captain**: A.G.Wakely. **Overseas Players**: T.Bavuma, Faheem Ashraf (T20 only) and J.O.Holder. **2019 Beneficiary**: None. **Head Groundsman**: Craig Harvey. **Scorer**: Tony Kingston. ‡ New registration. NQ Not qualified for England

‡NOBAVUMA, Temba, b Cape Town, South Africa 17 May 1990. Cousin of P.V.Mntungwa (Boland 2017-18). RHB, RM. Gauteng 2008-09 to 2013-14. Lions 2010-11 to date. Cape Cobras 2017-18. Tests (SA): 36 (2014-15 to 2018-19); HS 102* v E (Cape Town) 2015-16; BB 1-29 v A (Perth) 2016-17. LOI (SA): 2 (2016-17 to 2017-18); HS 113 v Ire (Benoni) 2016-17. F-c Tours (SA): E 2017; A 2014 (SA A), 2016 (SA A), 2016-17; NZ 2016-17; I 2015 (SA A); SL 2018; B 2015; Ire 2012 (SA A). HS 162 SA A v Aus A (Townsville) 2014. BB 2-34 Gauteng v NW (Potchefstroom) 2010-11. LO HS 117* Lions v Titans (Potchefstroom) 2018-19. LO BB –. T20 HS 79*.

BUCK, Nathan Liam (Newbridge HS; Ashby S), b Leicester 26 Apr 1991. 6'2" RHB, RMF. Squad No 11. Leicestershire 2009-14; cap 2011. Lancashire 2015-16. Northamptonshire 2017. F-c Tour (EL): WI 2010-11. HS 43 v Derbys (Derby) 2017. BB 6-34 v Durham (Chester-le-St) 2017. LO HS 21 Le v Glamorgan (Leicester) 2009 (P40). LO BB 4-39 EL v Sri Lanka A (Dambulla) 2011-12. T20 HS 11*. T20 BB 4-26.

COBB, Joshua James (Oakham S), b Leicester 17 Aug 1990. Son of R.A.Cobb (Leics and N Transvaal 1980-89). 5'11½". RHB, OB. Squad No 4. Leicestershire 2007-14; l-o captain 2014. Northamptonshire debut 2015; cap 2018. HS 148* Le v Middx (Lord's) 2008. Nh HS 96 v Durham (Chester-le-St) 2017. BB 2-11 Le v Glos (Leicester) 2008. Nh BB 2-44 v Loughborough MCCU (Northampton) 2017. LO HS 137 Le v Lancs (Manchester) 2012 (CB40). LO BB 3-34 Le v Glos (Leicester) 2013 (Y40). T20 HS 103. T20 BB 4-22.

COTTON, Benjamin David (Clayton Hall C; Stoke-on-Trent SFC), b Stoke-on-Trent, Staffs 13 Sep 1993. 6'4". RHB, RMF. Derbyshire 2014-17. Northamptonshire 2018. HS 43 v Leics (Derby) 2015. Nh HS 24* and BB 5-48 v Sussex (Northampton) 2018. LO HS 18* v Yorks (Scarborough) 2014 (RLC). LO BB 4-43 v Worcs (Worcester) 2016 (RLC). T20 HS 30*. T20 BB 2-14.

CURRAN, Benjamin Jack (Wellington C), b Northampton 7 Jun 1996. Son of K.M.Curran (Glos, Natal, Northants, Boland and Zimbabwe 1980-81 to 1999); grandson of K.P.Curran (Rhodesia 1947-48 to 1954-55); younger brother of T.K.Curran (*see SURREY*) and elder brother of S.M.Curran (*see SURREY*). LHB, OB. Debut (Northamptonshire) 2018. Nottinghamshire 2nd XI 2016. Surrey 2nd XI 2016. Warwickshire 2nd XI 2017. Leicestershire 2nd XI 2017. HS 83* v Sussex (Northampton) 2018. T20 HS 29.

‡NQ**FAHEEM ASHRAF**, b Punjab, Pakistan 16 Jan 1994. RHB, RFM. Faisalabad 2013-14. Faisalabad Wolves 2014-15. National Bank 2015-16. Habib Bank 2016-17 to date. Joins Northamptonshire in 2019 for T20 only. **Tests** (P): 4 (2018 to 2018-19); HS 83 v Ire (Dublin) 2018 – on debut; BB 3-42 v SA (Johannesburg) 2018-19. **LOI** (P): 18 (2017 to 2018-19); HS 23 v NZ (Wellington) 2017-18; BB 5-22 v Z (Bulawayo) 2018. **IT20** (P): 25 (2017 to 2018-19); HS 21 v A (Harare) 2018; BB 3-5 v Scot (Edinburgh) 2018. HS 116 Faisalabad v Multan (Faisalabad) 2013-14 – on debut. BB 6-65 HB v KRL (Karachi) 2016-17. LO HS 71 Faisalabad W v Hyderabad Hawks (Lahore) 2014-15. LO BB 5-22 (*see LOI*). T20 HS 54*. T20 BB 6-19.

‡NQ**HOLDER, Jason** Omar, b St George, Barbados 5 Nov 1991. RHB, RMF. Barbados 2008-09 to date. CC&C 2011-12. IPL: CSK 2013 to 2013-14. SH 2014. KKR 2016. **Tests** (WI): 37 (2014 to 2018-19, 29 as captain); HS 202* v E (Bridgetown) 2018-19; BB 6-59 v B (Kingston) 2018. **LOI** (WI): 90 (2012-13 to 2018-19, 69 as captain); HS 99* v PNG (Harare) 2017-18; BB 5-27 v I (North Sound) 2017. **IT20** (WI): 11 (2013-14 to 2018-19, 3 as captain); HS 26* v P (Port of Spain) 2016-17; BB 2-27 v P (Bridgetown) 2016-17. F-c Tours (WI)(C=Captain): E 2017C; A 2015-16C; SA 2014-15; NZ 2017-18C; I 2018-19C; SL 2015-16C; Z 2017-18C; UAE (v P) 2016-17C. HS 202* (*see Tests*). BB 6-59 (*see Tests*). LO HS 99* (*see LOI*). LO BB 5-27 (*see LOI*). T20 HS 54. T20 BB 4-27.

HUTTON, Brett Alan (Worksop C), b Doncaster, Yorks 6 Feb 1993. 6'2". RHB, RM. Squad No 16. Nottinghamshire 2011-17. Northamptonshire debut 2018. HS 74 Nt v Durham (Nottingham) 2016. Nh HS 27 v Kent (Canterbury) 2018. BB 8-57 v Glos (Northampton) 2018. LO HS 34* v Leics (Northampton) 2018 (RLC). LO BB 3-72 Nt v Kent (Nottingham) 2015 (RLC). T20 HS 18*. T20 BB 2-28.

KEOGH, Robert Ian (Queensbury S; Dunstable C), b Luton, Beds 21 Oct 1991. 5'11". RHB, OB. Squad No 14. Debut (Northamptonshire) 2012. Bedfordshire 2009-10. HS 221 v Hants (Southampton) 2013. BB 9-52 (13-125 match) v Glamorgan (Northampton) 2016. LO HS 134 v Durham (Northampton) 2016 (RLC). LO BB 2-26 v Yorks (Leeds) 2018 (RLC). T20 HS 41*. T20 BB 2-27.

NQ**LEVI, Richard** Ernst, b Johannesburg, South Africa 14 Jan 1988. 5'11". RHB, RM. Squad No 88. W Province 2006-07 to 2016-17. Cape Cobras 2008-09 to 2015-16. Northamptonshire debut 2014 (Kolpak signing); cap 2017. IPL: MI 2012. **IT20** (SA): 13 (2011-12 to 2012-13); HS 117* v NZ (Hamilton) 2011-12. HS 168 v Essex (Northampton) 2015. LO HS 166 Cobras v Titans (Paarl) 2012-13. T20 HS 117*.

‡NQ**MUZARABANI, Blessing** (Churchill S), b Harare, Zimbabwe 2 Oct 1996. Younger brother of T.Muzarabani (Centrals, MWR, SR, ME, HME 2006-07 to 2017-18). 6'6". RHB, RFM. Rising Stars 2017-18. Joins Northamptonshire in 2019 on three-year Kolpak deal. **Tests** (Z): 1 (2017-18); HS 10 and BB – v SA (Port Elizabeth) 2017-18. **LOI** (Z): 18 (2017-18 to 2018); HS 7 v Scot (Bulawayo) 2017-18; BB 4-47 v Afg (Bulawayo) 2017-18. **IT20** (Z): 6 (2017-18 to 2018); HS 1* v A (Harare) 2018; BB 3-21 v A (Harare) 2018 – separate matches. HS 23 RS v Midlands Rhinos (Kwekwe) 2017-18. BB 5-32 RS v BMT (Kwekwe) 2017-18. LO HS 7 (*see LOI*). LO BB 4-47 (*see LOI*). T20 HS 1*. T20 BB 3-21.

NEWTON, Robert Irving (Framlingham C), b Taunton, Somerset 18 Jan 1990. 5'8". RHB, OB. Squad No 10. Debut (Northamptonshire) 2010; cap 2017. 1000 runs (1): 1060 (2017). HS 202* v Leics (Northampton) 2016. BB 1-82 v Derbys (Derby) 2017. LO HS 107 v Worcs (Northampton) 2017 (RLC). T20 HS 38.

PROCTER, Luke Anthony (Counthill S, Oldham), b Oldham 24 June 1988. 5'11". LHB, RM. Squad No 2. Lancashire 2010-17. Northamptonshire debut 2017. HS 137 v Hants (Manchester) 2016. Nh HS 94 v Leics (Leicester) 2017. BB 7-71 v Surrey (Liverpool) 2012. Nh BB 5-33 v Durham (Chester-le-St) 2017. LO HS 97 v West Indies A (Manchester) 2010. LO BB 3-29 v Unicorns (Colwyn Bay) 2010 (CB40). T20 HS 25*. T20 BB 3-22.

ROSSINGTON, Adam Matthew (Mill Hill S), b Edgware, Middx 5 May 1993. 5'11". RHB, WK, occ RM. Squad No 7. Middlesex 2010-14. Northamptonshire debut 2015. HS 138* v Sussex (Arundel) 2016. Won 2013 Walter Lawrence Trophy with 55-minute 55-century v Cambridge MCCU (Cambridge). LO HS 97 v Notts (Nottingham) 2016 (RLC). T20 HS 85.

SANDERSON, Ben William (Ecclesfield CS; Sheffield C), b Sheffield, Yorks 3 Jan 1989. 6'0". RHB, RMF. Squad No 26. Yorkshire 2008-10. Northamptonshire debut 2015; cap 2018. Shropshire 2013-15. HS 42 v Kent (Canterbury) 2015. 50 wkts (2); most – 60 (2018). BB 8-73 v Glos (Northampton) 2016. LO HS 19* and LO BB 3-36 v Durham (Chester-le-St) 2017 (RLC). T20 HS 12*. T20 BB 4-21.

SOLE, Thomas Barclay (Merchiston Castle S; Cardiff Met U), b Edinburgh, Scotland 12 Jun 1996. Younger brother of C.B.Sole (Scotland 2016 to 2017-18); son of D.M.B.Sole (Scotland Grand Slam-winning rugby union captain); nephew of C.R.Trembath (Gloucestershire 1982-84). RHB, OB. Squad No 90. Northamptonshire 2nd XI debut 2015. Awaiting f-c debut. **LOI** (Scot): 5 (2017-18); HS 20 v Ire (Dubai, ICCA) 2017-18; BB 4-15 v Hong Kong (Bulawayo) 2017-18. LO HS 54 v S Africans (Northampton) 2017. LO BB 4-15 *(see LOI)*. T20 HS 7*. T20 BB –.

THURSTON, Charles Oliver (Bedford S; Loughborough U), b Cambridge 17 Aug 1996. RHB, RM. Loughborough MCCU 2016-18. Northamptonshire debut 2018. Bedfordshire 2014-17. Middlesex 2nd XI 2013-14. Northamptonshire 2nd XI debut 2015. HS 126 LU v Northants (Northampton) 2017. Nh HS 29 v Sussex (Northampton) 2018. BB –. LO HS 53 v Yorks (Leeds) 2018 (RLC). T20 HS 41.

NQ**VASCONCELOS, Ricardo** Surrador (St Stithians), b Johannesburg, South Africa 27 Oct 1997. LHB, WK. Squad No 27. Boland 2016-17 to 2017-18. Northamptonshire debut 2018. South Africa U19 2016. Portuguese passport. HS 140 Boland v Namibia (Windhoek) 2017-18 and 140 v Middx (Northampton) 2018. LO HS 56 Boland v Namibia (Windhoek) 2017-18. T20 HS 45*.

WAKELY, Alexander George (Bedford S), b Hammersmith, London 3 Nov 1988. 6'2". RHB, RM. Squad No 8. Debut (Northamptonshire) 2007; cap 2012; captain 2015 to date. Bedfordshire 2004-05. HS 123 v Leics (Northampton) 2015. BB 2-62 v Somerset (Taunton) 2007. LO HS 109* v Lancs (Liverpool) 2017 (RLC). LO BB 2-14 v Lancs (Northampton) 2007 (P40). T20 HS 64. T20 BB –.

WHITE, Graeme Geoffrey (Stowe S), b Milton Keynes, Bucks 18 Apr 1987. 5'11". RHB, SLA. Squad No 87. Debut (Northamptonshire) 2006. Nottinghamshire 2010-13. HS 65 v Glamorgan (Colwyn Bay) 2007. BB 6-44 v Glamorgan (Northampton) 2016. LO HS 41* v Yorks (Leeds) 2018 (RLC). LO BB 6-37 v Lancs (Northampton) 2016 (RLC). T20 HS 34. T20 BB 5-22 Nt v Lancs (Nottingham) 2013 – Nt record.

ZAIB, Saif Ali (RGS High Wycombe), b High Wycombe, Bucks 22 May 1998. LHB, SLA. Squad No 5. Debut (Northamptonshire) 2015. Northamptonshire 2nd XI debut 2013, aged 15y 90d. HS 65* v Glamorgan (Swansea) 2016. BB 6-115 v Loughborough MCCU (Northampton) 2017 CC BB 5-148 v Leics (Northampton) 2016. LO HS 17 and LO BB 2-22 v South Africans (Northampton) 2017. T20 HS 6. T20 BB –.

(Having made a County 1st XI appearance in 2018, even if not formally contracted. Some may return in 2019.)

^NQ^BRACEWELL, Douglas Andrew John, b Tauranga, New Zealand 28 Sep 1990. Son of B.P.Bracewell (Central Districts, Otago, Northern Districts & NZ 1977-78 to 1989-90); nephew of J.G.Bracewell (Otago, Auckland & NZ 1978-79 to 1989-90), D.W.Bracewell (Canterbury and Central Districts 1974-75 to 1979-80) and M.A.Bracewell (Otago 1977-78); cousin of M.G.Bracewell (Otago and Wellington 2010-11 to date). RHB, RM. Central Districts 2008-09 to date. Northamptonshire 2018. IPL: DD 2012. **Tests** (NZ): 27 (2011-12 to 2016); HS 47 v SL (Dunedin) 2015-16; BB 6-40 v A (Hobart) 2011-12. **LOI** (NZ): 19 (2011-12 to 2018-19); HS 57 v I (Mt Maunganui) 2018-19; BB 4-55 v WI (Whangarei) 2017-18. **IT20** (NZ): 18 (2011-12 to 2018-19); HS 44 v SL (Auckland) 2018-19; BB 3-25 v Z (Harare) 2011-12. F-c Tours (NZ): E 2013, 2015; A 2011-12, 2015-16; SA 2012-13, 2016; WI 2012; I 2012, 2013-14 (NZA); SL 2012-13, 2013-14 (NZA); Z 2011-12; B 2013-14. Nh HS 105 CD v Otago (Queenstown) 2014-15. Nh HS 81 and Nh BB 4-71 v Warwks (Birmingham) 2018. BB 7-35 CD v Canterbury (Rangiora) 2012-13. LO HS 80 CD v ND (Whangarei) 2015-16. LO BB 4-43 CD v Canterbury (Rangiora) 2010-11. T20 HS 44. T20 BB 3-21.

CROOK, Steven Paul (Rostrevor C; Magill U), b Modbury, S Australia 28 May 1983. Younger brother of A.R.Crook (S Australia, Aus Academy, Lancashire, Northamptonshire 1998-99 to 2008). 5'11". RHB, RFM. UK passport. Lancashire 2003-05. Northamptonshire 2005-18; cap 2013; testimonial 2018. Middlesex 2011-12. HS 145 v Worcs (Worcester) 2016. BB 5-48 M v Lancs (Lord's) 2012. Nh BB 5-71 v Essex (Northampton) 2009. LO HS 100 SJD v PDSC (Savar) 2013-14. LO BB 5-36 v Warwks (Northampton) 2013 (Y40). T20 HS 63. T20 BB 3-19.

DUCKETT, B.M. – see NOTTINGHAMSHIRE.

GLEESON, R.J. – see LANCASHIRE.

^NQ^KLEINVELDT, Rory Keith, b Cape Town, South Africa 15 Mar 1983. Cousin of M.C.Kleinveldt (W Province 2010-11 to date). Nephew of J.Kleinveldt (W Province and Transvaal 1979-80 to 1982-83). 6'2". RHB, RFM W Province 2002-03 to 2005-06. Cape Cobras 2005-06 to date. Hampshire 2008 (1 game). Northamptonshire 2015-18; cap 2016. **Tests** (SA): 4 (2012-13); HS 17* v A (Brisbane) 2012-13; BB 3-65 v A (Adelaide) 2012-13. **LOI** (SA): 10 (2012-13 to 2013); HS 43 v E (Oval) 2013; BB 4-22 v P (Bloemfontein) 2012-13. **IT20** (SA): 6 (2008-09 to 2012-13); HS 22 v P (Centurion) 2012-13; BB 3-18 v NZ (Durban) 2012-13. F-c Tours (SA A): A 2012-13 (SA); I 2007-08; SL 2010. HS 115* WP v KZN (Chatsworth) 2005-06. Nh HS 97 v Derbys (Northampton) 2016. 50 wkts (2); most – 57 (2015). BB 9-65 (13-98 match) v Notts (Northampton) 2017. LO HS 128 v Notts (Nottingham) 2016 (RLC). LO BB 4-22 (see LOI). T20 HS 46. T20 BB 3-14.

^NQ^PRASANNA, Seekkuge (Rewatha C), b Balapitiya, Sri Lanka 27 Jun 1985. 5'9". RHB, LB. Sri Lanka Army 2006-07 to date. Kandurata 2008-09 to 2009-10. Northamptonshire 2016-18. **Tests** (SL): 1 (2011); HS 5 and BB – v A (Pallekele) 2011. **LOI** (SL): 40 (2011 to 2018-19); HS 95 v Ire (Dublin) 2016; BB 3-32 v A (Colombo, RPS) 2011. **IT20** (SL): 20 (2013-14 to 2017-18); HS 37* v SA (Cape Town) 2016-17; BB 2-45 v P (Dubai, DSC) 2013-14. F-c Tour (SL A): E 2011. Nh HS 89 SL Army v SLPA (Panagoda) 2018-19. Nh HS 31 v Worcs (Northampton) 2016. 50 wkts (0+4); most – 71 (2008-09). BB 8-59 (12-95 match) SL Army v Bloomfield (Panagoda) 2008-09. NH BB 5-97 v Glos (Bristol) 2016. LO HS 95 (see LOI). LO BB 6-23 SL A v EL (Worcester) 2011. T20 HS 53. T20 BB 4-19.

WADE, Gareth (Prudhoe Community HS; Sunderland U), b Hexham, Northumberland 11 Jan 1991. RHB, RMF. Northamptonshire 2017-18. Northumberland 2014 to date. HS 1* and BB 1-75 v Pakistanis (Northampton) 2018. T20 BB –.

NORTHAMPTONSHIRE 2018

RESULTS SUMMARY

	Place	Won	Lost	Drew	Tied	Aband	NR
Specsavers County Champ (2nd Division)	9th	4	8	1		1	
All First-Class Matches		4	9	1		2	
Royal London One-Day Cup (North Group)	7th	2	5				1
Vitality Blast (North Group)	9th	2	11		1		

SPECSAVERS COUNTY CHAMPIONSHIP AVERAGES

BATTING AND FIELDING

Cap		M	I	NO	HS	Runs	Avge	100	50	Ct/St
2013	S.P.Crook	5	9	–	92	351	39.00	–	3	2
	B.J.Curran	5	9	1	83*	251	31.37	–	2	3
	R.S.Vasconcelos	10	18	–	140	554	30.77	1	4	14/1
2012	A.G.Wakely	12	22	1	106	600	28.57	1	4	4
2017	R.I.Newton	4	7	–	46	183	26.14	–	–	1
2017	R.E.Levi	11	20	1	75	492	25.89	–	2	15
2016	B.M.Duckett	8	16	1	133	375	25.00	1	1	5
	A.M.Rossington	11	19	1	58	419	23.27	–	3	34
	L.A.Procter	10	20	1	70	442	23.26	–	3	2
	D.A.J.Bracewell	3	6	1	81	113	22.60	–	1	2
	C.O.Thurston	2	4	–	29	78	19.50	–	–	1
	S.A.Zaib	7	11	1	57	163	16.30	–	1	–
	B.D.Cotton	2	4	2	24*	32	16.00	–	–	2
2018	J.J.Cobb	5	10	–	30	140	14.00	–	–	–
	S.Prasanna	2	4	–	27	42	10.50	–	–	–
	N.L.Buck	9	15	2	20	135	10.38	–	–	–
	B.A.Hutton	12	20	2	27	184	10.22	–	–	9
	R.I.Keogh	4	7	–	29	69	9.85	–	–	3
2018	B.W.Sanderson	13	21	13	36	72	9.00	–	–	3
2016	R.K.Kleinveldt	3	5	–	21	45	9.00	–	–	1
	R.J.Gleeson	4	7	1	26	38	6.33	–	–	–

BOWLING

	O	M	R	W	Avge	Best	5wI	10wM
B.D.Cotton	44	13	101	10	10.10	5-48	1	–
R.J.Gleeson	90.3	19	256	16	16.00	6-79	1	–
B.W.Sanderson	422	112	1002	60	16.70	5-16	2	–
R.K.Kleinveldt	95.1	14	282	14	20.14	4-51	–	–
L.A.Procter	101.1	29	341	14	24.35	5-33	1	–
S.Prasanna	72	7	247	10	24.70	4-49	–	–
N.L.Buck	196.5	29	782	31	25.22	4-51	–	–
B.A.Hutton	367.2	86	1143	45	25.40	8-57	3	–
D.A.J.Bracewell	93	19	304	11	27.63	4-71	–	–
Also bowled:								
S.P.Crook	32.2	5	146	8	18.25	4-51		

J.J.Cobb 3.4-0-28-0; R.I.Keogh 53.5-205-2; S.A.Zaib 26.4-8-52-2.

The First-Class Averages (pp 230–245) give the records of Northamptonshire players in all first-class county matches (Northamptonshire's other opponents being the Pakistanis), with the exception of R.J.Gleeson and C.O.Thurston, whose first-class figures for Northamptonshire are as above, and:
B.M.Duckett 9-18-1-133-416-24.47-1-1-5ct. Did not bowl.

NORTHAMPTONSHIRE RECORDS

FIRST-CLASS CRICKET

Highest Total	For 781-7d		v	Notts	Northampton	1995
	V 701-7d		by	Kent	Beckenham	2017
Lowest Total	For 12		v	Glos	Gloucester	1907
	V 33		by	Lancashire	Northampton	1977
Highest Innings	For 331*	M.E.K.Hussey	v	Somerset	Taunton	2003
	V 333	K.S.Duleepsinhji	for	Sussex	Hove	1930

Highest Partnership for each Wicket

1st	375	R.A.White/M.J.Powell	v	Glos	Northampton	2002
2nd	344	G.Cook/R.J.Boyd-Moss	v	Lancashire	Northampton	1986
3rd	393	A.Fordham/A.J.Lamb	v	Yorkshire	Leeds	1990
4th	370	R.T.Virgin/P.Willey	v	Somerset	Northampton	1976
5th	401	M.B.Loye/D.Ripley	v	Glamorgan	Northampton	1998
6th	376	R.Subba Row/A.Lightfoot	v	Surrey	The Oval	1958
7th	293	D.J.G.Sales/D.Ripley	v	Essex	Northampton	1999
8th	179	A.J.Hall/J.D.Middlebrook	v	Surrey	The Oval	2011
9th	156	R.Subba Row/S.Starkie	v	Lancashire	Northampton	1955
10th	148	B.W.Bellamy/J.V.Murdin	v	Glamorgan	Northampton	1925

Best Bowling	For 10-127	V.W.C.Jupp	v	Kent	Tunbridge W	1932
(Innings)	V 10- 30	C.Blythe	for	Kent	Northampton	1907
Best Bowling	For 15- 31	G.E.Tribe	v	Yorkshire	Northampton	1958
(Match)	V 17- 48	C.Blythe	for	Kent	Northampton	1907

Most Runs – Season	2198	D.Brookes (av 51.11)	1952
Most Runs – Career	28980	D.Brookes (av 36.13)	1934-59
Most 100s – Season	8	R.A.Haywood	1921
Most 100s – Career	67	D.Brookes	1934-59
Most Wkts – Season	175	G.E.Tribe (av 18.70)	1955
Most Wkts – Career	1102	E.W.Clark (av 21.26)	1922-47
Most Career W-K Dismissals	810	K.V.Andrew (653 ct; 157 st)	1953-66
Most Career Catches in the Field	469	D.S.Steele	1963-84

LIMITED-OVERS CRICKET

Highest Total	50ov	425		v	Notts	Nottingham	2016
	40ov	324-6		v	Warwicks	Birmingham	2013
	T20	231-5		v	Warwicks	Birmingham	2018
Lowest Total	50ov	62		v	Leics	Leicester	1974
	40ov	41		v	Middlesex	Northampton	1972
	T20	47		v	Durham	Chester-le-St[2]	2011
Highest Innings	50ov	161	D.J.G.Sales	v	Yorkshire	Northampton	2006
	40ov	172*	W.Larkins	v	Warwicks	Luton	1983
	T20	111*	L.Klusener	v	Worcs	Kidderminster	2007
Best Bowling	50ov	7-10	C.Pietersen	v	Denmark	Brondby	2005
	40ov	7-39	A.Hodgson	v	Somerset	Northampton	1976
	T20	6-21	A.J.Hall	v	Worcs	Northampton	2008

NOTTINGHAMSHIRE

Formation of Present Club: March/April 1841
Substantial Reorganisation: 11 December 1866
Inaugural First-Class Match: 1864
Colours: Green and Gold
Badge: Leaping stag
County Champions (since 1890): (6) 1907, 1929,
1981, 1987, 2005, 2010
NatWest Trophy Winners: (1) 1987
Benson and Hedges Cup Winners: (1) 1989
Sunday League Winners: (1) 1991
Yorkshire Bank 40 Winners: (1) 2013
Royal London Cup Winners: (1) 2017
Twenty20 Cup Winners: (1) 2017

NOTTINGHAMSHIRE
COUNTY CRICKET CLUB

Chief Executive: Lisa Pursehouse, Trent Bridge, West Bridgford, Nottingham NG2 6AG •
Tel: 0115 982 3000 • Email: questions@nottsccc.co.uk • Web: www.trentbridge.co.uk •
Twitter: @TrentBridge (72,678 followers)

Director of Cricket: Mick Newell. **Head Coach**: Peter Moores. **Assistant Head Coach**:
Paul Franks. **Bowling Coach**: Andy Pick. **Captains**: S.J.Mullaney (f-c & l-o) and
D.T.Christian (T20). **Overseas Player**: D.T.Christian. **2019 Testimonial**: S.C.J.Broad.
Head Groundsman: Steve Birks. **Scorer**: Roger Marshall and Anne Cusworth. ‡ New
registration. [NQ] Not qualified for England.

BALL, Jacob Timothy ('Jake') (Meden CS), b Mansfield 14 Mar 1991. Nephew of
B.N.French (Notts and England 1976-95). 6'0". RHB, RFM. Squad No 28. Debut
(Nottinghamshire) 2011; cap 2016. MCC 2016. **Tests**: 4 (2016 to 2017-18); HS 31 and BB
1-47 v I (Mumbai) 2016-17. **LOI**: 18 (2016-17 to 2018); HS 28 v B (Dhaka) 2016-17; BB
5-51 v B (Dhaka) 2016-17 – different games. **IT20**: 2 (2018); HS – ; BB 1-39 v I (Bristol)
2018. F-c Tours: A 2017-18; I 2016-17. HS 49* v Warwks (Nottingham) 2015. 50 wkts (1):
54 (2016). BB 6-49 v Sussex (Nottingham) 2015. Hat-trick v Middx (Nottingham) 2016. LO
HS 28 (*see LOI*). BB 5-51 (*see LOI*). T20 HS 8*. T20 BB 3-27.

BLATHERWICK, Jack Morgan (Holgate Ac, Hucknall; Central C, Nottingham), b Nottingham 4 June 1998. RHB, RMF. Squad No 47. Awaiting f-c debut. Nottinghamshire 2nd XI
debut 2016. England U19 2017. LO HS 3* v Warwks (Nottingham) 2018 (RLC). LO BB – .

BROAD, Stuart Christopher John (Oakham S), b Nottingham 24 Jun 1986. 6'6". LHB,
RFM. Squad No 8. Son of B.C.Broad (Glos, Notts, OFS and England 1979-94). Debut
(Leicestershire) 2005; cap 2007. Nottinghamshire debut/cap 2008; testimonial 2019. Big
Bash: HH 2016-17. YC 2006. *Wisden* 2009. **ECB Test Central Contract 2018-19. Tests**:
126 (2007-08 to 2018-19); HS 169 v P (Lord's) 2010, sharing in record Test and UK f-c 8th
wkt partnership of 332 with I.J.L.Trott; 50 wkts (2); most – 62 (2013); BB 8-15 v A
(Nottingham) 2015. Hat-tricks: v I (Nottingham) 2011, and v SL (Leeds) 2014. **LOI**: 121
(2006 to 2015-16, 3 as captain); HS 45* v I (Manchester) 2007; BB 5-23 v SA (Nottingham)
2008. **IT20**: 56 (2006 to 2013-14, 27 as captain); HS 18* v SA (Chester-le-St) 2012 and 18*
v A (Melbourne) 2013-14; BB 4-24 v NZ (Auckland) 2012-13. F-c Tours: A 2010-11,
2013-14, 2017-18; SA 2009-10, 2015-16; WI 2005-06 (Eng A), 2008-09, 2014-15, 2018-19;
NZ 2007-08, 2012-13, 2017-18; I 2008-09, 2012-13, 2016-17; SL 2007-08, 2011-12,
2018-19; B 2006-07 (Eng A), 2009-10, 2016-17; UAE 2011-12 (v P), 2015-16 (v P). HS 169
(*see Tests*). CC HS 91* Le v Derbys (Leicester) 2007. Nt HS 60 v Worcs (Nottingham) 2009.
BB 8-15 (*see Tests*). CC BB 8-52 (11-131 match) Nt v Warwks (Birmingham) 2010. LO HS
45* (*see LOI*). LO BB 5-23 (*see LOI*). T20 HS 18*. T20 BB 4-24.

CARTER, Matthew (Branston S), b Lincoln 26 May 1996. Younger brother of A.Carter (*see WORCESTERSHIRE*). RHB, OB. Squad No 20. Debut (Nottinghamshire) 2015, taking 7-56 v Somerset (Taunton) – the best debut figures for Nt since 1914. Nottinghamshire 2nd XI debut 2013. Lincolnshire 2013-17. HS 33 v Sussex (Hove) 2017. BB 7-56 (10-195 match) (*see above*). LO HS 17 v Kent (Nottingham) 2018 (RLC). LO BB 4-40 v Warwks (Nottingham) 2018 (RLC). T20 HS 16*. T20 BB 1-25.

‡**CHAPPELL**, Zachariah John ('**Zak**') (Stamford S), b Grantham, Lincs 21 Aug 1996. 6'4". RHB, RFM. Squad No 32. Leicestershire 2015-18. HS 96 Le v Derbys (Derby) 2015. BB 6-44 Le v Northants (Northampton) 2018. LO HS 59* Le v Durham (Gosforth) 2017 (RLC). LO BB 3-45 Le v Durham (Leicester) 2018. T20 HS 16. T20 BB 3-23.

ᴺᴼ**CHRISTIAN**, Daniel Trevor, b Camperdown, NSW, Australia 4 May 1983. RHB, RFM. Squad No 54. S Australia 2007-08 to 2012-13. Hampshire 2010. Gloucestershire 2013; cap 2013. Victoria 2013-14 to 2017-18. Nottinghamshire debut 2016, having joined in 2015 for l-o and T20 only; cap 2015; captain 2016 to date (T20 only). IPL: DC 2011-12. RCB 2013. RPS 2017. DD 2018. Big Bash: BH 2011-12 to 2014-15. HH 2015-16 to 2017-18. MR 2018-19. **LOI** (A): 19 (2011-12 to 2013-14); HS 39 v I (Adelaide) 2011-12; BB 5-31 v SL (Melbourne) 2011-12. **IT20** (A): 16 (2009-10 to 2017-18); HS 9 v I (Ranchi) 2017-18; BB 3-27 v WI (Gros Islet) 2011-12. HS 131* SA v NSW (Adelaide) 2011-12. CC HS 36 and CC BB 2-115 H v Somerset (Taunton) 2010. Nt HS 31 v Hants (Southampton) 2016. BB 5-24 SA v WA (Perth) (2009-10). Nt BB 1-22 v Warwks (Birmingham) 2016. LO HS 117 Vic v NSW (Sydney) 2013-14. LO BB 6-48 SA v Vic (Geelong) 2010-11. T20 HS 129 M v Kent (Canterbury) 2014 – M record. T20 BB 5-14.

‡**CLARKE, Joe** Michael (Llanfyllin HS), b Shrewsbury, Shrops 26 May 1996. 5'11". RHB, WK. Squad No 33. Worcestershire 2015-18. MCC 2017. Worcestershire 2nd XI debut 2013. Shropshire 2012-13. England U19 2014. F-c Tours (EL): WI 2017-18; UAE 2016-17 (v Afg). 1000 runs (1): 1325 (2016). HS 194 Wo v Derbys (Worcester) 2016. BB –. LO HS 131* Wo v Glos (Worcester) 2015 (RLC). T20 HS 124*.

COUGHLIN, Paul (St Robert of Newminster Catholic CS, Washington), b Sunderland, Co Durham 23 Oct 1992. Elder brother of J.Coughlin (*see DURHAM*); nephew of T.Harland (Durham 1974-78). 6'3". RHB, RM. Squad No 29. Durham 2012-17. Joined Nottinghamshire in 2018, but awaiting f-c debut. Northumberland 2011. F-c Tour (EL): WI 2017-18. HS 85 Du v Lancs (Chester-le-St) 2014, sharing Du record 9th wkt partnership of 150 with P.Mustard. BB 5-49 (10-133 match) Du v Northants (Chester-le-St) 2017. LO HS 22 Du v Notts (Nottingham) 2017 (RLC) and 22 Du v Lancs (Chester-le-St) 2017 (RLC). LO BB 3-36 Du v Worcs (Worcester) 2017 (RLC). T20 HS 53. T20 BB 5-42.

DUCKETT, Ben Matthew (Stowe S), b Farnborough, Kent 17 Oct 1994. 5'7". LHB, WK, occ OB. Squad No 17. Northamptonshire 2013-18; cap 2016. Nottinghamshire debut 2018. MCC 2017. Big Bash: HH 2018-19. Northamptonshire 2nd XI debut 2011. England U19 2012-13. PCA 2016. YC 2016. *Wisden* 2016. **Tests**: 4 (2016-17); HS 56 v B (Dhaka) 2016-17. **LOI**: 3 (2016-17); HS 63 v B (Chittagong) 2016-17. F-c Tours: I 2016-17; B 2016-17. 1000 runs (2); most – 1338 (2016). HS 282* Nh v Sussex (Northampton) 2016. Nt HS 80 v Yorks (Nottingham) 2018. BB 1-21 Nh v Kent (Beckenham) 2017. LO HS 220* EL v SL A (Canterbury) 2016. T20 HS 96.

FLETCHER, Luke Jack (Henry Mellish S, Nottingham), b Nottingham 18 Sep 1988. 6'6". RHB, RMF. Squad No 19. Debut (Nottinghamshire) 2008; cap 2014. Surrey 2015 (on loan). Derbyshire 2016 (on loan). HS 92 v Hants (Southampton) 2009 and 92 v Durham (Chester-le-St) 2017. BB 5-27 v Worcs (Worcester) 2018. LO HS 53* v Kent (Nottingham) 2018 (RLC). LO BB 4-20 v Worcs (Nottingham) 2018 (RLC). T20 HS 27. T20 BB 4-30.

FOOTITT, Mark Harold Alan (Carlton le Willows S; West Notts C), b Nottingham 25 Nov 1985. 6'2". RHB, LFM. Squad No 7. Nottinghamshire debut 2005, returned in 2017. Derbyshire 2010-18; cap 2014. Surrey 2016-17. MCC 2006. F-c Tour: SA 2015-16. HS 34 De v Leics (Leicester) 2015. Nt HS 21* v Essex (Nottingham) 2018. 50 wkts (2); most – 84 (2014). BB 7-62 Sy v Lancs (Oval) 2016. Nt BB 5-45 v West Indies A (Nottingham) 2006. LO HS 11* De v Notts (Nottingham) 2014 (RLC). LO BB 5-28 De v Scotland (Edinburgh) 2013 (Y40). T20 HS 2*. T20 BB 3-22.

GURNEY, Harry Frederick (Garendon HS; Loughborough GS; Leeds U), b Nottingham 25 Oct 1986. 6'2". RHB, LFM. Squad No 11. Leicestershire 2007-11. Nottinghamshire debut 2012; cap 2014. MCC 2014. Bradford/Leeds UCCE 2006-07 (not f-c). **LOI**: 10 (2014 to 2014-15); HS 6* v SL (Colombo, RPS) 2014-15; BB 4-55 v SL (Lord's) 2014. **IT20**: 2 (2014); BB 2-26 v SL (Oval) 2014. HS 42* v Sussex (Hove) 2017. BB 6-25 v Lancs (Manchester) 2018. Hat-trick v Sussex (Hove) 2013. LO HS 13* v Durham (Chester-le-St) 2012 (CB40). LO BB 5-24 Le v Hants (Leicester) 2010 (CB40). T20 HS 6. T20 BB 4-17.

HALES, Alexander Daniel (Chesham HS), b Hillingdon, Middx 3 Jan 1989. 6'5". RHB, OB, occ WK. Squad No 10. Debut (Nottinghamshire) 2008; cap 2011. Agreed white-ball-only contract in 2018. Worcestershire 2014 (1 game, on loan). Buckinghamshire 2006-07. IPL: SH 2018. Big Bash: MR 2012-13. AS 2013-14. HH 2014-15. **ECB L-O Central Contract 2018-19. Tests**: 11 (2015-16 to 2016); HS 94 v SL (Lord's) 2016; BB – . **LOI**: 70 (2014 to 2018-19); HS 171* v P (Nottingham) 2016. **IT20**: 60 (2011 to 2018-19); HS 116* v SL (Chittagong) 2014-15 – E record. 1000 runs (3); most – 1127 (2011). HS 236 v Yorks (Nottingham) 2015. BB 2-63 v Yorks (Nottingham) 2009. LO HS 187* v Surrey (Lord's) 2017 (RLC) – Nt record. T20 HS 116*.

JAMES, Lyndon Wallace (Oakham S), b Worksop 27 Dec 1998. RHB, RMF. Debut (Nottinghamshire) 2018. Nottinghamshire 2nd XI debut 2017. HS 13 and BB 3-54 v Essex (Nottingham) 2018 – only 1st XI appearance.

LIBBY, Jacob ('**Jake**') Daniel (Plymouth C; UWIC), b Plymouth, Devon 3 Jan 1993. 5'9". RHB, OB. Squad No 2. Cardiff MCCU 2014. Nottinghamshire debut 2014, scoring 108 v Sussex (Nottingham). Northamptonshire 2016 (on loan). Cornwall 2011-14. HS 144 v Durham (Chester-le-St) 2016. BB 1-13 Nh v Leics (Leicester) 2016. Nt BB 1-23 v Yorks (Nottingham) 2018. T20 HS 58.

MOORES, Thomas James (Loughborough GS), b Brighton, Sussex 4 Sep 1996. Son of P.Moores (Worcestershire, Sussex & OFS 1983-98); nephew of S.Moores (Cheshire 1995). LHB, WK. Squad No 23. Lancashire 2016 (on loan). Nottinghamshire debut 2016. Nottinghamshire 2nd XI debut 2014. HS 103 v Somerset (Taunton) 2018. LO HS 76 v Leics (Leicester) 2018 (RLC). T20 HS 80*.

MULLANEY, Steven John (St Mary's RC S, Astley), b Warrington, Cheshire 19 Nov 1986. 5'9". RHB, RM. Squad No 5. Lancashire 2006-08. Nottinghamshire debut 2010, scoring 100* v Hants (Southampton); cap 2013; captain 2018 to date. F-c Tour (EL): I 2018-19. 1000 runs (1): 1148 (2016). HS 168 v Kent (Nottingham) 2017. BB 5-32 v Glos (Nottingham) 2017. LO HS 124 v Durham (Chester-le-St) 2018 (RLC). LO BB 4-29 v Kent (Nottingham) 2013 (Y40). T20 HS 55. T20 BB 4-19.

NASH, Christopher David (Collyer's SFC; Loughborough U), b Cuckfield, Sussex 19 May 1983. 5'11". RHB, OB. Squad No 3. Sussex 2002-17; cap 2008; testimonial 2017. Nottinghamshire debut 2018. Loughborough UCCE 2003-04. British U 2004. 1000 runs (4); most – 1321 (2009). HS 184 Sx v Leics (Leicester) 2010. Nt HS 139 and Nt BB 2-4 v Worcs (Nottingham) 2018. BB 4-12 Sx v Glamorgan (Cardiff) 2010. LO HS 124* Sx v Kent (Canterbury) 2011 (CB40). LO BB 4-40 Sx v Yorks (Hove) 2009 (FPT). T20 HS 112*. T20 BB 4-7.

PATEL, Samit Rohit (Worksop C), b Leicester 30 Nov 1984. Elder brother of A.Patel (Derbyshire and Notts 2007-11). 5'8". RHB, SLA. Squad No 21. Debut (Nottinghamshire) 2002; cap 2008; testimonial 2017. MCC 2014, 2016. PCA 2017. **Tests**: 6 (2011-12 to 2015-16); HS 42 v P (Sharjah) 2015-16; BB 2-27 v SL (Galle) 2011-12. **LOI**: 36 (2008 to 2012-13); HS 70* v I (Mohali) 2011-12; BB 5-41 v SA (Oval) 2008. **IT20**: 18 (2011 to 2012-13); HS 67 v SL (Pallekele) 2012-13; BB 2-6 v Afg (Colombo, RPS) 2012-13. F-c Tours: NZ 2008-09 (Eng A); I 2012-13; SL 2011-12; UAE 2015-16 (v P). 1000 runs (2); most – 1125 (2014). HS 257* v Glos (Bristol) 2017. BB 7-68 (11-111 match) v Hants (Southampton) 2011. LO HS 129* v Warwks (Nottingham) 2013 (Y40). LO BB 6-13 v Ireland (Dublin) 2009 (FPT). T20 HS 90*. T20 BB 4-20.

SLATER, Benjamin Thomas (Netherthorpe S; Leeds Met U), b Chesterfield, Derbys 26 Aug 1991. 5'10". LHB, OB. Squad No 26. Debut (Leeds/Bradford MCCU) 2012. Southern Rocks 2012-13. Derbyshire 2013-18. Nottinghamshire debut 2018. HS 119 De v Leics (Derby) 2014, also scored 104 in same match. Nt HS 109 v Yorks (Nottingham) 2018. BB –. LO HS 148* v Northants (Northampton) 2016 (RLC). T20 HS 57.

WOOD, Luke (Portland CS, Worksop), b Sheffield, Yorks 2 Aug 1995. 5'9". LHB, LFM. Squad No 14. Debut (Nottinghamshire) 2014. England U19 2014 (on loan). Nottinghamshire 2nd XI debut 2012. England U19 2014. HS 100 v Sussex (Nottingham) 2015. BB 5-40 v Cambridge MCCU (Cambridge) 2016. CC BB 4-31 v Northants (Northampton) 2017. LO HS 52 and LO BB 2-44 v Leics (Leicester) 2016 (RLC). T20 HS 11. T20 BB 2-15.

RELEASED/RETIRED

(Having made a County 1st XI appearance in 2018)

NOBRATHWAITE, Kraigg Clairmonte (Combermere S), b Belfield, St Michael, Barbados 1 Dec 1992. RHB, OB. Barbados 2008-09 to date. Sagicor High Performance Centre 2014. Yorkshire 2017. Nottinghamshire 2018; cap 2018. **Tests** (WI): 56 (2011 to 2018-19); HS 212 v B (Kingstown) 2014; BB 6-29 v SL (Colombo, PSS) 2015-16. **LOI** (WI): 10 (2016-17); HS 78 v Z (Bulawayo) 2016-17; BB 1-56 v SL (Bulawayo) 2016-17. F-c Tours (WI): E 2010 (WI A), 2017; A 2015-16; SA 2014-15; NZ 2013-14, 2017-18; I 2011-12, 2013-14 (WI A), 2018-19; SL 2014-15 (WI A), 2015-16; Z 2017-18; B 2011-12, 2018-19; UAE (v P) 2016-17. HS 212 (*see Tests*). Nt HS 71 v Yorks (Nottingham) 2018. BB 6-29 (*see Tests*). LO HS 108 Barb v ICC Americas (Lucas Street) 2016-17. LO BB 2-54 WI A v SL A (Dambulla) 2014-15.

FRAINE, W.A.R. – *see YORKSHIRE.*

MILNES, M.E. – *see KENT.*

ROOT, W.T. – *see GLAMORGAN.*

^{NO}**SODHI**, Inderbir Singh ('**Ish**'), b Ludhiana, Punjab, India 31 Oct 1992. RHB, LBG. Northern Districts 2012-13 to date. Nottinghamshire 2017-18 (T20 only). Big Bash: AS 2016-17. **Tests** (NZ): 17 (2013-14 to 2017-18); HS 63 v P (Abu Dhabi) 2014-15; BB 4-60 v Z (Bulawayo) 2016. **LOI** (NZ): 30 (2015 to 2018-19); HS 24 v P (Abu Dhabi) 2018-19; BB 4-58 v E (Dunedin) 2017-18. **IT20** (NZ): 33 (2014 to 2018-19); HS 15 v P (Auckland) 2017-18; BB 3-18 v I (Nagpur) 2015-16. F-c Tours (NZ): WI 2014; I 2013-14, 2016-17, 2017-18 (NZ A); SL 2013-14 (NZ A); Z 2016; B 2013-14 (NZ A). UAE 2014-15 (v P), 2018-19 (v P). HS 82* ND v Otago (Dunedin) 2014-15. BB 7-30 (12-62 match) ND v Wellington (Wellington) 2017-18. LO HS 44* ND v CD (Whangarei) 2017-18. LO BB 4-10 NZ A v SL A (Bristol) 2014. T20 HS 51. T20 BB 6-11.

^{NO}**TAYLOR**, Luteru *Ross* Poutoa Lote (Palmerston Northh BHS; Wairarapa C), b Lower Hutt, Wellington, New Zealand 8 Mar 1984. 6'0". RHB, OB. Central Districts 2002-03 to date. Sussex 2016. Nottinghamshire 2018; cap 2018. IPL: RCB 2007-08 to 2009-10. RR 2011. DD 2012-14. PW 2013. **Tests** (NZ): 92 (2007-08 to 2018-19, 14 as captain); HS 290 v A (Perth) 2015-16; BB 2-4 v I (Ahmedabad) 2010-11. **LOI** (NZ): 218 (2005-06 to 2018-19, 20 as captain); 1000 runs (1): 1046 (2015); HS 181* v E (Dunedin) 2017-18; BB –. **IT20** (NZ): 88 (2006-07 to 2018-19, 13 as captain); HS 63 v WI (Auckland) 2008-09. F-c Tours (NZ) (C=Captain): E 2008, 2013, 2015; A 2008-09, 2011-12C, 2015-16; SA 2004 (NZ A), 2007-08, 2016; WI 2012C; I 2010-11, 2012C, 2014, 2016-17; SL 2009, 2012-13C; Z 2011-12C, 2016; B 2008-09, 2013-14 (NZ A). UAE 2014-15 (v P), 2018-19 (v P). HS 290 (*see Tests*). CC HS 146 v Essex (Chelmsford) 2018. BB 2-4 (*see Tests*). LO HS 181* (*see LOI*). LO BB 1-13 CD v Canterbury (Christchurch) 2005-06. T20 HS 111*. T20 BB 3-28.

WESSELS, M.H. – *see WORCESTERSHIRE*.

B.M.Kitt left the staff without making a County 1st XI appearance in 2018.

MIDDLESEX RELEASED/RETIRED (continued from p 155)

^{NO}**FRANKLIN**, James Edward Charles (Wellington C; Victoria U), Wellington, New Zealand 7 Nov 1980. 6'4½". LHB, LM. Irish passport. Wellington 1998-99 to 2014-15. Gloucestershire 2004-10; cap 2004. Glamorgan 2006; cap 2006. Nottinghamshire 2014; cap 2014. Middlesex 2015-17; cap 2015; captain (f-c & l-o) 2017 (l-o only in 2016). IPL: MI 2011-12. Big Bash: AS 2011-12. **Tests** (NZ): 31 (2000-01 to 2012-13); HS 122* v SA (Cape Town) 2006-07; BB 6-119 v A (Auckland) 2004-05. Hat-trick v B (Dhaka) 2004-05. **LOI** (NZ): 110 (2000-01 to 2013); HS 98* v I (Bangalore) 2010-11; BB 5-42 v E (Chester-le-St) 2004. **IT20** (NZ): 38 (2005-06 to 2013); HS 60 v Z (Hamilton) 2011-12; BB 4-15 v E (Hamilton) 2012-13. F-c Tours (NZ): E 2004; A 2004-05; SA 2004-05 (NZ A), 2005-06, 2012-13; I 2012; SL 2012-13; Z 2005, 2010-11 (NZ A); B 2004-05. HS 219 Wellington v Auckland (Auckland) 2008-09. HS 135 v Worcs (Uxbridge) 2015. BB 7-14 Gs v Derbys (Bristol) 2010. M BB 4-40 v Surrey (Lord's) 2017. Hat-tricks (*see above*) and Gs v Derbys (Cheltenham) 2009, also scoring 109 in same match. LO HS 133* Gs v Derbys (Bristol) 2010 (CB40). LO BB 5-42 (*see LOI*). T20 HS 90. T20 BB 5-21.

FULLER, J.K. – *see HAMPSHIRE*.

LACE, T.C. – *on loan to DERBYSHIRE for 2019*.

PATEL, Ravi Hasmukh (Merchant Taylors', Northwood; Loughborough U), b Harrow 4 Aug 1991. 5'8". RHB, SLA. Middlesex 2010-18. Loughborough MCCU 2011. Essex 2015 (on loan). HS 26* v Warwks (Uxbridge) 2013. BB 7-81 (12-173 match) v Somerset (Taunton) 2017. LO HS 24* v Somerset (Taunton) 2018 (RLC). LO BB 4-58 v. Sussex (Hove) 2018 (RLC). T20 HS 12. T20 BB 4-18.

N.R.D.Compton left the staff without making a County 1st XI appearance in 2018.

NOTTINGHAMSHIRE 2018

RESULTS SUMMARY

	Place	Won	Lost	Drew	Aband	NR
Specsavers County Champ (1st Division)	6th	4	8	2		
All First-Class Matches		4	8	2	1	
Royal London One-Day Cup (North Group)	QF	5	3			1
Vitality Blast (North Group)	QF	8	7			

SPECSAVERS COUNTY CHAMPIONSHIP AVERAGES

BATTING AND FIELDING

Cap		M	I	NO	HS	Runs	Avge	100	50	Ct/St
	B.T.Slater	4	8	–	109	349	43.62	1	1	1
2018	K.C.Brathwaite	4	8	1	71	296	42.28	–	3	1
2018	L.R.P.L.Taylor	8	15	–	146	506	33.73	1	4	13
2013	S.J.Mullaney	11	20	–	130	601	30.05	1	4	11
	T.J.Moores	13	22	1	103	616	29.33	1	2	39
2014	M.H.Wessels	12	23	3	75*	568	28.40	–	4	14
	B.M.Duckett	3	5	–	80	133	26.60	–	1	1
	J.D.Libby	14	27	2	100*	662	26.48	1	4	6
2008	S.R.Patel	14	26	1	76	639	25.56	–	6	5
	C.D.Nash	9	17	–	139	383	22.52	1	2	4
	M.E.Milnes	6	10	5	43	100	20.00	–	–	4
	M.H.A.Footitt	3	5	3	21*	38	19.00	–	–	1
	L.Wood	6	10	2	35*	137	17.12	–	–	5
	W.T.Root	6	12	–	36	196	16.33	–	–	3
2016	J.T.Ball	6	10	2	44*	130	16.25	–	–	2
2008	S.C.J.Broad	5	8	–	38	123	15.37	–	–	2
2014	L.J.Fletcher	13	23	1	43	304	13.81	–	–	6
2014	H.F.Gurney	11	16	10	29*	73	12.16	–	–	1
	M.Carter	4	8	–	22	76	9.50	–	–	4

Also batted (1 match each): W.A.R.Fraine 19, 30; L.W.James 1, 13.

BOWLING

	O	M	R	W	Avge	Best	5wI	10wM
S.C.J.Broad	117.3	31	352	18	19.55	4- 41	–	–
J.T.Ball	171.5	38	623	28	22.25	5- 43	2	–
L.J.Fletcher	347.3	86	977	38	25.71	5- 27	1	–
H.F.Gurney	325.3	52	1137	42	27.07	6- 25	2	–
M.Carter	153.2	28	525	16	32.81	5-113	1	–
S.J.Mullaney	114	21	402	11	36.54	4- 68	–	–
L.Wood	110.1	15	411	10	41.10	3- 66	–	–
S.R.Patel	305.5	66	896	19	47.15	6-114	1	–
M.E.Milnes	153	26	527	11	47.90	4- 44	–	–

Also bowled:

M.H.A.Footitt   66.4   9   276   6   46.00   3- 69   –   –

K.C.Brathwaite 2-0-10-0; L.W.James 15-1-68-3; J.D.Libby 11.5-0-40-1; C.D.Nash 22-1-66-3; W.T.Root 9.3-1-55-3.

Nottinghamshire played no first-class fixtures outside the County Championship in 2018. The First-Class Averages (pp 230–245) give the records of Nottinghamshire players in all first-class county matches, with the exception of S.C.J.Broad, B.M.Duckett, M.H.A.Footitt, W.A.R.Fraine, B.T.Slater and L.Wood, whose first-class figures for Nottinghamshire are as above.

NOTTINGHAMSHIRE RECORDS

FIRST-CLASS CRICKET

Highest Total	For	791		v	Essex	Chelmsford	2007
	V	781-7d		by	Northants	Northampton	1995
Lowest Total	For	13		v	Yorkshire	Nottingham	1901
	V	16		by	Derbyshire	Nottingham	1879
		16		by	Surrey	The Oval	1880
Highest Innings	For	312*	W.W.Keeton	v	Middlesex	The Oval	1939
	V	345	C.G.Macartney	for	Australians	Nottingham	1921

Highest Partnership for each Wicket

1st	406*	D.J.Bicknell/G.E.Welton	v	Warwicks	Birmingham	2000
2nd	398	A.Shrewsbury/W.Gunn	v	Sussex	Nottingham	1890
3rd	367	W.Gunn/J.R.Gunn	v	Leics	Nottingham	1903
4th	361	A.O.Jones/J.R.Gunn	v	Essex	Leyton	1905
5th	359	D.J.Hussey/C.M.W.Read	v	Essex	Nottingham	2007
6th	372*	K.P.Pietersen/J.E.Morris	v	Derbyshire	Derby	2001
7th	301	C.C.Lewis/B.N.French	v	Durham	Chester-le-St[2]	1993
8th	220	G.F.H.Heane/R.Winrow	v	Somerset	Nottingham	1935
9th	170	J.C.Adams/K.P.Evans	v	Somerset	Taunton	1994
10th	152	E.B.Alletson/W.Riley	v	Sussex	Hove	1911
	152	U.Afzaal/A.J.Harris	v	Worcs	Nottingham	2000

Best Bowling	For	10-66	K.Smales	v	Glos	Stroud	1956
(Innings)	V	10-10	H.Verity	for	Yorkshire	Leeds	1932
Best Bowling	For	17-89	F.C.L.Matthews	v	Northants	Nottingham	1923
(Match)	V	17-89	W.G.Grace	for	Glos	Cheltenham	1877

Most Runs – Season	2620	W.W.Whysall	(av 53.46)		1929
Most Runs – Career	31592	G.Gunn	(av 35.69)		1902-32
Most 100s – Season	9	W.W.Whysall			1928
	9	M.J.Harris			1971
	9	B.C.Broad			1990
Most 100s – Career	65	J.Hardstaff jr			1930-55
Most Wkts – Season	181	B.Dooland	(av 14.96)		1954
Most Wkts – Career	1653	T.G.Wass	(av 20.34)		1896-1920
Most Career W-K Dismissals	983	C.M.W.Read	(939 ct; 44 st)		1998-2017
Most Career Catches in the Field	466	A.O.Jones			1892-1914

LIMITED-OVERS CRICKET

Highest Total	50ov	445-8		v	Northants	Nottingham	2016
	40ov	296-7		v	Somerset	Taunton	2002
	T20	227-3		v	Derbyshire	Nottingham	2017
Lowest Total	50ov	74		v	Leics	Leicester	1987
	40ov	57		v	Glos	Nottingham	2009
	T20	91		v	Lancashire	Manchester	2006
Highest Innings	50ov	187*	A.D.Hales	v	Surrey	Lord's	2017
	40ov	150*	A.D.Hales	v	Worcs	Nottingham	2009
	T20	113*	D.T.Christian	v	Northants	Northampton	2018
Best Bowling	50ov	6-10	K.P.Evans	v	Northumb	Jesmond	1994
	40ov	6-12	R.J.Hadlee	v	Lancashire	Nottingham	1980
	T20	5-22	G.G.White	v	Lancashire	Nottingham	2013

SOMERSET

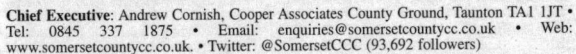

Formation of Present Club: 18 August 1875
Inaugural First-Class Match: 1882
Colours: Black, White and Maroon
Badge: Somerset Dragon
County Champions: (0); best – 2nd (Div 1) 2001, 2010, 2012, 2016
Gillette/NatWest/C&G Trophy Winners: (3) 1979, 1983, 2001
Benson and Hedges Cup Winners: (2) 1981, 1982
Sunday League Winners: (1) 1979
Twenty20 Cup Winners: (1) 2005

Chief Executive: Andrew Cornish, Cooper Associates County Ground, Taunton TA1 1JT •
Tel: 0845 337 1875 • Email: enquiries@somersetcountycc.co.uk • Web:
www.somersetcountycc.co.uk. • Twitter: @SomersetCCC (93,692 followers)

Director of Cricket: Andy Hurry. **Head Coach**: Jason Kerr. **Academy Director**: Steve
Snell. **Captains**: T.B.Abell (f-c and l-o) and L.Gregory (T20). **Overseas Players**: Azhar Ali
and J.E.Taylor (T20 only). **2019 Testimonial**: None. **Groundsman**: Simon Lee. **Scorer**: tbc.
‡ New registration. NQ Not qualified for England.

ABELL, Thomas Benjamin (Taunton S; Exeter U), b Taunton 5 Mar 1994. 5'10". RHB,
RM. Squad No 28. Debut (Somerset) 2014; captain 2017 to date; cap 2018. HS 135 v Lancs
(Manchester) 2016. BB 4-43 v Lancs (Manchester) 2018. Hat-trick v Notts (Nottingham)
2018. LO HS 106 v Sussex (Taunton) 2016 (RLC). T20 HS 48.

NQ**AZHAR ALI**, b Lahore, Pakistan 19 Feb 1985. RHB, LB. Squad No 79. Lahore Blues
2001-02. KRL 2002-03 to 2011-12. Lahore 2003-04. SNGPL 2012-13 to date. Somerset
debut 2018. **Tests** (P): 73 (2010 to 2018-19, 1 as captain); HS 302* v WI (Dubai, DSC)
2016-17; BB 2-35 v SL (Pallekele) 2015. **LOI** (P): 53 (2011 to 2017-18, 31 as captain); HS
102 v Z (Lahore) 2015; BB 2-26 v E (Dubai, DSC) 2015-16. F-c Tours (P): E 2010, 2016,
2018; A 2016-17 (PA), 2016-17; SA 2012-13, 2018-19; WI 2011, 2016-17; NZ 2010-11,
2016-17; SL 2009 (PA), 2012, 2014, 2015; Z 2011, 2013; B 2011-12, 2014-15; Ire 2018. HS
302* (*see* Tests). Sm HS 125 v Worcs (Worcester) 2018 – on debut. BB 4-34 KRL v
Peshawar (Peshawar) 2002-03. Sm BB 1-5 v Essex (Taunton) 2018. LO HS 132* SNGPL v
Lahore Blues (Islamabad) 2015-16. LO BB 5-23 Lahore Whites v Peshawar (Karachi) 2001
– on debut. T20 HS 72. T20 BB 3-10.

BANTON, Thomas (Bromsgrove S), b Chiltern, Bucks 11 Nov 1998. Son of C.Banton
(Nottinghamshire 1995). 6'2". RHB, WK. Squad No 18. Debut (Somerset) 2018.
Warwickshire 2nd XI 2015. Somerset 2nd XI debut 2016. England U19 2018. HS 30 v
Surrey (Taunton) 2018. LO HS 40 v Essex (Chelmsford) 2018 (RLC). T20 HS 29*.

BARTLETT, George Anthony (Millfield S), b Frimley, Surrey 14 Mar 1998. 6'0". RHB,
OB. Squad No 14. Debut (Somerset) 2017. Somerset 2nd XI debut 2015. England U19 2016
to 2017. HS 110 v Lancs (Manchester) 2018.

BESS, Dominic Mark (Blundell's S), b Exeter, Devon 22 Jul 1997. Cousin of Z.G.G.Bess
(Devon 2015 to date) and J.J.Bess (Devon 2007 to date). RHB, OB. Squad No 22. Debut
(Somerset) 2016. MCC 2018. Somerset 2nd XI debut 2013. Devon 2015-16. **Tests**: 2
(2018); HS 57 v P (Lord's) 2018; BB 3-33 v P (Leeds) 2018. F-c Tours (EL): WI 2017-18;
I 2018-19. HS 107 MCC v Essex (Bridgetown) 2018. HS 92 v Hants (Taunton) 2018. BB
7-117 (10-162 match) v Hants (Taunton) 2017. LO HS 24* South v North (Cave Hill)
2017-18. LO BB 3-35 EL v P A (Abu Dhabi) 2018-19. T20 HS 1. T20 BB 1-31.

‡**BROOKS, Jack** Alexander (Wheatley Park S), b Oxford 4 Jun 1984. 6'2''. RHB, RFM. Squad No 70. Northamptonshire 2009-12; cap 2012. Yorkshire 2013-18; cap 2013. Oxfordshire 2004-09. F-c Tour (EL): SA 2014-15. HS 109* Y v Lancs (Manchester) 2017. 50 wkts (4); most – 71 (2014). BB 6-65 Y v Middx (Lord's) 2016. LO HS 10 Nh v Middx (Uxbridge) 2009 (P40). LO BB 3-30 Y v Hants (Southampton) 2014 (RLC). T20 HS 33*. T20 BB 5-21.

BYROM, Edward James (St John's C, Harare), b Harare, Zimbabwe 17 Jun 1997. 5'11''. LHB, OB. Squad No 97. Irish passport. Debut (Somerset) 2017. Rising Stars 2017-18. Somerset 2nd XI debut 2015. HS 152 RS v MT (Kwekwe) 2017-18. Sm HS 56 v Middx (Taunton) 2017. BB –.

NQDAVEY, Joshua Henry (Culford S), b Aberdeen, Scotland 3 Aug 1990. 5'11''. RHB, RMF. Squad No 38. Middlesex 2010-12. Scotland 2011-12 to 2016. Somerset debut 2015. Suffolk 2014. **LOI** (Scot): 29 (2010 to 2017); HS 64 v Afg (Sharjah) 2012-13; BB 6-28 v Afg (Abu Dhabi) 2014-15. **IT20** (Scot): 14 (2012 to 2016-17); HS 24 v Z (Nagpur) 2015-16; BB 4-34 v Netherlands (Abu Dhabi) 2016-17. HS 72 M v Oxford MCCU (Oxford) 2010 – on debut. CC HS 61 M v Glos (Bristol) 2010. Sm HS 47 v Middx (Lord's) 2017. BB 5-65 v Yorks (Leeds) 2018. LO HS 91 Scot v Warwks (Birmingham) 2011 (CB40). LO BB 6-28 (*see LOI*). T20 HS 24. T20 BB 4-34.

DAVIES, Steven Michael (King Charles I S, Kidderminster), b Bromsgrove, Worcs 17 Jun 1986. 5'10''. LHB, WK. Squad No 11. Worcestershire 2005-09. Surrey 2010-16; cap 2011. Somerset debut/cap 2017. MCC 2006-07, 2011. **LOI**: 8 (2009-10 to 2010-11); HS 87 v P (Chester-le-St) 2010. **IT20**: 5 (2008-09 to 2010-11); HS 33 v P (Cardiff) 2010. F-c Tours: A 2010-11; B 2006-07 (Eng A); UAE 2011-12 (v P). 1000 runs (6); most – 1147 (2016). HS 200* Sy v Glamorgan (Cardiff) 2015. Sm HS 142 v Surrey (Taunton) 2017. LO HS 127* Sy v Hants (Oval) 2013 (Y40). T20 HS 99*.

GILCHRIST, Nathan Nicholas (St Stithian's C; King's C, Taunton), Harare, Zimbabwe 11 Jun 2000. RHB, RFM. Squad No 21. Somerset 2nd XI debut 2016. Awaiting 1st XI debut.

GREEN, Benjamin George Frederick (Exeter S), b Exeter, Devon 28 Sep 1997. 6'2''. RHB, RFM. Squad No 54. Debut (Somerset) 2018. Somerset 2nd XI debut 2014. Devon 2014-18. England U19 2014-15 to 2017. HS 26 and BB 1-8 v Hants (Southampton) 2018. LO HS 26* v Kent (Canterbury) 2018 (RLC). LO BB 1-52 v Hants (Southampton) 2018 (RLC). T20 HS 12*.

GREGORY, Lewis (Hele's S, Plympton), b Plymouth, Devon 24 May 1992. 6'0''. RHB, RMF. Squad No 24. Debut (Somerset) 2011; cap 2015; T20 captain 2018 to date. MCC 2017. Devon 2008. HS 137 v Middx (Lord's) 2017. BB 6-47 (11-122 match) v Northants (Northampton) 2014. LO HS 105* v Durham (Taunton) 2014 (RLC). LO BB 4-23 v Essex (Chelmsford) 2016 (RLC). T20 HS 62. T20 BB 4-15.

GROENEWALD, Timothy Duncan (Maritzburg C; South Africa U), b Pietermaritzburg, South Africa 10 Jan 1984. 6'0''. RHB, RFM. Squad No 5. Debut Cambridge UCCE 2006. Warwickshire 2006-08. Derbyshire 2009-14; cap 2011. Somerset debut 2014; cap 2016. Sm HS 78 Wa v Bangladesh A (Birmingham) 2008. CC HS 76 Wa v Durham (Chester-le-St) 2006. Sm HS 47 v New Zealanders (Taunton) 2015. BB 6-50 De v Surrey (Croydon) 2009. Sm BB 5-58 v Warwks (Birmingham) 2017. Hat-trick De v Essex (Chelmsford) 2014. LO HS 57 v Warwks (Birmingham) 2014 (RLC). LO BB 4-22 De v Worcs (Worcester) 2011 (CB40). T20 HS 41. T20 BB 4-21.

HILDRETH, James Charles (Millfield S), b Milton Keynes, Bucks 9 Sep 1984. 5'10'', RHB, RMF. Squad No 25. Debut (Somerset) 2003; cap 2007; testimonial 2017. MCC 2015. F-c Tour (EL): WI 2010-11. 1000 runs (7); most – 1620 (2015). HS 303* v Warwks (Taunton) 2009. BB 2-39 v Hants (Taunton) 2004. LO HS 159 v Glamorgan (Taunton) 2018 (RLC). LO BB 2-26 v Worcs (Worcester) 2008 (FPT). T20 HS 107*. T20 BB 3-24.

LAMMONBY, Thomas Alexander (Exeter S), b Exeter, Devon 2 Jun 2000. LHB, LM. Squad No 15. Somerset 2nd XI debut 2015. Devon 2016-18. England U19 2018-19. Awaiting 1st f-c debut.

LEACH, Matthew Jack (Bishop Fox's Community S, Taunton; Richard Huish C; UWIC), b Taunton 22 Jun 1991. 6'0''. LHB, SLA. Squad No 17. Cardiff MCCU 2012. Somerset debut 2012; cap 2017. MCC 2017. Dorset 2011. **Tests**: 4 (2017-18 to 2018-19); HS 16 v NZ (Christchurch) 2017-18; BB 5-83 v SL (Pallekele) 2018-19. F-c Tours (EL): WI 2017-18 (EL); NZ 2018-19; SL 2016-17 (EL), 2018-19; UAE 2016-17 (v Afg)(EL). HS 66 v Lancs (Manchester) 2018. 50 wkts (2); most – 68 (2016). BB 8-85 (10-112 match) v Essex (Taunton) 2018. LO HS 18 v Surrey (Oval) 2014 (RLC). LO BB 3-7 EL v UAE (Dubai, DSC) 2016-17.

OVERTON, Craig (West Buckland S), b Barnstaple, Devon 10 Apr 1994. Twin brother of Jamie Overton (*see below*). 6'5''. RHB, RMF. Squad No 12. Debut (Somerset) 2012; cap 2016. MCC 2017. Devon 2010-11. **Tests**: 3 (2017-18); HS 41* and BB 3-105 v A (Adelaide) 2017-18. F-c Tours: A 2017-18; NZ 2018-19; SL 138 v Hants (Taunton) 2016. BB 6-74 v Warwks (Birmingham) 2015. Hat-trick v Notts (Nottingham) 2018. LO HS 60* EL v SL A (Dambulla) 2016-17. LO BB 4-27 v Surrey (Oval) 2018 (RLC). T20 HS 35*. T20 BB 3-17.

OVERTON, Jamie (West Buckland S), b Barnstaple, Devon 10 Apr 1994. Twin brother of Craig Overton (*see above*). 6'5''. RHB, RFM. Squad No 8. Debut (Somerset) 2012. Devon 2011. F-c Tour (EL): UAE 2018-19 (v P A). HS 56 v Warwks (Birmingham) 2014. BB 6-95 v Middx (Taunton) 2013. LO HS 40* v Glos (Taunton) 2016 (RLC). LO BB 4-42 v Durham (Chester-le-St) 2012 (CB40). T20 HS 31. T20 BB 5-47.

ROUSE, Timothy David (Kingswood S, Bath; Cardiff U), b Sheffield, Yorks 9 Apr 1996. Younger brother of H.P.Rouse (Leeds/Bradford MCCU 2013-15). 5'11''. RHB, OB. Squad No 44. Cardiff MCCU 2015-17. Somerset debut 2016. Somerset 2nd XI debut 2012. No 1st XI appearances in 2018. HS 69 v Yorks (Scarborough) 2017. BB 2-31 CfU v Glamorgan (Cardiff) 2017. T20 HS 9.

SALE, Oliver Richard Trethowan (Sherborne S), b Newcastle-under-Lyme, Staffs 30 Sep 1995. 6'1''. RHB, RFM. Squad No 82. Somerset 2nd XI debut 2014. Awaiting f-c debut. T20 HS 1.

[NQ]**TAYLOR, Jerome** Everton, b St Elizabeth, Jamaica 22 Jun 1984. 5'11''. RHB, RF. Squad No 74. Jamaica 2002-03 to date. Leicestershire 2007. Sussex 2017 (l-o only). Somerset debut 2018 (T20 only). IPL: PW 2011. Big Bash: HH 2018-19. **Tests** (WI): 46 (2003 to 2015-16); HS 106 v NZ (Dunedin) 2008-09; BB 6-47 v A (Kingston) 2015. **LOI** (WI): 90 (2003 to 2017); HS 43* v SA (Durban) 2007-08; BB 5-48 v Z (Bulawayo) 2007-08. **IT20** (WI): 30 (2005-06 to 2017-18); HS 21 v P (Dubai, DSC) 2016-17; BB 3-6 v SA (Port Elizabeth) 2007-08. F-c Tours (WI): E 2007, 2009; A 2009-10, 2015-16; SA 2007-08, 2014-15; NZ 2005-06, 2008-09; P 2006-07; SL 2015-16; Z 2003-04. HS 106 (*see Tests*). CC HS 40 Le v Derbys (Leicester) 2007. CC BB 8-59 Jamaica v T&T (Port of Spain) 2002-03. CC BB 6-35 Le v Middx (Southgate) 2007. LO HS 43* (*see LOI*). LO BB 5-40 Jamaica v Guyana (Bridgetown) 2016-17. T20 HS 21. T20 BB 5-10.

TREGO, Peter David (Wyvern CS, W-s-M), b Weston-super-Mare 12 Jun 1981. 6'0''. RHB, RMF. Squad No 7. Debut (Somerset) 2000; cap 2007; benefit 2015. Kent 2003. Middlesex 2005. C Districts 2013-14. MCC 2013. Herefordshire 2005. 1000 runs (1): 1070 (2016). HS 154* v Lancs (Manchester) 2016, sharing Sm record 8th wkt partnership of 236 with R.C.Davies. 50 wkts (1): 50 (2012). BB 7-84 (11-153 match) v Yorks (Leeds) 2014. LO HS 147 v Glamorgan (Taunton) 2010 (CB40). LO BB 5-40 EL v WI A (Worcester) 2010. T20 HS 94*. T20 BB 4-27.

TRESCOTHICK, Marcus Edward (Sir Bernard Lovell S), b Keynsham 25 Dec 1975. 6'2". LHB, RM, occ WK. Squad No 2. Debut (Somerset) 1993; cap 1999; joint captain 2002; benefit 2008; captain 2010-15; testimonial 2018. PCA 2000, 2009, 2011. *Wisden* 2004. MBE 2005. **Tests**: 76 (2000 to 2006, 2 as captain); HS 219 v SA (Oval) 2003; BB 1-34 v P (Karachi) 2000-01. **LOI**: 123 (2000 to 2006, 10 as captain); HS 137 v P (Lord's) 2001; BB 2-7 v Z (Manchester) 2000. **IT20**: 3 (2005 to 2006); HS 72 v SL (Southampton) 2006. F-c Tours: A 2002-03; SA 2004-05; WI 2003-04; NZ 1999-00 (Eng A), 2001-02; I 2001-02, 2005-06 (*part*); P 2000-01, 2005-06; SL 2000-01, 2003-04; B 1999-00 (Eng A), 2003-04. 1000 runs (8); most – 1817 (2009). HS 284 v Northants (Northampton) 2007. BB 4-36 (inc hat-trick) v Young A (Taunton) 1995. CC BB 4-82 v Yorks (Leeds) 1998. Hat-trick 1995 (*see above*). LO HS 184 v Glos (Taunton) 2008 (P40) – Sm l-o record. LO BB 4-50 v Northants (Northampton) 2000 (NL). T20 HS 108*.

NQ**VAN DER MERWE, Roelof** Erasmus (Pretoria HS), b Johannesburg, South Africa 31 Dec 1984. RHB, SLA. Squad No 52. Northerns 2006-07 to 2013-14. Titans 2007-08 to 2014-15. Netherlands 2015 to date. Somerset debut 2016; cap 2018. IPL: RCB 2009 to 2009-10. DD 2011-13. Big Bash: BH 2011-12. **LOI** (SA): 13 (2008-09 to 2010); HS 12 v I (Gwalior) 2009-10; BB 3-27 v Z (Centurion) 2009-10. **IT20** (SA/Neth): 28 (13 for SA 2008-09 to 2010; 15 for Neth 2015 to 2018-19); HS 48 v A (Centurion) 2009-10; BB 2-3 v Ire (Dharamsala) 2015-16. HS 205* Titans v Warriors (Benoni) 2014-15. Sm HS 102* v Hants (Taunton) 2016. BB 4-22 v Middx (Taunton) 2017. LO HS 165* v Surrey (Taunton) 2017 (RLC). LO BB 5-26 Titans v Knights (Centurion) 2012-13. T20 HS 89*. T20 BB 3-13.

NQ**VAN MEEKEREN, Paul** Adriaan, b Amsterdam, Netherlands 15 Jan 1993. RHB, RMF. Squad No 47. Netherlands 2013 to date. Somerset debut 2016. **LOI** (Neth); 4 (2013 to 2018); HS 15* v SA (Amstelveen) 2013; BB 1-21 v Nepal (Amstelveen) 2018. **IT20** (Neth): 25 (2013 to 2018-19); HS 18 v Hong Kong (Dubai, DSC) 2016-17; BB 4-11 v Ire (Dharamsala) 2015-16. HS 34 Neth v PNG (Amstelveen) 2015. Sm HS 6 v Lancs (Manchester) 2018. BB 4-60 v Essex (Chelmsford) 2017. LO HS 15* (*see LOI*). LO BB 3-22 Neth v UAE (Amstelveen) 2017. T20 HS 18. T20 BB 4-11.

WALLER, Maximilian Thomas Charles (Millfield S; Bournemouth U), b Salisbury, Wiltshire 3 March 1988. 6'0". RHB, LB. Squad No 10. Debut (Somerset) 2009. Dorset 2007-08. HS 28 v Hants (Southampton) 2009. BB 3-33 v Cardiff MCCU (Taunton Vale) 2012. CC BB 2-27 v Sussex (Hove) 2009. LO HS 25* v Glamorgan (Taunton) 2013 (Y40). LO BB 3-37 v Glos (Bristol) 2017 (RLC). T20 HS 17. T20 BB 4-16.

RELEASED/RETIRED

(Having made a County 1st XI appearance in 2018)

NQ**ANDERSON, Corey** James, b Christchurch, New Zealand 13 Dec 1990. LHB, LMF. Canterbury 2006-07 to 2009-10. Northern Districts 2011-12 to 2017-18. Somerset 2017-18 (T20 only). IPL: MI 2014-15. DD 2017. RCB 2018. **Tests** (NZ): 13 (2013-14 to 2015-16); HS 116 v B (Dhaka) 2013-14; BB 3-47 v WI (Hamilton) 2013-14. **LOI** (NZ): 49 (2013 to 2017); HS 131* v WI (Queenstown) 2013-14; BB 5-63 v I (Auckland) 2013-14. **IT20** (NZ): 31 (2012-13 to 2018-19); HS 94* v B (Mt Maunganui) 2014-15; BB 2-17 v P (Wellington) 2015-16. F-c Tours (NZ): E 2015; I 2013-14 (NZA); SL 2013-14 (NZA); B 2013-14; UAE 2014-15 (v P). HS 167 ND v Otago (Hamilton) 2012-13. BB 5-22 ND v Canterbury (Hamilton) 2009-10. LO HS 131* (*see LOI*). LO BB 5-26 ND v Canterbury (Hamilton) 2009-10. T20 HS 95*. T20 BB 2-17.

RELEASED/RETIRED continued on p 181

SOMERSET 2018

RESULTS SUMMARY

	Place	Won	Lost	Tied	Drew	NR
Specsavers County Champ (1st Division)	2nd	7	2	1	4	
All First-Class Matches		7	2	1	4	
Royal London One-Day Cup (South Group)	4th	4	3			1
Vitality Blast (South Group)	SF	11	5			

SPECSAVERS COUNTY CHAMPIONSHIP AVERAGES
BATTING AND FIELDING

Cap		M	I	NO	HS	Runs	Avge	100	50	Ct/St
	M.T.Renshaw	6	11	1	112	513	51.30	3	1	5
2007	J.C.Hildreth	14	26	2	184	1089	45.37	3	6	13
2018	T.B.Abell	14	26	4	132*	883	40.13	1	5	2
	Azhar Ali	7	13	1	125	402	33.50	1	2	2
2017	S.M.Davies	14	25	2	92*	756	32.86	–	5	38/3
	G.A.Bartlett	6	11	–	110	306	27.81	1	–	2
1999	M.E.Trescothick	10	18	–	100	491	27.27	1	4	16
	D.M.Bess	7	11	1	92	226	22.60	–	1	3
2015	L.Gregory	12	21	2	65	411	21.63	–	3	12
	E.J.Byrom	8	15	–	54	309	20.60	–	2	2
	J.Overton	8	12	2	55	197	19.70	–	1	5
2016	C.Overton	11	18	1	80	331	19.47	–	1	9
	J.H.Davey	11	17	6	36	206	18.72	–	–	3
2016	T.D.Groenewald	7	11	5	36*	91	15.16	–	–	2
2017	M.J.Leach	11	16	2	66	174	12.42	–	1	5
2007	P.D.Trego	2	4	–	39	46	11.50	–	–	1
	B.G.F.Green	2	4	–	26	43	10.75	–	–	3

Also batted: T.Banton (2 matches) 30, 4, 3 (1 ct); P.A.van Meekeren (1) 6, 0*; R.E.van der Merwe (1 – cap 2018) 0; M.T.C.Waller (1) 0.

BOWLING

	O	M	R	W	Avge	Best	5wI	10wM
M.J.Leach	255.4	57	722	30	24.06	8- 85	3	2
T.D.Groenewald	173	41	509	21	24.23	4- 85	–	–
J.Overton	177.3	34	646	26	24.84	4- 25	–	–
L.Gregory	305.5	75	928	37	25.08	4- 33	–	–
J.H.Davey	290.4	73	862	34	25.35	5- 65	1	–
T.B.Abell	121.4	23	492	19	25.89	4- 43	–	–
C.Overton	321.3	72	1014	37	27.40	4- 27	–	–
D.M.Bess	204.1	51	602	11	54.72	3- 81	–	–

Also bowled:

R.E.van der Merwe	51	13	143	5	28.60	4-138		

Azhar Ali 11-3-20-1; G.A.Bartlett 3.2-0-27-0; E.J.Byrom 10-1-39-0; B.G.F.Green 7-3-17-1; M.T.Renshaw 3-1-11-0; P.D.Trego 41-7-146-3; P.A.van Meekeren 20-3-67-1.

Somerset played no first-class fixtures outside the County Championship in 2018. The First-Class Averages (pp 230–245) give the records of Somerset players in all first-class county matches, with the exceptions of Azhar Ali, D.M.Bess and M.J.Leach, whose first-class figures for Somerset are as above.

SOMERSET RECORDS

FIRST-CLASS CRICKET

Highest Total	For 850-7d		v	Middlesex	Taunton	2007
	V 811		by	Surrey	The Oval	1899
Lowest Total	For 25		v	Glos	Bristol	1947
	V 22		by	Glos	Bristol	1920
Highest Innings	For 342	J.L.Langer	v	Surrey	Guildford	2006
	V 424	A.C.MacLaren	for	Lancashire	Taunton	1895

Highest Partnership for each Wicket

1st	346	L.C.H.Palairet/ H.T.Hewett	v	Yorkshire	Taunton	1892
2nd	450	N.R.D.Compton/J.C.Hildreth	v	Cardiff MCCU	Taunton Vale	2012
3rd	319	P.M.Roebuck/M.D.Crowe	v	Leics	Taunton	1984
4th	310	P.W.Denning/I.T.Botham	v	Glos	Taunton	1980
5th	320	J.D.Francis/I.D.Blackwell	v	Durham UCCE	Taunton	2005
6th	265	W.E.Alley/K.E.Palmer	v	Northants	Northampton	1961
7th	279	R.J.Harden/G.D.Rose	v	Sussex	Taunton	1997
8th	236	P.D.Trego/R.C.Davies	v	Lancashire	Manchester	2016
9th	183	C.H.M.Greetham/H.W.Stephenson	v	Leics	Weston-s-Mare	1963
	183	C.J.Tavaré/N.A.Mallender	v	Sussex	Hove	1990
10th	163	I.D.Blackwell/N.A.M.McLean	v	Derbyshire	Taunton	2003

Best Bowling	For 10- 49	E.J.Tyler	v	Surrey	Taunton	1895
(Innings)	V 10- 35	A.Drake	for	Yorkshire	Weston-s-Mare	1914
Best Bowling	For 16- 83	J.C.White	v	Worcs	Bath	1919
(Match)	V 17-137	W.Brearley	for	Lancashire	Manchester	1905

Most Runs – Season	2761	W.E.Alley	(av 58.74)	1961
Most Runs – Career	21142	H.Gimblett	(av 36.96)	1935-54
Most 100s – Season	11	S.J.Cook		1991
Most 100s – Career	52	M.E.Trescothick		1993-2018
Most Wkts – Season	169	A.W.Wellard	(av 19.24)	1938
Most Wkts – Career	2165	J.C.White	(av 18.03)	1909-37
Most Career W-K Dismissals	1007	H.W.Stephenson	(698 ct; 309 st)	1948-64
Most Career Catches in the Field	433	M.E.Trescothick		1993-2018

LIMITED-OVERS CRICKET

Highest Total	50ov	413-4		v	Devon	Torquay	1990
	40ov	377-9		v	Sussex	Hove	2003
	T20	250-3		v	Glos	Taunton	2006
Lowest Total	50ov	58		v	Middlesex	Southgate	2000
	40ov	58		v	Essex	Chelmsford	1977
	T20	82		v	Kent	Taunton	2010
Highest Innings	50ov	177	S.J.Cook	v	Sussex	Hove	1990
	40ov	184	M.E.Trescothick	v	Glos	Taunton	2008
	T20	151*	C.H.Gayle	v	Kent	Taunton	2015
Best Bowling	50ov	8-66	S.R.G.Francis	v	Derbyshire	Derby	2004
	40ov	6-16	Abdur Rehman	v	Notts	Taunton	2012
	T20	6- 5	A.V.Suppiah	v	Glamorgan	Cardiff	2011

SURREY

Formation of Present Club: 22 August 1845
Inaugural First-Class Match: 1864
Colours: Chocolate
Badge: Prince of Wales' Feathers
County Champions (since 1890): (19) 1890, 1891, 1892, 1894, 1895, 1899, 1914, 1952, 1953, 1954, 1955, 1956, 1957, 1958, 1971, 1999, 2000, 2002, 2018
Joint Champions: (1) 1950
NatWest Trophy Winners: (1) 1982
Benson and Hedges Cup Winners: (3) 1974, 1997, 2001
Pro 40/National League (Div 1) Winners: (1) 2003
Sunday League Winners: (1) 1996
Clydesdale Bank 40 Winners: (1) 2011
Twenty20 Cup Winners: (1) 2003

Chief Executive: Richard Gould, The Kia Oval, London, SE11 5SS • Tel: 0203 946 1000 • Email: enquiries@surreycricket.com • Web: www.kiaoval.com • Twitter: @surreycricket (86,625 followers)

Director of Cricket: Alec Stewart. **Head Coach**: Michael Di Venuto. **Assistant Coach**: Richard Johnson. **Captains**: R.J.Burns (f-c and l-o) and J.W.Dernbach (T20). **Overseas Players**: D.Elgar and A.J.Finch. **2019 Testimonial**: J.W.Dernbach. **Head Groundsman**: Lee Fortiss. **Scorer**: Philip Makepeace. ‡ New registration. ^{NQ} Not qualified for England.

ATKINSON, Angus ('**Gus**') Alexander Patrick (Bradfield C), b Chelsea, Middx 19 Jan 1998. 6'2". RHB, RM. Squad No 37. Surrey 2nd XI debut 2016. Awaiting 1st XI debut.

BATTY, Gareth Jon (Bingley GS), b Bradford, Yorks 13 Oct 1977. Younger brother of J.D.Batty (Yorkshire and Somerset 1989-96). 5'11". RHB, OB. Squad No 13. Yorkshire 1997. Surrey debut 1999; cap 2011; captain 2015-17; testimonial 2017. Worcestershire 2002-09. MCC 2012. **Tests**: 9 (2003-04 to 2016-17); HS 38 v SL (Kandy) 2003-04; BB 3-55 v SL (Galle) 2003-04. Took wicket with his third ball in Test cricket. **LOI**: 10 (2002-03 to 2008-09); HS 17 v WI (Bridgetown) 2008-09; BB 2-40 v WI (Gros Islet) 2003-04. **IT20**: 1 (2008-09); HS 4 v WI (Port of Spain) 2008-09. F-c Tours: WI 2003-04, 2005-06; NZ 2008-09 (Eng A); I 2016-17; SL 2002-03 (ECB Acad), 2003-04; B 2003-04, 2016-17. HS 133 Wo v Surrey (Oval) 2004. Sy HS 110* v Hants (Southampton) 2016, sharing Sy record 8th wkt partnership of 222* with B.T.Foakes. 50 wkts (2); most – 60 (2003). BB 8-68 v Essex (Chelmsford) 2014. Hat-trick v Derbys (Oval) 2015. LO HS 83* v Yorks (Oval) 2001 (NL). LO BB 5-35 Wo v Hants (Southampton) 2009 (FPT). T20 HS 87. T20 BB 4-13.

BORTHWICK, Scott George (Farringdon Community Sports C, Sunderland), b Sunderland, Co Durham 19 Apr 1990. 5'9". LHB, LBG. Squad No 6. Durham 2009-16. Wellington 2015-16 to 2016-17. Surrey debut 2017; cap 2018. **Tests**: 1 (2013-14); HS 4 and BB 3-33 v A (Sydney) 2013-14. **LOI**: 2 (2011 to 2011-12); HS 15 v Ire (Dublin) 2011; BB –. **IT20**: 1 (2011); HS 14 and BB 1-15 v WI (Oval) 2011. F-c Tours: A 2013-14; SL 2013-14 (EL). 1000 runs (5); most – 1390 (2015). HS 216 Du v Middx (Chester-le-St) 2014, sharing Du record 2nd wkt partnership of 274 with M.D.Stoneman. Sy HS 175* and Sy BB 2-35 v West Indies A (Oval) 2018. BB 6-70 Du v Surrey (Oval) 2013. LO HS 87 and LO BB 5-38 Du v Leics (Leicester) 2015 (RLC). T20 HS 62. T20 BB 4-18.

BURNS, Rory Joseph (City of London Freemen's S), b Epsom 26 Aug 1990. 5'10". LHB, WK, occ RM. Squad No 17. Debut (Surrey) 2011; cap 2014; captain 2018 to date. MCC 2016. MCC Univs 2010. **Tests**: 6 (2018-19); HS 84 v WI (Bridgetown) 2018-19. 1000 runs (5); most – 1402 (2018). HS 219* v Hants (Oval) 2017. BB 1-18 v Middx (Lord's) 2013. LO HS 95 v Glos (Bristol) 2015 (RLC). T20 HS 50.

‡**CLARK, Jordan** (Sedbergh S), b Whitehaven, Cumbria 14 Oct 1990. Elder brother of G.Clark (*see DURHAM*). 6'4''. RHB, RMF, occ WK. Lancashire 2015-18. HS 140 La v Surrey (Oval) 2017. BB 5-58 La v Yorks (Manchester) 2018. Hat-trick La v Yorks (Manchester) 2018 dismissing J.E.Root, K.S.Williamson and J.M.Bairstow. LO HS 79* and LO BB 4-34 La v Worcs (Manchester) 2017 (RLC). T20 HS 44. T20 BB 4-22.

CLARKE, Rikki (Broadwater SS; Godalming C), b Orsett, Essex 29 Sep 1981. 6'4''. RHB, RMF. Squad No 81. Debut (Surrey) 2002, scoring 107* v Cambridge U (Cambridge); cap 2005. Derbyshire cap/captain 2008. Warwickshire 2008-17; cap 2011. MCC 2006, 2016. YC 2002. **Tests**: 2 (2003-04); HS 55 and BB 2-7 v B (Chittagong) 2003-04. **LOI**: 20 (2003 to 2006); HS 39 v P (Lord's) 2006; BB 2-28 v B (Dhaka) 2003-04. F-c Tours: WI 2003-04, 2005-06; SL 2002-03 (ECB Acad), 2004-05; B 2003-04. 1000 runs (1): 1027 (2006). HS 214 v Somerset (Guildford) 2006. BB 7-55 v Somerset (Oval) 2017. Took seven catches in an innings Wa v Lancs (Liverpool) 2011 to equal world record. LO HS 98* v Derbys (Derby) 2002 (NL). LO BB 5-26 Wa v Worcs (Birmingham) 2016 (RLC). T20 HS 79*. T20 BB 4-16

CURRAN, Samuel Matthew (Wellington C), b Northampton 3 Jun 1998. Son of K.M.Curran (Glos, Natal, Northants, Boland and Zimbabwe 1980-81 to 1999), grandson of K.P.Curran (Rhodesia 1947-48 to 1954-55), younger brother of T.K.Curran (*see below*). 5'9''. LHB, LMF. Squad No 58. Debut (Surrey) 2015, taking 5-101 v Kent (Oval); cap 2018. Surrey 2nd XI debut 2013. YC 2018. **ECB Test Central Contract 2018-19. Tests**: 9 (2018 to 2018-19); HS 78 v I (Southampton) 2018; BB 4-74 v I (Birmingham) 2018. **LOI**: 2 (2018 to 2018-19); HS 15 and BB 2-44 v A (Manchester) 2018. F-c Tours: WI 2018-19; SL 2016-17 (EL), 2018-19; UAE 2016-17 (v Afg)(EL). HS 96 v Lancs (Oval) 2016. BB 7-58 v Durham (Chester-le-St) 2016. LO HS 57 v Glos (Oval) 2016 (RLC). LO BB 4-32 v Northants (Oval) 2015 (RLC). T20 HS 50. T20 BB 4-13.

CURRAN, Thomas Kevin (Hilton C, Durban), b Cape Town, South Africa 12 Mar 1995. Son of K.M.Curran (Glos, Natal, Northants, Boland and Zimbabwe 1980-81 to 1999), grandson of K.P.Curran (Rhodesia 1947-48 to 1954-55), elder brother of S.M.Curran (*see above*). 6'0''. RHB, RFM. Squad No 59. Debut (Surrey) 2014; cap 2016. IPL: KKR 2018. Big Bash: SS 2018-19. **ECB Incremental Contract 2018-19. Tests**: 2 (2017-18); HS 39 v A (Sydney) 2017-18; BB 1-65 v A (Melbourne) 2017-18. **LOI**: 10 (2017 to 2018-19); HS 35 v A (Adelaide) 2017-18; BB 5-35 v A (Perth) 2017-18. **IT20**: 10 (2017 to 2018-19); HS 6 v A (Hobart) 2017-18; BB 4-36 v WI (Gros Islet) 2018-19. F-c Tours: A 2017-18; SL 2016-17 (EL); UAE 2016-17 (v Afg)(EL). HS 60 v Leics (Leicester) 2015. 50 wkts (1): 76 (2015). BB 7-20 v Glos (Oval) 2015. LO HS 44 v Yorks (Oval) 2015 (RLC). LO BB 5-16 EL v UAE (Dubai, DSC) 2016-17. T20 HS 62. T20 BB 4-35.

DERNBACH, Jade Winston (St John the Baptist S), b Johannesburg, South Africa 3 Mar 1986. 6'1½''. RHB, RFM. Squad No 16. Italian passport. UK resident since 1998. Debut (Surrey) 2003; cap 2011; captain 2018 to date (T20 only); testimonial 2019. **LOI**: 24 (2011 to 2013); HS 5 v SL (Leeds) 2011; BB 4-45 v P (Dubai) 2011-12. **IT20**: 34 (2011 to 2013-14); HS 12 v I (Colombo, RPS) 2012-13; BB 4-22 v I (Manchester) 2011. F-c Tour (EL): WI 2010-11. HS 56* v Northants (Northampton) 2010. 50 wkts (1): 51 (2010). BB 6-47 v Leics (Leicester) 2009. LO HS 31 v Somerset (Taunton) 2010 (CB40). BB 6-35 v Glos (Lord's) 2015 (RLC). T20 HS 24*. T20 BB 4-22.

DUNN, Matthew Peter (Bearwood C, Wokingham), b Egham 5 May 1992. 6'1''. LHB, RFM. Squad No 4. Debut (Surrey) 2010. MCC 2015. HS 31* v Kent (Guildford) 2014. BB 5-48 v Glos (Oval) 2014. LO HS –. LO BB 2-32 Eng Dev XI v SL A (Manchester) 2011. T20 HS 2. BB 3-8.

NQELGAR, Dean, b Welkom, OFS, South Africa 11 Jun 1987. 5'8". LHB, SLA. Squad No 64. Free State 2005-06 to 2010-11. Eagles 2006-07 to 2009-10. Knights 2010-11 to 2013-14. Somerset 2013-17; cap 2017. Titans 2014-15 to date. Surrey debut 2015. **Tests** (SA): 56 (2012-13 to 2018-19); 1000 runs (1): 1128 (2017); HS 199 v B (Potchefstroom) 2017-18; BB 4-22 v I (Mohali) 2015-16. **LOI** (SA): 8 (2012 to 2018-19); HS 42 v E (Oval) 2012; BB 1-11 v E (Southampton) 2012. F-c Tours (SA): E 2017; A 2012-13, 2016 (SA A), 2016-17; NZ 2016-17; I 2015-16; SL 2010 (SA A), 2014, 2018; Z 2014; B 2010 (SA A), 2015; UAE (v P) 2013-14; Ire 2012 (SA A). 1000 runs (0+2); most – 1193 (2009-10). HS 268 SA A v Aus A (Pretoria) 2013. CC HS 158 Sm v Middx (Lord's) 2017. Sy HS 110 v Somerset (Taunton) 2018. BB 4-22 (*see Tests*). CC BB 1-4 Sm v Essex (Taunton) 2017. LO HS 137 Titans v Lions (Potchefstroom) 2018-19. LO BB 4-37 Titans v Dolphins (Durban) 2018-19. T20 HS 79*. T20 BB 4-23.

NQFINCH, Aaron James, b Colac, Victoria, Australia 17 Nov 1986. 5'9". RHB, SLA. Squad No 15. Victoria 2007-08 to date. Yorkshire 2014-15. Surrey debut 2016; cap 2018. IPL: RR: 2009-10. DD 2011-12. PW 2013. SH 2014. MI 2015. GL 2016-17. KXIP 2018. Big Bash: MR 2011-12 to date. **Tests** (A): 5 (2018-19); HS 62 v P (Dubai, DSC) 2018-19; BB –. **LOI** (A): 104 (2012-13 to 2018-19); HS 148 v Scotland (Edinburgh) 2013; BB 1-2 v I (Pune) 2013-14. **IT20** (A): 52 (2010-11 to 2018-19); HS 172 v Z (Harare) 2018 – world record IT20 score. F-c Tours (Aus A): SA/Z 2013; Z 2011; UAE 2018-19 (v P)(A). HS 288* Cricket A v New Zealanders (Sydney) 2015-16. CC HS 110 Y v Warwks (Birmingham) 2014 and 110 v Warwks (Guildford) 2016. BB 1-0 Vic v WA (Perth) 2013-14. CC BB 1-20 Y v Sussex (Arundel) 2014. LO HS 154 Vic v Q (Brisbane) 2012-13. LO BB 2-44 Aus A v EL (Hobart) 2012-13. T20 HS 172. T20 BB 1-9.

FOAKES, Benjamin Thomas (Tendring TC), b Colchester, Essex 15 Feb 1993. 6'1". RHB, WK. Squad No 7. Essex 2011-14. Surrey debut 2015; cap 2016. MCC 2016. **Tests**: 5 (2018-19); HS 107 v SL (Galle) 2018-19 – on debut. F-c Tours: WI 2017-18 (EL), 2018-19; SL 2013-14 (EL), 2016-17 (EL), 2018-19; UAE 2016-17 (v Afg)(EL). HS 141* v Hants (Southampton) 2016, sharing Sy record 8th wkt partnership of 222* with G.J.Batty. LO HS 92 v Somerset (Taunton) 2016 (RLC). T20 HS 75*.

HARINATH, Arun (Tiffin Boys GS; Loughborough U), b Sutton 26 Mar 1987. 5'11". LHB, OB. Squad No 10. Loughborough UCCE 2007-09. Surrey debut 2009; cap 2016. Leicestershire 2017 (on loan). MCC 2008. Buckinghamshire 2007-08. HS 154 v Derbys (Derby) 2013. BB 2-1 v Glamorgan (Colwyn Bay) 2014. LO HS 52 v Derbys (Oval) 2013 (Y40). LO BB –.

JACKS, William George (St George's C, Weybridge), b Chertsey 21 Nov 1998. 6'1". RHB, RM. Squad No 9. Debut (Surrey) 2018. Surrey 2nd XI debut 2016. England U19 2016-17 to 2017. F-c Tour (EL): I 2018-19. HS 63 EL v I A (Wayanad) 2018-19. Sy HS 53 v Essex (Oval) 2018. BB –. LO HS 121 v Glos (Oval) 2018 (RLC). LO BB 2-33 EL v I A (Karyavattom) 2018-19. T20 HS 53. T20 BB –.

NQMcKERR, Conor (St John's C, Johannesburg), b Johannesburg, South Africa 19 Jan 1998. 6'6". RHB, RFM. Squad No 83. UK passport. Derbyshire 2017 (on loan), taking wkt of J.D.Libby with 4th ball in f-c cricket. Surrey debut 2017. Surrey 2nd XI debut 2016. UK passport. HS 29 v Yorks (Oval) 2018. BB 5-54 (10-141 match) De v Northants (Northampton) 2017. Sy BB 4-26 v Notts (Oval) 2018.

MEAKER, Stuart Christopher (Cranleigh S), b Durban, South Africa 21 Jan 1989. Moved to UK in 2001. 6'1". RHB, RFM. Squad No 18. Debut (Surrey) 2008; cap 2012. Auckland 2017-18. **LOI**: 2 (2011-12); HS 1 and BB 1-45 v I (Mumbai) 2011-12. **IT20**: 2 (2012-13); BB 1-28 v I (Pune) 2011-12. F-c Tour: I 2012-13. HS 94 v Bangladeshis (Oval) 2010. CC HS 72 v Essex (Colchester) 2009. 50 wkts (1): 51 (2012). BB 8-52 (11-167 match) v Somerset (Oval) 2012. LO HS 21* v Glamorgan (Oval) 2012 (CB40). LO BB 4-37 v Kent (Oval) 2017 (RLC). T20 HS 17. T20 BB 4-30.

NQMORKEL, Morne (Hoerskool, Vereeniging), b Vereeniging, South Africa 6 Oct 1984. Younger brother of J.A.Morkel (Easterns, Titans, Durham and South Africa 1999-00 to 2015-16). 6'4''. LHB, RF. Squad No 65. Easterns 2003-04 to 2017-18. Titans 2004-05 to 2017-18. Yorkshire 2008 (1 match). Surrey debut/cap 2018 (Kolpak signing). IPL: RR 2009 to 2009-10. DD 2011-13. KKR 2014-16. **Tests** (SA): 86 (2006-07 to 2017-18); HS 40 v A (Sydney) 2008-09 and 40 v NZ (Wellington) 2016-17; BB 6-23 v NZ (Wellington) 2011-12. **LOI** (SA): 114 (+ 3 Africa XI 2007) (2007 to 2017-18); HS 32* v WI (Bridgetown) 2016; BB 5-21 v A (Perth) 2014-15. **IT20** (SA): 41 (+ 3 World XI 2017) (2007 to 2017); HS 8* v P (Johannesburg) 2013-14; BB 4-17 v NZ (Durban) 2007. F-c Tours (SA): E 2008, 2012, 2017; A 2008-09, 2012-13; WI 2010; NZ 2011-12, 2016-17; I 2007-08, 2009-10, 2015-16; SL 2014; Z 2014; B 2007-08, 2015; UAE (v P) 2010-11, 2013-14. HS 82* (and 11-56 match) Titans v Warriors (E London) 2005-06. Sy HS 29 v Yorks (Scarborough) 2018 and 29 v Lancs (Oval) 2018. 50 wkts (1): 63 (2018). BB 6-23 (*see Tests*). Sy BB 6-57 v Lancs (Oval) 2018. LO HS 35 Easterns v Northerns (Pretoria) 2005-06. LO BB 5-21 (*see LOI*). T20 HS 23*. T20 BB 4-17.

PATEL, Ryan Samir (Whitgift S), b Sutton 26 Oct 1997. 5'10''. LHB, RMF. Squad No 26. Debut (Surrey) 2017. Surrey 2nd XI debut 2016. England U19 2017. HS 81 v Hants (Southampton) 2017. BB 6-5 v Somerset (Guildford) 2018.

‡PLUNKETT, Liam Edward (Nunthorpe SS; Teesside Tertiary C), b Middlesbrough, Yorks 6 Apr 1985. 6'3''. RHB, RF. Squad No 28. Durham 2003-07. Dolphins 2007-08. Yorkshire 2013-17; cap 2013. MCC 2017. IPL: DD 2018. Big Bash: MS 2018-19. **ECB L-O Central Contract 2018-19. Tests**: 13 (2005-06 to 2014); HS 55* v I (Lord's) 2014; BB 5-64 v SL (Leeds) 2014. **LOI**: 78 (2005-06 to 2018-19); HS 56 v P (Lahore) 2005-06. BB 5-52 v WI (Bristol) 2017. **IT20**: 22 (2006 to 2018-19); HS 18 v WI (Chester-le-St) 2017; BB 3-21 v P (Dubai, DSC) 2015-16. F-c Tours (EL): SA 2014-15; WI 2010-11; NZ 2008-09; I 2005-06 (E), 2007-08; P 2005-06 (E); SL 2013-14. HS 126 Y v Hants (Leeds) 2016. 50 wkts (3); most – 60 (2009). BB 6-33 Y v Leeds/Bradford MCCU (Leeds) 2013 on Y debut. CC BB 6-63 (11-119 match) Du v Worcs (Chester-le-St) 2009. LO HS 72 Du v Somerset (Chester-le-St) 2008 (P40). LO BB 5-52 (*see LOI*). T20 HS 41. T20 BB 5-31.

POPE, Oliver John Douglas (Cranleigh S), b Chelsea, Middx 2 Jan 1998. 5'9''. RHB, WK. Squad No 32. Debut (Surrey) 2017; cap 2018. Surrey 2nd XI debut 2015. England U19 2016 to 2016-17. **Tests**: 2 (2018); HS 28 v I (Lord's) 2018. F-c Tour (EL): I 2018-19. 1000 runs (1): 1098 (2018). HS 158* v Yorks (Oval) 2018. LO HS 93* EL v P A (Abu Dhabi) 2018-19. T20 HS 46.

ROY, Jason Jonathan (Whitgift S), b Durban, South Africa 21 Jul 1990. 6'0''. RHB, RM. Squad No 20. Debut (Surrey) 2010; cap 2014. IPL: GL 2017. DD 2018. Big Bash: ST 2014-15. SS 2016-17 to 2017-18. **ECB L-O Central Contract 2018-19. LOI**: 73 (2015 to 2018-19); HS 180 v A (Melbourne) 2017-18 – E record. **IT20**: 32 (2014 to 2018-19); HS 78 v NZ (Delhi) 2015-16. 1000 runs (1): 1078 (2014). HS 143 v Lancs (Oval) 2015. BB 3-9 v Glos (Bristol) 2014. LO HS 180 (*see LOI*). LO BB –. T20 HS 122* v Somerset (Oval) 2015 – Sy record. T20 BB 1-23.

SMITH, Jamie Luke (Whitgift S), b Epsom 12 Jul 2000. 5'10''. RHB, WK. Squad No 11. Surrey 2nd XI debut. England U19 2018-19. Awaiting f-c debut. T20 HS 7*.

STONEMAN, Mark Daniel (Whickham CS), b Newcastle upon Tyne, Northumb 26 Jun 1987. 5'10''. LHB, OB. Squad No 23. Durham 2007-16; captain (l-o only) 2015-16. Surrey debut 2017; cap 2018. **Tests**: 11 (2017 to 2018); HS 60 v NZ (Christchurch) 2017-18. F-c Tour: A 2017-18; NZ 2017-18. 1000 runs (5); most – 1481 (2017). HS 197 v Essex (Guildford) 2017. BB –. LO HS 144* v Notts (Lord's) 2017 (RLC). LO BB 1-8 Du v Derbys (Derby) 2016 (RLC). T20 HS 89*.

VAN DEN BERGH, Frederick Oliver Edward (Whitgift S, Croydon; Hatfield C, Durham U), b Farnborough, Kent 14 Jun 1992. 6'0". RHB, SLA. Squad No 5. Debut (Surrey) 2011. Durham MCCU 2013-14. HS 34 and BB 4-84 DU v Notts (Nottingham) 2013. Sy HS 16* v Leeds/Bradford MCCU (Oval) 2012. CC HS 5 and CC BB 3-84 v Yorks (Oval) 2017. Sy BB 3-79 v Cambridge MCCU (Cambridge) 2011. LO HS 29* v Sussex (Oval) 2014 (RLC). LO BB –. T20 HS 19*. T20 BB –.

VIRDI, Guramar Singh ('**Amar**') (Guru Nanak Sikh Ac, Hayes), b Chiswick, Middx 19 Jul 1998. 5'10". RHB, OB. Squad No 19. Debut (Surrey) 2017. Surrey 2nd XI debut 2016. England U19 2016 to 2017. HS 21* v Somerset (Taunton) 2018. BB 6-105 v Worcs (Oval) 2018.

RELEASED/RETIRED

(Having made a County 1st XI appearance in 2018)

NQ**De BRUYN, Theunis** Booysen, b Pretoria, South Africa 8 Oct 1992. RHB, RMF. Northerns 2013-14. Titans 2013-14 to date. Knights 2016-17 to 2017-18. Surrey 2018. **Tests** (SA): 9 (2016-17 to 2018-19); HS 101 v SL (Colombo, SSC) 2018; BB –. **IT20** (SA): 2 (2016-17); HS 19 v SL (Centurion) 2016-17. F-c Tours (SA): E 2017; NZ 2016-17; I 2015 (SAA); SL 2018; Z 2016 (SAA). HS 202* SA A v EL (Paarl) 2014-15. Sy HS 38 v Yorks (Scarborough) 2018. BB 2-24 SA v EL (Worcester) 2017. LO HS 152* Titans v Warriors (Port Elizabeth) 2014-15. LO BB 2-37 SA A v Aus Nat Perf XI (Mackay) 2016. T20 HS 100. T20 BB 1-28.

NQ**MADDINSON, Nicolas** James, Shoalhaven, NSW, Australia 21 Dec 1991. LHB, SLA. New South Wales 2010-11 to 2017-18. Victoria 2018-19. Surrey 2018 (T20 only). IPL: RCB 2014-15. Big Bash: SS 2011-12 to 2017-18. MS 2018-19. **Tests** (A): 3 (2016-17); HS 22 v P (Melbourne) 2016-17; BB –. **IT20** (A): 6 (2013-14 to 2018); HS 34 v I (Rajkot) 2013-14. F-c Tours (Aus A): E/Ire 2013; SA/Z 2013; I 2015. HS 181 Aus A v Glos (Bristol) 2013 – on UK debut. BB 2-10 NSW v SA (Coffs Harbour) 2015-16. LO HS 137 NSW v Tas (Perth) 2017-18. LO BB 4-28 Vic v WA (Melbourne, St K) 2018-19. T20 HS 85. T20 BB –.

PILLANS, M.W. – see YORKSHIRE.

SOMERSET RELEASED/RETIRED (continued from p 174)

NQ**MYBURGH, Johannes** Gerhardus (Pretoria BHS; U of SA), b Pretoria, South Africa 22 Oct 1980. Elder brother of S.J.Myburgh (Northerns, KZN and Netherlands 2005-06 to date), brother-in-law of F.de Wet (Northerns, NW, Lions, Hampshire, Dolphins and South Africa 2001-02 to 2011-12). 5'7". RHB, OB. Northerns 1997-98 to 2006-07. Titans 2004-05. Canterbury 2007-08 to 2009-10. Hampshire 2011. Durham 2012. Somerset 2014-16. EU qualified through wife's visa. HS 203 Northerns B v Easterns (Pretoria) 1997-98. Sm HS 150 v Durham MCCU (Taunton Vale) 2015. CC HS 118 v Durham (Taunton) 2015. BB 4-56 Canterbury v ND (Hamilton) 2008-09. Sm BB 3-57 v Yorks (Taunton) 2015. LO HS 112 Canterbury v Auckland (Christchurch) 2009-10. LO BB 2-22 Canterbury v CD (Christchurch) 2009-10. T20 HS 103*. T20 BB 3-16.

RENSHAW, M.T. – see KENT.

F.R.Trenouth left the staff without making a County 1st XI appearance in 2018.

SURREY 2018

	Place	Won	Lost	Drew	NR
Specsavers County Champ (1st Division)	1st	10	1	3	
All First-Class Matches		10	1	4	
Royal London One-Day Cup (South Group)	5th	4	3		1
Vitality Blast (South Group)	5th	7	5		2

SPECSAVERS COUNTY CHAMPIONSHIP AVERAGES
BATTING AND FIELDING

Cap		M	I	NO	HS	Runs	Avge	100	50	Ct/St
2018	O.J.D.Pope	13	16	2	158*	986	70.42	4	1	21
2014	R.J.Burns	14	22	1	193	1359	64.71	4	7	11
2018	S.G.Borthwick	8	12	1	83	444	40.36	–	5	13
	D.Elgar	7	10	–	110	387	38.70	1	2	6
2016	B.T.Foakes	12	18	1	90	624	36.70	–	4	37/1
2018	M.D.Stoneman	13	21	1	144	660	33.00	1	4	4
2005	R.Clarke	13	17	1	111	500	31.25	1	2	19
	R.S.Patel	9	13	3	48	255	25.50	–	–	4
2018	S.M.Curran	7	10	1	70	209	23.22	–	1	2
	C.McKerr	5	5	2	29	64	21.33	–	–	–
	W.G.Jacks	6	8	–	53	168	21.00	–	1	8
2016	T.K.Curran	4	5	–	43	81	16.20	–	–	–
2018	M.Morkel	10	13	2	29	172	15.63	–	–	1
2011	J.W.Dernbach	10	13	2	31	129	11.72	–	–	2
	G.S.Virdi	14	16	8	21*	68	8.50	–	–	5

Also batted: T.B.de Bruyn (2 matches) 0, 38, 8* (2 ct); M.P.Dunn (2) 0, 9*, 1 (2 ct); A.J.Finch (2 – cap 2018) 2, 43, 32 (1 ct); A.Harinath (2 – cap 2016) 48, 1, 7 (1 ct); S.C.Meaker (1 – cap 2012) 13 (1 ct); J.J.Roy (2 – cap 2014) 63, 5, 128.

BOWLING

	O	M	R	W	Avge	Best	5wI	10wM
M.Morkel	315.4	82	845	59	14.32	6- 57	4	–
T.K.Curran	120.4	30	312	19	16.42	5- 28	1	–
C.McKerr	67.2	13	246	13	18.92	4- 26	–	–
R.Clarke	363.1	87	1012	47	21.53	5- 29	1	–
S.M.Curran	192.2	37	608	25	24.32	6- 54	1	1
J.W.Dernbach	285.5	65	929	32	29.03	4- 49	–	–
G.S.Virdi	360.3	46	1184	39	30.35	6-105	1	–

Also bowled:

R.S.Patel	87.1	14	279	8	34.87	6- 5	1	–

S.G.Borthwick 18-1-67-0; M.P.Dunn 44.3-10-171-3; S.C.Meaker 22-1-93-0.

The First-Class Averages (pp 230–245) give the records of Surrey players in all first-class county matches (Surrey's other opponents being West Indies A), with the exception of R.J.Burns, S.M.Curran and O.J.D.Pope, whose first-class figures for Surrey are as above, and:

M.D.Stoneman 14-23-1-144-705-32.04-1-4-5ct. Did not bowl.

SURREY RECORDS

FIRST-CLASS CRICKET

Highest Total	For 811		v	Somerset	The Oval	1899
	V 863		by	Lancashire	The Oval	1990
Lowest Total	For 14		v	Essex	Chelmsford	1983
	V 16		by	MCC	Lord's	1872
Highest Innings	For 357*	R.Abel	v	Somerset	The Oval	1899
	V 366	N.H.Fairbrother	for	Lancashire	The Oval	1990

Highest Partnership for each Wicket

1st	428	J.B.Hobbs/A.Sandham	v	Oxford U	The Oval	1926
2nd	371	J.B.Hobbs/E.G.Hayes	v	Hampshire	The Oval	1909
3rd	413	D.J.Bicknell/D.M.Ward	v	Kent	Canterbury	1990
4th	448	R.Abel/T.W.Hayward	v	Yorkshire	The Oval	1899
5th	318	M.R.Ramprakash/Azhar Mahmood	v	Middlesex	The Oval	2005
6th	298	A.Sandham/H.S.Harrison	v	Sussex	The Oval	1913
7th	262	C.J.Richards/K.T.Medlycott	v	Kent	The Oval	1987
8th	222*	B.T.Foakes/G.J.Batty	v	Hampshire	Southampton[2]	2016
9th	168	E.R.T.Holmes/E.W.J.Brooks	v	Hampshire	The Oval	1936
10th	173	A.Ducat/A.Sandham	v	Essex	Leyton	1921

Best Bowling	For	10-43	T.Rushby	v	Somerset	Taunton	1921
(Innings)	V	10-28	W.P.Howell	for	Australians	The Oval	1899
Best Bowling	For	16-83	G.A.R.Lock	v	Kent	Blackheath	1956
(Match)	V	15-57	W.P.Howell	for	Australians	The Oval	1899

Most Runs – Season	3246	T.W.Hayward	(av 72.13)		1906
Most Runs – Career	43554	J.B.Hobbs	(av 49.72)		1905-34
Most 100s – Season	13	T.W.Hayward			1906
	13	J.B.Hobbs			1925
Most 100s – Career	144	J.B.Hobbs			1905-34
Most Wkts – Season	252	T.Richardson	(av 13.94)		1895
Most Wkts – Career	1775	T.Richardson	(av 17.87)		1892-1904
Most Career W-K Dismissals	1221	H.Strudwick	(1035 ct; 186 st)		1902-27
Most Career Catches in the Field	605	M.J.Stewart			1954-72

LIMITED-OVERS CRICKET

Highest Total	50ov	496-4		v	Glos	The Oval	2007
	40ov	386-3		v	Glamorgan	The Oval	2010
	T20	250-6		v	Kent	Canterbury	2018
Lowest Total	50ov	74		v	Kent	The Oval	1967
	40ov	64		v	Worcs	Worcester	1978
	T20	88		v	Kent	The Oval	2012
Highest Innings	50ov	268	A.D.Brown	v	Glamorgan	The Oval	2002
	40ov	203	A.D.Brown	v	Hampshire	Guildford	1997
	T20	131*	A.J.Finch	v	Sussex	Hove	2018
Best Bowling	50ov	7-33	R.D.Jackman	v	Yorkshire	Harrogate	1970
	40ov	7-30	M.P.Bicknell	v	Glamorgan	The Oval	1999
	T20	6-24	T.J.Murtagh	v	Middlesex	Lord's	2005

SUSSEX

Formation of Present Club: 1 March 1839
Substantial Reorganisation: August 1857
Inaugural First-Class Match: 1864
Colours: Dark Blue, Light Blue and Gold
Badge: County Arms of Six Martlets
County Champions: (3) 2003, 2006, 2007
Gillette/NatWest/C&G Trophy Winners: (5) 1963, 1964,
1978, 1986, 2006
Pro 40/National League (Div 1) Winners: (2) 2008, 2009
Sunday League Winners: (1) 1982
Twenty20 Cup Winners: (1) 2009

Chief Executive: Rob Andrew, The 1st Central County Ground, Eaton Road, Hove BN3 3AN • Tel: 0844 264 0202 • Email: info@sussexcricket.co.uk • Web: www.sussexcricket.co.uk • Twitter: @SussexCCC (74,266 followers)

Director of Cricket: Keith Greenfield. **Head Coach**: Jason Gillespie. **Batting Coach**: Michael Yardy. **Captain**: B.C.Brown. **Overseas Players**: Mir Hamza and Rashid Khan. **2019 Testimonial**: None. **Head Groundsman**: Andy Mackay. **Scorer**: Mike Charman. ‡ New registration. ^{NQ} Not qualified for England.

ARCHER, Jofra Chioke (Christchurch Foundation), b Bridgetown, Barbados 1 Apr 1995. 6'3". RHB, RF. Squad No 22. Debut (Sussex) 2016; cap 2017. IPL: RR 2018. Big Bash: HH 2017-18 to date. Qualified for England at the start of the 2019 season. HS 81* v Northants (Northampton) 2017. 50 wkts (1): 61 (2017). BB 7-67 v Kent (Hove) 2017. LO HS 45 v Essex (Chelmsford) 2017 (RLC). LO BB 5-42 v Somerset (Taunton) 2016 (RLC). T20 HS 36. T20 BB 4-18.

BEER, William Andrew Thomas (Reigate GS; Collyer's C, Horsham), b Crawley 8 Oct 1988. 5'10". RHB, LB. Squad No 18. Debut (Sussex) 2008. HS 50* v Loughboro MCCU (Hove) 2018. CC HS 39 v Middx (Lord's) 2013. BB 6-29 (11-91 match) v South Africa A (Arundel) 2017. CC BB 3-31 v Worcs (Worcester) 2010. LO HS 45* v Durham (Hove) 2014 (RLC). LO BB 3-27 v Warwks (Hove) 2012 (CB40). T20 HS 37. T20 BB 3-14.

BRIGGS, Danny Richard (Isle of Wight C), b Newport, IoW, 30 Apr 1991. 6'2". RHB, SLA. Squad No 21. Hampshire 2009-15; cap 2012. Sussex debut 2016. LOI: 1 (2011-12); BB 2-39 v P (Dubai) 2011-12. **IT20**: 7 (2012 to 2013-14); HS 0*; BB 2-25 v A (Chester-le-St) 2013. F-c Tours (EL): WI 2010-11; I 2018-19. HS 120* v South Africa A (Arundel) 2017. CC HS 54 H v Glos (Bristol) 2013. BB 6-45 EL v Windward Is (Roseau) 2010-11. CC BB 6-65 H v Notts (Southampton) 2011. Sx BB 5-93 v Glos (Bristol) 2016. LO HS 25 and LO BB 4-32 H v Glamorgan (Cardiff) 2012 (CB40). T20 HS 13. T20 BB 5-19.

BROWN, Ben Christopher (Ardingly C), b Crawley 23 Nov 1988. 5'8". 6'1". RHB, WK. Squad No 26. Debut (Sussex) 2007; cap 2014; captain 2017 to date. 1000 runs (2); most – 1031 (2015, 2018). HS 163 v Durham (Hove) 2014. BB 1-48 v Essex (Colchester) 2016. LO HS 73* v Kent (Hove) 2018 (RLC). T20 HS 68.

BURGESS, Michael Gregory Kerran (Cranleigh S; Loughborough U), b Epsom, Surrey 8 Jul 1994. RHB, RM, occ WK. Squad No 5. Loughborough MCCU 2014-15. Leicestershire 2016. Sussex debut 2017. Surrey 2nd XI 2011-13. HS 146 v Notts (Hove) 2017. LO HS 58 v Glamorgan (Cardiff) 2018 (RLC). T20 HS 56.

184

EVANS, Laurie John (Whitgift S; The John Fisher S; St Mary's C, Durham U), b Lambeth, London 12 Oct 1987. 6'0". RHB, RM. Squad No 32. Durham UCCE 2007. MCC 2007. Surrey 2009-10. Warwickshire 2010-16. Northamptonshire 2016 (on loan). Sussex debut 2017. HS 213* and BB 1-29 Wa v Sussex (Birmingham) 2015, sharing Wa 6th wkt record partnership of 327 with T.R.Ambrose. Sx HS 34 v Northants (Northampton) 2018. LO HS 134* v Kent (Canterbury) 2017 (RLC). LO BB –. T20 HS 104*. T20 BB 1-5.

FINCH, Harry Zachariah (St Richard's Catholic C, Bexhill; Eastbourne C), b Hastings 10 Feb 1995. 5'8". RHB, RM. Squad No 6. Debut (Sussex) 2013. Sussex 2nd XI debut 2011. England U19 2012-13. HS 135* and BB 1-9 v Leeds/Bradford MCCU (Hove) 2016. CC HS 103 v Middx (Hove) 2018. CC BB 1-30 v Northants (Arundel) 2016. LO HS 108 v Hants (Hove) 2018 (RLC). LO BB –. T20 HS 35*.

GARTON, George Henry Simmons (Hurstpierpoint C), b Brighton 15 Apr 1997. 5'10½". LHB, LF. Squad No 15. Debut (Sussex) 2016. Sussex 2nd XI debut 2014. HS 22* v Middx (Hove) 2016. BB 3-20 v Durham (Chester-le-St) 2017. LO HS 7* v Somerset (Hove) 2017 (RLC). LO BB 4-43 EL v SL A (Canterbury) 2016. T20 HS 2*. T20 BB 4-16.

HAINES, Thomas Jacob (Tanbridge House S, Horsham; Hurstpierpoint C), b Crawley 28 Oct 1998. 5'10". LHB, RM. Squad No 20. Debut (Sussex) 2016. Sussex 2nd XI debut 2014. HS 124 v Durham (Arundel) 2018. BB 1-13 v Durham (Chester-le-St) 2018.

JORDAN, Christopher James (Comber Mere S, Barbados; Dulwich C), b Christ Church, Barbados 4 Oct 1988. 6'0". RHB, RFM. Squad No 8. Surrey 2007-12. Barbados 2011-12 to 2012-13. Sussex debut 2013; cap 2014. IPL: RCB 2016. SH 2017 to date. Big Bash: AS 2016-17. ST 2018-19. **Tests**: 8 (2014 to 2014-15); HS 35 v SL (Lord's) 2014; BB 4-18 v I (Oval) 2014. **LOI**: 31 (2013 to 2016); HS 38* v SL (Oval) 2014; BB 5-29 v SL (Manchester) 2014. **IT20**: 38 (2013-14 to 2018-19); HS 27* v WI (Bridgetown) 2013-14; BB 4-6 v WI (Basseterre) 2018-19 – E record. F-c Tour: WI 2014-15. HS 147 v Notts (Hove) 2017. 50 wkts (1): 61 (2013). BB 7-43 Barbados v CC&C (Bridgetown) 2012-13. Sx BB 6-48 v Yorks (Leeds) 2013. LO HS 55 v Surrey (Guildford) 2016 (RLC). LO BB 5-28 v Middx (Hove) 2016 (RLC). T20 HS 45*. T20 BB 4-6.

MILLS, Tymal Solomon (Mildenhall TC), b Dewsbury, Yorks 12 Aug 1992. 6'1". RHB, LF. Squad No 7. Essex 2011-14. Sussex debut 2015; has played T20 only since start of 2016. IPL: RCB 2017. Big Bash: BH 2016-17. HH 2017-18. **IT20**: 4 (+1 ICC World XI 2018) (2016 to 2016-17); HS 0; BB 1-27 v I (Kanpur) 2016-17. F-c Tour (EL): SL 2013-14. HS 31* EL v SL A (Colombo, RPS) 2013-14. CC HS 30 v Kent (Canterbury) 2014. Sx HS 8 v Worcs (Hove) 2015. BB 4-25 Ex v Glamorgan (Cardiff) 2012. Sx BB 2-28 v Hants (Southampton) 2014. LO HS 3* v Notts (Hove) 2015 (RLC). LO BB 3-23 Ex v Durham (Chelmsford) 2013 (Y40). T20 HS 8*. T20 BB 4-22.

‡**NOMIR HAMZA**, b Karachi, Pakistan 10 Sep 1992. LHB, LMF. Karachi Whites 2012-13 to 2013-14. Karachi Dolphins 2014-15. United Bank 2015-16 to 2017-18. National Bank 2018-19. **Tests** (P): 1 (2018-19); HS 4* and BB 1-40 v A (Abu Dhabi) 2018-19. HS 25 NBP v Peshawar (Faisalabad) 2018-19. BB 7-59 UB v SSGC (Sialkot) 2016-17. LO HS 49 KD v Rawalpindi Rams (Karachi) 2014-15. LO BB 4-27 KD v Hyderabad Hawks (Karachi) 2013-14. T20 HS 5. T20 BB 4-28.

NORASHID KHAN Arman, b Nangarhar, Afghanistan 20 Sep 1998. RHB, LBG. Squad No 1. Afghanistan 2016-17 to date. Sussex debut 2018 (T20 only). IPL: SH 2017 to date. Big Bash: AS 2017-18 to date. **Tests** (Afg): 2 (2018 to 2018-19); HS 12 v I (Bengalaru) 2018; BB 5-82 v Ire (Dehradun) 2018-19. **LOI** (Afg): 57 (2015-16 to 2018-19); HS 60* v Ire (Belfast) 2016; BB 7-18 v WI (Gros Islet) 2017 – 4th best analysis in all LOI. **IT20** (Afg): 38 (2015-16 to 2018-19); HS 33 v WI (Basseterre) 2017; BB 5-3 v Ire (Greater Noida) 2016-17 – joint 4th best analysis in all IT20. HS 52 and BB 8-74 (12-122 match) Afg v EL (Abu Dhabi) 2016-17. LO HS 60* (*see LOI*). LO BB 7-18 (*see LOI*). T20 HS 56*. T20 BB 5-3.

RAWLINS, Delray Millard Wendell (Bede's S, Upper Dicker), b Bermuda 14 Sep 1997. 6'1". LHB, SLA. Squad No 9. Debut (Sussex) 2017. MCC 2018. Sussex 2nd XI debut 2015. Oxfordshire 2017. England U19 2016-17. HS 96 v South Africa A (Arundel) 2017. CC HS 55 v Notts (Hove) 2017. BB 1-46 v Kent (Hove) 2017. LO HS 53 South v North (Bridgetown) 2017-18. LO BB 1-33 ECB v I A (Leeds) 2018. T20 HS 49.

ROBINSON, Oliver Edward (King's S, Canterbury), b Margate, Kent 1 Dec 1993. 6'1". RHB, RMF/OB. Squad No 25. Debut (Sussex) 2015. HS 110 v Durham (Chester-le-St) 2015, on debut, sharing Sx record 10th wkt partnership of 164 with M.E.Hobden. 50 wkts (1): 81 (2018). BB 7-23 v Loughboro MCCU (Hove) 2018. CC BB 7-58 v Middx (Hove) 2018. LO HS 30 v Kent (Canterbury) 2015 (RLC). LO BB 3-31 v Kent (Hove) 2018 (RLC). T20 HS 10. T20 BB 3-16.

SAKANDE, Abidine (Ardingly C; St John's C, Oxford), b Chester 22 Sep 1994. 6'1". RHB, RFM. Squad No 11. Oxford U 2014-15. Oxford MCCU 2015-16. Sussex debut 2016. Sussex 2nd XI debut 2011. HS 33 OU v Cambridge U (Cambridge) 2015. Sx HS 17 and BB 5-43 v South Africa A (Arundel) 2017. CC HS 7* v Glos (Hove) 2017. CC BB 3-44 v Northants (Northampton) 2018. LO HS 7* v South Africans (Hove) 2017. LO BB 2-53 v Somerset (Taunton) 2018 (RLC).

SALT, Philip Dean (Reed's S, Cobham), b Bodelwyddan, Denbighs 28 Aug 1996. 5'10". RHB, OB. Squad No 28. Debut (Sussex) 2013. Sussex 2nd XI debut 2014. HS 148 v Derbys (Hove) 2018. LO HS 81 v Middx (Hove) 2016 (RLC). T20 HS 74.

[NQ]**VAN ZYL, Stiaan**, b Cape Town, South Africa 19 Sep 1987. 5'11½". LHB, RM. Squad No 74. Boland 2006-07 to 2010-11. Cape Cobras 2007-08 to 2017-18. W Province 2014-15 to 2016-17. Sussex debut 2017 (Kolpak signing). **Tests** (SA): 12 (2014-15 to 2016); HS 101* v WI (Centurion) 2014-15 – on debut; BB 3-20 v E (Durban) 2015-16. F-c Tours (SA): A 2016 (SA A), I 2015 (SA A), 2015-16; SL 2010 (SA A); B 2010 (SA A), 2015; Ire 2012 (SA A). 1000 runs (1): 1023 (2017). HS 228 Cobras v Lions (Paarl) 2017-18. Sx 166* v Leics (Arundel) 2017. BB 5-32 Boland v Northerns (Paarl) 2010-11. Sx BB 3-16 v Glos (Hove) 2018. LO HS 114* Cobras v Eagles (Kimberley) 2009-10. LO BB 4-24 Boland v Gauteng (Stellenbosch) 2010-11. T20 HS 86*. T20 BB 2-14.

WELLS, Luke William Peter (St Bede's S, Upper Dicker), b Eastbourne 29 Dec 1990. Son of A.P.Wells (Border, Kent, Sussex and England 1981-2000); elder.brother of D.A.C.Wells (Oxford MCCU 2017); nephew of C.M.Wells (Border, Derbyshire, Sussex and WP 1979-96). 6'4". LHB, LB. Squad No 31. Debut (Sussex) 2010; cap 2016. Colombo CC 2011-12. 1000 runs (2); most – 1292 (2017). HS 258 v Durham (Hove) 2017. BB 4-81 v Leics (Leicester) 2015. LO HS 62 v Kent (Hove) 2018 (RLC). BB 3-19 v Netherlands (Amstelveen) 2011 (CB40). T20 HS 11.

[NQ]**WIESE, David** (Witbank HS), b Roodepoort, South Africa 18 May 1985. 6'3". RHB, RMF. Squad No 96. Easterns 2005-06 to 2011-12. Titans 2009-10 to 2016-17. Sussex debut/cap 2016 (Kolpak signing). IPL: RCB 2015-16. **LOI** (SA): 6 (2015 to 2015-16); HS 41* and BB 3-50 v E (Cape Town) 2015-16. **IT20** (SA): 20 (2013 to 2015-16); HS 28 v WI (Nagpur) 2015-16; BB 5-23 v WI (Durban) 2014-15. F-c Tour (SA A): A 2014. HS 208 Easterns v GW (Benoni) 2008-09. Sx HS 106 v Warwks (Birmingham) 2018. BB 6-58 Titans v Knights (Centurion) 2014-15. Sx BB 5-48 v Glos (Hove) 2018. LO HS 106 Easterns v FS (Bloemfontein) 2007-08. LO BB 5-25 Easterns v Boland (Benoni) 2010-11. T20 HS 71*. T20 BB 5-19.

WRIGHT, Luke James (Belvoir HS; Ratcliffe C; Loughborough U), b Grantham, Lincs 7 Mar 1985. Younger brother of A.S.Wright (Leicestershire 2001-02). 5'11". RHB, RMF. Squad No 10. Leicestershire 2003 (one f-c match). Sussex debut 2004; cap 2007; T20 captain & benefit 2015; captain 2016-17. IPL: PW 2012-13. Big Bash: MS 2011-12 to 2017-18. **LOI**: 50 (2007 to 2013-14); HS 52 v NZ (Birmingham) 2008; BB 2-34 v NZ (Bristol) 2008 and 2-34 v A (Southampton) 2010. **IT20**: 51 (2007-08 to 2013-14); HS 99* v Afg (Colombo, RPS) 2012-13; BB 2-24 v NZ (Hamilton) 2012-13. F-c Tour (EL): NZ 2008-09. 1000 runs (1): 1220 (2015). HS 226* v Worcs (Worcester) 2015, sharing Sx record 6th wkt partnership of 335 with B.C.Brown. BB 5-65 v Derbys (Derby) 2010. LO HS 143* EL v B A (Bristol) 2013. LO BB 4-12 v Middx (Hove) 2004 (NL). T20 HS 153* v Essex (Chelmsford) 2014 – Sx record. T20 BB 3-17.

RELEASED/RETIRED

(Having made a County 1st XI appearance in 2018)

BRUCE, Thomas Charles, b Te Kuiti, New Zealand 2 Aug 1991. RHB, OB. Central Districts 2014-15 to date. Sussex 2018 (T20 only). **IT20** (NZ): 14 (2016-17 to 2017-18); HS 59* v B (Mt Maunganui) 2016-17. F-c Tours (NZA): I 2017-18; UAE 2018-19 (v P A). HS 166* CD v ND (Hamilton) 2015-16. BB 2-17 CD v Canterbury (Nelson) 2015-16. LO HS 100 CD v ND (New Plymouth) 2016-17. LO BB 1-13 CD v Wellington (Lincoln) 2018-19. T20 HS 88*. T20 BB 1-11.

NQ**SHARMA, Ishant**, b Delhi, India 2 Sep 1988. RHB, RFM. Delhi 2006-07 to date. Sussex 2018; cap 2018. IPL: KKR 2007-08 to 2009-10. DC 2011. SH 2013-15. RPS 2016. KXIP 2017. **Tests** (I): 90 (2007 to 2018-19); HS 31* v SL (Galle) 2010; BB 7-74 v E (Lord's) 2014. **LOI** (I): 80 (2007 to 2015-16); HS 13 v SL (Colombo, RPS) 2009; BB 4-34 v SL (Cuttack) 2014-15. **IT20** (I): 14 (2007-08 to 2013-14); HS 5* v SL (Nagpur) 2009-10; BB 2-34 v B (Nottingham) 2009. F-c Tours (I): E 2007, 2011, 2014, 2018; A 2007-08, 2011-12, 2014-15, 2018-19; SA 2010-11, 2013-14, 2017-18; WI 2011, 2016; NZ 2008-09, 2013-14; SL 2008, 2010, 2015; B 2007, 2009-10, 2015. HS 66 v Leics (Leicester) 2018. BB 7-24 (11-51 match) Delhi v Orissa (Delhi) 2008-09. Sx BB 4-52 v Kent (Canterbury) 2018. LO HS 31 Delhi v Punjab (Mohali) 2010-11. LO BB 5-21 Delhi v Vidarbha (Delhi) 2015-16. T20 HS 9. T20 BB 5-12.

WHITTINGHAM, S.G. – *see GLOUCESTERSHIRE*.

A:P.Barton and J.W.Jenner left the staff during the season without making a County 1st XI appearance in 2018.

SUSSEX 2018

RESULTS SUMMARY

	Place	Won	Lost	Drew	NR
Specsavers County Champ (2nd Division)	3rd	6	4	4	
All First-Class Matches		6	4	5	
Royal London One-Day Cup (South Group)	8th	2	4		2
Vitality Blast (South Group)	Finalist 9	4			4

SPECSAVERS COUNTY CHAMPIONSHIP AVERAGES
BATTING AND FIELDING

Cap		M	I	NO	HS	Runs	Avge	100	50	Ct/St
2014	B.C.Brown	14	24	3	116	912	43.42	1	7	52/1
2016	D.Wiese	13	20	4	106	538	33.62	1	2	2
	T.J.Haines	7	10	–	124	319	31.90	1	1	2
	P.D.Salt	14	24	–	148	739	30.79	2	2	11
	M.G.K.Burgess	12	19	1	101*	551	30.61	1	2	4
	H.Z.Finch	14	24	–	103	722	30.08	1	5	23
2016	L.W.P.Wells	14	24	1	102*	607	26.39	1	4	3
	S.van Zyl	5	9	–	45	237	26.33	–	–	1
2018	I.Sharma	4	6	2	66	102	25.50	–	1	1
2014	C.J.Jordan	8	13	–	68	299	23.00	–	2	5
2007	L.J.Wright	9	16	–	88	338	21.12	–	1	1
	D.R.Briggs	12	20	7	46	234	18.00	–	–	5
2017	J.C.Archer	8	13	3	33	170	17.00	–	–	6
	O.E.Robinson	14	22	3	52	294	15.47	–	1	5

Also played (1 match each): W.A.T.Beer did not bat; L.J.Evans 34, 0 (1 ct); G.H.S.Garton 22* (1 ct); D.M.W.Rawlins 0, 0; A.Sakande 0*, 1*; S.G.Whittingham 0*.

BOWLING

	O	M	R	W	Avge	Best	5wI	10wM
J.C.Archer	273.5	67	750	42	17.85	5-69	1	–
O.E.Robinson	485	92	1381	74	18.66	7-58	4	1
I.Sharma	114.3	19	346	15	23.06	4-52	–	–
D.Wiese	339.1	65	1041	41	25.39	5-48	1	–
D.R.Briggs	279.5	51	764	28	27.28	4-70	–	–
C.J.Jordan	191.1	32	598	20	29.90	3-23	–	–

Also bowled:
L.W.P.Wells | 125.2 | 14 | | 378 | 8 | 47.25 | 4-81 | – | –

W.A.T.Beer 26-3-88-1; B.C.Brown 3-2-1-0; M.G.K.Burgess 6-1-14-0; G.H.S.Garton 27-2-103-1; T.J.Haines 29-8-74-1; A.Sakande 22-1-91-3; P.D.Salt 9-2-32-1; S.van Zyl 48-12-127-3; S.G.Whittingham 16-2-61-2.

The First-Class Averages (pp 230–245) give the records of Sussex players in all first-class county matches (Sussex's other opponents being Loughborough MCCU), with the exception of I.Sharma, whose first-class figures for Sussex are as above.

SUSSEX RECORDS

FIRST-CLASS CRICKET

Highest Total	For 742-5d		v	Somerset	Taunton	2009
	V 726		by	Notts	Nottingham	1895
Lowest Total	For 19		v	Surrey	Godalming	1830
	19		v	Notts	Hove	1873
	V 18		by	Kent	Gravesend	1867
Highest Innings	For 344*	M.W.Goodwin	v	Somerset	Taunton	2009
	V 322	E.Paynter	for	Lancashire	Hove	1937

Highest Partnership for each Wicket

1st	490	E.H.Bowley/J.G.Langridge	v	Middlesex	Hove	1933
2nd	385	E.H.Bowley/M.W.Tate	v	Northants	Hove	1921
3rd	385*	M.H.Yardy/M.W.Goodwin	v	Warwicks	Hove	2006
4th	363	M.W.Goodwin/C.D.Hopkinson	v	Somerset	Taunton	2009
5th	297	J.H.Parks/H.W.Parks	v	Hampshire	Portsmouth	1937
6th	335	L.J.Wright/B.C.Brown	v	Durham	Hove	2014
7th	344	K.S.Ranjitsinhji/W.Newham	v	Essex	Leyton	1902
8th	291	R.S.C.Martin-Jenkins/M.J.G.Davis	v	Somerset	Taunton	2002
9th	178	H.W.Parks/A.F.Wensley	v	Derbyshire	Horsham	1930
10th	164	O.E.Robinson/M.E.Hobden	v	Durham	Chester-le-St^2	2015

Best Bowling	For	10- 48	C.H.G.Bland	v	Kent	Tonbridge	1899
(Innings)	V	9- 11	A.P.Freeman	for	Kent	Hove	1922
Best Bowling	For	17-106	G.R.Cox	v	Warwicks	Horsham	1926
(Match)	V	17- 67	A.P.Freeman	for	Kent	Hove	1922

Most Runs – Season	2850	J.G.Langridge	(av 64.77)	1949
Most Runs – Career	34150	J.G.Langridge	(av 37.69)	1928-55
Most 100s – Season	12	J.G.Langridge		1949
Most 100s – Career	76	J.G.Langridge		1928-55
Most Wkts – Season	198	M.W.Tate	(av 13.47)	1925
Most Wkts – Career	2211	M.W.Tate	(av 17.41)	1912-37
Most Career W-K Dismissals	1176	H.R.Butt	(911 ct; 265 st)	1890-1912
Most Career Catches in the Field	779	J.G.Langridge		1928-55

LIMITED-OVERS CRICKET

Highest Total	50ov	384-9		v	Ireland	Belfast	1996
	40ov	399-4		v	Worcs	Horsham	2011
	T20	242-5		v	Glos	Bristol	2016
Lowest Total	50ov	49		v	Derbyshire	Chesterfield	1969
	40ov	59		v	Glamorgan	Hove	1996
	T20	67		v	Hampshire	Hove	2004
Highest Innings	50ov	158*	M.W.Goodwin	v	Essex	Chelmsford	2006
	40ov	163	C.J.Adams	v	Middlesex	Arundel	1999
	T20	153*	L.J.Wright	v	Essex	Chelmsford	2014
Best Bowling	50ov	6- 9	A.I.C.Dodemaide	v	Ireland	Downpatrick	1990
	40ov	7-41	A.N.Jones	v	Notts	Nottingham	1986
	T20	5-11	Mushtaq Ahmed	v	Essex	Hove	2005

WARWICKSHIRE

Formation of Present Club: 8 April 1882
Substantial Reorganisation: 19 January 1884
Inaugural First-Class Match: 1894
Colours: Dark Blue, Gold and Silver
Badge: Bear and Ragged Staff
County Champions: (7) 1911, 1951, 1972, 1994, 1995, 2004, 2012
Gillette/NatWest Trophy Winners: (5) 1966, 1968, 1989, 1993, 1995
Benson and Hedges Cup Winners: (2) 1994, 2002
Sunday League Winners: (3) 1980, 1994, 1997
Clydesdale Bank 40 Winners: (1) 2010
Royal London Cup Winners: (1) 2015
Twenty20 Cup Winners: (1) 2014

Chief Executive: Neil Snowball, Edgbaston Stadium, Edgbaston, Birmingham, B5 7QU • Tel: 0844 635 1902 • Email: info@edgbaston.com • Web: www.edgbaston.com • Twitter: @CricketingBears (55,641 followers)

Sport Director: Paul Farbrace. **1st Team Coach**: Jim Troughton. **Batting Coach**: Tony Frost. **Bowling Coach**: Graeme Welch. **Captain**: J.S.Patel. **Vice-Captain**: D.P.Sibley. **Overseas Players**: A.C.Agar (T20 only) and J.S.Patel. **2019 Testimonial**: None. **Head Groundsman**: Gary Barwell. **Scorer**: Mel Smith. ‡ New registration. NQ Not qualified for England.

‡NQAGAR, Ashton Charles (De La Salle C), b Melbourne, Australia 14 Oct 1993. Elder brother of W.A.Agar (S Australia, Victoria (l-o only) and AS 2016-17 to date). LHB, SLA. W Australia 2012-13 to date. Middlesex 2018 (T20 only). Big Bash: PS 2013-14 to date. Tests (A): 4 (2013 to 2017); HS 98 v E (Nottingham) 2013 – on debut, a record score for a No 11, sharing a then world record 10th wkt partnership of 163 with P.J.Hughes; BB 3-46 v B (Dhaka) 2017. **LOI** (A): 9 (2015 to 2018); HS 46 v E (Cardiff) 2018; BB 2-48 v E (Chester-le-St) 2018. **IT20** (A): 15 (2015-16 to 2018-19); HS 29 v E (Birmingham) 2018; BB 3-27 v NZ (Auckland) 2017-18. F-c Tours (A): E 2013; I 2012-13, 2015 (Aus A); B 2017; Ire/Scot 2013 (Aus A). HS 106 WA v Tas (Perth) 2015-16. BB 6-110 (10-141 match) WA v NSW (Sydney) 2016-17. LO HS 64 WA v Tas (Sydney, NS) 2014-15. LO BB 5-39 Aus A v I A (Chennai) 2015. T20 HS 68. T20 BB 3-17.

AMBROSE, Timothy Raymond (Merewether HS, NSW; TAFE C), b Newcastle, NSW, Australia 1 Dec 1982. ECB qualified – British/EU passport. 5'7''. RHB, WK. Squad No 11. Sussex 2001-05; cap 2003. Warwickshire debut 2006; cap 2007; benefit 2016. Tests: 11 (2007-08 to 2008-09); HS 102 v NZ (Wellington) 2007-08. **LOI**: 5 (2008); HS 6 v NZ (Oval) 2008. **IT20**: 1 (2008); HS –. F-c Tours: WI 2008-09; NZ 2007-08. HS 251* v Worcs (Worcester) 2007. LO HS 135 v Durham (Birmingham) 2007 (FPT). T20 HS 77.

BANKS, Liam (Newcastle-under-Lyme S & SFC), b Newcastle-under-Lyme, Staffs 3 Jun 1999. 5'10''. RHB, RM. Squad No 8. Debut (Warwickshire) 2017. Warwickshire 2nd XI debut 2015. England U19 2017 to 2018. No 1s XI appearances in 2018. HS 29 v Yorks (Leeds) 2017.

BELL, Ian Ronald (Princethorpe C), b Walsgrave-on-Sowe 11 Apr 1982. 5'9''. RHB, RM. Squad No 4. Debut (Warwickshire) 1999; cap 2001; benefit 2011; captain 2016-17. MCC 2004, 2016. YC 2004. MBE 2005. *Wisden* 2007. **Tests**: 118 (2004 to 2015-16); 1000 runs (1): 1005 (2013); HS 235 v I (Oval) 2011; BB 1-33 v P (Faisalabad) 2005-06. **LOI**: 161 (2004-05 to 2014-15); 1000 runs (1): 1080 (2007); HS 141 v A (Hobart) 2014-15; BB 3-9 v Z (Bulawayo) 2004-05 – taking a wicket with his third ball in LOI. **IT20**: 8 (2006 to 2014); HS 60* v NZ (Manchester) 2008. F-c Tours: A 2006-07, 2010-11, 2013-14; SA 2009-10; WI 2000-01 (Eng A), 2008-09, 2014-15; NZ 2007-08, 2012-13; I 2005-06, 2008-09, 2012-13; P 2005-06; SL 2002-03 (ECB Acad), 2004-05, 2007-08, 2011-12; B 2009-10; UAE 2011-12 (v P), 2015-16 (v P). 1000 runs (5); most – 1714 (2004). HS 262* v Sussex (Horsham) 2004. BB 4-4 v Middx (Lord's) 2004. LO HS 158 EL v I A (Worcester) 2010. LO BB 5-41 v Essex (Chelmsford) 2003 (NL). T20 HS 131. T20 BB 1-12.

BROOKES, Henry James Hamilton (Tudor Grange Acad, Solihull), b Solihull 21 Aug 1999. 6'3''. RHB, RMF. Squad No 10. Debut (Warwickshire) 2017. Warwickshire 2nd XI debut 2016. England U19 2016-17 to 2017. HS 70 v Northants (Northampton) 2018. BB 4-54 v Northants (Birmingham) 2018. LO HS 1* v Notts (Nottingham) 2018 (RLC). LO BB 3-57 v Worcs (Birmingham) 2018 (RLC). T20 HS 9. T20 BB 2-28.

HAIN, Samuel Robert (Southport S, Gold Coast), b Hong Kong 16 July 1995. 5'10''. RHB, OB. Squad No 16. Debut (Warwickshire) 2014; cap 2018. MCC 2018. Warwickshire 2nd XI debut 2011. UK passport (British parents). HS 208 v Northants (Birmingham) 2014. LO HS 145* EL v WI A (Derby) 2018. T20 HS 95.

HANNON-DALBY, Oliver James (Brooksbank S, Leeds Met U), b Halifax, Yorkshire 20 Jun 1989. 6'7''. LHB, RMF. Squad No 20. Yorkshire 2008-12. Warwickshire debut 2013. HS 40 v Somerset (Taunton) 2014. BB 5-68 Y v Warwks (Birmingham) and 5-68 Y v Somerset (Leeds) 2010 – in consecutive matches. Wa BB 4-29 v Hants (Birmingham) 2017. LO HS 21* Y v Warwks (Scarborough) 2012 (CB40). LO BB 5-27 v Glamorgan (Birmingham) 2015 (RLC). T20 HS 14*. T20 BB 4-20.

HOSE, Adam John (Carisbrooke S), b Newport, IoW 25 Oct 1992. 6'2''. RHB, RMF. Squad No 21. Somerset 2016-17. Warwickshire debut 2018. HS 68 Sm v Yorks (Taunton) 2016 and 68 v Durham MCCU (Birmingham) 2018. LO HS 101* Sm v Glos (Bristol) 2017 (RLC). T20 HS 76.

LAMB, Matthew James (North Bromsgrove HS; Bromsgrove S), b Wolverhampton, Staffs 19 July 1996. 6'1''. RHB, RM. Squad No 7. Debut (Warwickshire) 2016. Warwickshire 2nd XI debut 2015. HS 79 v Derbys (Birmingham) 2018. BB 1-19 v Somerset (Birmingham) 2017. LO HS 47 v West Indies A (Birmingham) 2018. LO BB –.

MELLOR, Alexander James (Westwood C, Leek; Staffordshire U), b Stoke-on-Trent, Staffs 22 Jul 1991. 5'10''. LHB, WK. Squad No 15. Derbyshire 2016. Warwickshire debut 2016. Staffordshire 2014-15. HS 59 v Oxford MCCU (Oxford) 2017. CC HS 44 De v Essex (Derby) 2016. LO HS 3* v West Indies A (Birmingham) 2018. T20 HS 18*.

‡**MILES, Craig** Neil (Bradon Forest S, Swindon; Filton C, Bristol), b Swindon, Wilts 20 July 1994. Brother of A.J.Miles (Cardiff MCCU 2012). 6'4''. RHB, RMF. Squad No 34. Gloucestershire 2011-18; cap 2011. HS 62* Gs v Worcs (Cheltenham) 2014. 50 wkts (3); most – 58 (2018). Hat-trick Gs v Essex (Cheltenham) 2016. LO HS 16 Gs v Somerset (Taunton) 2016 (RLC). LO BB 4-29 Gs v Yorks (Scarborough) 2015 (RLC). T20 HS 8. T20 BB 3-25.

‡**NORWELL, Liam** Connor (Redruth SS), b Bournemouth, Dorset 27 Dec 1991. 6'3''. RHB, RMF. Squad No 24. Gloucestershire 2011-18, taking 6-46 v Derbys (Bristol) on debut; cap 2011. HS 102 Gs v Derbys (Bristol) 2016. 50 wkts (2); most – 68 (2015). BB 8-43 (10-95 match) Gs v Leics (Leicester) 2017. LO HS 16 Gs v Somerset (Bristol) 2017 (RLC). LO BB 6-52 Gs v Leics (Leicester) 2012 (CB40). T20 HS 2*. T20 BB 3-27.

PANAYI, George David (Shrewsbury S), b Enfield, Middx 23 Sep 1997. 6'3". RHB, RFM. Squad No 33. Debut (Warwickshire) 2017. Warwickshire 2nd XI debut 2015. England U19 2017. HS 16 and BB 3-41 v Lancs (Birmingham) 2017. LO BB –.

NOPATEL, Jeetan Shashi, b Wellington, New Zealand 7 May 1980. 5'10". RHB, OB. Squad No 5. Wellington 1999-00 to date. Warwickshire debut 2009; cap 2012; captain 2018 to date. *Wisden* 2014. **Tests** (NZ): 24 (2006-07 to 2016-17); HS 47 v I (Kolkata) 2016-17; BB 5-110 v WI (Napier) 2008-09. **LOI** (NZ): 43 (2005 to 2017); HS 34 v SL (Kingston) 2006-07; BB 3-11 v SA (Mumbai, BS) 2006-07. **IT20** (NZ): 11 (2005-06 to 2008-09); HS 5 v E (Auckland) 2007-08; BB 3-20 v SA (Johannesburg) 2005-06. F-c Tours (NZ): E 2008; SA 2005-06, 2012-13; I 2010-11, 2012, 2016-17; SL 2009, 2012-13; Z 2010-11, 2011-12; B 2008-09. HS 120 v Yorks (Birmingham) 2009. 50 wkts (6); most – 66 (2016). BB 7-38 v Somerset (Taunton) 2015. LO HS 50 v Kent (Birmingham) 2013 (Y40). LO BB 5-43 v Somerset (Birmingham) 2016 (RLC). T20 HS 34*. T20 BB 4-11.

POLLOCK, Edward John (RGS Worcester; Shrewsbury S; Collingwood C, Durham U), b High Wycombe, Bucks 10 Jul 1995. Son of A.J.Pollock (Cambridge U 1982-84); younger brother of A.W.Pollock (Cambridge MCCU & U 2013-15). 5'10". LHB, OB. Squad No 28. Durham MCCU 2015-17. Awaiting Warwickshire f-c debut. Durham 2nd XI 2015. Warwickshire 2nd XI debut 2015. Herefordshire 2014-16. HS 52 DU v Glos (Bristol) 2017. LO HS 56 v Notts (Nottingham) 2018 (RLC). T20 HS 66.

RHODES, William Michael Henry (Cottingham HS, Cottingham SFC, Hull), Nottingham 2 Mar 1995. 6'2". LHB, RMF. Squad No 35. Yorkshire 2014-15 to 2016. Essex 2016 (on loan). Warwickshire debut 2018. England U19 2014. HS 137 and Wa BB 1-1 v Glos (Birmingham) 2018. BB 3-42 Y v Middx (Leeds) 2015. LO HS 69 v Worcs (Birmingham) 2018 (RLC) and 69 v West Indies A (Birmingham) 2018. LO BB 2-22 Y v Essex (Chelmsford) 2015 (RLC). T20 HS 45. T20 BB 3-27.

SIBLEY, Dominic Peter (Whitgift S, Croydon), b Epsom, Surrey 5 Sep 1995. 6'0". RHB, OB. Squad No 45. Surrey 2013-17. Warwickshire debut 2017. England U19 2012-13 to 2014. HS 242 Sy v Yorks (Oval) 2013. Wa HS 144* v Sussex (Hove) 2018. BB 2-103 Sy v Hants (Southampton) 2016. Wa BB –. LO HS 115 v West Indies A (Birmingham) 2018. LO BB 1-20 Sy v Essex (Chelmsford) 2016 (RLC). T20 HS 74*. T20 BB 2-33.

SIDEBOTTOM, Ryan Nathan, b Shepparton, Victoria, Australia 14 Aug 1989. UK passport. 6'0". RHB, RMF. Squad No 22. Victoria 2012-13. Warwickshire debut 2017. HS 13 v Hants (Birmingham) 2017. BB 6-35 (10-96 match) v Northants (Northampton) 2018.

STONE, Oliver Peter (Thorpe St Andrew HS), b Norwich, Norfolk 9 Oct 1993. 6'1". RHB, RF. Squad No 6. Northamptonshire 2012-16. Warwickshire debut 2017. Norfolk 2011. **LOI:** 4 (2018-19); HS 9* and BB 1-23 v SL (Dambulla) 2018-19. HS 60 Nh v Kent (Northampton) 2016. Wa HS 42* v Glamorgan (Colwyn Bay) 2018. BB 8-80 v Sussex (Birmingham) 2018. LO HS 24* Nh v Derbys (Derby) 2015 (RLC). LO BB 4-71 v Worcs (Birmingham) 2018 (RLC). T20 HS 8*. T20 BB 3-22.

THOMASON, Aaron Dean (Barr Beacon S, Walsall), b Birmingham 26 Jun 1997. 5'10". RHB, RMF. Squad No 26. Warwickshire 2nd XI debut 2014. England U19 2015. Awaiting f-c debut. LO HS 28 v Durham (Birmingham) 2017 (RLC). LO BB 4-45 v Notts (Nottingham) 2018 (RLC). T20 HS 42. T20 BB 3-33.

THOMSON, Alexander Thomas (Kings S, Macclesfield; Denstone C; Cardiff Met U), b Macclesfield, Cheshire 30 Oct 1993. 6'2". RHB, OB. Squad No 29. Cardiff MCCU 2014-16. Warwickshire debut 2017. Staffordshire 2013-16. HS 26 v Hants (Birmingham) 2017. BB 6-138 CfU v Hants (Southampton) 2016. Wa BB –. LO HS 19 and LO BB 3-53 v West Indies A (Birmingham) 2018. T20 HS 14. T20 BB 4-35.

WOAKES, Christopher Roger (Barr Beacon Language S, Walsall), b Birmingham 2 March 1989. 6'2". RHB, RFM. Squad No 19. Debut (Warwickshire) 2006; cap 2009. Wellington 2012-13. MCC 2009. IPL: KKR 2017. RCB 2018. Big Bash: ST 2013-14. Herefordshire 2006-07. *Wisden* 2016. **ECB Test & LO Central Contract 2018-19. Tests:** 26 (2013 to 2018); HS 137* v I (Lord's) 2018; BB 6-70 v P (Lord's) 2016. **LOI:** 84 (2010-11 to 2018-19); HS 95* v SL (Nottingham) 2016; BB 6-45 v A (Brisbane) 2010-11. **IT20:** 8 (2010-11 to 2015-16); HS 37 v P (Sharjah) 2015-16; BB 2-40 v P (Dubai, DSC) 2015-16. F-c Tours: A 2017-18; SA 2015-16; WI 2010-11 (EL); NZ 2017-18; I 2016-17; SL 2013-14 (EL); B 2016-17; UAE 2015-16 (v P). HS 152* v Derbys (Derby) 2013. 50 wkts (3); most – 59 (2016). BB 9-36 v Durham (Birmingham) 2016. LO HS 95* *(see LOI)*. LO BB 6-45 *(see LOI)*. T20 HS 57*. T20 BB 4-21.

YATES, Robert Michael (Warwick S), b Solihull 19 Sep 1999. 6'0". LHB, OB. Warwickshire 2nd XI debut 2017. Staffordshire 2018. Awaiting 1st XI debut.

RELEASED/RETIRED

(Having made a County 1st XI appearance in 2018)

BARKER, K.H.D. – *see HAMPSHIRE.*

[NQ]**DE GRANDHOMME, Colin**, b Harare, Zimbabwe 22 Jul 1986. Son of L.L.de Grandhomme (Rhodesia B and Zimbabwe 1979-80 to 1987-88). RHB, RMF. Zimbabwe A 2005-06. Auckland 2006-07 to 2017-18. N Districts 2018-19. Warwickshire 2017-18 (T20 only). IPL: KKR 2017. RCB 2018. **Tests** (NZ): 17 (2016-17 to 2018-19); HS 105 v WI (Wellington) 2017-18; BB 6-41 v P (Christchurch) 2016-17 – on debut. **LOI** (NZ): 28 (2011-12 to 2018-19); HS 74* v P (Hamilton) 2017-18; BB 3-26 v I (Hamilton) 2018-19. **IT20** (NZ): 25 (2011-12 to 2018-19); HS 50 v I (Auckland) 2018-19; BB 2-22 v SA (Auckland) 2016-17. F-c Tours: E 2014 (NZ A); SA 2005-06 (Z U23); UAE 2018-19 (v P). HS 144* Auckland v Otago (Auckland) 2016-17. BB 6-24 Auckland v Wellington (Auckland) 2013-14. LO HS 151 NZ A v Northants (Northampton) 2014. LO BB 4-37 Auckland v Wellington (Wellington) 2015-16. T20 HS 72*. T20 BB 3-4.

DOUTHWAITE, Daniel Alexander (Reed's S, Cobham), b Kingston-upon-Thames, Surrey 8 Feb 1997. RHB, RMF. Awaiting f-c debut. Surrey 2nd XI 2015-16. Sussex 2nd XI 2016. LO HS 38* and LO BB 3-43 v West Indies A (Birmingham) 2018. T20 BB 1-7.

[NQ]**ELLIOTT, Grant** David (St Stithians) b Johannesburg, South Africa 21 Mar 1979. 6'1". RHB, RMF. Debut Transvaal B 1996-97. Griqualand West 1999-00 to 2000-01. Gauteng 2001-02 to 2002-03. Wellington 2005-06 to 2013-14. Surrey 2009 (1 match). Leicestershire 2015 (T20 only). Warwickshire 2017-18 (T20 only); T20 captain 2018. Qualified for NZ in 2007. **Tests** (NZ): 5 (2007-08 to 2009-10); HS 25 v P (Dunedin) 2009-10. BB 2-8 v P (Wellington) 2009-10. **LOI** (NZ): 83 (2008 to 2015-16); HS 115 v A (Sydney) 2008-09; BB 4-31 v E (Johannesburg) 2009-10. **IT20** (NZ): 16 (2008-09 to 2015-16, +1 for World XI); HS 27 v A (Dharamsala) 2015-16; BB 4-22 v SL (Auckland) 2015-16. F-c Tours (NZ): E 2008; A 2008-09; B 2008-09. HS 196* Wellington v Auckland (Wellington) 2007-08. CC HS 22 Sy v Middx (Oval) 2009. BB 5-33 Wellington v ND (Whangarei) 2013-14. LO HS 115 *(see LOI)*. LO BB 5-34 Wellington v Otago (Wellington) 2007-08. T20 HS 70. T20 BB 4-15.

POYSDEN, J.E. – *see YORKSHIRE.*

^{NQ}**RANKIN, William Boyd** (Strabane GS; Harper Adams UC), b Londonderry, Co Derry, N Ireland 5 Jul 1984. Brother of R.J.Rankin (Ireland U19 2003-04). 6'8". LHB, RFM. Ireland 2006-07 to date. Derbyshire 2007. Warwickshire 2008-17; cap 2013. Became available for England in 2012, before rejoining Ireland in 2015-16. **Tests** (E/Ire): 2 (1 for E 2013-14, 1 for Ire 2018); HS 17 and BB 2-75 Ire v P (Dublin) 2018. **LOI** (E/Ire): 65 (58 for Ire 2006-07 to 2018-19, 7 for E 2013 to 2013-14); HS 18* Ire v SL (Dublin) 2016; BB 4-15 Ire v UAE (Harare) 2017-18. **IT20** (E/Ire): 36 (34 for Ire 2009 to 2018-19, 2 for E 2013); HS 16* Ire v UAE (Abu Dhabi) 2015-16; BB 3-16 Ire v UAE (Dubai, DSC) 2016-17. F-c Tour: A 2013-14. HS 56* v Worcs (Birmingham) 2015. 50 wkts (1): 55 (2011). BB 6-55 v Yorks (Leeds) 2015. LO HS 18* v Northants (Northampton) 2013 (Y40) and *see LOI*. LO BB 4-15 (*see LOI*). T20 HS 16*. T20 BB 4-9.

SUKHJIT SINGH ('**Sunny**') (George Dixon International S, Birmingham; South & City C), b India 30 Mar 1996. 5'10". LHB, SLA. Warwickshire 2017-18. Warwickshire 2nd XI debut 2014. HS 16* and BB 6-144 v Hants (Southampton) 2017.

TROTT, Ian Jonathan Leonard (Rondebosch BHC; Stellenbosch U), b Cape Town, South Africa 22 Apr 1981. Stepbrother of K.C.Jackson (WP and Boland 1988-89 to 2001-02). 6'0". RHB, RM. Boland 2000-01. W Province 2001-02. EU/British passport. Warwickshire 2003-18, scoring 134 v Sussex (Birmingham) on debut; cap 2005; benefit 2014. Otago 2005-06. *Wisden* 2010. **Tests**: 52 (2009 to 2014-15); 1000 runs (2); most – 1325 (2010); HS 226 v B (Lord's) 2010; scored 119 v A (Oval) 2009 on debut; BB 1-5 v SL (Lord's) 2011. **LOI**: 68 (2009 to 2013); 1000 runs (1): 1315 (2011) – E record; HS 137 v A (Sydney) 2010-11; BB 2-31 v A (Adelaide) 2010-11. **IT20**: 7 (2007 to 2009-10); HS 51 v SA (Centurion) 2009-10. F-c Tours: A 2010-11, 2013-14; SA 2009-10, 2014-15 (EL); WI 2014-15; NZ 2008-09 (EL), 2012-13; I 2007-08 (EL), 2012-13; SL 2011-12; B 2009-10; UAE 2011-12 (v P). 1000 runs (9); most – 1400 (2009). HS 226 (*see Tests*). Wa HS 219* v Middx (Lord's) 2016. BB 7-39 v Kent (Canterbury) 2003. LO HS 137 (*see LOI*). LO BB 4-55 v Hants (Lord's) 2005 (CGT). T20 HS 86*. T20 BB 2-19.

UMEED, Andrew Robert Isaac (High School of Glasgow), b Glasgow 19 Apr 1996. 6'1". RHB, LB. Scotland 2015. Warwickshire debut 2016, scoring 101 v Durham (Birmingham). Warwickshire 2nd XI debut 2014. HS 113 v Lancs (Birmingham) 2017. LO HS 28 v West Indies A (Birmingham) 2018.

WRIGHT, C.J.C. – *see LEICESTERSHIRE.*

WARWICKSHIRE 2018

RESULTS SUMMARY

	Place	Won	Lost	Drew	Tied	NR
Specsavers County Champ (2nd Division)	1st	9	2	3		
All First-Class Matches		9	2	4		
Royal London One-Day Cup (North Group)	4th	4	2			2
Vitality Blast (North Group)	6th	6	7		1	

SPECSAVERS COUNTY CHAMPIONSHIP AVERAGES
BATTING AND FIELDING

Cap		M	I	NO	HS	Runs	Avge	100	50	Ct/St
2001	I.R.Bell	14	23	4	204	1027	54.05	5	2	13
	M.J.Lamb	3	4	1	79	151	50.33	–	1	1
2005	I.J.L.Trott	14	23	3	170*	935	46.75	2	6	11
	W.M.H.Rhodes	14	23	1	137	972	44.18	4	4	5
	D.P.Sibley	14	23	2	144*	777	37.00	4	1	18
2018	S.R.Hain	12	17	1	90	566	35.37	–	6	9
2007	T.R.Ambrose	14	20	1	103	656	34.52	1	3	57
	H.J.H.Brookes	5	6	1	70	165	33.00	–	2	3
	A.J.Hose	3	6	1	65	126	25.20	–	1	1
2013	C.J.C.Wright	14	18	2	72	342	21.37	–	2	3
2013	K.H.D.Barker	10	14	2	58	218	18.16	–	1	1
	O.P.Stone	7	8	2	42*	86	14.33	–	–	–
2012	J.S.Patel	14	19	3	32	184	11.50	–	–	4
	R.N.Sidebottom	9	12	6	10*	30	5.00	–	–	5
	O.J.Hannon-Dalby	4	7	–	13	29	4.14	–	–	–

Also batted: J.E.Poysden (1 match) 0; C.R.Woakes (2 – cap 2009) 7, 6, 73* (1 ct).

BOWLING

	O	M	R	W	Avge	Best	5wI	10wM
O.P.Stone	160.2	26	525	43	12.20	8-80	3	1
K.H.D.Barker	254.1	69	672	40	16.80	5-32	2	–
O.J.Hannon-Dalby	103.4	22	329	15	21.93	4-61	–	–
H.J.H.Brookes	142	22	470	21	22.38	4-54	–	–
J.S.Patel	431.4	108	1276	56	22.78	7-83	4	2
R.N.Sidebottom	185	40	637	25	25.48	6-35	1	1
C.J.C.Wright	373.2	67	1279	41	31.19	5-32	1	–

Also bowled:

J.E.Poysden	23.2	2	73	5	14.60	5-29	1	–

M.J.Lamb 6-1-22-0; W.M.H.Rhodes 56-12-182-1; C.R.Woakes 51-6-225-4.

The First-Class Averages (pp 230–245) give the records of Warwickshire players in all first-class county matches (Warwickshire's other opponents being Durham MCCU), with the exception of J.E.Poysden and C.R.Woakes, whose first-class figures for Warwickshire are as above.

WARWICKSHIRE RECORDS

FIRST-CLASS CRICKET

Highest Total	For 810-4d		v	Durham	Birmingham	1994
	V 887		by	Yorkshire	Birmingham	1896
Lowest Total	For 16		v	Kent	Tonbridge	1913
	V 15		by	Hampshire	Birmingham	1922
Highest Innings	For 501*	B.C.Lara	v	Durham	Birmingham	1994
	V 322	I.V.A.Richards	for	Somerset	Taunton	1985

Highest Partnership for each Wicket

1st	377*	N.F.Horner/K.Ibadulla	v	Surrey	The Oval	1960
2nd	465*	J.A.Jameson/R.B.Kanhai	v	Glos	Birmingham	1974
3rd	327	S.P.Kinneir/W.G.Quaife	v	Lancashire	Birmingham	1901
4th	470	A.I.Kallicharran/G.W.Humpage	v	Lancashire	Southport	1982
5th	335	J.O.Troughton/T.R.Ambrose	v	Hampshire	Birmingham	2009
6th	327	L.J.Evans/T.R.Ambrose	v	Sussex	Birmingham	2015
7th	289*	I.R.Bell/T.Frost	v	Sussex	Horsham	2004
8th	228	A.J.W.Croom/R.E.S.Wyatt	v	Worcs	Dudley	1925
9th	233	I.J.L.Trott/J.S.Patel	v	Yorkshire	Birmingham	2009
10th	214	N.V.Knight/A.Richardson	v	Hampshire	Birmingham	2002

Best Bowling	For	10-41	J.D.Bannister	v	Comb Servs	Birmingham	1959
(Innings)	V	10-36	H.Verity	for	Yorkshire	Leeds	1931
Best Bowling	For	15-76	S.Hargreave	v	Surrey	The Oval	1903
(Match)	V	17-92	A.P.Freeman	for	Kent	Folkestone	1932

Most Runs – Season	2417	M.J.K.Smith	(av 60.42)	1959
Most Runs – Career	35146	D.L.Amiss	(av 41.64)	1960-87
Most 100s – Season	9	A.I.Kallicharran		1984
	9	B.C.Lara		1994
Most 100s – Career	78	D.L.Amiss		1960-87
Most Wkts – Season	180	W.E.Hollies	(av 15.13)	1946
Most Wkts – Career	2201	W.E.Hollies	(av 20.45)	1932-57
Most Career W-K Dismissals	800	E.J.Smith	(662 ct; 138 st)	1904-30
Most Career Catches in the Field	422	M.J.K.Smith		1956-75

LIMITED-OVERS CRICKET

Highest Total	50ov	392-5		v	Oxfordshire	Birmingham	1984
	40ov	321-7		v	Leics	Birmingham	2010
	T20	242-2		v	Derbyshire	Birmingham	2015
Lowest Total	50ov	94		v	Glos	Bristol	2000
	40ov	59		v	Yorkshire	Leeds	2001
	T20	73		v	Somerset	Taunton	2013
Highest Innings	50ov	206	A.I.Kallicharran	v	Oxfordshire	Birmingham	1984
	40ov	137	I.R.Bell	v	Yorkshire	Birmingham	2005
	T20	158*	B.B.McCullum	v	Derbyshire	Birmingham	2015
Best Bowling	50ov	7-32	R.G.D.Willis	v	Yorkshire	Birmingham	1981
	40ov	6-15	A.A.Donald	v	Yorkshire	Birmingham	1995
	T20	5-19	N.M.Carter	v	Worcs	Birmingham	2005

WORCESTERSHIRE

Formation of Present Club: 11 March 1865
Inaugural First-Class Match: 1899
Colours: Dark Green and Black
Badge: Shield Argent a Fess between three Pears Sable
County Championships: (5) 1964, 1965, 1974, 1988, 1989
NatWest Trophy Winners: (1) 1994
Benson and Hedges Cup Winners: (1) 1991
Pro 40/National League (Div 1) Winners: (1) 2007
Sunday League Winners: (3) 1971, 1987, 1988
Twenty20 Cup Winners: (1) 2018

Chief Executive: Matt Rawnsley, County Ground, Blackfinch New Road, Worcester, WR2 4QQ • Tel: 01905 748474 Email: info@wccc.co.uk • Web: www.wccc.co.uk • Twitter : @WorcsCCC (62,805 followers)

Head of Player and Coaches Development: Kevin Sharp. **Head Bowling Coach**: Alan Richardson. **First Team Coach**: Alex Gidman. **Captain**: J.Leach. **Overseas Players**: C.J.Ferguson and M.J.Guptill (T20 only). **2019 Testimonial**: J.D.Shantry. **Head Groundsman**: Tim Packwood. **Scorer**: Sue Drinkwater (home) and Philip Mellish (away). ‡ New registration. NQ Not qualified for England.

Worcestershire revised their capping policy in 2002 and now award players with their County Colours when they make their Championship debut.

ALI, Moeen Munir (Moseley S), b Birmingham, Warwks 18 Jun 1987. Brother of A.K.Ali (Worcs, Glos and Leics 2000-12), cousin of Kabir Ali (Worcs, Rajasthan, Hants and Lancs 1999-2014). 6'0". LHB, OB. Squad No 8. Warwickshire 2005-06. Worcestershire debut 2007. Moors SC 2011-12. MT 2012-13. MCC 2012. IPL: RCB 2018. PCA 2013. *Wisden* 2014. **ECB Test & L-O Central Contract 2018-19. Tests**: 58 (2014 to 2018-19); 1000 runs (1): 1078 (2016); HS 155* v SL (Chester-le-St) 2016; BB 6-53 v SA (Lord's) 2017. Hat-trick v SA (Oval) 2017. **LOI**: 92 (2013-14 to 2018-19); HS 128 v Scotland (Christchurch) 2014-15; BB 4-46 v A (Manchester) 2018. **IT20**: 25 (2013-14 to 2018-19); HS 72* v A (Cardiff) 2015; BB 2-21 v I (Kanpur) 2016-17. F-c Tours: A 2013-14; SA 2015-16; WI 2014-15, 2018-19; NZ 2017-18; I 2016-17; SL 2013-14 (EL), 2018-19; B 2016-17; UAE 2015-16 (v P). 1000 runs (2); most – 1420 (2013). HS 250 v Glamorgan (Worcester) 2013. BB 6-29 (12-96 match) v Lancs (Manchester) 2012. LO HS 158 v Sussex (Horsham) 2011 (CB40). LO BB 4-33 v Notts (Nottingham) 2018 (RLC). T20 HS 115. T20 BB 5-34.

BARNARD, Edward George (Shrewsbury S), b Shrewsbury, Shrops 20 Nov 1995. Younger brother of M.R.Barnard (Oxford MCCU 2010). 6'1". RHB, RMF. Squad No 30. Debut (Worcestershire) 2015. Shropshire 2012. England U19 2012-13 to 2014. HS 75 v Durham (Worcester) 2017. BB 6-37 (11-89 match) v Somerset (Taunton) 2018. LO HS 51 v Somerset (Taunton) 2015 (RLC). LO BB 3-37 v Derbys (Derby) 2017 (RLC). T20 HS 34*. T20 BB 3-29.

BROWN, Patrick Rhys (Bourne GS, Lincs), b Peterborough, Cambs 23 Aug 1998. 6'2". RHB, RMF. Squad No 36. Debut (Worcestershire) 2017. Worcestershire 2nd XI debut 2016. Lincolnshire 2016. HS 5* v Sussex (Worcester) 2017. BB 2-15 v Leics (Worcester) 2017. LO HS 0*. LO BB 3-53 v Kent (Worester) 2018 (RLC). T20 HS 0. T20 BB 4-21.

COX, Oliver Ben (Bromsgrove S), b Wordsley, Stourbridge 2 Feb 1992. 5'10". RHB, WK. Squad No 10. Debut (Worcestershire) 2009. MCC 2017. HS 124 v Glos (Cheltenham) 2017. LO HS 122* v Kent (Worcester) 2018 (RLC). T20 HS 59*.

DELL, Joshua Jamie (Cheltenham C), b Tenbury Wells 26 Sep 1997. RHB, RMF. Awaiting f-c debut. Worcestershire 2nd XI debut 2015. England U19 2016. LO HS 46 v West Indies A (Worcester) 2018.

D'OLIVEIRA, Brett Louis (Worcester SFC), b Worcester 28 Feb 1992. Son of D.B.D'Oliveira (Worcs 1982-95), grandson of B.L.D'Oliveira (Worcs, EP and England 1964-80). 5'9". RHB, LB. Squad No 15. Debut (Worcestershire) 2012. MCC 2018. HS 202* v Glamorgan (Cardiff) 2016. BB 5-48 v Durham (Chester-le-St) 2015. LO HS 79 North v South (Bridgetown) 2017-18. LO BB 3-35 v Warwks (Worcester) 2013 (Y40). T20 HS 64. T20 BB 4-26.

FELL, Thomas Charles (Oakham S; Oxford Brookes U), b Hillingdon, Middx 17 Oct 1993. 6'1". RHB, WK, occ OB. Squad No 29. Oxford MCCU 2013. Worcestershire debut 2013. 1000 runs (1): 1127 (2015). HS 171 v Middx (Worcester) 2015. LO HS 116* v Lancs (Worcester) 2016 (RLC). T20 HS 23.

[NO]**FERGUSON, Callum** James, b North Adelaide, Australia 21 Nov 1984. RHB, RM. Squad No 5. S Australia 2004-05 to date. Worcestershire debut 2018 (l-o and T20 only). IPL: PW 2011-12. Big Bash: AS 2011-12 to 2013-14. MR 2014-15 to 2016-17. ST 2017-18 to date. **Tests** (A): 1 (2016-17); HS 3 v SA (Hobart) 2016-17. **LOI** (A): 30 (2008-09 to 2010-11); HS 71* v E (Oval) 2009. **IT20** (A): 3 (2008-09 to 2009); HS 8 (twice). F-c Tours (Aus A): I 2015; Z 2011. HS 213 SA v Tas (Hobart) 2015-16. BB 2-32 SA v Tas (Hobart) 2013-14. LO HS 192 v Leics (Worcester) 2018 (RLC) – Wo record on county debut. LO BB 1-8 SA v Vic (Sydney, BO) 2015-16. T20 HS 193*.

FINCH, Adam William (Kingswinford S; Oldswinford Hospital SFC), b Wordsley, Stourbridge 28 May 2000. RHB, RMF. Squad No 61. Worcestershire 2nd XI debut 2017. England U19 2018 to 2018-19. Awaiting 1st XI debut.

[NO]**GUPTILL, Martin** James (Avondale C), b Auckland, New Zealand 30 Sep 1986. 6'3". RHB, OB. Auckland 2005-06 to date. Derbyshire 2011-15; cap 2012. Worcestershire debut 2018. Lancashire l-o and T20 only 2016. IPL: MI 2016. KXIP 2017. Big Bash: ST 2012-13. **Tests** (NZ): 47 (2008-09 to 2016-17); HS 189 v B (Hamilton) 2009-10; BB 3-11 v Z (Bulawayo) 2016. **LOI** (NZ): 169 (2008-09 to 2018-19); HS 237* v WI (Wellington) 2014-15, 2nd highest score in all LOI; BB 2-6 v I (Delhi) 2016-17. **IT20** (NZ): 76 (2008-09 to 2018-19); HS 105 v A (Auckland) 2017-18; BB – . F-c Tours (NZ): E 2013, 2015; A 2011-12, 2015-16; SA 2012-13, 2016; WI 2012; I 2008-09 (NZ A), 2010-11, 2012, 2016-17; SL 2009, 2012-13; Z 2010-11 (NZ A), 2011-12, 2016. HS 227 De v Glos (Bristol) 2015. Wo HS 111 v Lancs (Worcester) 2018. BB 3-11 (see Tests). Wo BB 1-12 v Notts (Nottingham) 2018. LO HS 237* (see LOI). LO BB 2-6 (see LOI). T20 HS 120*. T20 BB –.

HAYNES, Jack Alexander (Malvern C), b Worcester 30 Jan 2001. Son of G.R.Haynes (Worcestershire 1991-99); younger brother of J.L.Haynes (Worcestershire 2nd XI 2015-16). RHB, OB. Worcestershire 2nd XI debut 2016. England U19 2018. Awaiting f-c debut. LO HS 33 v West Indies A (Worcester) 2018.

LEACH, Joseph (Shrewsbury S; Leeds U), b Stafford 30 Oct 1990. Elder brother of S.G.Leach (Oxford MCCU 2014-16). 6'1". RHB, RMF. Squad No 23. Leeds/Bradford MCCU 2012. Worcestershire debut 2012; captain 2017 to date. Staffordshire 2008-09. HS 114 v Glos (Cheltenham) 2013. 50 wkts (3); most – 69 (2017). BB 6-73 v Warwks (Birmingham) 2015. LO HS 63 v Yorks (Leeds) 2016 (RLC). LO BB 4-30 v Northants (Worcester) 2015 (RLC). T20 HS 24. T20 BB 5-33.

198

MILTON, Alexander Geoffrey (Malvern C; Cardiff U), b Redhill, Surrey 19 May 1996. 5'7". RHB, LB, occ WK. Cardiff MCCU 2016-18. Worcestershire debut 2018. Worcestershire 2nd XI debut 2012. Glamorgan 2nd XI 2015. Herefordshire 2016. HS 104* v Somerset (Worcester) 2018 – on county f-c debut, sharing record 10th wkt partnership of 136 with S.J.Magoffin. LO HS 0.

MITCHELL, Daryl Keith Henry (Prince Henry's HS; University C, Worcester), b Badsey, near Evesham 25 Nov 1983. 5'10". RHB, RM. Squad No 27. Debut (Worcestershire) 2005; captain 2011-16; benefit 2016. Mountaineers 2011-12. MCC 2015. 1000 runs (5); most – 1334 (2014). HS 298 v Somerset (Taunton) 2009. BB 4-49 v Yorks (Leeds) 2009. LO HS 107 v Sussex (Hove) 2013 (Y40). LO BB 4-19 v Northants (Milton Keynes) 2014 (RLC). T20 HS 68*. T20 BB 5-28.

MORRIS, Charles Andrew John (King's C, Taunton; Oxford Brookes U), b Hereford 6 Jul 1992. 6'0". RHB, RMF. Squad No 31. Oxford MCCU 2012-14. Worcestershire debut 2013. Devon 2011-12. RHB 33* OU v Warwks (Oxford) 2013. Wo HS 25* v Australians (Worcester) 2013. CC HS 24 v Glos (Worcester) 2014 and 24 v Sussex (Hove) 2015. 50 wkts (2); most – 56 (2014). BB 5-54 v Derbys (Derby) 2014. LO HS 16* v Northants (Milton Keynes) 2014 (RLC). LO BB 4-33 v Durham (Gosforth) 2018 (RLC). T20 HS 3. T20 BB 2-30.

NQPARNELL, Wayne Dillon (Grey HS), b Port Elizabeth, South Africa 30 Jul 1989. 6'1". LHB, LFM. Squad No 7. E Province 2006-07 to 2010-11. Warriors 2008-09 to 2014-15. Kent 2009-17. Sussex 2011. Cape Cobras 2015-16 to 2016-17. Worcestershire debut 2018. Glamorgan 2015 (T20 only). IPL: PW 2011-13. DD 2014. **Tests** (SA): 6 (2009-10 to 2017-18); HS 23 and BB 4-51 v SL (Johannesburg) 2016-17. **LOI** (SA): 65 (2008-09 to 2017); HS 56 v P (Sharjah) 2013-14; BB 5-48 v E (Cape Town) 2009-10. **IT20** (SA): 40 (2008-09 to 2017); HS 29* v A (Johannesburg) 2011-12; BB 4-13 v WI (Oval) 2009. F-c Tours (SA A): A 2016; I 2009-10 (SA), 2015; Ire 2012. HS 111* Cobras v Warriors (Paarl) 2015-16. CC HS 90 K v Glamorgan (Canterbury) 2018. Wo HS 58* v Yorks (Worcester) 2018. BB 7-51 Cobras v Dolphins (Cape Town) 2015-16. CC BB 4-23 v Hants (Worcester) 2018. LO HS 129 Warriors v Lions (Potchefstroom) 2013-14. LO BB 6-51 Warriors v Knights (Kimberley) 2013-14. T20 HS 99. T20 BB 4-13.

PENNINGTON, Dillon Young (Wrekin C), b Shrewsbury, Shrops 26 Feb 1999. RHB, RMF. Squad No 22. Debut (Worcestershire) 2018. Worcestershire 2nd XI debut 2017. HS 37 v Somerset (Worcester) 2018. BB 4-53 v Yorks (Scarborough) 2018. LO HS 4* and LO BB 5-67 v West Indies A (Worcester) 2018. T20 HS 6*. T20 BB 4-9.

RHODES, George Harry (Chase HS & SFC, Malvern), b Birmingham 26 Oct 1993. Son of S.J.Rhodes (Yorkshire, Worcestershire & England 1981-2004) and grandson of W.E.Rhodes (Nottinghamshire 1961-64). 6'0". RHB, OB. Squad No 34. Debut (Worcestershire) 2016. HS 59 v Essex (Chelmsford) 2016. BB 2-83 v Kent (Canterbury) 2016. LO HS 95 v West Indies A (Worcester) 2018. LO BB 2-34 v Yorks (Leeds) 2016 (RLC). T20 HS 17*. T20 BB 4-13.

SCRIMSHAW, George Louis Sheridan (John Taylor HS, Burton), b Burton-on-Trent, Staffs 10 Feb 1998. 6'6". RHB, RMF. Squad No 9. Worcestershire 2nd XI debut 2016. Awaiting f-c debut. Missed entire 2018 season through injury. T20 HS 1*. T20 BB 1-20.

TONGUE, Joshua Charles (King's S, Worcester; Worcester SFC), b Redditch 15 Nov 1997. 6'5". RHB, RM. Squad No 24. Debut (Worcestershire) 2016. Worcestershire 2nd XI debut 2015. HS 41 and BB 6-97 v Glamorgan (Worcester) 2017. LO HS 11* v Surrey (Worcester) 2017 (RLC). LO BB 2-46 v Lancs (Manchester) 2017 (RLC). T20 HS 2*. T20 BB 2-32.

TWOHIG, Benjamin Jake (Malvern C), b Dewsbury, Yorks 13 Apr 1998. 5'9". RHB, SLA. Squad No 42. Debut (Worcestershire) 2018. Worcestershire 2nd XI debut 2014. HS 35 v Notts (Nottingham) 2018. BB 2-47 v Yorks (Worcester) 2018. LO HS 1 and LO BB – v West Indies A (Worcester) 2018.

‡**WESSELS, Mattheus Hendrik ('Riki')** (Woodridge C, Pt Elizabeth; Northampton U), b Marogudoore, Queensland, Australia 12 Nov 1985. Left Australia when 2 months old. Qualified for England after gaining a UK passport in July 2016. Son of K.C.Wessels (OFS, Sussex, WP, NT, Q, EP, GW, Australia and South Africa 1973-74 to 1999-00). 5'11". RHB, WK. MCC 2004. Northamptonshire 2005-09. Nondescripts 2007-08. MWR 2009-10 to 2011-12. Nottinghamshire 2011-18; cap 2014. Big Bash: SS 2014-15. 1000 runs (2); most – 1213 (2014). HS 202* Nt v Sussex (Nottingham) 2017. BB 1-10 MWR v MT (Bulawayo) 2009-10. LO HS 146 Nt v Northants (Nottingham) 2016 (RLC). LO BB 1-0 MWR v MT (Bulawayo) 2009-10. T20 HS 110.

WESTBURY, Oliver ('Olly') Edward (Ellowes Hall Sports C, Dudley; Shrewsbury S), b Dudley, Warwicks 2 Jul 1997. 5'10". RHB, OB. Squad No 19. Debut (Worcestershire) 2018. Worcestershire 2nd XI debut 2014. England U19 2016. HS 22 v Essex (Chelmsford) 2018. BB –. LO HS 8 v West Indies A (Worcester) 2018. T20 HS 24.

WHITELEY, Ross Andrew (Repton S), b Sheffield, Yorks 13 Sep 1988. 6'2". LHB, LM. Squad No 44. Derbyshire 2008-13. Worcestershire debut 2013. HS 130* De v Kent (Derby) 2011. Wo HS 101 v Yorks (Scarborough) 2015. BB 2-6 De v Hants (Derby) 2012. Wo BB 1-2 v Lancs (Worcester) 2018. LO HS 77 v Yorks (Worcester) 2015 (RLC). LO BB 1-17 De v Unicorns (Wormsley) 2012 (CB40). T20 HS 91*. T20 BB 1-10.

ZAIN-UL-HASSAN (Pedmore Tech C, Stourbridge), b Islamabad, Pakistan 28 Oct 2000. LHB, RM. Awaiting f-c debut. Worcestershire 2nd XI debut 2017. LO HS 9* v West Indies A (Worcester) 2018. LO BB –.

RELEASED/RETIRED

(Having made a County 1st XI appearance in 2018)

CARTER, Andrew (Lincoln C), b Lincoln 27 Aug 1988. 6'4". Elder brother of M.Carter (see NOTTINGHAMSHIRE). RHB, RM. Nottinghamshire 2009-15. Essex 2010 (on loan). Glamorgan 2015 (on loan). Derbyshire 2016. Hampshire 2016 (on loan). Northamptonshire 2017. Worcestershire 2018 (T20 only). Lincolnshire 2007-17. HS 39 De v Glamorgan (Derby) 2016. BB 5-40 Ex v Kent (Canterbury) 2010. LO HS 12 Nt v Sussex (Hove) 2009 (P40). LO BB 4-45 Nt v Durham (Nottingham) 2012 (CB40). T20 HS 5*. T20 BB 4-20.

CLARKE, J.M. – see NOTTINGHAMSHIRE.

NQ**HEAD, Travis** Michael, b Adelaide, Australia 29 Dec 1993. 5'9". LHB, OB. S Australia 2011-12 to date. Yorkshire 2016. Worcestershire 2018. IPL: RCB 2016-17. Big Bash: AS 2012-13 to date. **Tests**: 8 (2018-19); HS 161 v SL (Canberra) 2018-19; BB – . **LOI** (A): 42 (2016 to 2018-19); HS 128 v P (Adelaide) 2016-17; BB 2-22 v SL (Pallekele) 2016. **IT20** (A): 16 (2015-16 to 2018); HS 48* v I (Guwahati) 2017-18; BB 1-16 v SL (Adelaide) 2016-17. F-c Tours (A): I 2015 (Aus A), 2018-19 (Aus A); UAE 2018-19 (v P). HS 192 SA v Tas (Adelaide) 2015-16. CC HS 62 v Essex (Worcester) 2018. BB 3-42 SA v NSW (Adelaide) 2015-16. LO HS 202 SA v WA (Sydney) 2015-16. LO BB 2-9 SA v NSW (Brisbane) 2014-15. T20 HS 101*. T20 BB 3-16.

NQ**MAGOFFIN, Stephen** James (Indooropilly HS; Curtin U, Perth), b Corinda, Queensland, Australia 17 Dec 1979. 6'4". LHB, RFM. W Australia 2004-05 to 2010-11. Surrey 2007. Worcestershire 2008-18. Queensland 2011-12. Sussex 2012-17; cap 2013. HS 79 WA v Tas (Perth) 2008-09. CC HS 51 Sx v Northants (Northampton) 2014. Wo HS 43 v Somerset (Worcester) 2018, sharing Wo record 10th wkt partnership of 136 with A.G.Milton. 50 wkts (5); most – 73 (2015). BB 8-20 (12-31 match) Sx v Somerset (Horsham) 2013. Wo BB 4-49 v Northants (Northampton) 2017. LO HS 24* Wo v Hants (Southampton) 2008 (FPT). LO BB 4-58 Sy v Kent (Oval) 2007 (FPT). T20 HS 11*. T20 BB 2-15.

J.D.Shantry left the staff without making a County 1st XI appearance in 2018.

WORCESTERSHIRE 2018

RESULTS SUMMARY

	Place	Won	Lost	Drew	Aband	NR
Specsavers County Champ (1st Division)	8th	2	10	2		
All First-Class Matches		2	10	2	1	
Royal London One-Day Cup (North Group)	SF	6	3			
Vitality Blast (North Group)	Winners	12	4			1

SPECSAVERS COUNTY CHAMPIONSHIP AVERAGES
BATTING AND FIELDING

Cap†		M	I	NO	HS	Runs	Avge	100	50	Ct/St
2007	M.M.Ali	3	5	–	219	383	76.60	1	2	–
2018	M.J.Guptill	2	4	–	111	170	42.50	1	–	3
2018	W.D.Parnell	6	10	3	58*	273	39.00	–	3	1
2005	D.K.H.Mitchell	14	26	–	178	957	36.80	4	1	21
2015	J.M.Clarke	14	26	1	177*	853	34.12	3	1	8
2018	T.M.Head	6	11	1	62	339	33.90	–	2	2
2013	R.A.Whiteley	6	11	–	91	364	33.09	–	2	8
2013	T.C.Fell	13	24	–	89	652	27.16	–	4	7
2015	E.G.Barnard	13	24	2	66	516	23.45	–	3	9
2018	A.G.Milton	7	13	2	104*	250	22.72	1	–	6/1
2009	O.B.Cox	12	22	1	65	372	17.71	–	2	35
2014	C.A.J.Morris	4	7	5	9*	31	15.50	–	–	–
2012	B.L.D'Oliveira	10	19	–	65	276	14.52	–	1	1
2018	B.J.Twohig	7	13	2	35	145	13.18	–	–	3
2017	J.C.Tongue	11	19	3	34	201	12.56	–	–	2
2018	O.E.Westbury	2	4	–	22	49	12.25	–	–	1
2008	S.J.Magoffin	6	10	3	43	65	9.28	–	–	1
2018	D.Y.Pennington	8	14	3	37	94	8.54	–	–	4
2012	J.Leach	5	9	–	18	66	7.33	–	–	1
2016	G.H.Rhodes	3	6	–	12	22	3.66	–	–	2

Also batted (1 match each): P.R.Brown (cap 2017) 2* (1 ct); L.Wood (cap 2018) 65*, 13.

BOWLING

	O	M	R	W	Avge	Best	5wI	10wM
M.M.Ali	107.5	20	334	18	18.55	6-49	2	–
J.Leach	157.5	28	508	23	22.08	4-42	–	–
E.G.Barnard	368.3	93	1138	49	23.22	6-37	4	1
J.C.Tongue	304.4	52	1011	40	25.27	5-53	2	–
W.D.Parnell	154.4	22	582	18	32.33	4-23	–	–
D.Y.Pennington	187	34	778	22	35.36	4-53	–	–
S.J.Magoffin	202	55	593	16	37.06	3-70	–	–
B.J.Twohig	161	18	598	10	59.80	2-47	–	–

Also bowled:

C.A.J.Morris	108.4	15	372	9	41.33	3-20	–	–

P.R.Brown 20-3-67-1; B.L.D'Oliveira 51-3-208-4; M.J.Guptill 4-1-17-1; T.M.Head 43-6-162-1; D.K.H.Mitchell 62-9-200-4; O.E.Westbury 1-0-6-0; R.A.Whiteley 36.2-4-115-3 L.Wood 32-6-108-1.

Worcestershire played no first-class fixtures outside the County Championship in 2018. The First-Class Averages (pp 230–245) give the records of Worcestershire players in all first-class county matches, with the exception of M.M.Ali, A.G.Milton and L.Wood, whose first-class figures for Worcestershire are as above.

† Worcestershire revised their capping policy in 2002 and now award players with their County Colours when they make their Championship debut.

WORCESTERSHIRE RECORDS

FIRST-CLASS CRICKET

Highest Total	For	701-6d		v	Surrey	Worcester	2007
	V	701-4d		by	Leics	Worcester	1906
Lowest Total	For	24		v	Yorkshire	Huddersfield	1903
	V	30		by	Hampshire	Worcester	1903
Highest Innings	For	405*	G.A.Hick	v	Somerset	Taunton	1988
	V	331*	J.D.B.Robertson	for	Middlesex	Worcester	1949

Highest Partnership for each Wicket

1st	309	H.K.Foster/F.L.Bowley	v	Derbyshire	Derby	1901
2nd	316	S.C.Moore/V.S.Solanki	v	Glos	Cheltenham	2008
3rd	438*	G.A.Hick/T.M.Moody	v	Hampshire	Southampton[1]	1997
4th	330	B.F.Smith/G.A.Hick	v	Somerset	Taunton	2006
5th	393	E.G.Arnold/W.B.Burns	v	Warwicks	Birmingham	1909
6th	265	G.A.Hick/S.J.Rhodes	v	Somerset	Taunton	1988
7th	256	D.A.Leatherdale/S.J.Rhodes	v	Notts	Nottingham	2002
8th	184	S.J.Rhodes/S.R.Lampitt	v	Derbyshire	Kidderminster	1991
9th	181	J.A.Cuffe/R.D.Burrows	v	Glos	Worcester	1907
10th	136	A.G.Milton/S.J.Magoffin	v	Somerset	Worcester	2018

Best Bowling	For	9- 23	C.F.Root	v	Lancashire	Worcester	1931
(Innings)	V	10- 51	J.Mercer	for	Glamorgan	Worcester	1936
Best Bowling	For	15- 87	A.J.Conway	v	Glos	Moreton-in-M	1914
(Match)	V	17-212	J.C.Clay	for	Glamorgan	Swansea	1937

Most Runs – Season	2654	H.H.I.H.Gibbons	(av 52.03)		1934
Most Runs – Career	34490	D.Kenyon	(av 34.18)		1946-67
Most 100s – Season	10	G.M.Turner			1970
	10	G.A.Hick			1988
Most 100s – Career	106	G.A.Hick			1984-2008
Most Wkts – Season	207	C.F.Root	(av 17.52)		1925
Most Wkts – Career	2143	R.T.D.Perks	(av 23.73)		1930-55
Most Career W-K Dismissals	1095	S.J.Rhodes	(991 ct; 104 st)		1985-2004
Most Career Catches in the Field	528	G.A.Hick			1984-2008

LIMITED-OVERS CRICKET

Highest Total	50ov	404-3		v	Devon	Worcester	1987
	40ov	376-6		v	Surrey	The Oval	2010
	T20	227-6		v	Northants	Kidderminster	2007
Lowest Total	50ov	58		v	Ireland	Worcester	2009
	40ov	86		v	Yorkshire	Leeds	1969
	T20	53		v	Lancashire	Manchester	2016
Highest Innings	50ov	192	C.J.Ferguson	v	Leics	Worcester	2018
	40ov	160	T.M.Moody	v	Kent	Worcester	1991
	T20	127	T.Kohler-Cadmore	v	Durham	Worcester	2004
Best Bowling	50ov	7-19	N.V.Radford	v	Beds	Bedford	1991
	40ov	6-16	Shoaib Akhtar	v	Glos	Worcester	2005
	T20	5-24	A.Hepburn	v	Notts	Worcester	2017

YORKSHIRE

Formation of Present Club: 8 January 1863
Substantial Reorganisation: 10 December 1891
Inaugural First-Class Match: 1864
Colours: Dark Blue, Light Blue and Gold
Badge: White Rose
County Championships (since 1890): (32) 1893, 1896,
1898, 1900, 1901, 1902, 1905, 1908, 1912, 1919, 1922,
1923, 1924, 1925, 1931, 1932, 1933, 1935, 1937, 1938,
1939, 1946, 1959, 1960, 1962, 1963, 1966, 1967, 1968,
2001, 2014, 2015
Joint Champions: (1) 1949
Gillette/C&G Trophy Winners: (3) 1965, 1969, 2002
Benson and Hedges Cup Winners: (1) 1987
Sunday League Winners: (1) 1983
Twenty20 Cup Winners: (0); best – Finalist 2012

Chief Executive: Mark Arthur, Emerald Headingley Pavilion, Kirkstall Lane, Headingley,
Leeds, LS6 3DP • Tel: 0843 504 3099 • Email: cricket@yorkshireccc.com • Web:
www.yorkshireccc.com • Twitter: @Yorkshireccc (122,267 followers)

Director of Cricket: Martyn Moxon. **1st XI Coach**: Andrew Gale. **Batting Coach**: Paul
Grayson. **Bowling Coach**: Richard Pyrah. **Captain**: G.S.Ballance. **Overseas Player**: None.
2019 Testimonial: None. **Head Groundsman**: Andy Fogarty. **Scorer**: John Potter. ‡ New
registration. ᴺᴼ Not qualified for England.

BAIRSTOW, Jonathan Marc (St Peter's S, York; Leeds Met U), b Bradford 26 Sep 1989.
Son of D.L.Bairstow (Yorkshire, GW and England 1970-90); brother of A.D.Bairstow
(Derbyshire 1995). 6'0''. RHB, WK, occ RM. Squad No 21. Debut (Yorkshire) 2009; cap
2011. Inaugural winner of Young Wisden Schools Cricketer of the Year 2008. YC 2011.
ECB Test & L-O Central Contract 2018-19. Tests: 63 (2012 to 2018-19); 1000 runs (1):
1470 (2016); HS 167* v SL (Lord's) 2016. Took a world record 70 dismissals in 2016, as
well as scoring a record number of runs in a calendar year for a keeper. **LOI**: 59 (2011 to
2018-19); 1000 runs (1): 1025 (2018); HS 141* v WI (Southampton) 2017. **IT20**: 30 (2011
to 2018-19); HS 68 v WI (Gros Islet) 2018-19. F-c Tours: A 2013-14, 2017-18; SA 2014-15
(EL), 2015-16; WI 2010-11 (EL), 2018-19; NZ 2017-18; I 2012-13, 2016-17; SL 2013-14
(EL), 2018-19; B 2016-17; UAE 2015-16 (v P). 1000 runs (3); most – 1286 (2016). HS 246
v Hants (Leeds) 2016. LO HS 174 v Durham (Leeds) 2017 (RLC). T20 HS 102*.

BALLANCE, Gary Simon (Peterhouse S, Marondera, Zimbabwe; Harrow S; Leeds Met
U), b Harare, Zimbabwe 22 Nov 1989. Nephew of G.S.Ballance (Rhodesia B 1978-79) and
D.L.Houghton (Rhodesia/Zimbabwe 1978-79 to 1997-98). 6'0''. LHB, LB. Squad No 19.
Debut (Yorkshire) 2008; cap 2012; captain 2017 to 2018 (*part*). MWR 2010-11 to 2011-12.
Wisden 2014. **Tests**: 23 (2013-14 to 2017); HS 156 v I (Southampton) 2014; BB – . **LOI**: 16
(2013 to 2014-15); HS 79 v A (Melbourne) 2013-14. F-c Tours: A 2013-14; WI 2014-15; B
2016-17. 1000 runs (2+1); most – 1363 (2013). HS 210 MWR v SR (Masvingo) 2011-12. Y
HS 203* v Hants (Southampton) 2017. BB – . LO HS 152* v Northants (Northampton) 2013
(RLC). T20 HS 79.

BARNES, Edward (King James S, Knaresborough), b York 26 Nov 1997. 6'0''. RHB,
RFM. Squad No 62. Yorkshire 2nd XI debut 2016. England U19 2016. Awaiting 1st XI
debut.

BRESNAN, Timothy Thomas (Castleford HS and TC; Pontefract New C), b Pontefract 28 Feb 1985. 6'0". RHB, RFM. Squad No 16. Debut (Yorkshire) 2003; cap 2006; benefit 2014. MCC 2006, 2009. Big Bash: HH 2014-15. PS 2016-17 to 2017-18, *Wisden* 2011. **Tests**: 23 (2009 to 2013-14); HS 91 v B (Dhaka) 2009-10; BB 5-48 v I (Nottingham). **LOI**: 85 (2006 to 2015); HS 80 v SA (Centurion) 2009-10; BB 5-48 v I (Bangalore) 2010-11. **IT20**: 34 (2006 to 2013-14); HS 47* v WI (Bridgetown) 2013-14; BB 3-10 v P (Cardiff) 2010. F-c Tours: A 2010-11, 2013-14; I 2012-13; SL 2011-12; B 2006-07 (Eng A); 2009-10. HS 169* v Durham (Chester-le-St) 2015, sharing Y record 7th wkt partnership of 366* with J.M.Bairstow. BB 5-28 v Hants (Leeds) 2018. LO HS 95* v Notts (Scarborough) 2016 (RLC). BB 5-48 (*see LOI*). T20 HS 51. T20 BB 6-19 v Lancs (Leeds) 2017 – Y record.

BROOK, Harry Cherrington (Sedbergh S), b Keighley 22 Feb 1999. 5'11". RHB, RM. Squad No 88. Debut (Yorkshire) 2016. Yorkshire 2nd XI debut 2015. England U19 2016-17 to 2017. HS 124 v Essex (Chelmsford) 2018. BB 1-54 v Somerset (Scarborough) 2017. LO HS 24 v Lancs (Manchester) 2018 (RLC). T20 HS 44.

CARVER, Karl (Thirsk S & SFC), b Northallerton 26 Mar 1996. 5'10". LHB, SLA. Squad No 29. Debut (Yorkshire) 2014. Yorkshire 2nd XI debut 2013. HS 20 v Somerset (Taunton) 2017. BB 4-106 v MCC (Abu Dhabi) 2015-16. CC BB 2-10 v Essex (Chelmsford) 2017. LO HS 35* v Somerset (Scarborough) 2015 (RLC). LO BB 3-5 v Lancs (Manchester) 2016 (RLC). T20 HS 2. T20 BB 3-40.

COAD, Benjamin Oliver (Thirsk S & SFC), b Harrogate 10 Jan 1994. 6'2". RHB, RM. Squad No 10. Debut (Yorkshire) 2016; cap 2018. HS 33 v Notts (Leeds) 2018. 50 wkts (1): 53 (2017). BB 6-25 v Lancs (Leeds) 2017. LO HS 9 v Hants (Southampton) 2018 (RLC). LO BB 4-63 v Derbys (Leeds) 2017 (RLC). T20 HS 2*. T20 BB 2-24.

FISHER, Matthew David (Easingwold SS), b York 9 Nov 1997. 6'1". RHB, RFM. Squad No 7. Debut (Yorkshire) 2015. MCC 2018. Yorkshire 2nd XI debut 2013, aged 15y 201d. England U19 2014. HS 37 and BB 5-54 v Warwks (Leeds) 2017. LO HS 36* v Worcs (Worcester) 2017 (RLC). LO BB 3-32 v Leics (Leeds) 2015 (RLC). T20 HS 17*. T20 BB 5-22.

‡**FRAINE, William** Alan Richard (Silcoates S; Bromsgrove SFC; Durham U), b Hudders-field, Yorks 13 Jun 1996. 6'2". RHB, RM. Squad No 31. Durham MCCU 2017-18. Nottinghamshire 2018. Worcestershire 2nd XI 2015-16. Nottinghamshire 2nd XI 2017-18. Herefordshire 2016. HS 30 Nt v Surrey (Nottingham) 2018. LO HS 13 Nt v Lancs (Manchester) 2018 (RLC). T20 HS 14.

KOHLER-CADMORE, Tom (Malvern C), b Chatham, Kent 19 Aug 1994. 6'2". RHB, OB. Squad No 32. Worcestershire 2014-17. Yorkshire debut 2017; cap 2019. HS 169 Wo v Glos (Worcester) 2016. Y HS 106 v Notts (Nottingham) 2018. LO HS 164 v Durham (Chester-le-St) 2018 (RLC). T20 HS 127 Wo v Durham (Worcester) 2016 – Wo record, winning Walter Lawrence Trophy for fastest 100 (43 balls).

LEANING, Jack Andrew (Archbishop Holgate's S, York; York C), b Bristol, Glos 18 Oct 1993. 5'10". RHB, RMF. Squad No 34. Debut (Yorkshire) 2013; cap 2016. YC 2015. HS 123 v Somerset (Taunton) 2014. BB 2-30 v MCC (Abu Dhabi) 2015-16. CC BB 1-16 v Surrey (Scarborough) 2018. LO HS 131* v Leics (Leicester) 2016 (RLC). LO BB 5-22 v Unicorns (Leeds) 2013 (Y40). T20 HS 64. T20 BB –.

LOGAN, James Edwin Graham (Normanton Freestone HS; Pontefract New C), b Wakefield 12 Oct 1997. 6'1". LHB, SLA. Squad No 11. Debut (Yorkshire) 2018. Yorkshire 2nd XI debut 2014. HS 6 and BB – v Worcs (Worcester) 2018 – only 1st XI game.

LYTH, Adam (Caedmon S, Whitby; Whitby Community C), b Whitby 25 Sep 1987. 5'8". LHB, RM. Squad No 9. Debut (Yorkshire) 2007; cap 2010. MCC 2017. PCA 2014. *Wisden* 2014. **Tests**: 7 (2015); HS 107 v NZ (Leeds) 2015. F-c Tours (EL): SA 2014-15; WI 2010-11. 1000 runs (3); most – 1619 (2014). HS 251 v Lancs (Manchester) 2014, sharing in Y record 6th wicket partnership of 296 with A.U.Rashid. BB 2-9 v Middx (Scarborough) 2016. LO HS 144 v Lancs (Manchester) 2018 (RLC). LO BB 1-6 v Middx (Leeds) 2013 (Y40). T20 HS 161 v Northants (Leeds) 2017 – Y & UK record; 5th highest score in all T20 cricket. T20 BB 2-5.

‡^{NQ}**OLIVIER, Duanne**, b Groblersdal, South Africa 9 May 1992. RHB, RFM. Squad No 74. Free State 2010-11 to 2017-18. Knights 2013-14 to date. Derbyshire 2018. Joins Yorkshire in 2019 on three-year Kolpak deal. **Tests**: 10 (2016-17 to 2018-19); HS 10* v P (Cape Town) 2018-19; BB 6-37 (11-96 match) v P (Centurion) 2018-19. **LOI** (SA): 2 (2018-19); HS – ; BB 2-73 v P (Port Elizabeth) 2018-19. F-c Tours (SA): E 2017; A 2016 (SAA); I 2018 (SAA); Z 2016 (SAA). HS 72 FS v Namibia (Bloemfontein) 2014-15. CC HS 40* v Warwks (Birmingham) 2018. 50 wkts (0+3); most – 64 (2016-17). BB 6-37 (*see Tests*). CC BB 5-20 (10-125 match) De v Durham (Chester-le-St) 2018. LO HS 25* and LO BB 4-34 Knights v Lions (Kimberley) 2017-18. T20 HS 15*. T20 BB 4-28.

PATTERSON, Steven Andrew (Malet Lambert CS; St Mary's SFC, Hull; Leeds U), b Hull 3 Oct 1983. 6'4". RHB, RMF. Squad No 17. Debut (Yorkshire) 2005; cap 2012; testimonial 2017; captain 2018 (*part*) to date. Bradford/Leeds UCCE 2003 (not f-c). HS 63* v Warwks (Birmingham) 2016. 50 wkts (2); most – 53 (2012). BB 6-40 v Essex (Chelmsford) 2018. LO HS 25* v Worcs (Leeds) 2006 (P40). LO BB 6-32 v Derbys (Leeds) 2010. T20 HS 3*. T20 BB 4-30.

^{NQ}**PILLANS, Mathew** William (Pretoria BHS; U of Pretoria), b Durban, South Africa 4 Jul 1991. Qualifies for England in 2023, ancestral visa. 6'6". RHB, RF. Squad No 47. Northerns 2012-13. KwaZulu-Natal Inland 2013-14 to 2015-16. Dolphins 2013-14 to 2015-16. Surrey 2016-18. Leicestershire 2017 (on loan). Yorkshire debut 2018. HS 56 Le v Northants (Northampton) 2017. Y HS 8 v Notts (Nottingham) 2018. BB 6-67 (10-129 match) Dolphins v Knights (Durban) 2014-15. CC BB 3-63 Le v Sussex (Arundel) 2017. Y BB –. LO HS 20* KZN v NW (Pietermaritzburg) 2013-14. LO BB 3-14 KZN v Namibia (Pietermaritzburg) 2015-16. T20 HS 34*. T20 BB 3-15.

POYSDEN, Joshua Edward (Cardinal Newman S, Hove; Anglia RU), b Shoreham-by-Sea, Sussex 8 Aug 1991. 5'9". LHB, LB. Squad No 14. Cambridge MCCU 2011-13. Warwickshire 2015-18. Yorkshire debut 2018. Unicorns (l-o) 2013. HS 47 CU v Surrey (Cambridge) 2011. CC HS v Lancs (Manchester) 2018. BB 5-29 Wa v Glamorgan (Birmingham) 2018. Y BB 3-128 v Worcs (Scarborough) 2018. LO HS 10* Unicorns v Glos (Wormsley) 2013 (Y40). LO BB 3-33 Unicorns v Middx (Lord's) 2013 (Y40). T20 HS 9*. T20 BB 4-51.

RASHID, Adil Usman (Belle Vue S, Bradford), b Bradford 17 Feb 1988. 5'8". RHB, LBG. Squad No 3. Debut (Yorkshire) 2006; cap 2008; testimonial 2018. MCC 2007-09. Big Bash: AS 2015-16. YC 2007. Match double (114, 48, 8-157 and 2-45) for England U19 v India U19 (Taunton) 2006. **ECB TEST & L-O Central Contract 2018-19**. **Tests**: 19 (2015-16 to 2018-19), taking 5-64 v P (Abu Dhabi) on debut; HS 61 v P (Dubai, DSC) 2015-16; BB 5-49 v SL (Colombo, SSC) 2018-19. **LOI**: 83 (2009 to 2018-19); HS 69 v NZ (Birmingham) 2015; BB 5-27 v Ire (Bristol) 2017. **IT20**: 36 (2009 to 2018-19); HS 9* v SA (Nottingham) 2009; BB 3-11 v SL (Colombo, RPS) 2018-19. F-c Tours: WI 2010-11 (EL), 2018-19; I 2007-08 (EL), 2016-17; SL 2018-19. B 2006-07 (Eng A), 2016-17; UAE 2015-16 (v P). HS 180 v Somerset (Leeds) 2013. 50 wkts (2); most – 65 (2008). BB 7-107 v Hants (Southampton) 2008. LO HS 71 v Glos (Leeds) 2014 (RLC). LO BB 5-27 (*see LOI*). T20 HS 36*. T20 BB 4-19.

ROOT, Joseph Edward (King Ecgbert S, Sheffield; Worksop C), b Sheffield 30 Dec 1990. Elder brother of W.T.Root (*see GLAMORGAN*). 6'0". RHB, OB. Squad No 66. Debut (Yorkshire) 2010; cap 2012. YC 2012. **ECB Test & L-O Central Contract 2018-19. Tests:** 80 (2012-13 to 2018-19, 27 as captain); 1000 runs (2); most – 1477 (2016); HS 254 v P (Manchester) 2016; BB 2-9 v A (Lord's) 2013. **LOI:** 126 (2012-13 to 2018-19); HS 133* v B (Oval) 2018; BB 3-52 v Ire (Lord's) 2017. **IT20:** 31 (2012-13 to 2018-19); HS 90* v A (Southampton) 2013; BB 2-9 v WI (Kolkata) 2016. F-c Tours(C=Captain): A 2013-14, 2017-18C; SA 2015-16; WI 2014-15, 2018-19C; NZ 2012-13, 2017-18C; I 2012-13, 2016-17; SL 2018-19C; UAE 2015-16 (v P). 1000 runs (3); most – 1228 (2013). HS 254 (*see Tests*). CC HS 236 v Derbys (Leeds) 2013. BB 4-5 v Lancs (Manchester) 2018. LO HS 133* (*see LOI*). LO BB 3-52 (*see LOI*). T20 HS 92*. T20 BB 2-9.

SHAW, Joshua (Crofton HS, Wakefield; Skills Exchange C), b Wakefield, Yorks 3 Jan 1996. Son of C.Shaw (Yorkshire 1984-88). 6'1". RHB, RMF. Squad No 25. Gloucestershire 2016-17 (on loan); cap 2016. Yorkshire debut 2016. Yorkshire 2nd XI debut 2012. England U19 2012-13 to 2014. HS 42 v Somerset (Leeds) 2018. BB 5-79 Gs v Sussex (Bristol) 2016. Y BB 3-58 v Pakistan A (Leeds) 2016. T20 HS 1. T20 BB –.

SHUTT, Jack William (Kirk Balk S; Thomas Rotherham C), b Barnsley 24 Jun 1997. 6'0". RHB, OB. Squad No 24. Yorkshire 2nd XI debut 2016. Awaiting 1st XI debut.

TATTERSALL, Jonathan Andrew (King James S, Knaresborough), b Harrogate 15 Dec 1994. 5'8". RHB, LB. Squad No 12. Debut (Yorkshire) 2018. Yorkshire 2nd XI debut 2012. England U19 2012-13 to 2014. HS 70 v Surrey (Scarborough) 2018. LO HS 89 v Hants (Southampton) 2018 (RLC). T20 HS 53*.

THOMPSON, Jordan Aaron (Benton Park S), b Leeds 9 Oct 1996. 5'11". LHB, RM. Squad No 44. Yorkshire 2nd XI debut 2014. Awaiting f-c debut. T20 HS 12*. T20 BB 3-23.

WAITE, Matthew James (Brigshaw HS), b Leeds 24 Dec 1995. 6'0". RHB, RFM. Squad No 6. Debut (Yorkshire) 2017. Yorkshire 2nd XI debut 2014. HS 42 and BB 3-91 v Notts (Nottingham) 2018. LO HS 71 v Warwks (Birmingham) 2017 (RLC). LO BB 4-65 v Worcs (Worcester) 2017 (RLC). T20 HS 19*. T20 BB 1-6.

WARNER, Jared David (Kettleborough Park HS; Silcoates SFC), b Wakefield 14 Nov 1996. 6'1". RHB, RFM. Squad No 45. Yorkshire 2nd XI debut 2015. England U19 2014-15 to 2015. Awaiting 1st XI debut.

WILLEY, David Jonathan (Northampton S), b Northampton 28 Feb 1990. Son of P.Willey (Northants, Leics and England 1966-91). 6'1". LHB, LMF. Squad No 72. Northamptonshire 2009-15; cap 2013. Yorkshire debut/cap 2016. Bedfordshire 2008. IPL: CSK 2018. Big Bash: PS 2015-16 to date. **ECB L-O Central Contract 2018-19. LOI:** 42 (2015 to 2018); HS 50 v I (Lord's) 2018; BB 4-34 v SL (Cardiff) 2016. **IT20:** 27 (2015 to 2018-19); HS 29* v I (Manchester) 2018; BB 4-7 v WI (Basseterre) 2018-19. HS 104* Nh v Glos (Northampton) 2015. Y HS 34* v Somerset (Leeds) 2018. BB 5-29 (10-75 match) Nh v Glos (Northampton) 2011. Y BB 3-55 v Surrey (Leeds) 2016. LO HS 167 Nh v Warwks (Birmingham) 2013 (Y40). LO BB 5-62 EL v NZ A (Bristol) 2014. T20 HS 118. T20 BB 4-7.

RELEASED/RETIRED

(Having made a County 1st XI appearance in 2018)

AZEEM Muhammad **RAFIQ** (Holgate S Sports C; Barnsley C), b Karachi, Pakistan 27 Feb 1991. 5'11". RHB, OB. Yorkshire 2009-17. Derbyshire 2011 (on loan). SSGC 2018-19. HS 100 v Worcs (Worcester) 2009. BB 5-50 v Essex (Chelmsford) 2012. LO HS 52* v Leics (Leeds) 2017 (RLC). LO BB 5-30 v Bangladesh A (Leeds) 2013. T20 HS 21*. T20 BB 5-19.

BROOKS, J.A. – *see SOMERSET.*

HODD, Andrew John (Bexhill C; Loughborough U), b Chichester, Sussex 12 Jan 1984. 5'9''. RHB, WK. Sussex 2003-11. Surrey 2005 (1 match). Yorkshire 2012-18; cap 2016. HS 123 Sx v Yorks (Hove) 2007. Y HS 96* v Notts (Scarborough) 2016. LO HS 91 Sx v Lancs (Hove) 2010 (CB40). T20 HS 70.

LEES, A.Z. – *see DURHAM.*

PLUNKETT, L.E. – *see SURREY.*

NO**PUJARA, Cheteshwar** Arvindbhai, b Rajkot, India 25 Jan 1988. RHB, LB. Son of A.S.Pujara (Saurashtra 1976-77 to 1979-80), nephew of B.S.Pujara (Saurashtra 1983-84 to 1996-97). Saurashtra 2005-06 to date. Derbyshire 2014. Yorkshire 2015-18. Nottinghamshire 2017; cap 2017. IPL: KKR 2009-10. RCB 2011-13. KXIP 2014. **Tests** (I): 68 (2010-11 to 2018-19); 1000 runs (1): 1140 (2017); HS 206* v E (Ahmedabad) 2012-13. **LOI** (I): 5 (2013 to 2014); HS 27 v B (Dhaka) 2014. F-c Tours (I): E 2010 (I A), 2014, 2018; A 2006 (I A), 2014-15, 2018-19; SA 2010-11, 2013 (I A), 2013-14, 2017-18; WI 2012 (I A), 2016; NZ 2013-14; SL 2015, 2017; Z/Ken 2007-08 (I A). 1000 runs (0+3); most – 2064 (2016-17). HS 352 Saur v Karnataka (Rajkot) 2012-13. Y HS 133* v Hants (Leeds) 2015. BB 2-4 Saur v Rajasthan (Jaipur) 2007-08. LO HS 158* Ind B v India A (Rajkot) 2012-13. T20 HS 100*.

NO**RAVAL, Jeet** Ashokbhai, b Ahmedabad, India 22 May 1988. LHB, LBG. Auckland 2008-09 to date. Central Districts 2012-13. Yorkshire 2018. **Tests** (NZ): 18 (2016-17 to 2018-19); HS 132 v B (Hamilton) 2018-19. F-c Tours (NZ): I 2017-18 (NZA); UAE 2018-19 (v P). 1000 runs (0+1): 1016 (2015-16). Y HS 256 Auckland v CD (Auckland) 2008-09, in his 2nd f-c innings. Y HS 21 v Worcs (Worcester) 2018. BB 2-10 Auckland v CD (Auckland) 2009-10. LO HS 149 Auckland v Canterbury (Auckland) 2017-18. LO BB 2-8 Auckland v Wellington (Wellington) 2010-11. T20 HS 56.

WAINMAN, James Charles (Leeds GS), b Harrogate 25 Jan 1993. 6'4''. RHB, LMF. Awaiting f-c debut. LO HS 33 and LO BB 3-51 v Sri Lanka A (Leeds) 2014. T20 HS 12*. T20 BB 1-27.

NO**WILLIAMSON, Kane** Stuart (Tauranga Boys' C), b Tauranga, New Zealand 8 Aug 1990. Cousin of D.Cleaver (C Districts 2010-11 to date). 5'8''. RHB, OB. N Districts 2007-08 to date. Gloucestershire 2011-12; cap 2011. Yorkshire 2013-18. IPL: SH 2015-18. **Tests** (NZ): 72 (2010-11 to 2018-19, 24 as captain); 1000 runs (1): 1172 (2015); HS 242* v SL (Wellington) 2014-15; scored 131 v I (Ahmedabad) 2010-11 on debut; BB 4-44 v E (Auckland) 2012-13. **LOI** (NZ): 139 (2010 to 2018-19, 65 as captain); 1000 runs (1): 1376 (2015); HS 145* v SA (Kimberley) 2012-13; BB 4-22 v SA (Paarl) 2012-13. **IT20** (NZ): 57 (2011-12 to 2018-19, 39 as captain); HS 73* v B (Napier) 2016-17; BB 2-16 v B (Mt Maunganui) 2016-17. F-c Tours (NZ)(C=Captain): E 2013, 2015; A 2011-12, 2015-16; SA 2012-13, 2016C; WI 2012, 2014; I 2010-11, 2012, 2016-17C; SL 2012-13; Z 2011-12, 2016C; B 2013-14; UAE 2014-15 (v P), 2018-19C (v P). HS 284* ND v Wellington (Lincoln) 2011-12. Y HS 189 v Sussex (Scarborough) 2014. BB 5-75 ND v Canterbury (Christchurch) 2008-09. CC BB 3-58 Gs v Northants (Northampton) 2012. Y BB 2-44 v Sussex (Hove) 2013. LO HS 145* (*see LOI*). LO BB 5-51 ND v Auckland (Auckland) 2009-10. T20 HS 101*. T20 BB 3-33.

YORKSHIRE 2018

RESULTS SUMMARY

	Place	Won	Lost	Drew	Aband	NR
Specsavers County Champ (1st Division)	4th	5	5	3	1	
All First-Class Matches		5	5	3	2	
Royal London One-Day Cup (North Group)	SF	6	3			1
Vitality Blast (North Group)	5th	7	7			

SPECSAVERS COUNTY CHAMPIONSHIP AVERAGES

BATTING AND FIELDING

Cap		M	I	NO	HS	Runs	Avge	100	50	Ct/St
	T.Kohler-Cadmore	6	11	2	106	414	46.00	2	2	4
2011	J.M.Bairstow	3	6	–	95	263	43.83	–	3	9
2012	G.S.Ballance	12	23	–	194	906	39.39	3	4	4
	K.S.Williamson	3	6	–	87	218	36.33	–	3	3
	J.A.Tattersall	7	12	1	70	350	31.81	–	2	19
2016	A.J.Hodd	3	6	–	85	175	29.16	–	2	12
2010	A.Lyth	13	25	1	134*	656	27.33	1	2	16
2016	J.A.Leaning	8	16	2	68	371	26.50	–	2	9
	H.C.Brook	12	23	–	124	575	25.00	–	3	7
	J.Shaw	3	6	1	42	104	20.80	–	–	–
2006	T.T.Bresnan	12	22	3	80	385	20.26	–	2	9
2012	S.A.Patterson	8	13	2	45*	205	18.63	–	–	2
	B.O.Coad	9	15	7	33	135	16.87	–	–	–
2012	J.E.Root	3	6	–	35	97	16.16	–	–	2
	M.J.Waite	4	6	–	42	96	16.00	–	–	–
2013	J.A.Brooks	13	22	3	82	303	15.94	–	1	1
	C.A.Pujara	6	12	–	41	172	14.33	–	–	4
2016	D.J.Willey	2	4	1	34*	42	14.00	–	–	–
	M.D.Fisher	2	4	1	20*	39	13.00	–	–	1
	J.A.Raval	4	7	–	21	84	12.00	–	–	3
	J.E.Poysden	3	5	2	20*	25	8.33	–	–	–
2014	A.Z.Lees	4	8	–	39	50	6.25	–	–	1

Also batted (1 match each): K.Carver 1*, 0*; J.E.G.Logan 6 (1 ct); M.W.Pillans 8.

BOWLING

	O	M	R	W	Avge	Best	5wI	10wM
B.O.Coad	272.5	87	784	48	16.33	6- 81	3	1
S.A.Patterson	235	63	594	24	24.75	6- 40	1	–
T.T.Bresnan	279.5	48	969	35	27.68	5- 28	1	–
J.A.Brooks	346.3	51	1430	51	28.03	6- 94	5	–

Also bowled:

	O	M	R	W	Avge	Best	5wI	10wM
J.E.Root	20.4	7	37	5	7.40	4- 5	–	–
M.J.Waite	61	14	221	8	27.62	3- 91	–	–
D.J.Willey	67.2	13	217	6	36.16	3- 72	–	–
J.E.Poysden	52.2	1	259	7	37.00	3-128	–	–

H.C.Brook 22.1-5-67-0; M.D.Fisher 54-6-219-2; J.A.Leaning 19-3-57-1; J.E.G.Logan 12-3-44-0; A.Lyth 68-8-246-4; M.W.Pillans 30-5-130-0; J.Shaw 63-5-265-4; K.S.Williamson 2-0-9-0.

Yorkshire played no first-class fixtures outside the County Championship in 2018. The First-Class Averages (pp 230–245) give the records of Yorkshire players in all first-class county matches, with the exception of J.M.Bairstow, M.D.Fisher, A.Z.Lees, M.W.Pillans, J.E.Poysden, C.A.Pujara and J.E.Root, whose first-class figures for Yorkshire are as above.

YORKSHIRE RECORDS

FIRST-CLASS CRICKET

Highest Total	For 887		v	Warwicks	Birmingham	1896
	V 681-7d		by	Leics	Bradford	1996
Lowest Total	For 23		v	Hampshire	Middlesbrough	1965
	V 13		by	Notts	Nottingham	1901
Highest Innings	For 341	G.H.Hirst	v	Leics	Leicester	1905
	V 318*	W.G.Grace	for	Glos	Cheltenham	1876

Highest Partnership for each Wicket

1st	555	P.Holmes/H.Sutcliffe	v	Essex	Leyton	1932
2nd	346	W.Barber/M.Leyland	v	Middlesex	Sheffield	1932
3rd	346	J.J.Sayers/A.McGrath	v	Warwicks	Birmingham	2009
4th	372	J.E.Root/J.M.Bairstow	v	Surrey	Leeds	2016
5th	340	E.Wainwright/G.H.Hirst	v	Surrey	The Oval	1899
6th	296	A.Lyth/A.U.Rashid	v	Lancashire	Manchester	2014
7th	366*	J.M.Bairstow/T.T.Bresnan	v	Durham	Chester-le-St^2	2015
8th	292	R.Peel/Lord Hawke	v	Warwicks	Birmingham	1896
9th	246	T.T.Bresnan/J.N.Gillespie	v	Surrey	The Oval	2007
10th	149	G.Boycott/G.B.Stevenson	v	Warwicks	Birmingham	1982

Best Bowling	For 10-10	H.Verity	v	Notts	Leeds	1932
(Innings)	V 10-37	C.V.Grimmett	for	Australians	Sheffield	1930
Best Bowling	For 17-91	H.Verity	v	Essex	Leyton	1933
(Match)	V 17-91	H.Dean	for	Lancashire	Liverpool	1913

Most Runs – Season	2883	H.Sutcliffe	(av 80.08)	1932
Most Runs – Career	38558	H.Sutcliffe	(av 50.20)	1919-45
Most 100s – Season	12	H.Sutcliffe		1932
Most 100s – Career	112	H.Sutcliffe		1919-45
Most Wkts – Season	240	W.Rhodes	(av 12.72)	1900
Most Wkts – Career	3597	W.Rhodes	(av 16.02)	1898-1930
Most Career W-K Dismissals	1186	D.Hunter	(863 ct; 323 st)	1888-1909
Most Career Catches in the Field	665	J.Tunnicliffe		1891-1907

LIMITED-OVERS CRICKET

Highest Total	50ov	411-6	v	Devon	Exmouth	2004
	40ov	352-6	v	Notts	Scarborough	2001
	T20	260-4	v	Northants	Leeds	2017
Lowest Total	50ov	76	v	Surrey	Harrogate	1970
	40ov	54	v	Essex	Leeds	2003
	T20	90-9	v	Durham	Chester-le-St^2	2009
Highest Innings	50ov	175	T.M.Head	v	Leics	Leicester	2016
	40ov	191	D.S.Lehmann	v	Notts	Scarborough	2001
	T20	161	A.Lyth	v	Northants	Leeds	2017
Best Bowling	50ov	7-27	D.Gough	v	Ireland	Leeds	1997
	40ov	7-15	R.A.Hutton	v	Worcs	Leeds	1969
	T20	6-19	T.T.Bresnan	v	Lancashire	Leeds	2017

FIRST-CLASS UMPIRES 2019

† New appointment. See page ** for key to abbreviations.

BAILEY, Robert John (Biddulph HS), b Biddulph, Staffs 28 Oct 1963. 6'3''. RHB, OB. Northamptonshire 1982-99; cap 1985; benefit 1993; captain 1996-97. Derbyshire 2000-01; cap 2000. Staffordshire 1988. YC 1984. **Tests:** 4 (1988 to 1989-90); HS 43 v WI (Oval) 1988. **LOI:** 4 (1984-85 to 1989-90); HS 43* v SL (Oval) 1988. F-c Tours: SA 1991-92 (Nh); WI 1989-90; Z 1994-95 (Nh). 1000 runs (13); most – 1987 (1990). HS 224* Nh v Glamorgan (Swansea) 1986. BB 5-54 Nh v Notts (Northampton) 1993. F-c career: 374 matches; 21844 runs @ 40.52, 47 hundreds; 121 wickets @ 42.51; 272 ct. Appointed 2006. Umpired 22 LOI (2011 to 2018). **ICC International Panel 2011 to date.**

BAINTON, Neil Laurence, b Romford, Essex 2 October 1970. No f-c appearances. Appointed 2006.

BALDWIN, Paul Kerr, b Epsom, Surrey 18 Jul 1973. No f-c appearances. Umpired 18 LOI (2006 to 2009). Reserve List 2010-14. Appointed 2015.

†BLACKWELL, Ian David (Brookfield Community S), b Chesterfield, Derbys 10 Jun 1978. 6'2''. LHB, SLA. Derbyshire 1997-99. Somerset 2000-08; cap 2001; captain 2006 (*part*). Durham 2009-12. Warwickshire 2012 (on loan). MCC 2012. **Tests:** 1 (2005-06); HS 4 and BB-v I (Nagpur) 2005-06. **LOI:** 34 (2002-03 to 2005-06); HS 82 v I (Colombo) 2002-03; BB 3-26 v A (Adelaide) 2002-03. F-c Tour: I 2005-06. 1000 runs (3); most – 1256 (2005). HS 247* Sm v Derbys (Taunton) 2003 – off 156 balls and including 204 off 98 balls in reduced post-lunch session. BB 7-52 Du v Australia A (Chester-le-St) 2012. CC BB 7-85 Du v Lancs (Manchester) 2009. F-c career: 210 matches; 11595 runs @ 39.57, 27 hundreds; 398 wickets @ 35.91; 66 ct. Reserve List 2015-17. Appointed 2018.

BURNS, Michael (Walney CS), b Barrow-in-Furness, Lancs 6 Feb 1969. 6'0''. RHB, RM, WK. Warwickshire 1992-96. Somerset 1997-2005; cap 1999; captain 2003-04. 1000 runs (2); most – 1133 (2003). HS 221 Sm v Yorks (Bath) 2001. BB 6-54 Sm v Leics (Taunton) 2001. F-c career: 154 matches; 7648 runs @ 32.68, 8 hundreds; 68 wickets @ 42.42; 142 ct, 7 st. Appointed 2016.

COOK, Nicholas Grant Billson (Lutterworth GS), b Leicester 17 Jun 1956. 6'0''. RHB, SLA. Leicestershire 1978-85; cap 1982. Northamptonshire 1986-94; cap 1987; benefit 1995. **Tests:** 15 (1983 to 1989); HS 31 v A (Oval) 1989; BB 6-65 (11-83 match) v P (Karachi) 1983-84. **LOI:** 3 (1983-84 to 1989-90); HS – ; BB 2-18 v P (Peshawar) 1987-88. F-c Tours: NZ 1979-80 (DHR), 1983-84; P 1983-84, 1987-88; SL 1985-86 (Eng B); Z 1980-81 (Le), 1984-85 (EC). HS 75 Le v Somerset (Taunton) 1980. 50 wkts (8); most – 90 (1982). BB 7-34 (10-97 match) Nh v Essex (Chelmsford) 1992. F-c career: 356 matches; 3137 runs @ 11.66; 879 wickets @ 29.01; 197 ct. Appointed 2009.

DEBENHAM, Benjamin John, b Chelmsford, Essex 11 Oct 1967. LHB. No f-c appearances. Reserve List 2012-17. Appointed 2018.

EVANS, Jeffery Howard, b Llanelli, Carms 7 Aug 1954. No f-c appearances. Appointed 2001. Umpired in Indian Cricket League 2007-08.

GOUGH, Michael Andrew (English Martyrs RCS; Hartlepool SFC), b Hartlepool, Co Durham 18 Dec 1979. Son of M.P.Gough (Durham 1974-77). 6'5''. RHB, OB. Durham 1998-2003. F-c Tours (Eng A): NZ 1999-00; B 1999-00. HS 123 Du v CU (Cambridge) 1998. CC HS 103 Du v Essex (Colchester) 2002. BB 5-56 Du v Middx (Chester-le-St) 2001. F-c career: 67 matches; 2952 runs @ 25.44, 2 hundreds; 30 wickets @ 45.00; 57 ct. Reserve List 2006-08. Appointed 2009. Umpired 9 Tests (2016 to 2018-19) and 49 LOI (2013 to 2018-19). **ICC International Panel 2012 to date.**

GOULD, Ian James (Westgate SS, Slough), b Taplow, Bucks 19 Aug 1957. 5'8''. LHB, WK. Middlesex 1975 to 1980-81, 1996; cap 1977. Auckland 1979-80. Sussex 1981-90; cap 1981; captain 1987; benefit 1990. MCC YC. **LOI:** 18 (1982-83 to 1983); HS 42 v A (Sydney) 1982-83. F-c Tours: A 1982-83; P 1980-81 (Int); Z 1980-81 (M). HS 128 M v Worcs (Worcester) 1978. BB 3-10 Sx v Surrey (Oval) 1989. Middlesex coach 1991-2000. Reappeared in one match (v OU) 1996. F-c career: 298 matches; 8756 runs @ 26.05, 4 hundreds; 7 wickets @ 52.14; 603 dismissals (536 ct, 67 st). Appointed 2002. Umpired 74 Tests (2008-09 to 2018-19) and 135 LOI (2006 to 2018-19), including 2010-11 and 2014-15 World Cups. **ICC Elite Panel 2009 to date.**

HARTLEY, Peter John (Greenhead GS; Bradford C), b Keighley, Yorks 18 Apr 1960. 6'0''. RHB, RMF. Warwickshire 1982. Yorkshire 1985-97; cap 1987; benefit 1996. Hampshire 1998-2000; cap 1998. F-c Tours (Y): SA 1991-92; WI 1986-87; Z 1995-96. HS 127* Y v Lancs (Manchester) 1988. 50 wkts (7); most – 81 (1995). BB 9-41 (inc hat-trick, 4 wkts in 5 balls and 5 in 9; 11-68 match) v Derbys (Chesterfield) 1995. Hat-trick 1995. F-c career: 232 matches; 4321 runs @ 19.91, 2 hundreds; 683 wickets @ 30.21; 68 ct. Appointed 2003. Umpired 6 LOI (2007 to 2009). **ICC International Panel 2006-09.**

ILLINGWORTH, Richard Keith (Salts GS), b Bradford, Yorks 23 Aug 1963. 5'11''. RHB, SLA. Worcestershire 1982-2000; cap 1986; benefit 1997. Natal 1988-89. Derbyshire 2001. Wiltshire 2005. **Tests:** 9 (1991 to 1995-96); HS 28 v SA (Pt Elizabeth) 1995-96; BB 4-96 v WI (Nottingham) 1995. Took wicket of P.V.Simmons with his first ball in Tests – v WI (Nottingham) 1991. **LOI:** 25 (1991 to 1995-96); HS 14 v P (Melbourne) 1991-92; BB 3-33 v Z (Albury) 1991-92. F-c Tours: SA 1995-96; NZ 1991-92; P 1990-91 (Eng A); SL 1990-91 (Eng A); Z 1989-90 (Eng A), 1990-91 (Wo), 1993-94 (Wo), 1996-97 (Wo). HS 120* Wo v Warwks (Worcester) 1987 – as night-watchman. Scored 106 for England A v Z (Harare) 1989-90 – also as night-watchman. 50 wkts (5); most – 75 (1990). BB 7-50 Wo v OU (Oxford) 1985. F-c career: 376 matches; 7027 runs @ 22.45, 4 hundreds; 831 wickets @ 31.54; 161 ct. Appointed 2006. Umpired 41 Tests (2012-13 to 2018-19) and 59 LOI (2010 to 2018-19), including 2014-15 World Cup. **ICC Elite Panel 2013 to date.**

KETTLEBOROUGH, Richard Allan (Worksop C), b Sheffield, Yorks 15 Mar 1973. 6'0''. LHB, RM. Yorkshire 1994-97. Middlesex 1998-99. F-c Tour (Y): Z 1995-96. HS 108 Y v Essex (Leeds) 1996. BB 2-26 Y v Notts (Scarborough) 1996. F-c career: 33 matches; 1258 runs @ 25.16, 1 hundred; 3 wickets @ 81.00; 20 ct. Appointed 2006. Umpired 58 Tests (2010-11 to 2018-19) and 77 LOI (2009 to 2018-19), including 2010-11 and 2014-15 World Cups. **ICC Elite Panel 2011 to date.**

LLONG, Nigel James (Ashford North S), b Ashford, Kent 11 Feb 1969. 6'0''. LHB, OB. Kent 1990-98; cap 1993. F-c Tour (K): Z 1992-93. HS 130 K v Hants (Canterbury) 1996. BB 5-21 K v Middx (Canterbury) 1996. F-c career: 68 matches; 3024 runs @ 31.17, 6 hundreds; 35 wickets @ 35.97; 59 ct. Appointed 2002. Umpired 56 Tests (2007-08 to 2018-19) and 123 LOI (2006 to 2018-19), including 2010-11 and 2014-15 World Cups. **ICC Elite Panel 2012 to date.**

LLOYD, Graham David (Hollins County HS), b Accrington, Lancs 1 Jul 1969. Son of D.Lloyd (Lancs and England 1965-83). 5'9''. RHB, RM. Lancashire 1988-2002; cap 1992; benefit 2001. **LOI:** 6 (1996 to 1998-99); HS 22 v A (Oval) 1997. F-c Tours: A 1992-93 (Eng A); WI 1995-96 (La). 1000 runs (5); most – 1389 (1992). HS 241 La v Essex (Chelmsford) 1996. BB 1-4. F-c career: 203 matches; 11279 runs @ 38.23, 24 hundreds; 2 wickets @ 220.00; 140 ct. Reserve List 2009-13. Appointed 2014.

LLOYDS, Jeremy William (Blundell's S), b Penang, Malaya 17 Nov 1954. 6'0''. LHB, OB. Somerset 1979-84; cap 1982. Gloucestershire 1985-91; cap 1985. OFS 1983-84 to 1987-88. F-c Tour (Gl): SL 1986-87. 1000 runs (3); most – 1295 (1986). HS 132* Sm v Northants (Northampton) 1982. BB 7-88 Sm v Essex (Chelmsford) 1982. F-c career: 267 matches; 10679 runs @ 31.04, 10 hundreds; 333 wickets @ 38.86; 229 ct. Appointed 1998. Umpired 5 Tests (2003-04 to 2004-05) and 18 LOI (2000 to 2005-06). **ICC International Panel 2003-06.**

MALLENDER, Neil Alan (Beverley GS), b Kirk Sandall, Yorks 13 Aug 1961. 6'0". RHB, RFM. Northamptonshire 1980-86 and 1995-96; cap 1984. Somerset 1987-94; cap 1987; benefit 1994. Otago 1983-84 to 1992-93; captain 1990-91 to 1992-93. **Tests:** 2 (1992); HS 4 v P (Oval) 1992; BB 5-50 v P (Leeds) 1992 – on debut. F-c Tour (Nh): Z 1994-95. HS 100* Otago v CD (Palmerston N) 1991-92. UK HS 87* Sm v Sussex (Hove) 1990. 50 wkts (6); most – 56 (1983). BB 7-27 Otago v Auckland (Auckland) 1984-85. UK BB 7-41 Nh v Derbys (Northampton) 1982. F-c career: 345 matches; 4709 runs @ 17.18, 1 hundred; 937 wickets @ 26.31; 111 ct. Appointed 1999. Umpired 3 Tests (2003-04) and 22 LOI (2001 to 2003-04), including 2002-03 World Cup. **ICC Elite Panel 2004**.

MILLNS, David James (Garibaldi CS; N Notts C; Nottingham Trent U), b Clipstone, Notts 27 Feb 1965. 6'3". LHB, RF. Nottinghamshire 1988-89, 2000-01; cap 2000. Leicestershire 1990-99; cap 1991; benefit 1999. Tasmania 1994-95. Boland 1996-97. F-c Tours: A 1992-93 (Eng A); SA 1996-97 (Le). HS 121 Le v Northants (Northampton) 1997. 50 wkts (4); most – 76 (1994). BB 9-37 (12-91 match) Le v Derbys (Derby) 1991. F-c career: 171 matches; 3082 runs @ 22.01, 3 hundreds; 553 wickets @ 27.35; 76 ct. Reserve List 2007-08. Appointed 2009.

O'SHAUGHNESSY, Steven Joseph (Harper Green SS, Franworth), b Bury, Lancs 9 Sep 1961. 5'10½". RHB, RM. Lancashire 1980-87; cap 1985. Worcestershire 1988-89. Scored 100 in 35 min to equal world record for La v Leics (Manchester) 1983. 1000 runs (1): 1167 (1984). HS 159* La v Somerset (Bath) 1984. BB 4-66 La v Notts (Nottingham) 1982. F-c career: 112 matches; 3720 runs @ 24.31, 5 hundreds; 114 wickets @ 36.03; 57 ct. Reserve List 2009-10. Appointed 2011.

POLLARD, Paul Raymond (Gedling CS), b Carlton, Nottingham 24 Sep 1968. 5'11". LHB, RM. Nottinghamshire 1987-98; cap 1992. Worcestershire 1999-2001. F-c Tour (Nt): SA 1996-97. 1000 runs (3); most – 1463 (1993). HS 180 Nt v Derbys (Nottingham) 1993. BB 2-79 Nt v Glos (Bristol) 1993. F-c career: 192 matches; 9685 runs @ 31.44, 15 hundreds; 4 wkts @ 68.00; 158 ct. Reserve List 2012-17. Appointed 2018.

ROBINSON, Robert Timothy (Dunstable GS; High Pavement SFC; Sheffield U), b Sutton in Ashfield, Notts 21 Nov 1958. 6'0". RHB, RM. Nottinghamshire 1978-99; cap 1983; captain 1988-95; benefit 1992. *Wisden* 1985. **Tests:** 29 (1984-85 to 1989); HS 175 v A (Leeds) 1985. **LOI:** 26 (1984-85 to 1988); HS 83 v P (Sharjah) 1986-87. F-c Tours: A 1987-88; SA 1989-90 (Eng XI), 1996-97 (Nt); NZ 1987-88; WI 1985-86; I/SL 1984-85; P 1987-88. 1000 runs (14) inc 2000 (1): 2032 (1984). HS 220* Nt v Yorks (Nottingham) 1990. BB 1-22. F-c career: 425 matches; 27571 runs @ 42.15, 63 hundreds; 4 wickets @ 72.25; 257 ct. Appointed 2007. Umpired 15 LOI (2013 to 2018). **ICC International Panel 2012 to date.**

SAGGERS, Martin John (Springwood HS, King's Lynn; Huddersfield U), b King's Lynn, Norfolk 23 May 1972. 6'2". RHB, RMF. Durham 1996-98. Kent 1999-2009; cap 2001; benefit 2009. MCC 2004. Essex 2007 (on loan). Norfolk 1995-96. **Tests:** 3 (2003-04 to 2004); HS 1 and BB 2-29 v B (Chittagong) 2003 – on debut. F-c Tour: B 2003-04. HS 64 K v Worcs (Canterbury) 2004. 50 wkts (4); most – 83 (2002). BB 7-79 K v Durham (Chester-le-St) 2000. F-c career: 119 matches; 1165 runs @ 11.20; 415 wickets @ 25.33; 27 ct. Reserve List 2010-11. Appointed 2012.

TAYLOR, Billy Victor (Bitterne Park S, Southampton), b Southampton 11 Jan 1977. Younger brother of J.L.Taylor (Wiltshire 1998-2002). 6'3". LHB, RMF. Sussex 1999-2003. Hampshire 2004-09; cap 2006; testimonial 2010. Wiltshire 1996-98. HS 40 v Essex (Southampton) 2004. BB 6-32 v Middlesex (Southampton) 2006 (inc hat-trick). F-c career: 54 matches; 431 runs @10.26; 136 wickets @ 33.34; 6 ct. Reserve list 2011-16. Appointed 2017.

WARREN, Russell John (Kingsthorpe Upper S), b Northampton 10 Sep 1971. 6'1". RHB, OB, WK. Northamptonshire 1992-2002; cap 1995. Nottinghamshire 2003-06; cap 2004. 1000 runs (1): 1030 (2001). HS 201* Nh v Glamorgan (Northampton) 2001. F-c career: 146 matches; 7776 runs @ 36.67, 15 hundreds; 128 ct, 5 st. Reserve List: 2015-17. Appointed: 2018.

WHARF, Alexander George (Buttershaw Upper S; Thomas Danby C), b Bradford, Yorks 4 Jun 1975. 6'5". RHB, RMF. Yorkshire 1994-97. Nottinghamshire 1998-99. Glamorgan 2000-08, scoring 100* v OU (Oxford) on debut; cap 2000; benefit 2009. **LOI:** 13 (2004 to 2004-05); HS 9 v India (Lord's) 2004; BB 4-24 v Z (Harare) 2004-05. F-c Tour (Eng A): WI 2005-06. HS 128* Gm v Glos (Bristol) 2007. 50 wkts (1): 52 (2003). BB 6-59 Gm v Glos (Bristol) 2005. F-c career: 121 matches; 3570 runs @ 23.03, 6 hundreds; 293 wickets @ 37.34; 63 ct. Reserve List 2011-13. Appointed 2014. Umpired 2 LOI (2018). **ICC International Panel 2018.**

RESERVE FIRST-CLASS LIST: Tom Lungley, James D.Middlebrook, Mark Newell, Ian N.Ramage, Christopher M.Watts, Robert A.White.

Test Match and LOI statistics to 14 March 2019.

TOURING TEAMS REGISTER 2018

INDIA

Full Names	Birthdate	Birthplace	Team	Type	F-C Debut
ASHWIN, Ravichandran	17.09.86	Madras	Tamil Nadu	RHB/OB	2006-07
BUMRAH, Jasprit Jasbirsingh	06.12.93	Ahmedabad	Gujarat	RHB/RFM	2013-14
DHAWAN, Shikhar	05.12.85	Delhi	Delhi	LHB/OB	2004-05
JADEJA, Ravindrasinh Anirudsinh	06.12.88	Navagam-Khed	Saurashtra	LHB/SLA	2006-07
KARTHIK, Krishnakumar Dinesh	01.06.85	Madras	Tamil Nadu	RHB/WK	2002-03
KOHLI, Virat	05.11.88	Delhi	Delhi	RHB/RM	2006-07
KULDEEP YADAV	14.12.94	Kanpur	Uttar Pradesh	LHB/SLC	2014-15
MOHAMMED SHAMI	03.09.90	Jonagar	Bengal	RHB/RFM	2010-11
PANDYA, Hardik Himanshu	11.10.93	Choryasi	Baroda	RHB/RMF	2013-14
PANT, Rishabh Rajendra	04.10.97	Haridwar	Delhi	LHB/WK	2015-16
PUJARA, Cheteshwar Arvindbhai	25.01.88	Rajkot	Saurashtra	RHB/LB	2005-06
RAHANE, Ajinkya Madhukar	06.06.88	Ashwi Khurd	Mumbai	RHB/OB	2007-08
RAHUL, Kannur Lokesh	18.04.92	Bangalore	Karnataka	RHB/OB	2010-11
SHARMA, Ishant	02.09.88	Delhi	Delhi	RHB/RFM	2006-07
VIHARI, Gade Hanuma	13.10.93	Kakinada	Andhra	RHB/OB	2010-11
VIJAY, Murali	01.04.84	Madras	Tamil Nadu	RHB/OB	2006-07
YADAV, Umesh Tilak	25.10.87	Nagpur	Vidarbha	RHB/RFM	2008-09

INDIA A

Full Names	Birthdate	Birthplace	Team	Type	F-C Debut
AGARWAL, Mayank Anurag	16.02.91	Bangalore	Karnataka	RHB/OB	2013-14
BAWNE, Ankit Ramdas	17.12.92	Paitha	Maharashtra	RHB/OB	2007-08
EASWARAN, Abhimanyu Rangana'	06.09.95	Dehra Dun	Bengal	RHB/LB	2013-14
GURBANI, Rajneesh Naresh	28.01.93	Nagpur	Vidarbha	RHB/RM	2016-17
MOHAMMED SIRAJ	13.03.94	Hyderabad	Hyderabad	RHB/RMF	2015-16
NADEEM, Shahbaz	12.08.89	Patna	Jharkhand	RHB/SLA	2004-05
NAIR, Karun Kaladharan	06.12.91	Jodhpur	Karnataka	RHB/OB	2013-14
PANT, Rishabh Rajendra	04.10.97	Haridwar	Delhi	LHB/WK	2015-16

Full Names	Birthdate	Birthplace	Team	Type	F-C Debut
RAHANE, Ajinkya Madhukar	06.06.88	Ashwi Khurd	Mumbai	RHB/RM	2007-08
RAJPOOT, Ankit Singh	04.12.93	Kanpur	Uttar Pradesh	RHB/RM	2012-13
SAINI, Navdeep Amarjeet	23.11.92	Karnal	Delhi	RHB/RM	2013-14
SAMARTH, Ravikumar	22.01.93	Mysore	Karnataka	RHB/OB	2013-14
SHAW, Prithvi Pankaj	09.11.99	Thane	Mumbai	RHB/OB	2016-17
SHANKAR, Vijay	26.01.91	Tirunelveli	Tamil Nadu	RHB/OB	2012-13
SRIKAR BHARAT, Kona	03.10.93	Visakhapatnam	Andhra	RHB/WK	2012-13
VIHARI, Gade Hanuma	13.10.93	Kakinada	Andhra	RHB/OB	2010-11
VIJAY, Murali	01.04.84	Madras	Tamil Nadu	RHB/OB	2006-07
YADAV, Jayant	22.01.90	Delhi	Haryana	RHB/OB	2011-12

PAKISTAN

Full Names	Birthdate	Birthplace	Team	Type	F-C Debut
ASAD SHAFIQ	28.01.86	Karachi	Sui Northern	RHB/LB	2007-08
AZHAR ALI	19.02.85	Lahore	Sui Northern	RHB/LB	2001-02
BABAR AZAM	15.10.94	Lahore	Sui Northern	RHB/OB	2010-11
FAHEEM ASHRAF	16.01.94	Kasur	Habib Bank	RHB/RFM	2013-14
HARIS SOHAIL	09.01.89	Sialkot	ZT Bank	LHB/LM	2007-08
HASAN ALI	07.02.94	Punjab	Islamabad	RHB/RFM	2013-14
IMAM-UL-HAQ	12.12.95	Lahore	Habib Bank	LHB/LB	2012-13
MOHAMMAD ABBAS	10.03.90	Sialkot	Sui Northern	RHB/RMF	2008-09
MOHAMMAD AMIR	13.04.92	Gujar Khan	Sui Southern	LHB/LFM	2008-09
RAHAT ALI	12.09.88	Multan	Khan Research	RHB/LFM	2007-08
SAMI ASLAM	12.12.95	Lahore	Sui Southern	LHB/OB	2012-13
SARFRAZ AHMED	22.05.87	Karachi	PIA	RHB/WK	2005-06
SHADAB KHAN	04.10.98	Mianwali	Sui Northern	RHB/LBG	2016-17
USMAN SALAHUDDIN	02.12.90	Lahore	Lahore Whites	RHB/LB	2007-08

WEST INDIES A

Full Names	Birthdate	Birthplace	Team	Type	F-C Debut
AMBRIS, Sunil Walford	23.03.93	St Vincent	Windward Is	RHB/WK	2013-14
BLACKWOOD, Jermaine	20.11.91	St Elizabeth	Jamaica	RHB/OB	2011-12
BROOKS, Sharmarh Shaqad Joshua	01.10.88	St Michael	Barbados	RHB/LB	2006-07
CAMPBELL, John Dillon	21.08.31	St James	Jamaica	LHB/OB	2013-14
CORNWALL, Rakheem Rashawn Shane	01.02.93	Antigua	Leeward Is	RHB/OB	2014-15
HEMRAJ, Chanderpaul	03.09.93	Guyana	Guyana	LHB	2011-12
HOLDER, Chemar Keron	03.03.98	Barbados	Barbados	RHB/RFM	2017-18
LEWIS, Sherman Hakim	21.10.95	St Andrew	Windward Is	RHB/RMF	2016-17
REIFER, Raymon Anton	11.05.91	St Lucy	Guyana	LHB/LM	2010-11
SHEPHERD, Romario	26.11.94	Guyana	Guyana	RHB/RFM	2016-17
SINGH, Vishaul Anthony	12.01.89	Georgetown	Guyana	LHB/SLA	2008-09
SMITH, Odean Fabian	01.11.96	St Elizabeth	Jamaica	RHB/RM	2017-18
THOMAS, Devon Cuthbert	12.11.89	Bethesda	Leeward Is	RHB/WK	2007-08
THOMAS, Oshane Romaine	18.02.97	Jamaica	Jamaica	LHB/RMF	2016-17
WARRICAN, Jomel Andrel	20.05.92	Richmond Hill	Barbados	RHB/SLA	2011-12

THE 2018 FIRST-CLASS SEASON STATISTICAL HIGHLIGHTS

FIRST TO INDIVIDUAL TARGETS

1000 RUNS	R.J.Burns	Surrey	29 August
2000 RUNS	–	Most – 1402 R.J.Burns (England Lions, Surrey)	
50 WICKETS	O.E.Robinson	Sussex	30 August
100 WICKETS	–	Most – 81 O.E.Robinson (Sussex)	

TEAM HIGHLIGHTS († *Team record*)
HIGHEST INNINGS TOTALS

609-6d	India A v West Indies A	Beckenham
592	Surrey v Nottinghamshire	Nottingham
582-9d	Kent v Gloucestershire	Bristol

HIGHEST FOURTH INNINGS TOTAL

445	Warwickshire (set 519) v Kent	Tunbridge Wells

LOWEST INNINGS TOTALS

50	Yorkshire v Essex	Chelmsford
56	Middlesex v Kent	Canterbury
61†	Durham v Leicestershire (*1st inns*)	Leicester
62	Gloucestershire v Northamptonshire	Northampton
64	Kent v Gloucestershire	Canterbury
66	Durham v Leicestershire (*2nd inns*)	Leicester
67	Surrey v Essex	The Oval
71	Northamptonshire v Middlesex	Lord's
73	Lancashire v Nottinghamshire	Manchester
77	Somerset v Lancashire	Taunton
78	Glamorgan v Kent	Canterbury
85	Glamorgan v Sussex (*1st inns*)	Hove
88	Glamorgan v Sussex (*2nd inns*)	Hove

HIGHEST MATCH AGGREGATE

1403-31	Notts (499-9d & 249-4d) v Worcs (287 & 368-8)	Nottingham

TIED MATCH

Lancashire (99 & 170) tied with Somerset (192 & 77)	Taunton

LARGE MARGINS OF VICTORY

342 runs	Kent (241 & 281) beat Middlesex (56 & 124)	Canterbury
328 runs	Glos (202 & 402-4d) beat Leics (111 & 165)	Bristol
301 runs	Nottinghamshire (380 & 266) beat Essex (206 & 139)	Chelmsford
Inns & 194 runs	Leicestershire (321) beat Durham (61 & 66)	Leicester
Inns & 186 runs	Worcestershire (572-7d) beat Yorkshire (216 & 170)	Scarborough
Inns & 183 runs	Surrey (592) beat Nottinghamshire (210 & 199)	Nottingham
Inns & 172 runs	Kent (436) beat Glamorgan (186 & 78)	Canterbury
Inns & 159 runs	England (396-7d) beat India (107 & 130) (*2nd Test*)	Lord's
Inns & 154 runs	Sussex (327) beat Glamorgan (85 & 88)	Hove

NARROW MARGINS OF VICTORY

3 runs	Leics (191 & 237) beat Glamorgan (178 & 247)	Leicester
6 runs	Surrey (211 & 306) beat Lancashire (247 & 264)	The Oval
1 wkt	Middlesex (233 & 383-9) beat Leicestershire (427 & 186)	Leicester
1 wkt	Essex (477-8d & 134-9) beat Surrey (67 & 541)	The Oval
1 wkt	Derbyshire (222 & 234-9) beat Northants (255 & 199)	Northampton

VICTORY AFTER FOLLOWING ON

Durham (184 & 403) beat Leicestershire (440 & 101) by 46 runs   Chester-le-Street
Middlesex (187 & 374) beat Northamptonshire (346 & 184) by 31 runs   Northampton

MOST EXTRAS IN AN INNINGS

	B	LB	W	NB		
81	34	23	2	22	Durham (376) v Derbyshire	Chester-le-Street

Under ECB regulations, Test matches excluded, two penalty extras were scored for each no-ball.

BATTING HIGHLIGHTS
DOUBLE HUNDREDS

M.M.Ali	219	Worcestershire v Yorkshire	Scarborough
I.R.Bell	204	Warwickshire v Glamorgan	Colwyn Bay
C.D.J.Dent	214*	Gloucestershire v Leicestershire	Bristol
M.A.Naylor	202	Oxford University v Cambridge U	Oxford
D.J.Vilas	235*	Lancashire v Somerset	Manchester
J.M.Vince	201*	Hampshire v Somerset	Taunton

HUNDRED IN EACH INNINGS OF A MATCH

I.R.Bell	106*	115*	Warwickshire v Glamorgan	Birmingham
D.K.H.Mitchell	118	163	Worcestershire v Lancashire	Worester

FASTEST HUNDRED AGAINST GENUINE BOWLING

G.Stewart   (103) 71 balls Kent v Middlesex   Canterbury

MOST RUNS FROM BOUNDARIES IN AN INNINGS

Runs	6s	4s			
132	4	27	D.J.Vilas	Lancashire v Somerset	Manchester
132	4	27	M.M.Ali	Worcestershire v Yorkshire	Scarborough

HUNDRED ON FIRST-CLASS DEBUT IN BRITAIN

S.W.Ambris	128	West Indies A v India A	Beckenham
R.Samarth	137	India A v West Indies A	Beckenham
P.P.Shaw	188	India A v West Indies A	Beckenham

CARRYING BAT THROUGH COMPLETED INNINGS

B.A.Godleman	105*	Derbyshire v Middlesex	Lord's
J.R.Murphy	39*	Glamorgan (94) v Kent	Cardiff

LONG INNINGS (Qualification 600 mins and/or 400 balls)

Mins	Balls			
532	408	R.J.Burns (193)	Surrey v Worcestershire	The Oval
514	437	J.M.Vince (201*)	Hampshire v Somerset	Taunton

BATTING FOR AN HOUR OR MORE WITHOUT SCORING

I.A.A.Thomas   (1*)   60mins   Kent v Middlesex   Canterbury

NOTABLE PARTNERSHIPS

Qualifications: 1st-4th wkts: 250 runs; 5th-6th: 225; 7th: 200; 8th: 175; 9th: 150; 10th: 100.

Second Wicket

294	D.K.H.Mitchell/M.M.Ali	Worcestershire v Yorkshire	Scarborough
260	D.P.Sibley/I.R.Bell	Warwickshire v Kent	Tunbridge Wells

Third Wicket

259	A.N.Cook/J.E.Root	England v India (*5th Test*)	The Oval

Fourth Wicket

289	U.T.Khawaja/K.S.Carlson	Glamorgan v Derbyshire	Swansea

Fifth Wicket

294	R.S.Bopara/R.N.ten Doeschate	Essex v Somerset	Chelmsford
267	D.A.Escott/M.A.Naylor	Oxford U v Cambridge U	Oxford

Sixth Wicket

278†	M.J.Richardson/S.W.Poynter	Durham v Derbyshire	Derby

Ninth Wicket

171	G.S.Ballance/J.A.Brooks	Yorkshire v Worcestershire	Worcester

Tenth Wicket

136†	A.G.Milton/S.J.Magoffin	Worcestershire v Somerset	Worcester
100	G.Stewart/I.A.A.Thomas	Kent v Durham	Canterbury

Thomas made 1* in 63 mins, while Stewart completed a century in 71 balls.

BOWLING HIGHLIGHTS

EIGHT OR MORE WICKETS IN AN INNINGS

B.A.Hutton	8-57	Northamptonshire v Gloucestershire	Northampton
M.J.Leach	8-85	Somerset v Essex	Taunton
C.Rushworth	8-51	Durham v Sussex	Chester-le-Street
O.P.Stone	8-80	Warwickshire v Sussex	Birmingham

TEN OR MORE WICKETS IN A MATCH

K.J.Abbott	11- 71	Hampshire v Somerset	Southampton
E.G.Barnard	11- 89	Worcestershire v Somerset	Taunton
B.O.Coad	10-130	Yorkshire v Nottinghamshire	Leeds
M.J.J.Critchley	10-194	Derbyshire v Northamptonshire	Chesterfield
S.M.Curran	10-101	Surrey v Yorkshire	The Oval
G.T.Griffiths	10- 83	Leicestershire v Durham	Chester-le-Street
M.J.Henry (3)	12- 73	Kent v Durham	Chester-le-Street
	10-122	Kent v Sussex	Canterbury
	11-114	Kent v Northamptonshire	Canterbury
M.J.Leach (2)	10-112	Somerset v Essex	Taunton
	12-112	Somerset v Lancashire	Taunton
K.A.Maharaj	11-102	Lancashire v Somerset	Taunton
Mohammad Abbas	10- 52	Leicestershire v Durham	Leicester
D.Olivier	10-125	Derbyshire v Durham	Chester-le-Street
A.P.Palladino	10- 81	Derbyshire v Glamorgan	Derby
J.S.Patel (2)	10-170	Warwickshire v Derbyshire	Birmingham
	10-106	Warwickshire v Glamorgan	Colwyn Bay
J.A.Porter	11- 98	Essex v Worcestershire	Chelmsford
O.E.Robinson	10- 67	Sussex v Leicestershire	Hove
C.Rushworth	12-100	Durham v Sussex	Chester-le-Street
Shadab Khan	10-157	Pakistanis v Northamptonshire	Northampton
R.N.Sidebottom	10- 96	Warwickshire v Northamptonshire	Northampton
O.P.Stone	11- 96	Warwickshire v Durham	Birmingham

FIVE WICKETS IN AN INNINGS ON FIRST-CLASS DEBUT

B.W.M.Mike 5-37 Leicestershire v Sussex Hove

HAT-TRICK

K.J.Abbott	Hampshire v Worcestershire	Worcester
T.B.Abell	Somerset v Nottinghamshire	Nottingham
J.Clark	Lancashire v Yorkshire	Manchester

Dismissed J.E.Root, K.S.Williamson and J.M.Bairstow – first occasion that three batsmen, each with more than 3000 Test runs, have formed part of a hat-trick.

C.Overton	Somerset v Nottinghamshire	Nottingham

All three wickets were caught by M.E.Trescothick. It was also the first instance since 1996 of two team-mates taking hat-tricks in the same County Championship match.

175 RUNS CONCEDED IN AN INNINGS

R.A.Jadeja 47-3-179-3 India v England (*5th Test*) The Oval

MOST OVERS BOWLED IN AN INNINGS

S.R.Harmer 50-10-122-1 Essex v Surrey The Oval

WICKET-KEEPING HIGHLIGHTS

SIX WICKET-KEEPING DISMISSALS IN AN INNINGS

T.R.Ambrose	6ct	Warwickshire v Sussex	Birmingham
B.C.Brown	6ct	Sussex v Gloucestershire	Cheltenham
D.J.Vilas	5ct, 1st	Lancashire v Yorkshire	Manchester

NINE OR MORE WICKET-KEEPING DISMISSALS IN A MATCH

T.R.Ambrose	10ct	Warwickshire v Durham	Chester-le-Street
B.T.Foakes	9ct	Surrey v Nottinghamshire	The Oval

FIELDING HIGHLIGHTS

FOUR OR MORE CATCHES IN THE FIELD IN AN INNINGS

K.Noema-Barnett	4ct	Gloucestershire v Northamptonshire	Northampton
K.L.Rahul	4ct	India v England (*3rd Test*)	Nottingham
O.P.Rayner	4ct	Middlesex v Derbyshire	Derby

SIX OR MORE CATCHES IN THE FIELD IN A MATCH

K.L.Rahul	7ct	India v England (*3rd Test*)	Nottingham
D.K.H.Mitchell	6ct	Worcestershire v Hampshire	Worcester

SPECSAVERS COUNTY CHAMPIONSHIP 2018 FINAL TABLES

DIVISION 1

	P	W	L	T	D	Bonus Points Bat	Bonus Points Bowl	Deduct Points	Total Points
1 **SURREY** (3)	14	10	1	–	3	41	38		254
2 Somerset (6)	14	7	2	1	4	33	35	–	208
3 Essex (1)	14	7	4	–	3†	25	35	–	187
4 Yorkshire (4)	14	5	5	–	4†	25	33	–	158
5 Hampshire (5)	14	4	5	–	5	16	39	–	144
6 Nottinghamshire (-)	14	4	8	–	2	21	38	–	133
7 Lancashire (2)	14	3	7	1	3	23	40	1	133
8 Worcestershire (3)	14	2	10	–	2	23	39	–	104

DIVISION 2

	P	W	L	T	D	Bonus Points Bat	Bonus Points Bowl	Deduct Points	Total Points
1 Warwickshire (-)	14	9	2	–	3	41	42	–	242
2 Kent (5)	14	10	3	–	1	16	40	–	221
3 Sussex (4)	14	6	4	–	4	32	38	–	186
4 Middlesex (-)	14	7	4	–	3	14	38	–	179
5 Gloucestershire (6)	14	5	4	–	5	15	37	–	157
6 Leicestershire (10)	14	5	7	–	2	22	40	3	149
7 Derbyshire (8)	14	4	7	–	3	30	38	–	147
8 Durham (9)	14	4	7	–	3†	16	35	–	130
9 Northamptonshire (3)	14	4	8	–	2†	14	38	–	126
10 Glamorgan (7)	14	2	10	–	2	13	38	1	92

† Match abandoned without a ball being bowled.
Lancashire and Glamorgan deducted 1 point each for slow over rate.
Leicestershire deducted 3 points for slow over rates.

SCORING OF CHAMPIONSHIP POINTS 2018

(a) For a win, 16 points, plus any points scored in the first innings.

(b) In a tie, each side to score eight points, plus any points scored in the first innings.

(c) In a drawn match, each side to score five points, plus any points scored in the first innings (see also paragraph (e) below).

(d) If the scores are equal in a drawn match, the side batting in the fourth innings to score eight points plus any points scored in the first innings, and the opposing side to score three points plus any points scored in the first innings.

(e) First Innings Points (awarded only for performances **in the first 110 overs** of each first innings and retained whatever the result of the match).

    (i) A maximum of five batting points to be available as under:
        200 to 249 runs – 1 point; 250 to 299 runs – 2 points; 300 to 349 runs – 3 points; 350 to 399 runs – 4 points; 400 runs or over – 5 points.

    (ii) A maximum of three bowling points to be available as under:
        3 to 5 wickets taken – 1 point; 6 to 8 wickets taken – 2 points; 9 to 10 wickets taken – 3 points.

(f) If a match is abandoned without a ball being bowled, each side to score five points.

(g) The side which has the highest aggregate of points gained at the end of the season shall be the Champion County of their respective Division. Should any sides in the Championship table be equal on points, the following tie-breakers will be applied in the order stated: most wins, fewest losses, team achieving most points in contests between teams level on points, most wickets taken, most runs scored. At the end of the season, the top two teams from the Second Division will be promoted and the bottom two teams from the First Division will be relegated.

COUNTY CHAMPIONS

The English County Championship was not officially constituted until December 1889. Prior to that date there was no generally accepted method of awarding the title; although the 'least matches lost' method existed, it was not consistently applied. Rules governing playing qualifications were agreed in 1873 and the first unofficial points system 15 years later.

Research has produced a list of champions dating back to 1826, but at least seven different versions exist for the period from 1864 to 1889 (see *The Wisden Book of Cricket Records*). Only from 1890 can any authorised list of county champions commence.

That first official Championship was contested between eight counties: Gloucestershire, Kent, Lancashire, Middlesex, Nottinghamshire, Surrey, Sussex and Yorkshire. The remaining counties were admitted in the following seasons: 1891 – Somerset, 1895 – Derbyshire, Essex, Hampshire, Leicestershire and Warwickshire, 1899 – Worcestershire, 1905 – Northamptonshire, 1921 – Glamorgan, and 1992 – Durham.

The Championship pennant was introduced by the 1951 champions, Warwickshire, and the Lord's Taverners' Trophy was first presented in 1973. The first sponsors, Schweppes (1977-83), were succeeded by Britannic Assurance (1984-98), PPP Healthcare (1999-2000), CricInfo (2001), Frizzell (2002-05), Liverpool Victoria (2006-15) and Specsavers (from 2016). Based on their previous season's positions, the 18 counties were separated into two divisions in 2000. From 2000 to 2005 the bottom three Division 1 teams were relegated and the top three Division 2 sides promoted. This was reduced to two teams from the end of the 2006 season.

1890	Surrey	1935	Yorkshire	1979	Essex
1891	Surrey	1936	Derbyshire	1980	Middlesex
1892	Surrey	1937	Yorkshire	1981	Nottinghamshire
1893	Yorkshire	1938	Yorkshire	1982	Middlesex
1894	Surrey	1939	Yorkshire	1983	Essex
1895	Surrey	1946	Yorkshire	1984	Essex
1896	Yorkshire	1947	Middlesex	1985	Middlesex
1897	Lancashire	1948	Glamorgan	1986	Essex
1898	Yorkshire	1949 {	Middlesex	1987	Nottinghamshire
1899	Surrey	{	Yorkshire	1988	Worcestershire
1900	Yorkshire	1950 {	Lancashire	1989	Worcestershire
1901	Yorkshire	{	Surrey	1990	Middlesex
1902	Yorkshire	1951	Warwickshire	1991	Essex
1903	Middlesex	1952	Surrey	1992	Essex
1904	Lancashire	1953	Surrey	1993	Middlesex
1905	Yorkshire	1954	Surrey	1994	Warwickshire
1906	Kent	1955	Surrey	1995	Warwickshire
1907	Nottinghamshire	1956	Surrey	1996	Leicestershire
1908	Yorkshire	1957	Surrey	1997	Glamorgan
1909	Kent	1958	Surrey	1998	Leicestershire
1910	Kent	1959	Yorkshire	1999	Surrey
1911	Warwickshire	1960	Yorkshire	2000	Surrey
1912	Yorkshire	1961	Hampshire	2001	Yorkshire
1913	Kent	1962	Yorkshire	2002	Surrey
1914	Surrey	1963	Yorkshire	2003	Sussex
1919	Yorkshire	1964	Worcestershire	2004	Warwickshire
1920	Middlesex	1965	Worcestershire	2005	Nottinghamshire
1921	Middlesex	1966	Yorkshire	2006	Sussex
1922	Yorkshire	1967	Yorkshire	2007	Sussex
1923	Yorkshire	1968	Yorkshire	2008	Durham
1924	Yorkshire	1969	Glamorgan	2009	Durham
1925	Yorkshire	1970	Kent	2010	Nottinghamshire
1926	Lancashire	1971	Surrey	2011	Lancashire
1927	Lancashire	1972	Warwickshire	2012	Warwickshire
1928	Lancashire	1973	Hampshire	2013	Durham
1929	Nottinghamshire	1974	Worcestershire	2014	Yorkshire
1930	Lancashire	1975	Leicestershire	2015	Yorkshire
1931	Yorkshire	1976	Middlesex	2016	Middlesex
1932	Yorkshire	1977 {	Kent	2017	Essex
1933	Yorkshire	{	Middlesex	2018	Surrey
1934	Lancashire	1978	Kent		

COUNTY CHAMPIONSHIP RESULTS 2018

DIVISION 1

	ESSEX	HANTS	LANCS	NOTTS	SOM'T	SURREY	WORCS	YORKS
ESSEX		C'ford	C'ford	C'ford	C'ford*	C'ford	C'ford	C'ford
		E I/52	E 31	Nt 301	Drawn	Sy 10w	E I/129	Y 91
HANTS	So'ton		So'ton	So'ton	So'ton	So'ton	So'ton	So'ton*
	Drawn		La 8w	H 270	H 6w	Sy I/58	H 196	Drawn
LANCS	Man	Man		Man	Man	Man	S'port	Man
	E 5w	Drawn		Nt 6w	Drawn	Drawn	La 4w	Y 118
NOTTS	N'ham	N'ham	N'ham		N'ham	N'ham	N'ham*	N'ham
	E 8w	Nt 203	La I/67		Sm I/146		Drawn	
SOM'T	Taunton	Taunton	Taunton	Taunton		Taunton	Taunton	Taunton
	Sm 45	Drawn	Tied	Sm 6w		Drawn	Sm 83	Sm 118
SURREY	Oval	Oval	Oval*	Oval	G'ford		Oval	Oval
	E 1w	Sy 139	Sy 6	Sy I/125	Sy I/69		Drawn	Sy I/17
WORCS	Worcs	Worcs	Worcs	Worcs	Worcs	Worcs		Worcs
	E 32	H 114	Wo 202	Nt I/41	Sm 141	Sy 3w		Y 7w
YORKS	Leeds	Leeds	Leeds	Leeds	Leeds	Scar	Scar	
	Aband	Drawn	Y 95	Y 164	Sm 224	Sy 7w	Wo I/186	

DIVISION 2

	DERBYS	DURHAM	GLAM	GLOS	KENT	LEICS	MIDDX	N'HANTS	SUSSEX	WARWKS
DERBYS		Derby	Derby	Derby	Derby	Derby*	Derby	Derby		C'field
		Drawn	De 169	Gs 2w	K 6w	Le 6w	De 101	De 39		
DURHAM	C-le-St				C-le-St	C-le-St	C-le-St	C-le-St	C-le-St	C-le-St*
	Du 95				K 9w	Du 46	M 57	Nh 7w	Du 186	Wa 86
GLAM	Swan	Cardiff		Cardiff	Cardiff	Cardiff		Cardiff		Col B
	Drawn	Du I/30		Gs 9w	K 6w	Gm 132		Nh 233		Wa I/35
GLOS		Chelt	Bristol		Bristol	Bristol	Bristol	Bristol	Chelt	
		Gs 41	Gm 6w		Drawn	Gs 328	Drawn	Drawn	Sx 28	
KENT		Cant	Cant	Cant		Cant	Cant	Cant	Cant	Tun W
		K I/172	Drawn	Gs 5w		Le 10w	K 342	K 102	K 58	K 73
LEICS	Leics	Leics	Leics		Leics		Leics		Leics	Leics
	Drawn	Le I/194	Le 3		K 8w		M 1w		Drawn	Wa I/104
MIDDX	Lord's		Lord's	Lord's	Lord's			Lord's	Lord's	Lord's
	M 117		Drawn	Drawn	K 3w			M 160	M 55	M 18
N'HANTS	No'ton	No'ton		No'ton*	No'ton	No'ton	No'ton		No'ton	No'ton
	De 1w	Aband		Nh 10w	K 3w	Le 6w	M 31		Nh 6w	Wa I/48
SUSSEX	Hove	Arundel	Hove*	Hove		Hove	Hove			Hove
	Sx 243	Sx I/64	Sx I/154	Drawn		Sx 274	Sx 3w			Drawn
WARWKS	Birm	Birm	Birm	Birm	Birm			Birm	Birm	
	Wa 8w	Drawn	Wa 4w	Wa I/47	Wa I/34			Wa 6w	Drawn	

* = Floodlit match

COUNTY CHAMPIONSHIP FIXTURES 2019

DIVISION 1

	ESSEX	HANTS	KENT	NOTTS	SOM'T	SURREY	WARWKS	YORKS
ESSEX		C'ford	C'ford	C'ford	C'ford	C'ford	C'ford	C'ford
HANTS	So'ton		So'ton	Newport	So'ton	So'ton	So'ton	So'ton
KENT	Cant	Cant		Tun W	Cant	Beck	Cant	Cant
NOTTS	N'ham	Mansf'd	N'ham		N'ham	N'ham	N'ham	N'ham
SOM'T	Taunton	Taunton	Taunton	Taunton		Taunton	Taunton	Taunton
SURREY	Oval	Oval	Oval	Oval	G'ford		Oval	G'ford
WARWKS	Worcs	Birm	Birm	Birm	Birm	Birm		Birm
YORKS	Leeds	Leeds	Leeds	Scar	Leeds	Scar	York	

DIVISION 2

	DERBYS	DURHAM	GLAM	GLOS	LANCS	LEICS	MIDDX	N'HANTS	SUSSEX	WORCS
DERBYS		Derby	Derby	Derby	Derby		Derby	C'field	Derby	
DURHAM	C-le-St		C-le-St	C-le-St		C-le-St		C-le-St	C-le-St	C-le-St
GLAM	Swan			Newport	Col B	Cardiff	Cardiff	Cardiff		Cardiff
GLOS	Bristol		Bristol			Chelt	Chelt		Bristol	Bristol
LANCS	Man	Sedburgh				L'pool	Man	Man	Man	Man
LEICS	Leics	Leics		Leics	Leics		Leics	Leics		Leics
MIDDX	Lord's	Lord's	Radlett	N'wood	Lord's	Lord's			Lord's	
N'HANTS		No'ton	No'ton		No'ton	No'ton	No'ton		No'ton	No'ton
SUSSEX		Hove	Hove	Arundel		Hove	Hove	Hove		Hove
WORCS	Worcs	Worcs	Worcs	Worcs	Worcs		Worcs		Worcs	

ROYAL LONDON ONE-DAY CUP 2018

This latest format of limited-overs competition was launched in 2014, and is now the only List-A tournament played in the UK. The top team from each group went through to the semi-finals, with a home draw; the second team from each group (drawn at home) played off against the third team from the other division to qualify for the semi-finals. The winner is decided in the final at Lord's.

NORTH GROUP	P	W	L	T	NR	Pts	Net RR
1 Worcestershire (1)	8	6	2	–	–	12	+0.26
2 Nottinghamshire (3)	8	5	2	–	1	11	+0.67
3 Yorkshire (2)	8	5	2	–	1	11	+0.51
4 Warwickshire (9)	8	4	2	–	2	10	+0.44
5 Derbyshire (7)	8	4	4	–	–	8	–0.55
6 Lancashire (4)	8	3	4	–	1	7	+0.96
7 Northamptonshire (8)	8	2	5	–	1	5	–0.33
8 Leicestershire (6)	8	2	6	–	–	4	–0.70
9 Durham (5)	8	2	6	–	–	4	–1.08

SOUTH GROUP	P	W	L	T	NR	Pts	Net RR
1 Hampshire (6)	8	5	2	–	1	11	+0.32
2 Essex (1)	8	5	3	–	–	10	+0.79
3 Kent (9)	8	5	3	–	–	10	+0.01
4 Somerset (2)	8	4	3	–	1	9	+0.54
5 Surrey (3)	8	4	3	–	1	9	–0.84
6 Middlesex (8)	8	4	4	–	–	8	+0.08
7 Gloucestershire (7)	8	2	3	–	3	7	–0.25
8 Sussex (5)	8	2	4	–	2	6	+0.07
9 Glamorgan (4)	8	1	7	–	–	2	–0.78

Win = 2 points. Tie (T)/No Result (NR) = 1 point. 2017 positions in brackets.

Positions of counties finishing equal on points are decided by most wins or, if equal, the team with the higher net run rate (ie deducting from the average runs per over scored by that team in matches where a result was achieved, the average runs per over scored against that team); if still equal, the team that achieved the most points in the matches played between them. In the event the teams still cannot be separated, the winner will be decided by drawing lots.

Statistical Highlights in 2018

Highest total	409-7	Nottinghamshire v Leics	Leicester
Biggest victory (runs)	220	Kent (384-8) beat Surrey (164)	Beckenham
Most runs	696 (ave 87.00)	H.G.Kuhn (Kent)	
Highest innings	192	C.J.Ferguson	Worcestershire v Leics	Worcester
Most sixes inns	8	J.C.Hildreth	Somerset v Glamorgan	Taunton
Highest partnership	239	J.M.Clarke/C.J.Ferguson	Worcs v Northants	Worcester
Most wickets	18 (ave 18.22)	M.W.Parkinson (Lancashire)	
Best bowling	6-25	D.I.Stevens	Kent v Surrey	Beckenham
Most economical	10-1-23-3	D.R.Briggs	Sussex v Kent	Hove
	10-3-23-2	P.D.Trego	Somerset v Surrey	The Oval
Most expensive	9-0-96-1	G.J.Batty	Surrey v Kent	Beckenham
	10-0-96-2	B.W.Sanderson	Northamptonshire v Worcs	Worcester
Most w/k dismissals	18	O.B.Cox (Worcestershire)	
Most w/k dismissals (inns)	5	T.R.Ambrose	Warwickshire v Yorkshire	Leeds
Most catches	11	T.Kohler-Cadmore (Yorkshire)	
Most catches (inns)	4	M.T.C.Waller	Somerset v Glamorgan	Taunton

2018 ROYAL LONDON ONE-DAY CUP FINAL
HAMPSHIRE v KENT

At Lord's, London, on 30 June.
Result: **HAMPSHIRE** won by 61 runs.
Toss: Kent. Award: R.R.Rossouw.

HAMPSHIRE			Runs	Balls	4/6	Fall
T.P.Alsop	st Billings b Qayyum		72	75	11	1-136
R.R.Rossouw	c Blake b Denly		125	114	9/3	3-270
* J.M.Vince	c Denly b Qayyum		23	24	3	2-193
S.A.Northeast	not out		75	60	6/2	
L.A.Dawson	c Blake b Denly		8	7	–	4-287
† L.D.McManus	c Dickson b Denly		6	11	1	5-297
J.J.Weatherley	lbw b Denly		0	2	–	6-297
G.K.Berg	b Haggett		9	8	–/1	7-323
D.W.Steyn	not out		1	1	–	
C.P.Wood						
M.S.Crane						
Extras	(LB 2, NB 4, W 5)		11			
Total	(7 wkts; 50 overs)		**330**			

KENT			Runs	Balls	4/6	Fall
D.J.Bell-Drummond	b Wood		86	89	11	4-179
H.G.Kuhn	run out		32	39	4/1	1- 55
J.L.Denly	c Vince b Berg		12	23	1	2- 83
S.R.Dickson	c Rossouw b Crane		30	41	1/1	3-158
*†S.W.Billings	c Steyn b Berg		75	60	8/1	10-269
A.J.Blake	run out		9	9	–/1	5-190
D.I.Stevens	c Weatherley b Dawson		12	9	–/1	6-217
M.J.Henry	c Alsop b Steyn		0	2	–	7-218
C.J.Haggett	run out		1	3	–	8-241
H.W.Podmore	run out		1	1	–	9-257
Imran Qayyum	not out		3	8	–	
Extras	(B 1, LB 4, NB 2, W 1)		8			
Total	(47.1 overs)		**269**			

KENT	O	M	R	W	HAMPSHIRE	O	M	R	W
Podmore	9	0	54	0	Wood	9	0	43	1
Henry	9	0	64	0	Steyn	9	1	56	1
Haggett	3	0	34	1	Berg	9.1	1	43	2
Stevens	10	0	59	0	Dawson	10	1	48	1
Denly	10	1	57	4	Crane	7	0	53	1
Imran Qayyum	9	0	60	2	Vince	3	0	21	0

Umpires: N.G.B.Cook and D.J.Millns

SEMI-FINALS

At New Road, Worcester, on 17 June. Toss: Worcestershire. **KENT** won by two wickets.
Worcestershire 306-6 (50; O.B.Cox 122*, B.L.D'Oliveira 78, E.G.Barnard 50*). Kent 307-8
(49.4; H.G.Kuhn 127, A.P.Rouse 70, A.J.Blake 61, P.R.Brown 3-53). Award: H.G.Kuhn.
   At The Rose Bowl, Southampton, on 18 June. Toss: Yorkshire. **HAMPSHIRE** won by
107 runs. Hampshire 348-9 (50; J.M.Vince 171, S.A.Northeast 58). Yorkshire 241 (43.4;
J.A.Tattersall 89, L.A.Dawson 4-47, C.P.Wood 3-46). Award: J.M.Vince.

PRINCIPAL LIST A RECORDS 1963-2018

These records cover all the major limited-overs tournaments played by the counties since the inauguration of the Gillette Cup in 1963.

Highest Totals		496-4	Surrey v Glos	The Oval	2007
		445-8	Notts v Northants	Nottingham	2016
Highest Total Batting Second		429	Glamorgan v Surrey	The Oval	2002
Lowest Totals		23	Middlesex v Yorks	Leeds	1974
		36	Leics v Sussex	Leicester	1973
Largest Victory (Runs)		346	Somerset beat Devon	Torquay	1990
		304	Sussex beat Ireland	Belfast	1996
Highest Scores	268	A.D.Brown	Surrey v Glamorgan	The Oval	2002
	206	A.I.Kallicharran	Warwicks v Oxfords	Birmingham	1984
	203	A.D.Brown	Surrey v Hampshire	Guildford	1997
	201*	R.S.Bopara	Essex v Leics	Leicester	2008
	201	V.J.Wells	Leics v Berkshire	Leicester	1996
Fastest Hundred	36 balls	G.D.Rose	Somerset v Devon	Torquay	1990
	43 balls	R.R.Watson	Scotland v Somerset	Edinburgh	2003
	44 balls	M.A.Ealham	Kent v Derbyshire	Maidstone	1995
	44 balls	T.C.Smith	Lancashire v Worcs	Worcester	2012
	44 balls	D.I.Stevens	Kent v Sussex	Canterbury	2013
Most Sixes (Inns)	15	R.N.ten Doeschate	Essex v Scotland	Chelmsford	2013

Highest Partnership for each Wicket

1st	342	M.J.Lumb/M.H.Wessels	Notts v Northants	Nottingham	2016
2nd	302	M.E.Trescothick/C.Kieswetter	Somerset v Glos	Taunton	2008
3rd	309*	T.S.Curtis/T.M.Moody	Worcs v Surrey	The Oval	1994
4th	234*	D.Lloyd/C.H.Lloyd	Lancashire v Glos	Manchester	1978
5th	221*	R.R.Sarwan/M.A.Hardinges	Glos v Lancashire	Manchester	2005
6th	226	N.J.Llong/M.V.Fleming	Kent v Cheshire	Bowdon	1999
7th	170	D.R.Brown/A.F.Giles	Warwicks v Essex	Birmingham	2003
8th	174	R.W.T.Key/J.C.Tredwell	Kent v Surrey	The Oval	2007
9th	155	C.M.W.Read/A.J.Harris	Notts v Durham	Nottingham	1984
10th	82	G.Chapple/P.J.Martin	Lancashire v Worcs	Manchester	1996
Best Bowling	8-21	M.A.Holding	Derbyshire v Sussex	Hove	1988
	8-26	K.D.Boyce	Essex v Lancashire	Manchester	1971
	8-31	D.L.Underwood	Kent v Scotland	Edinburgh	1987
	8-66	S.R.G.Francis	Somerset v Derbys	Derby	2004
Four Wkts in Four Balls		A.Ward	Derbyshire v Sussex	Derby	1970
		S.M.Pollock	Warwickshire v Leics	Birmingham	1996
		V.C.Drakes	Notts v Derbyshire	Nottingham	1999
		D.A.Payne	Gloucestershire v Essex	Chelmsford	2010
		G.R.Napier	Essex v Surrey	Chelmsford	2013

Most Economical Analyses

8-8-0-0	B.A.Langford	Somerset v Essex	Yeovil	1969
8-7-1-1	D.R.Doshi	Notts v Northants	Northampton	1977
12-9-3-1	J.Simmons	Lancashire v Suffolk	Bury St Eds	1985
8-6-2-3	F.J.Titmus	Middlesex v Northants	Northampton	1972

Most Expensive Analyses

9-0-108-3	S.D.Thomas	Glamorgan v Surrey	The Oval	2002
10-0-107-0	J.W.Dernbach	Surrey v Essex	The Oval	2008
11-0-103-0	G.Welch	Warwicks v Lancs	Birmingham	1995
10-0-101-1	M.J.J.Critchley	Derbyshire v Worcs	Worcester	2016

Century and Five Wickets in an Innings

154*, 5-26	M.J.Procter	Glos v Somerset	Taunton	1972
206, 6-32	A.I.Kallicharran	Warwicks v Oxfords	Birmingham	1984
103, 5-41	C.L.Hooper	Kent v Essex	Maidstone	1993
125, 5-41	I.R.Bell	Warwicks v Essex	Chelmsford	2003

Most Wicket-Keeping Dismissals in an Innings

8 (8 ct)	D.J.S.Taylor	Somerset v British Us	Taunton	1982
8 (8 ct)	D.J.Pipe	Worcs v Herts	Hertford	2001

Most Catches in an Innings by a Fielder

5	J.M.Rice	Hampshire v Warwicks	Southampton	1978
5	D.J.G.Sales	Northants v Essex	Northampton	2007

VITALITY BLAST 2018

In 2018, the Twenty20 competition was sponsored by Vitality. Between 2003 and 2009, three regional leagues competed to qualify for the knockout stages, but this was reduced to two leagues in 2010, before returning to the three-division format in 2012. In 2014, the competition reverted to two regional leagues. (2017's positions in brackets.)

NORTH GROUP

	P	W	L	T	NR	Pts	Net RR
Worcestershire (8)	14	9	4	–	1	19	+0.59
Durham (9)	14	9	4	–	1	19	+0.55
Lancashire (7)	14	8	5	–	1	17	+0.68
Nottinghamshire (1)	14	8	6	–	–	16	+0.07
Yorkshire (5)	14	7	7	–	–	14	–0.03
Warwickshire (3)	14	6	7	1	–	13	+0.03
Derbyshire (2)	14	5	7	–	2	12	–0.04
Leicestershire (4)	14	5	8	–	1	11	–0.38
Northamptonshire (6)	14	2	11	1	–	5	–1.39

SOUTH GROUP

	P	W	L	T	NR	Pts	Net RR
Somerset (4)	14	10	4	–	–	20	+0.78
Kent (6)	14	8	2	–	4	20	+0.62
Sussex (5)	14	7	3	–	4	18	+0.73
Gloucestershire (9)	14	8	4	–	2	18	+0.38
Surrey (2)	14	7	5	–	2	16	+0.98
Glamorgan (1)	14	7	6	–	1	15	–0.14
Essex (8)	14	2	8	1	3	8	–1.03
Hampshire (3)	14	2	9	1	–	7	–0.82
Middlesex (7)	14	2	12	–	–	4	–1.12

QUARTER-FINALS: LANCASHIRE beat Kent by six wickets at Canterbury.
SUSSEX beat Durham by five wickets at Chester-le-Street.
WORCESTERSHIRE beat Gloucestershire by five wickets at Worcester.
SOMERSET beat Nottinghamshire by 19 runs at Taunton.

SEMI-FINALS: WORCESTERSHIRE beat Lancashire by 20 runs at Birmingham.
SUSSEX beat Somerset by 35 runs at Birmingham.

LEADING AGGREGATES AND RECORDS 2018

BATTING (550 runs)	M	I	NO	HS	Runs	Avge	100	50	R/100b	Sixes
L.J.Evans (Sussex)	15	14	5	96	614	68.22	–	7	135.8	17
A.J.Finch (Surrey)	9	9	5	131*	589	147.25	2	3	182.3	31
I.R.Bell (Warwks)	14	14	2	131	580	48.33	1	4	139.0	15

BOWLING (24 wkts)	O	M	R	W	Avge	BB	4w	R/Over
P.R.Brown (Worcs)	54.1	–	414	31	13.35	4-21	1	7.64
M.W.Parkinson (Lancs)	56.4	–	415	25	16.60	3-19	–	7.32
J.Overton (Somerset)	52.4	–	540	24	22.50	5-47	2	10.25

Highest total	250-6		Surrey v Kent	Canterbury
Highest innings	131*	A.J.Finch	Surrey v Sussex	Hove
Most sixes	34	C.J.Anderson (Somerset)		
Highest partnership	194	J.J.Roy/A.J.Finch	Surrey v Middlesex	The Oval
Best bowling	6-28	J.K.Fuller	Middlesex v Hampshire	Southampton
Most economical	4-1-6-4	R.A.J.Smith	Glamorgan v Middlesex	Richmond
Most expensive	4-0-62-1	T.E.Barber	Middlesex v Gloucestershire	Bristol
Most w/k dismissals	18	D.J.Vilas (Lancashire)		
Most catches	15	E.G.Barnard (Worcestershire)		
Most catches (inns)	4	M.T.C.Waller	Somerset v Nottinghamshire	Taunton
	4	E.J.G.Morgan	Middlesex v Essex	Lord's

226

2018 VITALITY BLAST FINAL
SUSSEX v WORCESTERSHIRE

At Edgbaston, Birmingham, on 15 September (floodlit).
Result: WORCESTERSHIRE won by five wickets.
Toss: Sussex. Award: O.B.Cox.

SUSSEX		Runs	Balls	4/6	Fall
P.D.Salt	run out	17	8	1/2	1- 19
* L.J.Wright	b Ali	33	25	3/2	2- 77
L.J.Evans	b Barnard	52	44	4/2	5-138
D.M.W.Rawlins	c Brown b Ali	21	16	–/2	3-121
D.Wiese	b Ali	6	6	1	4-131
† M.G.K.Burgess	not out	14	14	–/1	
J.C.Archer	c Barnard b Parnell	7	8	–	6-157
C.J.Jordan					
W.A.T.Beer					
D.R.Briggs					
T.S.Mills					
Extras	(LB 2, NB 2, W 3)	7			
Total	(6 wkts; 20 overs)	**157**			

WORCESTERSHIRE		Runs	Balls	4/6	Fall
J.M.Clarke	c Burgess b Briggs	33	27	4	1- 61
* M.M.Ali	c Salt b Beer	41	27	6/1	4- 90
T.C.Fell	c Wright b Beer	1	3	–	2- 62
B.L.D'Oliveira	st Burgess b Briggs	10	9	1	3- 80
† O.B.Cox	not out	46	27	5/2	
R.A.Whiteley	c Jordan b Archer	14	17	2	5-126
E.G.Barnard	not out	1	2	–	
W.D.Parnell					
D.K.H.Mitchell					
L.Wood					
P.R.Brown					
Extras	(B 5, LB 2, NB 2, W 3)	12			
Total	(5 wkts; 18.3 overs)	**158**			

WORCESTERSHIRE	O	M	R	W	SUSSEX	O	M	R	W
Wood	4	0	24	0	Archer	3.3	0	36	1
Parnell	3	0	32	1	Mills	3	0	26	0
Brown	4	0	15	0	Jordan	3	0	29	0
Barnard	3	0	28	1	Wiese	1	0	9	0
Ali	4	0	30	3	Briggs	4	0	19	2
D'Oliveira	1	0	15	0	Beer	4	0	32	2
Mitchell	1	0	11	0					

Umpires: M.J.Saggers and A.G.Wharf

TWENTY20 CUP WINNERS

2003	Surrey	2009	Sussex	2015	Lancashire
2004	Leicestershire	2010	Hampshire	2016	Northamptonshire
2005	Somerset	2011	Leicestershire	2017	Nottinghamshire
2006	Leicestershire	2012	Hampshire	2018	Worcestershire
2007	Kent	2013	Northamptonshire		
2008	Middlesex	2014	Warwickshire		

PRINCIPAL TWENTY20 CUP RECORDS 2003-18

Highest Total	260-4		Yorkshire v Northants	Leeds	2017
Highest Total Batting 2nd	231-5		Warwickshire v Northants	Birmingham	2018
Lowest Total	47		Northants v Durham	Chester-le-St	2011
Largest Victory (Runs)	143		Somerset v Essex	Chelmsford	2011
Largest Victory (Balls)	75		Hampshire v Glos	Bristol	2010
Highest Scores	161	A.Lyth	Yorkshire v Northants	Leeds	2017
	158*	B.B.McCullum	Warwickshire v Derbys	Birmingham	2015
	153*	L.J.Wright	Sussex v Essex	Chelmsford	2014
	152*	G.R.Napier	Essex v Sussex	Chelmsford	2008
	151*	C.H.Gayle	Somerset v Kent	Taunton	2015
Fastest Hundred	34 balls	A.Symonds	Kent v Middlesex	Maidstone	2004
Most Sixes (Innings)	16	G.R.Napier	Essex v Sussex	Chelmsford	2008
Most Runs in Career	3927	J.L.Denly	Kent, Middlesex		2004-18

Highest Partnership for each Wicket

1st	207	J.L.Denly/D.J.Bell-Drummond	Kent v Essex	Chelmsford	2017
2nd	186	J.L.Langer/C.L.White	Somerset v Glos	Taunton	2006
3rd	171	I.R.Bell/A.J.Hose	Warwickshire v Northants	Birmingham	2018
4th	159*	L.J.Wright/M.W.Machan	Sussex v Essex	Chelmsford	2014
5th	117*	M.N.W.Spriegel/G.C.Wilson	Surrey v Middlesex	Lord's	2012
6th	126*	C.S.MacLeod/J.W.Hastings	Durham v Northants	Chester-le-St	2014
7th	80	D.T.Christian/T.S.Roland-Jones	Middlesex v Kent	Canterbury	2014
8th	86*	J.A.Simpson/T.G.Southee	Middlesex v Hampshire	Southampton	2017
9th	69	C.J.Anderson/J.H.Davey	Somerset v Surrey	The Oval	2017
10th	59	H.H.Streak/J.E.Anyon	Warwickshire v Worcs	Birmingham	2005

Best Bowling

	6- 5	A.V.Suppiah	Somerset v Glamorgan	Cardiff	2011
	6-16	T.G.Southee	Essex v Glamorgan	Chelmsford	2011
	6-19	T.T.Bresnan	Yorkshire v Lancashire	Leeds	2017
	6-21	A.J.Hall	Northants v Worcs	Northampton	2008
	6-28	J.K.Fuller	Middlesex v Hampshire	Southampton	2018
Most Wkts in Career	156	Yasir Arafat	Hants, Kent, Lancs, Somerset, Surrey, Sussex		2006-16

Most Economical Innings Analyses (Qualification: 4 overs)

4-2-5-2	A.C.Thomas	Somerset v Hampshire	Southampton	2010
4-0-5-3	D.R.Briggs	Hampshire v Kent	Canterbury	2010
4-1-6-2	J.Louw	Northants v Warwicks	Birmingham	2004
4-0-6-1	M.W.Alleyne	Glos v Worcs	Worcester	2005
4-1-6-4	R.A.J.Smith	Glamorgan v Middlesex	Richmond	2018

Most Maiden Overs in an Innings

4-2-9-1	M.Morkel	Kent v Surrey	Beckenham	2007
4-2-5-2	A.C.Thomas	Somerset v Hampshire	Southampton	2010
4-2-14-1	S.M.Curran	Surrey v Sussex	Hove	2018

Most Expensive Innings Analyses

4-0-77-0	B.W.Sanderson	Northants v Yorkshire	Leeds	2017
4-0-67-1	R.J.Kirtley	Sussex v Essex	Chelmsford	2008
4-0-65-2	M.J.Hoggard	Yorkshire v Lancs	Leeds	2005
4-0-65-1	P.I.Walter	Essex v Kent	Chelmsford	2017

Most Wicket-Keeping Dismissals in Career

114	J.S.Foster	Essex		2003-17

Most Wicket-Keeping Dismissals in an Innings

5 (5 ct)	M.J.Prior	Sussex v Middlesex	Richmond	2006
5 (4 ct, 1 st)	G.L.Brophy	Yorkshire v Durham	Chester-le-St	2008
5 (3 ct, 2 st)	B.J.M.Scott	Worcs v Yorkshire	Worcester	2011
5 (4 ct, 1 st)	G.C.Wilson	Surrey v Hampshire	The Oval	2014
5 (5 ct)	N.J.O'Brien	Leics v Northants	Leicester	2014
5 (3 ct, 2 st)	J.A.Simpson	Middlesex v Surrey	Lord's	2014
5 (4 ct, 1 st)	C.B.Cooke	Glamorgan v Surrey	Cardiff	2016

Most Catches in Career

94	S.J.Croft	Lancashire		2006-18

Most Catches in an Innings by a Fielder

5	M.W.Machan	Sussex v Glamorgan	Hove	2016

YOUNG CRICKETER OF THE YEAR

This annual award, made by The Cricket Writers' Club, is currently restricted to players qualified for England, Andrew Symonds meeting that requirement at the time of his award, and under the age of 23 on 1st May. In 1986 their ballot resulted in a dead heat. Up to 1 April 2019 their selections have gained a tally of 2,734 international Test match caps (shown in brackets).

1950 R.Tattersall (16)	1974 P.H.Edmonds (51)	1997 B.C.Hollioake (2)
1951 P.B.H.May (66)	1975 A.Kennedy	1998 A.Flintoff (79)
1952 F.S.Trueman (67)	1976 G.Miller (34)	1999 A.J.Tudor (10)
1953 M.C.Cowdrey (114)	1977 I.T.Botham (102)	2000 P.J.Franks
1954 P.J.Loader (13)	1978 D.I.Gower (117)	2001 O.A.Shah (6)
1955 K.F.Barrington (82)	1979 P.W.G.Parker (1)	2002 R.Clarke (2)
1956 B.Taylor	1980 G.R.Dilley (41)	2003 J.M.Anderson (148)
1957 M.J.Stewart (8)	1981 M.W.Gatting (79)	2004 I.R.Bell (118)
1958 A.C.D.Ingleby-Mackenzie	1982 N.G.Cowans (19)	2005 A.N.Cook (161)
1959 G.Pullar (28)	1983 N.A.Foster (29)	2006 S.C.J.Broad (126)
1960 D.A.Allen (39)	1984 R.J.Bailey (4)	2007 A.U.Rashid (19)
1961 P.H.Parfitt (37)	1985 D.V.Lawrence (5)	2008 R.S.Bopara (13)
1962 P.J.Sharpe (12)	1986 { A.A.Metcalfe	2009 J.W.A.Taylor (7)
1963 G.Boycott (108)	J.J.Whitaker (1)	2010 S.T.Finn (36)
1964 J.M.Brearley (39)	1987 R.J.Blakey (2)	2011 J.M.Bairstow (63)
1965 A.P.E.Knott (95)	1988 M.P.Maynard (4)	2012 J.E.Root (80)
1966 D.L.Underwood (86)	1989 N.Hussain (96)	2013 B.A.Stokes (52)
1967 A.W.Greig (58)	1990 M.A.Atherton (115)	2014 A.Z.Lees
1968 R.M.H.Cottam (4)	1991 M.R.Ramprakash (52)	2015 J.A.Leaning
1969 A.Ward (5)	1992 I.D.K.Salisbury (15)	2016 B.M.Duckett (4)
1970 C.M.Old (46)	1993 M.N.Lathwell (2)	2017 D.W.Lawrence
1971 J.Whitehouse	1994 J.P.Crawley (37)	2018 S.M.Curran (4)
1972 D.R.Owen-Thomas	1995 A.Symonds (26 – Australia)	
1973 M.Hendrick (30)	1996 C.E.W.Silverwood (6)	

THE PROFESSIONAL CRICKETERS' ASSOCIATION

PLAYER OF THE YEAR

Founded in 1967, the Professional Cricketers' Association introduced this award, decided by their membership, in 1970. The award, now known as the Reg Hayter Cup, is presented at the PCA's Annual Awards Dinner in London.

1970 { M.J.Procter	1986 C.A.Walsh	2003 Mushtaq Ahmed
J.D.Bond	1987 R.J.Hadlee	2004 A.Flintoff
1971 L.R.Gibbs	1988 G.A.Hick	2005 A.Flintoff
1972 A.M.E.Roberts	1989 S.J.Cook	2006 M.R.Ramprakash
1973 P.G.Lee	1990 G.A.Gooch	2007 O.D.Gibson
1974 B.Stead	1991 Waqar Younis	2008 M.van Jaarsveld
1975 Zaheer Abbas	1992 C.A.Walsh	2009 M.E.Trescothick
1976 P.G.Lee	1993 S.L.Watkin	2010 N.M.Carter
1977 M.J.Procter	1994 B.C.Lara	2011 M.E.Trescothick
1978 J.K.Lever	1995 D.G.Cork	2012 N.R.D.Compton
1979 J.K.Lever	1996 P.V.Simmons	2013 M.M.Ali
1980 R.D.Jackman	1997 S.P.James	2014 A.Lyth
1981 R.J.Hadlee	1998 M.B.Loye	2015 C.Rushworth
1982 M.D.Marshall	1999 S.G.Law	2016 B.M.Duckett
1983 K.S.McEwan	2000 M.E.Trescothick	2017 S.R.Patel
1984 R.J.Hadlee	2001 D.P.Fulton	2018 J.L.Denly
1985 N.V.Radford	2002 M.P.Vaughan	

2018 FIRST-CLASS AVERAGES

These averages involve the 508 players who appeared in the 146 first-class matches played by 29 teams in England and Wales during the 2018 season.

'Cap' denotes the season in which the player was awarded a 1st XI cap by the county he represented in 2018. If he played for more than one county in 2018, the county(ies) who awarded him his cap is (are) underlined. Durham abolished both their capping and 'awards' system after the 2005 season. Glamorgan's capping system is based on a player's number of appearances. Gloucestershire now cap players on first-class debut. Worcestershire now award county colours when players make their Championship debut.

Team abbreviations: CU – Cambridge University/Cambridge MCCU; CfU – Cardiff MCCU; De – Derbyshire; Du – Durham; DU – Durham MCCU; E – England; EL – England Lions; Ex – Essex; Gm – Glamorgan; Gs – Gloucestershire; H – Hampshire; I – India; IA – India A; K – Kent; La – Lancashire; Le – Leicestershire; LU – Loughborough MCCU; M – Middlesex; Nh – Northamptonshire; Nt – Nottinghamshire; OU – Oxford University/Oxford MCCU; P – Pakistan(is); Sm – Somerset; Sy – Surrey; Sx – Sussex; Wa – Warwickshire; WIA – West Indies A; Wo – Worcestershire; Y – Yorkshire.

† Left-handed batsman. Cap: a dash (–) denotes a non-county player. A blank denotes uncapped by his current county.

BATTING AND FIELDING

	Cap	M	I	NO	HS	Runs	Avge	100	50	Ct/St
V.R.Aaron (Le)		3	5	1	8	14	3.50	–	–	–
K.J.Abbott (H)	2017	15	22	5	60*	436	25.64	–	2	–
T.B.Abell (Sm)	2018	14	26	4	132*	883	40.13	1	5	2
C.N.Ackermann (Le)		14	24	2	196*	876	39.81	2	3	10
H.D.Adair (OU)		1								–
† J.H.K.Adams (H)	2006	15	26	2	182*	764	31.83	2	1	15
M.A.Agarwal (IA)		2	4	–	68	69	17.25	–	1	3
† M.M.Ali (E/Wo)	2007	5	9	–	219	502	55.77	1	3	1
H.A.J.Allen (CfU)		2	1	–	4	4	4.00	–	–	–
† T.P.Alsop (H)		8	14	1	99	397	30.53	–	4	22
S.W.Ambris (WIA)		3	6	1	128	250	50.00	1	1	1
T.R.Ambrose (Wa)	2007	15	21	2	103	666	35.05	1	3	58
H.M.Amla (H)		5	9	–	112	492	54.66	2	3	2
† J.M.Anderson (E/La)	2003	10	14	8	11	34	5.66	–	–	2
M.K.Andersson (De/M)		4	8	2	34	83	13.83	–	–	2
J.C.Archer (Sx)	2017	8	13	3	33	170	17.00	–	–	6
U.Arshad (Le)		1	2	–	9	9	4.50	–	–	–
Asad Shafiq (P)	–	4	5	1	186*	294	73.50	1	1	4
R.Ashwin (I)	–	4	8	2	33*	126	21.00	–	–	1
S.J.S.Assani (CfU)		1								–
Azhar Ali (P/Sm)		11	20	1	125	503	26.47	1	3	2
Babar Azam (P)	–	3	3	1	68*	136	68.00	–	2	–
T.E.Bailey (La)	2018	15	22	2	66	308	15.40	–	1	6
J.M.Bairstow (E/Y)	2011	10	18	–	95	541	30.05	–	5	28/1
T.W.Balderson (CU)	–	1	2	1	2*	3	3.00	–	–	–
J.T.Ball (Nt)	2016	6	10	2	44*	130	16.25	–	–	1
† G.S.Ballance (Y)	2012	12	23	–	194	906	39.39	3	4	4
E.R.Bamber (M)		6	10	3	27*	76	10.85	–	–	2
T.Banton (Sm)		2	3	–	30	37	12.33	–	–	1
T.E.Barber (M)		2	3	1	3	3	1.50	–	–	–
† K.H.D.Barker (Wa)	2013	11	14	2	58	218	18.16	–	1	1
E.G.Barnard (Wo)	2015	13	24	2	66	516	23.45	–	3	9
G.A.Bartlett (Sm)		6	11	–	110	306	27.81	1	–	2
A.R.Bawne (IA)	–	1	2	1	43*	44	44.00	–	–	–
W.A.T.Beer (Sx)		2	1	1	50*	50	–	–	1	–

230

	Cap	M	I	NO	HS	Runs	Avge	100	50	Ct/St
I.R.Bell (Wa)	2001	15	24	4	204	1127	56.35	6	2	13
D.J.Bell-Drummond (K)	2015	14	25	2	61	437	19.00	–	1	3
G.K.Berg (H)	2016	10	14	2	84*	335	27.91	–	2	4
D.M.Bess (E/EL/Sm)		10	15	1	92	350	25.00	–	2	4
S.W.Billings (K)	2015	8	14	2	85	370	30.83	–	2	20/2
J.Blackwood (WIA)		2	4	–	67	158	39.50	–	2	2
† A.J.Blake (K)		2	2	–	28	31	15.50	–	–	–
J.J.Bohannon (La)		5	9	1	78*	255	31.87	–	2	2
R.S.Bopara (Ex)	2005	14	23	5	133*	776	43.11	2	4	8
S.G.Borthwick (Sy)	2018	9	13	2	175*	619	56.27	1	5	15
† J.W.R.Bowers (CU)	–	1	–	–	–	–	–	–	–	–
D.A.J.Bracewell (Nh)		3	6	1	81	113	22.60	–	1	2
† J.R.Bracey (Gs/LU)	2016	16	30	3	125*	819	30.33	2	2	16
K.C.Brathwaite (Nt)	2018	4	8	1	71	296	42.28	–	3	1
T.T.Bresnan (Y)	2006	12	22	3	80	385	20.26	–	2	9
A.D.F.Brewster (CfU)	–	2	1	–	7	7	7.00	–	–	–
D.D.W.Brierley (CU)	–	1	–	–	–	–	–	–	–	–
D.R.Briggs (Sx)		12	20	7	46	234	18.00	–	–	5
† S.C.J.Broad (E/Nt)	2008	12	18	–	38	212	11.77	–	–	5
T.M.J.Brock (OU)	–	1	2	–	2	2	1.00	–	–	–
† C.A.J.Brodrick (De)		1	2	–	19	19	9.50	–	–	2
H.C.Brook (Y)		12	23	–	124	575	25.00	1	3	7
H.J.H.Brookes (Wa)		5	6	1	70	165	33.00	–	2	3
J.A.Brooks (Y)	2013	13	22	3	82	303	15.94	–	1	1
S.S.J.Brooks (WIA)	–	3	4	1	122*	224	74.66	1	1	3
B.C.Brown (Sx)	2014	15	25	4	119*	1031	49.09	2	7	54/1
C.R.Brown (Gm)		6	12	–	33	95	7.91	–	–	3
K.R.Brown (La)	2015	2	4	–	43	67	16.75	–	–	1
P.R.Brown (Wo)	2017	1	1	1	2*	2	–	–	–	1
† N.L.J.Browne (Ex)	2015	11	18	–	100	514	28.55	1	3	8
N.L.Buck (Nh)		9	15	2	20	135	10.38	–	–	–
K.A.Bull (Gm)		4	8	3	30	76	15.20	–	–	2
† J.Bulpitt (CU)	–	1	–	–	–	–	–	–	–	–
J.J.Bumrah (I)	–	3	5	2	6	6	2.00	–	–	1
M.G.K.Burgess (Sx)		13	20	1	101*	559	29.42	1	2	4
† R.J.Burns (EL/Sy)	2014	15	24	1	193	1402	60.95	4	7	11
J.C.Buttler (E/La)	2018	8	14	1	106	572	44.00	1	5	8
† E.J.Byrom (Sm)		8	15	–	54	309	20.60	–	2	2
† J.D.Campbell (WIA)	–	3	6	–	61	208	34.66	–	2	5
† M.A.Carberry (Le)		4	6	–	73	193	32.16	–	1	1
L.J.Carey (Gm)		6	8	–	28	58	7.25	–	–	–
K.S.Carlson (Gm)		13	25	1	152	567	23.62	1	1	5
M.Carter (Nt)		4	8	–	22	76	9.50	–	–	4
H.W.R.Cartwright (M)		8	13	–	80	204	15.69	–	1	7
† K.Carver (Y)		1	2	1	1*	1	–	–	–	–
† S.Chanderpaul (La)	2010	8	13	–	65	257	19.76	–	2	1
L.J.Chapman (CU)	–	1	–	–	–	–	–	–	–	1
Z.J.Chappell (Le)		4	5	2	40	145	48.33	–	–	1
B.G.Charlesworth (Gs)	2018	6	9	1	77*	194	24.25	–	2	2
† D.Chohan (CU)	–	1	2	–	67	104	52.00	–	1	2
V.Chopra (Ex)	2018	7	13	–	61	201	15.46	–	1	7
G.Clark (Du)		12	22	–	64	460	20.90	–	2	9
J.Clark (La)		11	16	–	82	538	33.62	–	5	2
J.M.Clarke (Wo)	2015	14	26	1	177*	853	34.12	3	1	8
R.Clarke (Sy)	2005	13	17	1	111	500	31.25	1	1	19
† M.E.Claydon (K)	2016	1	2	–	5	5	2.50	–	–	–

231

	Cap	M	I	NO	HS	Runs	Avge	100	50	Ct/St
B.O.Coad (Y)	2018	9	15	7	33	135	16.87	–	–	–
J.J.Cobb (Nh)	2018	6	12	–	52	199	16.58	–	1	–
I.A.Cockbain (Gs)	2011	1	1	–	0	0	0.00	–	–	1
M.T.Coles (Ex)		4	5	1	10*	37	9.25	–	–	1
P.D.Collingwood (Du)	1998	11	20	–	47	299	14.95	–	–	12
T.G.L.Colverd (CU)	–	1	2	–	63	63	31.50	–	1	–
† A.N.Cook (E/EL/Ex)	2005	14	25	–	180	1041	41.64	2	6	22
S.C.Cook (Gm)		4	8	–	36	120	15.00	–	–	3
S.J.Cook (Ex)		10	11	7	14	56	14.00	–	–	1
C.B.Cooke (Gm)	2016	14	25	–	69	606	24.24	–	4	41/1
† J.M.Cooke (DU)	–	2	–	–	–	–	–	–	–	–
T.P.Corner (CU)	–	1	2	–	46	56	28.00	–	–	–
R.R.S.Cornwall (WIA)	–	1	2	–	40	40	20.00	–	–	2
† M.J.Cosgrove (Le)	2015	14	24	–	75	440	18.33	–	3	6
B.D.Cotton (Nh)		3	4	2	24*	32	16.00	–	–	2
J.Coughlin (Du)		2	4	–	19	42	10.50	–	–	1
O.B.Cox (Wo)	2009	12	22	1	65	372	17.71	–	2	35
Z.Crawley (K)		16	26	–	168	797	30.65	1	4	11
M.J.J.Critchley (De)		14	26	1	105	705	28.20	1	4	11
S.J.Croft (La)	2010	9	14	1	148*	424	32.61	1	2	10
S.P.Crook (Nh)	2013	6	11	–	92	361	32.81	–	3	3
J.O.Cross-Zamirski (CU)	–	1	2	1	1	1	1.00	–	–	1
T.N.Cullen (Gm)		2	4	–	20	29	7.25	–	–	7
† B.J.Curran (Nh)		5	9	1	83*	251	31.37	–	2	3
† S.M.Curran (E/EL/Sy)	2018	13	19	1	78	513	28.50	–	3	3
T.K.Curran (Sy)	2016	5	7	–	43	83	11.85	–	–	–
A.K.Dal (De)		4	7	–	25	107	15.28	–	–	2
J.H.Davey (Sm)		11	17	6	36	206	18.72	–	–	3
A.L.Davies (La)	2017	15	25	–	115	752	30.08	1	5	21/1
R.C.Davies (Du)		3	6	–	20	27	4.50	–	–	7
† S.M.Davies (Sm)	2017	14	25	2	92*	756	32.86	–	5	38/3
W.S.Davis (De)		1	1	–	6	6	6.00	–	–	–
M.J.Dawes (OU)	–	1	–	–	–	–	–	–	–	1
L.A.Dawson (H)	2013	11	18	2	72	398	24.87	–	1	6
T.B.de Bruyn (Sy)		2	3	1	38	46	23.00	–	–	2
M.de Lange (Gm)		3	5	1	90	142	35.50	–	2	1
† H.E.Dearden (Le)		10	18	2	74	357	22.31	–	2	6
J.L.Denly (K)	2008	16	26	2	119	954	39.75	4	3	3
† C.D.J.Dent (Gs)	2010	15	30	3	214*	903	33.44	1	4	11
J.W.Dernbach (Sy)	2011	10	13	2	31	129	11.72	–	–	2
A.C.H.Dewhurst (CU)	–	1	2	–	65	69	34.50	–	1	–
N.J.Dexter (Le)		12	20	3	87	585	34.41	–	3	9
† S.Dhawan (I)	–	4	8	–	44	162	20.25	–	–	2
S.R.Dickson (K)		16	28	1	134*	793	29.37	3	2	25
M.W.Dixon (Du)		1	1	1	8*	8	–	–	–	–
B.L.D'Oliveira (Wo)	2012	10	19	–	65	276	14.52	–	1	1
A.H.T.Donald (Gm)		4	7	1	27	67	11.16	–	–	2
G.S.Drissell (Gs)	2017	5	9	–	19	76	8.44	–	–	–
† B.M.Duckett (Nh/Nt)	2016	12	23	1	133	549	24.95	1	2	6
† M.P.Dunn (Sy)		2	3	1	9*	10	5.00	–	–	2
A.R.Easwaran (IA)	–	1	2	–	31	54	27.00	–	–	1
E.J.H.Eckersley (Le)	2013	7	12	–	74	220	18.33	–	2	26
F.H.Edwards (Sy)	2018	15	20	9	14	75	6.81	–	–	3
† D.Elgar (Sy)		7	10	–	110	387	38.70	1	2	6
† S.M.Ervine (De/H)	2005	4	7	1	65*	134	22.33	–	1	2
D.A.Escott (OU)	–	1	2	1	175	176	176.00	1	–	1

232

	Cap	M	I	NO	HS	Runs	Avge	100	50	Ct/St
S.S.Eskinazi (M)	2018	13	23	1	134	874	39.72	1	5	16
B.N.Evans (CfU)	–	2	1	–	0	0	0.00	–	–	–
L.J.Evans (Sx)		2	3	–	34	46	15.33	–	–	1
S.T.Evans (Le/LU)		5	8	1	33*	85	12.14	–	–	1
Faheem Ashraf (P)	–	3	4	–	37	50	12.50	–	–	1
M.J.Fanning (OU)	–	1	–	–	–	–	–	–	–	–
T.C.Fell (Wo)	2013	13	24	–	89	652	27.16	–	4	7
E.W.F.Fenwick (DU)	–	1	–	–	–	–	–	–	–	–
L.H.Ferguson (De)		5	10	2	16	51	6.37	–	–	4
A.J.Finch (Sx)	2018	2	3	–	43	77	25.66	–	–	1
H.Z.Finch (Sx)		15	25	–	103	802	32.08	1	6	25
S.T.Finn (M)	2009	4	6	–	27	50	8.33	–	–	1
M.D.Fisher (EL/Y)		3	5	1	20*	45	11.25	–	–	2
L.J.Fletcher (Nt)	2014	13	23	1	43	304	13.81	–	–	4
B.T.Foakes (Sy)	2016	12	18	1	90	624	36.70	–	4	37/1
M.H.A.Footitt (Dy/Nt)		4	7	4	21*	38	12.66	–	–	2
J.S.Foster (Ex)	2001	5	7	–	69	165	23.57	–	1	13/1
W.A.R.Fraine (DU/Nt)		3	2	–	30	49	24.50	–	–	–
J.K.Fuller (M)		8	16	3	71	242	18.61	–	1	3
† G.H.S.Garton (Sx)		1	1	1	22*	22	–	–	–	1
† W.R.S.Gidman (K)		5	4	–	19	27	6.75	–	–	2
A.F.Gleadall (De)		1	2	1	27*	29	29.00	–	–	–
R.J.Gleeson (La/Nh)		6	10	4	26	47	7.83	–	–	–
† J.S.D.Gnodde (OU)		2	2	1	18	22	22.00	–	–	–
B.A.Godleman (De)	2015	14	27	2	122	658	26.32	2	3	8
† B.W.M.Graves (DU)		2	2	–	–	–	–	–	–	–
B.G.F.Green (Sm)		2	4	–	26	43	10.75	–	–	3
S.R.Green (OU)		1	–	–	–	–	–	–	–	–
A.D.Greenidge (CU)		1	–	–	–	–	–	–	–	–
L.Gregory (Sm)	2015	12	21	2	65	411	21.63	–	3	12
G.T.Griffiths (Le)		12	18	8	40	225	22.50	–	–	2
T.D.Groenewald (Sm)	2016	7	11	5	36*	91	15.16	–	–	2
† N.R.T.Gubbins (EL/M)	2016	10	19	–	107	667	35.10	1	3	3
B.D.Guest (La)		1	2	–	8	8	4.00	–	–	–
C.J.Guest (CU)		1	–	–	–	–	–	–	–	–
M.J.Guptill (Wo)	2018	2	4	–	111	170	42.50	1	–	3
R.N.Gurbani (IA)		1	1	–	0	0	0.00	–	–	–
H.F.Gurney (Nt)	2014	11	16	10	29*	73	12.16	–	–	1
† C.J.Haggett (K)		3	4	–	31	53	13.25	–	–	1
S.R.Hain (Wa)	2018	12	17	1	90	566	35.37	–	6	9
H.Hameed (La)	2016	11	18	–	31	170	9.44	–	–	6
Hamidullah Qadri (De)		4	8	2	15*	33	5.50	–	–	2
M.A.H.Hammond (Gs)	2013	8	16	2	123*	476	34.00	2	2	6
N.A.Hammond (LU)		2	2	–	18	19	9.50	–	–	–
† J.S.Handley (CU)		1	–	–	–	–	–	–	–	–
G.T.Hankins (Gs)	2016	2	4	1	54*	76	25.33	–	1	3
† O.J.Hannon-Dalby (Wa)		4	7	–	13	29	4.14	–	–	–
G.H.I.Harding (Du)		1	2	–	7	7	3.50	–	–	–
A.Harinath (Sy)	2016	3	5	–	48	73	14.60	–	–	1
† Haris Sohail (P)	–	4	7	2	79	253	50.60	–	2	2
S.R.Harmer (Ex)	2018	14	20	3	102*	460	27.05	1	1	13
J.A.R.Harris (M)	2015	13	22	8	79*	460	32.42	–	3	6
G.J.Harte (Du)		8	15	–	114	382	25.46	2	–	4
Hasan Ali (P)	–	3	4	–	24	57	14.25	–	–	–
† Hasan Azad (LU)		2	3	–	33	54	18.00	–	–	–
T.M.Head (Wo)	2018	6	11	1	62	339	33.90	–	2	2

233

	Cap	M	I	NO	HS	Runs	Avge	100	50	Ct/St
T.D.Heathfield (OU)	–	1	–	–	–	–	–	–	–	–
T.G.Helm (M)		5	6	2	52	102	25.50	–	1	2
† C.Hemraj (WIA)	–	2	4	–	42	84	21.00	–	–	2
M.J.Henry (K)	2018	11	17	3	81	303	21.64	–	2	2
C.L.Herring (CfU)	–	1	1	–	9	9	9.00	–	–	2
R.F.Higgins (Gs)	2018	15	25	3	105	526	23.90	1	2	6
J.C.Hildreth (Sm)	2007	14	26	2	184	1089	45.37	3	6	13
L.J.Hill (Le)		9	15	2	85	241	18.53	–	1	29
A.J.Hodd (Y)	2016	3	6	–	85	175	29.16	–	2	12
M.G.Hogan (Gm)	2013	13	21	8	28	152	11.69	–	–	7
† M.D.E.Holden (M)		14	25	3	119*	643	29.22	1	3	4
C.K.Holder (WIA)	–	2	2	1	8	13	13.00	–	–	–
I.G.Holland (H)		7	11	1	31	135	13.50	–	–	3
P.J.Horton (Le)		12	22	1	88	594	28.28	–	5	3
A.J.Hose (Wa)		4	7	1	68	194	32.33	–	2	1
H.R.Hosein (De)		8	16	2	66*	376	26.85	–	3	12/1
B.A.C.Howell (Gs)	2012	14	25	1	89	693	28.87	–	5	9
A.L.Hughes (De)	2017	14	27	1	103	737	28.34	1	5	9
M.S.T.Hughes (OU)	–	1	2	–	11	15	7.50	–	–	–
M.D.Hunn (K)		1	–	–	–	–	–	–	–	–
B.A.Hutton (Nh)		13	22	2	27	198	9.90	–	–	9
E.R.B.Hyde (CU)	–	1	2	–	32	32	16.00	–	–	2
† Imam-ul-Haq (P)	–	4	7	2	61	187	37.40	–	2	–
W.G.Jacks (Sy)		7	10	1	53	225	25.00	–	1	8
† R.A.Jadeja (I)	–	1	2	1	86*	99	99.00	–	1	–
L.W.James (Nt)	–	1	2	–	13	14	7.00	–	–	–
A.Javid (La)		6	10	–	58	157	15.70	–	1	2
† K.K.Jennings (E/La)	2018	17	27	1	177	945	36.34	3	1	14
M.A.Jones (Du)		1	2	–	10	13	6.50	–	–	–
R.A.Jones (Le)		1	1	–	0	0	0.00	–	–	1
R.P.Jones (La)		6	9	1	68	175	21.87	–	1	7
C.J.Jordan (Sx)	2014	8	13	–	68	299	23.00	–	2	5
K.D.Karthik (I)	–	2	4	–	20	21	5.25	–	–	5
J.B.R.Keeping (CU)	–	1	–	–	–	–	–	–	–	–
R.I.Keogh (Nh)		5	9	–	29	92	10.22	–	–	3
† U.T.Khawaja (Gm)		4	8	–	126	420	52.50	3	–	2
D.Klein (Le)		5	9	3	94	202	33.66	–	1	2
R.K.Kleinveldt (Nh)	2016	3	5	–	21	45	9.00	–	–	1
T.Kohler-Cadmore (Y)		6	11	2	106	414	46.00	2	2	4
V.Kohli (I)	–	5	10	–	149	593	59.30	2	3	4
H.G.Kuhn (K)	2018	14	26	3	96*	780	33.91	–	6	21
† Kuldeep Yadav (I)	–	1	2	–	0	0	0.00	–	–	–
T.C.Lace (De)		4	8	–	43	219	27.37	–	–	1
† M.B.Lake (OU)		1	–	–	–	–	–	–	–	–
D.J.Lamb (La)		4	6	2	20*	57	14.25	–	–	1
M.J.Lamb (Wa)		3	4	1	79	151	50.33	–	1	1
† T.W.M.Latham (Du)		4	8	–	147	366	45.75	1	2	8
J.L.Lawlor (Gm)		3	6	–	21	49	8.16	–	–	3
D.W.Lawrence (Ex)	2017	13	22	1	124	505	24.04	1	1	10
J.Leach (Wo)	2012	5	9	–	18	66	7.33	–	–	1
M.J.Leach (EL/Sm)	2017	12	17	3	66	186	13.28	–	1	5
J.A.Leaning (Y)	2016	8	16	2	68	371	26.50	–	2	9
A.Z.Lees (Du/Y)	2014	10	19	–	69	306	16.10	–	1	4
B.J.Leighton (OU)		1	–	–	–	–	–	–	–	–
† T.J.Lester (La)	–	1	2	–	8	16	8.00	–	–	–
R.E.Levi (Nh)	2017	12	22	1	75	532	25.33	–	2	16

	Cap	M	I	NO	HS	Runs	Avge	100	50	Ct/St
S.H.Lewis (WIA)	–	3	4	1	18	28	9.33	–	–	–
J.D.Libby (Nt)		14	27	2	100*	662	26.48	1	4	6
C.J.Liddle (Gs)	2017	3	4	2	6*	11	5.50	–	–	–
A.M.Lilley (La)		1	1	–	28	28	28.00	–	–	–
L.S.Livingstone (La)	2017	10	16	2	48*	336	24.00	–	–	15
D.L.Lloyd (Gm)		10	18	2	119	474	29.62	1	3	3
† J.E.G.Logan (Y)		1	1	–	6	6	6.00	–	–	1
J.H.Ludlow (CfU)		2	1	–	19	19	19.00	–	–	2
† A.Lyth (Y)	2010	13	25	1	134*	656	27.33	1	2	16
B.J.McCarthy (Du)		6	11	1	43	111	11.10	–	–	2
C.M.MacDonell (DU)		2	1	1	22*	22	–	–	–	1
A.H.McGrath (DU)		2	–	–			–	–	–	–
C.McKerr (Sy)		5	5	2	29	64	21.33	–	–	–
L.D.McManus (H)		8	12	1	66	211	19.18	–	1	9
L.Machado (CfU)		2	1	–	7	7	7.00	–	–	–
W.L.Madsen (De)	2011	14	27	–	144	1016	37.62	2	7	25
† S.J.Magoffin (Wo)	2008	6	10	3	43	65	9.28	–	–	1
K.A.Maharaj (La)		3	5	–	38	66	13.20	–	–	2
S.Mahmood (La)		2	1	–	0	0	0.00	–	–	–
† D.J.Malan (E/EL/M)	2010	16	29	1	119	817	29.17	1	6	20
A.K.Markram (Du)		3	5	–	94	124	24.80	–	1	4
† S.E.Marsh (Gm)		4	7	–	111	203	29.00	1	1	1
J.D.Marshall (DU)		2	1	–	0	0	0.00	–	–	–
S.C.Meaker (Sy)	2012	2	2	–	13	18	9.00	–	–	2
J.M.Mennie (La)		7	11	4	68*	232	33.14	–	2	1
C.A.J.Meschede (Gm)		4	8	1	55	151	21.57	–	2	–
B.W.M.Mike (Le)		4	7	–	39	96	13.71	–	–	1
C.N.Miles (Gs)	2011	14	20	5	38*	201	13.40	–	–	4
M.E.Milnes (Nt)		6	10	5	43	100	20.00	–	–	4
A.G.Milton (CfU/Wo)	2018	9	14	2	104*	255	21.25	1	–	6/1
D.K.H.Mitchell (Wo)	2005	14	26	–	178	957	36.80	4	1	21
Mohammad Abbas (Le/P)	2018	13	19	7	32*	92	7.66	–	–	2
† Mohammad Amir (P)		4	5	2	24*	64	21.33	–	–	1
Mohammed Shami (I)		5	10	1	10*	27	3.00	–	–	2
Mohammed Siraj (IA)		2	3	–	11	12	4.00	–	–	1
T.J.Moores (Nt)		13	22	1	103	616	29.33	1	2	39
A.O.Morgan (Gm)		3	6	–	36	89	14.83	–	–	1
† E.J.G.Morgan (M)	2008	6	11	–	76	121	11.00	–	1	4
† M.Morkel (Sy)	2018	11	14	2	29	194	16.16	–	1	5
C.A.J.Morris (Wo)	2014	4	7	5	9*	31	15.50	–	–	–
S.J.Mullaney (Nt)	2013	11	20	–	130	601	30.05	1	4	11
† J.R.Murphy (Gm)		12	23	2	80	533	25.38	–	2	4
† T.J.Murtagh (M)	2008	12	19	4	40	200	13.33	–	–	3
† D.G.Murty (CU)		1	2	–	52	56	28.00	–	1	–
S.Nadeem (IA)		3	4	–	15	36	9.00	–	–	1
K.K.Nair (IA)		3	6	–	93	227	37.83	–	2	3
C.D.Nash (Nt)		9	17	–	139	383	22.52	1	2	4
M.A.Naylor (OU)		1	1	–	202	202	202.00	1	–	–
R.I.Newton (Nh)	2017	5	9	–	118	336	37.33	1	–	3
C.Nicholls (DU)		2	–	–			–	–	–	–
† K.Noema-Barnett (Gs)	2015	9	16	6	73*	327	32.70	–	2	12
S.A.Northeast (H)		11	19	–	129	479	25.21	1	1	5
L.C.Norwell (La)	2011	1	2	–	3	3	1.50	–	–	–
D.Olivier (De)		7	11	2	40*	78	8.66	–	–	1
G.Onions (La)	2018	13	19	4	41	135	9.00	–	–	1
C.Overton (Sm)	2016	11	18	1	80	331	19.47	–	1	9

235

	Cap	M	I	NO	HS	Runs	Avge	100	50	Ct/St
J.Overton (Sm)		8	12	2	55	197	19.70	–	1	5
A.P.Palladino (De)	2012	12	23	6	32	317	18.64	–	–	1
H.J.Palmer (CU)	–	1	–							
H.H.Pandya (I)	–	4	8	1	52*	164	23.42	–	1	
† R.R.Pant (I/IA)	–	5	10	1	114	351	39.00	1	3	25
C.F.Parkinson (Le)		12	19	1	48	252	14.00	–	–	11
M.W.Parkinson (La)		7	11	5	9*	35	5.83	–	–	1
† W.D.Parnell (Wo)	2018	6	10	3	58*	273	39.00	–	3	1
S.D.Parry (La)	2015	3	4	–	6	7	1.75	–	–	1
† A.R.Patel (Du)		4	7	1	95*	147	24.50	–	1	1
J.S.Patel (Wa)	2012	14	19	3	32	184	11.50	–	–	4
R.H.Patel (M)		2	4	–	20	33	8.25	–	–	1
† R.S.Patel (Sy)		10	15	3	48	350	29.16	–	–	4
S.R.Patel (Nt)	2008	14	26	1	76	639	25.6	–	6	5
S.A.Patterson (Y)	2012	8	13	2	45*	205	18.63	–	–	2
D.A.Payne (Gs)	2011	7	11	6	31	86	17.20	–	–	1
S.J.Pearce (CfU)	–	2	1	–	35	35	35.00	–	–	–
D.Y.Pennington (Wo)	2018	8	14	3	37	94	8.54	–	–	4
M.S.Pepper (Ex)		4	4	–	22	53	13.25	–	–	
W.J.N.Pereira (LU)	–	2	2	1	28*	28	28.00	–	–	
T.H.S.Pettman (OU)	–	2	1	1	54*	54	–	–	1	–
O.L.Pike (CfU)	–	2	1	1	0*	0	–	–	–	–
M.W.Pillans (Sy/Y)		2	2	–	10	18	9.00	–	–	1
M.J.Plater (DU)	–	2	1	1	9*	9	–	–	–	1
† J.H.Plom (Ex)		1	–	–						
H.W.Podmore (K)		15	22	7	53	285	19.00	–	1	2
O.J.D.Pope (E/EL/Sy)	2018	16	21	3	158*	1098	61.00	4	2	26
J.A.Porter (EL/Ex)	2015	15	18	3	31	88	5.86	–	–	3
M.J.Potts (Du)		1	2	1	36	51	51.00	–	–	
J.D.Powe (OU)	–	1	1	–	11	11	11.00	–	–	
S.W.Poynter (Du)		11	20	1	170	475	25.00	1	1	34/1
J.E.Poysden (Wa/Y)		4	6	2	20*	25	6.25	–	–	
S.Prasanna (Nh)		2	4	–	27	42	10.50	–	–	
R.D.Pringle (Du)		1	2	–	34	37	18.50	–	–	1
† L.A.Procter (Nh)		11	22	1	70	444	21.14	–	3	2
C.A.Pujara (I/Y)		10	20	1	132*	450	23.68	1	1	4
M.R.Quinn (Ex)		3	5	4	16	26	26.00	–	–	
A.J.W.Rackow (OU)	–	2	1	–	16	16	16.00	–	–	
A.M.Rahane (I/IA)	–	6	12	–	81	354	29.50	–	2	4
Rahat Ali (P)	–	2	2	1	14	14	14.00	–	–	
K.L.Rahul (I)	–	5	10	–	149	299	29.90	1	–	14
† B.A.Raine (Le)		11	17	–	65	371	21.82	–	1	5
A.S.Rajpoot (IA)	–	2	2	2	0*	0	–	–	–	
† R.Rampaul (De)		8	11	5	18*	51	8.50	–	–	2
A.U.Rashid (E)	–	5	8	2	33*	119	19.83	–	–	1
J.A.Raval (Y)		4	7	–	21	84	12.00	–	–	3
† D.M.W.Rawlins (Sx)		1	2	–	0	0	0.00	–	–	
O.P.Rayner (H/M)	2015	12	17	2	49	172	11.46	–	–	16
L.M.Reece (De)		6	11	1	157*	349	34.90	1	1	2
† R.A.Reifer (WIA)	–	3	5	1	52	74	18.50	–	1	–
† M.T.Renshaw (Sm)		6	11	1	112	513	51.30	3	1	5
G.H.Rhodes (Wo)	2016	3	6	–	12	22	3.66	–	–	2
† W.M.H.Rhodes (Wa)		15	24	1	137	974	42.34	4	4	5
M.J.Richardson (Du)		10	18	–	115	377	20.94	1	1	3
A.E.N.Riley (K)		6	6	3	23	56	18.66	–	–	6
N.J.Rimmington (Du)		7	13	1	61	255	21.25	–	1	1

	Cap	M	I	NO	HS	Runs	Avge	100	50	Ct/St
† S.E.Rippington (CU)	–	1	–	–	–	–	–	–	–	1
J.A.J.Rishton (LU)	–	2	2	1	32*	55	55.00	–	–	–
† W.J.R.Robertson (OU)	–	1	–	–	–	–	–	–	–	–
O.E.Robinson (Sx)		15	23	3	52	307	15.35	–	1	5
O.G.Robinson (K)		3	4	–	26	59	14.75	–	–	1
S.D.Robson (M)	2013	14	25	1	135	768	32.00	2	2	7
G.H.Roderick (Gs)	2013	13	23	2	85*	585	27.85	–	5	49
O.J.W.Rogers (OU)	–	1	1	–	13	13	13.00	–	–	–
T.S.Roland-Jones (M)	2012	3	4	–	46	79	19.75	–	–	–
W.J.L.Rollings (LU)	–	2	2	–	4	4	2.00	–	–	1
J.E.Root (E/Y)	2012	10	18	–	125	533	29.61	1	2	8
† W.T.Root (Nt)		6	12	–	36	196	16.33	–	–	3
A.M.Rossington (Nh)		12	21	1	90	551	27.55	–	4	34
† R.R.Rossouw (H)		10	18	3	120*	550	36.66	1	2	8
A.P.Rouse (K/Sy)		10	14	2	55	242	20.16	–	1	28
J.J.Roy (Sy)	2014	2	3	–	128	196	65.33	1	1	4
F.W.A.Ruffell (DU)	–	2	–	–	–	–	–	–	–	–
C.Rushworth (Du)		12	22	12	11*	72	7.20	–	–	2
A.M.C.Russell (DU)	–	1	–	–	–	–	–	–	–	–
N.A.Saini (IA)	–	2	3	1	4	5	2.50	–	–	–
A.Sakande (Sx)		2	2	1	1*	1	–	–	–	1
M.E.T.Salisbury (Du)		10	19	5	37	141	10.07	–	–	1
P.D.Salt (Sx)		15	25	–	148	747	29.88	2	2	12
A.G.Salter (Gm)		10	17	3	72*	204	14.57	–	1	8
R.Samarth (IA)	–	2	4	–	137	167	41.75	1	–	1
† Sami Aslam (P)	–	1	1	–	13	13	13.00	–	–	–
C.W.G.Sanders (LU)	–	2	2	–	56	62	31.00	–	1	–
B.W.Sanderson (Nh)	2018	13	21	13	36	72	9.00	–	–	3
Sarfraz Ahmed (P)	–	4	5	–	14	43	8.60	–	–	12/1
† D.W.Sayer (Le)		1	2	–	21	27	13.50	–	–	2
G.F.B.Scott (M)		1	2	–	13	16	8.00	–	–	–
B.M.A.Seabrook (CU)	–	1	–	–	–	–	–	–	–	–
N.J.Selman (Gm)		12	23	–	42	403	17.52	–	–	21
J.C.Seward (OU)	–	1	–	–	–	–	–	–	–	1
Shadab Khan (P)	–	4	5	–	56	122	24.40	–	2	1
V.Shankar (IA)	–	2	3	–	34	77	25.66	–	–	1
I.Sharma (I/Sx)	2018	9	15	3	66	144	12.00	–	1	1
J.Shaw (Y)		3	6	1	42	104	20.80	–	–	–
P.P.Shaw (IA)	–	2	4	–	188	250	62.50	1	1	4
R.Shepherd (WIA)	–	2	3	–	19	29	9.66	–	–	1
C.E.Shreck (Le)		2	2	–	26	26	13.00	–	–	–
D.P.Sibley (Wa)		15	24	2	144*	779	35.40	4	1	18
P.M.Siddle (Ex)		7	11	2	33*	158	17.55	–	–	2
R.N.Sidebottom (Wa)		10	12	6	10*	30	5.00	–	–	5
J.A.Simpson (M)	2011	9	15	1	42*	351	25.07	–	–	23/3
† V.A.Singh (WIA)	–	2	4	–	47	97	24.25	–	–	–
P.Sisodiya (Gm)		2	4	1	38	41	13.66	–	–	1
B.T.Slater (De/Nt)		13	25	1	109	1025	42.70	1	7	4
D.Smit (De)		4	8	2	45*	129	21.50	–	–	11
O.F.Smith (WIA)	–	1	1	–	30	30	30.00	–	–	2
R.A.J.Smith (Gm)		7	14	2	52*	246	20.50	–	1	1
W.R.Smith (Du)		9	17	–	90	357	21.00	–	2	5
O.C.Soames (H/LU)		6	9	–	29	90	10.00	–	–	1
V.V.S.Sohal (DU)	–	1	–	–	–	–	–	–	–	–
J.H.Sookias (DU)	–	1	–	–	–	–	–	–	–	3
K.Srikar Bharat (IA)	–	1	2	1	33*	35	35.00	–	–	6

237

	Cap	M	I	NO	HS	Runs	Avge	100	50	Ct/St
C.T.Steel (Du)		12	22	–	160	638	29.00	1	4	9
D.I.Stevens (K)	2005	12	19	3	89	319	19.68	–	2	2
G.Stewart (K)		11	17	1	103	414	25.87	1	2	3
D.W.Steyn (H)		5	7	1	25	65	10.83	–	–	1
P.R.Stirling (M)	2016	6	11	–	52	199	18.09	–	1	4
† B.A.Stokes (Du/E)		6	12	–	62	259	21.58	–	1	4
O.P.Stone (Wa)		8	8	2	42*	86	14.33	–	–	–
† M.D.Stoneman (E/Sy)	2018	15	25	1	144	718	29.91	1	4	5
J.Subramanyan (DU)		1	–	–	–	–	–	–	–	–
† Sukhjit Singh (Wa)		1	–	–	–	–	–	–	–	–
K.Suresh (CU)		1	2	–	18	23	11.50	–	–	–
J.A.Tattersall (Y)		7	12	1	70	350	31.81	–	2	19
B.J.Taylor (H)		1	2	–	16	21	10.50	–	–	–
J.M.R.Taylor (Gs)	2010	11	20	1	112	452	23.78	1	–	4
L.R.P.L.Taylor (Nt)	2018	8	15	–	146	506	33.73	1	4	13
M.D.Taylor (Gs)	2013	15	19	3	48	177	11.06	–	–	4
T.A.I.Taylor (Le)		1	2	–	26	31	15.50	–	–	–
R.N.ten Doeschate (Ex)	2006	13	21	3	173*	694	38.55	1	4	13
D.C.Thomas (WIA)		3	6	1	28	134	26.80	–	–	13
I.A.A.Thomas (K)		13	14	8	4*	17	2.83	–	–	6
† O.R.Thomas (WIA)		1	2	1	6*	8	8.00	–	–	–
C.O.Thurston (LU/Nh)		4	6	–	29	93	15.50	–	–	1
A.D.Tillcock (LU)		2	2	–	23	27	13.50	–	–	–
J.C.Tongue (Wo)	2017	11	19	3	34	201	12.56	–	–	2
P.D.Trego (Sm)	2007	2	4	–	39	46	11.50	–	–	1
† M.E.Trescothick (Sm)	1999	10	18	–	100	491	27.27	1	4	16
I.J.L.Trott (Wa)	2005	15	24	4	170*	1046	52.30	3	6	11
S.A.Turner (CU)		1	2	–	33	48	24.00	–	–	–
J.R.Turpin (CfU)		2	1	–	5	5	5.00	–	–	–
B.J.Twohig (Wo)	2018	7	13	2	35	145	13.18	–	–	3
Usman Salahuddin (P)		1	2	–	33	37	18.50	–	–	–
G.L.van Buuren (Gs)	2016	8	15	1	83	327	23.35	–	3	2
T.van der Gugten (Gm)	2018	10	18	5	60*	217	16.69	–	2	2
R.E.van der Merwe (Sm)		1	1	–	0	0	0.00	–	–	–
P.A.van Meekeren (Sm)		1	2	1	6	6	6.00	–	–	–
† S.van Zyl (Sx)		5	9	–	45	237	26.33	–	–	1
† R.S.Vasconcelos (Nh)		11	20	1	140	608	32.00	1	4	15/1
G.H.Vihari (I/IA)	–	3	6	–	68	175	29.14	–	2	2
M.Vijay (Ex/I/IA)		6	11	–	100	357	32.45	1	3	3
D.J.Vilas (La)	2018	15	24	2	235*	879	39.95	3	2	50/4
G.C.Viljoen (De)		12	22	2	60*	386	19.30	–	1	1
J.M.Vince (H)	2013	14	25	1	201*	962	40.08	3	2	5
G.S.Virdi (Sy)		15	17	8	21*	79	8.77	–	–	5
G.Wade (Nh)		1	2	1	1*	1	1.00	–	–	–
G.G.Wagg (Gm)	2013	4	8	–	33	102	12.75	–	–	–
† N.Wagner (Ex)		3	4	1	37	80	26.66	–	–	3
M.J.Waite (Y)		4	6	–	42	96	16.00	–	–	–
A.G.Wakely (Nh)	2012	12	22	1	106	600	28.57	1	4	4
M.T.C.Waller (Sm)		1	1	–	0	0	0.00	–	–	–
† P.I.Walter (Ex)		2	2	–	14	21	10.50	–	–	–
J.A.Warrican (WIA)		2	4	1	5	13	4.33	–	–	3
J.J.Weatherley (H)		13	22	1	126*	486	23.14	1	2	5
L.A.Webb (OU)		1	–	–	–	–	–	–	–	1
† W.J.Weighell (Du)		3	5	–	84	185	37.00	–	1	1
† L.W.P.Wells (Sx)	2016	15	25	1	102*	613	25.54	1	4	3
M.H.Wessels (Nt)	2014	12	23	3	75*	568	28.40	–	4	14

	Cap	M	I	NO	HS	Runs	Avge	100	50	Ct/St
O.E.Westbury (Wo)	2018	2	4	–	22	49	12.25	–	–	1
T.Westley (Ex)	2013	14	24	1	134	731	31.78	2	2	2
B.T.J.Wheal (H)		6	7	1	25*	63	10.50	–	–	7
A.J.A.Wheater (Ex)		9	14	3	68*	390	35.45	–	4	23/1
D.M.Wheeldon (De)		1	2	1	33*	35	35.00	–	–	–
R.G.White (M)		6	11	1	35	101	10.10	–	–	14
R.A.Whiteley (Wo)	2013	6	11	–	91	364	33.09	–	2	8
S.G.Whittingham (Sx)		2	1	1	0*	0	–	–	–	–
D.Wiese (Sx)	2016	13	20	4	106	538	33.62	1	2	2
† A.R.Wilkinson (OU)		1	–	–	–	–	–	–	–	–
D.J.Willey (Y)	2016	2	4	1	34*	42	14.00	–	–	–
K.S.Williamson (Y)		3	6	–	87	218	36.33	–	3	3
G.C.Wilson (Du)		8	14	1	66	357	27.46	–	2	16
N.J.Winder (CU)		1	2	–	8	9	4.50	–	–	–
C.R.Woakes (E/EL/Wa)	2009	6	9	2	137*	295	42.14	1	1	2
C.P.Wood (H)		3	5	1	26	56	14.00	–	–	2
† L.Wood (Nt/Wo)	2018	7	12	3	65*	215	23.88	–	1	5
M.A.Wood (Du/E)		5	9	2	61*	126	18.00	–	1	2
† A.J.Woodland (CfU)		2	1	–	1	1	1.00	–	–	2
D.J.Worrall (Gs)	2018	4	5	1	50	94	23.50	–	1	2
C.J.C.Wright (Wa)	2013	15	18	2	72	342	21.37	–	2	3
L.J.Wright (Sx)	2007	10	17	–	88	349	20.52	–	1	1
J.Yadav (IA)		3	6	2	23*	59	14.75	–	–	–
U.T.Yadav (I)		1	2	2	1*	1	–	–	–	–
† S.A.Zaib (Nh)		7	11	1	57	163	16.30	–	1	–

BOWLING

See BATTING AND FIELDING section for details of matches and caps

	Cat	O	M	R	W	Avge	Best	5wI	10wM
V.R.Aaron (Le)	RFM	86	11	359	9	39.88	4-65	–	–
K.J.Abbott (H)	RFM	348.3	70	1182	51	23.17	6-39	4	1
T.B.Abell (Sm)	RM	121.4	23	492	19	25.89	4-43	–	–
C.N.Ackermann (Le)	OB	43.3	5	137	9	15.22	2-26	–	–
J.H.K.Adams (H)	LM	1	0	3	0		–	–	
M.M.Ali (E/Wo)	OB	183.5	29	586	30	19.53	6-49	3	–
H.A.J.Allen (CfU)	SLA	17	0	101	0		–	–	
T.P.Alsop (H)	SLA	3	0	12	1	12.00	1-12	–	–
J.M.Anderson (E/La)	RFM	337.4	99	887	42	21.11	5-20	1	–
M.K.Andersson (De/M)	RM	70	5	239	12	19.91	4-25	–	–
J.C.Archer (Sx)	RF	273.5	67	750	42	17.85	5-69	1	–
U.Arshad (Le)	RMF	16	2	81	0		–	–	
Asad Shafiq (P)	LB	3	0	6	0		–	–	
R.Ashwin (I)	OB	139.4	30	360	11	32.72	4-62	–	–
S.J.S.Assani (CfU)	RMF	8	2	41	0		–	–	
Azhar Ali (P/Sm)	LB	11	3	20	1	20.00	1- 5	–	–
T.E.Bailey (La)	RMF	454.4	114	1281	65	19.70	5-53	1	–
T.W.Balderson (CU)	SLA	35	8	91	2	45.50	2-91	–	–
J.T.Ball (Nt)	RFM	171.5	38	623	28	22.25	5-43	1	–
E.R.Bamber (M)	RMF	203.5	37	567	28	20.25	4-81	–	–
T.E.Barber (M)	LFM	34	4	131	0		–	–	
K.H.D.Barker (Wa)	LMF	259.1	71	682	41	16.63	5-32	2	–
E.G.Barnard (Wo)	RMF	368.3	93	1138	49	23.22	6-37	4	1
G.A.Bartlett (Sm)	OB	3.2	0	27	0		–	–	
W.A.T.Beer (Sx)	LB	40	8	104	3	34.66	1- 7	–	–
D.J.Bell-Drummond (K)	RMF	7	3	8	2	4.00	1- 1	–	–

	Cat	O	M	R	W	Avge	Best	5wI	10wM
G.K.Berg (H)	RMF	200.1	41	654	15	43.60	5-130	1	–
D.M.Bess (E/EL/Sm)	OB	252.5	55	783	16	48.93	3- 33	–	–
J.J.Bohannon (La)	RMF	27	3	103	5	20.60	3- 46	–	–
R.S.Bopara (Ex)	RM	80.2	9	304	9	33.77	3- 30	–	–
S.G.Borthwick (Sy)	LBG	28.1	1	126	2	63.00	2- 35	–	–
D.A.J.Bracewell (Nh)	RM	93	19	304	11	27.63	4- 71	–	–
K.C.Brathwaite (Nh)	OB	2	0	10	0				
T.T.Bresnan (Wa)	RFM	279.5	48	969	35	27.68	5- 28	1	–
A.D.F.Brewster (CfU)	RFM	39	4	162	0				
D.R.Briggs (Sx)	SLA	279.5	51	764	28	27.28	4- 70	–	–
S.C.J.Broad (E/Nt)	RFM	324.2	86	967	41	23.58	4- 41	–	–
H.C.Brook (Y)	RM	32.1	5	67	0				
H.J.H.Brookes (Wa)	RMF	142	22	470	21	22.38	4- 54	–	–
J.A.Brooks (Y)	RFM	346.3	51	1430	51	28.03	6- 94	5	–
B.C.Brown (Sx)	(WK)	3	2	1	0				
P.R.Brown (Wo)	RMF	20	3	67	1	67.00	1- 53	–	–
N.L.J.Browne (Ex)	LB	1	0	4	0				
N.L.Buck (Nh)	RMF	196.5	22	782	31	25.22	4- 51	–	–
K.A.Bull (Gm)	OB	85.4	14	278	11	25.27	3- 36	–	–
J.Bulpitt (CU)	LM	12	3	32	0				
J.J.Bumrah (I)	RFM	133.2	31	363	14	25.92	5- 85	1	–
M.G.K.Burgess (Sx)	RM	6	1	14	0				
E.J.Byrom (Sm)	OB	10	1	39	0				
J.D.Campbell (WIA)	OB	12	1	45	1	45.00	1- 23	–	–
M.A.Carberry (Le)	RM	2	0	7	0				
L.J.Carey (Gm)	RFM	172	36	592	13	45.53	4-105	–	–
K.S.Carlson (Gm)	OB	1	0	5	0				
M.Carter (Nt)	OB	153.2	28	525	16	32.81	5-113	1	–
H.W.R.Cartwright (M)	RM	122.2	16	410	19	21.57	4- 33	–	–
L.J.Chapman (CU)	OB	13	1	65	1	65.00	1- 65	–	–
Z.J.Chappell (Le)	RFM	76	13	255	16	15.93	6- 44	1	–
B.G.Charlesworth (Gs)	RM/OB	21.1	7	47	4	11.75	3- 25	–	–
G.Clark (Du)	LB	13.5	0	51	2	25.50	1- 10	–	–
J.Clark (La)	RMF	217.1	28	730	26	28.07	5- 58	1	–
R.Clarke (Sy)	RMF	363.1	87	1012	47	21.53	5- 29	1	–
M.E.Claydon (K)	RMF	11.4	0	27	2	13.50	2- 27	–	–
B.O.Coad (Y)	RMF	272.5	87	784	48	16.33	6- 81	3	1
J.J.Cobb (Nh)	OB	14.4	1	67	0				
M.T.Coles (Ex)	RMF	124	27	393	13	30.23	5-123	1	–
P.D.Collingwood (Du)	RM	49	15	116	6	19.33	2- 25	–	–
S.J.Cook (Ex)	RFM	219.3	60	684	27	25.33	5- 28	1	–
J.M.Cooke (DU)	RFM	26	4	61	2	30.50	1- 26	–	–
R.R.S.Cornwall (WIA)	OB	11	0	66	0				
M.J.Cosgrove (Le)	RM	3	0	8	0				
B.D.Cotton (Nh)	RMF	44	13	101	10	10.10	5- 48	1	–
J.Coughlin (Du)	RM	35	3	139	3	46.33	2- 31	–	–
M.J.J.Critchley (De)	LB	285.5	14	1218	32	38.06	6-106	1	1
S.J.Croft (La)	RMF	7	2	11	0				
S.P.Crook (Nh)	RFM	58.2	7	235	12	19.58	4- 51	–	–
J.O.Cross-Zamirski (CU)	RMF	29	5	104	3	34.66	2- 96	–	–
S.M.Curran (E/EL/Sy)	LMF	303	55	970	45	21.55	6- 54	2	1
T.K.Curran (Sy)	RFM	120.4	30	312	19	16.42	5- 28	1	–
A.K.Dal (De)	RM	1	0	1	0				
J.H.Davey (Sm)	RMF	290.4	73	862	34	25.35	5- 65	1	–
W.S.Davis (De)	RFM	11	3	39	2	19.50	2- 39	–	–
M.J.Dawes (OU)	RM	45	15	114	1	114.00	1- 41	–	–

	Cat	O	M	R	W	Avge	Best	5wI	10wM
L.A.Dawson (H)	SLA	205.2	36	627	20	31.35	4-30	–	–
M.de Lange (Gm)	RF	114.4	22	383	16	23.93	5-62	1	–
J.L.Denly (K)	LB	160.1	28	426	23	18.52	4-36	–	–
C.D.J.Dent (Gs)	SLA	4	3	2	0				
J.W.Dernbach (Sy)	RFM	285.5	65	929	32	29.03	4-49	–	–
N.J.Dexter (Le)	RMF	169	40	494	18	27.44	3-17	–	–
M.W.Dixon (Du)	RF	28.2	6	108	2	54.00	2-99	–	–
B.L.D'Oliveira (Wo)	LB	51	3	208	4	52.00	2-44	–	–
G.S.Drissell (Gs)	OB	83	10	272	4	68.00	2-38	–	–
M.P.Dunn (Sy)	RFM	44.3	10	171	3	57.00	2-41	–	–
F.H.Edwards (M)	RFM	362.2	55	1443	54	26.72	6-50	2	–
S.M.Ervine (De/H)	RM	18	0	65	0				
D.A.Escott (OU)	LB	22.2	5	52	4	13.00	3-52	–	–
B.N.Evans (CfU)	RMF	40	10	141	5	28.20	4-53	–	–
S.T.Evans (Le/LU)		1	0	3	0				
Faheem Ashraf (P)	RFM	61	13	208	4	52.00	3-60	–	–
M.J.Fanning (OU)	RFM	17	5	46	0				
E.W.F.Fenwick (DU)		16	2	55	0				
L.H.Ferguson (De)	RF	164.3	22	618	18	34.33	4-56	–	–
S.T.Finn (M)	RFM	108	9	395	9	43.88	2-34	–	–
M.D.Fisher (EL/Y)	RFM	79	8	291	5	58.20	2-43	–	–
L.J.Fletcher (Nt)	RMF	347.3	86	977	38	25.71	5-27	1	–
M.H.A.Footitt (De/Nt)	LFM	81.4	11	333	7	47.57	3-69	–	–
J.K.Fuller (M)	RFM	227.2	25	845	28	30.17	4-49	–	–
G.H.S.Garton (Sx)	LF	27	2	103	1	103.00	1-46	–	–
W.R.S.Gidman (K)	RM	33.4	5	103	7	14.71	5-47	1	–
A.F.Gleadall (De)	RMF	13.3	1	59	1	59.00	1-20	–	–
R.J.Gleeson (La/Nh)	RFM	147.3	34	452	26	17.38	6-79	1	–
J.S.D.Gnodde (OU)	SLA	27	8	67	3	22.33	2-35	–	–
B.W.M.Graves (DU)	SLA	28	2	113	1	113.00	1-62	–	–
B.G.F.Green (Sm)	RFM	7	3	17	1	17.00	1- 8	–	–
S.R.Green (OU)	LM	1	1	0	0				
L.Gregory (Sm)	RMF	305.5	75	928	37	25.08	4-33	–	–
G.T.Griffiths (Le)	RMF	269	67	882	36	24.50	6-49	1	1
T.D.Groenewald (Sm)	RFM	173	41	509	21	24.23	4-85	–	–
C.J.Guest (CU)	OB	5	0	28	1	28.00	1-28	–	–
M.J.Guptill (Wo)	OB	4	1	17	1	17.00	1-12	–	–
R.N.Gurbani (IA)	RM	37	4	117	4	29.25	3-64	–	–
H.F.Gurney (Nt)	LFM	325.3	52	1137	42	27.07	6-25	2	–
C.J.Haggett (K)	RMF	29	11	85	6	14.16	2- 6	–	–
T.J.Haines (Sx)	RM	29	8	74	1	74.00	1-13	–	–
Hamidullah Qadri (De)	OB	78.1	7	319	8	39.87	3-66	–	–
M.A.H.Hammond (Gs)	OB	3	0	14	0				
J.S.Handley (CU)	LB	10.3	4	38	0				
O.J.Hannon-Dalby (Wa)	RMF	103.4	22	329	15	21.93	4-61	–	–
G.H.I.Harding (Du)	SLA	30	4	106	0				
Haris Sohail (P)	LM	15.4	0	50	1	50.00	1-16	–	–
S.R.Harmer (Ex)	OB	526.2	136	1394	57	24.45	6-87	3	–
J.A.R.Harris (M)	RFM	384.5	67	1253	61	20.54	7-83	3	–
G.J.Harte (Du)	RM	45.1	7	148	3	49.33	2-26	–	–
Hasan Ali (P)	RFM	69.4	14	219	7	31.28	4-51	–	–
T.M.Head (Wo)	OB	43	6	162	1	162.00	1-30	–	–
T.D.Heathfield (OU)	RMF	9	1	32	0				
T.G.Helm (M)	RMF	74.5	12	236	7	33.71	3-46	–	–
M.J.Henry (K)	RFM	382.4	83	1161	75	15.48	7-42	5	3
R.F.Higgins (Gs)	RM	359.5	102	892	48	18.58	5-21	2	–

	Cat	O	M	R	W	Avge	Best	5wI	10wM
M.G.Hogan (Gm)	RFM	393.3	101	1014	45	22.53	5- 49	2	–
M.D.E.Holden (M)	OB	40	3	145	1	145.00	1- 15	–	–
C.K.Holder (WIA)	RFM	73	4	312	8	39.00	4- 57	–	–
I.G.Holland (H)	RMF	151	42	389	15	25.93	3- 48	–	–
B.A.C.Howell (Gs)	RMF	28	5	122	4	30.50	2- 54	–	–
A.L.Hughes (De)	RM	87	19	255	10	25.50	4- 57	–	–
M.S.T.Hughes (OU)	RM	2	0	7	0				
B.A.Hutton (Nh)	RM	392.2	91	1212	46	26.34	8- 57	3	–
R.A.Jadeja (I)	SLA	77	3	258	7	36.85	4- 79	–	–
L.W.James (Nt)	RMF	15	1	68	3	22.66	3- 54	–	–
A.Javid (Le)	OB	26.2	3	78	2	39.00	1- 30	–	–
K.K.Jennings (E/La)	RM	21	0	113	0				
R.A.Jones (Le)	RMF	13	1	44	1	44.00	1- 39	–	–
R.P.Jones (La)	LB	7	0	20	1	20.00	1- 18	–	–
C.J.Jordan (Sx)	RFM	191.1	32	598	20	29.90	3- 23	–	–
R.I.Keogh (Nh)	OB	90.3	11	347	6	57.83	4-111	–	–
D.Klein (Le)	LMF	94	17	400	5	80.00	2- 23	–	–
R.K.Kleinveldt (Nh)	RMF	95.1	14	282	14	20.14	4- 51	–	–
Kuldeep Yadav (I)	SLC	9	1	44	0				
M.B.Lake (OU)	RM	9	2	26	0				
D.J.Lamb (La)	RM	28	1	146	0				
M.J.Lamb (Wa)	RM	6	1	22	0				
J.L.Lawlor (Gm)	OB	29.1	3	110	4	27.50	3- 59	–	–
D.W.Lawrence (Ex)	LB	3	0	15	0				
J.Leach (Wo)	RMF	157.5	28	508	23	22.08	4- 42	–	–
M.J.Leach (EL/Sm)	SLA	262.4	57	757	31	24.41	8- 85	3	2
J.A.Leaning (Y)	RMF	19	3	57	1	57.00	1- 16	–	–
B.J.Leighton (OU)	RM	26	4	79	3	26.33	2- 42	–	–
T.J.Lester (La)	LFM	27.1	2	78	3	26.00	2- 51	–	–
S.H.Lewis (WIA)	RMF	88.1	15	351	12	29.25	4- 35	–	–
J.D.Libby (Nt)	OB	11.5	0	40	1	40.00	1- 23	–	–
C.J.Liddle (Gs)	LFM	40	7	122	4	30.50	2- 23	–	–
A.M.Lilley (La)	OB	28.3	6	89	2	44.50	2- 52	–	–
L.S.Livingstone (La)	LB	86.5	18	214	7	30.57	3- 27	–	–
D.L.Lloyd (Gm)	OB	105.3	19	343	9	38.11	2- 31	–	–
J.E.G.Logan (Y)	SLA	12	3	44	0				
A.Lyth (Y)	RM	68	8	246	4	61.50	2- 97	–	–
B.J.McCarthy (Du)	RMF	130.3	21	460	14	32.85	4- 58	–	–
C.M.MacDonell (DU)	RFM	18	0	83	0				
A.H.McGrath (DU)	LM	29	6	89	1	89.00	1- 45	–	–
C.McKerr (Sy)	RFM	67.2	13	246	13	18.92	4- 26	–	–
W.L.Madsen (De)	OB	42.4	9	152	4	38.00	1- 9	–	–
S.J.Magoffin (Wo)	RFM	202	55	593	16	37.06	3- 70	–	–
K.A.Maharaj (La)	SLA	103.4	23	283	17	16.64	7- 37	1	1
S.Mahmood (La)	RFM	37	6	110	5	22.00	3- 53	–	–
D.J.Malan (E/EL/M)	LB	48	3	145	3	48.33	1- 15	–	–
A.K.Markram (Du)	OB	1.4	1	1	1	1.00	1- 1	–	–
S.C.Meaker (Sy)	RMF	44	5	158	2	79.00	1- 29	–	–
J.M.Mennie (La)	RMF	192.5	44	601	28	21.46	4- 43	–	–
C.A.J.Meschede (Gm)	RMF	76	8	327	9	36.33	2- 30	–	–
B.W.M.Mike (Le)	RM	87.2	10	385	19	20.26	5- 37	1	–
C.N.Miles (Gs)	RMF	341.1	65	1213	58	20.91	5- 50	2	–
M.E.Milnes (Nt)	RMF	153	26	527	11	47.90	4- 44	–	–
D.K.H.Mitchell (Wo)	RM	62	9	200	4	50.00	2- 21	–	–
Mohammad Abbas (Le/P)	RMF	433.1	124	1124	64	17.56	6- 48	5	1
Mohammad Amir (P)	LF	97.1	21	271	8	33.87	4- 36	–	–

	Cat	O	M	R	W	Avge	Best	5wI	10wM
Mohammed Shami (I)	RFM	172.4	25	622	16	38.87	4- 57	–	–
Mohammed Siraj (IA)	RMF	85.5	14	266	15	17.73	4- 64	–	–
A.O.Morgan (Gm)	SLA	12.1	2	46	0			–	–
M.Morkel (Sy)	RF	339.4	90	907	63	14.39	6- 57	4	–
C.A.J.Morris (Wo)	RMF	108.4	15	372	9	41.33	3- 20	–	–
S.J.Mullaney (Nt)	RM	114	21	402	11	36.54	4- 68	–	–
J.R.Murphy (Gm)	LFM	16.3	2	73	1	73.00	1- 41	–	–
T.J.Murtagh (M)	RFM	359.5	95	888	58	15.31	5- 38	2	–
S.Nadeem (IA)	SLA	105	16	332	12	27.66	3- 42	–	–
C.D.Nash (Nt)	OB	22	1	66	3	22.00	2- 4	–	–
K.Noema-Barnett (Gs)	RM	82.4	14	271	8	33.87	2- 34	–	–
L.C.Norwell (Gs)	RMF	9	3	20	0			–	–
D.Olivier (De)	RF	251.3	47	852	31	27.48	5- 20	2	1
G.Onions (La)	RFM	398.3	81	1275	59	21.61	6- 55	2	–
C.Overton (Sm)	RMF	321.3	72	1014	37	27.40	4- 27	–	–
J.Overton (Sm)	RFM	177.3	34	646	26	24.84	4- 25	–	–
A.P.Palladino (De)	RMF	369	94	1006	51	19.72	6- 29	3	1
H.H.Pandya (I)	RMF	64.1	7	247	10	24.70	5- 28	1	–
C.F.Parkinson (Le)	SLA	239	42	824	10	82.40	3- 50	–	–
M.W.Parkinson (La)	LB	170.1	30	512	18	28.44	5-101	1	–
W.D.Parnell (Wo)	LFM	154.4	22	582	18	32.33	4- 23	–	–
S.D.Parry (La)	SLA	97	14	274	3	91.33	2-101	–	–
A.R.Patel (Du)	SLA	99.4	33	235	18	13.05	7- 54	1	–
J.S.Patel (Wa)	OB	431.4	108	1276	56	22.78	7- 83	4	2
R.H.Patel (M)	SLA	48.2	9	177	6	29.50	3- 58	–	–
R.S.Patel (Sy)	RMF	97.1	16	309	8	38.62	6- 5	1	–
S.R.Patel (Nt)	SLA	305.5	66	896	19	47.15	6-114	1	–
S.A.Patterson (Y)	RMF	235	63	594	24	24.75	6- 40	1	–
D.A.Payne (Gs)	LMF	204.2	42	573	22	26.04	4- 25	–	–
S.J.Pearce (CfU)	LB	18.4	0	106	1	106.00	1- 74	–	–
D.Y.Pennington (Wo)	RMF	187	34	778	22	35.36	4- 53	–	–
W.J.N.Pereira (LU)	LFM	42	5	138	2	69.00	2- 55	–	–
T.H.S.Pettman (OU)	RFM	63	25	129	9	14.33	5- 41	1	–
O.L.Pike (CfU)	RMF	34	5	138	2	69.00	1- 35	–	–
M.W.Pillans (Sy/Y)	RF	49	8	198	3	66.00	3- 29	–	–
H.W.Podmore (K)	RMF	353.4	85	1037	45	23.04	6- 36	1	–
J.A.Porter (EL/Ex)	RFM	457.3	87	1508	61	24.72	7- 41	3	1
M.J.Potts (Du)	RM	5	0	37	1	37.00	1- 37	–	–
J.E.Poysden (Wa/Y)	LB	75.4	3	332	12	27.66	5- 29	1	–
S.Prasanna (Nh)	LB	72	7	247	10	24.70	4- 49	–	–
R.D.Pringle (Du)	OB	28	2	74	3	24.66	3- 31	–	–
L.A.Procter (Nh)	RM	117.1	22	411	14	29.35	5- 33	1	–
M.R.Quinn (Ex)	RMF	101	19	306	12	25.50	3- 23	–	–
Rahat Ali (P)	LFM	35	7	110	4	27.50	2- 25	–	–
B.A.Raine (Le)	RMF	395.1	90	1146	51	22.47	4- 44	–	–
A.S.Rajpoot (IA)	RM	61.1	21	161	7	23.00	4- 76	–	–
R.Rampaul (De)	RFM	183.3	35	651	13	50.07	3- 53	–	–
A.U.Rashid (E)	LB	87	10	309	10	30.90	3-101	–	–
O.P.Rayner (H/M)	OB	218.5	52	530	12	44.16	4- 54	–	–
L.M.Reece (De)	LM	64.1	13	186	11	16.90	7- 20	1	–
R.A.Reifer (WIA)	RMF	89.3	15	311	11	28.27	5- 50	1	–
M.T.Renshaw (Sm)	OB	3	1	11	0			–	–
W.M.H.Rhodes (Wa)	RMF	56	12	182	1	182.00	1- 0	–	–
A.E.N.Riley (K)	OB	136.2	33	341	9	37.88	4- 68	–	–
N.J.Rimmington (Du)	RFM	167.4	34	606	11	55.09	3- 39	–	–
S.E.Rippington (CU)	LM	20	1	90	1	90.00	1- 90	–	–

243

	Cat	O	M	R	W	Avge	Best	5wI	10wM
J.A.J.Rishton (LU)	RM	35	5	111	2	55.50	1- 44	–	–
W.J.R.Robertson (OU)	RM	3	1	7	1	7.00	1- 7	–	–
O.E.Robinson (Sx)	RMF	500.4	96	1412	81	17.43	7- 23	5	1
S.D.Robson (M)	LB	4	0	27	0				
O.J.W.Rogers (OU)	LB	7.1	1	13	1	13.00	1- 7	–	–
T.S.Roland-Jones (M)	RFM	21	0	98	2	49.00	1- 35	–	–
W.J.L.Rollings (LU)	RFM	38	5	139	2	69.50	2- 78	–	–
J.E.Root (E/Y)	OB	29.4	8	63	5	12.60	4- 5	–	–
W.T.Root (Nt)	OB	9.3	1	55	3	18.33	3- 37	–	–
F.W.A.Ruffell (DU)	RM	27	1	96	0				
C.Rushworth (Du)	RMF	386.4	83	1201	60	20.01	8- 51	3	1
A.M.C.Russell (DU)	RFM	12	2	34	1	34.00	1- 34	–	–
N.A.Saini (IA)	RM	84	18	284	6	47.33	2- 41	–	–
A.Sakande (Sx)	RFM	37.4	7	129	4	32.25	3- 44	–	–
M.E.T.Salisbury (Du)	RMF	293.1	54	1090	44	24.77	6- 37	1	–
P.D.Salt (Sx)	OB	9	2	32	1	32.00	1- 32	–	–
A.G.Salter (Gm)	OB	245	45	759	18	42.16	4- 80	–	–
C.W.G.Sanders (LU)	RFM	45	9	174	3	58.00	2- 67	–	–
B.W.Sanderson (Nh)	RMF	422	112	1002	60	16.70	5- 16	2	–
D.W.Sayer (Le)	LM	5	1	28	0				
G.F.B.Scott (M)	RM	12	3	23	0				
B.M.A.Seabrook (CU)	RM	6	1	25	0				
N.J.Selman (Gm)	RM	1	0	6	0				
Shadab Khan (P)	LBG	110.5	14	392	15	26.13	6- 77	1	–
V.Shankar (IA)	OB	27	0	109	2	54.50	1- 20	–	–
I.Sharma (I/Sx)	RFM	265.3	55	783	33	23.72	5- 51	1	–
J.Shaw (Y)	RMF	63	5	265	4	66.25	2- 72	–	–
R.Shepherd (WIA)	RFM	40.1	5	171	4	42.75	1- 30	–	–
P.M.Siddle (Ex)	RFM	234.4	47	607	37	16.40	5- 37	3	–
R.N.Sidebottom (Wa)	RMF	187	40	644	25	25.76	6- 35	1	1
P.Sisodiya (Gm)	SLA	63.2	12	151	7	21.57	3- 54	–	–
O.F.Smith (WIA)	RM	24	3	99	3	33.00	2- 15	–	–
R.A.J.Smith (Gm)	RM	155.3	24	593	20	29.65	5- 87	1	–
W.R.Smith (Du)	OB	66.1	6	204	4	51.00	2- 10	–	–
V.V.S.Sohal (DU)	OB	12	0	56	0				
C.T.Steel (Du)	LB	46.2	4	202	9	22.44	2- 7	–	–
D.I.Stevens (K)	RM	295.4	76	799	42	19.02	6- 26	2	–
G.Stewart (K)	RMF	164.5	26	505	22	22.95	6- 22	1	–
D.W.Steyn (H)	RF	142.3	30	382	20	19.10	5- 66	1	–
P.R.Stirling (M)	OB	24	3	81	2	40.50	2- 62	–	–
B.A.Stokes (Du/E)	RMF	181.2	33	599	25	23.96	5- 52	1	–
O.P.Stone (Wa)	RF	161.2	26	529	43	12.30	8- 80	3	1
J.Subramanyan (DU)	LB	18	1	67	1	67.00	1- 67	–	–
K.Suresh (CU)	RFM	37.1	3	173	3	57.66	3-172	–	–
B.J.Taylor (H)	OB	16	4	50	2	25.00	2- 50	–	–
M.D.Taylor (Gs)	LMF	358	66	1186	51	23.25	5- 15	2	–
T.A.I.Taylor (Le)	RMF	34	11	92	6	15.33	4- 15	–	–
D.C.Thomas (WIA)	RM	14	1	60	1	60.00	1- 60	–	–
I.A.A.Thomas (K)	RMF	196	34	662	25	26.48	5- 91	1	–
O.R.Thomas (WIA)	RMF	24	2	130	3	43.33	3- 66	–	–
C.O.Thurston (LU/Nh)	RM	3	0	16	0				
A.D.Tillcock (LU)	SLA	41	4	93	1	93.00	1- 53	–	–
J.C.Tongue (Wo)	RM	304.4	52	1011	40	25.27	5- 53	2	–
P.D.Trego (Sm)	RMF	41	7	146	3	48.66	2- 63	–	–
S.A.Turner (CU)		10	0	50	0				
J.R.Turpin (CfU)	RM	30.2	5	129	2	64.50	1- 49	–	–

	Cat	O	M	R	W	Avge	Best	5wI	10wM
B.J.Twohig (Wo)	SLA	161	18	598	10	59.80	2- 47	–	–
G.L.van Buuren (Gs)	SLA	72	8	246	4	61.50	3- 74	–	–
T.van der Gugten (Gm)	RFM	287	69	936	43	21.76	7- 42	2	–
R.E.van der Merwe (Sm)	SLA	51	13	143	5	28.60	4-138	–	–
P.A.van Meekeren (Sm)	RMF	20	3	67	1	67.00	1- 67	–	–
S.van Zyl (Sx)	RM	48	12	127	3	42.33	3- 16	–	–
G.H.Vihari (I/IA)	OB	10.3	1	38	3	12.66	3- 37	–	–
M.Vijay (E/I/IA)	OB	3	0	11	0			–	–
G.C.Viljoen (De)	RF	356.1	55	1225	38	32.23	4- 51	–	–
J.M.Vince (H)	RM	5	1	17	0			–	–
G.S.Virdi (Sy)	OB	383.3	47	1263	40	31.57	6-105	1	–
G.Wade (Nh)	RMF	28	4	118	1	118.00	1- 75	–	–
G.G.Wagg (Gm)	LM	82.4	13	258	8	32.25	3- 25	–	–
N.Wagner (Ex)	LMF	109	9	421	9	46.77	3-122	–	–
M.J.Waite (H)	RFM	61	14	221	8	27.62	3- 91	–	–
P.I.Walter (Ex)	LMF	11	1	39	2	19.50	2- 21	–	–
J.A.Warrican (WIA)	SLA	28	3	137	1	137.00	1- 36	–	–
J.J.Weatherley (H)	OB	14	1	65	2	32.50	1- 2	–	–
W.J.Weighell (Du)	RMF	108.3	23	304	15	20.26	7- 32	1	–
L.W.P.Wells (Sx)	LB	136.2	14	399	8	49.87	4- 81	–	–
O.E.Westbury (Wo)	OB	1	0	6	0				
T.Westley (Ex)	OB	26	9	65	3	21.66	1- 0	–	–
B.T.J.Wheal (H)	RMF	114.5	17	462	11	42.00	2- 46	–	–
D.M.Wheeldon (De)	RFM	13	2	48	1	48.00	1- 12	–	–
R.A.Whiteley (Wo)	LM	36.2	4	115	3	38.33	1- 2	–	–
S.G.Whittingham (Sx)	RFM	25	2	117	4	29.25	2- 56	–	–
D.Wiese (Sx)	RMF	339.1	65	1041	41	25.39	5- 48	1	–
A.R.Wilkinson (OU)	LFM	4	0	18	1	18.00	1- 18	–	–
D.J.Willey (Y)	LMF	67.2	13	217	6	36.16	3- 72	–	–
K.S.Williamson (Y)	OB	2	0	9	0				
N.J.Winder (CU)	SLA	32	4	106	0				
C.R.Woakes (E/EL/Wa)	RFM	144	22	514	19	27.05	3- 55	–	–
C.P.Wood (H)	LM	72	13	268	6	44.66	2- 56	–	–
L.Wood (Nt/Wo)	LFM	142.1	21	519	11	47.18	3- 66	–	–
M.A.Wood (Du/E)	RF	136.4	31	374	19	19.68	6- 46	2	–
A.J.Woodland (CfU)	RM	11	0	49	0				
D.J.Worrall (Gs)	RFM	119.1	33	348	16	21.75	4- 45	–	–
C.J.C.Wright (Wa)	RFM	378.2	68	1292	41	31.51	5- 32	1	–
J.Yadav (I)	OB	103.3	13	368	5	73.60	2- 23	–	–
U.T.Yadav (I)	RFM	24	3	76	3	25.33	2- 20	–	–
S.A.Zaib (Nh)	SLA	26.4	8	52	2	26.00	2- 24	–	–

FIRST-CLASS CAREER RECORDS

Compiled by Philip Bailey

The following career records are for all players who appeared in first-class and county cricket during the 2018 season, and are complete to the end of that season. Some players who did not appear in 2018 but may do so in 2019 are included.

BATTING AND FIELDING

'1000' denotes instances of scoring 1000 runs in a season. Where these have been achieved outside the British Isles they are shown after a plus sign.

	M	I	NO	HS	Runs	Avge	100	50	1000	Ct/St
Aaron, V.R.	51	78	17	72	693	11.36	–	1	–	11
Abbott, K.J.	100	139	26	97*	2198	19.45	–	8	–	17
Abell, T.B.	59	107	12	135	3055	32.15	4	18	–	35
Ackermann, C.N.	104	182	18	196*	6717	40.95	16	38	0+1	88
Adair, H.R.D.	1	–	–	–	–	–	–	–	–	0
Adams, J.H.K.	233	409	30	262*	14134	37.29	25	73	5	189
Agar, A.C.	50	73	9	106	1689	26.39	2	9	–	19
Agarwal, M.A.	40	68	6	304*	2997	48.33	7	17	0+1	25
Ali, A.M.	15	25	1	80	639	26.62	–	3	–	6
Ali, M.M.	184	313	27	250	10908	38.13	20	68	2	105
Allen, H.A.J.	2	1	–	4	4	4.00	–	–	–	0
Alsop, T.P.	33	56	1	117	1482	26.94	1	12	–	46
Ambris, S.W.	44	76	6	231	2189	31.27	6	9	–	63/3
Ambrose, T.R.	239	363	34	251*	10950	33.28	17	65	–	639/40
Amla, H.M.	231	384	29	311*	17444	49.13	52	85	0+2	182
Anderson, C.J.	53	89	10	167	2862	36.22	4	13	–	39
Anderson, J.M.	234	300	120	81	1766	9.81	–	1	–	135
Andersson, M.K.	6	12	2	34	99	9.90	–	–	–	6
Archer, J.C.	28	41	9	81*	1003	31.34	–	6	–	19
Arshad, U.	18	23	1	84	557	25.31	–	3	–	6
Asad Shafiq	125	212	17	223	7623	39.09	20	36	0+1	112
Ashar Zaidi	112	179	13	202	6019	36.25	12	29	0+1	84
Ashwin, R.	105	145	26	124	3719	31.25	6	19	–	41
Assani, S.J.S.	1	–	–	–	–	–	–	–	–	1
Azeem Rafiq	38	45	5	100	866	21.65	1	4	–	14
Azhar Ali	168	293	26	302*	10636	39.83	34	44	–	136
Babar Azam	44	72	7	266	2301	35.40	2	17	–	28
Bailey, T.E.	46	64	11	66	904	17.05	–	3	–	9
Bairstow, J.M.	170	278	32	246	11117	45.19	23	60	3	444/20
Balderson, T.W.	1	2	1	2*	3	3.00	–	–	–	0
Ball, J.T.	52	79	12	49*	897	13.38	–	–	–	7
Ballance, G.S.	145	238	22	210	10268	47.53	35	48	3+1	115
Bamber, E.R.	6	10	3	27*	76	10.85	–	–	–	2
Bancroft, C.T.	76	139	11	228*	4910	38.35	11	20	–	101/1
Banton, T.	2	3	–	30	37	12.33	–	–	–	1
Barber, T.E.	2	3	1	3	3	1.50	–	–	–	0
Barker, K.H.D.	113	150	25	125	3554	28.43	6	16	–	33
Barnard, E.G.	46	69	12	75	1599	28.05	–	10	–	24
Bartlett, G.A.	10	18	1	110	406	22.55	1	–	–	5
Batty, G.J.	253	374	64	133	7276	23.47	3	30	–	161
Bavuma, T.	121	200	28	162	6439	37.43	12	35	–	60
Bawne, A.R.	79	123	19	258*	5411	52.02	17	28	–	36
Beer, W.A.T.	16	17	4	50*	338	26.00	–	1	–	5

246

	M	I	NO	HS	Runs	Avge	100	50	1000	Ct/St
Bell, I.R.	307	516	55	262*	20256	43.93	57	103	5	233
Bell-Drummond, D.J.	97	164	14	206*	4825	32.16	9	24	1	40
Berg, G.K.	122	184	22	130*	4845	29.90	2	27	–	65
Bess, D.M.	24	37	5	107	777	24.28	1	3	–	16
Billings, S.W.	61	89	9	171	2641	33.01	3	13	–	157/11
Blackwood, J.	81	148	8	147	4439	31.70	4	30	–	81
Blake, A.J.	40	62	6	105*	1374	24.53	1	6	–	23
Bohannon, J.J.	5	9	1	78*	255	31.87	–	2	–	2
Bopara, R.S.	210	341	39	229	12251	40.56	29	52	1	108
Borthwick, S.G.	150	251	25	216	8375	37.05	17	46	4	200
Bowers, J.W.R.	1	–	–	–	–	–	–	–	–	0
Bracewell, D.A.J.	89	135	19	105	3087	26.61	2	16	–	44
Bracey, J.R.	23	40	4	156	1282	35.61	3	5	–	22
Brathwaite, C.R.	39	64	9	109	1522	27.67	1	9	–	20
Brathwaite, K.C.	130	231	18	212	8765	41.15	21	47	–	81
Bravo, D.J.	100	180	7	197	5302	30.64	8	30	–	89
Bresnan, T.T.	194	264	41	169*	6456	28.95	6	33	–	101
Brewster, A.D.F.	4	2	1	7	8	8.00	–	–	–	0
Brierley, D.D.W.	2	2	–	12	12	6.00	–	–	–	0
Briggs, D.R.	101	128	34	120*	1654	17.59	1	1	–	36
Broad, S.C.J.	199	275	38	169	4909	20.71	1	24	–	70
Brodrick, C.A.J.	2	3	–	52	71	23.66	–	1	–	3
Brook, H.C.	17	30	–	124	657	21.90	1	3	–	8
Brookes, H.J.H.	6	8	1	70	180	25.71	–	2	–	3
Brooks, J.A.	119	145	49	109*	1609	16.76	1	4	–	29
Brooks, S.S.J.	64	106	12	166	3236	34.42	5	19	–	57
Brown, B.C.	125	195	30	163	6495	39.36	15	36	2	343/16
Brown, C.R.	10	19	–	35	249	13.10	–	–	–	3
Brown, K.R.	85	140	6	132	3572	26.65	2	22	–	52
Brown, P.R.	5	6	4	5*	14	7.00	–	–	–	2
Browne, N.L.J.	76	124	9	255	4821	41.92	14	20	3	56
Bruce, T.C.	33	58	7	166*	2268	44.47	4	16	–	51
Buck, N.L.	83	117	31	43	1058	12.30	–	–	–	15
Bull, K.A.	11	18	6	31	145	12.08	–	–	–	3
Bulpitt, J.	1	–	–	–	–	–	–	–	–	0
Bumrah, J.J.	32	39	23	16*	130	8.12	–	–	–	12
Burgess, M.G.K.	26	38	3	146	1336	38.17	2	6	–	27
Burnham, J.T.A.	26	44	4	135	1018	25.45	1	6	–	9
Burns, J.A.	96	168	-11	202*	6305	40.15	15	35	–	84
Burns, R.J.	107	184	14	219*	7601	44.71	15	42	5	93
Buttler, J.C.	89	140	13	144	4165	32.79	5	25	–	176/2
Byrom, E.J.	19	36	–	152	915	25.41	1	3	–	7
Campbell, J.D.	55	103	3	156	2984	29.84	3	17	–	61
Carberry, M.A.	208	363	25	300*	13868	41.02	35	67	4	94
Carey, L.J.	20	27	3	54	289	12.04	–	1	–	4
Carlson, K.S.	26	47	2	191	1263	28.06	3	3	–	10
Carter, A.	36	41	14	39	307	11.37	–	–	–	8
Carter, M.	9	16	1	33	140	9.33	–	–	–	8
Cartwright, H.W.R.	41	67	6	170*	2297	37.65	3	11	–	16
Carver, K.	8	13	6	20	108	15.42	–	–	–	4
Chanderpaul, S.	385	626	108	303*	27545	53.17	77	144	1+1	193
Chapman, L.J.	3	4	–	13	18	4.50	–	–	–	2
Chappell, Z.J.	14	21	4	96	532	31.29	–	2	–	1
Charlesworth, B.G.	6	9	1	77*	194	24.25	–	2	–	2
Chohan, D.	4	8	–	83	225	28.12	–	2	–	3
Chopra, V.	186	305	20	233*	9977	35.00	20	50	3	220

	M	I	NO	HS	Runs	Avge	100	50	1000	Ct/St
Christian, D.T.	83	141	17	131*	3783	30.50	5	16	–	90
Clark, G.	30	55	–	109	1464	26.61	1	10	–	21
Clark, J.	42	59	4	140	1616	29.38	1	9	–	6
Clarke, J.M.	61	105	8	194	3836	39.54	12	14	1	29
Clarke, R.	238	358	40	214	10426	32.78	17	54	1	356
Claydon, M.E.	102	130	28	77	1561	15.30	–	4	–	11
Coad, B.O.	24	33	13	33	281	14.05	–	–	–	1
Cobb, J.J.	119	205	22	148*	4702	25.69	3	27	–	50
Cockbain, I.A.	51	86	6	151*	2382	29.77	4	13	–	35
Coetzer, K.J.	94	156	11	219	4404	30.37	8	19	–	46
Coles, M.T.	111	147	20	103*	2508	19.74	1	12	–	58
Collingwood, P.D.	306	527	52	206	16938	35.65	35	85	3	352
Colverd, T.G.L.	6	12	–	64	226	18.83	–	2	–	3
Cook, A.N.	289	513	36	294	22604	47.38	63	107	8+1	306
Cook, S.C.	213	393	32	390	14403	39.89	44	57	0+4	133
Cook, S.J.	19	19	11	14	60	7.50	–	–	–	1
Cooke, C.B.	77	133	16	171	4110	35.12	4	27	–	123/2
Cooke, J.M.	4	2	–	21	28	14.00	–	–	–	6
Corner, T.P.	1	2	–	46	56	28.00	–	–	–	0
Cornwall, R.R.S.	44	77	4	101*	1682	23.04	1	8	–	38
Cosgrove, M.J.	208	370	19	233	14279	40.68	35	81	4	130
Cotton, B.D.	23	33	11	43	346	15.72	–	–	–	5
Coughlin, J.	3	5	–	19	42	8.40	–	–	–	1
Coughlin, P.	32	51	7	85	1168	26.54	–	7	–	13
Cox, O.B.	101	165	22	124	3981	27.83	3	23	–	267/12
Crane, M.S.	32	45	17	29	321	11.46	–	–	–	9
Crawley, Z.	21	33	–	168	934	28.30	1	5	–	15
Critchley, M.J.J.	32	54	5	137*	1480	30.20	3	6	–	16
Croft, S.J.	165	258	23	156	7791	33.15	13	44	–	172
Crook, S.P.	106	146	19	145	4043	31.83	5	22	–	36
Cross-Zamirski, J.O.	1	2	1	1	1	1.00	–	–	–	1
Cullen, T.N.	8	13	–	42	183	14.07	–	–	–	15/1
Curran, B.J.	5	9	1	83*	251	31.37	–	2	–	3
Curran, S.M.	47	70	8	96	1790	28.87	–	13	–	13
Curran, T.K.	58	79	10	60	1211	17.55	–	5	–	20
Dal, A.K.	4	7	–	25	107	15.28	–	–	–	2
Davey, J.H.	26	42	8	72	626	18.41	–	3	–	11
Davies, A.L.	65	100	4	140*	3298	34.35	4	21	1	156/15
Davies, R.C.	23	31	1	86	442	14.73	–	3	–	43/6
Davies, S.M.	210	348	34	200*	12409	39.51	23	58	6	484/30
Davis, W.S.	13	17	4	25	112	8.61	–	–	–	2
Dawes, M.J.	2	1	1	0*	0	–	–	–	–	1
Dawson, L.A.	142	233	25	169	6677	32.10	8	35	1	139
Dearden, H.E.	23	43	2	87	838	20.43	–	4	–	20
de Bruyn, T.B.	54	93	9	202*	3852	45.85	10	17	–	53
de Grandhomme, C.	94	154	19	144*	4895	36.25	11	29	–	94
de Lange, M.	74	99	15	90	1323	15.75	–	3	–	32
Delport, C.S.	61	106	6	163	3206	32.06	3	19	–	36
Denly, J.L.	189	325	23	227	10986	36.37	27	54	4	78
Dent, C.D.J.	129	232	22	268	7894	37.59	14	47	3	148
Dernbach, J.W.	113	139	47	56*	871	9.46	–	1	–	17
de Villiers, A.B.	141	238	23	278*	10689	49.71	25	60	0+1	275/6
Dewhurst, A.C.H.	2	4	–	91	163	40.75	–	2	–	1
Dexter, N.J.	153	257	30	163*	7875	34.69	17	37	–	97
Dhawan, S.	121	200	10	224	8338	43.88	24	29	0+1	120
Dickinson, C.M.	4	6	–	99	211	35.16	–	2	–	4

	M	I	NO	HS	Runs	Avge	100	50	1000	Ct/St
Dickson, S.R.	57	94	7	318	3068	35.26	7	13	–	46
Dixon, M.W.	13	13	4	22	76	8.44	–	–	–	1
D'Oliveira, B.L.	52	92	2	202*	2495	27.72	6	6	–	25
Donald, A.H.T.	39	71	4	234	2056	30.68	2	13	1	31
Drissell, G.S.	6	10	–	19	76	7.60	–	–	–	0
Duckett, B.M.	74	127	7	282*	4643	38.69	14	21	2	59/3
Dunn, M.P.	36	38	18	31*	143	7.15	–	–	–	7
Easwaran, A.R.	32	58	5	150*	2282	43.05	7	11	–	35
Eckersley, E.J.H.	108	193	12	158	5779	31.92	14	19	1	175/3
Edwards, F.H.	123	173	65	40	757	7.00	–	–	–	23
Elgar, D.	178	309	25	268	12542	44.16	38	46	0+2	142
Elliott, G.D.	83	134	7	196*	3883	30.57	8	20	–	46
Ervine, S.M.	229	358	43	237*	11390	36.15	22	57	1	195
Escott, D.A.	3	6	1	175	373	74.60	2	–	–	5
Eskinazi, S.S.	38	67	4	179	2346	37.23	5	11	–	32
Evans, B.N.	2	1	–	0	0	0.00	–	–	–	0
Evans, L.J.	60	103	6	213*	3020	31.13	5	16	–	49
Evans, S.T.	8	12	1	114	248	22.54	1	–	–	2
Faheem Ashraf	38	54	7	116	1432	30.46	2	5	–	18
Fanning, M.J.	1	–	–	–	–	–	–	–	–	0
Faulkner, J.P.	63	95	12	121	2566	30.91	2	15	–	26
Fell, T.C.	73	126	5	171	3672	30.34	5	16	1	56
Fenwick, E.W.F.	1	–	–	–	–	–	–	–	–	0
Ferguson, C.J.	120	223	20	213	7910	38.96	17	42	–	63
Ferguson, L.H.	38	53	20	41	424	12.84	–	–	–	13
Finch, A.J.	76	126	6	288*	4338	36.15	7	27	–	69
Finch, H.Z.	39	63	5	135*	1728	29.79	3	11	–	50
Finn, S.T.	149	182	59	56	1111	9.03	–	1	–	47
Fisher, M.D.	9	12	2	37	131	13.10	–	–	–	3
Fletcher, L.J.	104	152	27	92	1820	14.56	–	4	–	26
Foakes, B.T.	90	137	25	141*	4552	40.64	8	24	–	174/15
Footitt, M.H.A.	96	124	39	34	678	7.97	–	–	–	26
Foster, J.S.	289	427	52	212	13761	36.69	23	70	1	839/62
Fraine, W.A.R.	5	5	–	30	97	19.40	–	–	–	0
Franklin, J.E.C.	206	321	46	219	9780	35.56	22	44	–	107
Fuller, J.K.	49	64	8	93	1101	19.66	–	5	–	20
Garton, G.H.S.	10	11	3	22*	101	12.62	–	–	–	4
Gidman, W.R.S.	83	125	21	143	3673	35.31	5	21	1	38
Gleadall, A.F.	1	2	1	27*	29	29.00	–	–	–	0
Gleeson, R.J.	24	30	12	31	219	12.16	–	–	–	6
Gnodde, J.S.D.	5	8	2	54	113	18.83	–	1	–	4
Godleman, B.A.	141	253	13	204	7667	31.94	17	36	1	95
Graves, B.W.M.	3	1	–	0	0	0.00	–	–	–	0
Green, B.G.F.	2	4	–	26	43	10.75	–	–	–	3
Green, S.R.	1	–	–	–	–	–	–	–	–	0
Greenidge, A.D.	3	4	–	22	35	8.75	–	–	–	1
Gregory, L.	71	104	11	137	1942	20.88	1	7	–	35
Griffiths, G.T.	18	26	11	40	262	17.46	–	–	–	2
Groenewald, T.D.	131	187	63	78	2275	18.34	–	6	–	42
Gubbins, N.R.T.	57	101	2	201*	3492	35.27	6	23	1	23
Guest, B.D.	1	2	–	8	8	4.00	–	–	–	0
Guest, C.J.	3	4	–	9	21	5.25	–	–	–	2
Guptill, M.J.	107	194	13	227	6825	37.70	14	36	–	116
Gurbani, R.N.	12	15	4	22*	59	5.36	–	–	–	6
Gurney, H.F.	103	131	63	42*	424	6.23	–	–	–	12
Haggett, C.J.	41	54	13	80	926	22.58	–	2	–	10

	M	I	NO	HS	Runs	Avge	100	50	1000	Ct/St
Hain, S.R.	60	92	8	208	2845	33.86	8	13	–	46
Haines, T.J.	9	13	–	124	331	25.46	1	1	–	3
Hales, A.D.	107	182	6	236	6655	37.81	13	38	3	84
Hameed, H.	53	91	8	122	2566	30.91	4	14	1	30
Hamidullah Qadri	7	14	6	15*	53	6.62	–	–	–	4
Hammond, M.A.H.	11	19	2	123*	510	30.00	2	2	–	7
Hammond, N.A.	2	2	–	18	19	9.50	–	–	–	0
Handley, S.	1	–	–	–	–	–	–	–	–	0
Hankins, G.T.	24	39	2	116	938	25.35	1	6	–	29
Hannon-Dalby, O.J.	57	68	23	40	294	6.53	–	–	–	5
Harding, G.H.I.	2	3	–	7	7	2.33	–	–	–	0
Harinath, A.	75	131	6	154	3870	30.96	6	21	–	20
Haris Sohail	64	99	14	211*	4316	50.77	11	27	0+1	31
Harmer, S.R.	123	187	39	102*	3781	25.54	2	20	–	117
Harris, J.A.R.	134	192	45	87*	3265	22.21	–	15	–	40
Harte, G.J.	8	15	–	114	382	25.46	2	–	–	4
Hasan Ali	33	48	15	50*	532	16.12	–	1	–	12
Hasan Azad	8	10	1	99	306	34.00	–	2	–	2
Head, T.M.	68	126	4	192	4385	35.94	7	28	–	27
Heathfield, T.D.	3	2	2	12*	12	–	–	–	–	0
Helm, T.G.	22	30	7	52	343	14.91	–	1	–	8
Hemphrey, C.R.	22	41	3	118	1260	33.15	4	6	–	15
Hemraj, C.	19	35	1	90	930	27.35	–	6	–	13
Henry, M.J.	57	75	14	81	1330	21.80	–	5	–	22
Herring, C.L.	14	17	2	114*	305	20.33	1	–	–	37/1
Higgins, R.F.	19	32	3	105	655	22.58	1	2	–	6
Hildreth, J.C.	248	409	31	303*	16433	43.47	44	74	7	206
Hill, L.J.	33	59	7	126	1227	23.59	1	4	–	68/2
Hodd, A.J.	114	163	25	123	3809	27.60	4	23	–	278/23
Hogan, M.G.	144	206	79	57	2004	15.77	–	2	–	75
Holden, M.D.E.	25	44	4	153	1401	35.02	3	6	–	9
Holder, C.K.	4	4	1	8	18	6.00	–	–	–	0
Holder, J.O.	61	95	10	110	2077	24.43	2	9	–	40
Holland, I.G.	17	25	5	58*	393	19.65	–	2	–	4
Horton, P.J.	203	346	25	209	11557	36.00	23	64	3	188/1
Hose, A.J.	8	15	1	68	406	29.00	–	4	–	2
Hosein, H.R.	31	52	10	108	1259	29.97	1	9	–	75/2
Howell, B.A.C.	76	121	13	163	3009	27.86	2	16	–	40
Hughes, A.L.	58	101	10	142	2699	29.65	5	12	–	41
Hughes, M.S.T.	4	8	–	116	406	50.75	2	1	–	2
Hunn, M.D.	20	16	11	32*	94	18.80	–	–	–	8
Hutton, B.A.	46	73	8	74	1168	17.96	–	4	–	25
Hyde, E.R.B.	1	2	–	32	32	16.00	–	–	–	2
Imam-ul-Haq	39	70	12	200*	2060	35.51	4	12	–	26
Imran Qayyum	5	7	2	39	40	8.00	–	–	–	3
Imran Tahir	194	246	62	77*	2617	14.22	–	4	–	81
Ingram, C.A.	111	195	17	190	6641	37.30	14	30	–	75
Jacks, W.G.	7	10	1	53	225	25.00	–	1	–	8
Jadeja, R.A.	89	131	19	331	4999	44.63	8	24	–	80
James, L.W.	1	2	–	13	14	7.00	–	–	–	0
Javid, A.	38	61	6	133	1247	22.67	2	4	–	18
Jennings, K.K.	113	200	11	221*	6417	33.95	17	21	1	76
Jones, M.A.	1	2	–	10	13	6.50	–	–	–	0
Jones, R.A.	59	90	17	62	895	12.26	–	2	–	22
Jones, R.P.	13	21	3	106*	474	26.33	1	1	–	13
Jordan, C.J.	102	142	21	147	2999	24.78	2	14	–	119

	M	I	NO	HS	Runs	Avge	100	50	1000	Ct/St
Karthik, K.D.	160	243	19	213	9239	41.24	27	41	0+1	382/44
Karunaratne, F.D.M.	151	261	21	212	11248	46.86	37	48	0+1	156/1
Keeping, J.B.R.	1	–	–	–	–	–	–	–	–	1
Keogh, R.I.	64	106	8	221	2796	28.53	7	7	–	18/1
Khawaja, U.T.	126	220	20	214	8698	43.49	25	43	0+1	93
Klein, D.	58	85	18	94	1268	18.92	–	5	–	19
Kleinveldt, R.K.	146	205	23	115*	3609	19.82	1	16	–	71
Klinger, M.	182	321	33	255	11320	39.30	30	49	1+2	179
Kohler-Cadmore, T.	46	77	6	169	2328	32.78	6	12	–	52
Kohli, V.	103	170	15	243	8396	54.16	30	27	0+1	98
Kuhn, H.G.	158	277	27	244*	10623	42.49	23	53	0+1	358/18
Kuldeep Yadav	25	33	4	117	756	26.06	1	5	–	11
Lace, T.C.	4	8	–	43	219	27.37	–	–	–	2
Lake, M.B.	7	11	1	66	147	14.70	–	1	–	1
Lamb, D.J.	4	6	2	20*	57	14.25	–	–	–	1
Lamb, J.L.	11	20	1	79	482	25.36	–	3	–	4
Latham, T.W.M.	93	164	11	261	6358	41.55	13	40	–	117/1
Lawlor, J.L.	9	14	2	81	310	25.83	–	3	–	6
Lawrence, D.W.	54	86	8	161	2894	37.10	8	11	1	42
Leach, J.T.	75	111	12	114	2452	24.76	2	16	–	21
Leach, M.J.	67	89	22	66	841	12.55	–	2	–	23
Leaning, J.A.	59	95	10	123	2640	31.05	4	13	–	48
Lees, A.Z.	95	163	12	275*	5091	33.71	12	23	2	66
Leighton, B.J.	1	–	–	–	–	–	–	–	–	0
Lester, T.J.	11	13	7	8	22	3.66	–	–	–	7
Levi, R.E.	100	166	16	168	5544	36.96	10	31	–	85
Lewis, S.H.	17	27	12	18	79	5.26	–	–	–	4
Libby, J.D.	50	86	6	144	2385	29.81	5	10	–	16
Liddle, C.J.	34	36	18	53	208	11.55	–	1	–	8
Lilley, A.M.	14	18	5	63	426	32.76	–	2	–	4
Livingstone, L.S.	43	71	13	224	2356	40.62	6	10	–	61
Lloyd, D.L.	55	93	11	119	2271	27.69	4	7	–	18
Logan, J.E.G.	1	1	–	6	6	6.00	–	–	–	1
Ludlow, J.H.	2	1	–	19	19	19.00	–	–	–	2
Lyth, A.	161	270	12	251	9858	38.20	23	50	3	204
McCarthy, B.J.	20	31	7	51*	471	19.62	–	1	–	9
MacDonell, C.M.	8	11	4	91	347	49.57	–	2	–	2
McGrath, A.H.	3	1	–	12	12	12.00	–	–	–	0
McKerr, C.	9	9	3	29	98	16.33	–	–	–	0
MacLeod, C.S.	28	41	6	84	904	25.82	–	5	–	20
McManus, L.D.	32	46	5	132*	1147	27.97	1	5	–	63/9
Machado, L.	2	1	–	7	7	7.00	–	–	–	0
Maddinson, N.J.	72	127	7	181	4170	34.75	8	20	–	57
Madsen, W.L.	170	304	22	231*	11047	39.17	28	58	5	162
Magoffin, S.J.	160	217	57	79	2657	16.60	–	5	–	35
Maharaj, K.A.	108	148	26	114*	2535	20.77	2	7	–	37
Mahmood, S.	7	8	5	9	18	6.00	–	–	–	1
Malan, D.J.	174	298	20	182*	10170	36.58	21	56	2	181
Markram, A.K.	51	87	5	182	3747	45.69	10	18	0+1	50
Marsh, S.E.	147	259	22	182	9423	40.61	25	45	–	127
Marshall, J.D.	4	4	1	41*	85	28.33	–	–	–	1
Maxwell, G.J.	59	100	9	278	3738	41.07	7	20	–	47
Meaker, S.C.	89	117	24	94	1445	15.53	–	6	–	20
Mellor, A.J.	9	16	1	59	282	18.80	–	1	–	15
Mennie, J.M.	65	109	19	79*	1654	18.37	–	8	–	26
Meschede, C.A.J.	70	101	13	107	2250	25.56	2	13	–	23

	M	I	NO	HS	Runs	Avge	100	50	1000	Ct/St
Mike, B.W.M.	4	7	–	39	96	13.71	–	–	–	2
Miles, C.N.	68	94	14	62*	1343	16.78	–	5	–	17
Mills, T.S.	32	38	15	31*	260	11.30	–	–	–	9
Milne, A.F.	29	43	13	97	717	23.90	–	4	–	10
Milnes, M.E.	8	12	5	43	109	15.57	–	–	–	6
Milton, A.G.	10	15	2	104*	267	20.53	1	–	–	6/1
Mir Hamza	52	62	27	24	217	6.20	–	–	–	10
Mitchell, D.K.H.	192	347	37	298	12507	40.34	35	48	6	263
Mohammad Abbas	83	122	44	40	550	7.05	–	–	–	22
Mohammad Amir	59	89	14	66	1161	15.48	–	2	–	12
Mohammad Nabi	33	53	4	117	1275	26.02	2	5	–	20
Mohammed Shami	57	80	23	51*	723	12.68	–	1	–	14
Moores, T.J.	20	34	1	103	818	24.78	1	2	–	46
Morgan, A.O.	17	31	5	103*	556	21.38	1	1	–	5
Morgan, E.J.G.	99	164	16	209*	4912	33.18	11	23	1	75/1
Morkel, M.	137	167	32	82*	1895	14.03	–	4	–	48
Morris, C.A.J.	48	67	38	33*	305	10.51	–	–	–	12
Mujeeb Zadran	1	2	–	15	18	9.00	–	–	–	5
Mullaney, S.J.	122	204	8	168	6602	33.68	13	36	1	117
Munro, C.	48	74	4	281	3611	51.58	13	15	–	21
Murphy, J.R.	18	32	2	80	669	22.30	–	2	–	6
Murtagh, T.J.	218	289	83	74*	3923	19.04	–	10	–	62
Murty, D.G.	1	2	–	52	56	28.00	–	1	–	0
Muzarabani, B.	6	12	2	23	138	13.80	–	–	–	2
Myburgh, J.G.	108	190	23	203	6841	40.96	16	39	–	61
Nadeem, S.	96	134	4	85	1937	14.90	–	7	–	43
Nair, K.K.	61	97	9	328	4496	51.09	13	17	–	50
Nash, C.D.	193	331	19	184	11807	37.84	24	61	4	118
Naylor, M.A.	2	3	–	202	221	73.66	1	–	–	0
Newton, R.I.	87	152	11	202*	5161	36.60	13	23	1	27
Nicholls, C.	1	–	–	–	–	–	–	–	–	0
Nicholls, H.M.	61	104	8	145*	3521	36.67	6	21	–	54
Nijjar, A.S.S	11	14	5	53	235	26.11	–	1	–	1
Noema-Barnett, K.	82	123	19	107	2893	27.81	2	17	–	47
Northeast, S.A.	149	255	18	191	9060	38.22	20	46	3	78
Norwell, L.C.	68	86	34	102	703	13.51	1	1	–	15
Olivier, D.	83	105	28	72	1014	13.16	–	3	–	23
Onions, G.	183	238	85	65	2035	13.30	–	1	–	34
Overton, C.	76	111	15	138	2074	21.60	1	8	–	46
Overton, J.	53	73	19	56	963	17.83	–	5	–	9
Palladino, A.P.	155	223	47	106	2781	15.80	1	7	–	40
Palmer, H.J.	5	8	–	32	123	15.37	–	–	–	4
Panayi, G.D.	2	3	–	16	17	5.66	–	–	–	0
Pandya, H.H.	28	45	1	108	1278	29.04	1	9	–	14
Pant, R.R.	26	40	2	308	1906	50.15	5	8	–	81/7
Parkinson, C.F.	21	32	7	75	435	17.40	–	1	–	4
Parkinson, M.W.	16	22	9	13	71	5.46	–	–	–	3
Parnell, W.D.	68	93	11	111*	2297	28.01	2	14	–	21
Parry, S.D.	26	32	2	44	452	15.06	–	–	–	7
Patel, A.R.	27	37	7	110*	1310	43.66	1	11	–	13
Patel, J.S.	272	361	74	120	6169	21.49	3	26	–	137
Patel, R.H.	26	38	17	26*	220	10.47	–	–	–	7
Patel, R.S.	14	21	3	81	520	28.88	–	1	–	6
Patel, S.R.	212	345	18	257*	11976	36.62	26	59	4	134
Patterson, S.A.	140	165	41	63*	2044	16.48	–	3	–	25
Payne, D.A.	83	102	34	67*	1423	20.92	–	6	–	27

	M	I	NO	HS	Runs	Avge	100	50	1000	Ct/St
Pearce, S.J.	2	1	–	35	35	35.00	–	–	–	0
Pennington, D.Y.	8	14	3	37	94	8.54	–	–	–	4
Pepper, M.S.	2	4	–	22	53	13.25	–	–	–	0
Pereira, W.J.N.	2	2	1	28*	28	28.00	–	–	–	0
Perera, N.L.T.C.	33	52	6	113*	1409	30.63	1	8	–	24
Pettman, T.H.S.	3	3	1	54*	88	44.00	–	1	–	0
Pike, O.L.	3	1	1	0*	0	–	–	–	–	0
Pillans, M.W.	41	58	5	56	727	13.71	–	1	–	20
Plater, M.J.	2	1	1	9*	9	–	–	–	–	1
Plom, J.H.	1	–	–	–	–	–	–	–	–	0
Plunkett, L.E.	155	213	39	126	4376	25.14	3	22	–	86
Podmore, H.W.	27	40	11	66*	494	17.03	–	2	–	6
Pollock, E.J.	5	7	1	52	184	30.66	–	1	–	1
Pope, O.J.D.	22	31	6	158*	1368	54.72	5	3	1	29
Porter, J.A.	67	78	28	34	324	6.48	–	–	–	21
Potts, M.J.	6	8	3	53*	120	24.00	–	1	–	0
Powe, J.D.	1	1	–	11	11	11.00	–	–	–	7
Poynter, S.W.	36	56	2	170	1281	23.72	2	3	–	103/3
Poysden, J.E.	14	14	4	47	96	9.60	–	–	–	2
Prasanna, S.	104	167	7	81	3479	21.74	–	20	–	74
Pringle, R.D.	37	58	8	99	1292	25.84	–	8	–	22
Procter, L.A.	79	126	7	137	3549	29.82	3	20	–	19
Pujara, C.A.	177	291	35	352	13801	53.91	45	46	0+3	120/1
Quinn, M.R.	30	39	9	50	324	10.80	–	1	–	5
Rackow, A.J.W.	3	3	–	95	134	44.66	–	1	–	1
Rahane, A.M.	117	199	21	265*	9158	51.44	29	38	0+3	122
Rahat Ali	72	68	36	35*	346	6.65	–	–	–	21
Rahul, K.L.	68	115	4	337	5411	48.74	14	27	0+2	77
Raine, B.A.	64	105	9	72	1979	20.61	–	8	–	15
Rajpoot, A.	40	53	20	19	125	3.78	–	–	–	8
Rampaul, R.	77	113	27	64*	1119	13.01	–	2	–	22
Rankin, W.B.	106	126	51	56*	697	9.29	–	1	–	28
Rashid, A.U.	171	244	40	180	6696	32.82	10	37	–	79
Rashid Khan	5	6	1	52	144	28.80	–	1	–	0
Raval, J.A.	95	170	10	256	6317	39.48	14	30	0+1	103
Rawlins, D.M.W.	7	12	–	96	245	20.41	–	2	–	0
Rayner, O.P.	141	187	30	143*	3251	20.70	2	13	–	189
Reece, L.M.	47	83	7	168	2584	34.00	4	18	–	23
Reifer, R.A.	62	104	12	108*	2400	26.08	1	12	–	30
Renshaw, M.T.	42	79	5	184	3035	41.01	10	10	–	36
Rhodes, G.H.	17	32	4	59	675	24.10	–	4	–	9
Rhodes, W.M.H.	34	52	3	137	1667	34.02	4	7	–	14
Richardson, K.W.	30	48	4	49	641	14.56	–	–	–	9
Richardson, M.J.	102	174	11	148	4816	29.54	6	26	2	181/5
Riley, A.E.N.	58	72	26	34	485	10.54	–	–	–	33
Rimmington, N.J.	46	66	14	102*	989	19.01	1	2	–	12
Rippington, S.E.	3	4	2	2*	2	1.00	–	–	–	1
Rishton, J.A.J.	2	2	1	32*	55	55.00	–	–	–	0
Robertson, W.J.R.	1	–	–	–	–	–	–	–	–	0
Robinson, O.E.	42	62	11	110	1094	21.45	1	4	–	14
Robinson, O.G.	3	4	–	26	59	14.75	–	–	–	1
Robson, S.D.	142	251	17	231	8850	37.82	21	35	2	134
Roderick, G.H.	82	132	17	171	4147	36.06	5	30	–	224/4
Rogers, O.J.W.	1	1	–	13	13	13.00	–	–	–	0
Roland-Jones, T.S.	102	141	26	103*	2488	21.63	1	9	–	30
Rollings, W.J.L.	2	2	–	4	4	2.00	–	–	–	1

253

	M	I	NO	HS	Runs	Avge	100	50	1000	Ct/St
Root, J.E.	131	227	22	254	10068	49.11	23	56	3	120
Root, W.T.	14	24	1	133	697	30.30	2	2	–	3
Rossington, A.M.	63	102	10	138*	3100	33.69	6	20	–	133/9
Rossouw, R.R.	97	171	9	319	6743	41.62	19	28	0+1	116
Rouse, A.P.	34	48	4	95*	1070	24.31	–	5	–	106/4
Roy, J.J.	80	130	11	143	4572	38.42	9	21	1	72
Ruffell, F.W.A.	2	–	–	–	–	–	–	–	–	0
Rushworth, C.	112	159	48	57	1394	12.55	–	1	–	24
Russell, A.M.C.	1	–	–	–	–	–	–	–	–	0
Saini, N.A.	34	37	14	42*	227	9.86	–	–	–	12
Sakande, A.	11	13	5	33	104	13.00	–	–	–	4
Salisbury, M.E.T.	26	43	10	37	298	9.03	–	–	–	4
Salt, P.D.	22	35	1	148	950	27.94	2	3	–	14
Salter, A.G.	54	84	17	88	1582	23.61	–	8	–	28
Samarth, R.	45	78	4	235	3187	43.06	9	15	–	46
Sami Aslam	52	90	2	221	3110	35.34	8	13	–	33
Sanders, C.W.G.	2	2	–	56	62	31.00	–	1	–	0
Sanderson, B.W.	45	60	24	42	259	7.19	–	–	–	9
Sarfraz Ahmed	141	221	42	213*	7233	40.40	10	50	–	437/49
Sayer, D.W.	1	2	–	21	27	13.50	–	–	–	2
Scott, G.F.B.	5	7	2	16*	53	10.60	–	–	–	2
Seabrook, B.M.A.	1	–	–	–	–	–	–	–	–	0
Selman, N.J.	37	69	4	142*	1775	27.30	6	5	–	44
Seward, J.C.	1	–	–	–	–	–	–	–	–	1
Shadab Khan	12	16	1	132	452	30.13	1	3	–	7
Shankar, V.	34	45	8	111	1748	47.24	5	10	–	23
Sharif, S.M.	9	12	4	60	229	28.62	–	1	–	5
Sharma, I.	128	163	62	66	884	8.75	–	1	–	27
Shaw, J.	24	32	7	42	298	11.92	–	–	–	5
Shaw, P.P.	12	23	1	188	1262	57.36	6	5	–	9
Shepherd, R.	11	14	2	53	211	17.58	–	1	–	4
Short, D.J.M.	9	17	–	66	401	23.58	–	2	–	7
Sibley, D.P.	51	87	9	242	2622	33.61	6	14	–	43
Siddle, P.M.	150	199	35	103*	2790	17.01	1	5	–	48
Sidebottom, R.N.	17	26	12	13	56	4.00	–	–	–	5
Simpson, J.A.	140	221	33	143	5827	30.99	5	33	–	430/24
Singh, V.A.	61	105	9	161	3238	33.72	8	12	–	39
Siraj, M.	17	24	3	26	119	5.66	–	–	–	3
Sisodiya, P.	2	4	1	38	41	13.66	–	–	–	1
Slater, B.T.	69	129	6	119	4003	32.54	4	24	1	24
Smit, D.	137	208	37	156*	6077	35.53	9	33	0+1	362/22
Smith, O.F.	3	4	1	54	125	41.66	–	1	–	4
Smith, R.A.J.	26	37	6	57*	620	20.00	–	2	–	4
Smith, T.M.J.	43	59	12	80	1055	22.44	–	2	–	12
Smith, W.R.	181	309	21	210	9343	32.44	17	37	1	114
Snater, S.	3	4	1	50*	73	24.33	–	1	–	1
Soames, O.C.	6	9	–	29	90	10.00	–	–	–	1
Sodhi, I.S.	62	94	14	82*	1737	21.71	–	9	–	28
Sohal, V.V.S.	1	–	–	–	–	–	–	–	–	0
Sookias, J.H.	1	–	–	–	–	–	–	–	–	3
Sowter, N.A.	1	2	–	37	37	18.50	–	–	–	0
Srikar Bharat, K.	48	80	4	308	2745	36.11	4	16	–	166/19
Steel, C.T.	31	55	2	224	1852	34.94	3	11	–	16
Stevens, D.I.	290	456	29	208	15036	35.21	33	77	3	194
Stevenson, R.A.	4	5	1	30	73	18.25	–	–	–	0
Stewart, G.	12	19	2	103	429	25.23	1	2	–	3

	M	I	NO	HS	Runs	Avge	100	50	1000	Ct/St
Steyn, D.W.	136	165	37	82	1767	13.80	–	4	–	30
Stirling, P.R.	65	102	4	146	2706	27.61	5	14	–	37
Stoinis, M.P.	49	84	6	170	2559	32.80	4	16	–	19
Stokes, B.A.	121	203	9	258	6569	33.86	14	33	–	81
Stone, O.P.	34	42	10	60	532	16.62	–	1	–	14
Stoneman, M.D.	176	307	8	197	10474	35.03	22	54	5	83
Subramanyan, J.	1	–	–	–	–	–	–	–	–	0
Sukhjit Singh	6	8	2	16*	18	3.00	–	–	–	1
Suresh, K.	1	2	–	18	23	11.50	–	–	–	0
Tattersall, J.A.	7	12	1	70	350	31.81	–	2	–	19
Taylor, B.J.	6	10	3	36	133	19.00	–	–	–	2
Taylor, J.E.	98	152	22	106	1538	11.83	1	1	–	23
Taylor, J.M.R.	68	105	9	156	2950	30.72	7	8	–	36
Taylor, L.R.P.L.	159	269	22	290	10693	43.29	25	56	–	202
Taylor, M.D.	43	57	21	48	447	12.41	–	–	–	7
Taylor, T.A.I.	26	41	6	80	618	17.65	–	2	–	5
ten Doeschate, R.N.	174	256	38	259*	10283	47.16	27	48	1	110
Thomas, D.C.	80	143	5	172	3822	27.69	5	16	–	168/2
Thomas, I.A.A.	33	44	22	13	114	5.18	–	–	–	9
Thomas, O.R.	6	10	2	18	43	5.37	–	–	–	0
Thomson, A.T.	6	7	–	26	113	16.14	–	–	–	2
Thurston, C.O.	8	10	–	126	236	23.60	1	–	–	2
Tillcock, A.D.	4	4	1	23	59	19.66	–	–	–	3
Tongue, J.C.	26	37	6	41	339	10.93	–	–	–	8
Topley, R.J.W.	34	41	19	16	94	4.27	–	–	–	4
Trego, P.D.	217	322	37	154*	9510	33.36	15	54	1	87
Trescothick, M.E.	385	665	36	284	26089	41.47	66	127	8	550
Trevaskis, L.	1	2	–	9	14	7.00	–	–	–	0
Trott, I.J.L.	281	468	47	226	18662	44.32	46	92	9	223
Turner, S.A.	1	2	–	33	48	24.00	–	–	–	0
Turpin, J.R.	4	2	1	5	5	5.00	–	–	–	1
Twohig, B.J.	7	13	2	35	145	13.18	–	–	–	3
Tye, A.J.	9	–	–	10	52	5.20	–	–	–	1
Umeed, A.R.I.	15	25	1	113	497	20.70	2	–	–	13
Usman Salahuddin	100	164	26	161*	6366	46.13	20	34	0+2	66
van Beek, L.V.	36	51	9	111*	1000	23.80	1	4	–	25
van Buuren, G.L.	75	119	18	235	4348	43.04	10	26	–	42
van den Bergh, F.O.E.	7	9	1	34	62	7.75	–	–	–	1
van der Gugten, T.	35	52	11	60*	517	12.60	–	3	–	6
van der Merwe, R.E.	63	102	14	205*	3052	34.68	6	18	–	46
van Meekeren, P.A.	8	14	3	34	106	9.63	–	–	–	2
van Zyl, S.	162	271	39	228	10201	43.96	24	46	1+1	95
Vasconcelos, R.S.	22	41	3	140	1252	32.94	3	8	–	28/4
Vihari, G.H.	62	96	15	302*	4996	58.77	14	24	0+1	61/1
Vijay, M.	127	213	7	266	8960	43.49	25	37	0+1	108
Vilas, D.J.	138	214	25	244	7614	40.28	19	33	–	370/19
Viljoen, G.C.	113	160	19	72	2100	14.89	–	7	–	31
Vince, J.M.	155	258	19	240	9188	38.44	23	35	2	133
Virdi, G.S.	18	21	9	21*	97	8.08	–	–	–	5
Wade, D.	2	2	1	1*	1	1.00	–	–	–	0
Wagg, G.G.	151	224	22	200	5386	26.66	4	31	–	49
Wagner, N.	153	205	44	70	2740	17.01	–	7	–	44
Wahab Riaz	131	186	29	84	2499	15.91	–	8	–	38
Waite, M.J.	5	8	–	42	118	14.75	–	–	–	0
Wakely, A.G.	134	217	15	123	6317	31.27	8	35	–	84
Waller, M.T.C.	9	10	1	28	91	10.11	–	–	–	5

	M	I	NO	HS	Runs	Avge	100	50	1000	Ct/St
Walter, P.I.	10	10	3	68*	240	34.28	–	1	–	0
Warrican, J.A.	50	64	19	71*	516	11.46	–	1	–	29
Watt, M.R.J.	4	3	1	81*	128	64.00	–	1	–	2
Weatherley, J.J.	23	37	1	126*	817	22.69	1	3	–	6
Webb, L.A.	3	4	–	32	68	17.00	–	–	–	1
Weighell, W.J.	12	20	4	84	469	29.31	–	3	–	3
Wells, L.W.P.	125	208	12	258	7159	36.52	18	30	3	57
Wells, T.J.	17	27	2	87*	522	20.88	–	2	–	8
Wessels, M.H.	197	327	29	202*	10740	36.04	22	55	2	311/16
Westbury, O.E.	2	4	–	22	49	12.25	–	–	–	1
Westley, T.	164	272	20	254	9151	36.31	20	44	1	104
Wheal, B.T.J.	25	29	8	25*	157	7.47	–	–	–	11
Wheater, A.J.A.	127	189	23	204*	6066	36.54	11	35	–	206/11
Wheeldon, D.M.	1	2	1	33*	35	35.00	–	–	–	0
White, G.G.	39	55	5	65	659	13.18	–	2	–	12
White, R.G.	12	17	1	69	211	13.18	–	1	–	20
Whiteley, R.A.	77	126	12	130*	3152	27.64	3	16	–	55
Whittingham, S.G.	15	16	6	22	68	6.80	–	–	–	3
Wiese, D.	108	171	20	208	5087	33.68	10	26	–	68
Wilkinson, A.R.	3	2	–	12	12	6.00	–	–	–	0
Willey, D.J.	66	93	11	104*	2179	26.57	2	14	–	14
Williamson, K.S.	131	226	17	284*	10039	48.03	28	52	–	122
Wilson, G.C.	104	161	22	160*	4761	34.25	3	29	–	189/5
Winder, N.J.	2	3	–	8	10	3.33	–	–	–	0
Woakes, C.R.	140	207	48	152*	5620	35.34	10	23	–	59
Wood, C.P.	43	62	6	105*	1326	23.67	1	6	–	14
Wood, L.	30	47	11	100	989	27.47	1	3	–	11
Wood, M.A.	49	81	16	72*	1369	21.06	–	5	–	12
Woodland, A.J.	2	1	–	1	1	1.00	–	–	–	2
Worrall, D.J.	39	58	24	50	359	10.55	–	1	–	13
Wright, C.J.C.	146	187	42	77	2699	18.61	–	11	–	25
Wright, L.J.	144	223	23	226*	7622	38.11	17	38	1	58
Yadav, J.	50	77	12	211	1931	29.70	3	7	–	28
Yadav, U.T.	75	88	40	128*	733	15.27	1	1	–	29
Zahir Khan	7	6	5	1*	1	1.00	–	–	–	1
Zaib, S.A.	13	19	3	65*	331	20.68	–	2	–	3
Zampa, A.	35	58	7	74	1111	21.78	–	6	–	9

BOWLING

'50wS' denotes instances of taking 50 or more wickets in a season. Where these have been achieved outside the British Isles they are shown after a plus sign.

	Runs	Wkts	Avge	Best	5wI	10wM	50wS
Aaron, V.R.	4493	135	33.28	6- 63	4	–	–
Abbott, K.J.	8093	370	21.87	8- 45	24	3	2+1
Abell, T.B.	621	22	28.22	4- 43	–	–	–
Ackermann, C.N.	1905	48	39.68	3- 45	–	–	–
Adams, J.H.K.	721	13	55.46	2- 16	–	–	–
Agar, A.C.	5203	133	39.12	6-110	5	2	–
Agarwal, M.A.	217	3	72.33	2- 18	–	–	–
Ali, A.M.	86	1	86.00	1- 10	–	–	–
Ali, M.M.	12794	325	39.36	6- 29	12	2	–
Allen, H.A.J.	101	0			–	–	–
Alsop, T.P.	78	3	26.00	2- 59	–	–	–
Ambrose, T.R.	1	1	1.00	1- 0	–	–	–
Amla, H.M.	277	1	277.00	1- 10	–	–	–

256

	Runs	Wkts	Avge	Best	5wI	10wM	50wS
Anderson, C.J.	1675	40	41.87	5- 22	1	–	–
Anderson, J.M.	23096	909	25.40	7- 42	44	6	4
Andersson, M.K.	239	12	19.91	4- 25	–	–	–
Archer, J.C.	3071	131	23.44	7- 67	5	1	1
Arshad, U.	1036	36	28.77	4- 78	–	–	–
Asad Shafiq	307	5	61.40	2- 20	–	–	–
Ashar Zaidi	2803	94	29.81	4- 50	–	–	–
Ashwin, R.	13290	493	26.95	7- 59	39	10	0+1
Assani, S.J.S.	41	0					
Azeem Rafiq	2804	71	39.49	5- 50	1	–	–
Azhar Ali	1961	46	42.63	4- 34	–	–	–
Babar Azam	423	5	84.60	1- 13	–	–	–
Bailey, T.E.	4039	155	26.05	5- 12	6	1	1
Bairstow, J.M.	1	0					
Balderson, T.W.	91	2	45.50	2- 91	–	–	–
Ball, J.T.	4530	173	26.18	6- 49	6	–	1
Ballance, G.S.	154	0					
Bamber, E.R.	567	28	20.25	4- 81	–	–	–
Bancroft, C.T.	67	1	67.00	1- 67	–	–	–
Barber, T.E.	131	0					
Barker, K.H.D.	9122	359	25.40	6- 40	14	1	3
Barnard, E.G.	4093	143	28.62	6- 37	4	1	–
Bartlett, G.A.	27	0					
Batty, G.J.	21678	656	33.04	8- 68	26	3	2
Bavuma, T.	311	7	44.42	2- 34	–	–	–
Bawne, A.R.	275	4	68.75	2- 25	–	–	–
Beer, W.A.T.	1002	32	31.31	6- 29	2	1	–
Bell, I.R.	1615	47	34.36	4- 4	–	–	–
Bell-Drummond, D.J.	72	2	36.00	1- 1	–	–	–
Berg, G.K.	8057	254	31.72	6- 56	5	–	–
Bess, D.M.	2110	78	27.05	7-117	7	1	–
Billings, S.W.	4	0					
Blackwood, J.	438	10	43.80	3- 44	–	–	–
Blake, A.J.	129	3	43.00	2- 9	–	–	–
Bohannon, J.J.	103	5	20.60	3- 46	–	–	–
Bopara, R.S.	9107	248	36.72	5- 49	3	–	–
Borthwick, S.G.	7708	202	38.15	6- 70	3	–	–
Bracewell, D.A.J.	9156	274	33.41	7- 35	8	–	–
Brathwaite, C.R.	2098	88	23.84	7- 90	2	–	–
Brathwaite, K.C.	1087	22	49.40	6- 29	1	–	–
Bravo, D.J.	5918	177	33.43	6- 11	7	–	–
Bresnan, T.T.	16830	546	30.82	5- 28	9	–	–
Brewster, A.D.F.	353	3	117.66	2- 87	–	–	–
Briggs, D.R.	8867	261	33.97	6- 45	8	–	–
Broad, S.C.J.	19434	706	27.52	8- 15	27	3	–
Brook, H.C.	132	1	132.00	1- 54	–	–	–
Brookes, H.J.H.	513	21	24.42	4- 54	–	–	–
Brooks, J.A.	11869	434	27.34	6- 65	19	–	4
Brooks, S.S.J.	548	7	78.28	2- 68	–	–	–
Brown, B.C.	94	1	94.00	1- 48	–	–	–
Brown, C.R.	14	0					
Brown, K.R.	65	2	32.50	2- 30	–	–	–
Brown, P.R.	266	7	38.00	2- 15	–	–	–
Browne, N.L.J.	175	0					
Bruce, T.C.	570	16	35.62	2- 17	–	–	–
Buck, N.L.	7684	225	34.15	6- 34	7	–	–
Bull, K.A.	761	20	38.05	4- 62	–	–	–

257

	Runs	Wkts	Avge	Best	5wI	10wM	50wS
Bulpitt, J.	32	0					
Bumrah, J.J.	2972	117	25.40	6- 29	8	–	–
Burgess, M.G.K.	14	0					
Burns, J.A.	48	1	48.00	1- 0	–	–	–
Burns, R.J.	127	2	63.50	1- 18	–	–	–
Buttler, J.C.	11	0					
Byrom, E.J.	39	0					
Campbell, J.D.	1576	55	28.65	7- 73	2	–	–
Carberry, M.A.	1081	17	63.58	2- 85	–	–	–
Carey, L.J.	1982	61	32.49	4- 85	–	–	–
Carlson, K.S.	183	6	30.50	5- 28	1	–	–
Carter, A.	3200	108	29.62	5- 40	2	–	–
Carter, M.	1197	33	36.27	7- 56	2	1	–
Cartwright, H.W.R.	1393	38	36.65	4- 33	–	–	–
Carver, K.	543	18	30.16	4-106	–	–	–
Chanderpaul, S.	2537	60	42.28	4- 48	–	–	–
Chapman, L.J.	323	9	35.88	6- 78	1	–	–
Chappell, Z.J.	1026	31	33.09	6- 44	1	–	–
Charlesworth, B.G.	47	4	11.75	3- 25	–	–	–
Chopra, V.	128	0					
Christian, D.T.	5679	163	34.84	5- 24	3	–	–
Clark, G.	51	2	25.50	1- 10	–	–	–
Clark, J.	2728	78	34.97	5- 58	1	–	–
Clarke, J.M.	22	0					
Clarke, R.	14459	460	31.43	7- 55	5	–	–
Claydon, M.E.	9129	280	32.60	6-104	8	–	2
Coad, B.O.	2030	103	19.70	6- 25	7	2	1
Cobb, J.J.	1516	17	89.17	2- 11	–	–	–
Cockbain, I.A.	44	1	44.00	1- 23	–	–	–
Coetzer, K.J.	414	7	59.14	2- 16	–	–	–
Coles, M.T.	10255	348	29.46	6- 51	12	2	2
Collingwood, P.D.	6396	166	38.53	5- 52	2	–	–
Colverd, T.G.L.	2	0					
Cook, A.N.	211	7	30.14	3- 13	–	–	–
Cook, S.C.	482	11	43.81	3- 42	–	–	–
Cook, S.J.	1395	53	26.32	5- 18	3	–	–
Cooke, J.M.	308	3	102.66	1- 26	–	–	–
Cornwall, R.R.S.	5135	202	25.42	8-108	14	1	0+1
Cosgrove, M.J.	2357	52	45.32	3- 3	–	–	–
Cotton, B.D.	1741	47	37.04	5- 48	1	–	–
Coughlin, J.	184	5	36.80	2- 31	–	–	–
Coughlin, P.	2244	75	29.92	5- 49	2	1	–
Crane, M.S.	3605	77	46.81	5- 35	2	–	–
Critchley, M.J.J.	2286	42	54.42	6-106	1	1	–
Croft, S.J.	2914	71	41.04	6- 41	1	–	–
Crook, S.P.	8211	207	39.66	5- 48	3	–	–
Cross-Zamirski, J.O.	104	3	34.66	2- 96	–	–	–
Curran, S.M.	3784	131	28.88	7- 58	6	1	–
Curran, T.K.	5495	192	28.61	7- 20	7	1	1
Dal, A.K.	1	0					
Davey, J.H.	1637	59	27.74	5- 65	1	–	–
Davis, W.S.	1263	40	31.57	7-146	1	–	–
Dawes, M.J.	165	2	82.50	1- 26	–	–	–
Dawson, L.A.	6632	189	35.08	7- 51	3	–	–
Dearden, H.E.	95	2	47.50	1- 0	–	–	–
de Bruyn, T.B.	427	11	38.81	2- 24	–	–	–
de Grandhomme, C.	4488	151	29.72	6- 24	2	–	–

258

	Runs	Wkts	Avge	Best	5wI	10wM	50wS
de Lange, M.	8218	279	29.45	7- 23	11	2	–
Delport, C.S.	723	14	51.64	2- 10	–	–	–
Denly, J.L.	2295	62	37.01	4- 36	–	–	–
Dent, C.D.J.	795	8	99.37	2- 21	–	–	–
Dernbach, J.W.	10139	311	32.60	6- 47	10	–	1
de Villiers, A.B.	138	2	69.00	2- 49	–	–	–
Dexter, N.J.	5385	166	32.43	6- 63	6	–	–
Dhawan, S.	142	3	47.33	2- 30	–	–	–
Dickson, S.R.	44	2	22.00	1- 15	–	–	–
Dixon, M.W.	1232	29	42.48	5-124	1	–	–
D'Oliveira, B.L.	1981	37	53.54	5- 48	1	–	–
Drissell, G.S.	330	4	82.50	2- 38	–	–	–
Duckett, B.M.	49	1	49.00	1- 21	–	–	–
Dunn, M.P.	3576	99	36.12	5- 48	3	–	–
Easwaran, A.R.	126	2	63.00	1- 20	–	–	–
Eckersley, E.J.H.	67	2	33.50	2- 29	–	–	–
Edwards, F.H.	12485	405	30.82	7- 87	23	2	1
Elgar, D.	2621	51	51.39	4- 22	–	–	–
Elliott, G.D.	3378	92	36.71	5- 33	1	–	–
Ervine, S.M.	11901	280	42.50	6- 82	5	–	–
Escott, D.A.	157	10	15.70	6- 71	1	–	–
Evans, B.N.	141	5	28.20	4- 53	–	–	–
Evans, L.J.	259	2	129.50	1- 29	–	–	–
Evans, S.T.	24	0					
Faheem Ashraf	2972	110	27.01	6- 65	5	–	–
Fanning, M.J.	46	0					
Faulkner, J.P.	4759	192	24.78	5- 5	5	–	–
Fell, T.C.	17	0					
Fenwick, E.W.F.	55	0					
Ferguson, C.J.	99	2	49.50	2- 32	–	–	–
Ferguson, L.H.	3503	142	24.66	7- 34	11	1	–
Finch, A.J.	310	5	62.00	1- 0	–	–	–
Finch, H.Z.	109	2	54.50	1- 9	–	–	–
Finn, S.T.	15381	531	28.96	9- 37	13	1	2
Fisher, M.D.	789	20	39.45	5- 54	1	–	–
Fletcher, L.J.	8728	308	28.33	5- 27	4	–	–
Foakes, B.T.	6	0					
Footitt, M.H.A.	9227	352	26.21	7- 62	21	1	2
Foster, J.S.	128	1	128.00	1-122	–	–	–
Franklin, J.E.C.	13504	479	28.19	7- 14	14	1	–
Fuller, J.K.	4662	141	33.06	6- 24	5	1	–
Garton, G.H.S.	942	24	39.25	3- 20	–	–	–
Gidman, W.R.S.	5156	219	23.54	6- 15	10	1	2
Gleadall, A.F.	59	1	59.00	1- 20	–	–	–
Gleeson, R.J.	2053	93	22.07	6- 79	5	–	–
Gnodde, J.S.D.	208	4	52.00	2- 35	–	–	–
Godleman, B.A.	35	0					
Graves, B.W.M.	119	1	119.00	1- 62	–	–	–
Green, B.G.F.	17	1	17.00	1- 8	–	–	–
Green, S.R.	0	0					
Gregory, L.	5694	204	27.91	6- 47	9	1	–
Griffiths, G.T.	1316	44	29.90	6- 49	1	1	–
Groenewald, T.D.	11313	383	29.53	6- 50	15	–	–
Gubbins, N.R.T.	52	0					
Guest, C.J.	171	1	171.00	1- 28	–	–	–
Guptill, M.J.	670	11	60.90	3- 11	–	–	–
Gurbani, R.N.	1190	60	19.83	7- 68	5	1	–

	Runs	Wkts	Avge	Best	5wI	10wM	50wS
Gurney, H.F.	9472	310	30.55	6- 25	8	–	–
Haggett, C.J.	3008	89	33.79	4- 15	–	–	–
Hain, S.R.	31	0					
Haines, T.J.	82	1	82.00	1- 13	–	–	–
Hales, A.D.	173	3	57.66	2- 63	–	–	–
Hameed, H.	21	0					
Hamidullah Qadri	607	18	33.72	5- 60	1	–	–
Hammond, M.A.H.	210	1	210.00	1- 96	–	–	–
Handley, S.	38	0					
Hankins, G.T.	13	0					
Hannon-Dalby, O.J.	4426	124	35.69	5- 68	2	–	–
Harding, G.H.I.	292	4	73.00	4-111	–	–	–
Harinath, A.	195	5	39.00	2- 1	–	–	–
Haris Sohail	191	7	27.28	3- 1	–	–	–
Harmer, S.R.	14314	495	28.91	9- 95	23	4	2+1
Harris, J.A.R.	12978	462	28.09	9- 34	15	2	3
Harte, G.J.	148	3	49.33	2- 26	–	–	–
Hasan Ali	3479	138	25.21	8-107	8	2	–
Hasan Azad	2	0					
Head, T.M.	2150	33	65.15	3- 42	–	–	–
Heathfield, T.D.	159	3	53.00	1- 26	–	–	–
Helm, T.G.	1693	54	31.35	5- 59	1	–	–
Hemphrey, C.R.	396	6	66.00	2- 56	–	–	–
Hemraj, C.	47	2	23.50	1- 7	–	–	–
Henry, M.J.	5993	242	24.76	7- 42	12	3	1
Higgins, R.F.	1173	60	19.55	5- 21	2	–	–
Hildreth, J.C.	492	6	82.00	2- 39	–	–	–
Hill, L.J.	6	0					
Hodd, A.J.	21	0					
Hogan, M.G.	13378	548	24.41	7- 92	22	2	3
Holden, M.D.E.	348	5	69.60	2- 59	–	–	–
Holder, C.K.	524	18	29.11	5- 57	1	–	–
Holder, J.O.	3878	151	25.68	6- 59	7	1	–
Holland, I.G.	818	35	23.37	4- 16	–	–	–
Horton, P.J.	80	2	40.00	2- 6	–	–	–
Howell, B.A.C.	2960	89	33.25	5- 57	1	–	–
Hughes, A.L.	1496	32	46.75	4- 46	–	–	–
Hughes, M.S.T.	94	2	47.00	1- 16	–	–	–
Hunn, M.D.	1647	46	35.80	5- 99	1	–	–
Hutton, B.A.	4345	152	28.58	8- 57	7	2	–
Imam-ul-Haq	58	1	58.00	1- 4	–	–	–
Imran Qayyum	481	12	40.08	3-158	–	–	–
Imran Tahir	20881	784	26.63	8- 42	53	11	2+2
Ingram, C.A.	2133	50	42.66	4- 16	–	–	–
Jadeja, R.A.	9019	381	23.67	7- 31	27	7	0+3
James, L.W.	68	3	22.66	3- 54	–	–	–
Javid, A.	433	5	86.60	1- 1	–	–	–
Jennings, K.K.	863	28	30.82	3- 37	–	–	–
Jones, R.A.	5320	163	32.63	7-115	5	–	–
Jones, R.P.	20	1	20.00	1- 18	–	–	–
Jordan, C.J.	9758	304	32.09	7- 43	9	–	1
Karthik, K.D.	130	0					
Karunaratne, F.D.M.	398	3	132.66	1- 6	–	–	–
Keogh, R.I.	2940	71	41.40	9- 52	1	1	–
Khawaja, U.T.	99	1	99.00	1- 21	–	–	–
Klein, D.	5573	196	28.43	8- 72	10	1	–
Kleinveldt, R.K.	12490	450	27.75	9- 65	20	2	2

	Runs	Wkts	Avge	Best	5wI	10wM	50wS
Klinger, M.	3	0					
Kohli, V.	330	3	110.00	1- 19	–	–	–
Kuhn, H.G.	12	0					
Kuldeep Yadav.	2913	90	32.36	6- 79	3	–	0+1
Lake, M.B.	354	7	50.57	2- 41	–	–	–
Lamb, D.J.	146	0					
Lamb, M.J.	88	3	29.33	1- 19	–	–	–
Latham, T.W.M.	18	1	18.00	1- 7	–	–	–
Lawlor, J.L.	264	7	37.71	3- 59	–	–	–
Lawrence, D.W.	292	9	32.44	2- 63	–	–	–
Leach, J.	6980	269	25.94	6- 73	12	1	3
Leach, M.J.	5673	218	26.02	8- 85	16	3	2
Leaning, J.A.	327	4	81.75	2- 30	–	–	–
Lees, A.Z.	77	2	38.50	2- 51	–	–	–
Leighton, B.J.	79	3	26.33	2- 42	–	–	–
Lester, T.J.	899	12	74.91	3- 50	–	–	–
Lewis, S.H.	1277	49	26.06	5- 64	1	–	–
Libby, J.D.	264	4	66.00	1- 13	–	–	–
Liddle, C.J.	2326	48	48.45	3- 42	–	–	–
Lilley, A.M.	1385	38	36.44	5- 23	2	–	–
Livingstone, L.S.	963	24	40.12	6- 52	1	–	–
Lloyd, D.L.	2375	51	46.56	3- 36	–	–	–
Logan, J.E.G.	44	0					
Lyth, A.	1536	33	46.54	2- 9	–	–	–
McCarthy, B.J.	1899	62	30.62	6- 63	2	–	–
MacDonell, C.M.	391	2	195.50	2- 57	–	–	–
McGrath, A.H.	197	5	39.40	4-108	–	–	–
McKerr, C.	638	28	22.78	5- 54	2	1	–
MacLeod, C.S.	444	16	27.75	4- 66	–	–	–
Maddinson, N.J.	296	7	42.28	2- 10	–	–	–
Madsen, W.L.	1520	29	52.41	3- 45	–	–	–
Magoffin, S.J.	14091	597	23.60	8- 20	27	4	5
Maharaj, K.A.	10733	404	26.56	9-129	22	4	–
Mahmood, S.	554	21	26.38	4- 50	–	–	–
Malan, D.J.	2292	55	41.67	5- 61	1	–	–
Markram, A.K.	241	3	80.33	1- 1	–	–	–
Marsh, S.E.	155	2	77.50	2- 20	–	–	–
Maxwell, G.J.	2651	60	44.18	4- 42	–	–	–
Meaker, S.C.	8701	279	31.18	8- 52	11	2	1
Mennie, J.M.	6399	241	26.55	7- 96	6	–	0+1
Meschede, C.A.J.	5310	142	37.39	5- 84	1	–	–
Mike, B.W.M.	385	19	20.26	5- 37	1	–	–
Miles, C.N.	6805	255	26.68	6- 63	13	1	3
Mills, T.S.	2008	55	36.50	4- 25	–	–	–
Milne, A.F.	2805	84	33.39	5- 47	2	–	–
Milnes, M.E.	635	14	45.35	4- 44	–	–	–
Mir Hamza	4701	258	18.22	7- 59	25	6	0+1
Mitchell, D.K.H.	1216	27	45.03	4- 49	–	–	–
Mohammad Abbas	7635	377	20.25	8- 46	30	8	1+2
Mohammad Amir	5190	219	23.69	7- 61	11	2	0+1
Mohammad Nabi	1989	87	22.86	6- 33	3	–	–
Mohammed Shami	6254	221	28.29	7- 79	9	2	–
Morgan, A.O.	895	15	59.66	2- 37	–	–	–
Morgan, E.J.G.	90	2	45.00	2- 24	–	–	–
Morkel, M.	13028	523	24.91	6- 23	20	2	1
Morris, C.A.J.	4429	136	32.56	5- 54	2	–	2
Mujeeb Zadran	75	1	75.00	1- 75	–	–	–

	Runs	Wkts	Avge	Best	5wI	10wM	50wS
Mullaney, S.J.	3264	95	34.35	5- 32	1	–	–
Munro, C.	1640	58	28.27	4- 36	–	–	–
Murphy, J.R.	208	3	69.33	2- 90	–	–	–
Murtagh, T.J.	19613	760	25.80	7- 82	30	4	7
Muzarabani, B.	372	18	20.66	5- 32	1	–	–
Myburgh, J.G.	2160	45	48.00	4- 56	–	–	–
Nadeem, S.	10801	364	29.67	7- 45	14	3	0+2
Nair, K.K.	628	13	48.30	2- 11	–	–	–
Nash, C.D.	3271	78	41.93	4- 12	–	–	–
Newton, R.I.	107	1	107.00	1- 82	–	–	–
Nicholls, H.M.	24	0					
Nijjar, A.S.S.	739	16	46.18	2- 33	–	–	–
Noema-Barnett, K.	4337	128	33.88	4- 20	–	–	–
Northeast, S.A.	147	1	147.00	1- 60	–	–	–
Norwell, L.C.	6690	248	26.97	8- 43	10	3	2
Olivier, D.	7506	331	22.67	6- 60	18	3	0+2
Onions, G.	17702	678	26.10	9- 67	28	3	8
Overton, C.	6402	239	26.78	6- 74	4	–	–
Overton, J.	4250	129	32.94	6- 95	2	–	–
Palladino, A.P.	12569	437	28.76	7- 53	16	1	3
Panayi, G.D.	141	4	35.25	3- 41	–	–	–
Pandya, H.H.	1384	41	33.75	5- 28	2	–	–
Pant, R.R.	9	1	9.00	1- 9	–	–	–
Parkinson, C.F.	1911	41	46.60	8-148	1	1	–
Parkinson, M.W.	1183	42	28.16	5- 49	2	–	–
Parnell, W.D.	6035	198	30.47	7- 51	6	1	–
Parry, S.D.	1716	50	34.32	5- 23	2	–	–
Patel, A.R.	2635	97	27.16	7- 54	5	–	–
Patel, J.S.	26798	813	32.96	7- 38	34	5	6
Patel, R.H.	2549	81	31.46	7- 81	3	1	–
Patel, R.S.	437	10	43.70	6- 5	1	–	–
Patel, S.R.	12558	322	39.00	7- 68	5	1	–
Patterson, S.A.	10359	372	27.84	6- 40	7	–	2
Payne, D.A.	7101	220	32.27	6- 26	3	–	–
Pearce, S.J.	106	1	106.00	1- 74	–	–	–
Pennington, D.Y.	778	22	35.36	4- 53	–	–	–
Pereira, W.J.N.	138	2	69.00	2- 55	–	–	–
Perera, N.L.T.C.	2299	56	41.05	5- 69	1	–	–
Pettman, T.H.S.	313	13	24.07	5- 41	1	–	–
Pike, O.L.	220	5	44.00	3- 82	–	–	–
Pillans, M.W.	3651	129	28.30	6- 67	3	1	0+1
Plunkett, L.E.	14273	452	31.57	6- 33	11	1	3
Podmore, H.W.	2005	76	26.38	6- 36	1	–	–
Porter, J.A.	6452	270	23.89	7- 41	10	2	4
Potts, M.J.	502	15	33.46	3- 48	–	–	–
Poysden, J.E.	1084	33	32.84	5- 29	2	–	–
Prasanna, S.	11200	511	21.91	8- 59	37	8	0+4
Pringle, R.D.	2360	61	38.68	7-107	2	1	–
Procter, L.A.	3097	89	34.79	7- 71	3	–	–
Pujara, C.A.	146	5	29.20	2- 4	–	–	–
Quinn, M.R.	3175	113	28.09	7- 76	1	1	–
Rahane, A.M.	75	0					
Rahat Ali	6158	248	24.83	6- 40	10	–	0+1
Rahul, K.L.	83	0					
Raine, B.A.	5741	207	27.73	6- 66	5	–	2
Rajpoot, A.	3802	128	29.70	6- 68	5	1	–
Rampaul, R.	6839	219	31.22	7- 51	9	1	–

	Runs	Wkts	Avge	Best	5wI	10wM	50wS
Rankin, W.B.	9205	347	26.52	6- 55	9	–	1
Rashid, A.U.	17494	500	34.98	7-107	19	1	2
Rashid Khan	681	37	18.40	8- 74	4	1	–
Raval, J.A.	1004	20	50.20	2- 10	–	–	–
Rawlins, D.M.W.	161	1	161.00	1- 46	–	–	–
Rayner, O.P.	9936	298	33.34	8- 46	10	1	1
Reece, L.M.	1201	33	36.39	7- 20	1	–	–
Reifer, R.A.	3365	129	26.08	6- 74	5	–	–
Renshaw, M.T.	57	1	57.00	1- 12	–	–	–
Rhodes, G.H.	465	6	77.50	2- 83	–	–	–
Rhodes, W.M.H.	1011	26	38.88	3- 42	–	–	–
Richardson, K.W.	3105	98	31.68	5- 69	1	–	–
Richardson, M.J.	13	0					
Riley, A.E.N.	4586	126	36.39	7-150	5	–	1
Rimmington, N.J.	3789	116	32.66	5- 27	3	–	–
Rippington, S.E.	267	7	38.14	3- 51	–	–	–
Rishton, J.A.J.	111	2	55.50	1- 44	–	–	–
Robertson, W.J.R.	7	1	7.00	1- 7	–	–	–
Robinson, O.E.	3912	165	23.70	7- 23	7	1	1
Robson, S.D.	137	2	68.50	1- 4	–	–	–
Rogers, O.J.W.	13	1	13.00	1- 7	–	–	–
Roland-Jones, T.S.	9343	366	25.52	6- 50	16	3	2
Rollings, W.J.L.	139	2	69.50	2- 78	–	–	–
Root, J.E.	1747	39	44.79	4- 5	–	–	–
Root, W.T.	107	6	17.83	3- 29	–	–	–
Rossington, A.M.	66	0					
Rossouw, R.R.	70	3	23.33	1- 1	–	–	–
Roy, J.J.	495	14	35.35	3- 9	–	–	–
Ruffell, F.W.A.	96	0					
Rushworth, C.	9959	419	23.76	9- 52	21	3	4
Russell, A.M.C.	34	1	34.00	1- 34	–	–	–
Saini, N.A.	2688	102	26.35	6- 32	2	–	–
Sakande, A.	857	27	31.74	5- 43	1	–	–
Salisbury, M.E.T.	2356	71	33.18	6- 37	1	–	–
Salt, P.D.	32	1	32.00	1- 32	–	–	–
Salter, A.G.	4027	82	49.10	4- 80	–	–	–
Samarth, R.	366	4	91.50	2- 67	–	–	–
Sami Aslam	24	0					
Sanders, C.W.G.	174	3	58.00	2- 67	–	–	–
Sanderson, B.W.	3479	172	20.22	8- 73	9	1	2
Sarfraz Ahmed	5	0					
Sayer, D.W.	28	0					
Scott, G.F.B.	144	2	72.00	2- 67	–	–	–
Seabrook, B.M.A.	25	0					
Selman, N.J.	14	0					
Shadab Khan	1372	53	25.88	6- 77	2	1	–
Shankar, V.	1265	29	43.62	4- 52	–	–	–
Sharif, S.M.	654	18	36.33	4- 94	–	–	–
Sharma, I.	12215	411	29.72	7- 24	13	2	–
Shaw, J.	2396	59	40.61	5- 79	2	–	–
Shaw, P.P.	10	0					
Shepherd, R.	830	30	27.66	5- 40	1	–	–
Short, D.J.M.	545	16	34.06	3- 78	–	–	–
Sibley, D.P.	264	4	66.00	2-103	–	–	–
Siddle, P.M.	14121	512	27.58	8- 54	20	–	0+1
Sidebottom, R.N.	1247	49	25.44	6- 35	1	1	–
Simpson, J.A.	21	0					

263

	Runs	Wkts	Avge	Best	5wI	10wM	50wS
Singh, V.A.	39	0					
Siraj, M.	1499	72	20.81	5- 52	1	–	–
Sisodiya, P.	151	7	21.57	3- 54	–	–	–
Slater, B.T.	113	0					
Smit, D.	3501	106	33.02	7- 27	3	–	–
Smith, O.F.	226	6	37.66	2- 15	–	–	–
Smith, R.A.J.	2064	58	35.58	5- 87	1	–	–
Smith, T.M.J.	3641	74	49.20	4- 35	–	–	–
Smith, W.R.	1598	32	49.93	3- 34	–	–	–
Snater, S.	324	12	27.00	5- 88	2	–	–
Sodhi, I.S.	7167	203	35.30	7- 30	12	2	–
Sohal, V.V.S.	56	0					
Sowter, N.A.	25	1	25.00	1- 23	–	–	–
Steel, C.T.	595	18	33.05	2- 7	–	–	–
Stevens, D.I.	12083	463	26.09	8- 75	21	1	3
Stevenson, R.A.	270	3	90.00	1- 15	–	–	–
Stewart, G.	594	24	24.75	6- 22	1	–	–
Steyn, D.W.	14025	600	23.37	8- 41	35	7	0+2
Stirling, P.R.	1089	25	43.56	2- 27	–	–	–
Stoinis, M.P.	1951	42	46.45	4- 82	–	–	–
Stokes, B.A.	8389	281	29.85	7- 67	7	1	–
Stone, O.P.	2809	116	24.21	8- 80	5	1	–
Stoneman, M.D.	150	0					
Subramanyan, J.	67	1	67.00	1- 67	–	–	–
Sukhjit Singh	452	17	26.58	6-144	2	–	–
Suresh, K.	173	3	57.66	3-172	–	–	–
Taylor, B.J.	544	13	41.84	4- 64	–	–	–
Taylor, J.E.	8081	300	26.93	8- 59	15	2	–
Taylor, J.M.R.	3290	75	43.86	4- 16	–	–	–
Taylor, L.R.P.L.	378	6	63.00	2- 4	–	–	–
Taylor, M.D.	3974	113	35.16	5- 15	4	–	1
Taylor, T.A.I.	2427	70	34.67	6- 61	2	–	–
ten Doeschate, R.N.	7172	212	33.83	6- 20	7	–	–
Thomas, D.C.	450	12	37.50	2- 50	–	–	–
Thomas, I.A.A.	2124	70	30.34	5- 91	1	–	–
Thomas, O.R.	449	11	40.81	3- 66	–	–	–
Thomson, A.T.	326	9	36.22	6-138	1	–	–
Thurston, C.O.	16	0					
Tillcock, A.D.	244	1	244.00	1- 53	–	–	–
Tongue, J.C.	2272	91	24.96	6- 97	4	–	–
Topley, R.J.W.	3401	127	26.77	6- 29	7	2	–
Trego, P.D.	13973	382	36.57	7- 84	5	1	1
Trescothick, M.E.	1551	36	43.08	4- 36	–	–	–
Trevaskis, L.	126	1	126.00	1- 69	–	–	–
Trott, I.J.L.	3487	70	49.81	7- 39	1	–	–
Turner, S.A.	50	0					
Turpin, J.R.	281	6	46.83	2- 44	–	–	–
Twohig, B.J.	598	10	59.80	2- 47	–	–	–
Tye, A.J.	991	27	36.70	3- 47	–	–	–
Umeed, A.R.I.	73	2	36.50	1- 19	–	–	–
Usman Salahuddin	78	0					
van Beek, L.V.	3054	106	28.81	6- 46	6	1	–
van Buuren, G.L.	2469	84	29.39	4- 12	–	–	–
van den Bergh, F.O.E.	667	15	44.46	4- 84	–	–	–
van der Gugten, T.	3399	138	24.63	7- 42	10	1	1
van der Merwe, R.E.	4342	123	35.30	4- 22	–	–	–
van Meekeren, P.A.	785	21	37.38	4- 60	–	–	–

	Runs	Wkts	Avge	Best	5wI	10wM	50wS
van Zyl, S.	2535	68	37.27	5- 32	1	–	–
Vihari, G.H.	784	22	35.63	3- 17	–	–	–
Vijay, M.	588	11	53.45	3- 46	–	–	–
Vilas, D.J.	3	0					
Viljoen, G.C.	11749	438	26.82	8- 90	25	5	0+1
Vince, J.M.	1014	22	46.09	5- 41	1	–	–
Virdi, G.S.	1534	46	33.34	6-105	1	–	–
Wade, G.	218	2	109.00	1- 75	–	–	–
Wagg, G.G.	14973	437	34.26	6- 29	12	1	2
Wagner, N.	17128	628	27.27	7- 39	30	2	0+2
Wahab Riaz	12558	436	28.80	9- 59	16	5	0+2
Waite, M.J.	291	11	26.45	3- 91	–	–	–
Wakely, A.G.	426	6	71.00	2- 62	–	–	–
Waller, M.T.C.	493	10	49.30	3- 33	–	–	–
Walter, P.I.	540	13	41.53	3- 44	–	–	–
Warrican, J.A.	4079	209	19.51	8- 34	15	3	0+1
Watt, M.R.J.	322	8	40.25	3- 60	–	–	–
Weatherley, J.J.	161	3	53.66	1- 2	–	–	–
Weighell, W.J.	1250	43	29.06	7- 32	2	–	–
Wells, L.W.P.	2601	54	48.16	4- 81	–	–	–
Wells, T.J.	858	19	45.15	4- 46	–	–	–
Wessels, M.H.	130	3	43.33	1- 10	–	–	–
Westbury, O.E.	6	0					
Westley, T.	2635	59	44.66	4- 55	–	–	–
Wheal, B.T.J.	2080	56	37.14	6- 51	1	–	–
Wheater, A.J.A.	86	1	86.00	1- 86	–	–	–
Wheeldon, D.M.	48	1	48.00	1- 12	–	–	–
White, G.G.	2730	65	42.00	6- 44	1	–	–
Whiteley, R.A.	1761	32	55.03	2- 6	–	–	–
Whittingham, S.G.	1389	46	30.19	5- 70	2	–	–
Wiese, D.	8524	312	27.32	6- 58	8	1	–
Wilkinson, A.R.	277	8	34.62	3- 35	–	–	–
Willey, D.J.	5100	167	30.53	5- 29	5	1	–
Williamson, K.S.	3644	85	42.87	5- 75	1	–	–
Wilson, G.C.	89	0					
Winder, N.J.	177	0					
Woakes, C.R.	12182	474	25.70	9- 36	19	4	3
Wood, C.P.	3174	105	30.22	5- 39	3	–	–
Wood, L.	2496	73	34.19	5- 40	1	–	–
Wood, M.A.	4219	151	27.94	6- 46	8	–	–
Woodland, A.J.	49	0					
Worrall, D.J.	4376	152	28.78	6- 96	5	–	–
Wright, C.J.C.	13608	406	33.51	6- 22	11	–	1
Wright, L.J.	4862	120	40.51	5- 65	3	–	–
Yadav, J.	4427	134	33.03	7- 64	6	1	–
Yadav, U.T.	7175	228	31.46	7- 74	9	–	–
Zahir Khan	447	34	13.14	5- 31	1	–	–
Zaib, S.A.	397	13	30.53	6-115	2	–	–
Zampa, A.	4629	100	46.29	6- 62	2	1	–

LIMITED-OVERS CAREER RECORDS

Compiled by Philip Bailey

The following career records, to the end of the 2018 season, include all players currently registered with first-class counties. These records are restricted to performances in limited-overs matches of 'List A' status as defined by the Association of Cricket Statisticians and Historians now incorporated by ICC into their Classification of Cricket. The following matches qualify for List A status and are included in the figures that follow: Limited-Overs Internationals; Other International matches (e.g. Commonwealth Games, 'A' team internationals); Premier domestic limited-overs tournaments in Test status countries; Official tourist matches against the main first-class teams.

The following matches do NOT qualify for inclusion: World Cup warm-up games; Tourist matches against first-class teams outside the major domestic competitions (e.g. Universities, Minor Counties etc.); Festival, pre-season friendly games and Twenty20 Cup matches.

	M	Runs	Avge	HS	100	50	Wkts	Avge	Best	Econ
Abbott, K.J.	94	470	18.07	56	–	1	121	29.97	4-21	5.16
Abell, T.B.	14	383	38.30	106	1	1	–	–	–	–
Ackermann, C.N.	71	1739	32.81	92	–	13	37	36.64	4-48	4.60
Agar, A.C.	35	489	22.22	64	–	1	44	32.43	5-39	5.14
Ali, A.M.	16	313	22.35	88	–	3	1	124.00	1-31	6.52
Ali, M.M.	198	4879	29.04	158	11	20	146	42.30	4-33	5.31
Alsop, T.P.	38	1114	30.94	116	2	6	–	–	–	–
Ambrose, T.R.	178	4006	32.30	135	3	23	–	–	–	170/34
Anderson, J.M.	255	373	9.32	28	–	–	352	28.41	5-23	4.83
Archer, J.C.	14	192	24.00	45	–	–	21	30.71	5-42	5.29
Arshad, U.	14	56	18.66	25	–	–	9	52.33	3-50	6.23
Azhar Ali	158	5723	47.29	132*	15	34	62	35.04	5-23	5.43
Bailey, T.E.	14	80	16.00	33	–	–	18	35.38	3-31	6.05
Bairstow, J.M.	118	3881	41.28	174	9	17	–	–	–	73/8
Ball, J.T.	87	184	8.76	28	–	–	104	34.58	5-51	5.81
Ballance, G.S.	103	4066	49.58	152*	7	25	–	–	–	–
Bancroft, C.T.	41	1224	36.00	176	1	9	–	–	–	35/1
Banton, T.	7	70	11.66	40	–	–	–	–	–	–
Barber, T.E.	7	1	0.16	1	–	–	9	35.77	3-62	6.44
Barker, K.H.D.	62	560	20.00	56	–	1	69	32.79	4-33	5.79
Barnard, E.G.	35	464	20.93	51	–	2	46	32.69	3-37	5.96
Batty, G.J.	265	2354	15.48	83*	–	5	246	32.58	5-35	4.64
Bavuma, T.	79	1802	30.03	113	2	7	0	–	–	8.00
Beer, W.A.T.	53	349	15.17	45*	–	–	47	40.82	3-27	5.17
Bell, I.R.	318	11130	41.22	158	13	79	33	34.48	5-41	5.29
Bell-Drummond, D.J.	85	3197	41.51	171*	5	22	0	–	–	6.35
Berg, G.K.	90	1314	23.89	75	–	7	77	35.85	4-24	5.44
Bess, D.M.	7	55	13.75	24*	–	–	8	41.62	3-61	6.28
Billings, S.W.	84	2538	40.93	175	5	18	–	–	–	78/8
Blake, A.J.	97	1924	30.06	116	1	11	3	24.66	2-13	5.28
Blatherwick, J.M.	2	5	–	3*	–	–	0	–	–	8.50
Bohannon, J.	5	54	18.00	25	–	–	0	–	–	6.60
Bopara, R.S.	315	9666	40.78	201*	15	59	240	28.62	5-63	5.30
Borthwick, S.G.	99	1350	22.13	87	–	7	69	40.18	5-38	6.05
Bresnan, T.T.	273	3104	21.40	95*	–	9	309	34.09	5-48	5.23
Briggs, D.R.	90	284	11.83	25	–	–	97	35.56	4-32	5.12
Broad, S.C.J.	151	620	11.92	45*	–	–	216	30.51	5-23	5.27
Brook, H.C.	7	68	13.60	24	–	–	–	–	–	–
Brookes, H.J.H.	7	1	–	1*	–	–	9	27.22	3-57	5.50

266

	M	Runs	Avge	HS	100	50	Wkts	Avge	Best	Econ
Brooks, J.A.	36	49	4.90	10	–	–	37	34.48	3-30	4.83
Brown, B.C.	66	930	23.84	73*	–	6	–	–	–	61/10
Brown, C.R.	3	163	54.33	98	–	1	–	–	–	–
Brown, P.R.	6	0	–	0*	–	–	7	34.42	3-53	6.39
Browne, N.L.J.	21	557	30.94	99	–	3	–	–	–	–
Buck, N.L.	53	122	8.71	21	–	–	57	39.22	4-39	6.24
Bull, K.A.	2	–	–	–	–	–	1	48.00	1-40	5.53
Burgess, M.G.K.	18	352	22.00	58	–	2	–	–	–	9/0
Burnham, J.T.A.	5	69	17.25	26	–	–	–	–	–	–
Burns, J.A.	61	1923	34.96	154	3	11	–	–	–	–
Burns, R.J.	49	1524	37.17	95	–	11	–	–	–	–
Butchart, D.N.	1	12	12.00	12	–	–	–	–	–	–
Buttler, J.C.	186	5313	45.41	129	8	34	–	–	–	198/30
Carey, L.J.	11	32	16.00	12	–	–	8	63.00	2-57	5.74
Carlson, K.S.	12	316	28.72	63	–	2	1	47.00	1-30	6.71
Carter, A.	23	35	5.83	12	–	–	31	25.77	4-45	6.20
Carter, M.	5	28	7.00	17	–	–	13	15.23	4-40	4.60
Carver, K.	15	52	–	35*	–	–	14	31.42	3- 5	5.43
Chappell, Z.J.	12	122	17.42	59*	–	1	11	48.90	3-45	5.92
Chopra, V.	109	4368	44.12	160	9	28	0	–	–	6.00
Christian, D.T.	119	2844	32.68	117	2	14	107	33.50	6-48	5.52
Clark, G.	26	576	23.04	114	1	1	3	6.00	3-18	4.50
Clark, J.	46	835	32.11	79*	–	4	31	42.22	4-34	6.24
Clarke, J.M.	48	1390	33.09	131*	3	7	–	–	–	19/2
Clarke, R.	229	4061	25.54	98*	–	21	150	37.89	5-26	5.43
Claydon, M.E.	107	271	8.21	19	–	–	136	31.97	5-31	5.59
Coad, B.O.	17	15	15.00	9	–	–	20	37.40	4-63	5.87
Cobb, J.J.	89	2908	37.28	137	6	19	32	49.90	3-34	5.87
Cockbain, I.A.	65	1539	34.20	108*	2	9	–	–	–	–
Coetzer, K.J.	157	5022	37.20	156	10	29	4	114.50	1- 2	6.46
Coles, M.T.	76	545	14.34	100	1	1	130	22.48	6-32	5.64
Cook, A.N.	160	5851	39.80	137	12	34	0	–	–	3.33
Cook, S.J.	8	2	2.00	1*	–	–	5	55.60	1-21	4.21
Cooke, C.B.	80	2270	35.46	137*	2	14	–	–	–	47/3
Cosgrove, M.J.	152	4637	32.65	121	4	38	18	63.38	2-21	6.41
Cotton, B.D.	30	71	17.75	18*	–	–	32	37.06	4-43	5.59
Coughlin, P.	26	166	11.85	22	–	–	18	50.83	3-36	5.61
Cox, O.B.	66	1133	26.97	122*	1	4	–	–	–	69/8
Crane, M.S.	30	68	17.00	21*	–	–	53	29.49	4-30	6.10
Crawley, Z.	14	342	26.30	99*	–	2	–	–	–	–
Critchley, M.J.J.	34	461	21.95	64	–	1	25	51.84	4-48	6.64
Croft, S.J.	147	3736	34.27	127	2	28	60	39.16	4-24	5.45
Curran, S.M.	50	595	21.25	57	–	1	68	30.63	4-32	5.53
Curran, T.K.	64	490	18.84	44	–	–	98	27.11	5-16	5.57
Davey, J.H.	73	1132	23.10	91	–	5	89	26.52	6-28	5.46
Davies, A.L.	39	1104	33.45	147	1	5	–	–	–	39/10
Davies, S.M.	184	5645	35.50	127*	9	35	–	–	–	147/42
Davis, W.S.	1	–	–	–	–	–	–	–	–	–
Dawson, L.A.	148	3221	32.53	113*	2	17	142	31.30	6-47	4.78
Dearden, H.E.	2	37	18.50	31	–	–	–	–	–	–
de Lange, M.	79	573	14.32	53	–	1	139	25.84	5-49	5.46
Dell, J.J.	1	46	46.00	46	–	–	–	–	–	–
Delport, C.S.	107	2765	30.38	169*	3	15	38	42.00	4-42	6.09
Denly, J.L.	151	4668	36.18	150*	8	23	46	23.86	4-35	5.05
Dent, C.D.J.	61	1559	30.56	151*	3	4	12	34.33	4-43	5.64

	M	Runs	Avge	HS	100	50	Wkts	Avge	Best	Econ
Dernbach, J.W.	144	242	7.56	31	–	–	228	27.10	6-35	5.90
de Villiers, A.B.	263	11123	53.47	176	29	63	7	28.85	2-15	6.31
Dexter, N.J.	108	2070	29.57	135*	2	9	48	48.25	4-22	5.65
Dickinson, J.W.	1	0	0.00	0	–	–	1	87.00	1-87	8.70
Dickson, S.R.	38	956	29.87	99	–	8	–	–	–	–
D'Oliveira, B.L.	57	919	25.52	79	–	5	44	43.20	3-35	5.24
Donald, A.H.T.	23	293	14.65	53	–	1	–	–	–	–
Douthwaite, D.A.	1	38	–	38*	–	–	3	14.33	3-43	4.30
Drissell, G.S.	1	0	0.00	0	–	–	0	–	–	6.42
Duckett, B.M.	61	2049	40.98	220*	3	14	–	–	–	32/3
Dunn, M.P.	1	–	–	–	–	–	2	16.00	2-32	5.33
Edwards, F.H.	89	138	8.62	21*	–	–	115	29.91	6-22	5.18
Elgar, D.	144	4991	42.65	131*	5	38	51	48.00	3-43	5.42
Eskinazi, S.S.	8	169	24.14	49	–	–	–	–	–	3/0
Evans, L.J.	55	1400	36.84	134*	2	4	0	–	–	8.83
Evans, S.T.	1	20	20.00	20	–	–	–	–	–	–
Faheem Ashraf	55	603	17.22	71	–	2	83	24.01	5-22	5.08
Fell, T.C.	36	1149	37.06	116*	1	10	–	–	–	–
Ferguson, C.J.	154	4984	41.88	192	9	30	1	22.00	1- 8	4.40
Finch, A.J.	172	6250	38.58	154	15	38	7	45.28	2-44	5.38
Finch, H.Z.	28	961	41.78	108	1	7	0	–	–	9.00
Finn, S.T.	141	368	10.82	42*	–	–	198	28.98	5-33	5.13
Fisher, M.D.	34	228	28.50	36*	–	–	32	42.68	3-32	5.92
Fletcher, L.J.	67	357	17.85	53*	–	1	64	40.12	4-20	5.63
Foakes, B.T.	65	1552	34.48	92	–	14	–	–	–	76/7
Footitt, M.H.A.	36	28	4.66	11*	–	–	47	29.51	5-28	6.25
Fraine, W.A.R.	3	27	13.50	13	–	–	–	–	–	–
Fuller, J.K.	52	597	22.11	45	–	–	70	29.74	6-35	5.78
Funnell, J.H.	1	1	–	1*	–	–	1	67.00	1-67	9.57
Garton, G.H.S.	16	20	6.66	7*	–	–	20	36.30	4-43	6.48
Gleadall, A.F.	1	–	–	–	–	–	0	–	–	7.33
Gleeson, R.J.	21	53	6.62	13	–	–	28	29.14	5-47	5.82
Godleman, B.A.	60	2026	39.72	137	3	11	–	–	–	–
Green, B.G.F.	3	35	35.00	26*	–	–	1	70.00	1-52	6.36
Gregory, L.	56	782	23.00	105*	1	4	79	26.31	4-22	6.16
Griffiths, G.T.	16	24	24.00	15*	–	–	22	30.77	4-30	5.65
Groenewald, T.D.	103	731	19.75	57	–	2	116	32.74	4-22	5.57
Gubbins, N.R.T.	46	1647	37.43	141	5	8	–	–	–	–
Guptill, M.J.	214	8269	43.75	237*	23	43	5	21.00	2- 6	5.47
Gurney, H.F.	92	60	5.45	13*	–	–	113	33.48	5-24	5.86
Haggett, C.J.	38	337	16.85	45	–	–	47	35.36	4-59	5.92
Hain, S.R.	42	2271	68.81	145*	9	12	–	–	–	–
Hales, A.D.	167	6053	38.55	187*	17	30	0	–	–	15.00
Hameed, H.	11	388	43.11	88	–	3	–	–	–	–
Hamidullah Qadri	3	4	4.00	4	–	–	1	61.00	1-31	6.00
Hammond, M.A.H.	3	0	0.00	0	–	–	5	19.40	2-18	5.10
Hankins, G.T.	10	418	46.44	92	–	4	–	–	–	–
Hannon-Dalby, O.J.	37	82	13.66	21*	–	–	54	32.40	5-27	6.32
Harding, G.H.I.	8	23	–	18*	–	–	6	71.83	2-52	5.90
Harinath, A.	7	108	21.60	52	–	1	0	–	–	5.33
Harmer, S.R.	77	909	20.65	44*	–	–	74	41.37	4-42	5.08
Harris, J.A.R.	59	300	11.11	32	–	–	80	29.06	4-38	5.72
Harte, G.J.	5	140	35.00	48	–	–	3	30.33	2-35	5.35
Haynes, J.A.	1	33	33.00	33	–	–	–	–	–	–
Helm, T.G.	31	179	13.76	30	–	–	37	32.29	5-33	5.49

	M	Runs	Avge	HS	100	50	Wkts	Avge	Best	Econ
Hemphrey, C.R.	6	97	16.16	26	–	–	1	67.00	1-18	3.94
Higgins, R.F.	24	445	24.72	81*	–	2	14	32.64	4-50	5.52
Hildreth, J.C.	201	5324	34.79	159	7	23	6	30.83	2-26	7.40
Hill, L.J.	33	607	22.48	86	–	3	–	–	–	18/2
Hogan, M.G.	66	159	15.90	27	–	–	99	29.06	5-44	5.05
Holden, M.D.E.	5	187	62.33	71	–	2	1	41.00	1-29	3.41
Holder, J.O.	126	1868	23.64	99*	–	8	184	26.48	5-27	5.01
Holland, I.G.	2	11	–	11*	–	–	3	39.00	2-57	6.15
Horton, P.J.	115	2868	30.83	111*	3	14	1	7.00	1- 7	3.50
Hose, A.J.	29	761	33.08	101*	1	4	–	–	–	–
Hosein, H.R.	4	42	42.00	40	–	–	–	–	–	1/1
Howell, B.A.C.	76	1789	36.51	122	1	11	64	35.42	3-37	5.08
Hughes, A.L.	56	695	23.16	96*	–	2	36	44.44	3-31	5.46
Hutton, B.A.	13	146	24.33	34*	–	–	15	44.13	3-72	6.40
Imran Qayyum	19	53	6.62	18	–	–	20	40.60	4-33	5.01
Ingram, C.A.	186	7584	47.40	142	18	48	40	33.62	4-39	5.44
Jacks, W.G.	9	282	35.25	121	1	1	1	109.00	1-12	6.05
Javid, A.	43	613	27.86	43	–	–	27	47.51	4-42	5.94
Jennings, K.K.	58	1855	41.22	139	4	12	11	54.63	2-19	6.13
Jones, M.A.	5	194	38.80	87	–	2	–	–	–	–
Jones, R.P.	3	19	9.50	17	–	–	–	–	–	–
Jordan, C.J.	78	607	15.17	55	–	1	117	29.01	5-28	5.68
Karunaratne, F.D.M.	118	3514	34.45	132	5	22	3	15.33	2-13	4.31
Keogh, R.I.	38	913	29.45	134	1	8	5	148.00	2-26	5.52
Klein, D.	26	118	11.80	26	–	–	37	26.05	5-35	4.76
Klinger, M.	177	7451	49.34	166*	18	44	–	–	–	–
Kohler-Cadmore, T.	45	1455	33.83	164	3	7	–	–	–	–
Kuhn, H.G.	161	4491	34.02	141*	12	21	–	–	–	175/22
Lamb, D.J.	2	5	–	4*	–	–	4	27.00	2-51	5.40
Lamb, M.J.	3	61	20.33	47	–	–	0	–	–	9.00
Lawrence, D.W.	20	400	23.52	115	1	–	6	54.50	3-35	5.40
Leach, J.	38	539	26.95	63	–	1	43	39.97	4-30	6.04
Leach, M.J.	16	22	7.33	18	–	–	21	30.52	3- 7	4.66
Leaning, J.A.	45	1033	31.30	131*	2	5	9	26.22	5-22	5.55
Lees, A.Z.	46	1172	29.30	102	1	8	–	–	–	–
Levi, R.E.	130	4412	38.03	166	8	28	–	–	–	–
Liddle, C.J.	75	126	6.00	18	–	–	110	26.52	5-18	5.89
Lilley, A.M.	12	36	9.00	16	–	–	15	22.60	4-30	5.21
Livingstone, L.S.	48	1424	38.48	129	1	10	22	34.03	3-51	5.04
Lloyd, D.L.	38	702	22.64	92	–	3	17	42.17	5-53	5.96
Lyth, A.	115	3564	35.64	144	5	16	4	86.50	1- 6	6.07
McManus, L.D.	32	430	21.50	47	–	–	–	–	–	24/8
Madsen, W.L.	96	2869	39.84	138	4	18	14	25.28	3-27	4.82
Mahmood, S.	14	47	47.00	27*	–	–	17	34.88	5-60	6.20
Malan, D.J.	143	4938	41.84	185*	10	24	38	30.26	4-25	5.73
Marsh, S.E.	147	5857	43.38	186	15	31	1	31.00	1-14	5.16
Maxwell, G.J.	137	3649	33.78	146	4	24	75	37.29	4-46	5.37
Meaker, S.C.	69	115	7.18	21*	–	–	75	35.13	4-37	6.16
Mellor, A.J.	3	3	–	3*	–	–	–	–	–	1/0
Meschede, C.A.J.	52	462	14.90	45	–	–	51	34.56	4- 5	5.55
Mike, B.W.M.	1	10	10.00	10	–	–	0	–	–	15.33
Miles, C.N.	35	76	7.60	16	–	–	43	34.62	4-29	6.18
Mills, T.S.	43	7	1.75	3*	–	–	22	35.77	3-23	5.97
Milne, A.F.	73	392	17.81	45	–	–	103	30.00	5-61	5.27
Milton, A.G.	1	0	0.00	0	–	–	–	–	–	0/0

	M	Runs	Avge	HS	100	50	Wkts	Avge	Best	Econ
Mir Hamza	52	176	19.55	49	–	–	71	30.19	4-27	5.07
Mitchell, D.K.H.	128	3297	34.34	107	3	22	75	35.42	4-19	5.54
Mohammad Abbas	47	124	7.75	15*	–	–	63	27.87	4-31	4.70
Mohammad Amir	65	385	20.26	73*	–	2	94	27.09	5-36	4.60
Mohammad Nabi	141	3439	30.16	146	3	15	162	29.80	5-12	4.22
Moores, T.J.	12	285	31.66	76	–	1	–	–	–	10/3
Morgan, A.O.	3	32	16.00	29	–	–	2	40.50	2-49	5.78
Morgan, E.J.G.	334	10030	37.28	161	19	58	0	–	–	7.00
Morkel, M.	150	374	9.84	35	–	–	226	26.13	5-21	4.94
Morris, C.A.J.	26	49	12.25	16*	–	–	29	37.06	4-33	5.97
Mujeeb Zadran	30	44	7.33	15	–	–	52	20.88	5-50	3.85
Mullaney, S.J.	111	2240	33.93	124	2	15	95	33.43	4-29	5.16
Murphy, J.R.	3	25	8.33	10	–	–	0	–	–	6.40
Murtagh, T.J.	194	792	10.42	35*	–	–	252	29.46	4-14	5.04
Muzarabani, B.	19	16	2.00	7	–	–	19	40.21	4-47	5.49
Nash, C.D.	124	3391	30.54	124*	2	22	45	32.82	4-40	5.52
Newton, R.I.	42	1072	29.77	107	1	5	–	–	–	–
Nijjar, A.S.S.	3	21	21.00	21	–	–	1	107.00	1-39	5.09
Northeast, S.A.	96	2706	33.40	132	3	15	–	–	–	–
Norwell, L.C.	17	47	5.87	16	–	–	23	31.13	6-52	5.50
Olivier, D.	42	184	12.26	25*	–	–	58	23.98	4-34	5.01
Onions, G.	91	162	7.36	30*	–	–	104	31.00	4-45	5.11
Overton, C.	58	543	17.51	60*	–	1	70	34.54	4-27	5.41
Overton, J.	30	277	18.46	40*	–	–	40	31.10	4-42	6.51
Palladino, A.P.	56	267	10.68	31	–	–	54	37.00	5-49	5.37
Panayi, G.D.	1	–	–	–	–	–	0	–	–	8.50
Parkinson, C.F.	8	122	30.50	52*	–	1	2	210.50	1-34	6.37
Parkinson, M.W.	16	30	15.00	15*	–	–	30	22.63	5-68	4.85
Parnell, W.D.	156	1954	24.73	129	2	5	211	30.02	6-51	5.43
Parry, S.D.	95	341	12.62	31	–	–	115	30.10	5-17	5.03
Patel, J.S.	218	748	9.46	50	–	1	267	30.46	5-43	4.65
Patel, S.R.	236	6060	35.02	129*	7	33	217	32.84	6-13	5.38
Patterson, S.A.	90	231	13.58	25*	–	–	114	28.60	6-32	5.07
Payne, D.A.	59	108	10.80	23	–	–	101	23.06	7-29	5.64
Pennington, D.Y.	3	7	7.00	4*	–	–	8	22.25	5-67	6.84
Pillans, M.W.	12	79	19.75	20*	–	–	16	21.50	3-14	4.91
Plunkett, L.E.	194	1577	20.75	72	–	3	254	30.25	5-52	5.50
Podmore, H.W.	10	8	8.00	6*	–	–	10	49.90	4-57	6.80
Pollock, E.J.	9	174	24.85	56	–	1	–	–	–	–
Pope, O.J.D.	16	367	36.70	68	–	3	–	–	–	–
Porter, J.A.	21	13	6.50	6	–	–	28	27.64	4-29	5.10
Potts, M.J.	2	31	15.50	30	–	–	3	27.66	3-69	8.30
Poynter, S.W.	42	566	20.21	109	1	–	–	–	–	37/2
Poysden, J.E.	24	33	4.71	10*	–	–	24	39.37	3-33	5.96
Pringle, R.D.	40	492	15.87	125	1	–	14	65.64	2-39	5.58
Procter, L.A.	37	535	26.75	97	–	4	18	41.44	3-29	6.11
Quinn, M.R.	32	124	17.71	36	–	–	44	34.95	4-71	5.74
Raine, B.A.	20	330	20.62	83	–	1	20	47.05	3-31	6.00
Rampaul, R.	178	632	11.70	86*	–	1	268	24.61	5-48	4.88
Rashid, A.U.	186	1584	19.80	71	–	2	255	30.39	5-27	5.38
Rashid Khan	54	697	21.78	60*	–	3	122	14.72	7-18	3.94
Rawlins, D.M.W.	6	133	22.16	53	–	1	1	161.00	1-33	5.96
Rayner, O.P.	61	508	22.08	61	–	1	53	38.05	4-35	5.15
Reece, L.M.	32	598	26.00	92	–	4	14	45.00	4-35	6.09
Renshaw, M.T.	16	504	33.60	88	–	5	0	–	–	4.50

	M	Runs	Avge	HS	100	50	Wkts	Avge	Best	Econ
Rhodes, G.H.	7	102	34.00	95	–	1	5	48.60	2-34	6.39
Rhodes, W.M.H.	23	390	22.94	69	–	2	12	37.08	2-22	5.50
Richardson, K.W.	70	358	11.93	36	–	–	115	27.60	6-48	5.10
Richardson, M.J.	25	1089	54.45	111	2	9	–	–	–	12/0
Riley, A.E.N.	33	61	8.71	21*	–	–	32	34.31	4-40	5.13
Rimmington, N.J.	56	534	17.80	55	–	1	74	31.58	4-34	4.72
Robinson, O.E.	14	122	17.42	30	–	–	14	40.57	3-31	5.91
Robinson, O.G.	1									1/0
Robson, S.D.	16	407	29.07	88	–	2	–	–	–	–
Roderick, G.H.	43	882	31.50	104	1	6	–	–	–	42/4
Roland-Jones, T.S.	71	553	19.06	65	–	1	113	24.29	4-10	5.09
Root, J.E.	153	5923	47.76	133*	14	35	32	54.46	3-52	5.61
Root, W.T.	16	387	38.70	107*	1	1	3	65.00	1-27	6.80
Rossington, A.M.	43	1197	37.40	97	–	10	–	–	–	28/5
Rossouw, R.R.	142	5258	39.53	156	12	30	1	44.00	1-17	5.86
Rouse, A.P.	31	551	29.00	75*	–	3	–	–	–	28/2
Roy, J.J.	156	5313	37.15	180	13	27	0	–	–	12.00
Rushworth, C.	72	188	12.53	38*	–	–	111	24.90	5-31	5.28
Sakande, A.	5	8	8.00	7*	–	–	5	45.00	2-53	7.06
Salisbury, M.E.T.	7	6	6.00	5*	–	–	5	42.60	4-55	6.45
Salt, P.D.	9	253	28.11	81	–	2	–	–	–	–
Salter, A.G.	36	371	20.61	51	–	1	17	67.94	2-41	5.38
Sanderson, B.W.	25	54	13.50	19*	–	–	23	40.65	3-36	6.03
Scott, G.F.B.	2	6	3.00	4	–	–	0	–	–	9.33
Selman, N.J.	9	242	26.88	92	–	1	–	–	–	–
Sharif, S.M.	62	354	13.61	34	–	–	86	27.75	5-33	5.02
Short, D.J.M.	17	350	31.81	119*	1	1	13	36.92	3-53	5.45
Sibley, D.P.	14	301	30.10	115	1	–	1	62.00	1-20	6.88
Siddle, P.M.	52	230	12.77	62	–	1	57	34.70	4-27	4.54
Simpson, J.A.	84	1355	25.56	82*	–	7	–	–	–	70/16
Slater, B.T.	32	1296	51.84	148*	4	6	–	–	–	–
Smit, D.	123	2135	31.86	109	1	11	45	38.06	4-39	4.89
Smith, R.A.J.	16	70	8.75	14	–	–	14	41.00	4-76	6.80
Smith, T.M.J.	73	468	23.40	65	–	1	57	41.94	4-26	5.48
Smith, W.R.	118	2782	29.59	120*	3	20	14	40.71	2-19	5.65
Snater, S.	15	56	8.00	23*	–	–	13	37.92	5-60	5.21
Sole, T.B.	7	78	26.00	54	–	1	8	35.50	4-15	4.65
Sowter, N.A.	10	79	15.80	29	–	–	11	37.00	3-43	5.17
Spencer, M.T.	1						0	–	–	5.40
Steel, C.T.	11	181	20.11	77	–	1	0	–	–	9.40
Stevens, D.I.	311	7571	29.69	147	7	46	157	31.75	6-25	4.79
Stevenson, R.A.	3	0	0.00	0	–	–	2	71.00	1-28	7.10
Stewart, G.	5	69	23.00	44	–	–	8	19.00	3-17	3.76
Stirling, P.R.	180	5969	35.74	177	15	25	65	40.27	6-55	4.97
Stokes, B.A.	139	3686	34.77	164	7	18	119	31.35	5-61	5.73
Stone, O.P.	25	113	22.60	24*	–	–	23	38.86	4-71	5.40
Stoneman, M.D.	74	2601	40.01	144*	6	16	1	8.00	1- 8	12.00
Swindells, H.J.	2	28	28.00	28	–	–	–	–	–	–
Tattersall, J.A.	8	143	35.75	89	–	2	–	–	–	6/1
Taylor, B.J.	17	355	35.50	69	–	3	15	42.33	4-26	4.56
Taylor, J.E.	128	474	9.87	43*	–	–	192	27.11	5-40	5.08
Taylor, J.M.R.	42	836	30.96	68	–	7	29	35.20	4-38	5.17
Taylor, M.D.	22	38	19.00	16	–	–	15	64.06	3-48	5.87
Taylor, T.A.I.	5	–	–	–	–	–	5	45.00	3-48	6.19
ten Doeschate, R.N.	219	5826	45.51	180	11	30	173	30.29	5-50	5.76

	M	Runs	Avge	HS	100	50	Wkts	Avge	Best	Econ
Thomas, I.A.A.	21	18	6.00	6	–	–	31	31.09	4-30	5.58
Thomason, A.D.	16	153	21.85	28	–	–	13	31.38	4-45	7.20
Thomson, A.T.	1	19	19.00	19	–	–	3	17.66	3-53	5.30
Thurston, C.O.	1	53	53.00	53	–	1	–	–	–	
Tongue, J.C.	7	12	12.00	11*	–	–	8	37.37	2-46	6.57
Trego, P.D.	187	4573	32.66	147	9	25	171	32.50	5-40	5.56
Trescothick, M.E.	372	12229	37.28	184	28	63	57	28.84	4-50	4.90
Twohig, B.J.	1	1	1.00	1	–	–	0	–	–	5.50
van Beek, L.V.	52	405	14.46	64*	–	2	58	30.01	6-18	5.52
van Buuren, G.L.	63	1312	29.15	119*	1	6	48	31.52	5-35	4.74
van den Bergh, F.O.E.	3	29	–	29*	–	–	0	–	–	4.69
van der Gugten, T.	53	327	15.57	36	–	–	64	34.23	5-24	5.53
van der Merwe, R.E.	173	2652	26.52	165*	1	10	237	25.89	5-26	4.82
van Meekeren, P.A.	42	118	9.83	15*	–	–	39	29.94	3-22	4.73
van Zyl, S.	116	3350	35.63	114*	5	18	20	46.35	4-24	5.26
Vasconcelos, R.S.	19	439	24.38	56	–	2	–	–	–	16/2
Vilas, D.J.	150	4174	35.67	120	8	19	–	–	–	149/26
Vince, J.M.	122	4205	39.29	178	8	20	2	62.00	1-18	5.63
Wagg, G.G.	132	1853	19.71	62*	–	3	147	34.36	4-35	5.90
Waite, M.J.	11	246	35.14	71	–	1	13	32.61	4-65	6.18
Wakely, A.G.	81	2191	32.22	109*	2	14	5	26.20	2-14	5.77
Waller, M.T.C.	58	109	15.57	25*	–	–	45	37.68	3-37	5.65
Walter, P.I.	6	37	18.50	19	–	–	12	22.25	4-37	6.25
Watt, M.R.J.	24	145	13.18	31*	–	–	28	31.00	3-21	4.26
Weatherley, J.J.	19	497	33.13	105*	1	3	8	27.62	4-25	4.05
Weighell, W.J.	10	48	12.00	23	–	–	20	27.45	5-57	6.45
Wells, L.W.P.	26	232	11.60	62	–	1	10	38.40	3-19	5.27
Wessels, M.H.	170	4451	30.69	146	4	25	1	48.00	1- 0	5.87
Westbury, O.E.	1	8	8.00	8	–	–	–	–	–	
Westley, T.	80	2480	35.42	134	5	18	20	41.50	4-60	4.95
Wheal, B.T.J.	23	60	8.57	18*	–	–	37	24.16	4-38	4.88
Wheater, A.J.A.	80	1713	28.55	135	2	9	–	–	–	41/12
Wheeldon, D.M.	7	28	5.60	14	–	–	5	48.40	3-31	5.52
White, G.G.	84	539	15.40	41*	–	–	92	28.94	6-37	5.06
White, R.G.	1	12	12.00	12	–	–	–	–	–	1/0
Whiteley, R.A.	71	1319	25.86	77	–	9	12	40.08	4-58	6.63
Whittingham, S.G.	5	6	6.00	3*	–	–	10	20.90	3-35	4.76
Wiese, D.	140	3185	33.88	108	1	18	127	35.92	5-25	5.32
Willey, D.J.	121	1606	23.97	167	3	5	131	31.64	5-62	5.65
Woakes, C.R.	153	1692	24.17	95*	–	4	183	33.20	6-45	5.47
Wood, C.P.	75	383	13.20	41	–	–	104	26.89	5-22	5.35
Wood, L.	3	56	56.00	52	–	1	3	29.66	2-44	5.56
Wood, M.A.	62	79	6.07	15*	–	–	73	35.21	4-33	5.31
Worrall, D.J.	26	43	14.33	16	–	–	31	38.45	5-62	5.24
Wright, C.J.C.	99	229	10.90	42	–	–	100	35.68	4-20	5.58
Wright, L.J.	204	4717	31.87	143*	10	17	111	38.11	4-12	5.34
Zaib, S.A.	8	56	11.20	17	–	–	3	42.66	2-22	6.40
Zain-ul-Hassan	1	9	–	9*	–	–	0	–	–	6.71
Zampa, A.	59	465	17.22	66	–	3	83	33.26	4-18	5.39

FIRST-CLASS CRICKET RECORDS

To the end of the 2018 season

TEAM RECORDS
HIGHEST INNINGS TOTALS

1107	Victoria v New South Wales	Melbourne	1926-27
1059	Victoria v Tasmania	Melbourne	1922-23
952-6d	Sri Lanka v India	Colombo	1997-98
951-7d	Sind v Baluchistan	Karachi	1973-74
944-6d	Hyderabad v Andhra	Secunderabad	1993-94
918	New South Wales v South Australia	Sydney	1900-01
912-8d	Holkar v Mysore	Indore	1945-46
910-6d	Railways v Dera Ismail Khan	Lahore	1964-65
903-7d	England v Australia	The Oval	1938
900-6d	Queensland v Victoria	Brisbane	2005-06
887	Yorkshire v Warwickshire	Birmingham	1896
863	Lancashire v Surrey	The Oval	1990
860-6d	Tamil Nadu v Goa	Panjim	1988-89
850-7d	Somerset v Middlesex	Taunton	2007

Excluding penalty runs in India, there have been 35 innings totals of 800 runs or more in first-class cricket. Tamil Nadu's total of 860-6d was boosted to 912 by 52 penalty runs.

HIGHEST SECOND INNINGS TOTAL

770	New South Wales v South Australia	Adelaide	1920-21

HIGHEST FOURTH INNINGS TOTAL

654-5	England (set 696 to win) v South Africa	Durban	1938-39

HIGHEST MATCH AGGREGATE

2376-37	Maharashtra v Bombay	Poona	1948-49

RECORD MARGIN OF VICTORY

Innings and 851 runs: Railways v Dera Ismail Khan   Lahore   1964-65

MOST RUNS IN A DAY

721	Australians v Essex	Southend	1948

MOST HUNDREDS IN AN INNINGS

6	Holkar v Mysore	Indore	1945-46

LOWEST INNINGS TOTALS

12	†Oxford University v MCC and Ground	Oxford	1877
12	Northamptonshire v Gloucestershire	Gloucester	1907
13	Auckland v Canterbury	Auckland	1877-78
13	Nottinghamshire v Yorkshire	Nottingham	1901
14	Surrey v Essex	Chelmsford	1983
15	MCC v Surrey	Lord's	1839
15	†Victoria v MCC	Melbourne	1903-04
15	†Northamptonshire v Yorkshire	Northampton	1908
15	Hampshire v Warwickshire	Birmingham	1922

† Batted one man short

There have been 28 instances of a team being dismissed for under 20.

LOWEST MATCH AGGREGATE BY ONE TEAM

34 (16 and 18) Border v Natal   East London   1959-60

LOWEST COMPLETED MATCH AGGREGATE BY BOTH TEAMS

105	MCC v Australians	Lord's	1878

FEWEST RUNS IN AN UNINTERRUPTED DAY'S PLAY
Australia (80) v Pakistan (15-2)   Karachi   1956-57

TIED MATCHES

Before 1949 a match was considered to be tied if the scores were level after the fourth innings, even if the side batting last had wickets in hand when play ended. Law 22 was amended in 1948 and since then a match has been tied only when the scores are level after the fourth innings has been completed. There have been 61 tied first-class matches, five of which would not have qualified under the current law. The most recent are:

Windward Is (117 & 241) v Guyana (194 & 164)	Providence	2017-18
Chilaw Marians (293 & 117) v Burgher Recreation (316 & 94)	Katunayake	2017-18
Bloomfield (163 & 206) v Sri Lanka Army (171 & 198)	Colombo, MSC	2017-18
Lancashire (99 & 170) v Somerset (192 & 77)	Taunton	2018

BATTING RECORDS
35,000 RUNS IN A CAREER

	Career	I	NO	HS	Runs	Avge	100
J.B.Hobbs	1905-34	1315	106	316*	**61237**	50.65	197
F.E.Woolley	1906-38	1532	85	305*	**58969**	40.75	145
E.H.Hendren	1907-38	1300	166	301*	**57611**	50.80	170
C.P.Mead	1905-36	1340	185	280*	**55061**	47.67	153
W.G.Grace	1865-1908	1493	105	344	**54896**	39.55	126
W.R.Hammond	1920-51	1005	104	336*	**50551**	56.10	167
H.Sutcliffe	1919-45	1088	123	313	**50138**	51.95	149
G.Boycott	1962-86	1014	162	261*	**48426**	56.83	151
T.W.Graveney	1948-71/72	1223	159	258	**47793**	44.91	122
G.A.Gooch	1973-2000	990	75	333	**44846**	49.01	128
T.W.Hayward	1893-1914	1138	96	315*	**43551**	41.79	104
D.L.Amiss	1960-87	1139	126	262*	**43423**	42.86	102
M.C.Cowdrey	1950-76	1130	134	307	**42719**	42.89	107
A.Sandham	1911-37/38	1000	79	325	**41284**	44.82	107
G.A.Hick	1983/84-2008	871	84	405*	**41112**	52.23	136
L.Hutton	1934-60	814	91	364	**40140**	55.51	129
M.J.K.Smith	1951-75	1091	139	204	**39832**	41.84	69
W.Rhodes	1898-1930	1528	237	267*	**39802**	30.83	58
J.H.Edrich	1956-78	979	104	310*	**39790**	45.47	103
R.E.S.Wyatt	1923-57	1141	157	232	**39405**	40.04	85
D.C.S.Compton	1936-64	839	88	300	**38942**	51.85	123
G.E.Tyldesley	1909-36	961	106	256*	**38874**	45.46	102
J.T.Tyldesley	1895-1923	994	62	295*	**37897**	40.60	86
K.W.R.Fletcher	1962-88	1167	170	228*	**37665**	37.77	63
C.G.Greenidge	1970-92	889	75	273*	**37354**	45.88	92
J.W.Hearne	1909-36	1025	116	285*	**37252**	40.98	96
L.E.G.Ames	1926-51	951	95	295	**37248**	43.51	102
D.Kenyon	1946-67	1159	59	259	**37002**	33.63	74
W.J.Edrich	1934-58	964	92	267*	**36965**	42.39	86
J.M.Parks	1949-76	1227	172	205*	**36673**	34.76	51
M.W.Gatting	1975-98	861	123	258	**36549**	49.52	94
D.Denton	1894-1920	1163	70	221	**36479**	33.37	69
G.H.Hirst	1891-1929	1215	151	341	**36323**	34.13	60
I.V.A.Richards	1971/72-93	796	63	322	**36212**	49.40	114
A.Jones	1957-83	1168	72	204*	**36049**	32.89	56
W.G.Quaife	1894-1928	1203	185	255*	**36012**	35.37	72
R.E.Marshall	1945/46-72	1053	59	228*	**35725**	35.94	68
M.R.Ramprakash	1987-2012	764	93	301*	**35659**	53.14	114
G.Gunn	1902-32	1061	82	220	**35208**	35.96	62

HIGHEST INDIVIDUAL INNINGS

501*	B.C.Lara	Warwickshire v Durham	Birmingham	1994
499	Hanif Mohammed	Karachi v Bahawalpur	Karachi	1958-59
452*	D.G.Bradman	New South Wales v Queensland	Sydney	1929-30
443*	B.B.Nimbalkar	Maharashtra v Kathiawar	Poona	1948-49
437	W.H.Ponsford	Victoria v Queensland	Melbourne	1927-28
429	W.H.Ponsford	Victoria v Tasmania	Melbourne	1922-23
428	Aftab Baloch	Sind v Baluchistan	Karachi	1973-74
424	A.C.MacLaren	Lancashire v Somerset	Taunton	1895
405*	G.A.Hick	Worcestershire v Somerset	Taunton	1988
400*	B.C.Lara	West Indies v England	St John's	2003-04
394	Naved Latif	Sargodha v Gujranwala	Gujranwala	2000-01
390	S.C.Cook	Lions v Warriors	East London	2009-10
385	B.Sutcliffe	Otago v Canterbury	Christchurch	1952-53
383	C.W.Gregory	New South Wales v Queensland	Brisbane	1906-07
380	M.L.Hayden	Australia v Zimbabwe	Perth	2003-04
377	S.V.Manjrekar	Bombay v Hyderabad	Bombay	1990-91
375	B.C.Lara	West Indies v England	St John's	1993-94
374	D.P.M.D.Jayawardena	Sri Lanka v South Africa	Colombo	2006
369	D.G.Bradman	South Australia v Tasmania	Adelaide	1935-36
366	N.H.Fairbrother	Lancashire v Surrey	The Oval	1990
366	M.V.Sridhar	Hyderabad v Andhra	Secunderabad	1993-94
365*	C.Hill	South Australia v NSW	Adelaide	1900-01
365*	G.St A.Sobers	West Indies v Pakistan	Kingston	1957-58
364	L.Hutton	England v Australia	The Oval	1938
359*	V.M.Merchant	Bombay v Maharashtra	Bombay	1943-44
359*	S.B.Gohel	Gujarat v Orissa	Jaipur	2016-17
359	R.B.Simpson	New South Wales v Queensland	Brisbane	1963-64
357*	R.Abel	Surrey v Somerset	The Oval	1899
357	D.G.Bradman	South Australia v Victoria	Melbourne	1935-36
356	B.A.Richards	South Australia v W Australia	Perth	1970-71
355*	G.R.Marsh	W Australia v S Australia	Perth	1989-90
355*	K.P.Pietersen	Surrey v Leicestershire	The Oval	2015
355	B.Sutcliffe	Otago v Auckland	Dunedin	1949-50
353	V.V.S.Laxman	Hyderabad v Karnataka	Bangalore	1999-00
352	W.H.Ponsford	Victoria v New South Wales	Melbourne	1926-27
352	C.A.Pujara	Saurashtra v Karnataka	Rajkot	2012-13
351*	S.M.Gugale	Maharashtra v Delhi	Mumbai	2016-17
351	K.D.K.Vithanage	Tamil Union v SL Air	Katunayake	2014-15
350	Rashid Israr	Habib Bank v National Bank	Lahore	1976-77

There have been 220 triple hundreds in first-class cricket, W.V.Raman (313) and Arjan Kripal Singh (302*) for Tamil Nadu v Goa at Panjim in 1988-89 providing the only instance of two batsmen scoring 300 in the same innings.

MOST HUNDREDS IN SUCCESSIVE INNINGS

6	C.B.Fry	Sussex and Rest of England	1901
6	D.G.Bradman	South Australia and D.G.Bradman's XI	1938-39
6	M.J.Procter	Rhodesia	1970-71

TWO DOUBLE HUNDREDS IN A MATCH

244	202* A.E.Fagg	Kent v Essex	Colchester	1938

TRIPLE HUNDRED AND HUNDRED IN A MATCH

333	123	G.A.Gooch	England v India	Lord's	1990
319	105	K.C.Sangakkara	Sri Lanka v Bangladesh	Chittagong	2013-14

DOUBLE HUNDRED AND HUNDRED IN A MATCH MOST TIMES

4	Zaheer Abbas	Gloucestershire	1976-81

TWO HUNDREDS IN A MATCH MOST TIMES

8	Zaheer Abbas	Gloucestershire and PIA	1976-82
8	R.T.Ponting	Tasmania, Australia and Australians	1992-2006
7	W.R.Hammond	Gloucestershire, England and MCC	1927-45
7	M.R.Ramprakash	Middlesex, Surrey	1990-2010

MOST HUNDREDS IN A SEASON

18	D.C.S.Compton	1947	16	J.B.Hobbs	1925

100 HUNDREDS IN A CAREER

	Total		100th Hundred	
	Hundreds	Inns	Season	Inns
J.B.Hobbs	197	1315	1923	821
E.H.Hendren	170	1300	1928-29	740
W.R.Hammond	167	1005	1935	679
C.P.Mead	153	1340	1927	892
G.Boycott	151	1014	1977	645
H.Sutcliffe	149	1088	1932	700
F.E.Woolley	145	1532	1929	1031
G.A.Hick	136	871	1998	574
L.Hutton	129	814	1951	619
G.A.Gooch	128	990	1992-93	820
W.G.Grace	126	1493	1895	1113
D.C.S.Compton	123	839	1952	552
T.W.Graveney	122	1223	1964	940
D.G.Bradman	117	338	1947-48	295
I.V.A.Richards	114	796	1988-89	658
M.R.Ramprakash	114	764	2008	676
Zaheer Abbas	108	768	1982-83	658
A.Sandham	107	1000	1935	871
M.C.Cowdrey	107	1130	1973	1035
T.W.Hayward	104	1138	1913	1076
G.M.Turner	103	792	1982	779
J.H.Edrich	103	979	1977	945
L.E.G.Ames	102	951	1950	915
G.E.Tyldesley	102	961	1934	919
D.L.Amiss	102	1139	1986	1081

MOST 400s: 2 – B.C.Lara, W.H.Ponsford

MOST 300s or more: 6 – D.G.Bradman; 4 – W.R.Hammond, W.H.Ponsford

MOST 200s or more: 37 – D.G.Bradman; 36 – W.R.Hammond; 22 – E.H.Hendren

MOST RUNS IN A MONTH

1294 (avge 92.42)	L.Hutton	Yorkshire	June 1949

MOST RUNS IN A SEASON

Runs			I	NO	HS	Avge	100	Season
3816	D.C.S.Compton	Middlesex	50	8	246	90.85	18	1947
3539	W.J.Edrich	Middlesex	52	8	267*	80.43	12	1947
3518	T.W.Hayward	Surrey	61	8	219	66.37	13	1906

The feat of scoring 3000 runs in a season has been achieved 28 times, the most recent instance being by W.E.Alley (3019) in 1961. The highest aggregate in a season since 1969 is 2755 by S.J.Cook in 1991.

1000 RUNS IN A SEASON MOST TIMES

28   W.G.Grace (Gloucestershire), F.E.Woolley (Kent)

HIGHEST BATTING AVERAGE IN A SEASON

(Qualification: 12 innings)

Avge			I	NO	HS	Runs	100	Season
115.66	D.G.Bradman	Australians	26	5	278	2429	13	1938
106.50	K.C.Sangakkara	Surrey	16	2	200	1491	8	2017
104.66	D.R.Martyn	Australians	14	5	176*	942	5	2001
103.54	M.R.Ramprakash	Surrey	24	2	301*	2278	8	2006
102.53	G.Boycott	Yorkshire	20	5	175*	1538	6	1979
102.00	W.A.Johnston	Australians	17	16	28*	102	–	1953
101.70	G.A.Gooch	Essex	30	3	333	2746	12	1990
101.30	M.R.Ramprakash	Surrey	25	5	266*	2026	10	2007
100.12	G.Boycott	Yorkshire	30	5	233	2503	13	1971

FASTEST HUNDRED AGAINST AUTHENTIC BOWLING

35 min	P.G.H.Fender	Surrey v Northamptonshire	Northampton	1920

FASTEST DOUBLE HUNDRED

113 min	R.J.Shastri	Bombay v Baroda	Bombay	1984-85

FASTEST TRIPLE HUNDRED

181 min	D.C.S.Compton	MCC v NE Transvaal	Benoni	1948-49

MOST SIXES IN AN INNINGS

23	C.Munro	Central Districts v Auckland	Napier	2014-15

MOST SIXES IN A MATCH

23	C.Munro	Central Districts v Auckland	Napier	2014-15

MOST SIXES IN A SEASON

80	I.T.Botham	Somerset and England		1985

MOST BOUNDARIES IN AN INNINGS

72	B.C.Lara	Warwickshire v Durham	Birmingham	1994

MOST RUNS OFF ONE OVER

36	G.St A.Sobers	Nottinghamshire v Glamorgan	Swansea	1968
36	R.J.Shastri	Bombay v Baroda	Bombay	1984-85

Both batsmen hit for six all six balls of overs bowled by M.A.Nash and Tilak Raj respectively.

MOST RUNS IN A DAY

390*	B.C.Lara	Warwickshire v Durham	Birmingham	1994

There have been 19 instances of a batsman scoring 300 or more runs in a day.

LONGEST INNINGS

1015 min	R.Nayyar (271)	Himachal Pradesh v Jammu & Kashmir	Chamba	1999-00

HIGHEST PARTNERSHIPS FOR EACH WICKET

First Wicket

561	Waheed Mirza/Mansoor Akhtar	Karachi W v Quetta	Karachi	1976-77
555	P.Holmes/H.Sutcliffe	Yorkshire v Essex	Leyton	1932
554	J.T.Brown/J.Tunnicliffe	Yorkshire v Derbys	Chesterfield	1898

Second Wicket

580	Rafatullah Mohmand/Aamer Sajjad	WAPDA v SSGC	Sheikhupura	2009-10
576	S.T.Jayasuriya/R.S.Mahanama	Sri Lanka v India	Colombo	1997-98
480	D.Elgar/R.R.Rossouw	Eagles v Titans	Centurion	2009-10
475	Zahir Alam/L.S.Rajput	Assam v Tripura	Gauhati	1991-92
465*	J.A.Jameson/R.B.Kanhai	Warwickshire v Glos	Birmingham	1974

Third Wicket

624	K.C.Sangakkara/D.P.M.D.Jayawardena	Sri Lanka v South Africa	Colombo	2006
594*	S.M.Gugale/A.R.Bawne	Maharashtra v Delhi	Mumbai	2016-17
539	S.D.Jogiyani/R.A.Jadeja	Saurashtra v Gujarat	Surat	2012-13
523	M.A.Carberry/N.D.McKenzie	Hampshire v Yorkshire	Southampton	2011

Fourth Wicket

577	V.S.Hazare/Gul Mahomed	Baroda v Holkar	Baroda	1946-47
574*	C.L.Walcott/F.M.M.Worrell	Barbados v Trinidad	Port-of-Spain	1945-46
502*	F.M.M.Worrell/J.D.C.Goddard	Barbados v Trinidad	Bridgetown	1943-44
470	A.I.Kallicharran/G.W.Humpage	Warwickshire v Lancs	Southport	1982

Fifth Wicket

520*	C.A.Pujara/R.A.Jadeja	Saurashtra v Orissa	Rajkot	2008-09
494	Marchall Ayub/Mehrab Hossain Jr	Central Zone v East Zone	Bogra	2012-13
479	Misbah-ul-Haq/Usman Arshad	Sui NGP v Lahore Shalimar	Lahore	2009-10
464*	M.E.Waugh/S.R.Waugh	NSW v W Australia	Perth	1990-91
423	Mosaddek Hossain/Al-Amin	Barisal v Rangpur	Savar	2014-15
420	Mohd. Ashraful/Marshall Ayub	Dhaka v Chittagong	Chittagong	2006-07
410*	A.S.Chopra/S.Badrinath	India A v South Africa A	Delhi	2007-08
405	S.G.Barnes/D.G.Bradman	Australia v England	Sydney	1946-47
401	M.B.Loye/D.Ripley	Northants v Glamorgan	Northampton	1998

Sixth Wicket

487*	G.A.Headley/C.C.Passailaigue	Jamaica v Tennyson's	Kingston	1931-32
428	W.W.Armstrong/M.A.Noble	Australians v Sussex	Hove	1902
417	W.P.Saha/L.R.Shukla	Bengal v Assam	Kolkata	2010-11
411	R.M.Poore/E.G.Wynyard	Hampshire v Somerset	Taunton	1899

Seventh Wicket

460	Bhupinder Singh jr/P.Dharmani	Punjab v Delhi	Delhi	1994-95
371	M.R.Marsh/S.M.Whiteman	Australia A v India A	Brisbane	2014
366*	J.M.Bairstow/T.T.Bresnan	Yorkshire v Durham	Chester-le-Street	2015

Eighth Wicket

433	V.T.Trumper/A.Sims	Australians v C'bury	Christchurch	1913-14
392	A.Mishra/J.Yadav	Haryana v Karnataka	Hubli	2012-13
332	I.J.L.Trott/S.C.J.Broad	England v Pakistan	Lord's	2010

Ninth Wicket

283	J.Chapman/A.Warren	Derbys v Warwicks	Blackwell	1910
268	J.B.Commins/N.Boje	SA 'A' v Mashonaland	Harare	1994-95
261	W.L.Madsen/T.Poynton	Derbys v Northants	Northampton	2012
251	J.W.H.T.Douglas/S.N.Hare	Essex v Derbyshire	Leyton	1921

Tenth Wicket

307	A.F.Kippax/J.E.H.Hooker	NSW v Victoria	Melbourne	1928-29
249	C.T.Sarwate/S.N.Banerjee	Indians v Surrey	The Oval	1946
239	Aqil Arshad/Ali Raza	Lahore Whites v Hyderabad	Lahore	2004-05

BOWLING RECORDS – 2000 WICKETS IN A CAREER

	Career	Runs	Wkts	Avge	100w
W.Rhodes	1898-1930	69993	4187	16.71	23
A.P.Freeman	1914-36	69577	3776	18.42	17
C.W.L.Parker	1903-35	63817	3278	19.46	16
J.T.Hearne	1888-1923	54352	3061	17.75	15
T.W.J.Goddard	1922-52	59116	2979	19.84	16
W.G.Grace	1865-1908	51545	2876	17.92	10
A.S.Kennedy	1907-36	61034	2874	21.23	15
D.Shackleton	1948-69	53303	2857	18.65	20
G.A.R.Lock	1946-70/71	54709	2844	19.23	14
F.J.Titmus	1949-82	63313	2830	22.37	16
M.W.Tate	1912-37	50571	2784	18.16	13+1
G.H.Hirst	1891-1929	51282	2739	18.72	15

	Career	Runs	Wkts	Avge	100w
C.Blythe	1899-1914	42136	**2506**	16.81	14
D.L.Underwood	1963-87	49993	**2465**	20.28	10
W.E.Astill	1906-39	57783	**2431**	23.76	9
J.C.White	1909-37	43759	**2356**	18.57	14
W.E.Hollies	1932-57	48656	**2323**	20.94	14
F.S.Trueman	1949-69	42154	**2304**	18.29	12
J.B.Statham	1950-68	36999	**2260**	16.37	13
R.T.D.Perks	1930-55	53771	**2233**	24.07	16
J.Briggs	1879-1900	35431	**2221**	15.95	12
D.J.Shepherd	1950-72	47302	**2218**	21.32	12
E.G.Dennett	1903-26	42571	**2147**	19.82	12
T.Richardson	1892-1905	38794	**2104**	18.43	10
T.E.Bailey	1945-67	48170	**2082**	23.13	9
R.Illingworth	1951-83	42023	**2072**	20.28	10
F.E.Woolley	1906-38	41066	**2068**	19.85	8
N.Gifford	1960-88	48731	**2068**	23.56	4
G.Geary	1912-38	41339	**2063**	20.03	11
D.V.P.Wright	1932-57	49307	**2056**	23.98	10
J.A.Newman	1906-30	51111	**2032**	25.15	9
A.Shaw	1864-97	24580	**2026+1**	12.12	9
S.Haigh	1895-1913	32091	**2012**	15.94	11

ALL TEN WICKETS IN AN INNINGS

This feat has been achieved 81 times in first-class matches (excluding 12-a-side fixtures).
Three Times: A.P.Freeman (1929, 1930, 1931)
Twice: V.E.Walker (1859, 1865); H.Verity (1931, 1932); J.C.Laker (1956)

Instances since 1945:

W.E.Hollies	Warwickshire v Notts	Birmingham	1946
J.M.Sims	East v West	Kingston on Thames	1948
J.K.R.Graveney	Gloucestershire v Derbyshire	Chesterfield	1949
T.E.Bailey	Essex v Lancashire	Clacton	1949
R.Berry	Lancashire v Worcestershire	Blackpool	1953
S.P.Gupte	President's XI v Combined XI	Bombay	1954-55
J.C.Laker	Surrey v Australians	The Oval	1956
K.Smales	Nottinghamshire v Glos	Stroud	1956
G.A.R.Lock	Surrey v Kent	Blackheath	1956
J.C.Laker	England v Australia	Manchester	1956
P.M.Chatterjee	Bengal v Assam	Jorhat	1956-57
J.D.Bannister	Warwicks v Combined Services	Birmingham (M & B)	1959
A.J.G.Pearson	Cambridge U v Leicestershire	Loughborough	1961
N.I.Thomson	Sussex v Warwickshire	Worthing	1964
P.J.Allan	Queensland v Victoria	Melbourne	1965-66
I.J.Brayshaw	Western Australia v Victoria	Perth	1967-68
Shahid Mahmood	Karachi Whites v Khairpur	Karachi	1969-70
E.E.Hemmings	International XI v W Indians	Kingston	1982-83
P.Sunderam	Rajasthan v Vidarbha	Jodhpur	1985-86
S.T.Jefferies	Western Province v OFS	Cape Town	1987-88
Imran Adil	Bahawalpur v Faisalabad	Faisalabad	1989-90
G.P.Wickremasinghe	Sinhalese v Kalutara	Colombo	1991-92
R.L.Johnson	Middlesex v Derbyshire	Derby	1994
Naeem Akhtar	Rawalpindi B v Peshawar	Peshawar	1995-96
A.Kumble	India v Pakistan	Delhi	1998-99
D.S.Mohanty	East Zone v South Zone	Agartala	2000-01
O.D.Gibson	Durham v Hampshire	Chester-le-Street	2007
M.W.Olivier	Warriors v Eagles	Bloemfontein	2007-08
Zulfiqar Babar	Multan v Islamabad	Multan	2009-10

MOST WICKETS IN A MATCH

19	J.C.Laker	England v Australia	Manchester	1956

MOST WICKETS IN A SEASON

Wkts		Season	Matches	Overs	Mdns	Runs	Avge
304	A.P.Freeman	1928	37	1976.1	423	5489	18.05
298	A.P.Freeman	1933	33	2039	651	4549	15.26

The feat of taking 250 wickets in a season has been achieved on 12 occasions, the last instance being by A.P.Freeman in 1933. 200 or more wickets in a season have been taken on 59 occasions, the last being by G.A.R.Lock (212 wickets, average 12.02) in 1957.

The highest aggregates of wickets taken in a season since the reduction of County Championship matches in 1969 are as follows:

Wkts		Season	Matches	Overs	Mdns	Runs	Avge
134	M.D.Marshall	1982	22	822	225	2108	15.73
131	L.R.Gibbs	1971	23	1024.1	295	2475	18.89
125	F.D.Stephenson	1988	22	819.1	196	2289	18.31
121	R.D.Jackman	1980	23	746.2	220	1864	15.40

Since 1969 there have been 50 instances of bowlers taking 100 wickets in a season.

MOST HAT-TRICKS IN A CAREER

7	D.V.P.Wright
6	T.W.J.Goddard, C.W.L.Parker
5	S.Haigh, V.W.C.Jupp, A.E.G.Rhodes, F.A.Tarrant

ALL-ROUND RECORDS
THE 'DOUBLE'

3000 runs and 100 wickets: J.H.Parks (1937)

2000 runs and 200 wickets: G.H.Hirst (1906)

2000 runs and 100 wickets: F.E.Woolley (4), J.W.Hearne (3), W.G.Grace (2), G.H.Hirst (2), W.Rhodes (2), T.E.Bailey, D.E.Davies, G.L.Jessop, V.W.C.Jupp, J.Langridge, F.A.Tarrant, C.L.Townsend, L.F.Townsend

1000 runs and 200 wickets: M.W.Tate (3), A.E.Trott (2), A.S.Kennedy

Most Doubles: 16 – W.Rhodes; 14 – G.H.Hirst; 10 – V.W.C.Jupp

Double in Debut Season: D.B.Close (1949) – aged 18, the youngest to achieve this feat.

The feat of scoring 1000 runs and taking 100 wickets in a season has been achieved on 305 occasions, R.J.Hadlee (1984) and F.D.Stephenson (1988) being the only players to complete the 'double' since the reduction of County Championship matches in 1969.

WICKET-KEEPING RECORDS
1000 DISMISSALS IN A CAREER

	Career	Dismissals	Ct	St
R.W.Taylor	1960-88	**1649**	1473	176
J.T.Murray	1952-75	**1527**	1270	257
H.Strudwick	1902-27	**1497**	1242	255
A.P.E.Knott	1964-85	**1344**	1211	133
R.C.Russell	1981-2004	**1320**	1192	128
F.H.Huish	1895-1914	**1310**	933	377
B.Taylor	1949-73	**1294**	1083	211
S.J.Rhodes	1981-2004	**1263**	1139	124
D.Hunter	1889-1909	**1253**	906	347
H.R.Butt	1890-1912	**1228**	953	275
J.H.Board	1891-1914/15	**1207**	852	355
H.Elliott	1920-47	**1206**	904	302
J.M.Parks	1949-76	**1181**	1088	93
R.Booth	1951-70	**1126**	948	178
L.E.G.Ames	1926-51	**1121**	703	418

	Career	Dismissals	Ct	St
C.M.W.Read	1997-2017	**1104**	1051	53
D.L.Bairstow	1970-90	**1099**	961	138
G.Duckworth	1923-47	**1096**	753	343
H.W.Stephenson	1948-64	**1082**	748	334
J.G.Binks	1955-75	**1071**	895	176
T.G.Evans	1939-69	**1066**	816	250
A.Long	1960-80	**1046**	922	124
G.O.Dawkes	1937-61	**1043**	895	148
R.W.Tolchard	1965-83	**1037**	912	125
W.L.Cornford	1921-47	**1017**	675	342

MOST DISMISSALS IN AN INNINGS

9	(8ct, 1st)	Tahir Rashid	Habib Bank v PACO	Gujranwala	1992-93
9	(7ct, 2st)	W.R.James	Matabeleland v Mashonaland CD	Bulawayo	1995-96
8	(8ct)	A.T.W.Grout	Queensland v W Australia	Brisbane	1959-60
8	(8ct)	D.E.East	Essex v Somerset	Taunton	1985
8	(8ct)	S.A.Marsh	Kent v Middlesex	Lord's	1991
8	(6ct, 2st)	T.J.Zoehrer	Australians v Surrey	The Oval	1993
8	(7ct, 1st)	D.S.Berry	Victoria v South Australia	Melbourne	1996-97
8	(7ct, 1st)	Y.S.S.Mendis	Bloomfield v Kurunegala Youth	Colombo	2000-01
8	(7ct, 1st)	S.Nath	Assam v Tripura (on debut)	Gauhati	2001-02
8	(8ct)	J.N.Batty	Surrey v Kent	The Oval	2004
8	(8ct)	Golam Mabud	Sylhet v Dhaka	Dhaka	2005-06
8	(8ct)	D.C.de Boorder	Otago v Wellington	Wellington	2009-10
8	(8ct)	R.S.Second	Free State v North West	Bloemfontein	2011-12
8	(8ct)	T.L.Tsolekile	South Africa A v Sri Lanka A	Durban	2012

MOST DISMISSALS IN A MATCH

14	(11ct, 3st)	I.Khaleel	Hyderabad v Assam	Guwahati	2011-12
13	(11ct, 2st)	W.R.James	Matabeleland v Mashonaland CD	Bulawayo	1995-96
12	(8ct, 4st)	E.Pooley	Surrey v Sussex	The Oval	1868
12	(9ct, 3st)	D.Tallon	Queensland v NSW	Sydney	1938-39
12	(9ct, 3st)	H.B.Taber	NSW v South Australia	Adelaide	1968-69
12	(12ct)	P.D.McGlashan	Northern Districts v Central Districts	Whangarei	2009-10
12	(11ct, 1st)	T.L.Tsolekile	Lions v Dolphins	Johannesburg	2010-11
12	(12ct)	Kashif Mahmood	Lahore Shalimar v Abbottabad	Abbottabad	2010-11
12	(12ct)	R.S.Second	Free State v North West	Bloemfontein	2011-12

MOST DISMISSALS IN A SEASON

128	(79ct, 49st)	L.E.G.Ames			1929

FIELDING RECORDS
750 CATCHES IN A CAREER

1018	F.E.Woolley	1906-38	784	J.G.Langridge	1928-55
887	W.G.Grace	1865-1908	764	W.Rhodes	1898-1930
830	G.A.R.Lock	1946-70/71	758	C.A.Milton	1948-74
819	W.R.Hammond	1920-51	754	E.H.Hendren	1907-38
813	D.B.Close	1949-86			

MOST CATCHES IN AN INNINGS

7	M.J.Stewart	Surrey v Northamptonshire	Northampton	1957
7	A.S.Brown	Gloucestershire v Nottinghamshire	Nottingham	1966
7	R.Clarke	Warwickshire v Lancashire	Liverpool	2011

MOST CATCHES IN A MATCH

10	W.R.Hammond	Gloucestershire v Surrey	Cheltenham	1928
9	R.Clarke	Warwickshire v Lancashire	Liverpool	2011

MOST CATCHES IN A SEASON

78	W.R.Hammond		1928	77	M.J.Stewart		1957

ENGLAND LIMITED-OVERS INTERNATIONALS 2018

AUSTRALIA v ENGLAND

LIMITED-OVERS INTERNATIONALS

Melbourne Cricket Ground, 14 January. Toss: England. **ENGLAND** won by five wickets. Australia 304-8 (50; A.J.Finch 107, M.P.Stoinis 60, M.R.Marsh 50, L.E.Plunkett 3-71). England 308-5 (48.5; J.J.Roy 180, J.E.Root 91*). Award: J.J.Roy.
J.J.Roy's 180 was an England LOI record score.

Woolloongabba, Brisbane, 19 January. Toss: Australia. **ENGLAND** won by four wickets. Australia 270-9 (50; A.J.Finch 106). England 274-6 (44.2; J.M.Bairstow 60, A.D.Hales 57, M.A.Starc 4-59). Award: J.E.Root.

Sydney Cricket Ground, 21 January. Toss: Australia. **ENGLAND** won by 16 runs. England 302-6 (50; J.C.Buttler 100*, C.R.Woakes 53*). Australia 286-6 (50; A.J.Finch 62, M.P.Stoinis 56, M.R.Marsh 55). Award: J.C.Buttler.

Adelaide Oval, 26 January. Toss: Australia. **AUSTRALIA** won by three wickets. England 196 (44.5; C.R.Woakes 78, P.J.Cummins 4-24, A.J.Tye 3-33, J.R.Hazlewood 3-39). Australia 197-7 (37; T.M.Head 96, A.U.Rashid 3-49). Award: P.J.Cummins.

Perth Stadium, 28 January. Toss: Australia. **ENGLAND** won by 12 runs. England 259 (47.4; J.E.Root 62, A.J.Tye 5-46). Australia 247 (48.2; M.P.Stoinis 87, T.K.Curran 5-35, M.M.Ali 3-55). Award: T.K.Curran. Series award: J.E.Root.

TRANS-TASMAN TWENTY20 INTERNATIONAL TRI-SERIES

Bellerive Oval, Hobart, 7 February. Toss: Australia. **AUSTRALIA** won by five wickets. England 155-9 (20; D.J.Malan 50, G.J.Maxwell 3-10). Australia 161-5 (18.3; G.J.Maxwell 103*, D.J.Willey 3-28). Award: G.J.Maxwell.

Melbourne Cricket Ground, 10 February. Toss: Australia. **AUSTRALIA** won by seven wickets. England 137-7 (20; K.W.Richardson 3-33). Australia 138-3 (14.3). Award: K.W.Richardson.

Westpac Stadium, Wellington, 13 February. Toss: England. **NEW ZEALAND** won by 12 runs. New Zealand 196-5 (20; K.S.Williamson 72, M.J.Guptill 65). England 184-9 (20; D.J.Malan 59). Award: K.S.Williamson.

Seddon Park, Hamilton, 18 February. Toss: New Zealand. **ENGLAND** won by 2 runs. England 194-7 (20; E.J.G.Morgan 80*, D.J.Malan 53, T.A.Boult 3-50). New Zealand 192-4 (20; M.J.Guptill 62, C.Munro 57). Award: E.J.G.Morgan.

NEW ZEALAND v ENGLAND

LIMITED-OVERS INTERNATIONALS

Seddon Park, Hamilton, 25 February. Toss: New Zealand. **NEW ZEALAND** won by three wickets. England 284-8 (50; J.C.Buttler 79, J.E.Root 71). New Zealand 287-7 (49.2; L.R.P.L.Taylor 113, T.W.M.Latham 79). Award: L.R.P.L.Taylor.

Bay Oval, Mount Maunganui, 28 February. Toss: England. **ENGLAND** won by six wickets. New Zealand 223 (49.4; M.J.Santner 63*, M.J.Guptill 50). England 225-4 (37.5; B.A.Stokes 63*, E.J.G.Morgan 62). Award: B.A.Stokes.

Westpac Stadium, Wellington, 3 March. Toss: New Zealand. **ENGLAND** won by 4 runs. England 234 (50; I.S.Sodhi 3-53). New Zealand 230-8 (50; K.S.Williamson 112*, M.M.Ali 3-36). Award: M.M.Ali.

University Oval, Dunedin, 7 March. Toss: New Zealand. **NEW ZEALAND** won by five wickets. England 335-9 (50; J.M.Bairstow 138, J.E.Root 102, I.S.Sodhi 4-58). New Zealand 339-5 (49.3; L.R.P.L.Taylor 181*, T.W.M.Latham 71). Award: L.R.P.L.Taylor.

Hagley Oval, Christchurch, 10 March. Toss: England. **ENGLAND** won by seven wickets. New Zealand 223 (49.5; M.J.Santner 67, H.M.Nicholls 55, C.R.Woakes 3-32, A.U.Rashid 3-42). England 229-3 (32.4; J.M.Bairstow 104, A.D.Hales 61). Award: J.M.Bairstow. Series award: C.R.Woakes.

SCOTLAND v ENGLAND

LIMITED-OVERS INTERNATIONAL

Raeburn Place, Edinburgh, 10 June. Toss: England. **SCOTLAND** won by 6 runs. Scotland 371-5 (50; C.S.MacLeod 140*, K.J.Coetzer 58, H.G.Munsey 55). England 365 (48.5; J.M.Bairstow 105, A.D.Hales 52, M.R.J.Watt 3-55). Award: C.S.MacLeod.

ENGLAND v AUSTRALIA

ROYAL LONDON LIMITED-OVERS INTERNATIONALS

The Oval, London, 13 June. Toss: Australia. **ENGLAND** won by three wickets. Australia 214 (47; G.J.Maxwell 62, L.E.Plunkett 3-42, M.M.Ali 3-43). England 218-7 (44; E.J.G.Morgan 69, J.E.Root 50). Award: M.M.Ali.

Sophia Gardens, Cardiff, 16 June. Toss: Australia. **ENGLAND** won by 38 runs. England 342-8 (50; J.J.Roy 120, J.C.Buttler 91*). Australia 304 (47.1; S.E.Marsh 131, L.E.Plunkett 4-53, A.U.Rashid 3-70). Award: J.J.Roy.

Trent Bridge, Nottingham, 19 June. Toss: Australia. **ENGLAND** won by 242 runs. England 481-6 (50; A.D.Hales 147, J.M.Bairstow 139, J.J.Roy 82, E.J.G.Morgan 67, J.A.Richardson 3-92). Australia 239 (37; T.M.Head 51, A.U.Rashid 4-47, M.M.Ali 3-28). Award: A.D.Hales.
England's total was a world record in LOIs; the winning margin of 242 runs was a record for England.

Riverside Ground, Chester-le-Street, 21 June. Toss: Australia. **ENGLAND** won by six wickets. Australia 310-8 (50; S.E.Marsh 101, A.J.Finch 100, T.M.Head 63, D.J.Willey 4-43). England 314-4 (44.4; J.J.Roy 101, J.M.Bairstow 79, J.C.Buttler 54*). Award: J.J.Roy. England debut: C.Overton.

Old Trafford, Manchester, 24 June. Toss: Australia. **ENGLAND** won by one wicket. Australia 205 (34.4; T.M.Head 56, M.M.Ali 4-46). England 208-9 (48.3; J.C.Buttler 110*, B.Stanlake 3-35, K.W.Richardson 3-51). Award: J.C.Buttler. Series award: J.C.Buttler. England debut: S.M.Curran.

VITALITY TWENTY20 INTERNATIONAL

Edgbaston, Birmingham, 27 June. Toss: Australia. **ENGLAND** won by 28 runs. England 221-5 (20; J.C.Buttler 61). Australia 193 (19.4; A.J.Finch 84, A.U.Rashid 3-27, C.J.Jordan 3-42). Award: A.U.Rashid.

ENGLAND v INDIA

VITALITY TWENTY20 INTERNATIONALS

Old Trafford, Manchester, 3 July. Toss: India. **INDIA** won by eight wickets. England 159-8 (20; J.C.Buttler 69, Kuldeep Yadav 5-24). India 162-3 (18.2; K.L.Rahul 101*). Award: Kuldeep Yadav.

Sophia Gardens, Cardiff, 6 July. Toss: England. **ENGLAND** won by five wickets. India 148-5 (20). England 149-5 (19.4; A.D.Hales 58*). Award: A.D.Hales. England debut: J.T.Ball.

County Ground, Bristol, 8 July. Toss: India. **INDIA** won by seven wickets. England 198-9 (20; J.J.Roy 67, H.H.Pandya 4-38). India 201-3 (18.4; R.G.Sharma 100*). Award: R.G.Sharma. Series award: R.G.Sharma.

ROYAL LONDON LIMITED-OVERS INTERNATIONALS

Trent Bridge, Nottingham, 12 July. Toss: India. **INDIA** won by eight wickets. England 268 (49.5; J.C.Buttler 53, B.A.Stokes 50, Kuldeep Yadav 6-25). India 269-2 (40.1; R.G.Sharma 137*, V.Kohli 75). Award: Kuldeep Yadav.

Lord's, London, 14 July. Toss: England. **ENGLAND** won by 86 runs. England 322-7 (50; J.E.Root 113*, E.J.G.Morgan 53, D.J.Willey 50, Kuldeep Yadav 3-68). India 236 (50; L.E.Plunkett 4-46). Award: J.E.Root.

Headingley, Leeds, 17 July. Toss: England. **ENGLAND** won by eight wickets. India 256-8 (50; V.Kohli 71, D.J.Willey 3-40, A.U.Rashid 3-49). England 260-2 (44.3; J.E.Root 100*, E.J.G.Morgan 88*). Award: A.U.Rashid. Series award: J.E.Root.

SRI LANKA v ENGLAND

LIMITED-OVERS INTERNATIONALS

Rangiri Dambulla International Stadium, 10 October. Toss: Sri Lanka. **NO RESULT**. England 92-2 (15). England debut: O.P.Stone.

Rangiri Dambulla International Stadium, 13 October. Toss: Sri Lanka. **ENGLAND** won by 31 runs (D/L method). England 278-9 (50; E.J.G.Morgan 92, J.E.Root 71, S.L.Malinga 5-44). Sri Lanka 140-5 (29; C.R.Woakes 3-26). Award: E.J.G.Morgan.

Pallekele International Cricket Stadium, Kandy, 17 October. Toss: England. **ENGLAND** won by seven wickets. Sri Lanka 150-9 (21; A.U.Rashid 4-36, T.K.Curran 3-17). England 153-3 (18.3/21; E.J.G.Morgan 58*). Award: A.U.Rashid.

Pallekele International Cricket Stadium, Kandy, 20 October. Toss: England. **ENGLAND** won by 18 runs (D/L method). Sri Lanka 273-7 (M.D.Shanaka 66, D.P.D.N.Dickwella 52). England 132-2 (27). Award: E.J.G.Morgan.

R.Premadasa Stadium, Colombo, 23 October. Toss: Sri Lanka. **SRI LANKA** won by 219 runs (D/L method). Sri Lanka 366-6 (50; D.P.D.N.Dickwella 95, L.D.Chandimal 80, B.K.G.Mendis 56). England 132-2 (26.1; B.A.Stokes 67, M.K.P.A.D.Perera 4-19, P.V.D.Chameera 3-20). Award: D.P.D.N.Dickwella. Series award: E.J.G.Morgan.

TWENTY20 INTERNATIONAL

R.Premadasa Stadium, Colombo, 27 October. Toss: Sri Lanka. **ENGLAND** won by 30 runs. England 187-8 (20; J.J.Roy 69). Sri Lanka 157 (20; N.L.T.C.Perera 57, J.L.Denly 4-19, A.U.Rashid 3-11). Award: J.L.Denly.

ENGLAND RESULTS IN 2018

	P	W	L	T	NR
Limited Overs	24	17	6	–	1
Twenty20	9	4	5	–	–
Overall	33	21	11	–	1

600 RUNS IN LIMITED-OVERS INTERNATIONALS IN 2018

	P	I	NO	HS	Runs	Ave	100	50	S/Rate
J.M.Bairstow	22	22	–	139	1025	46.59	4	2	118.22
J.E.Root	24	24	8	113*	946	59.12	3	5	83.93
J.J.Roy	22	22	–	180	894	40.63	3	1	105.05
E.J.G.Morgan	22	22	4	92	756	42.00	–	7	93.79
J.C.Buttler	23	18	5	110*	671	51.61	2	4	113.53

20 WICKETS IN LIMITED-OVERS INTERNATIONALS IN 2018

	P	O	M	Runs	W	Ave	Best	4wI	Econ
A.U.Rashid	24	213.0	1	1154	42	27.47	4-36	2	5.41
M.M.Ali	24	195.5	3	1000	29	34.48	4-46	1	5.10

LIMITED-OVERS INTERNATIONALS CAREER RECORDS

These records, complete to 2 March 2019 (except for Ireland and Afghanistan to 5 March 2019), include all players registered for county cricket for the 2018 season at the time of going to press, plus those who have appeared in LOI matches for ICC full member countries since 1 December 2017.

ENGLAND – BATTING AND FIELDING

	M	I	NO	HS	Runs	Avge	100	50	Ct/St
M.M.Ali	92	74	11	128	1645	26.11	3	5	28
T.R.Ambrose	5	5	1	6	10	2.50	–	–	3
J.M.Anderson	194	79	43	28	273	7.58	–	–	53
J.M.Bairstow	59	54	8	141*	2118	46.04	6	8	24/2
J.T.Ball	18	6	2	28	38	9.50	–	–	5
G.S.Ballance	16	15	1	79	279	21.21	–	2	8
G.J.Batty	10	8	2	17	30	5.00	–	–	4
I.R.Bell	161	157	14	141	5416	37.87	4	35	54
S.W.Billings	15	12	–	62	271	22.58	–	2	13
R.S.Bopara	120	109	21	101*	2695	30.62	1	14	35
S.G.Borthwick	2	2	–	15	18	9.00	–	–	–
T.T.Bresnan	85	64	20	80	871	19.79	–	1	20
D.R.Briggs	1	–	–	–	–	–	–	–	–
S.C.J.Broad	121	68	25	45*	529	12.30	–	–	27
J.C.Buttler	127	105	22	150	3387	40.80	7	18	155/28
R.Clarke	20	13	–	39	144	11.07	–	–	11
A.N.Cook	92	92	4	137	3204	36.40	5	19	36
S.M.Curran	2	2	–	15	17	8.50	–	–	–
T.K.Curran	13	8	5	35	71	23.66	–	–	4
S.M.Davies	8	8	–	87	244	30.50	–	1	8
L.A.Dawson	3	2	–	10	14	7.00	–	–	–
J.L.Denly	9	9	–	67	268	29.77	–	2	5
J.W.Dernbach	24	8	1	5	19	2.71	–	–	5
B.M.Duckett	3	3	–	63	123	41.00	–	2	–
S.T.Finn	69	30	13	35	136	8.00	–	–	15
H.F.Gurney	10	6	4	6*	15	7.50	–	–	1
A.D.Hales	70	67	3	171	2419	37.79	6	14	27
C.J.Jordan	31	21	7	38*	169	12.07	–	–	19
S.C.Meaker	2	2	–	1	2	1.00	–	–	–
E.J.G.Morgan †	194	180	27	124*	6069	39.66	11	38	68
G.Onions	4	1	–	1	1	1.00	–	–	–
C.Overton	1	–	–	–	–	–	–	–	2
S.D.Parry	2	–	–	–	–	–	–	–	–
S.R.Patel	36	22	7	70*	482	32.13	–	1	7
L.E.Plunkett	78	45	15	56	584	19.46	–	1	25
A.U.Rashid	83	36	9	69	529	19.59	–	1	25
T.S.Roland-Jones	1	1	1	37*	37	–	–	–	–
J.E.Root	126	119	19	133*	5090	50.90	14	29	57
J.J.Roy	73	71	2	180	2661	38.56	7	12	29
B.A.Stokes	79	68	11	102*	2088	36.63	3	14	39
O.P.Stone	4	1	1	9*	9	–	–	–	–
M.E.Trescothick	123	122	6	137	4335	37.37	12	21	49
J.M.Vince	6	5	–	51	131	26.20	–	1	4
D.J.Willey	42	25	12	50	245	18.84	–	1	19
C.R.Woakes	84	57	18	95*	1039	26.64	–	4	35
M.A.Wood	40	13	8	13	45	9.00	–	–	9
L.J.Wright	50	39	4	52	707	20.20	–	2	18

ENGLAND – BOWLING

	O	M	R	W	Avge	Best	4wI	R/Over
M.M.Ali	702.4	10	3668	78	47.02	4-46	1	5.22
J.M.Anderson	1597.2	125	7861	269	29.22	5-23	13	4.92
J.T.Ball	157.5	5	980	21	46.66	5-51	1	6.20
G.J.Batty	73.2	1	366	5	73.20	2-40	–	4.99
I.R.Bell	14.4	0	88	6	14.66	3- 9	–	6.00
R.S.Bopara	310	11	1523	40	38.07	4-38	1	4.91
S.G.Borthwick	9	0	72	0	–	–	–	8.00
T.T.Bresnan	703.3	35	3813	109	34.98	5-48	4	5.42
D.R.Briggs	10	0	39	2	19.50	2-39	–	3.90
S.C.J.Broad	1018.1	56	5364	178	30.13	5-23	10	5.26
R.Clarke	78.1	3	415	11	37.72	2-28	–	5.30
S.M.Curran	12	0	90	2	45.00	2-44	–	7.50
T.K.Curran	92.5	3	581	18	32.27	5-35	1	6.25
L.A.Dawson	14	0	96	3	32.00	2-70	–	6.85
J.W.Dernbach	205.4	6	1308	31	42.19	4-45	1	6.35
S.T.Finn	591.4	38	2996	102	29.37	5-33	6	5.06
H.F.Gurney	75.5	4	432	11	39.27	4-55	1	5.69
C.J.Jordan	255.2	5	1521	43	35.37	5-29	1	5.95
S.C.Meaker	19	1	110	2	55.00	1-43	–	5.78
G.Onions	34	1	185	4	46.25	2-58	–	5.44
C.Overton	7	0	55	0	–	–	–	7.85
S.D.Parry	19	2	92	4	23.00	3-32	–	4.84
S.R.Patel	197.5	4	1091	24	45.45	5-41	1	5.51
L.E.Plunkett	604.3	14	3557	116	30.66	5-52	6	5.88
A.U.Rashid	681.4	6	3807	128	29.74	5-27	9	5.58
T.S.Roland-Jones	7	2	34	1	34.00	1-34	–	4.85
J.E.Root	223.4	2	1299	20	64.95	3-52	–	5.80
B.A.Stokes	417.3	6	2562	63	40.66	5-61	2	6.13
O.P.Stone	16	0	97	1	97.00	1-23	–	6.06
M.E.Trescothick	38.4	0	219	4	54.75	2- 7	–	5.66
D.J.Willey	293.3	15	1665	48	34.68	4-34	2	5.67
C.R.Woakes	654	32	3669	116	31.62	6-45	10	5.61
M.A.Wood	331.1	11	1851	41	45.14	4-33	2	5.58
L.J.Wright	173	2	884	15	58.93	2-34	–	5.10

† *E.J.G.Morgan has also made 23 appearances for Ireland (see below).*

AUSTRALIA – BATTING AND FIELDING

	M	I	NO	HS	Runs	Avge	100	50	Ct/St
A.C.Agar	9	8	1	46	144	20.57	–	–	4
J.P.Behrendorff	3	1	1	1*	1	–	–	–	–
J.A.Burns	6	6	–	69	146	24.33	–	1	2
A.T.Carey	10	10	1	47	282	31.33	–	–	7
D.T.Christian	19	18	5	39	273	21.00	–	–	10
M.J.Cosgrove	3	3	–	74	112	37.33	–	1	–
N.M.Coulter-Nile	23	16	5	34	148	13.45	–	–	7
P.J.Cummins	43	24	10	36	166	11.85	–	–	6
J.P.Faulkner	69	52	22	116	1032	34.40	1	4	21
C.J.Ferguson	30	25	9	71*	663	41.43	–	5	7
A.J.Finch	100	96	1	148	3444	36.25	11	18	47
P.S.P.Handscomb	12	11	–	82	319	29.00	–	3	7
J.R.Hazlewood	44	13	11	11*	37	18.50	–	–	13
T.M.Head	42	39	2	128	1273	34.40	1	10	12
U.T.Khawaja	22	21	2	98	633	33.31	–	6	5
C.A.Lynn	4	4	–	44	75	18.75	–	–	3
N.M.Lyon	17	9	6	30	62	20.66	–	–	3
M.R.Marsh	53	49	9	102*	1428	35.70	1	11	25

AUSTRALIA – BATTING AND FIELDING (continued)

	M	I	NO	HS	Runs	Avge	100	50	Ct/St
S.E.Marsh	63	62	2	151	2536	42.26	7	13	18
G.J.Maxwell	91	82	9	102	2367	32.42	1	16	54
M.G.Neser	2	2	–	6	8	4.00	–	–	–
T.D.Paine	35	35	3	111	890	27.81	1	5	51/4
J.A.Richardson	7	5	1	16	39	9.75	–	–	1
K.W.Richardson	18	8	3	19	45	9.00	–	–	4
D.J.M.Short	4	4	1	47*	83	27.66	–	–	1
P.M.Siddle	20	6	3	10*	31	10.33	–	–	1
S.P.D.Smith	108	94	12	164	3431	41.84	8	19	62
B.Stanlake	7	5	2	2	4	1.33	–	–	1
M.A.Starc	75	38	16	52*	280	12.72	–	1	19
M.P.Stoinis	25	25	5	146*	844	42.20	1	5	7
A.J.Turner	1	1	–	21	21	21.00	–	–	1
A.J.Tye	7	7	3	19	57	14.25	–	–	1
D.A.Warner	106	104	4	179	4343	43.43	14	17	49
C.L.White	91	77	16	105	2072	33.96	2	11	37
A.Zampa	35	17	4	22	97	7.46	–	–	8

AUSTRALIA – BOWLING

	O	M	R	W	Avge	Best	4wI	R/Over
A.C.Agar	72	2	414	8	51.75	2-48	–	5.75
J.P.Behrendorff	28.2	3	137	3	45.66	2-39	–	4.83
D.T.Christian	121.1	4	595	20	29.75	5-31	1	4.91
M.J.Cosgrove	5	0	13	1	13.00	1- 1	–	2.60
N.M.Coulter-Nile	197.2	7	1057	40	26.42	4-48	1	5.35
P.J.Cummins	374	19	1979	65	30.44	4-24	4	5.29
J.P.Faulkner	535.1	12	2962	96	30.85	4-32	4	5.53
A.J.Finch	26.2	0	137	2	68.50	1- 2	–	5.20
J.R.Hazlewood	382.2	25	1811	72	25.15	6-52	4	4.73
T.M.Head	127.3	0	737	12	61.41	2-22	–	5.78
N.M.Lyon	157	10	771	18	42.83	4-44	1	4.91
M.R.Marsh	283.2	6	1564	44	35.54	5-33	2	5.52
G.J.Maxwell	336.4	7	1885	46	40.97	4-46	2	5.59
M.G.Neser	16.4	1	120	2	60.00	2-46	–	7.20
J.A.Richardson	67	5	383	13	29.46	4-26	1	5.71
K.W.Richardson	155.5	10	854	27	31.62	5-68	1	5.48
D.J.M.Short	7	0	59	0	–	–	–	8.42
P.M.Siddle	150.1	10	743	17	43.70	3-55	–	4.94
S.P.D.Smith	174.2	1	931	27	34.48	3-16	–	5.34
B.Stanlake	59	3	324	7	46.28	3-35	–	5.49
M.A.Starc	626.5	34	3109	145	21.44	6-28	14	4.95
M.P.Stoinis	166.4	1	1005	22	45.68	3-16	–	6.03
A.J.Tye	64.3	1	392	12	32.66	5-46	1	6.07
D.A.Warner	1	0	8	0	–	–	–	8.00
C.L.White	55.1	2	351	12	29.25	3- 5	–	6.36
A.Zampa	291.4	3	1631	44	37.06	3-16	–	5.59

SOUTH AFRICA – BATTING AND FIELDING

	M	I	NO	HS	Runs	Avge	100	50	Ct/St
K.J.Abbott	28	13	4	23	76	8.44	–	–	7
H.M.Amla	174	171	12	159	7910	49.74	27	37	83
T.Bavuma	2	2	–	113	161	80.50	1	–	1
F.Behardien	59	49	14	70	1074	30.68	–	6	27
C.J.Dala	2	2	1	5	8	8.00	–	–	1
Q.de Kock	101	101	5	178	4249	44.26	13	18	142/7
M.de Lange	4	–	–	–	–	–	–	–	–

	M	I	NO	HS	Runs	Avge	100	50	Ct/St
A.B.de Villiers	223	213	39	176	9427	54.17	25	52	171/5
F.du Plessis	129	123	17	185	4848	45.73	10	31	67
J.P.Duminy	192	174	39	150*	5016	37.15	4	27	77
D.Elgar	8	7	1	42	104	17.33	–	–	4
B.E.Hendricks	2	1	1	2*	2	–	–	–	–
R.R.Hendricks	14	14	1	102	413	31.76	1	2	10
Imran Tahir	94	31	13	29	145	8.05	–	–	18
C.A.Ingram	31	29	3	124	843	32.42	3	3	12
C.Jonker	2	2	–	25	31	15.50	–	–	–
H.Klaasen	14	13	2	59	251	22.81	–	1	16/3
K.A.Maharaj	4	2	–	17	25	12.50	–	–	–
A.K.Markram	16	16	–	66	407	25.43	–	1	6
D.A.Miller	116	103	29	139	2831	38.25	5	12	56
M.Morkel	114	45	17	32*	239	8.53	–	–	29
C.H.Morris	34	23	3	62	393	19.65	–	1	6
P.W.A.Mulder	8	7	3	19*	57	14.25	–	–	3
L.T.Ngidi	13	6	5	19*	34	34.00	–	–	4
D.Olivier	2	–	–	–	–	–	–	–	–
W.D.Parnell	65	38	14	56	508	21.16	–	1	12
D.Paterson	4	–	–	–	–	–	–	–	2
A.L.Phehlukwayo	39	23	11	69*	376	31.33	–	1	10
D.Pretorius	16	7	1	50	101	16.83	–	1	5
K.Rabada	62	23	10	26	198	15.23	–	–	18
R.R.Rossouw	36	35	3	132	1239	38.71	3	7	22
T.Shamsi	13	3	2	0*	0	0.00	–	–	2
D.W.Steyn	122	49	12	60	361	9.75	–	1	28
H.E.van der Dussen	5	4	2	93	241	120.50	–	3	4
R.E.van der Merwe	13	7	3	12	39	9.75	–	–	3
D.Wiese	6	6	1	41*	102	20.40	–	–	4
K.Zondo	5	5	1	54	142	35.50	–	1	1

SOUTH AFRICA – BOWLING

	O	M	R	W	Avge	Best	4wI	R/Over
K.J.Abbott	217.1	13	1051	34	30.91	4-21	1	4.83
F.Behardien	124.4	2	719	14	51.35	3-19	–	5.76
C.J.Dala	17	0	121	1	121.00	1-57	–	7.11
M.de Lange	34.5	1	198	10	19.80	4-46	1	5.68
A.B.de Villiers	32	0	202	7	28.85	2-15	–	6.31
F.du Plessis	32	0	189	2	94.50	1- 8	–	5.90
J.P.Duminy	569.3	9	3045	67	45.44	4-16	1	5.34
D.Elgar	16	1	67	2	33.50	1-11	–	4.18
B.E.Hendricks	16	0	81	1	81.00	1-50	–	5.06
R.R.Hendricks	7	0	47	1	47.00	1-13	–	6.71
Imran Tahir	813.3	35	3806	153	24.87	7-45	9	4.67
C.A.Ingram	1	0	17	0	–	–	–	17.00
K.A.Maharaj	31.1	0	166	6	27.66	3-25	–	5.32
A.K.Markram	8	0	56	2	28.00	2-18	–	7.00
M.Morkel	930	45	4595	180	25.52	5-21	9	4.94
C.H.Morris	252	5	1415	35	40.42	4-31	2	5.61
P.W.A.Mulder	47	0	275	8	34.37	2-59	–	5.85
L.T.Ngidi	107.4	9	599	26	23.03	4-51	2	5.56
D.Olivier	19	0	124	3	41.33	2-73	–	6.52
W.D.Parnell	485.1	20	2738	94	29.12	5-48	5	5.64
D.Paterson	34.5	0	217	4	54.25	3-44	–	6.22
A.L.Phehlukwayo	269	13	1520	51	29.80	4-22	3	5.65
D.Pretorius	134.2	5	642	24	26.75	3- 5	–	4.77

	O	M	R	W	Avge	Best	4wI	R/Over
K.Rabada	528.2	34	2643	98	26.96	6-16	7	5.00
R.R.Rossouw	7.3	0	44	1	44.00	1-17	–	5.86
T.Shamsi	114.3	4	619	17	36.41	4-33	1	5.40
D.W.Steyn	1025.3	69	5013	193	25.97	6-39	7	4.88
R.E.van der Merwe	117.3	2	561	17	33.00	3-27	–	4.77
D.Wiese	49	0	316	9	35.11	3-50	–	6.44

WEST INDIES – BATTING AND FIELDING

	M	I	NO	HS	Runs	Avge	100	50	Ct/St
F.A.Allen	4	4	–	10	25	6.25	–	–	–
R.R.Beaton	2	2	1	12*	15	15.00	–	–	–
D.Bishoo	42	25	10	29*	164	10.93	–	–	7
C.R.Brathwaite	33	29	2	50	389	14.40	–	1	10
D.M.Bravo	102	98	11	124	2784	32.00	3	18	31
J.D.Campbell	5	4	–	30	69	17.25	–	–	–
R.L.Chase	11	9	1	33*	117	14.62	–	–	4
S.S.Cottrell	10	5	3	8	14	7.00	–	–	4
F.H.Edwards	50	22	14	13	73	9.12	–	–	4
S.T.Gabriel	18	13	7	12*	21	3.50	–	–	1
C.H.Gayle	286	280	17	215	10096	38.38	25	50	119
C.Hemraj	6	6	–	32	82	13.66	–	–	2
S.O.Hetmyer	25	24	–	127	899	40.86	4	2	13
J.O.Holder	90	73	17	99*	1471	26.26	–	7	35
K.A.Hope	7	6	–	46	138	23.00	–	–	1
S.D.Hope	49	45	6	146*	1777	45.56	4	8	47/8
A.S.Joseph	16	8	5	29*	104	34.66	–	–	5
E.Lewis	35	32	1	176*	1010	32.58	2	3	12
O.C.McCoy	2	1	1	0*	0	–	–	–	–
N.O.Miller	50	27	13	51	284	20.28	–	1	18
J.N.Mohammed	28	24	1	91*	551	23.95	–	4	3
A.R.Nurse	45	36	13	44	449	19.52	–	–	14
K.M.A.Paul	11	9	2	36	115	16.42	–	–	5
N.Pooran	1	1	–	0	0	0.00	–	–	1
K.O.A.Powell	46	44	–	83	1005	22.84	–	9	14
R.Powell	34	31	3	101	670	23.92	1	2	14
R.Rampaul	92	40	11	86*	362	12.48	–	1	14
K.A.J.Roach	80	52	32	34	276	13.80	–	–	18
A.D.Russell	52	44	9	92*	998	28.51	–	4	11
M.N.Samuels	207	196	26	133*	5606	32.97	10	30	50
J.E.Taylor	90	42	9	43*	278	8.42	–	–	20
O.R.Thomas	9	3	1	0*	0	0.00	–	–	–
C.A.K.Walton	9	8	–	19	53	6.62	–	–	9/1
K.O.K.Williams	8	5	4	16*	19	19.00	–	–	–

WEST INDIES – BOWLING

	O	M	R	W	Avge	Best	4wI	R/Over
F.A.Allen	23	0	131	0	–	–	–	5.69
R.R.Beaton	17	1	102	1	102.00	1-60	–	6.00
D.Bishoo	337	8	1668	38	43.89	3-30	–	4.94
C.R.Brathwaite	246.4	11	1352	31	43.61	5-27	2	5.48
J.D.Campbell	1	0	13	0	–	–	–	13.00
R.L.Chase	26.5	2	149	3	49.66	2-47	–	5.55
S.S.Cottrell	64.4	0	402	15	26.80	5-46	1	6.21
F.H.Edwards	356.2	23	1812	60	30.20	6-22	2	5.08
S.T.Gabriel	139.5	5	782	23	34.00	3-17	–	5.59
C.H.Gayle	1214.3	38	5788	165	35.07	5-46	4	4.76

	O	M	R	W	Avge	Best	4wI	R/Over
C.Hemraj	1.1	0	9	0	–	–	–	7.71
J.O.Holder	710	40	3934	119	33.05	5-27	6	5.54
A.S.Joseph	126.1	3	818	24	34.08	5-56	2	6.48
O.C.McCoy	14	0	109	4	27.25	2-38	–	7.78
N.O.Miller	354.1	16	1660	45	36.88	4-43	2	4.68
J.N.Mohammed	24.2	1	131	0	–	–	–	5.38
A.R.Nurse	351.4	6	1817	42	43.26	4-62	1	5.16
K.M.A.Paul	84.4	1	498	11	45.27	2-29	–	5.88
R.Powell	40.5	0	243	3	81.00	1- 7	–	5.95
R.Rampaul	672.1	33	3434	117	29.35	5-49	10	5.10
K.A.J.Roach	661.1	47	3312	114	29.05	6-27	6	5.00
A.D.Russell	362.4	13	2128	65	32.73	4-35	5	5.86
M.N.Samuels	848.3	23	4127	89	46.37	3-12	–	4.86
J.E.Taylor	723.3	35	3780	128	29.53	5-48	4	5.22
O.R.Thomas	57.1	0	413	15	27.53	5-21	1	7.22
K.O.K.Williams	55	0	293	9	32.55	4-43	1	5.32

NEW ZEALAND – BATTING AND FIELDING

	M	I	NO	HS	Runs	Avge	100	50	Ct/St
T.D.Astle	9	5	2	49	79	26.33	–	–	2
T.A.Boult	79	35	20	21*	144	9.60	–	–	23
D.A.J.Bracewell	19	12	2	57	158	15.80	–	1	3
N.T.Broom	39	39	4	109*	943	26.94	1	5	9
M.S.Chapman	5	5	1	124*	160	40.00	1	–	1
C.de Grandhomme	28	21	6	74*	443	29.53	–	1	8
L.H.Ferguson	27	13	6	19	58	8.28	–	–	8
M.J.Guptill	169	166	18	237*	6440	43.51	16	34	82
M.J.Henry	43	16	6	48*	193	19.30	–	–	14
T.W.M.Latham	85	79	8	137	2395	33.73	4	14	58/7
A.F.Milne	40	17	7	36	168	16.80	–	–	21
C.Munro	51	47	1	87	1146	24.91	–	7	20
J.D.S.Neesham	49	42	9	74	1015	30.75	–	5	19
H.M.Nicholls	41	39	10	124*	1029	35.48	1	8	16
J.S.Patel	43	15	8	34	95	13.57	–	–	13
M.J.Santner	59	46	16	67	826	27.53	–	2	22
T.L.Seifert	3	2	–	22	33	16.50	–	–	7/1
I.S.Sodhi	30	12	2	24	62	6.20	–	–	7
T.G.Southee	139	84	31	55	669	12.62	–	1	39
L.R.P.L.Taylor	218	203	37	181*	8026	48.34	20	47	137
B.J.Watling	28	25	2	96*	573	24.91	–	5	20
K.S.Williamson	139	133	12	145*	5554	45.90	11	37	54
G.H.Worker	10	10	2	58	272	34.00	–	3	5

NEW ZEALAND – BOWLING

	O	M	R	W	Avge	Best	4wI	R/Over
T.D.Astle	45	1	246	10	24.60	3-33	–	5.46
T.A.Boult	715	54	3632	147	24.70	7-34	10	5.07
D.A.J.Bracewell	155.2	15	798	23	34.69	4-55	1	5.13
C.de Grandhomme	165	4	834	18	46.33	3-26	–	5.05
L.H.Ferguson	233.2	3	1310	46	28.47	5-45	2	5.61
M.J.Guptill	18.1	0	98	4	24.50	2- 6	–	5.39
M.J.Henry	370.1	22	2045	78	26.21	5-30	8	5.52
A.F.Milne	300.1	7	1581	41	38.56	3-49	–	5.26
C.Munro	91	1	472	7	67.42	2-10	–	5.18
J.D.S.Neesham	240.5	2	1522	44	34.59	4-42	2	6.31
J.S.Patel	335.4	9	1691	49	34.51	3-11	–	5.03

NEW ZEALAND – BOWLING (continued)

	O	M	R	W	Avge	Best	4wI	R/Over
M.J.Santner	446.1	8	2187	63	34.71	5-50	1	4.90
I.S.Sodhi	252	9	1395	39	35.76	4-58	1	5.53
T.G.Southee	1161.1	72	6303	185	34.07	7-33	7	5.42
L.R.P.L.Taylor	7	0	35	0	–	–	–	5.00
K.S.Williamson	229.3	2	1246	35	35.60	4-22	1	5.42
G.H.Worker	1	0	5	0	–	–	–	5.00

INDIA – BATTING AND FIELDING

	M	I	NO	HS	Runs	Avge	100	50	Ct/St
K.K.Ahmed	8	3	1	5	9	4.50	–	–	1
J.J.Bumrah	45	6	2	10*	11	2.75	–	–	15
Y.S.Chahal	40	6	3	18*	34	11.33	–	–	10
D.L.Chahar	1	1	–	12	12	12.00	–	–	–
S.Dhawan	124	123	7	137	5178	44.63	15	27	60
M.S.Dhoni	336	284	81	183*	10300	50.73	9	71	309/117
S.S.Iyer	6	5	–	88	210	42.00	–	2	3
R.A.Jadeja	148	98	33	87	1990	30.61	–	10	52
K.M.Jadhav	55	36	13	120	1083	47.08	2	5	26
K.D.Karthik	91	77	21	79	1738	31.03	–	9	61/7
S.Kaul	3	2	–	1	1	0.50	–	–	1
V.Kohli	223	215	37	183	10577	59.42	39	49	108
Kuldeep Yadav	40	14	9	19	78	15.60	–	–	4
B.Kumar	103	47	15	53*	476	14.87	–	1	24
Mohammed Shami	60	26	13	25	118	9.07	–	–	21
Mohammed Siraj	1	–	–	–	–	–	–	–	–
M.K.Pandey	23	18	6	104*	440	36.66	1	2	6
H.H.Pandya	45	29	4	83	731	29.24	–	4	19
R.R.Pant	3	2	–	24	41	20.50	–	–	3
A.M.Rahane	90	87	3	111	2962	35.26	3	24	48
K.L.Rahul	13	12	3	100*	317	35.22	1	2	6
S.K.Raina	226	194	35	116*	5615	35.31	5	36	102
A.T.Rayudu	53	48	14	124*	1674	49.23	3	10	17
V.Shankar	5	1	–	45	45	45.00	–	–	4
R.G.Sharma	202	196	31	264	7845	47.54	22	39	73
Shubman Gill	2	2	–	9	16	8.00	–	–	–
S.N.Thakur	5	2	1	22*	22	22.00	–	–	3
Washington Sundar	1	–	–	–	–	–	–	–	1
U.T.Yadav	75	24	14	18*	79	7.90	–	–	22

INDIA – BOWLING

	O	M	R	W	Avge	Best	4wI	R/Over
K.K.Ahmed	63	2	338	11	30.72	3-13	–	5.36
J.J.Bumrah	378.4	26	1699	80	21.23	5-27	5	4.48
Y.S.Chahal	352.1	12	1692	71	23.83	6-42	5	4.80
D.L.Chahar	4	0	37	1	37.00	1-37	–	9.25
M.S.Dhoni	6	0	31	1	31.00	1-14	–	5.16
S.S.Iyer	1	0	2	0	–	–	–	2.00
R.A.Jadeja	1248.1	49	6088	171	35.60	5-36	8	4.87
K.M.Jadhav	165.5	1	820	26	31.53	3-23	–	4.94
S.Kaul	27	0	179	0	–	–	–	6.62
V.Kohli	106.5	1	665	4	166.25	1-15	–	6.22
Kuldeep Yadav	343	10	1636	79	20.70	6-25	5	4.76
B.Kumar	820.5	65	4094	114	35.91	5-42	4	4.98
Mohammed Shami	509.3	33	2782	110	25.29	4-35	6	5.46
Mohammed Siraj	10	0	76	0	–	–	–	7.60
H.H.Pandya	315.4	4	1748	44	39.72	3-31	–	5.53

INDIA – BOWLING (continued)

	O	M	R	W	Avge	Best	4wI	R/Over
S.K.Raina	354.2	5	1811	36	50.30	3-34	–	5.11
A.T.Rayudu	20.1	1	124	3	41.33	1- 5	–	6.14
V.Shankar	19	0	100	0	–	–	–	5.26
R.G.Sharma	98.5	2	515	8	64.37	2-27	–	5.21
S.N.Thakur	35.5	0	218	6	36.33	4-52	1	6.08
Washington Sundar	10	0	65	1	65.00	1-65	–	6.50
U.T.Yadav	593	23	3565	106	33.63	4-31	4	6.01

PAKISTAN – BATTING AND FIELDING

	M	I	NO	HS	Runs	Avge	100	50	Ct/St
Aamer Yamin	4	3	2	62	95	95.00	–	1	–
Asif Ali	11	8	1	50*	200	28.57	–	1	2
Azhar Ali	53	53	3	102	1845	36.90	3	12	8
Babar Azam	59	57	9	125*	2462	51.29	8	10	29
Faheem Ashraf	18	11	2	23	104	11.55	–	–	5
Fakhar Zaman	31	31	4	210*	1442	53.40	3	9	12
Haris Sohail	26	25	3	89*	960	43.63	–	10	9
Hasan Ali	44	22	6	59	203	12.68	–	2	12
Hussain Talat	1	1	–	2	2	2.00	–	–	–
Imad Wasim	36	24	11	63*	570	43.84	–	4	9
Imam-ul-Haq	21	21	3	128	1090	60.55	5	5	4
Junaid Khan	71	28	15	25	63	4.84	–	–	7
Mohammad Amir	49	27	9	73*	352	19.55	–	2	6
Mohammad Hafeez	208	206	15	140*	6302	32.99	11	36	79
Mohammad Nawaz[3]	14	12	3	53	199	22.11	–	–	4
Mohammad Rizwan	27	24	7	75*	474	27.88	–	3	28
Rumman Raees	9	4	1	16	27	9.00	–	–	2
Sarfraz Ahmed	101	76	17	105	1942	32.91	2	9	98/23
Shadab Khan	34	16	6	54	294	29.40	–	3	7
Shaheen Shah Afridi	10	4	3	14*	15	15.00	–	–	1
Shoaib Malik	279	250	40	143	7379	35.13	9	43	95
Umar Amin	16	16	1	59	271	18.06	–	1	6
Usman Khan	12	1	–	0	0	0.00	–	–	3
Yasir Shah	19	9	3	32*	102	17.00	–	–	5

PAKISTAN – BOWLING

	O	M	R	W	Avge	Best	4wI	R/Over
Aamer Yamin	26	1	154	2	77.00	1-38	–	5.92
Azhar Ali	43	0	260	4	65.00	2-26	–	6.04
Faheem Ashraf	112.3	6	505	18	28.05	5-22	1	4.48
Fakhar Zaman	18.3	0	88	1	88.00	1-19	–	4.75
Haris Sohail	88	0	503	10	50.30	3-45	–	5.71
Hasan Ali	354.1	13	1862	77	24.18	5-34	4	5.25
Hussain Talat	2	0	16	0	–	–	–	8.00
Imad Wasim	255.3	4	1152	30	38.40	5-14	1	4.50
Junaid Khan	554.1	32	2896	104	27.84	4-12	4	5.22
Mohammad Amir	403.1	28	1912	60	31.86	4-28	1	4.74
Mohammad Hafeez	1244.5	47	5138	137	37.50	4-41	1	4.12
Mohammad Nawaz[3]	112.3	2	583	16	36.43	4-42	1	5.18
Rumman Raees	77.1	2	464	14	33.14	3-49	–	6.01
Sarfraz Ahmed	2	0	15	0	–	–	–	7.50
Shadab Khan	271.1	6	1304	47	27.74	4-28	3	4.80
Shaheen Shah Afridi	76.5	4	368	19	19.36	4-38	2	4.78
Shoaib Malik	1311.2	38	6102	156	39.11	4-19	1	4.65
Sohail Khan	111	4	597	19	31.42	5-55	1	5.37
Umar Amin	7	0	24	0	–	–	–	3.42

	O	M	R	W	Avge	Best	4wI	R/Over
Usman Khan	81	4	402	23	17.47	5-34	3	4.96
Yasir Shah	158.3	3	807	19	42.47	6-26	2	5.09

SRI LANKA – BATTING AND FIELDING

	M	I	NO	HS	Runs	Avge	100	50	Ct/St
M.A.Aponso	9	7	4	4	10	3.33	–	–	–
P.V.D.Chameera	23	14	7	19*	93	13.28	–	–	4
L.D.Chandimal	146	132	21	111	3599	32.42	4	22	59/7
D.M.de Silva	28	26	4	84	593	26.95	–	4	18
P.W.H.de Silva	9	7	1	22	63	10.50	–	–	4
D.P.D.N.Dickwella	49	46	1	116	1555	34.55	2	9	33/7
A.N.P.R.Fernando	34	15	10	7	27	5.40	–	–	6
D.A.S.Gunaratne	31	25	4	114*	575	27.38	1	1	10
M.D.Gunathilleke	36	35	1	116	1102	32.41	1	8	12
G.S.N.F.G.Jayasuriya	9	7	1	31	83	13.83	–	–	1
N.G.R.P.Jayasuriya	2	2	1	11*	11	11.00	–	–	–
F.D.M.Karunaratne	17	13	1	60	190	15.83	–	1	4
C.B.R.L.S.Kumara	8	5	3	7*	16	8.00	–	–	2
D.S.M.Kumara	1	1	–	7	7	7.00	–	–	–
R.A.S.Lakmal	81	44	19	26	205	8.20	–	–	19
S.L.Malinga	213	109	34	56	534	7.12	–	1	30
A.D.Mathews	203	173	46	139*	5380	42.36	2	37	50
B.K.G.Mendis	57	55	2	102	1424	26.86	1	12	29
S.S.Pathirana	18	14	1	56	332	25.53	–	1	4
M.D.K.Perera	13	12	–	30	152	12.66	–	–	2
M.D.K.J.Perera	85	81	5	135	2242	29.50	4	11	32/2
M.K.P.A.D.Perera	30	23	5	50*	276	15.33	–	1	13
N.L.T.C.Perera	148	115	16	140	2091	21.12	1	10	57
S.Prasanna	40	37	3	95	421	12.38	–	2	7
C.A.K.Rajitha	3								
W.S.R.Samarawickrama	6	6	–	54	132	22.00	–	1	1
P.A.D.L.R.Sandakan	19	10	4	6	28	4.66	–	–	7
M.D.Shanaka	19	16	1	66	327	21.80	–	2	2
W.U.Tharanga	232	220	17	174*	6936	34.16	15	37	49
H.D.R.L.Thirimanne	117	97	12	139*	2946	34.65	4	20	37

SRI LANKA – BOWLING

	O	M	R	W	Avge	Best	4wI	R/Over
M.A.Aponso	70.3	1	377	10	37.70	4-18	1	5.34
P.V.D.Chameera	149.1	7	796	19	41.89	3-20	–	5.33
D.M.de Silva	86	0	464	10	46.40	2-35	–	5.39
P.W.H.de Silva	43.1	0	296	9	32.88	3-15	–	6.05
A.N.P.R.Fernando	259.2	13	1591	38	41.86	3-28	–	6.13
D.A.S.Gunaratne	139	3	723	22	32.86	3-10	–	5.20
M.D.Gunathilleke	49	1	288	6	48.00	3-48	–	5.87
G.S.N.F.G.Jayasuriya	29	0	150	2	75.00	1-15	–	5.17
N.G.R.P.Jayasuriya	16	0	95	0			–	5.93
F.D.M.Karunaratne	1.4	0	11	0			–	6.60
C.B.R.L.S.Kumara	51.4	0	396	8	49.50	2-34	–	7.66
D.S.M.Kumara	6.1	1	26	3	8.66	3-26	–	4.21
R.A.S.Lakmal	614.2	35	3321	105	31.62	4-13	3	5.40
S.L.Malinga	1715.2	97	9159	318	28.80	6-38	18	5.33
A.D.Mathews	845.1	54	3901	114	34.21	6-20	–	4.61
B.K.G.Mendis	3.2	0	28	0			–	8.40
S.S.Pathirana	127.3	2	720	15	48.00	3-37	–	5.64
M.D.K.Perera	76	0	409	13	31.46	3-48	–	5.38

SRI LANKA – BOWLING (continued)

	O	M	R	W	Avge	Best	4wI	R/Over
M.K.P.A.D.Perera	240.2	4	1239	46	26.93	6-29	4	5.15
N.L.T.C.Perera	878.4	25	5170	165	31.33	6-44	9	5.88
S.Prasanna	324.1	9	1767	32	33.28	3-32	–	5.45
C.A.K.Rajitha	15.5	0	92	2	46.00	1-21	–	5.81
P.A.D.L.R.Sandakan	141.5	0	918	17	54.00	4-52	1	6.47
M.D.Shanaka	36	0	219	7	31.28	5-43	1	6.08
H.D.R.L.Thirimanne	17.2	0	94	3	31.33	2-36	–	5.42

A.N.P.R.Fernando is also known as N.Pradeep; D.S.M.Kumara is also known as D.S.K.Madushanka; M.K.P.A.D.Perera is also known as A.Dananjaya.

ZIMBABWE – BATTING AND FIELDING

	M	I	NO	HS	Runs	Avge	100	50	Ct/St
R.P.Burl	13	11	2	30*	139	15.44	–	–	6
B.B.Chari	10	10	–	39	131	13.10	–	–	3/1
T.L.Chatara	62	41	17	23	159	6.62	–	–	6
C.J.Chibhabha	103	103	2	99	2389	23.65	–	16	33
E.Chigumbura	210	195	26	117	4289	25.37	2	19	72
T.S.Chisoro	18	15	6	42*	134	14.88	–	–	6
A.G.Cremer	96	71	20	58	744	14.58	–	1	37
C.R.Ervine	84	81	11	130*	2176	31.08	2	12	39
K.M.Jarvis	40	28	7	37	153	7.28	–	–	8
T.Kamunhukamwe	2	2	–	34	37	18.50	–	–	–
H.Masakadza	204	203	4	178*	5604	28.16	5	34	71
W.P.Masakadza	17	10	1	15	53	5.88	–	–	4
P.S.Masvaure	2	2	–	39	40	20.00	–	–	–
B.A.Mavuta	5	5	1	20	52	13.00	–	–	2
S.F.Mire	40	40	–	112	840	21.00	1	3	11
P.J.Moor	42	39	3	52	698	19.38	–	3	20/1
C.B.Mpofu	80	39	19	6	46	2.30	–	–	11
R.C.Murray	5	5	1	47	108	27.00	–	–	3
T.K.Musakanda	15	15	1	60	304	21.71	–	1	11
B.Muzarabani	18	15	7	7	16	2.00	–	–	7
R.Ngarava	9	6	1	10	14	2.80	–	–	1
L.N.Roche	3	2	–	4	4	2.00	–	–	1
Sikandar Raza	88	85	13	141	2477	34.40	3	13	36
B.R.M.Taylor	188	187	15	145*	6156	35.79	10	36	118/29
D.T.Tiripano	24	18	5	44	199	15.30	–	–	3
B.V.Vitori	24	14	3	20*	86	7.81	–	–	4
M.N.Waller	79	72	6	99*	1259	19.07	–	5	22
S.C.Williams	122	118	16	129*	3395	33.28	2	29	43
C.Zhuwao	9	9	–	45	154	17.11	–	–	1

ZIMBABWE – BOWLING

	O	M	R	W	Avge	Best	4wI	R/Over
R.P.Burl	13.4	0	81	2	40.50	1- 2	–	5.92
T.L.Chatara	506.1	39	2636	85	31.01	4-33	1	5.20
C.J.Chibhabha	277.5	12	1615	35	46.14	4-25	1	5.81
E.Chigumbura	694.1	23	4057	95	42.70	4-28	1	5.84
T.S.Chisoro	128	7	556	20	27.80	3-16	–	4.34
A.G.Cremer	780	28	3597	119	30.22	6-46	7	4.61
K.M.Jarvis	322.4	15	1812	45	40.26	4-37	1	5.61
H.Masakadza	304.2	5	1622	39	41.58	3-39	–	5.32
W.P.Masakadza	143.1	8	734	21	34.95	4-21	1	5.12
P.S.Masvaure	3	0	19	0	–	–	–	6.33
B.A.Mavuta	39	0	220	5	44.00	2-48	–	5.64

ZIMBABWE – BOWLING (continued)

	O	M	R	W	Avge	Best	4wI	R/Over
S.F.Mire	69.3	0	433	7	61.85	3-49	–	6.23
C.B.Mpofu	627.5	40	3407	88	38.71	6-52	3	5.42
T.K.Musakanda	2	0	11	0	–	–	–	5.50
B.Muzarabani	131	4	733	18	40.72	4-47	1	5.59
R.Ngarava	62.5	2	409	8	51.12	2-37	–	6.50
L.N.Roche	23	1	157	2	78.50	1-54	–	6.82
Sikandar Raza	412.2	16	1999	53	37.71	3-21	–	4.84
B.R.M.Taylor	66	0	406	9	45.11	3-54	–	6.15
D.T.Tiripano	150.2	7	885	20	44.25	5-63	1	5.88
B.V.Vitori	198.5	4	1149	32	35.90	5-20	2	5.77
M.N.Waller	111	0	566	10	56.60	2-44	–	5.09
S.C.Williams	612	21	3008	60	50.13	3-15	–	4.91
C.Zhuwao	3.1	0	21	0	–	–	–	6.63

BANGLADESH – BATTING AND FIELDING

	M	I	NO	HS	Runs	Avge	100	50	Ct/St
Abu Hider	2	1	–	1	1	1.00	–	–	1
Abul Hasan	7	3	–	7	11	3.66	–	–	1
Anumul Haque	37	34	–	120	1038	30.52	3	3	10
Ariful Haque	1	–	–	–	–	–	–	–	–
Fazle Mahmud	2	2	–	0	0	0.00	–	–	1
Imrul Kayes	78	78	2	144	2434	32.02	4	16	21
Liton Das	27	27	1	121	508	19.53	1	1	15/3
Mahmudullah	171	148	38	128*	3673	33.39	3	20	57
Mashrafe Mortaza	203	149	26	51*	1738	14.13	–	1	57
Mehedi Hasan	25	16	2	51	291	20.78	–	1	7
Mohammad Mithun	15	13	2	63	360	32.72	–	4	5
Mohammad Saifuddin	10	7	1	50	175	29.16	–	1	1
Mominul Haque	28	26	1	60	557	22.28	–	3	4
Mosaddek Hossain	24	20	9	50*	341	31.00	–	1	9
Mushfiqur Rahim	201	187	31	144	5392	34.56	6	32	164/42
Mustafizur Rahman	43	21	15	18*	57	9.50	–	–	8
Nasir Hossain	65	52	8	100	1281	29.11	1	6	34
Nazmul Hossain	3	3	–	7	20	6.66	–	–	2
Nazmul Islam	5	1	–	7	7	7.00	–	–	2
Rubel Hossain	96	49	23	17	123	4.73	–	–	17
Sabbir Rahman	57	51	5	102	1212	26.34	1	5	30
Sanjamul Islam	3	1	–	19	19	19.00	–	–	–
Shakib Al Hasan	195	183	24	134*	5577	35.07	7	40	45
Soumya Sarkar	41	40	3	127*	1274	34.43	2	7	20
Tamim Iqbal	189	187	8	154	6460	36.08	11	44	48

BANGLADESH – BOWLING

	O	M	R	W	Avge	Best	4wI	R/Over
Abu Hider	18	2	89	3	29.66	2-50	–	4.94
Abul Hasan	36	1	244	0	–	–	–	6.77
Ariful Haque	3	0	17	0	–	–	–	5.66
Fazle Mahmud	3	0	16	0	–	–	–	5.33
Mahmudullah	677.4	14	3501	76	46.06	3- 4	–	5.16
Mashrafe Mortaza	1692.2	121	8106	258	31.41	6-26	8	4.78
Mehedi Hasan	207.1	9	912	26	35.07	4-29	1	4.40
Mohammad Saifuddin	70	4	373	7	53.28	3-45	–	5.32
Mominul Haque	39	1	190	7	27.14	2-13	–	4.87
Mosaddek Hossain	90.2	1	454	11	41.27	3-13	–	5.02
Mustafizur Rahman	354.4	19	1672	77	21.71	6-43	5	4.71
Nasir Hossain	209.2	4	988	24	41.16	3-26	–	4.71

BANGLADESH – BOWLING (continued)

	O	M	R	W	Avge	Best	4wI	R/Over
Nazmul Islam	44	0	224	5	44.80	2-38	–	5.09
Rubel Hossain	714.4	25	4019	122	32.94	6-26	8	5.62
Sabbir Rahman	46.2	0	313	3	104.33	1-12	–	6.75
Sanjamul Islam	25	–	79	5	15.80	2-22	–	3.16
Shakib Al Hasan	1649.5	81	7333	247	29.68	5-47	9	4.44
Soumya Sarkar	22	0	123	1	123.00	1-19	–	5.59
Tamim Iqbal	1	0	13	0	–	–	–	13.00

IRELAND – BATTING AND FIELDING

	M	I	NO	HS	Runs	Avge	100	50	Ct/St
A.Balbirnie	53	50	4	145*	1393	30.28	3	7	17
J.Cameron-Dow	2	–	–	–	–	–	–	–	–
P.K.D.Chase	25	16	6	14	35	3.50	–	–	5
G.H.Dockrell	80	51	22	62*	527	18.17	–	2	33
E.C.Joyce †	61	60	8	160*	2151	41.36	5	12	21
A.R.McBrine	35	21	9	79	250	20.83	–	1	16
B.J.McCarthy	24	15	3	16*	82	6.83	–	–	8
J.A.McCollum	1	1	–	0	0	0.00	–	–	–
E.J.G.Morgan	23	23	2	115	744	35.42	1	5	9
T.J.Murtagh	48	30	9	23*	161	7.66	–	–	14
K.J.O'Brien	131	119	15	142	3203	30.79	2	16	57
N.J.O'Brien	103	101	9	109	2581	28.05	1	18	90/14
W.T.S.Porterfield	125	122	3	139	3726	31.31	11	15	59
S.W.Poynter	19	17	4	36	177	13.61	–	–	19/1
W.B.Rankin †	56	25	15	18*	64	6.40	–	–	15
Simi Singh	13	12	1	45	160	14.54	–	–	8
P.R.Stirling	103	100	2	177	3455	35.25	7	17	39
G.C.Wilson	99	93	11	113	1974	24.07	1	12	66/10

IRELAND – BOWLING

	O	M	R	W	Avge	Best	4wI	R/Over
A.Balbirnie	10	0	68	2	34.00	1-26	–	6.80
J.Cameron-Dow	11	0	73	1	73.00	1-37	–	6.63
P.K.D.Chase	206.2	2	1356	34	39.88	3-33	–	6.57
G.H.Dockrell	650.1	29	3006	86	34.95	4-24	4	4.62
A.R.McBrine	286.5	14	1292	36	35.88	3-38	–	4.50
B.J.McCarthy	207	7	1189	48	24.77	5-46	3	5.74
T.J.Murtagh	412.3	38	1858	60	30.96	4-30	4	4.50
K.J.O'Brien	681.3	29	3575	112	31.91	4-13	5	5.24
W.B.Rankin	464	36	2209	79	27.96	4-15	3	4.76
Simi Singh	86	3	333	11	30.27	3-15	–	3.87
P.R.Stirling	386.4	8	1849	40	46.22	6-55	2	4.78

† E.C.Joyce also made 17 appearances for England, and W.B.Rankin also made 7 appearances for England.

AFGHANISTAN – BATTING AND FIELDING

	M	I	NO	HS	Runs	Avge	100	50	Ct/St
Afsar Zazai	17	16	1	60	264	17.60	–	2	20/2
Aftab Alam	20	12	8	16*	61	15.25	–	–	6
Asghar Stanikzai	97	91	7	101	1877	22.34	1	9	21
Dawlat Zadran	74	50	26	47*	502	20.91	–	–	14
Gulbadin Naib	51	43	8	82*	806	23.02	–	5	9
Hashmatullah Shahidi	28	28	5	97*	747	32.47	–	6	6
Hazratullah Zazai	5	5	–	67	141	28.20	–	1	1
Ihsanullah	16	16	2	57*	307	21.92	–	3	10

	M	I	NO	HS	Runs	Avge	100	50	Ct/St
Ikram Ali Khil	1	1	1	5*	5	–	–	–	–
Javed Ahmadi	41	38	–	81	947	24.92	–	7	10
Mohammad Nabi	109	97	11	116	2461	28.61	1	12	50
Mohammad Shahzad	78	78	3	131*	2556	34.08	5	13	59/25
Mujeeb Zadran	26	10	4	15	40	6.66	–	–	2
Najibullah Zadran	52	48	8	104*	1193	29.82	1	8	31
Nasir Jamal	16	14	1	53	352	27.07	–	3	4
Noor Ali Zadran	45	45	1	114	1139	25.88	1	7	15
Rahmat Shah	56	52	2	114	1790	35.80	3	13	13
Rashid Khan	55	40	8	60*	695	21.71	–	3	17
Samiullah Shinwari	80	70	10	96	1737	28.95	–	11	21
Sayed Shirzad	1	–	–	–	–	–	–	–	–
Shafiqullah	24	21	2	56	430	22.63	–	2	11/3
Shapoor Zadran	43	27	17	17	67	6.70	–	–	5
Sharafuddin Ashraf	14	9	3	21	53	8.83	–	–	2

AFGHANISTAN – BOWLING

	O	M	R	W	Avge	Best	4wI	R/Over
Aftab Alam	156.3	10	772	27	28.59	3-48	–	4.93
Asghar Stanikzai	23.1	1	91	3	30.33	1- 1	–	3.92
Dawlat Zadran	565.1	41	3001	103	29.13	4-22	3	5.30
Gulbadin Naib	259.4	9	1339	39	34.33	4-27	2	5.15
Hashmatullah Shahidi	3	0	25	0	–	–	–	8.33
Javed Ahmadi	60.5	0	294	8	36.75	4-37	1	4.83
Mohammad Nabi	863	35	3682	116	31.74	4-30	2	4.26
Mujeeb Zadran	238	22	908	48	18.91	5-50	3	3.81
Najibullah Zadran	5	0	30	0	–	–	–	6.00
Nasir Jamal	1	0	7	0	–	–	–	7.00
Rahmat Shah	69.2	2	410	12	34.16	5-32	1	5.91
Rashid Khan	456.1	25	1782	120	14.85	7-18	8	3.90
Samiullah Shinwari	343.5	10	1698	45	37.73	4-31	–	4.93
Shapoor Zadran	322.3	34	1543	43	35.88	4-24	2	4.78
Sharafuddin Ashraf	99.2	2	414	12	34.50	3-29	–	4.16

ASSOCIATES – BATTING AND FIELDING

	M	I	NO	HS	Runs	Avge	100	50	Ct/St
J.H.Davey (Scotland)	29	26	5	64	471	22.42	–	2	9
M.A.Jones (Scotland)	5	5	–	87	194	38.80	–	2	2
F.J.Klaassen (Neth)	2	2	–	13	24	12.00	–	–	–
R.A.J.Smith (Scotland)	2	1	–	10	10	10.00	–	–	–
R.N.ten Doeschate (Neth)	33	32	9	119	1541	67.00	5	9	13
T.van der Gugten (Neth)	4	2	–	2	4	2.00	–	–	–
P.A.van Meekeren (Neth)	4	3	3	15*	30	–	–	–	–
B.T.J.Wheal (Scotland)	11	6	3	14	16	5.33	–	–	3
S.G.Whittingham (Scot)	4	3	2	3*	6	6.00	–	–	3

ASSOCIATES – BOWLING

	O	M	R	W	Avge	Best	4wI	R/Over
J.H.Davey	199.5	18	1014	47	21.57	6-28	3	5.07
F.J.Klaassen	20	2	68	6	11.33	3-30	–	3.40
R.A.J.Smith	15	0	97	1	97.00	1-34	–	6.46
R.N.ten Doeschate	263.2	18	1327	55	24.12	4-31	3	5.03
T.van der Gugten	21	3	85	8	10.62	5-24	1	4.04
P.A.van Meekeren	26	0	131	2	65.50	1-21	–	5.03
B.T.J.Wheal	96.3	9	410	19	21.57	3-34	–	4.24
S.G.Whittingham	33.5	2	174	7	24.85	3-58	–	5.14

LIMITED-OVERS INTERNATIONALS RESULTS

1970-71 to 2 March 2019

This chart excludes all matches involving multinational teams.

Team	Opponents	Matches	Won													Tied	NR
			E	A	SA	WI	NZ	I	P	SL	Z	B	Ire	Afg	Ass		
England	Australia	147	61	81	–	–	–	–	–	–	–	–	–	–	–	2	3
	South Africa	59	26	–	29	–	–	–	–	–	–	–	–	–	–	1	3
	West Indies	101	51	–	–	44	–	–	–	–	–	–	–	–	–	–	6
	New Zealand	89	40	–	–	–	43	–	–	–	–	–	–	–	–	2	4
	India	99	41	–	–	–	–	53	–	–	–	–	–	–	–	2	3
	Pakistan	82	49	–	–	–	–	–	31	–	–	–	–	–	–	–	2
	Sri Lanka	74	36	–	–	–	–	–	–	35	–	–	–	–	–	1	2
	Zimbabwe	30	21	–	–	–	–	–	–	–	8	–	–	–	–	–	1
	Bangladesh	20	16	–	–	–	–	–	–	–	–	4	–	–	–	–	–
	Ireland	9	7	–	–	–	–	–	–	–	–	–	1	–	–	–	1
	Afghanistan	1	1	–	–	–	–	–	–	–	–	–	–	–	–	–	–
	Associates	15	13	–	–	–	–	–	–	–	–	–	–	0	1	–	1
Australia	South Africa	99	–	48	47	–	–	–	–	–	–	–	–	–	–	3	1
	West Indies	139	–	73	–	60	–	–	–	–	–	–	–	–	–	3	3
	New Zealand	136	–	90	–	–	39	–	–	–	–	–	–	–	–	–	7
	India	132	–	74	–	–	–	48	–	–	–	–	–	–	–	–	10
	Pakistan	98	–	62	–	–	–	–	32	–	–	–	–	–	–	1	3
	Sri Lanka	96	–	60	–	–	–	–	–	32	–	–	–	–	–	–	4
	Zimbabwe	30	–	27	–	–	–	–	–	–	2	–	–	–	–	–	1
	Bangladesh	20	–	18	–	–	–	–	–	–	–	1	–	–	–	–	1
	Ireland	5	–	4	–	–	–	–	–	–	–	–	0	–	–	–	1
	Afghanistan	2	–	2	–	–	–	–	–	–	–	–	–	0	–	–	–
	Associates	16	–	16	–	–	–	–	–	–	–	–	–	–	0	–	–
S Africa	West Indies	61	–	–	44	15	–	–	–	–	–	–	–	–	–	1	1
	New Zealand	70	–	–	41	–	24	–	–	–	–	–	–	–	–	–	5
	India	83	–	–	46	–	–	34	–	–	–	–	–	–	–	–	3
	Pakistan	78	–	–	50	–	–	–	27	–	–	–	–	–	–	–	1
	Sri Lanka	71	–	–	38	–	–	–	–	31	–	–	–	–	–	1	1
	Zimbabwe	41	–	–	38	–	–	–	–	–	2	–	–	–	–	–	1
	Bangladesh	20	–	–	17	–	–	–	–	–	–	3	–	–	–	–	–
	Ireland	5	–	–	5	–	–	–	–	–	–	–	0	–	–	–	–
	Associates	18	–	–	18	–	–	–	–	–	–	–	–	–	0	–	–
W Indies	New Zealand	64	–	–	–	30	27	–	–	–	–	–	–	–	–	–	7
	India	126	–	–	–	62	–	59	–	–	–	–	–	–	–	2	3
	Pakistan	133	–	–	–	70	–	–	60	–	–	–	–	–	–	3	–
	Sri Lanka	56	–	–	–	28	–	–	–	25	–	–	–	–	–	–	3
	Zimbabwe	48	–	–	–	36	–	–	–	–	10	–	–	–	–	1	1
	Bangladesh	34	–	–	–	21	–	–	–	–	–	11	–	–	–	–	2
	Ireland	7	–	–	–	5	–	–	–	–	–	–	1	–	–	–	1
	Afghanistan	5	–	–	–	1	–	–	–	–	–	–	–	3	–	–	1
	Associates	19	–	–	–	18	–	–	–	–	–	–	–	–	1	–	–
N Zealand	India	106	–	–	–	–	45	55	–	–	–	–	–	–	–	1	5
	Pakistan	106	–	–	–	–	48	–	54	–	–	–	–	–	–	1	3
	Sri Lanka	98	–	–	–	–	48	–	–	41	–	–	–	–	–	1	8
	Zimbabwe	38	–	–	–	–	27	–	–	–	9	–	–	–	–	1	1
	Bangladesh	34	–	–	–	–	24	–	–	–	–	10	–	–	–	–	–
	Ireland	4	–	–	–	–	4	–	–	–	–	–	0	–	–	–	–
	Afghanistan	1	–	–	–	–	1	–	–	–	–	–	–	0	–	–	–
	Associates	12	–	–	–	–	12	–	–	–	–	–	–	–	0	–	–
India	Pakistan	131	–	–	–	–	–	54	73	–	–	–	–	–	–	–	4
	Sri Lanka	158	–	–	–	–	–	90	–	56	–	–	–	–	–	1	11
	Zimbabwe	63	–	–	–	–	–	51	–	–	10	–	–	–	–	–	2
	Bangladesh	35	–	–	–	–	–	29	–	–	–	5	–	–	–	–	1
	Ireland	3	–	–	–	–	–	3	–	–	–	–	0	–	–	–	–
	Afghanistan	2	–	–	–	–	–	2	–	–	–	–	–	0	–	–	–
	Associates	24	–	–	–	–	–	22	–	–	–	–	–	0	1	–	1
Pakistan	Sri Lanka	153	–	–	–	–	–	–	90	58	–	–	–	–	–	1	4
	Zimbabwe	59	–	–	–	–	–	–	52	–	4	–	–	–	–	1	2
	Bangladesh	36	–	–	–	–	–	–	31	–	–	5	–	–	–	–	–

	Opponents	Matches	E	A	SA	WI	NZ	I	P	SL	Z	B	Ire	Afg	Ass	Tied	NR
	Ireland	7							5				1			1	
	Afghanistan	3							3					0			
	Associates	21							21						0		
Sri Lanka	Zimbabwe	57								44	11						2
	Bangladesh	45								36		7					2
	Ireland	4								4			0				
	Afghanistan	3								2				1			
	Associates	16								15					1		
Zimbabwe	Bangladesh	72									28	44					
	Ireland	10									6		3			1	
	Afghanistan	25									10			15			
	Associates	44									34				7	1	2
Bangladesh	Ireland	9										6	2				1
	Afghanistan	7										4		3			
	Associates	26										18			8		
Ireland	Afghanistan	22											10	11			1
	Associates	56											43		9	2	2
Afghanistan	Associates	37												23	13		1
Associates	Associates	128													123		5
		4093	362	555	373	390	342	498	479	379	134	118	61	56	165	37	144

MERIT TABLE OF ALL L-O INTERNATIONALS

	Matches	Won	Lost	Tied	No Result	% Won (exc NR)
South Africa	605	373	210	6	16	63.32
Australia	920	555	322	9	34	62.64
India	962	499	414	9	40	54.12
Pakistan	907	479	401	8	19	53.94
Afghanistan	108	56	48	1	3	53.33
England	726	362	330	8	26	51.71
West Indies	793	390	365	10	28	50.98
Sri Lanka	831	379	410	5	37	47.73
New Zealand	758	342	370	6	40	47.63
Ireland	141	61	69	3	8	45.86
Bangladesh	358	118	233	–	7	33.61
Zimbabwe	517	134	365	7	11	26.48
Associate Members (v Full*)	304	42	253	3	6	14.09

* Results of games between two Associate Members and those involving multi-national sides are excluded from this list; Associate Members have participated in 432 LOIs, 128 LOIs being between Associate Members.

TEAM RECORDS
HIGHEST TOTALS

† Batting Second

481-6	(50 overs)	England v Australia	Nottingham	2018
444-3	(50 overs)	England v Pakistan	Nottingham	2016
443-9	(50 overs)	Sri Lanka v Netherlands	Amstelveen	2006
439-2	(50 overs)	South Africa v West Indies	Johannesburg	2014-15
438-9†	(49.5 overs)	South Africa v Australia	Johannesburg	2005-06
438-4	(50 overs)	South Africa v India	Mumbai	2015-16
434-4	(50 overs)	Australia v South Africa	Johannesburg	2005-06
418-5	(50 overs)	South Africa v Zimbabwe	Potchefstroom	2006-07
418-5	(50 overs)	India v West Indies	Indore	2011-12
418-6	(50 overs)	England v West Indies	St George's	2018-19
417-6	(50 overs)	Australia v Afghanistan	Perth	2014-15

414-7	(50 overs)	India v Sri Lanka	Rajkot	2009-10
413-5	(50 overs)	India v Bermuda	Port of Spain	2006-07
411-8†	(50 overs)	Sri Lanka v India	Rajkot	2009-10
411-4	(50 overs)	South Africa v Ireland	Canberra	2014-15
408-5	(50 overs)	South Africa v West Indies	Sydney	2014-15
408-9	(50 overs)	England v New Zealand	Birmingham	2015
404-5	(50 overs)	India v Sri Lanka	Kolkata	2014-15
402-2	(50 overs)	New Zealand v Ireland	Aberdeen	2008
401-3	(50 overs)	India v South Africa	Gwalior	2009-10
399-6	(50 overs)	South Africa v Zimbabwe	Benoni	2010-11
399-9	(50 overs)	England v South Africa	Bloemfontein	2015-16
399-1	(50 overs)	Pakistan v Zimbabwe	Bulawayo	2018
398-5	(50 overs)	Sri Lanka v Kenya	Kandy	1995-96
398-5	(50 overs)	New Zealand v England	The Oval	2015
397-5	(44 overs)	New Zealand v Zimbabwe	Bulawayo	2005
393-6	(50 overs)	New Zealand v West Indies	Wellington	2014-15
392-6	(50 overs)	South Africa v Pakistan	Pretoria	2006-07
392-4	(50 overs)	India v New Zealand	Christchurch	2008-09
392-4	(50 overs)	India v Sri Lanka	Mohali	2017-18
391-4	(50 overs)	England v Bangladesh	Nottingham	2005
389	(48 overs)	West Indies v England	St George's	2018-19
387-5	(50 overs)	India v England	Rajkot	2008-09
385-7	(50 overs)	Pakistan v Bangladesh	Dambulla	2010
384-6	(50 overs)	South Africa v Sri Lanka	Centurion	2016-17
383-6	(50 overs)	India v Australia	Bangalore	2013-14
381-6	(50 overs)	India v England	Cuttack	2016-17
378-5	(50 overs)	Australia v New Zealand	Canberra	2016-17
377-6	(50 overs)	Australia v South Africa	Basseterre	2006-07
377-8	(50 overs)	Sri Lanka v Ireland	Dublin	2016
377-5	(50 overs)	India v West Indies	Mumbai (BS)	2018-19
376-2	(50 overs)	India v New Zealand	Hyderabad, India	1999-00
376-9	(50 overs)	Australia v Sri Lanka	Sydney	2014-15
375-3	(50 overs)	Pakistan v Zimbabwe	Lahore	2015
375-5	(50 overs)	India v Sri Lanka	Colombo (RPS)	2017

The highest score for Zimbabwe is 351-7 (v Kenya, Mombasa, 2008-09), for Afghanistan is 338 (v Ire, Greater Noida, 2016-17), for Ireland is 331-8 (v Z, Hobart, 2014-15) and 331-6 (v Scotland, Dubai, 2017-18) and for Bangladesh 329-6 (v P, Dhaka, 2014-15).

HIGHEST MATCH AGGREGATES

872-13	(99.5 overs)	South Africa v Australia	Johannesburg	2005-06
825-15	(100 overs)	India v Sri Lanka	Rajkot	2009-10
807-16	(98 overs)	West Indies v England	St George's	2018-19

LARGEST RUNS MARGINS OF VICTORY

290 runs	New Zealand beat Ireland	Aberdeen	2008
275 runs	Australia beat Afghanistan	Perth	2014-15
272 runs	South Africa beat Zimbabwe	Benoni	2010-11
258 runs	South Africa beat Sri Lanka	Paarl	2011-12
257 runs	India beat Bermuda	Port of Spain	2006-07
257 runs	South Africa beat West Indies	Sydney	2014-15
256 runs	Australia beat Namibia	Potschefstroom	2002-03
256 runs	India beat Hong Kong	Karachi	2008
255 runs	Pakistan beat Ireland	Dublin	2016
245 runs	Sri Lanka beat India	Sharjah	2000-01
244 runs	Pakistan beat Zimbabwe	Bulawayo	2018
243 runs	Sri Lanka beat Bermuda	Port of Spain	2006-07
242 runs	England beat Australia	Nottingham	2018
234 runs	Sri Lanka beat Pakistan	Lahore	2008-09
233 runs	Pakistan beat Bangladesh	Dhaka	1999-00
232 runs	Australia beat Sri Lanka	Adelaide	1984-85
231 runs	South Africa beat Netherlands	Mohali	2010-11

229 runs	Australia beat Netherlands	Basseterre	2006-07
226 runs	Ireland beat UAE	Harare	2017-18
224 runs	Australia beat Pakistan	Nairobi	2002
224 runs	India beat West Indies	Mumbai (BS)	2018-19
221 runs	South Africa beat Netherlands	Basseterre	2006-07

LOWEST TOTALS (Excluding reduced innings)

35	(18.0 overs)	Zimbabwe v Sri Lanka	Harare	2003-04
36	(18.4 overs)	Canada v Sri Lanka	Paarl	2002-03
38	(15.4 overs)	Zimbabwe v Sri Lanka	Colombo (SSC)	2001-02
43	(19.5 overs)	Pakistan v West Indies	Cape Town	1992-93
43	(20.1 overs)	Sri Lanka v South Africa	Paarl	2011-12
44	(24.5 overs)	Zimbabwe v Bangladesh	Chittagong	2009-10
45	(40.3 overs)	Canada v England	Manchester	1979
45	(14.0 overs)	Namibia v Australia	Potchefstroom	2002-03
54	(26.3 overs)	India v Sri Lanka	Sharjah	2000-01
54	(23.2 overs)	West Indies v South Africa	Cape Town	2003-04
54	(13.5 overs)	Zimbabwe v Afghanistan	Harare	2016-17
55	(28.3 overs)	Sri Lanka v West Indies	Sharjah	1986-87
58	(18.5 overs)	Bangladesh v West Indies	Dhaka	2010-11
58	(17.4 overs)	Bangladesh v India	Dhaka	2014
58	(16.1 overs)	Afghanistan v Zimbabwe	Sharjah	2015-16
61	(22.0 overs)	West Indies v Bangladesh	Chittagong	2011-12
63	(25.5 overs)	India v Australia	Sydney	1980-81
63	(18.3 overs)	Afghanistan v Scotland	Abu Dhabi	2014-15
64	(35.5 overs)	New Zealand v Pakistan	Sharjah	1985-86
65	(24.0 overs)	USA v Australia	Southampton	2004
65	(24.3 overs)	Zimbabwe v India	Harare	2005
67	(31.0 overs)	Zimbabwe v Sri Lanka	Harare	2008-09
67	(24.4 overs)	Canada v Netherlands	King City	2013
67	(24.0 overs)	Sri Lanka v England	Manchester	2014
67	(25.1 overs)	Zimbabwe v Pakistan	Bulawayo	2018
68	(31.3 overs)	Scotland v West Indies	Leicester	1999
69	(28.0 overs)	South Africa v Australia	Sydney	1993-94
69	(22.5 overs)	Zimbabwe v Kenya	Harare	2005-06
69	(23.5 overs)	Kenya v New Zealand	Chennai	2010-11
70	(25.2 overs)	Australia v England	Birmingham	1977
70	(26.3 overs)	Australia v New Zealand	Adelaide	1985-86
70	(23.5 overs)	West Indies v Australia	Perth	2012-13
70	(24.4 overs)	Bangladesh v West Indies	St George's	2014

The lowest for England is 86 (v A, Manchester, 2001) and for Ireland is 77 (v SL, St George's, 2007).

LOWEST MATCH AGGREGATES

73-11	(23.2 overs)	Canada (36) v Sri Lanka (37-1)	Paarl	2002-03
75-11	(27.2 overs)	Zimbabwe (35) v Sri Lanka (40-1)	Harare	2003-04
78-11	(20.0 overs)	Zimbabwe (38) v Sri Lanka (40-1)	Colombo (SSC)	2001-02

BATTING RECORDS

6000 RUNS IN A CAREER

		LOI	I	NO	HS	Runs	Avge	100	50
S.R.Tendulkar	I	463	452	41	200*	18426	44.83	49	96
K.C.Sangakkara	SL/Asia/ICC	404	380	41	169	14234	41.98	25	93
R.T.Ponting	A/ICC	.375	365	39	164	13704	42.03	30	82
S.T.Jayasuriya	SL/Asia	445	433	18	189	13430	32.36	28	68
D.P.M.D.Jayawardena	SL/Asia	448	418	39	144	12650	33.37	19	77
Inzamam-ul-Haq	P/Asia	378	350	53	137*	11739	39.52	10	83
J.H.Kallis	SA/Afr/ICC	328	314	53	139	11579	44.36	17	86
S.C.Ganguly	I/Asia	311	300	23	183	11363	41.02	22	72
R.S.Dravid	I/Asia/ICC	344	318	40	153	10889	39.16	12	83
V.Kohli	I	223	215	37	183	10577	59.42	39	49

		LOI	I	NO	HS	Runs	Avge	100	50
M.S.Dhoni	I/Asia	339	287	82	183*	**10474**	51.09	10	71
B.C.Lara	WI/ICC	299	289	32	169	**10405**	40.48	19	63
T.M.Dilshan	SL	330	303	41	161*	**10290**	39.27	22	47
C.H.Gayle	WI/ICC	289	283	17	215	**10151**	38.16	25	51
Mohammad Yousuf	P/Asia	288	272	40	141*	**9720**	41.71	15	64
A.C.Gilchrist	A/ICC	287	279	11	172	**9619**	35.89	16	55
A.B.de Villiers	SA/Afr	228	218	39	176	**9577**	53.50	25	53
M.Azharuddin	I	334	308	54	153*	**9378**	36.92	7	58
P.A.de Silva	SL	308	296	30	145	**9284**	34.90	11	64
Saeed Anwar	P	247	244	19	194	**8824**	39.21	20	43
S.Chanderpaul	WI	268	251	40	150	**8778**	41.60	11	59
Yuvraj Singh	I/Asia	304	278	40	150	**8701**	36.55	14	52
D.L.Haynes	WI	238	237	28	152*	**8648**	41.37	17	57
M.S.Atapattu	SL	268	259	32	132*	**8529**	37.57	11	59
M.E.Waugh	A	244	236	20	173	**8500**	39.35	18	50
V.Sehwag	I/Asia/ICC	251	245	9	219	**8273**	35.05	15	38
H.H.Gibbs	SA	248	240	16	175	**8094**	36.13	21	37
Shahid Afridi	P/Asia/ICC	398	369	27	124	**8064**	23.57	6	39
S.P.Fleming	NZ/ICC	280	269	21	134*	**8037**	32.40	8	49
L.R.P.L.Taylor	NZ	218	203	37	181*	**8026**	48.34	20	47
M.J.Clarke	A	245	223	44	130	**7981**	44.58	8	58
H.M.Amla	SA	174	171	12	159	**7910**	49.74	27	37
R.G.Sharma	I	202	196	31	264	**7845**	47.54	22	39
S.R.Waugh	A	325	288	58	120*	**7569**	32.90	3	45
A.Ranatunga	SL	269	255	47	131*	**7456**	35.84	4	49
Javed Miandad	P	233	218	41	119*	**7381**	41.70	8	50
Shoaib Malik	P	279	250	40	143	**7379**	35.13	9	43
Younus Khan	P	265	255	23	144	**7249**	31.24	7	48
Salim Malik	P	283	256	38	102	**7170**	32.88	5	47
N.J.Astle	NZ	223	217	14	145*	**7090**	34.92	16	41
G.C.Smith	SA/Afr	197	194	10	141	**6989**	37.98	10	47
W.U.Tharanga	SL/Asia	233	221	17	174*	**6945**	34.04	15	37
M.G.Bevan	A	232	196	67	108*	**6912**	53.58	6	46
E.J.G.Morgan	E/Ire	217	203	29	124*	**6813**	39.15	12	43
G.Kirsten	SA	185	185	19	188*	**6798**	40.95	13	45
A.Flower	Z	213	208	16	145	**6786**	35.34	4	55
I.V.A.Richards	WI	187	167	24	189*	**6721**	47.00	11	45
G.W.Flower	Z	221	214	18	142*	**6571**	33.52	6	40
Ijaz Ahmed	P	250	232	29	139*	**6564**	32.33	10	37
A.R.Border	A	273	252	39	127*	**6524**	30.62	3	39
Tamim Iqbal	B	189	187	8	154	**6460**	36.08	11	44
M.J.Guptill	NZ	169	166	18	237*	**6440**	43.51	16	34
Mohammad Hafeez	P	208	206	15	140*	**6302**	32.99	11	36
R.B.Richardson	WI	224	217	30	122	**6248**	33.41	5	44
B.R.M.Taylor	Z	188	187	15	145*	**6156**	35.79	10	36
M.L.Hayden	A/ICC	161	155	15	181*	**6133**	43.80	10	36
B.B.McCullum	NZ	260	228	28	166	**6083**	30.41	5	32
D.M.Jones	A	164	161	25	145	**6068**	44.61	7	46

The most runs for Ireland is 3723 by W.T.S.Porterfield (121 innings) and for Afghanistan 2551 by Mohammad Shahzad (77 innings).

HIGHEST INDIVIDUAL INNINGS

264	R.G.Sharma	India v Sri Lanka	Kolkata	2014-15
237*	M.J.Guptill	New Zealand v West Indies	Wellington	2014-15
219	V.Sehwag	India v West Indies	Indore	2011-12
215	C.H.Gayle	West Indies v Zimbabwe	Canberra	2014-15
210*	Fakhar Zaman	Pakistan v Zimbabwe	Bulawayo	2018
209	R.G.Sharma	India v Australia	Bangalore	2013-14
208*	R.G.Sharma	India v Sri Lanka	Mohali	2017-18
200*	S.R.Tendulkar	India v South Africa	Gwalior	2009-10
194*	C.K.Coventry	Zimbabwe v Bangladesh	Bulawayo	2009

194	Saeed Anwar	Pakistan v India	Madras	1996-97
189*	I.V.A.Richards	West Indies v England	Manchester	1984
189*	M.J.Guptill	New Zealand v England	Southampton	2013
189	S.T.Jayasuriya	Sri Lanka v India	Sharjah	2000-01
188*	G.Kirsten	South Africa v UAE	Rawalpindi	1995-96
186*	S.R.Tendulkar	India v New Zealand	Hyderabad	1999-00
185*	S.R.Watson	Australia v Bangladesh	Dhaka	2010-11
185	F.du Plessis	South Africa v Sri Lanka	Cape Town	2016-17
183*	M.S.Dhoni	India v Sri Lanka	Jaipur	2005-06
183	S.C.Ganguly	India v Sri Lanka	Taunton	1999
183	V.Kohli	India v Pakistan	Dhaka	2011-12
181*	M.L.Hayden	Australia v New Zealand	Hamilton	2006-07
181*	L.R.P.L.Taylor	New Zealand v England	Dunedin	2017-18
181	I.V.A.Richards	West Indies v Sri Lanka	Karachi	1987-88
180*	M.J.Guptill	New Zealand v South Africa	Hamilton	2016-17
180	J.J.Roy	England v Australia	Melbourne	2017-18
179	D.A.Warner	Australia v Pakistan	Adelaide	2016-17
178*	H.Masakadza	Zimbabwe v Kenya	Harare	2009-10
178	D.A.Warner	Australia v Afghanistan	Perth	2014-15
178	Q.de Kock	South Africa v Australia	Centurion	2016-17
177	P.R.Stirling	Ireland v Canada	Toronto	2010
176*	E.Lewis	West Indies v England	The Oval	2017
176	A.B.de Villiers	South Africa v Bangladesh	Paarl	2017-18
175*	Kapil Dev	India v Zimbabwe	Tunbridge Wells	1983
175	H.H.Gibbs	South Africa v Australia	Johannesburg	2005-06
175	S.R.Tendulkar	India v Australia	Hyderabad, India	2009-10
175	V.Sehwag	India v Bangladesh	Dhaka	2010-11
175	C.S.MacLeod	Scotland v Canada	Christchurch	2013-14
174*	W.U.Tharanga	Sri Lanka v India	Kingston	2013
173	M.E.Waugh	Australia v West Indies	Melbourne	2000-01
173	D.A.Warner	Australia v South Africa	Cape Town	2016-17
172*	C.B.Wishart	Zimbabwe v Namibia	Harare	2002-03
172	A.C.Gilchrist	Australia v Zimbabwe	Hobart	2003-04
172	L.Vincent	New Zealand v Zimbabwe	Bulawayo	2005
171*	G.M.Turner	New Zealand v East Africa	Birmingham	1975
171*	R.G.Sharma	India v Australia	Perth	2015-16
171	A.D.Hales	England v Pakistan	Nottingham	2016
170*	L.Ronchi	New Zealand v Sri Lanka	Dunedin	2014-15

The highest for Bangladesh is 154 by Tamim Iqbal (v Z, Bulawayo, 2009) and for Afghanistan 131* by Mohammad Shahzad (v Z, Sharjah, 2015-16).

HUNDRED ON DEBUT

D.L.Amiss	103	England v Australia	Manchester	1972
D.L.Haynes	148	West Indies v Australia	St John's	1977-78
A.Flower	115*	Zimbabwe v Sri Lanka	New Plymouth	1991-92
Salim Elahi	102*	Pakistan v Sri Lanka	Gujranwala	1995-96
M.J.Guptill	122*	New Zealand v West Indies	Auckland	2008-09
C.A.Ingram	124	South Africa v Zimbabwe	Bloemfontein	2010-11
R.J.Nicol	108*	New Zealand v Zimbabwe	Harare	2011-12
P.J.Hughes	112	Australia v Sri Lanka	Melbourne	2012-13
M.J.Lumb	106	England v West Indies	North Sound	2013-14
M.S.Chapman	124*	Hong Kong v UAE	Dubai	2015-16
K.L.Rahul	100*	India v Zimbabwe	Harare	2016
T.Bavuma	113	South Africa v Ireland	Benoni	2016-17
Imam-ul-Haq	100	Pakistan v Sri Lanka	Abu Dhabi	2017-18
R.R.Hendricks	102	South Africa v Sri Lanka	Pallekele	2018

Shahid Afridi scored 102 for P v SL, Nairobi, 1996-97, in his second match having not batted in his first.

Fastest 100	31 balls	A.B.de Villiers (149)	SA v WI	Johannesburg	2014-15
Fastest 50	16 balls	A.B.de Villiers (149)	SA v WI	Johannesburg	2014-15

15 HUNDREDS

		Inns	100	E	A	SA	WI	NZ	I	P	SL	Z	B	Ire	Afg	Ass
S.R.Tendulkar	I	452	49	2	9	5	4	5	–	5	8	5	1	–	–	5
V.Kohli	I	215	39	3	6	4	7	5	–	2	8	1	3	–	–	
R.T.Ponting	A	365	30*	5	–	2	2	6	6	1	4	1	1	–	–	1
S.T.Jayasuriya	SL	433	28	4	2	–	1	5	7	3	–	1	4	–	–	1
H.M.Amla	SA	171	27	2	1	–	5	2	2	3	5	3	2	1	–	1
A.B.de Villiers	SA	218	25	2	1	–	5	1	6	3	2	3	1	–	–	1
C.H.Gayle	WI	283	25	4	–	3	–	2	4	3	1	3	1	–	–	4
K.C.Sangakkara	SL	380	25	4	2	2	–	2	6	2	–	–	5	–	–	2
R.G.Sharma	I	196	22	1	7	2	2	1	–	1	5	1	2	–	–	
S.C.Ganguly	I	300	22	1	1	2	–	2	–	2	4	3	1	–	4	
T.M.Dilshan	SL	303	22	2	1	2	–	3	4	2	–	2	4	–	–	2
H.H.Gibbs	SA	240	21	2	3	–	2	3	2	4	2	1	2	–	–	1
L.R.P.L.Taylor	NZ	203	20	5	2	1	1	–	2	3	2	2	2	–	–	
Saeed Anwar	P	244	20	–	1	–	1	4	4	–	7	2	–	–	–	
B.C.Lara	WI	289	19	1	3	3	–	2	5	2	1	1	–	–	1	
D.P.M.D.Jayawardena	SL	418	19*	5	–	1	4	–	3	1	–	1	3	–	1	1
M.E.Waugh	A	236	18	1	–	2	3	1	3	3	1	3	–	–	–	1
D.L.Haynes	WI	237	17	2	6	–	–	2	2	4	1	–	–	–	–	
J.H.Kallis	SA	314	17	1	1	–	4	3	2	1	3	1	–	–	1	
M.J.Guptill	NZ	166	16	2	1	2	2	–	1	1	2	2	3	–	–	
N.J.Astle	NZ	217	16	2	1	1	1	–	5	2	–	3	–	–	1	
A.C.Gilchrist	A	279	16*	2	–	2	–	2	1	1	6	1	–	–	–	
S.Dhawan	I	123	15	–	2	3	2	–	–	1	4	1	–	1	1	
W.U.Tharanga	SL	221	15	3	1	1	1	1	1	2	–	3	1	–	–	1
V.Sehwag	I	245	15	1	–	–	2	6	–	2	2	–	1	–	–	1
Mohammad Yousuf	P	273	15	–	1	2	2	1	1	–	3	3	3	–	–	

* = Includes hundred scored against multi-national side. The most for England is 14 by J.E.Root (in 119 innings), for Zimbabwe 10 by B.R.M.Taylor (187), for Bangladesh 11 by Tamim Iqbal (187), for Ireland 11 by W.T.S.Porterfield (121), and for Afghanistan 5 by Mohammad Shahzad (77).

HIGHEST PARTNERSHIP FOR EACH WICKET

1st	304	Imam-ul-Haq/Fakhar Zaman	Pakistan v Zimbabwe	Bulawayo	2018
2nd	372	C.H.Gayle/M.N.Samuels	West Indies v Zimbabwe	Canberra	2014-15
3rd	258	D.M.Bravo/D.Ramdin	West Indies v Bangladesh	Basseterre	2014
4th	275*	M.Azharuddin/A.Jadeja	India v Zimbabwe	Cuttack	1997-98
5th	256*	D.A.Miller/J.P.Duminy	South Africa v Zimbabwe	Hamilton	2014-15
6th	267*	G.D.Elliott/L.Ronchi	New Zealand v Sri Lanka	Dunedin	2014-15
7th	177	J.C.Buttler/A.U.Rashid	England v New Zealand	Birmingham	2015
8th	138*	J.M.Kemp/A.J.Hall	South Africa v India	Cape Town	2006-07
9th	132	A.D.Mathews/S.L.Malinga	Sri Lanka v Australia	Melbourne	2010-11
10th	106*	I.V.A.Richards/M.A.Holding	West Indies v England	Manchester	1984

BOWLING RECORDS
200 WICKETS IN A CAREER

		LOI	Balls	R	W	Avge	Best	5w	R/Over
M.Muralitharan	SL/Asia/ICC	350	18811	12326	534	23.08	7-30	10	3.93
Wasim Akram	P	356	18186	11812	502	23.52	5-15	6	3.89
Waqar Younis	P	262	12698	9919	416	23.84	7-36	13	4.68
W.P.J.U.C.Vaas	SL/Asia	322	15775	11014	400	27.53	8-19	4	4.18
Shahid Afridi	P/Asia/ICC	398	17620	13632	395	34.51	7-12	9	4.62
S.M.Pollock	SA/Afr/ICC	303	15712	9631	393	24.50	6-35	5	3.67
G.D.McGrath	A/ICC	250	12970	8391	381	22.02	7-15	7	3.88
B.Lee	A	221	11185	8877	380	23.36	5-22	9	4.76
A.Kumble	I/Asia	271	14496	10412	337	30.89	6-12	2	4.30
S.T.Jayasuriya	SL	445	14874	11871	323	36.75	6-29	4	4.78
S.L.Malinga	SL	214	10316	9182	318	28.87	6-38	8	5.34
J.Srinath	I	229	11935	8847	315	28.08	5-23	3	4.44
D.L.Vettori	NZ/ICC	295	14060	9674	305	31.71	5- 7	2	4.12
S.K.Warne	A/ICC	194	10642	7541	293	25.73	5-33	1	4.25

		LOI	Balls	R	W	Avge	Best	5w	R/Over
Saqlain Mushtaq	P	169	8770	6275	288	21.78	5-20	6	4.29
A.B.Agarkar	I	191	9484	8021	288	27.85	6-42	2	5.07
Z.Khan	I/Asia	200	10097	8301	282	29.43	5-42	1	4.93
J.H.Kallis	SA/Afr/ICC	328	10750	8680	273	31.79	5-30	2	4.84
A.A.Donald	SA	164	8561	5926	272	21.78	6-23	2	4.15
J.M.Anderson	E	194	9584	7861	269	29.22	5-23	2	4.92
Abdul Razzaq	P/Asia	265	10941	8564	269	31.83	6-35	3	4.69
Harbhajan Singh	I/Asia	236	12479	8973	269	33.35	5-31	3	4.31
M.Ntini	SA/ICC	173	8687	6559	266	24.65	6-22	4	4.53
Mashrafe Mortaza	B/Asia	205	10249	8214	259	31.71	6-26	1	4.80
Kapil Dev	I	225	11202	6945	253	27.45	5-43	1	3.72
Shoaib Akhtar	P/Asia/ICC	163	7764	6169	247	24.97	6-16	4	4.76
Shakib Al Hasan	B	195	9899	7333	247	29.68	5-47	1	4.44
K.D.Mills	NZ	170	8230	6485	240	27.02	5-25	1	4.72
M.G.Johnson	A	153	7489	6038	239	25.26	6-31	3	4.83
H.H.Streak	Z/Afr	189	9468	7129	239	29.82	5-32	1	4.51
D.Gough	E/ICC	159	8470	6209	235	26.42	5-44	2	4.39
C.A.Walsh	WI	205	10822	6918	227	30.47	5- 1	1	3.83
C.E.L.Ambrose	WI	176	9353	5429	225	24.12	5-17	4	3.48
Abdur Razzak	B	153	7965	6065	207	29.29	5-29	4	4.56
C.J.McDermott	A	138	7460	5018	203	24.71	5-44	1	4.03
C.Z.Harris	NZ	250	10667	7613	203	37.50	5-42	1	4.28
C.L.Cairns	NZ/ICC	215	8168	6594	201	32.80	5-42	1	4.84

The most wickets for Ireland is 112 by K.J.O'Brien (120 matches) and for Afghanistan 119 by Rashid Khan (54).

BEST FIGURES IN AN INNINGS

8-19	W.P.J.U.C.Vaas	Sri Lanka v Zimbabwe	Colombo (SSC)	2001-02
7-12	Shahid Afridi	Pakistan v West Indies	Providence	2013
7-15	G.D.McGrath	Australia v Namibia	Potchefstroom	2002-03
7-18	Rashid Khan	Afghanistan v West Indies	Gros Islet	2017
7-20	A.J.Bichel	Australia v England	Port Elizabeth	2002-03
7-30	M.Muralitharan	Sri Lanka v India	Sharjah	2000-01
7-33	T.G.Southee	New Zealand v England	Wellington	2014-15
7-34	T.A.Boult	New Zealand v West Indies	Christchurch	2017-18
7-36	Waqar Younis	Pakistan v England	Leeds	2001
7-37	Aqib Javed	Pakistan v India	Sharjah	1991-92
7-45	Imran Tahir	South Africa v West Indies	Basseterre	2016
7-51	W.W.Davis	West Indies v Australia	Leeds	1983
6- 4	S.T.R.Binny	India v Bangladesh	Dhaka	2014
6-12	A.Kumble	India v West Indies	Calcutta	1993-94
6-13	B.A.W.Mendis	Sri Lanka v India	Karachi	2008
6-14	G.J.Gilmour	Australia v England	Leeds	1975
6-14	Imran Khan	Pakistan v India	Sharjah	1984-85
6-14	M.F.Maharoof	Sri Lanka v West Indies	Mumbai	2006-07
6-15	C.E.H.Croft	West Indies v England	Kingstown	1980-81
6-16	Shoaib Akhtar	Pakistan v New Zealand	Karachi	2001-02
6-16	K.Rabada	South Africa v Bangladesh	Dhaka	2015
6-18	Azhar Mahmood	Pakistan v West Indies	Sharjah	1999-00
6-19	H.K.Olonga	Zimbabwe v England	Cape Town	1999-00
6-19	S.E.Bond	New Zealand v Zimbabwe	Harare	2005
6-20	B.C.Strang	Zimbabwe v Bangladesh	Nairobi	1997-98
6-20	A.D.Mathews	Sri Lanka v India	Colombo (RPS)	2009-10
6-22	F.H.Edwards	West Indies v Zimbabwe	Harare	2003-04
6-22	M.Ntini	South Africa v Australia	Cape Town	2005-06
6-23	A.A.Donald	South Africa v Kenya	Nairobi	1996-97
6-23	A.Nehra	India v England	Durban	2002-03
6-23	S.E.Bond	New Zealand v Australia	Port Elizabeth	2002-03
6-24	Imran Tahir	South Africa v Zimbabwe	Bloemfontein	2018-19
6-25	S.B.Styris	New Zealand v West Indies	Port of Spain	2002
6-25	W.P.J.U.C.Vaas	Sri Lanka v Bangladesh	Pietermaritzburg	2002-03
6-25	Kuldeep Yadav	India v England	Nottingham	2018
6-26	Waqar Younis	Pakistan v Sri Lanka	Sharjah	1989-90

6-26	Mashrafe Mortaza	Bangladesh v Kenya	Nairobi	2006
6-26	Rubel Hossain	Bangladesh v New Zealand	Dhaka	2013-14
6-26	Yasir Shah	Pakistan v Zimbabwe	Harare	2015-16
6-27	Naved-ul-Hasan	Pakistan v India	Jamshedpur	2004-05
6-27	C.R.D.Fernando	Sri Lanka v England	Colombo (RPS)	2007-08
6-27	M.Kartik	India v Australia	Mumbai	2007-08
6-27	K.A.J.Roach	West Indies v Netherlands	Delhi	2010-11
6-27	S.P.Narine	West Indies v South Africa	Providence	2016
6-28	H.K.Olonga	Zimbabwe v Kenya	Bulawayo	2002-03
6-28	J.H.Davey	Scotland v Afghanistan	Abu Dhabi	2014-15
6-28	M.A.Starc	Australia v New Zealand	Auckland	2014-15
6-29	B.P.Patterson	West Indies v India	Nagpur	1987-88
6-29	S.T.Jayasuriya	Sri Lanka v England	Moratuwa	1992-93
6-29	B.A.W.Mendis	Sri Lanka v Zimbabwe	Harare	2008-09
6-29	M.K.P.A.D.Perera	Sri Lanka v South Africa	Colombo (RPS)	2018
6-30	Waqar Younis	Pakistan v New Zealand	Auckland	1993-94
6-31	P.D.Collingwood	England v Bangladesh	Nottingham	2005
6-31	M.G.Johnson	Australia v Sri Lanka	Pallekele	2011
6-33	T.A.Boult	New Zealand v Australia	Hamilton	2016-17
6-34	Zahoor Khan	UAE v Ireland	Dubai (ICCA)	2016-17
6-35	S.M.Pollock	South Africa v West Indies	East London	1998-99
6-35	Abdul Razzaq	Pakistan v Bangladesh	Dhaka	2001-02

The best figures for Ireland are 6-55 by P.R.Stirling (v Afg, Greater Noida, 2016-17).

HAT-TRICKS

Jalaluddin	Pakistan v Australia	Hyderabad	1982-83
B.A.Reid	Australia v New Zealand	Sydney	1985-86
C.Sharma	India v New Zealand	Nagpur	1987-88
Wasim Akram	Pakistan v West Indies	Sharjah	1989-90
Wasim Akram	Pakistan v Australia	Sharjah	1989-90
Kapil Dev	India v Sri Lanka	Calcutta	1990-91
Aqib Javed	Pakistan v India	Sharjah	1991-92
D.K.Morrison	New Zealand v India	Napier	1993-94
Waqar Younis	Pakistan v New Zealand	East London	1994-95
Saqlain Mushtaq	Pakistan v Zimbabwe	Peshawar	1996-97
E.A.Brandes	Zimbabwe v England	Harare	1996-97
A.M.Stuart	Australia v Pakistan	Melbourne	1996-97
Saqlain Mushtaq	Pakistan v Zimbabwe	The Oval	1999
W.P.J.U.C.Vaas	Sri Lanka v Zimbabwe	Colombo (SSC)	2001-02
Mohammad Sami	Pakistan v West Indies	Sharjah	2001-02
W.P.J.U.C.Vaas[1]	Sri Lanka v Bangladesh	Pietermaritzburg	2002-03
B.Lee	Australia v Kenya	Durban	2002-03
J.M.Anderson	England v Pakistan	The Oval	2003
S.J.Harmison	England v India	Nottingham	2004
C.K.Langeveldt	South Africa v West Indies	Bridgetown	2004-05
Shahadat Hossain	Bangladesh v Zimbabwe	Harare	2006
J.E.Taylor	West Indies v Australia	Mumbai	2006-07
S.E.Bond	New Zealand v Australia	Hobart	2006-07
S.L.Malinga[2]	Sri Lanka v South Africa	Providence	2006-07
A.Flintoff	England v West Indies	St Lucia	2008-09
M.F.Maharoof	Sri Lanka v India	Dambulla	2010
Abdur Razzak	Bangladesh v Zimbabwe	Dhaka	2010-11
K.A.J.Roach	West Indies v Netherlands	Delhi	2010-11
S.L.Malinga	Sri Lanka v Kenya	Colombo (RPS)	2010-11
S.L.Malinga	Sri Lanka v Australia	Colombo (RPS)	2011
D.T.Christian	Australia v Sri Lanka	Melbourne	2011-12
N.L.T.C.Perera	Sri Lanka v Pakistan	Colombo (RPS)	2012
C.J.McKay	Australia v England	Cardiff	2013
Rubel Hossain	Bangladesh v New Zealand	Dhaka	2013-14
P.Utseya	Zimbabwe v South Africa	Harare	2014
Taijul Islam	Bangladesh v Zimbabwe	Dhaka	2014-15
S.T.Finn	England v Australia	Melbourne	2014-15
J.P.Duminy	South Africa v Sri Lanka	Sydney	2014-15

K.Rabada	South Africa v Bangladesh	Mirpur	2015		
J.P.Faulkner	Australia v Sri Lanka	Colombo (RPS)	2016		
Taskin Ahmed	Bangladesh v Sri Lanka	Dambulla	2016-17		
P.W.H.de Silva	Sri Lanka v Zimbabwe	Galle	2017		
Kuldeep Yadav	India v Australia	Kolkata	2017-18		
D.S.K.Madushanka	Sri Lanka v Bangladesh	Dhaka	2017-18		
Imran Tahir	South Africa v Zimbabwe	Bloemfontein	2018-19		
T.A.Boult	New Zealand v Pakistan	Abu Dhabi	2018-19		

[1] The first three balls of the match. Took four wickets in opening over (W W W 4 wide W 0).
[2] Four wickets in four balls.

WICKET-KEEPING RECORDS
150 DISMISSALS IN A CAREER

Total			LOI	Ct	St
482†‡	K.C.Sangakkara	Sri Lanka/Asia/ICC	360	384	98
472‡	A.C.Gilchrist	Australia/ICC	287	417	55
432	M.S.Dhoni	India/Asia	339	312	120
424	M.V.Boucher	South Africa/Africa	295	402	22
287‡	Moin Khan	Pakistan	219	214	73
242†‡	B.B.McCullum	New Zealand	185	227	15
233	I.A.Healy	Australia	168	194	39
220‡	Rashid Latif	Pakistan	166	182	38
206‡	R.S.Kaluwitharana	Sri Lanka	187	131	75
204‡	P.J.L.Dujon	West Indies	169	183	21
204	Mushfiqur Rahim	Bangladesh	201	162	42
189	R.D.Jacobs	West Indies	147	160	29
188	D.Ramdin	West Indies	139	181	7
187	Kamran Akmal	Pakistan	154	156	31
183	J.C.Buttler	England	127	155	28
181	B.J.Haddin	Australia	126	170	11
165	D.J.Richardson	South Africa	122	148	17
165†‡	A.Flower	Zimbabwe	213	133	32
163†‡	A.J.Stewart	England	170	148	15
154‡	N.R.Mongia	India	140	110	44
152	Q.de Kock	South Africa	102	144	8

† Excluding catches taken in the field. ‡ Excluding matches when not wicket-keeper.
The most for Ireland is 96 by N.J.O'Brien (103 matches) and for Afghanistan 82 by Mohammad Shahzad (77).

SIX DISMISSALS IN AN INNINGS

6	(6ct)	A.C.Gilchrist	Australia v South Africa	Cape Town	1999-00
6	(6ct)	A.J.Stewart	England v Zimbabwe	Manchester	2000
6	(5ct/1st)	R.D.Jacobs	West Indies v Sri Lanka	Colombo (RPS)	2001-02
6	(6ct)	A.C.Gilchrist	Australia v England	Sydney	2002-03
6	(6ct)	A.C.Gilchrist	Australia v Namibia	Potchefstroom	2002-03
6	(6ct)	A.C.Gilchrist	Australia v Sri Lanka	Colombo (RPS)	2003-04
6	(6ct)	M.V.Boucher	South Africa v Pakistan	Cape Town	2006-07
6	(5ct/1st)	M.S.Dhoni	India v England	Leeds	2007
6	(6ct)	A.C.Gilchrist	Australia v India	Baroda	2007-08
6	(5ct/1st)	A.C.Gilchrist	Australia v India	Sydney	2007-08
6	(6ct)	M.J.Prior	England v South Africa	Nottingham	2008
6	(6ct)	J.C.Buttler	England v South Africa	The Oval	2013
6	(6ct)	M.H.Cross	Scotland v Canada	Christchurch	2013-14
6	(5ct/1st)	Q.de Kock	South Africa v New Zealand	Mt Maunganui	2014-15
6	(6ct)	Sarfraz Ahmed	Pakistan v South Africa	Auckland	2014-15

FIELDING RECORDS

100 CATCHES IN A CAREER

Total			LOI		Total			LOI
218	D.P.M.D.Jayawardena	Sri Lanka/Asia	448		118	T.M.Dilshan	Sri Lanka	330
160	R.T.Ponting	Australia/ICC	375		113	Inzamam-ul-Haq	Pakistan/Asia	378
156	M.Azharuddin	India	334		111	S.R.Waugh	Australia	325
140	S.R.Tendulkar	India	463		109	R.S.Mahanama	Sri Lanka	213
137	L.R.P.L.Taylor	New Zealand	218		108	P.D.Collingwood	England	197
133	S.P.Fleming	New Zealand/ICC	280		108	V.Kohli	India	223
131	J.H.Kallis	South Africa/Africa/ICC	328		108	M.E.Waugh	Australia	244
130	Younus Khan	Pakistan	265		108	H.H.Gibbs	South Africa	248
130	M.Muralitharan	Sri Lanka/Asia/ICC	350		108	S.M.Pollock	South Africa/Africa/ICC	303
127	A.R.Border	Australia	273		106	M.J.Clarke	Australia	245
127	Shahid Afridi	Pakistan/Asia/ICC	398		105	M.E.K.Hussey	Australia	185
124	R.S.Dravid	India/Asia/ICC	344		105	G.C.Smith	South Africa/Africa	197
123	S.T.Jayasuriya	Sri Lanka/Asia	445		105	J.N.Rhodes	South Africa	245
120	C.L.Hooper	West Indies	227		102	S.K.Raina	India	226
120	C.H.Gayle	West Indies/ICC	289		100	I.V.A.Richards	West Indies	187
120	B.C.Lara	West Indies/ICC	299		100	S.C.Ganguly	India/Asia	311

The most for Zimbabwe is 86 by G.W.Flower (221), for Bangladesh 57 by Mahmudullah (171) and Mashrafe Mortaza (203), for Ireland 59 by W.T.S.Porterfield (124), and for Afghanistan 50 by Mohammad Nabi (108).

FIVE CATCHES IN AN INNINGS

5	J.N.Rhodes	South Africa v West Indies	Bombay (BS)	1993-94

APPEARANCE RECORDS

250 MATCHES

463	S.R.Tendulkar	India		295	M.V.Boucher	South Africa/Africa
448	D.P.M.D.Jayawardena	Sri Lanka/Asia		295	D.L.Vettori	New Zealand/ICC
445	S.T.Jayasuriya	Sri Lanka/Asia		289	C.H.Gayle	West Indies/ICC
404	K.C.Sangakkara	Sri Lanka/Asia/ICC		288	Mohammad Yousuf	Pakistan/Asia
398	Shahid Afridi	Pakistan/Asia/ICC		287	A.C.Gilchrist	Australia/ICC
378	Inzamam-ul-Haq	Pakistan/Asia		283	Salim Malik	Pakistan
375	R.T.Ponting	Australia/ICC		280	S.P.Fleming	New Zealand/ICC
356	Wasim Akram	Pakistan		279	Shoaib Malik	Pakistan
350	M.Muralitharan	Sri Lanka/Asia/ICC		273	A.R.Border	Australia
344	R.S.Dravid	India/Asia/ICC		271	A.Kumble	India/Asia
339	M.S.Dhoni	India/Asia		269	A.Ranatunga	Sri Lanka
334	M.Azharuddin	India		268	M.S.Atapattu	Sri Lanka
330	T.M.Dilshan	Sri Lanka		268	S.Chanderpaul	West Indies
328	J.H.Kallis	South Africa/Africa/ICC		265	Abdul Razzaq	Pakistan/Asia
325	S.R.Waugh	Australia		265	Younus Khan	Pakistan
322	W.P.J.U.C.Vaas	Sri Lanka/Asia		262	Waqar Younis	Pakistan
311	S.C.Ganguly	India/Asia		260	B.B.McCullum	New Zealand
308	P.A.de Silva	Sri Lanka		251	V.Sehwag	India/Asia/ICC
304	Yuvraj Singh	India/Asia		250	C.Z.Harris	New Zealand
303	S.M.Pollock	South Africa/Africa/ICC		250	Ijaz Ahmed	Pakistan
299	B.C.Lara	West Indies/ICC		250	G.D.McGrath	Australia/ICC

The most for England is 197 by P.D.Collingwood, for Zimbabwe 221 by G.W.Flower, for Bangladesh 203 by Mohammad Ashraful, for Ireland 130 by K.J.O'Brien, and for Afghanistan 108 by Mohammad Nabi.

The most consecutive appearances is 185 by S.R.Tendulkar for India (Apr 1990-Apr 1998).

100 MATCHES AS CAPTAIN

LOI			W	L	T	NR	% Won (exc NR)
230	R.T.Ponting	Australia/ICC	165	51	2	12	75.68
218	S.P.Fleming	New Zealand	98	106	1	13	47.80
200	M.S.Dhoni	India	110	74	5	11	58.20
193	A.Ranatunga	Sri Lanka	89	95	1	8	48.10
178	A.R.Border	Australia	107	67	1	3	61.14
174	M.Azharuddin	India	90	76	2	6	53.57
150	G.C.Smith	South Africa/Africa	92	51	1	6	63.88
147	S.C.Ganguly	India/Asia	76	66	–	5	53.52
139	Imran Khan	Pakistan	75	59	1	4	55.55
138	W.J.Cronje	South Africa	99	35	1	3	73.33
129	D.P.M.D.Jayawardena	Sri Lanka	71	49	1	8	58.67
125	B.C.Lara	West Indies	59	59	–	7	50.42
118	S.T.Jayasuriya	Sri Lanka	66	47	2	3	57.39
109	Wasim Akram	Pakistan	66	41	2	–	60.55
106	A.D.Mathews	Sri Lanka	49	51	1	5	48.51
106	S.R.Waugh	Australia	67	35	3	1	63.80
105	I.V.A.Richards	West Indies	67	36	–	2	65.04
103	A.B.de Villers	South Africa	59	39	1	4	59.59
101	W.T.S.Porterfield	Ireland	44	49	2	6	46.31

The most for England is 95 by A.N.Cook, for Zimbabwe 86 by A.D.R.Campbell, for Bangladesh 73 by Mashrafe Mortaza, and for Afghanistan 53 by Asghar Afghan.

150 LOI UMPIRING APPEARANCES

209	R.E.Koertzen	South Africa	09.12.1992	to	09.06.2010
200	B.F.Bowden	New Zealand	23.03.1995	to	06.02.2016
196	Alim Dar	Pakistan	16.02.2000	to	11.12.2018
181	S.A.Bucknor	West Indies	18.03.1989	to	29.03.2009
174	D.J.Harper	Australia	14.01.1994	to	19.03.2011
174	S.J.A.Taufel	Australia	13.01.1999	to	02.09.2012
172	D.R.Shepherd	England	09.06.1983	to	12.07.2005
154	R.B.Tiffin	Zimbabwe	25.10.1992	to	22.07.2018

ICC CRICKET WORLD CUP RECORDS

Previous winners:

1975	West Indies	1979	West Indies
1983	India	1987-88	Australia
1991-92	Pakistan	1995-96	Sri Lanka
1999	Australia	2002-03	Australia
2006-07	Australia	2010-11	India
2014-15	Australia		

TEAM RECORDS
HIGHEST TOTALS

417-6 (50)	Australia v Afghanistan	Perth	2014-15
413-5 (50)	India v Bermuda	Port of Spain	2006-07
411-4 (50)	South Africa v Ireland	Canberra	2014-15
408-5 (50)	South Africa v West Indies	Sydney	2014-15

England's highest score is 338-8 (50; v India, Bengalaru, 2010-11)

LOWEST TOTALS

36 (18.4)	Canada v Sri Lanka	Paarl	2002-03
45 (40.3)	Canada v England	Manchester	1979
45 (14)	Namibia v Australia	Potchefstroom	2002-03

England's lowest score is 93 (36.2; v Australia, Leeds, 1975)

LARGEST MARGINS OF VICTORY

275 runs	Australia (417-6) v Afghanistan (142)	Perth	2014-15
257 runs	India (413-5) v Bermuda (156)	Port of Spain	2006-07
257 runs	South Africa (408-5) v West Indies (151)	Sydney	2014-15
256 runs	Australia (301-6) v Namibia (45)	Potchefstroom	2002-03

There have been 11 victories in World Cup history by ten wickets.

BATTING RECORDS
MOST RUNS IN WORLD CUP MATCHES

2278 (ave 56.95)	S.R.Tendulkar	India	1992-2011
1743 (ave 45.86)	R.T.Ponting	Australia	1996-2011
1532 (ave 56.74)	K.C.Sangakkara	Sri Lanka	2003-2015

MOST RUNS IN A WORLD CUP TOURNAMENT

673 (ave 61.18)	S.R.Tendulkar	India	2002-03
659 (ave 73.22)	M.L.Hayden	Australia	2006-07

HIGHEST SCORES

237*	M.J.Guptill	New Zealand v West Indies	Wellington	2014-15
215	C.H.Gayle	West Indies v Zimbabwe	Canberra	2014-15
188*	G.Kirsten	South Africa v UAE	Rawalpindi	1995-96
183	S.C.Ganguly	India v Sri Lanka	Taunton	1999
181	I.V.A.Richards	West Indies v Sri Lanka	Karachi	1987-88

The highest score for England is 158 by A.J.Strauss (v India, Bengalaru, 2010-11)

FASTEST HUNDRED

51 balls	G.J.Maxwell (102)	Australia v Sri Lanka	Sydney	2014-15

MOST SIXES IN AN INNINGS

16	C.H.Gayle (215)	West Indies v Zimbabwe	Canberra	2014-15

HIGHEST PARTNERSHIP FOR EACH WICKET

1st	282	W.U.Tharanga/T.M.Dilshan	Sri Lanka v Zimbabwe	Pallekele	2010-11
2nd	372	C.H.Gayle/M.N.Samuels	West Indies v Zimbabwe	Canberra	2014-15
3rd	237*	R.S.Dravid/S.R.Tendulkar	India v Kenya	Bristol	1999
4th	204	M.J.Clarke/B.J.Hodge	Australia v Netherlands	Basseterre	2006-07
5th	256*	D.A.Miller/J.P.Duminy	South Africa v Zimbabwe	Hamilton	2014-15
6th	162	K.J.O'Brien/A.P.Cusack	Ireland v England	Bengalaru	2010-11
7th	107	Shaiman Anwar/Amjad Javed	UAE v Ireland	Brisbane	2014-15
7th	107	Amjad Javed/Nasir Aziz	UAE v West Indies	Napier	2014-15
8th	117	D.L.Houghton/I.P.Butchart	Zimbabwe v New Zealand	Hyderabad	1987-88
9th	126*	Kapil Dev/S.M.H.Kirmani	India v Zimbabwe	Tunbridge Wells	1983
10th	71	A.M.E.Roberts/J.Garner	West Indies v India	Manchester	1983

BOWLING RECORDS – MOST WICKETS IN WORLD CUP MATCHES

71 (ave 18.19)	G.D.McGrath	Australia	1996-2007
68 (ave 19.63)	M.Muralitharan	Sri Lanka	1996-2011
55 (ave 23.83)	Wasim Akram	Pakistan	1987-2003

MOST WICKETS IN A WORLD CUP TOURNAMENT

26 (ave 13.73)	G.D.McGrath	Australia	2006-07
23 (ave 14.39)	W.P.J.U.C.Vaas	Sri Lanka	2002-03
23 (ave 15.26)	M.Muralitharan	Sri Lanka	2006-07
23 (ave 20.30)	S.W.Tait	Australia	2006-07

BEST BOWLING FIGURES IN AN INNINGS

7-15	G.D.McGrath	Australia v Namibia	Potchefstroom	2002-03
7-20	A.J.Bichel	Australia v England	Port Elizabeth	2002-03
7-33	T.G.Southee	New Zealand v England	Wellington	2014-15
7-51	W.W.Davis	West Indies v Australia	Leeds	1983

The best figures for England are 5-39 by V.J.Marks (v Sri Lanka, Taunton, 1983)

MOST ECONOMICAL BOWLING ANALYSIS (Min 10 overs)

O	M	R	W				
12	8	6	1	B.S.Bedi	India v East Africa	Leeds	1975
10	5	8	4	C.M.Old	England v Canada	Manchester	1979
10	4	8	2	C.E.L.Ambrose	West Indies v Scotland	Leicester	1999

MOST EXPENSIVE BOWLING ANALYSIS

O	M	R	W				
12	1	105	2	M.C.Snedden	New Zealand v England	The Oval	1983
10	2	104	1	J.O.Holder	West Indies v South Africa	Sydney	2014-15
10	1	101	2	Dawlat Zadran	Afghanistan v Australia	Perth	2014-15

WICKET-KEEPING RECORDS – MOST DISMISSALS IN WORLD CUP MATCHES

54 (41ct, 13st)	K.C.Sangakkara	Sri Lanka	2003-2015
52 (45ct, 7st)	A.C.Gilchrist	Australia	1999-2007

MOST DISMISSALS IN AN INNINGS

6 (6ct)	A.C.Gilchrist	Australia v Namibia	Potchefstroom	2002-03
6 (6ct)	Sarfraz Ahmed	Pakistan v South Africa	Auckland	2001-15

FIELDING RECORDS – MOST CATCHES IN WORLD CUP MATCHES

28	R.T.Ponting	Australia	1996-2011
18	S.T.Jayasuriya	Sri Lanka	1992-2007

MOST CATCHES IN AN INNINGS

4	M.Kaif	India v Sri Lanka	Johannesburg	2002-03
4	Soumya Sarkar	Bangladesh v Scotland	Nelson	2014-15
4	Umar Akmal	Pakistan v Ireland	Adelaide	2014-15

ENGLAND TWENTY20 INTERNATIONALS CAREER RECORDS

These records, complete to 4 April 2019, include all players registered for county cricket for the 2019 season at the time of going to press.

BATTING AND FIELDING

	M	I	NO	HS	Runs	Avge	100	50	Ct/St
M.M.Ali	25	22	6	72*	235	14.68	–	1	7
T.R.Ambrose	1	–	–	–	–	–	–	–	1/1
J.M.Anderson	19	4	3	1*	1	1.00	–	–	3
J.M.Bairstow	30	25	6	68	513	27.00	–	3	24/2
J.T.Ball	2	–	–	–	–	–	–	–	1
G.J.Batty	1	1	–	4	4	4.00	–	–	–
I.R.Bell	8	8	1	60*	188	26.85	–	1	4
S.W.Billings†	20	17	–	87	310	18.23	–	2	13/1
R.S.Bopara	38	35	10	65*	711	28.44	–	3	7
S.G.Borthwick	1	1	–	14	14	14.00	–	–	1
T.T.Bresnan	34	22	9	47*	216	16.61	–	–	10
D.R.Briggs	7	1	1	0*	0	–	–	–	1
S.C.J.Broad	56	26	10	18*	118	7.37	–	–	21
J.C.Buttler	66	58	11	73*	1260	26.80	–	7	23/4
A.N.Cook	4	4	–	26	61	15.25	–	–	1
M.S.Crane	2	–	–	–	–	–	–	–	–
T.K.Curran	10	4	3	6	10	10.00	–	–	1
S.M.Davies	5	5	–	33	102	20.40	–	–	2/1
L.A.Dawson	6	2	1	10	17	17.00	–	–	2
J.L.Denly	9	8	–	30	72	9.00	–	–	2
J.W.Dernbach	34	7	2	12	24	4.80	–	–	8
S.T.Finn	21	3	3	8*	14	–	–	–	6
H.F.Gurney	2	–	–	–	–	–	–	–	–
A.D.Hales	60	60	7	116*	1664	31.01	1	8	32
C.J.Jordan	38	23	10	27*	168	12.92	–	–	21
L.S.Livingstone	2	2	–	16	16	8.00	–	–	–
D.J.Malan	5	5	–	78	250	50.00	–	4	1
S.C.Meaker	2	–	–	–	–	–	–	–	1
T.S.Mills†	4	1	–	0	0	0.00	–	–	1
E.J.G.Morgan	80	78	15	85*	1753	27.82	–	9	35
S.D.Parry	5	1	–	1	1	1.00	–	–	2
S.R.Patel	18	14	2	67	189	15.75	–	1	3
L.E.Plunkett	22	11	4	18	42	6.00	–	–	7
A.U.Rashid	36	14	8	9*	47	7.83	–	–	10
J.E.Root	31	29	5	90*	846	35.25	–	5	18
J.J.Roy	32	32	–	78	743	23.21	–	4	5
B.A.Stokes	23	20	5	38	232	15.46	–	–	9
M.E.Trescothick	3	3	–	72	166	55.33	–	2	2
J.M.Vince	7	7	–	46	194	27.71	–	–	4
D.J.Willey	27	19	7	29*	166	13.83	–	–	11
C.R.Woakes	8	7	4	37	91	30.33	–	–	1
M.A.Wood	5	2	2	5*	10	–	–	–	–
L.J.Wright	51	45	5	99*	759	18.97	–	4	14

BOWLING

	O	M	R	W	Avge	Best	4wI	R/Over
M.M.Ali	60.2	0	519	15	34.60	2-21	–	8.60
J.M.Anderson	70.2	1	552	18	30.66	3-23	–	7.84
J.T.Ball	7	0	83	2	41.50	1-39	–	11.85
G.J.Batty	3	0	17	0	–	–	–	5.66
R.S.Bopara	53.4	1	387	16	24.18	4-10	1	7.21
S.G.Borthwick	4	0	15	1	15.00	1-15	–	3.75
T.T.Bresnan	110.3	1	887	24	36.95	3-10	–	8.02
D.R.Briggs	18	0	199	5	39.80	2-25	–	11.05
S.C.J.Broad	195.3	2	1491	65	22.93	4-24	1	7.62
M.S.Crane	8	0	62	1	62.00	1-38	–	7.75
T.K.Curran	31	0	280	11	25.45	4-36	1	9.03
L.A.Dawson	20	0	152	5	30.40	3-27	–	7.60
J.L.Denly	10	0	70	7	10.00	4-19	1	7.00
J.W.Dernbach	117	1	1020	39	26.15	4-22	1	8.71
S.T.Finn	80	0	583	27	21.59	3-16	–	7.28
H.F.Gurney	8	0	55	3	18.33	2-26	–	6.87
C.J.Jordan	134.4	0	1156	46	25.13	4- 6	2	8.58
D.J.Malan	2	0	27	1	27.00	1-27	–	13.50
S.C.Meaker	7.5	0	70	2	35.00	1-28	–	8.93
T.S.Mills	16	0	116	3	38.66	1-27	–	7.25
S.D.Parry	16	0	138	3	46.00	2-33	–	8.62
S.R.Patel	42	0	321	7	45.85	2- 6	–	7.64
L.E.Plunkett	79.2	1	627	25	25.08	3-21	–	7.90
A.U.Rashid	118	1	863	36	23.97	3-11	–	7.31
J.E.Root	14	0	139	6	23.16	2- 9	–	9.92
B.A.Stokes	55.4	1	496	10	49.60	3-26	–	8.91
D.J.Willey	89.5	0	736	34	21.64	4- 7	1	8.19
C.R.Woakes	27	0	253	7	36.14	2-40	–	9.37
M.A.Wood	17.3	0	148	11	13.45	3- 9	–	8.45
L.J.Wright	55	0	465	18	25.83	2-24	–	8.45

† S.W.Billings and T.S.Mills also played one game for an ICC World XI v West Indies at Lord's in 2018.

INTERNATIONAL TWENTY20 RECORDS

MATCH RESULTS

2004-05 to 14 March 2019

	Opponents	Matches	E	A	SA	WI	NZ	I	P	SL	Z	B	Ire	Afg	Ass	Tied	NR
England	Australia	16	6	9	–	–	–	–	–	–	–	–	–	–	–	–	1
	South Africa	15	6	–	8	–	–	–	–	–	–	–	–	–	–	–	1
	West Indies	18	7	–	–	11	–	–	–	–	–	–	–	–	–	–	–
	New Zealand	16	10	–	–	–	5	–	–	–	–	–	–	–	–	–	1
	India	14	7	–	–	–	–	7	–	–	–	–	–	–	–	–	–
	Pakistan	14	9	–	–	–	–	–	4	–	–	–	–	–	–	1	–
	Sri Lanka	9	5	–	–	–	–	–	–	4	–	–	–	–	–	–	–
	Zimbabwe	1	1	–	–	–	–	–	–	–	0	–	–	–	–	–	–
	Bangladesh	0	0	–	–	–	–	–	–	–	–	0	–	–	–	–	–
	Ireland	1	0	–	–	–	–	–	–	–	–	–	0	–	–	–	1
	Afghanistan	2	2	–	–	–	–	–	–	–	–	–	–	0	–	–	–
	Associates	2	0	–	–	–	–	–	–	–	–	–	–	–	2	–	–
Australia	South Africa	18	–	11	7	–	–	–	–	–	–	–	–	–	–	–	–
	West Indies	11	–	5	–	6	–	–	–	–	–	–	–	–	–	–	–
	New Zealand	9	–	7	–	–	1	–	–	–	–	–	–	–	–	1	–
	India	20	–	8	–	–	–	11	–	–	–	–	–	–	–	–	1
	Pakistan	20	–	7	–	–	–	–	12	–	–	–	–	–	–	1	–
	Sri Lanka	13	–	5	–	–	–	–	–	8	–	–	–	–	–	–	–
	Zimbabwe	3	–	2	–	–	–	–	–	–	1	–	–	–	–	–	–
	Bangladesh	4	–	4	–	–	–	–	–	–	–	0	–	–	–	–	–
	Ireland	1	–	1	–	–	–	–	–	–	–	–	0	–	–	–	–
	Afghanistan	0	–	0	–	–	–	–	–	–	–	–	–	0	–	–	–
	Associates	1	–	1	–	–	–	–	–	–	–	–	–	–	0	–	–
S Africa	West Indies	10	–	–	6	4	–	–	–	–	–	–	–	–	–	–	–
	New Zealand	15	–	–	11	–	4	–	–	–	–	–	–	–	–	–	–
	India	13	–	–	5	–	–	8	–	–	–	–	–	–	–	–	–
	Pakistan	14	–	–	8	–	–	–	6	–	–	–	–	–	–	–	–
	Sri Lanka	10	–	–	5	–	–	–	–	5	–	–	–	–	–	–	–
	Zimbabwe	5	–	–	5	–	–	–	–	–	0	–	–	–	–	–	–
	Bangladesh	6	–	–	6	–	–	–	–	–	–	0	–	–	–	–	–
	Ireland	0	–	–	0	–	–	–	–	–	–	–	0	–	–	–	–
	Afghanistan	2	–	–	2	–	–	–	–	–	–	–	–	0	–	–	–
	Associates	2	–	–	2	–	–	–	–	–	–	–	–	–	0	–	–
W Indies	New Zealand	13	–	–	–	3	6	–	–	–	–	–	–	–	–	3	1
	India	11	–	–	–	5	–	5	–	–	–	–	–	–	–	–	1
	Pakistan	14	–	–	–	3	–	–	11	–	–	–	–	–	–	–	–
	Sri Lanka	9	–	–	–	3	–	–	–	6	–	–	–	–	–	–	–
	Zimbabwe	3	–	–	–	2	–	–	–	–	1	–	–	–	–	–	–
	Bangladesh	12	–	–	–	6	–	–	–	–	–	5	–	–	–	–	1
	Ireland	4	–	–	–	2	–	–	–	–	–	–	1	–	–	–	1
	Afghanistan	4	–	–	–	3	–	–	–	–	–	–	–	1	–	–	–
	Associates	0	–	–	–	0	–	–	–	–	–	–	–	–	0	–	–
N Zealand	India	11	–	–	–	–	8	3	–	–	–	–	–	–	–	–	–
	Pakistan	21	–	–	–	–	8	–	13	–	–	–	–	–	–	–	–
	Sri Lanka	16	–	–	–	–	8	–	–	6	–	–	–	–	–	1	1
	Zimbabwe	6	–	–	–	–	6	–	–	–	0	–	–	–	–	–	–
	Bangladesh	7	–	–	–	–	7	–	–	–	–	0	–	–	–	–	–
	Ireland	1	–	–	–	–	1	–	–	–	–	–	0	–	–	–	–
	Afghanistan	0	–	–	–	–	0	–	–	–	–	–	–	0	–	–	–
	Associates	3	–	–	–	–	3	–	–	–	–	–	–	–	0	–	–
India	Pakistan	8	–	–	–	–	–	6	1	–	–	–	–	–	–	1	–
	Sri Lanka	16	–	–	–	–	–	11	–	5	–	–	–	–	–	–	–
	Zimbabwe	7	–	–	–	–	–	5	–	–	2	–	–	–	–	–	–
	Bangladesh	8	–	–	–	–	–	8	–	–	–	0	–	–	–	–	–
	Ireland	3	–	–	–	–	–	3	–	–	–	–	0	–	–	–	–
	Afghanistan	2	–	–	–	–	–	2	–	–	–	–	–	0	–	–	–
	Associates	2	–	–	–	–	–	1	–	–	–	–	–	–	0	–	1

Opponents		Matches	E	A	SA	WI	NZ	I	Won P	SL	Z	B	Ire	Afg	Ass	Tied	NR
Pakistan	Sri Lanka	18	–	–	–	–	–	–	13	5	–	–	–	–	–	–	–
	Zimbabwe	11	–	–	–	–	–	–	11	–	0	–	–	–	–	–	–
	Bangladesh	10	–	–	–	–	–	–	8	–	–	2	–	–	–	–	–
	Ireland	1	–	–	–	–	–	–	1	–	–	–	0	–	–	–	–
	Afghanistan	1	–	–	–	–	–	–	1	–	–	–	–	0	–	–	–
	Associates	7	–	–	–	–	–	–	7	–	–	–	–	–	0	–	–
Sri Lanka	Zimbabwe	3	–	–	–	–	–	–	–	3	0	–	–	–	–	–	–
	Bangladesh	11	–	–	–	–	–	–	–	7	–	4	–	–	–	–	–
	Ireland	1	–	–	–	–	–	–	–	1	–	–	0	–	–	–	–
	Afghanistan	1	–	–	–	–	–	–	–	1	–	–	–	0	–	–	–
	Associates	4	–	–	–	–	–	–	–	4	–	–	–	–	0	–	–
Zimbabwe	Bangladesh	9	–	–	–	–	–	–	–	–	4	5	–	–	–	–	–
	Ireland	1	–	–	–	–	–	–	–	–	0	–	1	–	–	–	–
	Afghanistan	7	–	–	–	–	–	–	–	–	0	–	–	7	–	–	–
	Associates	6	–	–	–	–	–	–	–	–	5	–	–	–	0	1	–
Bangladesh	Ireland	5	–	–	–	–	–	–	–	–	–	3	1	–	–	–	1
	Afghanistan	4	–	–	–	–	–	–	–	–	–	1	–	3	–	–	–
	Associates	9	–	–	–	–	–	–	–	–	–	6	–	–	3	–	–
Ireland	Afghanistan	15	–	–	–	–	–	–	–	–	–	–	3	12	–	–	–
	Associates	42	–	–	–	–	–	–	–	–	–	–	23	–	15	1	3
Afghanistan	Associates	33	–	–	–	–	–	–	–	–	–	–	–	26	7	–	–
Associates	Associates	83	–	–	–	–	–	–	–	–	–	–	–	–	80	–	3
		748	**53**	**60**	**65**	**48**	**57**	**70**	**88**	**55**	**13**	**26**	**29**	**49**	**107**	**10**	**18**

MATCH RESULTS SUMMARY

	Matches	Won	Lost	Tied	NR	% Won (ex NR)
Afghanistan	71	49	22	0	0	69.01
Pakistan	139	88	48	3	0	63.30
India	115	70	41	1	3	62.50
South Africa	110	65	44	0	1	59.63
Australia	116	60	52	2	2	52.63
England	108	53	50	1	4	50.96
Sri Lanka	111	55	54	1	1	50.00
New Zealand	118	57	53	5	3	49.56
West Indies	109	48	54	3	4	45.71
Ireland	75	29	39	1	6	42.02
Bangladesh	85	26	57	0	2	31.32
Associates (v Full)	111	27	78	2	4	25.23
Zimbabwe	62	13	48	1	0	20.96

Results of games between two Associate Members and Pakistan's three IT20s v a World XI in 2017 (W2, L1) and West Indies' IT20 v an ICC World XI in 2018 (W1) are excluded from these figures.

INTERNATIONAL TWENTY20 RECORDS

(To 14 March 2019)

TEAM RECORDS

HIGHEST INNINGS TOTALS

† Batting Second

278-3	Afghanistan v Ireland	Dehradun	2018-19
263-3	Australia v Sri Lanka	Pallekele	2016
260-6	Sri Lanka v Kenya	Johannesburg	2007-08
260-5	India v Sri Lanka	Indore	2017-18
248-6	Australia v England	Southampton	2013
245-6	West Indies v India	Lauderhill	2016
245-5†	Australia v New Zealand	Auckland	2017-18
244-4†	India v West Indies	Lauderhill	2016

243-5	New Zealand v West Indies	Mt Maunganui	2017-18
243-6	New Zealand v Australia	Auckland	2017-18
241-6	South Africa v England	Centurion	2009-10
236-6†	West Indies v South Africa	Johannesburg	2014-15
233-8	Afghanistan v Ireland	Greater Noida	2016-17
231-7	South Africa v West Indies	Johannesburg	2014-15
230-8†	England v South Africa	Mumbai	2015-16
229-4	South Africa v England	Mumbai	2015-16
229-2	Australia v Zimbabwe	Harare	2018
225-7	Ireland v Afghanistan	Abu Dhabi	2013-14
224-4	South Africa v Bangladesh	Potchefstroom	2017-18
221-5	Australia v England	Sydney	2006-07
221-3	Scotland v Netherlands	Amstelveen	2018
221-5	England v Australia	Birmingham	2018

The highest total for Pakistan is 205-3 (v West Indies, Karachi, 2017-18), for Zimbabwe 200-2 (v New Zealand, Hamilton, 2011-12) and for Bangladesh is 215-5 (v Sri Lanka, Colombo (RPS), 2017-18).

LOWEST COMPLETED INNINGS TOTALS

† Batting Second

39 (10.3)	Netherlands v Sri Lanka	Chittagong	2013-14
45† (11.5)	West Indies v England	Basseterre	2018-19
53 (14.3)	Nepal v Ireland	Belfast	2015
56† (18.4)	Kenya v Afghanistan	Sharjah	2013-14
60† (15.3)	New Zealand v Sri Lanka	Chittagong	2013-14
60† (13.4)	West Indies v Pakistan	Karachi	2017-18
67 (17.2)	Kenya v Ireland	Belfast	2008
68† (16.4)	Ireland v West Indies	Providence	2009-10
69† (17.0)	Hong Kong v Nepal	Chittagong	2013-14
69† (17.4)	Nepal v Netherlands	Amstelveen	2015
70	Bermuda v Canada	Belfast	2008
70† (15.4)	Bangladesh v New Zealand	Kolkata	2015-16
70† (12.3)	Ireland v India	Dublin	2018
71 (19.0)	Kenya v Ireland	Dubai	2011-12
71 (13.2)	Ireland v Afghanistan	Dubai	2016-17
71 (13.0)	West Indies v England	Basseterre	2018-19
72 (17.1)	Afghanistan v Bangladesh	Dhaka	2013-14
72	Nepal v Hong Kong	Colombo (PSS)	2014-15
73 (16.5)	Kenya v New Zealand	Durban	2007-08
73† (16.4)	UAE v Netherlands	Dubai	2015-16
74 (17.3)	India v Australia	Melbourne	2007-08
74† (19.1)	Pakistan v Australia	Dubai	2012
75† (19.2)	Canada v Zimbabwe	King City (NW)	2008-09

The lowest total for England is 80 (v India, Colombo (RPS), 2012-13), for Australia 79 (v England, Southampton, 2005), for South Africa 98 (v Sri Lanka, Colombo (RPS), 2018), for Sri Lanka 82 (v India, Visakhapatnam, 2015-16), and for Zimbabwe 84 (v New Zealand, Providence, 2010).

LARGEST RUNS MARGIN OF VICTORY

172 runs	Sri Lanka beat Kenya	Johannesburg	2007
143 runs	Pakistan beat West Indies	Karachi	2017-18
143 runs	India beat Ireland	Dublin	2018
137 runs	England beat West Indies	Basseterre	2018-19
130 runs	South Africa beat Scotland	The Oval	2009

There have been 14 victories by ten wickets.

BATTING RECORDS
1500 RUNS IN A CAREER

Runs			M	I	NO	HS	Avge	50	R/100B
2331	R.G.Sharma	I	94	86	14	118	32.37	20	137.6
2272	M.J.Guptill	NZ	76	74	7	105	33.91	16	132.7
2263	V.Kohli	I	67	62	17	90*	50.28	20	137.4
2263	Shoaib Malik	P	111	104	30	75	30.58	7	124.0
2140	B.B.McCullum	NZ	71	70	10	123	35.66	15	136.2
1936	Mohammad Shahzad	Afg	65	65	3	118*	31.22	13	134.8
1908	Mohammad Hafeez	P	89	86	8	86	24.46	10	116.1
1889	T.M.Dilshan	SL	80	79	12	104*	28.19	14	120.5
1858	J.P.Duminy	SA	78	72	23	96*	37.91	11	124.3
1792	D.A.Warner	A	70	70	3	90*	26.74	13	140.1
1753	E.J.G.Morgan	E	80	78	15	85*	27.82	9	130.1
1690	Umar Akmal	P	82	77	14	94	26.82	8	122.9
1672	A.B.de Villiers	SA	78	75	11	79*	26.12	10	135.1
1671	A.J.Finch	A	52	52	7	172	37.13	11	155.8
1644	A.D.Hales	E	60	60	7	116*	31.01	9	136.6
1627	C.H.Gayle	WI	58	54	4	117	32.54	15	142.8
1617	M.S.Dhoni	I	98	85	42	56	37.60	2	126.1
1613	Tamim Iqbal	B/Wd	75	75	5	103*	23.04	7	116.6
1611	M.N.Samuels	WI	67	65	10	89*	29.29	10	116.2
1605	S.K.Raina	I	78	66	11	101	29.18	6	134.8
1579	L.R.P.L.Taylor	NZ	88	80	19	63	25.88	5	121.0
1516	H.Masakadza	Z	58	58	2	93*	27.07	10	117.0
1514	G.J.Maxwell	A	59	53	9	145*	34.40	9	158.2
1505	K.S.Williamson	NZ	57	55	7	73*	31.35	9	121.7

The most for Ireland is 1433 by P.R.Stirling (57 innings).

HIGHEST INDIVIDUAL INNINGS

Score	Balls				
172	76	A.J.Finch	A v Z	Harare	2018
162*	62	Hazratullah Zazai	Afg v Ire	Dehradun	2018-19
156	63	A.J.Finch	A v E	Southampton	2013
145*	65	G.J.Maxwell	A v SL	Pallekele	2016
125*	62	E.Lewis	WI v I	Kingston	2017
124*	71	S.R.Watson	A v I	Sydney	2015-16
123	58	B.B.McCullum	NZ v B	Pallekele	2012-13
122	60	Babar Hayat	HK v Oman	Fatullah	2015-16
119	56	F.du Plessis	SA v WI	Johannesburg	2014-15
118*	67	Mohammad Shahzad	Afg v Z	Sharjah	2015-16
118	43	R.G.Sharma	I v SL	Indore	2017-18
117*	51	R.E.Levi	SA v NZ	Hamilton	2011-12
117*	68	Shaiman Anwar	UAE v PNG	Abu Dhabi	2017
117	57	C.H.Gayle	WI v SA	Johannesburg	2007-08
116*	56	B.B.McCullum	NZ v A	Christchurch	2009-10
116*	64	A.D.Hales	E v SL	Chittagong	2013-14
114*	70	M.van Wyk	SA v WI	Durban	2014-15
113*	55	G.J.Maxwell	A v I	Bengalaru	2018-19
111*	62	Ahmed Shehzad	P v B	Dhaka	2013-14
111*	61	R.G.Sharma	I v WI	Lucknow	2018-19
110*	51	K.L.Rahul	I v WI	Lauderhill	2016
109*	58	C.Munro	NZ v I	Rajkot	2017-18
106	66	R.G.Sharma	I v SA	Dharamsala	2015-16
105	54	M.J.Guptill	NZ v A	Auckland	2017-18
104*	57	T.M.Dilshan	SL v A	Pallekele	2011
104	53	C.Munro	NZ v WI	Mt Maunganui	2017-18

103*	63	Tamim Iqbal	B v Oman	Dharmasala	2015-16
103*	58	G.J.Maxwell	A v E	Hobart	2017-18
103	59	R.Sandaruwan	Kuw v Bah	Al Amerat	2018-19
101*	69	M.J.Guptill	NZ v SA	East London	2012-13
101*	36	D.A.Miller	SA v B	Potchefstroom	2017-18
101*	54	K.L.Rahul	I v E	Manchester	2018
101	60	S.K.Raina	I v SA	Gros Islet	2009-10
101	54	C.Munro	NZ v B	Mt Maunganui	2016-17
100*	48	C.H.Gayle	WI v E	Mumbai	2015-16
100*	56	R.G.Sharma	I v E	Bristol	2018
100	64	D.P.M.D.Jayawardena	SL v Z	Providence	2009-10
100	58	R.D.Berrington	Sc v B	The Hague	2012
100	49	E.Lewis	WI v I	Lauderhill	2016

The highest score for Zimbabwe is 94 by S.F.Mire (v P, Harare, 2018) and for Ireland 91 by P.R.Stirling (v Afg, Dehradun, 2018-19).

MOST SIXES IN AN INNINGS

16	Hazratullah Zazai (162*)	Afg v Ire	Dehradun	2018-19
14	A.J.Finch (156)	A v E	Southampton	2013
13	R.E.Levi (117*)	SA v NZ	Hamilton	2011-12
12	E.Lewis (125*)	WI v I	Kingston	2017

HIGHEST PARTNERSHIP FOR EACH WICKET

1st	236	Hazratullah Zazai/Usmann Ghani	Afg v Ire	Dehradun	2018-19
2nd	166	D.P.M.D.Jayawardena/K.C.Sangakkara	SL v WI	Bridgetown	2009-10
3rd	152	A.D.Hales/E.J.G.Morgan	E v SL	Chittagong	2013-14
4th	161	D.A.Warner/G.J.Maxwell	A v SA	Johannesburg	2015-16
5th	119*	Shoaib Malik/Misbah-ul-Haq	P v A	Johannesburg	2007-08
6th	101*	C.L.White/M.E.K.Hussey	A v SL	Bridgetown	2009-10
7th	91	P.D.Collingwood/M.H.Yardy	E v WI	The Oval	2007
8th	80	P.L.Mommsen/S.M.Sharif	Sc v Ne	Edinburgh	2015
9th	66	D.J.Bravo/J.E.Taylor	WI v P	Dubai	2016-17
10th	38	Mohammad Adnan/Usman Ali	Saud v Qat	Al Amerat	2018-19

BOWLING RECORDS
55 WICKETS IN A CAREER

Wkts			Matches	Overs	Mdns	Runs	Avge	Best	R/Over
98	Shahid Afridi	P/Wd	99	361.2	4	2396	24.44	4-11	6.63
94	S.L.Malinga	SL	70	249.5	–	1834	19.51	5-31	7.34
88	Shakib Al Hasan	B	72	261.5	1	1775	20.17	5-20	6.77
85	Umar Gul	P	60	200.3	2	1443	16.97	5- 6	7.19
85	Saeed Ajmal	P	64	238.2	2	1516	17.83	4-19	6.36
75	Rashid Khan	Afg	38	144.0	1	867	11.56	5- 3	6.02
69	Mohammad Nabi	Afg	68	238.4	5	1705	24.71	4-10	7.14
67	T.G.Southee	NZ	58	204.0	2	1748	26.08	5-18	8.56
66	B.A.W.Mendis	SL	39	147.3	5	952	14.42	6- 8	6.45
66	K.M.D.N.Kulasekara	SL	58	205.1	6	1530	23.18	4-31	7.45
65	S.C.J.Broad	E	56	195.3	2	1491	22.93	4-24	7.62
63	G.H.Dockrell	Ire	60	187.4	1	1270	20.15	4-20	6.76
62	Imran Tahir	SA/Wd	37	136.5	–	927	14.95	5-23	6.77
58	D.W.Steyn	SA	42	150.1	2	1009	17.39	4- 9	6.71
58	K.J.O'Brien	Ire	73	150.3	–	1134	19.55	4-45	7.53
58	N.L.McCullum	NZ	63	187.1	–	1278	22.03	4-16	6.82
56	S.Badree	WI/Wd	52	191.0	4	1180	21.07	4-15	6.17
55	Mohammad Amir	P	42	156.0	5	1066	19.38	4-13	6.83

The most wickets for Australia is 48 by S.R.Watson (58 matches), for India 52 by R.Ashwin (46 matches) and for Zimbabwe 35 by A.G.Cremer (29 matches).

BEST FIGURES IN AN INNINGS

6- 8	B.A.W.Mendis	SL v Z	Hambantota	2012-13
6-16	B.A.W.Mendis	SL v A	Pallekele	2011
6-25	Y.S.Chahal	I v E	Bangalore	2016-17
5- 3	H.M.R.K.B.Herath	SL v NZ	Chittagong	2013-14
5- 3	Rashid Khan	Afg v Ire	Greater Noida	2016-17
5- 6	Umar Gul	P v NZ	The Oval	2009
5- 6	Umar Gul	P v SA	Centurion	2012-13
5-13	Elias Sunny	B v Ire	Belfast	2012
5-13	Samiullah Shenwari	Afg v Ken	Sharjah	2013-14
5-14	Imad Wasim	P v WI	Dubai	2016-17
5-15	K.M.A.Paul	WI v B	Dhaka	2018-19
5-18	T.G.Southee	NZ v P	Auckland	2010-11
5-19	R.McLaren	SA v WI	North Sound	2009-10
5-19	Ahsan Malik	Neth v SA	Chittagong	2013-14
5-20	N.Odhiambo	Ken v Sc	Nairobi (Gym)	2009-10
5-20	Shakib Al Hasan	B v WI	Dhaka	2018-19
5-22	Mustafizur Rahman	B v NZ	Kolkata	2015-16
5-23	D.Wiese	SA v WI	Durban	2014-15
5-23	Imran Tahir	SA v Z	East London	2018-19
5-24	A.C.Evans	Sc v Neth	Edinburgh	2015
5-24	Imran Tahir	SA v NZ	Auckland	2016-17
5-24	B.Kumar	I v SA	Johannesburg	2017-18
5-24	Kuldeep Yadav	I v E	Manchester	2018
5-24	Ibrahim Hassan	Mald v Bah	Al Amerat	2018-19

The best figures for England are 4-6 by C.J.Jordan (v WI, Basseterre, 2018-19), for Australia 5-27 by J.P.Faulkner (v P, Mohali, 2015-16), for Zimbabwe 4-28 by W.P.Masakadza (v Sc, Nagpur, 2015-16), and for Ireland 4-11 by A.R.Cusack (v WI, Kingston, 2013-14).

HAT-TRICKS

B.Lee	Australia v Bangladesh	Melbourne	2007-08
J.D.P.Oram	New Zealand v Sri Lanka	Colombo (RPS)	2009
T.G.Southee	New Zealand v Pakistan	Auckland	2010-11
N.L.T.C.Perera	Sri Lanka v India	Ranchi	2015-16
S.L.Malinga	Sri Lanka v Bangladesh	Colombo (RPS)	2016-17
Faheem Ashraf	Pakistan v Sri Lanka	Abu Dhabi	2017-18
Rashid Khan	Afghanistan v Ireland	Dehradun	2018-19

WICKET-KEEPING RECORDS
25 DISMISSALS IN A CAREER

Dis			Matches	Ct	St
91	M.S.Dhoni	India	89	57	34
60	Kamran Akmal	Pakistan	54	28	32
58	D.Ramdin	West Indies	68	38	20
58	Mushfiqur Rahim	Bangladesh	77	30	28
54	Mohammad Shahzad	Afghanistan	65	26	28
45	K.C.Sangakkara	Sri Lanka	56	25	20
44	Q.de Kock	South Africa	35	35	9
42	Sarfraz Ahmed	Pakistan	54	32	10
32†	B.B.McCullum	New Zealand	71	24	8
30‡	L.Ronchi	Aus/ICC/N Zealand	33	24	6
28†	A.B.de Villiers	South Africa	78	21	7
27	W.Barresi	Netherlands	40	26	1
25	N.J.O'Brien	Ireland	30	15	10
25†	G.C.Wilson	Ireland	61	21	4
25†	J.C.Buttler	England	66	21	4

† Excluding catches taken in the field. ‡ L.Ronchi played 3 matches for Australia.

319

MOST DISMISSALS IN AN INNINGS

| 5 (3 ct, 2 st) | Mohammad Shahzad | Afghanistan v Oman | Abu Dhabi | 2015-16 |
| 5 (5 ct) | M.S.Dhoni | India v England | Bristol | 2018 |

FIELDING RECORDS
25 CATCHES IN A CAREER

Total			Matches	Total			Matches
50	Shoaib Malik	Pakistan	111	35	E.J.G.Morgan	England	80
45	D.A.Miller	South Africa	67	35	R.G.Sharma	India	94
44†	A.B.de Villiers	South Africa	78	34	J.P.Duminy	South Africa	78
44	L.R.P.L.Taylor	New Zealand	88	33	G.H.Dockrell	Ireland	60
42	S.K.Raina	India	78	33	V.Kohli	India	67
41	D.A.Warner	Australia	70	32	A.D.Hales	England	60
40	M.J.Guptill	New Zealand	76	31	D.J.G.Sammy	W Indies/Wld	68
38	Umar Akmal	Pakistan	82	30	G.J.Maxwell	Australia	59
37	Mohammad Nabi	Afghanistan	68	30	N.L.T.C.Perera	ICC/Sri Lanka	68
35	D.J.Bravo	West Indies	66	30	Shahid Afridi	Pakistan	99

† Excluding catches taken as a wicket-keeper.

MOST CATCHES IN AN INNINGS

4	D.J.G.Sammy	West Indies v Ireland	Providence	2009-10
4	P.W.Borren	Netherlands v Bangladesh	The Hague	2012
4	C.J.Anderson	New Zealand v South Africa	Port Elizabeth	2012-13
4	L.D.Chandimal	Sri Lanka v Bangladesh	Chittagong	2013-14
4	A.M.Rahane	India v England	Birmingham	2014
4	Babar Hayat	Hong Kong v Afghanistan	Dhaka	2015-16
4	D.A.Miller	South Africa v Pakistan	Cape Town	2018-19

APPEARANCE RECORDS
70 APPEARANCES

111	Shoaib Malik	Pakistan/ICC		78	S.K.Raina	India
99	Shahid Afridi	Pakistan/ICC		77	Mushfiqur Rahim	Bangladesh
98	M.S.Dhoni	India		76	M.J.Guptill	New Zealand
94	R.G.Sharma	India		76	Mahmudullah	Bangladesh
89	Mohammad Hafeez	Pakistan		76	N.L.T.C.Perera	Sri Lanka/World
88	L.R.P.L.Taylor	New Zealand		75	Tamim Iqbal	Bangladesh/World
82	Umar Akmal	Pakistan		73	K.J.O'Brien	Ireland
80	T.M.Dilshan	Sri Lanka		72	A.D.Mathews	Sri Lanka
80	E.J.G.Morgan	England		71	B.B.McCullum	New Zealand
78	A.B.de Villiers	South Africa		70	S.L.Malinga	Sri Lanka
78	J.P.Duminy	South Africa		70	D.A.Warner	Australia

The most for West Indies is 68 by D.Ramdin, for Zimbabwe 58 by H.Masakadza, and for Afghanistan 68 by Mohammad Nabi.

30 MATCHES AS CAPTAIN

			W	L	T	NR	%age wins
72	M.S.Dhoni	India	41	28	1	2	58.57
56	W.T.S.Porterfield	Ireland	26	26	–	4	50.00
47	D.J.G.Sammy	West Indies	27	17	1	2	60.00
46	Asghar Stanikzai	Afghanistan	37	9	–	–	80.43
44	Shahid Afridi	ICC/Pakistan	19	24	1	–	43.18
39	F.du Plessis	South Africa	24	15	–	–	61.53
39	K.S.Williamson	New Zealand	19	19	–	1	50.00
37	P.W.Borren	Netherlands	21	15	–	1	58.33
37	E.J.G.Morgan	England	20	16	1	–	54.05
33	Sarfraz Ahmed	Pakistan	29	4	–	–	87.87
30	P.D.Collingwood	England	17	11	–	2	60.71

INDIAN PREMIER LEAGUE 2018

The 11th IPL tournament was held in India between 7 April and 27 May.

Team	P	W	L	T	NR	Pts	Net RR
1 Sunrisers Hyderabad (3)	14	9	5	–	–	18	+0.28
2 Chennai Super Kings (-)	14	9	5	–	–	18	+0.25
3 Kolkata Knight Riders (4)	14	8	6	–	–	16	–0.07
4 Rajasthan Royals (-)	14	7	7	–	–	14	–0.25
5 Mumbai Indians (1)	14	6	8	–	–	12	+0.31
6 Royal Challengers Bangalore (8)	14	6	8	–	–	12	+0.12
7 Kings XI Punjab (5)	14	6	8	–	–	12	–0.50
8 Delhi Capitals (-)	14	5	9	–	–	10	–0.22

1st Qualifying Match: At Wankhede Stadium, Mumbai, 22 May (floodlit). Toss: Chennai Super Kings. **CHENNAI SUPER KINGS** won by two wickets. Sunrisers Hyderabad 139-7 (20). Chennai Super Kings 140-8 (19.1; F.du Plessis 67*). Award: F.du Plessis.

Eliminator: At Eden Gardens, Kolkata, 23 May (floodlit). Toss: Rajasthan Royals. **KOLKATA KNIGHT RIDERS** won by 25 runs. Kolkata Knight Riders 169-7 (20; K.D.Karthik 52). Rajasthan Royals 144-4 (20; S.V.Samson 50). Award: A.D.Russell (KKR, 49* in 25b).

2nd Qualifying Match: At Eden Gardens, Kolkata, 25 May (floodlit). Toss: Kolkata Knight Riders. **SUNRISERS HYDERABAD** won by 14 runs. Sunrisers Hyderabad 174-7 (20). Kolkata Knight Riders 160-9 (20; Rashid Khan 3-19). Award: Rashid Khan.

FINAL: At Wankhede Stadium, Mumbai, 27 May (floodlit). Toss: Chennai Super Kings. **CHENNAI SUPER KINGS** won by eight wickets. Sunrisers Hyderabad 178-6 (20). Chennai Super Kings 181-2 (18.3; S.R.Watson 117*). Award: S.R.Watson. Series award: S.P.Narine (KKR).

IPL winners:	2008	Rajasthan Royals	2009	Deccan Chargers
	2010	Chennai Super Kings	2011	Chennai Super Kings
	2012	Kolkata Knight Riders	2013	Mumbai Indians
	2014	Kolkata Knight Riders	2015	Mumbai Indians
	2016	Sunrisers Hyderabad	2017	Mumbai Indians

TEAM RECORDS
HIGHEST TOTALS

263-5 (20)	Bangalore v Pune	Bangalore	2013
248-3 (20)	Bangalore v Gujarat	Bangalore	2016

LOWEST TOTALS

49 (9.4)	Bangalore v Kolkata	Kolkata	2017
58 (15.1)	Rajasthan v Bangalore	Cape Town	2009

LARGEST MARGINS OF VICTORY

146 runs	Mumbai (212-3) v Delhi (66)	Delhi	2017

There have been 11 victories in IPL history by ten wickets, the most recent being:

10 wickets	Bangalore (92-0) v Punjab (88)	Indore	2018

Delhi beat Punjab by ten wickets in a reduced game in 2009.

BATTING RECORDS
MOST RUNS IN IPL

4985	S.K.Raina	Chennai, Gujarat	2008-18
4948	V.Kohli	Bangalore	2008-18

800 RUNS IN A SEASON

Runs			Year	M	I	NO	HS	Ave	100	50	6s	4s	R/100B
973	V.Kohli	Bangalore	2016	16	16	4	113	81.08	4	7	38	83	152.0
848	D.A.Warner	Hyderabad	2016	17	17	3	93*	60.57	–	9	31	88	151.4

HIGHEST SCORES

Score	Balls				
175*	66	C.H.Gayle	Bangalore v Pune	Bangalore	2013
158*	73	B.B.McCullum	Kolkata v Bangalore	Bangalore	2008
133*	59	A.B.de Villiers	Bangalore v Mumbai	Mumbai	2015
129*	52	A.B.de Villiers	Bangalore v Mumbai	Bangalore	2016
128*	62	C.H.Gayle	Bangalore v Delhi	Delhi	2012
128*	63	R.R.Pant	Delhi v Hyderabad	Delhi	2018

K.P.Pietersen 103* (Delhi v Deccan at Delhi, 2012) and B.A.Stokes 103* (Pune v Gujarat at Pune, 2017) are the only England-qualified centurions in the IPL.

FASTEST HUNDRED

30 balls	C.H.Gayle (175*)	Bangalore v Pune	Bangalore	2013

MOST SIXES IN AN INNINGS

17	C.H.Gayle	Bangalore v Pune	Bangalore	2013

HIGHEST STRIKE RATE IN A SEASON (Qualification: 100 runs or more)

R/100B	Runs	Balls		
204.34	188	92	B.B.McCullum	Kolkata	2008

HIGHEST STRIKE RATE IN AN INNINGS (Qualification: 25 runs, 350+ strike rate)

R/100B	Runs	Balls			
422.2	38*	9	C.H.Morris	Delhi v Pune	Pune	2017
400.0	28	7	J.A.Morkel	Chennai v Bangalore	Chennai	2012
387.5	31	8	A.B.de Villiers	Bangalore v Pune	Bangalore	2013
385.7	27*	7	B.Akhil	Bangalore v Deccan	Hyderabad	2008
372.7	41	11	A.B.de Villiers	Bangalore v Mumbai	Bangalore	2015
350.0	35	10	C.H.Gayle	Bangalore v Hyderabad	Bangalore	2015
350.0	35*	10	S.N.Khan	Bangalore v Hyderabad	Bangalore	2016

BOWLING RECORDS
MOST WICKETS IN IPL

154	S.L.Malinga	Mumbai		2009-17
146	A.Mishra	Deccan, Delhi, Hyderabad		2008-18

25 WICKETS IN A SEASON

Wkts			Year	P	O	M	Runs	Avge	Best	4w	R/Over
32	D.J.Bravo	Chennai	2013	18	62.3	–	497	15.53	4-42	1	7.95
28	S.L.Malinga	Mumbai	2011	16	63.0	2	375	13.39	5-13	1	5.95
28	J.P.Faulkner	Rajasthan	2013	16	63.1	2	427	15.25	5-16	2	6.75
26	D.J.Bravo	Chennai	2015	17	52.2	–	426	16.38	3-22	–	8.14
26	B.Kumar	Hyderabad	2017	14	52.2	–	369	14.19	5-19	1	7.05
25	M.Morkel	Delhi	2012	16	63.0	1	453	18.12	4-20	1	7.19

BEST BOWLING FIGURES IN AN INNINGS

6-14	Sohail Tanvir	Rajasthan v Chennai	Jaipur	2008
6-19	A.Zampa	Pune v Hyderabad	Visakhapatnam	2016
5- 5	A.Kumble	Bangalore v Rajasthan	Cape Town	2009
5-12	I.Sharma	Deccan v Kochi	Kochi	2011
5-13	S.L.Malinga	Mumbai v Delhi	Delhi	2011

MOST ECONOMICAL BOWLING ANALYSIS

O	M	R	W				
4	1	6	0	F.H.Edwards	Deccan v Kolkata	Cape Town	2009
4	1	6	1	A.Nehra	Delhi v Punjab	Bloemfontein	2009

MOST EXPENSIVE BOWLING ANALYSIS

O	M	R	W				
4	0	70	0	Basil Thampi	Hyderabad v Bangalore	Bangalore	2018
4	0	66	0	I.Sharma	Hyderabad v Chennai	Hyderabad	2013

BIG BASH 2018-19

The seventh Big Bash tournament was held in Australia between 19 December and 17 February.

Team	P	W	L	T	NR	Pts	Net RR
1 Hobart Hurricanes (4)	14	10	4	–	–	20	+0.60
2 Melbourne Renegades (3)	14	8	6	–	–	16	+0.17
3 Sydney Sixers (5)	14	8	6	–	–	16	+0.04
4 Melbourne Stars (8)	14	7	7	–	–	14	–0.06
5 Brisbane Heat (7)	14	6	7	–	1	13	+0.24
6 Sydney Thunder (6)	14	6	7	–	1	13	0.0
7 Adelaide Strikers (2)	14	6	8	–	–	12	–0.47
8 Perth Scorchers (1)	14	4	10	–	–	8	–0.50

1st Semi-final: At Bellerive Oval, Hobart, 14 February (floodlit). Toss: Melbourne Stars. **MELBOURNE STARS** won by six wickets. Hobart Hurricanes 153-7 (20; B.R.McDermott 53, D.J.Worrall 4-23). Melbourne Stars 157-4 (18.5; Qais Ahmad 3-33). Award: D.J.Worrall.

2nd Semi-final: At Docklands Stadium, Melbourne, 15 February (floodlit). Toss: Melbourne Renegades. **MELBOURNE RENEGADES** won by three wickets. Sydney Sixers 180-3 (20; J.R.Philippe 52, D.P.Hughes 52). Melbourne Renegades 184-7 (19.5). Award: D.T.Christian (MR, 31* in 14b).

FINAL: At Docklands Stadium, Melbourne, 17 February. Toss: Melbourne Stars. **MELBOURNE RENEGADES** won by 13 runs. Melbourne Renegades 145-5 (20). Melbourne Stars 132-7 (20; B.R.Dunk 57). Award: D.T.Christian (MR, 38* in 30b, 2-33 and 2ct).

Big Bash winners:	2011-12 Sydney Sixers	2012-13 Brisbane Heat
	2013-14 Perth Scorchers	2014-15 Perth Scorchers
	2015-16 Sydney Thunder	2016-17 Perth Scorchers
	2017-18 Adelaide Strikers	

TEAM RECORDS
HIGHEST TOTALS

223-8 (20)	Hurricanes v Renegades	Melbourne (Dock)	2016-17
222-4 (20)	Renegades v Hurricanes	Melbourne (Dock)	2016-17

LOWEST TOTALS

57 (12.4)	Renegades v Stars	Melbourne (Dock)	2014-15
69 (15.2)	Scorchers v Stars	Perth	2012-13

LARGEST MARGINS OF VICTORY

112 runs	Renegades (57) v Stars (169-6)	Melbourne (Dock)	2014-15
10 wickets	Scorchers (171-0) v Renegades (170-4)	Melbourne (Dock)	2015-16
10 wickets	Strikers (154-5) v Hurricanes (158-0)	Adelaide	2018-19
10 wickets	Stars (156-8) v Heat (158-0)	Brisbane	2018-19

BATTING RECORDS
MOST RUNS IN BIG BASH

1947 (av 30.42)	M.Klinger	Strikers, Scorchers	2011-19
1945 (av 39.69)	C.A.Lynn	Heat	2011-19

MOST RUNS IN A SEASON

Runs		Year	M	I	NO	HS	Ave	100	50	6s	4s	R/100B
632	D.J.M.Short	Hurricanes 2018-19	15	15	3	96*	53.08	–	6	22	65	140.6

HIGHEST SCORES

Score	Balls				
122*	69	D.J.M.Short	Hurricanes v Heat	Brisbane	2017-18
117	60	L.J.Wright	Stars v Hurricanes	Hobart	2011-12

115	70	J.Weatherald		Strikers v Hurricanes	Adelaide	2017-18

FASTEST HUNDRED

39 balls	C.J.Simmons (102)	Scorchers v Strikers	Perth	2013-14

MOST SIXES IN AN INNINGS

11	C.H.Gayle (100*)	Thunder v Strikers	Sydney (SA)	2011-12
11	C.J.Simmons (112)	Scorchers v Sixers	Sydney	2013-14
11	C.A.Lynn (98*)	Heat v Scorchers	Perth	2016-17

HIGHEST STRIKE RATE IN AN INNINGS (Qualification: 25 runs, 325+ strike rate)

R/100B	Score	Balls			
377.7	34	9	D.T.Christian	Heat v Hurricanes	Hobart	2014-15
329.4	56	17	C.H.Gayle	Renegades v Strikers	Melbourne (Dk)	2015-16
327.2	36*	11	B.J.Rohrer	Renegades v Heat	Melbourne (Dk)	2013-14

HIGHEST PARTNERSHIPS

172	R.J.Quiney/L.J.Wright	Stars v Hurricanes	Hobart	2011-12
171*	S.E.Marsh/M.Klinger	Scorchers v Renegades	Melbourne (Dk)	2015-16
171	A.T.Carey/J.Weatherald	Strikers v Hurricanes	Adelaide	2017-18

BOWLING RECORDS
MOST WICKETS IN BIG BASH

95	B.Laughlin	Strikers, Hurricanes	2011-19
85	S.A.Abbott	Sixers, Thunder	2011-19

MOST WICKETS IN A SEASON

Wkts			Year	P	O	M	Runs	Avge	Best	4w	R/Over
24	K.W.Richardson	Renegades	2018-19	14	54.5	–	425	17.70	3-22	–	7.75

BEST BOWLING FIGURES IN AN INNINGS

6- 7	S.L.Malinga	Stars v Scorchers	Perth	2012-13
6-11	I.S.Sodhi	Strikers v Thunder	Sydney (Show)	2016-17
5-14	D.T.Christian	Hurricanes v Strikers	Hobart	2016-17

MOST ECONOMICAL BOWLING ANALYSIS

O	M	R	W				
4	2	3	3	M.G.Johnson	Scorchers v Stars	Perth	2016-17
4	1	7	6	S.L.Malinga	Stars v Scorchers	Perth	2012-13
4	1	7	1	Fawad Ahmed	Renegades v Heat	Melbourne (Dk)	2014-15
4	0	7	3	B.J.Dwarshuis	Sixers v Strikers	Sydney	2018-19

MOST EXPENSIVE BOWLING ANALYSIS

O	M	R	W				
4	0	60	0	D.J.Worrall	Stars v Hurricanes	Melbourne	2014-15
4	0	59	0	N.L.T.C.Perera	Renegades v Hurricanes	Melbourne (Dk)	2016-17
3.3	0	57	1	S.A.Abbott	Sixers v Strikers	Adelaide	2015-16

WICKET-KEEPING RECORDS
MOST DISMISSALS IN BIG BASH

38	M.S.Wade	Hurricanes, Renegades, Stars	2011-19

MOST DISMISSALS IN A SERIES

14	A.T.Carey	Strikers	2017-18

MOST DISMISSALS IN AN INNINGS

5 (5ct)	T.I.F.Triffitt	Scorchers v Renegades	Perth	2012-13

IRELAND INTERNATIONALS

The following players have played for Ireland in any format of international cricket since 1 December 2017 and are still available for selection. Details correct to 18 March 2019.

BALBIRNIE, Andrew (St Andrew's C, Dublin; UWIC), b Dublin 28 Dec 1990. 6'2". RHB, OB. Cardiff MCCU 2012-13. Ireland debut 2012. Middlesex 2012-15. Leinster 2017 to date. Ireland Wolves 2017-18. **Tests**: 2 (2018 to 2018-19); HS 82 v Afg (Dehradun) 2018-19. **LOI**: 55 (2010 to 2018-19); HS 145* v Afg (Dehradun) 2018-19; BB 1-26 v Afg (Dubai, DSC) 2014-15. **IT20**: 22 (2015 to 2018-19); HS 83 v Neth (Al Amerat) 2018-19. HS 205* Ire v Neth (Dublin) 2017. BB 4-23 Lein v North-West (Bready) 2017. LO HS 160* Ire W v B A (Dublin, CA) 2018. LO BB 1-26 (*see LOI*). T20 HS 83.

CAMERON-DOW, James, b Cape Town, South Africa 18 May 1990. LHB, SLA. Northern 2018. Ireland Wolves 2018-19. **Tests**: 1 (2018-19); HS 32* and BB 2-94 v Afg (Dehradun) 2018-19. **LOI**: 4 (2018-19); HS 7* and BB 3-32 (Dehradun) 2018-19. HS 76* Ire W v SL A (Hambantota) 2018-19. BB 7-77 Ire W v SL A (Colombo, SSC) 2018-19. LO HS 20 Ire W v SL A (Colombo, SSC) 2018-19. LO BB 3-32 (*see LOI*). T20 Hs 8*. T20 BB 1-15.

CHASE, Peter Karl David (Malahide Community S), b Dublin 9 Oct 1993. 6'4". RHB, RMF. Durham 2014, taking 5-64 v Notts (Chester-le-St) on debut. Ireland debut 2016. Leinster debut 2017. **LOI**: 25 (2014-15 to 2018); HS 14 v NZ (Dublin) 2017; BB 3-33 v B (Dublin) 2017. **IT20**: 12 (2018 to 2018-19); HS 4 v Afg (Bready) 2018; BB 4-35 v I (Dublin) 2018. HS 24 and BB 5-24 Leinster v NW (Bready) 2018. LO HS 22* Ire v SL A (Belfast) 2014. LO BB 5-42 Ire W v B A (Dublin, CA) 2018. T20 HS 9*. T20 BB 4-11.

DOCKRELL, George Henry (Gonzaga C, Dublin), b Dublin 22 Jul 1992. 6'3". RHB, SLA. Ireland 2010 to date. Somerset 2011-14. Sussex 2015. Leinster 2017 to date. Ireland Wolves 2017-18. **Tests**: 1 (2018-19); HS 39 and BB 2-63 v Afg (Dehradun) 2018-19. **LOI**: 82 (2009-10 to 2018-19); HS 62* v Afg (Sharjah) 2017-18; BB 4-24 v Scot (Belfast) 2013. **IT20**: 60 (2009-10 to 2018-19); HS 34* v Afg (Dehradun) 2018-19; BB 4-20 v Neth (Dubai) 2009-10. HS 92 Leinster v NW (Bready) 2018. BB 6-27 Sm v Middx (Taunton) 2012. LO HS 94* Leinster v Northern (Belfast) 2018. LO BB 5-21 Leinster v Northern (Dublin, V) 2018. T20 HS 40*. T20 BB 4-20.

GETKATE, Shane Charles, b Durban, South Africa 2 Oct 1991. Grandson of R.S.Getkate (Natal 1936-37). RHB, RMF. Northern debut 2017. Ireland Wolves 2017-18. Warwickshire 2nd XI 2011. MCC YC 2013-14. Northamptonshire 2nd XI 2014. **IT20**: 6 (2018-19); HS 24 v Afg (Dehradun) 2018-19; BB 2-15 v Scotland (Al Amerat) 2018-19. HS 70 Northern v Leinster (Comber) 2018. BB 4-62 Northern v Leinster (Dublin, CA) 2017. LO HS 86 Ire W v SL A (Colombo, SSC) 2018-19. LO BB 5-44 Northern v Leinster (Downpatrick) 2017. T20 HS 45. T20 BB 3-23.

KANE, Tyrone Edward (Catholic Uni S, Dublin; University C, Dublin), b Dublin 8 Jul 1994. RHB, RMF. Leinster debut 2017. Nottinghamshire 2nd XI 2016. **Tests**: 1 (2018); HS 14 v P (Dublin) 2018; BB – . **IT20**: 6 (2015 to 2018); HS 26* v Scot (Bready) 2015; BB 3-19 v PNG (Belfast) 2015. HS 75 and BB 3-45 Leinster v Northern (Dublin, CA) 2017. LO HS 57 Leinster v NW (Dublin, OL) 2018. LO BB 4-24 Ire W v B A (Wicklow) 2018. T20 HS 26*. T20 BB 5-22.

LITTLE, Joshua Brian, b Dublin 1 Nov 1999. RHB, LFM. Leinster debut 2018. Ireland Wolves 2018-19. **IT20**: 10 (2016 to 2018-19); HS 7 v Neth (Al Amerat) 2018-19; BB 2-20 v Afg (Bready) 2018. HS 27 Leinster v NW (Bready) 2018. BB 3-95 Leinster v Northern (Dublin) 2018. LO HS 2* and LO BB 2-7 Leinster v NW (Dublin, OL) 2018. T20 HS 7. T20 BB 3-17.

McBRINE, Andrew Robert, b Londonderry 30 Apr 1993. Son of A.McBrine (Ireland 1985-92), nephew of J.McBrine (Ireland 1986). LHB, OB. Ireland debut 2013. North-West debut 2017. Ireland Wolves 2017-18. **Tests:** 1 (2018-19); HS 4 and BB 2-77 v Afg (Dehradun) 2018-19. **LOI:** 37 (2014 to 2018-19); HS 79 v SL (Dublin) 2016; BB 3-38 v PNG (Harare) 2017-18. **IT20:** 19 (2013-14 to 2016-17); HS 14* v UAE (Dubai, DSC) 2016-17; BB 2-7 v PNG (Townsville) 2015-16. HS 77 NW v Northern (Comber) 2018. BB 4-35 NW v Northern (Bready) 2018. LO HS 89 Ire W v B A (Dublin, CA) 2018. LO BB 3-32 NW v Northern (Waringstown) 2017. T20 HS 52*. T20 BB 3-19.

McCARTHY, B.J. – *see DURHAM*.

McCOLLUM, James Alexander (Methodist C, Belfast), b Craigavon 1 Aug 1995. RHB, RM. Durham MCCU 2017. Northern debut 2017. Ireland Wolves 2018-19. **Tests:** 1 (2018-19); HS 39 v Afg (Dehradun) 2018-19. **LOI:** 1 (2018-19); HS 0 v Afg (Dehradun) 2018-19. HS 119* Northern v Leinster (Belfast) 2017. BB 5-32 Northern v NW (Bready) 2018. LO HS Ire W v SL A (Colombo, RPS) 2018-19. LO BB 1-14 Northern v NW (Eglinton) 2018. T20 HS 18.

MURTAGH, T.J. – *see MIDDLESEX*.

O'BRIEN, Kevin Joseph (Marian C, Dublin; Tallaght I of Tech), b Dublin 4 Mar 1984. RHB, RM. Son of B.A.O'Brien (Ireland 1966-81) and younger brother of N.J.O'Brien (Kent, Northamptonshire, Leicestershire, North-West and Leicestershire 2004-18). Ireland debut 2006-07. Nottinghamshire 2009. Surrey 2014. Leicestershire 2015-16 (l-o and T20 only). Leinster debut 2017. **Tests:** 2 (2018 to 2018-19); HS 118 v P (Dublin) 2018 – on debut; BB – . **LOI:** 133 (2006 to 2018-19, 4 as captain); HS 142 v Kenya (Nairobi) 2006-07; BB 4-13 v Neth (Amstelveen) 2013. **IT20:** 73 (2008 to 2018-19, 4 as captain); HS 74 v Afg (Dehradun) 2018-19; BB 4-45 v Afg (Greater Noida) 2016-17. HS 171* Ire v Kenya (Nairobi) 2008-09. BB 5-39 Ire v Canada (Toronto) 2010. LO HS 142 (*see LOI*). LO BB 4-13 (*see LOI*). T20 HS 119. T20 BB 4-22.

PORTERFIELD, William Thomas Stuart (Strabane GS; Leeds Met U), b Londonderry 6 Sep 1984. 5'11". LHB, OB. Ireland 2006-07 to date. Gloucestershire 2008-10; cap 2008. Warwickshire 2011-17; cap 2011. MCC 2007. North-West debut 2018. **Tests:** 2 (2018 to 2018-19, 2 as captain); HS 32 v P (Dublin) 2018. **LOI** (Ire): 127 (2006 to 2018-19, 104 as captain); HS 139 v UAE (Dubai, ICCA) 2017-18. **IT20** (Ire): 61 (2008 to 2018, 56 as captain); HS 72 v UAE (Abu Dhabi) 2015-16. HS 207 NW v Leinster (Bready) 2018. BB 1-29 Ire v Jamaica (Spanish Town) 2009-10. LO HS 139 (*see LOI*). T20 HS 127*.

POYNTER, S.W. – *see DURHAM*.

RANKIN, W.B. – *see WARWICKSHIRE*.

SINGH, Simranjit (**'Simi'**), b Bathlana, Punjab, India 4 Feb 1987. RHB, OB. Leinster debut 2017. Ireland debut 2017. Ireland Wolves 2017-18. **LOI:** 15 (2017 to 2018-19); HS 45 v Scot (Dubai, ICCA) 2017-18; BB 3-15 v UAE (Harare) 2017-18. **IT20:** 14 (2018 to 2018-19); HS 57* v Neth (Rotterdam) 2018; BB 3-15 v Oman (Al Amerat) 2018-19. HS 121 Ire W v B A (Sylhet) 2017-18. BB 3-39 Leinster v Northern (Comber) 2018. LO HS 121* Leinster v Northern (Dublin, V) 2018. LO BB 3-15 (*see LOI*). T20 HS 109. T20 BB 3-15.

STIRLING, P.R. – *see MIDDLESEX*.

THOMPSON, Stuart Robert (Limavady GS; U of Northumbria) b Eglinton, Londonderry 15 Aug 1991. LHB, RM. Ireland debut 2012. North-West debut 2017. Ireland Wolves 2017-18. Played county 2nd XI cricket for four counties 2012-15. **Tests:** 2 (2018 to 2018-19); HS 53 v P (Dublin) 2018; BB 3-28 v Afg (Dehradun) 2018-19. **LOI:** 20 (2013 to 2017); HS 39 v Scot (Dublin) 2014; BB 2-17 v WI (Kingston) 2013-14. **IT20:** 31 (2013-14 to 2018-19); HS 56 v Afg (Greater Noida) 2016-17; BB 4-18 v Neth (Al Amerat) 2018-19. HS 148 NW v Leinster (Dublin, SP) 2018. BB 3-32 NW v Northern (Eglinton) 2017. LO HS 68 Ire W v B A (Oak Hill) 2018. LO BB 3-51 Ire v SA A (Belfast) 2012. T20 HS 56. T20 BB 4-18.

TUCKER, Lorcan John, b Dublin 10 Sep 1996. RHB, WK. Leinster debut 2017. Ireland Wolves 2018-19. **IT20**: 7 (2016 to 2018-19); HS 22* v Oman (Al Amerat) 2018-19. HS 80 Ire W v SL A (Hambantota) 2018-19. LO HS 109 Ire W v SL A (Hambantota) 2018-19. T20 HS 44.

WILSON, G.C. – *see DERBYSHIRE.*

YOUNG, Craig Alexander (Strabane HS; North West IHE, Belfast), b Londonderry 4 Apr 1990. RHB, RM. Ireland debut 2013. North-West debut 2017. Ireland Wolves 2018-19. Sussex 2nd XI 2010-13. Hampshire 2nd XI 2016. **LOI**: 13 (2014 to 2017); HS 11 v Scot (Dublin) 2014; BB 5-46 v Scot (Dublin) 2014 – different matches. **IT20**: 16 (2015 to 2018); HS 2* v Hong Kong (Bready) 2016; BB 2-15 v PNG (Townsville) 2015-16. HS 23 and BB 5-37 NW v Northern (Eglinton) 2017. LO HS 26 Ire v SL A (Belfast) 2014. LO BB 5-46 (*see LOI*). T20 HS 5*. T20 BB 5-15.

INTERNATIONAL FIXTURES

Fri 3 May			**Sun 19 May**		
LOI	Dublin, Mal	Ireland v England	LOI	Stormont	Ireland v Afghanistan
Sun 5 May			**Tue 21 May**		
LOI	Dublin, CA	Ireland v West Indies	LOI	Stormont	Ireland v Afghanistan
Tue 7 May			**Mon 1 July**		
LOI	Dublin, CA	West Indies v Bangladesh	LOI	Bready	Ireland v Zimbabwe
Thu 9 May			**Thu 4 July**		
LOI	Dublin, Mal	Ireland v Bangladesh	LOI	Stormont	Ireland v Zimbabwe
Sat 11 May			**Sun 7 July**		
LOI	Dublin, Mal	Ireland v West Indies	LOI	Stormont	Ireland v Zimbabwe
Mon 13 May			**Wed 10 July**		
LOI	Dublin, Mal	West Indies v Bangladesh	IT20	Stormont	Ireland v Zimbabwe
Wed 15 May			**Fri 12 July**		
LOI	Dublin, CA	Ireland v Bangladesh	IT20	Bready	Ireland v Zimbabwe
Fri 17 May			**Sun 14 July**		
LOI	Dublin, Mal	Tri-Series Final	IT20	Bready	Ireland v Zimbabwe
			Wed 24 – Sat 27 July		
			TM	Lord's	**ENGLAND v IRELAND**

ENGLAND WOMEN INTERNATIONALS

The following players have either played for England since 21 October 2017 or have been awarded central contracts for 2019. Details correct to 21 February 2019.

BEAUMONT, Tamsin (**'Tammy'**) Tilley, b Dover, Kent 11 Mar 1991. RHB, WK. MBE 2018. Kent 2007 to date. Diamonds 2007-12. Sapphires 2008. Emeralds 2011-13. Surrey Stars 2016-17. Adelaide Strikers 2016-17 to 2017-18. Southern Vipers 2018. **Tests**: 3 (2013 to 2017-18); HS 70 v A (Sydney) 2017-18. **LOI**: 56 (2009-10 to 2018); HS 168* v P (Taunton) 2016. **IT20**: 62 (2009-10 to 2018-19); HS 116 v SA (Taunton) 2018.

BRUNT, Katherine Helen, b Barnsley, Yorks 2 Jul 1985. RHB, RMF. Yorkshire 2004 to date. Sapphires 2006-08. Diamonds 2011-12. Perth Scorchers 2015-16 to 2017-18. Yorkshire Diamonds 2016 to date. **Tests**: 11 (2004 to 2017-18); HS 52 v A (Worcester) 2005; BB 6-69 v A (Worcester) 2009. **LOI**: 112 (2004-05 to 2018); HS 72* v SA (Worcester) 2018; BB 5-18 v A (Wormsley) 2011. **IT20**: 65 (2005 to 2018); HS 42* v SA (Taunton) 2018; BB 3-6 v NZ (Lord's) 2009.

CROSS, Kathryn (**'Kate'**) Laura, b Manchester, Lancs 3 Oct 1991. RHB, RMF. Lancashire 2005 to date. Sapphires 2007-08. Emeralds 2012. W Australia 2017-18 to date. Brisbane Heat 2015-16. Lancashire Thunder 2016 to date. Perth Scorchers 2018-19. **Tests**: 3 (2013-14 to 2015); HS 4* v A (Canterbury) 2015; BB 3-29 v I (Wormsley) 2014. **LOI**: 15 (2013-14 to 2018); HS 4* v I (Scarborough) 2017; BB 5-24 v NZ (Lincoln) 2014-15. **IT20**: 4 (2013-14 to 2014-15); HS –; BB 2-27 v NZ (Whangarei) 2014-15.

DAVIDSON-RICHARDS, Alice Natica, b Tunbridge Wells, Kent 29 May 1994. RHB, RFM. Kent 2010 to date. Sapphires 2011-12. Emeralds 2013. Yorkshire Diamonds 2016 to date. **LOI**: 1 (2017-18); HS 9 v I (Nagpur) 2017-18. **IT20**: 5 (2017-18); HS 24 v A (Mumbai, BS) 2017-18; BB –.

DAVIES, Freya Ruth, b Chichester, Sussex 27 Oct 1995. RHB, RFM. Sussex 2012 to date. Western Storm 2016 to date.

DUNKLEY, Sophia Ivy R., b Lambeth, Surrey 16 Jul 1998. RHB, LB. Middlesex 2013 to date. Surrey Stars 2016 to date. **IT20**: 5 (2018-19); HS 35 v WI (Gros Islet) 2018-19.

ECCLESTONE, Sophie (Helsby HS), b Chester 6 May 1999. RHB, SLA. Cheshire 2013-14. Lancashire 2015 to date. Lancashire Thunder 2016 to date. **Tests**: 1 (2017-18); HS 8* and BB 3-107 v A (Sydney) 2017-18. **LOI**: 13 (2016-17 to 2018); HS 12* v SA (Worcester) 2018; BB 4-14 v I (Nagpur) 2017-18. **IT20**: 19 (2016 to 2018-19); HS 9* and BB 4-18 v NZ (Taunton) 2018.

ELWISS, Georgia Amanda, b Wolverhampton, Staffs 31 May 1991. RHB, RMF. Staffordshire 2004-10. Sapphires 2006-12. Diamonds 2008. Australia CT 2009-10 to 2010-11. Emeralds 2011. Sussex 2011 to date. Rubies 2013. Loughborough Lightning 2016 to date. Melbourne Stars 2017-18 to date. **Tests**: 2 (2015 to 2017-18); HS 46 v A (Canterbury) 2015; BB 1-40 v A (Sydney) 2017-18. **LOI**: 33 (2011-12 to 2018); HS 77 v P (Taunton) 2016; BB 3-17 v I (Wormsley) 2012. **IT20**: 13 (2011-12 to 2016); HS 18 v SA (Paarl) 2015-16; BB 2-9 v P (Chennai) 2015-16.

FARRANT, Natasha (**'Tash'**) Eleni (Sevenoaks S), b Athens, Greece 29 May 1996. LHB, LMF. Kent 2012 to date. Sapphires 2013. W Australia 2016-17. Southern Vipers 2016 to date. **LOI**: 1 (2013-14); HS 1* and BB 1-14 v WI (Port of Spain) 2013-14. **IT20**: 14 (2013 to 2018); HS 3* v A (Mumbai, BS) 2017-18; BB 2-15 v P (Loughborough) 2013.

GEORGE, Katie Louise, b Haywards Heath, Sussex 7 Apr 1999. LHB, LM. Hampshire 2013 to date. Southern Vipers 2016 to date. **LOI**: 2 (2018); HS 9 and BB 3-36 v NZ (Derby) 2018. **IT20**: 5 (2017-18 to 2018); HS 0; BB 1-22 v NZ (Bristol) 2018.

GORDON, Kirstie Louise, b Huntly, Aberdeenshire 20 Oct 1997. RHB, SLA. Nottinghamshire 2016 to date. Loughborough Lightning 2018. **IT20:** 5 (2018-19); HS 1* v A (North Sound) 2018-19; BB 3-16 v B (Gros Islet) 2018-19.

GUNN, Jennifer ('Jenny') Louise, b Nottingham 9 May 1986. MBE 2014. RHB, RMF. Nottinghamshire 2001-15. Emeralds 2006-08. S Australia 2006-07 to 2007-08. Diamonds 2007. W Australia 2008-09. Yorkshire 2011. Rubies 2012-13. Warwickshire 2016 to date. Yorkshire Diamonds 2016-17. Loughborough Lightning 2018. **Tests:** 11 (2004 to 2014); HS 62* and BB 5-19 v I (Wormsley) 2014. **LOI:** 143 (2003-04 to 2018); HS 73 v NZ (Taunton) 2007; BB 5-22 v P (Louth) 2013. **IT20:** 104 (2004 to 2018, 3 as captain); HS 69 v SL (Colombo, NCC) 2010-11; BB 5-18 v NZ (Bridgetown) 2013-14.

HARTLEY, Alexandra, b Blackburn, Lancs 26 Sep 1993. RHB, SLA. Lancashire 2008 to date. Emeralds 2011-13. Rubies 2012. Middlesex 2013-16. Tasmania 2018-19. Surrey Stars 2016-17. Lancashire Thunder 2018. Hobart Hurricanes 2018. **LOI:** 23 (2016 to 2017-18); HS 3* v I (Nagpur) 2017-18; BB 4-24 v WI (Kingston) 2016-17. **IT20:** 3 (2016 to 2017-18); HS 2* v I (Mumbai, BS) 2017-18; BB 2-19 v P (Chelmsford) 2016.

HAZELL, Danielle ('Danni'), b Durham 13 May 1988. RHB, OB. Durham 2002-04. Sapphires 2006-13. Emeralds 2007. Yorkshire 2008 to date. Diamonds 2011-12. Yorkshire Diamonds 2016. Melbourne Stars 2016-17. Lancashire Thunder 2017 to date. Adelaide Strikers 2018-19. **Tests:** 3 (2010-11 to 2013-14); HS 15 v A (Perth) 2013-14; BB 2-32 v A (Sydney) 2010-11. **LOI:** 53 (2009-10 to 2017-18); HS 45 v SL (Colombo, RPS) 2016-17; BB 4-32 v I (Nagpur) 2017-18. **IT20:** 85 (2009-10 to 2018-19); HS 18* v WI (Arundel) 2012; BB 4-12 v WI (Hove) 2012.

JONES, Amy Ellen, b Solihull, Warwicks 13 Jun 1993. RHB, WK. Warwickshire 2008 to date. Diamonds 2011. Emeralds 2012. Rubies 2013. W Australia 2017-18. Loughborough Lightning 2016 to date. Sydney Sixers 2016-17 to 2017-18. Perth Scorchers 2018-19. **LOI:** 29 (2012-13 to 2018); HS 94 v I (Nagpur) 2017-18. **IT20:** 29 (2013 to 2018); HS 53* v I (North Sound) 2018-19.

KNIGHT, Heather Clare, b Rochdale, Lancs 26 Dec 1990. RHB, OB. OBE 2018. Devon 2008-09. Emeralds 2008-13. Berkshire 2010 to date. Sapphires 2011-12. Tasmania 2014-15 to 2015-16. Hobart Hurricanes 2015-16 to date. Western Storm 2016 to date. *Wisden* 2017. **Tests:** 6 (2010-11 to 2017-18, 1 as captain); HS 157 v A (Wormsley) 2013; BB 1-7 v I (Wormsley) 2014. **LOI:** 86 (2009-10 to 2018, 31 as captain); HS 106 v P (Leicester) 2017; BB 5-26 v P (Leicester) 2016. **IT20:** 53 (2010-11 to 2018-19, 20 as captain); HS 51 v A (Canberra) 2017-18; BB 3-9 v I (North Sound) 2018-19.

MARSH, Laura Alexandra, b Pembury, Kent 5 Dec 1986. RHB, RMF/OB. Sussex 2003-10. Rubies 2006-07. Emeralds 2008. Sapphires 2011. Kent 2011 to date. New South Wales 2015-16. Otago 2015-16. Sydney Sixers 2015-16. Surrey Stars 2016 to date. **Tests:** 8 (2006 to 2017-18); HS 55 v A (Wormsley) 2013; BB 3-44 v I (Leicester) 2006. **LOI:** 95 (2006 to 2018); HS 67 v Ire (Kibworth) 2010; BB 5-15 v P (Sydney) 2008-09. **IT20:** 60 (2007 to 2016-17); HS 54 v P (Galle) 2012-13; BB 3-12 v P (Chennai) 2015-16.

SCIVER, Natalie Ruth (Epsom C), b Tokyo, Japan 20 Aug 1992. RHB, RM. Surrey 2010 to date. Rubies 2011. Emeralds 2012-13. Melbourne Stars 2015-16 to 2016-17. Surrey Stars 2016 to date. Perth Scorchers 2017-18. *Wisden* 2017. **Tests:** 4 (2013-14 to 2016-17); HS 49 and BB 1-30 v A (Perth) 2013-14. **LOI:** 53 (2013 to 2018); HS 137 v P (Leicester) 2017; BB 3-3 v WI (Bristol) 2017. **IT20:** 55 (2013 to 2018-19); HS 68* v A (Mumbai, BS) 2017-18; BB 4-15 v A (Cardiff) 2015.

SHRUBSOLE, Anya, b Bath, Somerset 7 Dec 1991. RHB, RMF. MBE 2018. Somerset 2004 to date. Rubies 2006-12. Emeralds 2006-13. Western Storm 2016 to date. Perth Scorchers 2016-17. *Wisden* 2017. **Tests:** 5 (2013 to 2017-18); HS 20 v A (Sydney) 2017-18; BB 4-51 v A (Perth) 2013-14. **LOI:** 55 (2008 to 2018, 1 as captain); HS 29 v NZ (Mt Maunganui) 2014-15; BB 6-46 v I (Lord's) 2017, in World Cup final. **IT20:** 59 (2008 to 2018-19); HS 29 v WI (Gros Islet) 2018-19; BB 5-11 v NZ (Wellington) 2011-12.

SMITH, Bryony Frances, b Sutton, Surrey 12 Dec 1997. RHB, OB. Surrey 2014 to date. Surrey Stars 2016 to date. **IT20**: 3 (2017-18); HS 15 v I (Mumbai, BS) 2017-18.

SMITH, Linsey Claire Neale, b Hillingdon, Middx 10 Mar 1995. LHB, SLA. Berkshire 2011-16. Rubies 2011-12. Sussex 2017 to date. Southern Vipers 2016-17. Loughborough Lightning 2018. **IT20**: 2 (2018-19); HS –; BB 1-17 v B (Gros Islet) 2018-19.

TAYLOR, Sarah Jane (Bede's S, Upper Dicker), b Whitechapel, London 20 May 1989. RHB, WK. Sussex 2004 to date. Rubies 2006-12. Emeralds 2008-13. Wellington 2010-11 to 2011-12. S Australia 2014-15 to 2015-16. Adelaide Strikers 2015-16. Lancashire Thunder 2017. Surrey Stars 2018. **Tests**: 9 (2006 to 2017-18); HS 40 v I (Wormsley) 2014. **LOI**: 118 (2006 to 2017-18); HS 147 v SA (Bristol) 2017. **IT20**: 89 (2006 to 2018); HS 77 v A (Chelmsford) 2013.

WILSON, Frances Claire, b Aldershot, Hants 7 Nov 1991. RHB, OB. Somerset 2006-14. Diamonds 2011. Emeralds 2012. Rubies 2013. Middlesex 2015 to date. Wellington 2016-17 to 2017-18. Western Storm 2016 to date. Sydney Thunder 2017-18. **Tests**: 1 (2017-18); HS 13 v A (Sydney) 2017-18. **LOI**: 20 (2010-11 to 2017-18); HS 81 v I (Derby) 2017. **IT20**: 14 (2010-11 to 2017-18); HS 43* v P (Southampton) 2016.

WINFIELD, Lauren, b York 16 Aug 1990. RHB, WK. Yorkshire 2007 to date. Diamonds 2011. Sapphires 2012. Rubies 2013. Brisbane Heat 2015-16 to 2016-17. Yorkshire Diamonds 2016 to date. Hobart Hurricanes 2017-18. **Tests**: 3 (2014 to 2017-18); HS 35 v I (Wormsley) 2014. **LOI**: 37 (2013 to 2018); HS 123 v P (Worcester) 2016. **IT20**: 23 (2013 to 2018-19); HS 74 v SA (Birmingham) 2014 and 74 v P (Bristol) 2016.

WYATT, Danielle ('Danni') Nicole, b Stoke-on-Trent, Staffs 22 Apr 1991. RHB, OB/RM. Staffordshire 2005-12. Emeralds 2006-08. Sapphires 2011-13. Victoria 2011-12 to 2015-16. Nottinghamshire 2013-15. Sussex 2016 to date. Melbourne Renegades 2015-16 to date. Lancashire Thunder 2016. Southern Vipers 2017 to date. **LOI**: 61 (2009-10 to 2018); HS 47 v I (Nagpur) 2017-18; BB 3-7 v SA (Cuttack) 2012-13. **IT20**: 88 (2009-10 to 2018-19); HS 124 v I (Mumbai, BS) 2017-18; BB 4-11 v SA (Basseterre) 2010.

WOMEN'S LIMITED-OVERS RECORDS

1973 to 15 March 2019
RESULTS SUMMARY

	Matches	Won	Lost	Tied	No Result	% Won (exc NR)
Australia	320	249	63	2	6	79.29
England	336	196	128	2	10	60.12
India	266	146	115	1	4	55.72
South Africa	187	93	84	2	8	51.95
New Zealand	335	170	157	2	6	51.67
West Indies	168	79	83	1	5	48.46
Sri Lanka	161	56	100	–	5	35.89
Trinidad & Tobago	6	2	4	–	–	33.33
Pakistan	157	46	109	–	2	29.67
Ireland	148	39	103	–	6	27.64
Bangladesh	36	8	26	–	2	23.52
Jamaica	5	1	4	–	–	20.00
Netherlands	101	19	81	–	1	19.00
Denmark	33	6	27	–	–	18.18
International XI	18	3	14	–	1	17.64
Young England	6	1	5	–	–	16.66
Scotland	8	1	7	–	–	12.50
Japan	5	–	5	–	–	0.00

TEAM RECORDS – HIGHEST INNINGS TOTALS

491-4 (50 overs)	New Zealand v Ireland	Dublin	2018
455-5 (50 overs)	New Zealand v Pakistan	Christchurch	1996-97
440-3 (50 overs)	New Zealand v Ireland	Dublin	2018
418 (49.5 overs)	New Zealand v Ireland	Dublin	2018
412-3 (50 overs)	Australia v Denmark	Mumbai	1997-98
397-4 (50 overs)	Australia v Pakistan	Melbourne	1996-97
378-5 (50 overs)	England v Pakistan	Worcester	2016

LARGEST RUNS MARGIN OF VICTORY

408 runs	New Zealand beat Pakistan	Christchurch	1996-97
374 runs	Australia beat Pakistan	Melbourne	1996-97

LOWEST INNINGS TOTALS

22 (23.4 overs)	Netherlands v West Indies	Deventer	2008
23 (24.1 overs)	Pakistan v Australia	Melbourne	1996-97
24 (21.3 overs)	Scotland v England	Reading	2001

BATTING RECORDS – 2500 RUNS IN A CAREER

Runs		Career	M	I	NO	HS	Avge	100	50
6720	M.Raj (I)	1999-2019	203	183	52	125*	51.29	7	52
5992	C.M.Edwards (E)	1997-2016	191	180	23	173*	38.16	9	46
4844	B.J.Clark (A)	1991-2005	118	114	12	229*	47.49	5	30
4814	K.L.Rolton (A)	1995-2009	141	132	32	154*	48.14	8	33
4400	S.R.Taylor (WI)	2008-2019	117	115	14	171	43.96	5	33
4392	S.W.Bates (NZ)	2006-2019	121	115	12	168	42.64	10	25
4101	S.C.Taylor (E)	1998-2011	126	120	18	156*	40.20	8	23
4064	D.A.Hockley (NZ)	1982-2000	118	115	18	117	41.89	4	34
3958	S.J.Taylor (E)	2006-2019	121	114	13	147	39.18	7	19
3821	A.E.Satterthwaite (NZ)	2007-2019	119	113	15	137*	38.98	6	21
3492	A.J.Blackwell (A)	2003-2017	144	124	27	114	36.00	3	25
3273	M.M.Lanning (A)	2011-2019	72	72	8	152*	51.14	12	11
3058	M.du Preez (SA)	2007-2019	121	113	19	116*	32.53	2	14
2919	H.M.Tiffen (NZ)	1999-2009	117	111	16	100	30.72	1	18
2856	A.Chopra (I)	1995-2012	127	112	21	100	31.38	1	16
2844	E.C.Drumm (NZ)	1992-2006	101	94	13	116	35.11	2	19
2833	D.J.S.Dottin (WI)	2008-2019	117	111	11	104*	28.33	1	19
2748	E.A.Perry (A)	2007-2019	103	81	28	107*	51.84	1	26

Runs		Career	M	I	NO	HS	Avge	100	50
2728	L.C.Sthalekar (A)	2001-2013	125	111	22	104*	30.65	2	16
2630	L.M.Keightley (A)	1995-2005	82	78	12	156*	39.84	4	21
2554	L.S.Greenway (E)	2003-2016	126	111	26	125*	30.04	1	12
2510	S.F.M.Devine (NZ)	2006-2019	102	89	11	145	32.17	5	12

HIGHEST INDIVIDUAL INNINGS

232*	A.C.Kerr	New Zealand v Ireland	Dublin	2018
229*	B.J.Clark	Australia v Denmark	Mumbai	1997-98
188	D.B.Sharma	India v Ireland	Potchefstroom	2017
178*	A.C.Jayangani	Sri Lanka v Australia	Bristol	2017
173*	C.M.Edwards	England v Ireland	Pune	1997-98
171*	H.Kaur	India v Australia	Derby	2017
171	S.R.Taylor	West Indies v Sri Lanka	Mumbai	2012-13
168*	T.T.Beaumont	England v Pakistan	Taunton	2016
168	S.W.Bates	New Zealand v Pakistan	Sydney	2008-09
157	R.H.Priest	New Zealand v Sri Lanka	Lincoln	2015-16
156*	L.M.Keightley	Australia v Pakistan	Melbourne	1996-97
156*	S.C.Taylor	England v India	Lord's	2006
154*	K.L.Rolton	Australia v Sri Lanka	Christchurch	2000-01
153*	J.Logtenberg	South Africa v Netherlands	Deventer	2007
152*	M.M.Lanning	Australia v Sri Lanka	Bristol	2017
151	K.L.Rolton	Australia v Ireland	Dublin	2005
151	S.W.Bates	New Zealand v Ireland	Dublin	2018

HIGHEST PARTNERSHIP FOR EACH WICKET

1st	320	D.B.Sharma/P.G.Raut	India v Ireland	Potchefstroom	2017
2nd	295	A.C.Kerr/L.M.Kasperek	New Zealand v Ireland	Dublin	2018
3rd	244	K.L.Rolton/L.C.Sthalekar	Australia v Ireland	Dublin	2005
4th	224*	J.Logtenberg//M.du Preez	South Africa v Netherlands	Deventer	2007
5th	188*	S.C.Taylor/J.Cassar	England v Sri Lanka	Lincoln	2000-01
6th	142	S.Luus/C.L.Tryon	South Africa v Ireland	Dublin	2016
7th	104*	S.J.Tsukigawa/N.J.Browne	New Zealand v England	Chennai	2006-07
8th	85*	S.L.Clarke/N.J.Shaw	England v Scotland	Reading	2001
9th	73	L.R.F.Askew/I.T.Guha	England v New Zealand	Chennai	2006-07
10th	76	A.J.Blackwell/K.M.Beams	Australia v India	Derby	2017

BOWLING RECORDS - 100 WICKETS IN A CAREER

	LOI	Balls	Runs	W	Avge	Best	4w	R/Over
J.Goswami (I)	2002-2019	177	8574	4653	218	21.34	6-31	8	3.25
C.L.Fitzpatrick (A)	1993-2007	109	6017	3023	180	16.79	5-14	11	3.01
A.Mohammed (WI)	2003-2019	117	5140	2898	146	19.84	7-14	11	3.38
L.C.Sthalekar (A)	2001-2013	125	5964	3646	146	24.97	5-35	2	3.66
N.David (I)	1995-2008	97	4892	2305	141	16.34	5-20	6	2.82
K.H.Brunt (E)	2005-2019	115	5679	3297	141	23.38	5-18	7	3.48
Sana Mir (P)	2005-2019	115	5672	3481	141	24.68	5-32	7	3.68
S.R.Taylor (WI)	2008-2019	117	4901	2684	137	19.59	4-17	5	3.28
J.L.Gunn (E)	2004-2018	143	5864	3788	135	28.05	5-22	6	3.87
E.A.Perry (A)	2007-2019	103	4798	3502	134	26.13	5-19	3	4.37
D.van Niekerk (SA)	2009-2019	99	4206	2469	128	19.28	5-17	8	3.52
S.Ismail (SA)	2007-2019	89	4339	2609	127	20.54	6-10	5	3.60
H.A.S.D.Siriwardene (SL)	2003-2019	112	5166	3327	119	27.95	4-11	6	3.86
L.A.Marsh (E)	2006-2018	95	4914	3184	118	26.98	5-15	4	3.88
M.Kapp (SA)	2009-2019	99	4287	2628	109	24.11	4-14	3	3.67
C.E.Taylor (E)	1988-2005	105	5140	2443	102	23.95	4-13	2	2.85
I.T.Guha (E)	2001-2013	83	3767	2345	101	23.21	5-14	4	3.73
N.Al Khadeer (I)	2002-2012	78	4036	2402	100	24.02	5-14	5	3.57

SIX OR MORE WICKETS IN AN INNINGS

7- 4	Sajjida Shah	Pakistan v Japan	Amsterdam	2003
7- 8	J.M.Chamberlain	England v Denmark	Haarlem	1991
7-14	A.Mohammed	West Indies v Pakistan	Dhaka	2011-12
7-24	S.Nitschke	Australia v England	Kidderminster	2005

6-10	J.Lord	New Zealand v India	Auckland	1981-82
6-10	M.Maben	India v Sri Lanka	Kandy	2003-04
6-10	S.Ismail	South Africa v Netherlands	Savar	2011-12
6-20	G.L.Page	New Zealand v Trinidad & T	St Albans	1973
6-20	D.B.Sharma	India v Sri Lanka	Ranchi	2015-16
6-20	Khadija Tul Kubra	Bangladesh v Pakistan	Cox's Bazar	2018-19
6-31	J.Goswami	India v New Zealand	Southgate	2011
6-32	B.H.McNeill	New Zealand v England	Lincoln, NZ	2007-08
6-36	S.Luus	South Africa v Ireland	Dublin	2016
6-46	A.Shrubsole	England v India	Lord's	2017

WICKET-KEEPING AND FIELDING RECORDS – 100 DISMISSALS IN A CAREER

Total			LOI	Ct	St
151	T.Chetty	South Africa	105	106	45
133	R.J.Rolls	New Zealand	104	89	44
131	S.J.Taylor	England	121	81	50
114	J.Smit	England	109	69	45
102	M.R.Aguilera	West Indies	112	76	26

SIX DISMISSALS IN AN INNINGS

6 (4ct, 2st)	S.L.Illingworth	New Zealand v Australia	Beckenham	1993
6 (1ct, 5st)	V.Kalpana	India v Denmark	Slough	1993
6 (2ct, 4st)	Batool Fatima	Pakistan v West Indies	Karachi	2003-04
6 (4ct, 2st)	Batool Fatima	Pakistan v Sri Lanka	Colombo (PSS)	2011

50 CATCHES IN THE FIELD IN A CAREER

Total			LOI	Career
63	S.W.Bates	New Zealand	121	2006-2019
63	J.Goswami	India	177	2002-2019
57	S.R.Taylor	West Indies	117	2008-2019
55	A.J.Blackwell	Australia	144	2003-2017
52	L.S.Greenway	England	126	2003-2016
52	C.M.Edwards	England	191	1997-2016
50	D.van Niekerk	South Africa	99	2009-2019
50	M.Raj	India	203	1999-2019

FOUR CATCHES IN THE FIELD IN AN INNINGS

4	Z.J.Goss	Australia v New Zealand	Adelaide	1995-96
4	J.L.Gunn	England v New Zealand	Lincoln, NZ	2014-15
4	Nahida Khan	Pakistan v Sri Lanka	Dambulla	2017-18

APPEARANCE RECORDS – 125 APPEARANCES

203	M.Raj	India	1999-2019
191	C.M.Edwards	England	1997-2016
177	J.Goswami	India	2002-2019
144	A.J.Blackwell	Australia	2003-2017
143	J.L.Gunn	England	2004-2018
141	K.L.Rolton	Australia	1995-2009
134	S.J.McGlashan	New Zealand	2002-2016
127	A.Chopra	India	1995-2012
126	L.S.Greenway	England	2003-2016
126	S.C.Taylor	England	1998-2011
125	N.J.Browne	New Zealand	2002-2014
125	L.C.Sthalekar	Australia	2001-2013

100 CONSECUTIVE APPEARANCES

| 109 | M.Raj | India | 17.04.2004 to 07.02.2013 |
| 101 | M.du Preez | South Africa | 08.03.2009 to 05.02.2018 |

100 MATCHES AS CAPTAIN

			Won	Lost	No Result	
126	M.Raj	India	77	46	3	2004-2019
117	C.M.Edwards	England	72	38	7	2005-2016
101	B.J.Clark	Australia	83	17	1	1994-2005

WOMEN'S INTERNATIONAL TWENTY20 RECORDS

2004 to 17 February 2019

MATCH RESULTS SUMMARY

	Matches	Won	Lost	Tied	NR	Win %
Zimbabwe	5	5	–	–	–	100.00
England	120	84	33	2	1	70.58
Australia	118	75	41	2	–	63.55
New Zealand	116	69	44	2	1	60.00
West Indies	115	66	42	5	2	58.40
India	101	53	46	–	2	53.53
South Africa	94	41	51	–	2	44.56
Pakistan	102	41	57	3	1	40.59
Bangladesh	58	17	41	–	–	29.31
Sri Lanka	90	23	63	–	4	26.74
Ireland	57	15	42	–	–	26.31
Associates (v Full Members)	32	1	30	–	1	3.22

WOMEN'S INTERNATIONAL TWENTY20 RECORDS
TEAM RECORDS – HIGHEST INNINGS TOTALS † Batting Second

250-3	England v South Africa	Taunton	2018
216-1	New Zealand v South Africa	Taunton	2018
210-5	Namibia v Lesotho	Gaborone	2018
209-4	Australia v England	Mumbai (BS)	2017-18
205-1	South Africa v Netherlands	Potchefstroom	2010-11
203-3	UAE v China	Bangkok	2018-19
199-3†	England v India	Mumbai (BS)	2017-18
198-4	India v England	Mumbai (BS)	2017-18
195-3	Australia v Pakistan	Kuala Lumpur	2018-19
194-5	India v New Zealand	Providence	2018-19
191-4	West Indies v Netherlands	Potchefstroom	2010-11
191-4	Australia v Ireland	Sylhet	2013-14

LOWEST COMPLETED INNINGS TOTALS † Batting Second

14† (10.0)	China v UAE	Bangkok	2018-19
18† (9.5)	Mexico v Brazil	Cundinamarca	2018
25 (11.0)	Mozambique v Namibia	Gaborone	2018
27† (13.4)	Malaysia v Thailand	Kuala Lumpur	2018
27† (11.1)	Indonesia v Nepal	Bangkok	2018-19
30† (18.4)	Malaysia v Pakistan	Kuala Lumpur	2018
30† (12.5)	Bangladesh v Pakistan	Cox's Bazar	2018-19

The lowest score for England is 87 (v Australia, Hove, 2015).

BATTING RECORDS – 1600 RUNS IN A CAREER

Runs			M	I	NO	HS	Avge	50	R/100B
3100	S.W.Bates	NZ	111	108	7	124*	30.69	22	112.2
2748	S.R.Taylor	WI	93	92	15	90	35.68	20	102.5†
2605	C.M.Edwards	E	95	93	14	92*	32.97	12	106.9
2368	D.J.S.Dottin	WI	110	108	19	112*	26.60	12	125.3†
2315	M.M.Lanning	A	85	82	14	126	34.04	13	116.5
2307	M.Raj	I	86	81	20	97*	37.81	17	96.7†
2175	S.J.Taylor	E	89	86	11	77	29.00	16	110.6
1955	S.F.M.Devine	NZ	83	80	10	73	27.92	10	125.1

334

Runs			M	I	NO	HS	Avge	50	R/100B
1910	H.Kaur	I	96	85	17	103	28.08	7	103.2†
1812	Bismah Maroof	P	95	89	17	65*	25.16	7	90.0
1699	D.van Niekerk	SA	76	67	10	90*	29.80	10	95.1

† *No information on balls faced for games at Roseau on 22 and 23 February 2012.*

HIGHEST INDIVIDUAL INNINGS

Score	Balls				
126	65	M.M.Lanning	A v Ire	Sylhet	2013-14
124*	66	S.W.Bates	NZ v SA	Taunton	2018
124	64	D.N.Wyatt	E v I	Mumbai (BS)	2017-18
117*	70	B.L.Mooney	A v E	Canberra	2017-18
116*	71	S.A.Fritz	SA v Neth	Potchefstroom	2010-11
116	52	T.T.Beaumont	E v SA	Taunton	2018
112*	45	D.J.S.Dottin	WI v SA	Basseterre	2010
112	67	D.J.S.Dottin	WI v SL	Coolidge	2017-18
103	51	H.Kaur	I v NZ	Providence	2018-19
100	57	D.N.Wyatt	A v A	Canberra	2017-18

HIGHEST PARTNERSHIP FOR EACH WICKET

1st	182	S.W.Bates/S.F.M.Devine	NZ v SA	Taunton	2018
2nd	121	H.K.Matthews/D.J.S.Dottin	WI v SL	Coolidge	2017-18
3rd	124	T.D.Smartt/S.A.C.A.King	WI v Neth	Potchefstroom	2010-11
3rd	124	K.J.Martin/A.E.Satterthwaite	NZ v WI	Mt Maunganui	2017-18
4th	147*	K.L.Rolton/K.A.Blackwell	A v E	Taunton	2005
5th	119*	M.M.Lanning/R.L.Haynes	A v NZ	Sydney	2018-19
6th	84	M.A.A.Sanjeewani/N.N.D.de Silva	SL v P	Colombo (SSC)	2017-18
7th	58	S.I.R.Dunkley/A.Shrubsole	E v WI	Gros Islet	2018-19
8th	39	L.E.Kaushalya/K.A.D.A.Kanchana	SL v I	Ranchi	2015-16
9th	33*	D.Hazell/H.L.Colvin	E v WI	Bridgetown	2013-14
10th	23*	L.N.McCarthy/E.J.Tice	Ire v SL	Dublin	2013

BOWLING RECORDS – 75 WICKETS IN A CAREER

Wkts			Matches	Overs	Mdns	Runs	Avge	Best	R/Over
115	A.Mohammed	WI	102	346.3	6	1917	16.66	5-10	5.53
100	E.A.Perry	A	102	324.5	6	1919	19.19	4-12	5.90
85	D.Hazell	E	85	317.3	6	1764	20.75	4-12	5.55
84	Sana Mir	P	100	354.2	8	1927	22.94	4-13	5.43
83	Nida Dar	P	91	285.1	7	1456	17.54	5-21	5.10
82	S.R.Taylor	WI	93	247.3	4	1348	16.43	4-12	5.44
81	A.Shrubsole	E	59	200.4	10	1110	13.70	5-11	5.53
80	S.F.M.Devine	NZ	83	218.1	6	1340	16.75	4-22	6.14
80	S.Ismail	SA	75	257.4	10	1528	19.10	5-30	5.93
75	J.L.Gunn	E	104	230.5	1	1487	19.82	5-18	6.44

BEST FIGURES IN AN INNINGS

6- 3	Mas Elysa	Mal v Chi	Bangkok	2018-19
6- 8	B.Mpedi	Bot v Les	Gaborone	2018
6-10	Zon Lin	Mya v Indo	Bangkok	2018-19
6-17	A.E.Satterthwaite	NZ v E	Taunton	2007
5- 4	C.Sutthiruang	Thai v Indo	Bangkok	2018-19
5- 5	D.J.S.Dottin	WI v B	Providence	2018-19
5- 8	S.Luus	SA v Ire	Chennai	2015-16
5-10	A.Mohammed	WI v SA	Cape Town	2009-10
5-10	M.Strano	A v NZ	Geelong	2016-17
5-11	A.Shrubsole	E v NZ	Wellington	2011-12

5-11	J.Goswami	I v A	Visakhapatnam	2011-12
5-12	A.Mohammed	WI v NZ	Bridgetown	2013-14
5-12	W.Liengprasert	Thai v SL	Kuala Lumpur	2018

HAT-TRICKS

Asmavia Iqbal	Pakistan v England	Loughborough	2012
Ekta Bisht	Sri Lanka v India	Colombo (NCC)	2012-13
M.Kapp	South Africa v Bangladesh	Potchefstroom	2013-14
N.R.Sciver	England v New Zealand	Bridgetown	2013-14
Sana Mir	Pakistan v Sri Lanka	Sharjah	2014-15
A.M.Peterson	New Zealand v Australia	Geelong	2016-17
M.Schutt	Australia v India	Mumbai (BS)	2017-18
Fahima Khatun	Bangladesh v UAE	Utrecht	2018
A.Mohammed	West Indies v South Africa	Tarouba	2018-19
A.Shrubsole	England v South Africa	Gros Islet	2018-19

WICKET-KEEPING RECORDS – 40 DISMISSALS IN A CAREER

Dis			Matches	Ct	St
73	S.J.Taylor	England	89	23	50
70	A.J.Healy	Australia	92	28	42
70	M.R.Aguilleira	West Indies	95	36	34
68	R.H.Priest	New Zealand	68	38	30
57	T.Chetty	South Africa	68	34	23
50	Batool Fatima	Pakistan	45	11	39
40	J.M.Fields	Australia	37	25	15

FIVE DISMISSALS IN AN INNINGS

5 (1ct, 4st)	Kycia A.Knight	West Indies v Sri Lanka	Colombo (RPS)	2012-13
5 (1ct, 4st)	Batool Fatima	Pakistan v Ireland	Dublin	2013
5 (1ct, 4st)	Batool Fatima	Pakistan v Ireland	Dublin	2013
5 (3ct, 2st)	B.Bezuuidenhout	New Zealand v Ireland	Dublin	2018

FIELDING RECORDS – 32 CATCHES IN A CAREER

Total			Matches	Total			Matches
58	J.L.Gunn	England	104	33	J.E.Cameron	Australia	64
54	L.S.Greenway	England	85	33	A.J.Blackwell	Australia	95
54	S.W.Bates	New Zealand	111	32	S.A.C.A.King	West Indies	76
38	H.Kaur	India	96	32	S.R.Taylor	West Indies	93

FOUR CATCHES IN AN INNINGS

4	L.S.Greenway	England v New Zealand	Chelmsford	2010
4	V.Krishnamurthy	India v Australia	Providence	2018-19

APPEARANCE RECORDS – 100 APPEARANCES

111	S.W.Bates	New Zealand	102	A.Mohammed	West Indies
110	D.J.S.Dottin	West Indies	102	E.A.Perry	Australia
104	J.L.Gunn	England	100	Sana Mir	Pakistan

50 MATCHES AS CAPTAIN

			W	L	T	NR	%age wins
93	C.M.Edwards	England	68	23	1	1	73.91
73	M.R.Aguilleira	West Indies	39	29	3	2	54.92
65	Sana Mir	Pakistan	26	36	2	1	40.62
64	S.W.Bates	New Zealand	39	24	1	–	60.93
53	M.M.Lanning	Australia	40	13	–	–	75.47
50	M.du Preez	South Africa	24	25	–	1	48.97

KIA SUPER LEAGUE 2018

The third Kia Super League tournament was held between 22 July and 27 August.

Team	P	W	L	T	NR	Pts	Net RR
1 Loughborough Lightning (4)	10	7	3	–	–	33	+1.36
2 Western Storm (3)	10	6	3	–	1	30	+0.91
3 Surrey Stars (2)	10	5	4	–	1	24	–0.40
4 Lancashire Thunder (6)	10	5	5	–	–	21	–0.82
5 Yorkshire Diamonds (5)	10	3	6	–	1	15	–0.29
6 Southern Vipers (1)	10	2	7	–	1	10	–0.49

4 points for a win, with a bonus point if the winning side has a run rate 1.25 times greater than the opposition. 2 points for no result/tie.

Semi-final: At County Ground, Hove, 27 August. Toss: Western Storm. **SURREY STARS** won by 9 runs. Surrey Stars 162-5 (20; N.R.Sciver 72*). Western Storm 153-6 (20; F.C.Wilson 58*). Award: N.R.Sciver.

FINAL: At County Ground, Hove, 27 August. Toss: Loughborough Lightning. **SURREY STARS** won by 66 runs. Surrey Stars 183-6 (20; L.Lee 104, N.R.Sciver 40). Loughborough Lightning 117 (18.3; M.K.Villiers 3-22, D.van Niekerk 3-37). Award: L.Lee.

Previous winners: 2016 Southern Vipers 2017 Western Storm

TEAM RECORDS – HIGHEST TOTALS

185-4 (20)	Storm v Thunder	Taunton	2018
183-6 (20)	Stars v Lightning	Hove	2018
180-2 (20)	Vipers v Lightning	Derby	2017

LOWEST TOTALS

64 (16.3)	Diamonds v Vipers	Southampton	2016
66 (16.4)	Stars v Diamonds	York	2018

LARGEST MARGINS OF VICTORY

95 runs	Diamonds (166-6) v Thunder (71)	Manchester	2016
10 wickets	Diamonds (160-7) v Storm (161-0)	York	2017

BATTING RECORDS – MOST RUNS IN A SEASON

421 (ave 60.14)	S.Mandhana	Western Storm	2018
368 (ave 46.00)	H.C.Knight	Western Storm	2018

HIGHEST SCORES

Score	Balls				
119*	72	S.W.Bates	Vipers v Lightning	Derby	2017
106*	65	R.H.Priest	Storm v Diamonds	York	2017
104	58	L.Lee	Stars v Lightning	Hove	2018
102	61	S.Mandhana	Storm v Thunder	Manchester	2018

HIGHEST STRIKE RATE IN AN INNINGS (Qualification: 30 runs, 240+ strike rate)

R/100B	Score	Balls				
273.6	52*	19	S.Mandhana	Storm v Lightning	Taunton	2018
240.0	48	20	S.Mandhana	Storm v Diamonds	Taunton	2018

BOWLING RECORDS – 16 WICKETS IN A SEASON

Wkts			Year	P	O	M	Runs	Avge	Best	4w	R/Over
17	K.L.Gordon	Lightning	2018	11	35.0	–	212	12.47	3-13	–	6.05
16	S.F.M.Devine	Lightning	2018	11	35.5	1	259	16.18	3-15	–	7.22

BEST BOWLING FIGURES IN AN INNINGS

5-23	A.Shrubsole	Storm v Diamonds	Leeds	2016
5-26	R.M.Farrell	Stars v Thunder	Manchester	2017
5-26	K.H.Brunt	Diamonds v Vipers	York	2018

PRINCIPAL WOMEN'S FIXTURES 2019

F   Floodlit match   LOI   Royal London Limited-overs International
IT20   Vitality Women's IT20   TM   Kia Women's Test Match
KSL   Kia Super League

Thu 6 June
LOI^F   Leicester   England v West Indies

Sun 9 June
LOI   Worcester   England v West Indies

Thu 13 June
LOI^F   Chelmsford   England v West Indies

Tue 18 June
IT20^F   Northampton   England v West Indies

Fri 21 June
IT20^F   Northampton   England v West Indies

Tue 25 June
IT20^F   Derby   England v West Indies

Tue 2 July
LOI^F   Leicester   England v Australia

Thu 4 July
LOI^F   Leicester   England v Australia

Sun 7 July
LOI   Canterbury   England v Australia

Thu 18 – Sun 21 July
TM   Taunton   ENGLAND v AUSTRALIA

Fri 26 July
IT20^F   Chelmsford   England v Australia

Sun 28 July
IT20   Hove   England v Australia

Wed 31 July
IT20^F   Bristol   England v Australia

Tue 6 August
KSL   Liverpool   Thunder v Vipers
KSL   Loughborough   Lightning v Storm
KSL^F   Leeds   Diamonds v Stars

Thu 8 August
KSL   Loughborough   Lightning v Vipers
KSL   Guildford   Stars v Thunder

Sat 10 August
KSL   Taunton   Storm v Thunder

Sun 11 August
KSL   Southampton   Vipers v Storm
KSL   Leeds   Diamonds v Lightning

Mon 12 August
KSL^F   The Oval   Stars v Vipers

Tue 13 August
KSL   Liverpool   Thunder v Diamonds
KSL   Bristol   Storm v Lightning

Thu 15 August
KSL^F   Hove   Vipers v Thunder
KSL   Guildford   Stars v Lightning
KSL   York   Diamonds v Storm

Sun 18 August
KSL   Chester BH   Thunder v Storm
KSL   Loughborough   Lightning v Diamonds
KSL   Arundel   Vipers v Stars

Tue 20 August
KSL^F   Manchester   Thunder v Lightning
KSL   Guildford   Stars v Diamonds
KSL   Bristol   Storm v Vipers

Wed 21 August
KSL^F   Southampton   Vipers v Diamonds
KSL^F   Taunton   Storm v Stars

Fri 23 August
KSL   Loughborough   Lightning v Stars
KSL   Scarborough   Diamonds v Thunder

Sun 25 August
KSL   Nottingham   Lightning v Thunder
KSL   Guildford   Stars v Storm
KSL   York   Diamonds v Vipers

Wed 28 August
KSL^F   tbc   Thunder v Stars
KSL^F   Southampton   Vipers v Lightning
KSL^F   Taunton   Storm v Diamonds

Sun 1 September
KSL   Hove   Semi-final and FINAL

MCCA FIXTURES 2019

Sun 5 May
	TWENTY20 COMPETITION
Carlisle	Cumberland v Cheshire (1)
Grantham	Lincolnshire v Northumberland (1)
Brockhampton	Herefordshire v Oxfordshire (2)
Whitchurch	Shropshire v Berkshire (2)
Peterborough	Cambridgeshire v Hertfordshire (3)
Werrington	Cornwall v Wiltshire (4)
Newbridge	Wales MC v Devon (4)

Sun 5 May
	KNOCK-OUT TROPHY
Manor Park	Norfolk v Suffolk

Mon 6 May
	TWENTY20 COMPETITION
Wargrave	Berkshire v Buckinghamshire (2)
Magdalen C Sch	Oxfordshire v Shropshire (2)
Welwyn Garden C	Hertfordshire v Bedfordshire (3)
Manor Park	Norfolk v Suffolk (3)
Sidmouth	Devon v Wiltshire (4)
Newport	Wales MC v Dorset (4)

Sun 12 May
	TWENTY20 COMPETITION
Woolpit	Suffolk v Cambridgeshire (3)

Sun 12 May
	KNOCK-OUT TROPHY
Ampthill	Bedfordshire v Oxfordshire
Toft	Cheshire v Northumberland
Bishop's Stortford	Hertfordshire v Staffordshire

Sun 19 May
	TWENTY20 COMPETITION
Nantwich	Cheshire v Staffordshire (1)
Jesmond	Northumberland v Cumberland (1)

Sun 26 May
	TWENTY20 COMPETITION
Penrith	Cumberland v Lincolnshire (1)
Rolleston	Staffordshire v Northumberland (1)
High Wycombe	Buckinghamshire v Oxfordshire (2)
Wrekin College	Shropshire v Herefordshire (2)
Dunstable	Bedfordshire v Suffolk (3)
Sawston	Cambridgeshire v Norfolk (3)
Wadebridge	Cornwall v Wales MC (4)
North Perrott	Dorset v Devon (4)

Sun 2 June
	KNOCK-OUT TROPHY
Bracebridge H	Lincs v Cheshire/N'berland (a)
Oswestry	Shropshire v Cumberland (b)
Eastnor	Herefordshire v Herts/Staffs (c)
Exning	Cambs v Norfolk/Suffolk (d)
Oratory School	Berkshire v Dorset (e)
Truro	Cornwall v Buckinghamshire (f)
Lisvane	Wales MC v Beds/Oxon (g)
Warminster	Wiltshire v Devon (h)

Sun 9 June
	TWENTY20 COMPETITION
tbc	Lincolnshire v Staffordshire (1)
Jesmond	Northumberland v Cheshire (1)
Colwall	Herefordshire v Buckinghamshire (2)
Banbury	Oxfordshire v Berkshire (2)
Manor Park	Norfolk v Bedfordshire (3)
Ipswich School	Suffolk v Hertfordshire (3)
Wimborne	Dorset v Cornwall (4)
Warminster	Wiltshire v Wales MC

Sun 16 June	**TWENTY20 COMPETITION**
New Brighton	Cheshire v Lincolnshire (1)
tbc	Staffordshire v Cumberland (1)
Falkland	Berkshire v Herefordshire (2)
Gerrards Cross	Buckinghamshire v Shropshire (2)
Bedford	Bedfordshire v Cambridgeshire (3)
Harpenden	Hertfordshire v Norfolk (3)
North Devon	Devon v Cornwall (4)
South Wilts	Wiltshire v Dorset (4)

Sun 23 – Tue 25 June	**MCCA CHAMPIONSHIP**
tbc	Cambridgeshire v Norfolk
Chester BH	Cheshire v Wiltshire
Truro	Cornwall v Oxfordshire
Colwall	Herefordshire v Berkshire
Bishop's Stortford	Hertfordshire v Buckinghamshire
Sleaford	Lincolnshire v Cumberland
Swalwell	Northumberland v Bedfordshire
Shrewsbury	Shropshire v Dorset
Sleaford	Suffolk v Staffordshire
Pontarddulais	Wales MC v Devon

Sun 30 June	**KNOCK-OUT TROPHY – Quarter-finals**
Match 1	Winner Match (a) v Winner Match (b)
Match 2	Winner Match (c) v Winner Match (d)
Match 3	Winner Match (e) v Winner Match (f)
Match 4	Winner Match (g) v Winner Match (h)

Sun 7 – Tue 9 July	**MCCA CHAMPIONSHIP**
Bedford Modern S	Bedfordshire v Hertfordshire
Falkland	Berkshire v Wales MC
High Wycombe	Buckinghamshire v Suffolk
Netherfield	Cumberland v Cambridgeshire
Bournemouth	Dorset v Cheshire
Eastnor	Herefordshire v Devon
Banbury	Oxfordshire v Shropshire
West Brom Dartmouth	Staffordshire v Lincolnshire
Corsham	Wiltshire v Cornwall

Sun 21 – Tue 23 July	**MCCA CHAMPIONSHIP**
Finchampstead	Berkshire v Cheshire
Chesham	Buckinghamshire v Northumberland
Wisbech	Cambridgeshire v Bedfordshire
Furness	Cumberland v Norfolk
Sandford	Devon v Wiltshire
Bashley	Dorset v Herefordshire
North Mymms	Hertfordshire v Staffordshire
Cleethorpes	Lincolnshire v Suffolk
Bridgnorth	Shropshire v Cornwall
Usk	Wales MC v Oxfordshire

Sun 4 – Tue 6 August	**MCCA CHAMPIONSHIP**
Flitwick	Bedfordshire v Buckinghamshire
Alderley Edge	Cheshire v Devon
Redruth	Cornwall v Dorset
Manor Park	Norfolk v Lincolnshire
Jesmond	Northumberland v Hertfordshire
The Parks	Oxfordshire v Herefordshire
Shifnal	Shropshire v Berkshire
Checkley	Staffordshire v Cumberland
Ipswich School	Suffolk v Cambridgeshire
South Wilts	Wiltshire v Wales MC

Sun 11 – Tue 13 August Manor Park	**MCCA CHAMPIONSHIP** Norfolk v Northumberland
Sun 11 August tbc tbc	**KNOCK-OUT TROPHY – Semi-finals** Winner Match 1 v Winner Match 2 Winner Match 3 v Winner Match 4
Sun 18 – Tue 20 August Luton Town & Ind Nantwich St Austell Sedbergh School Sidmouth North Perrott Brockhampton Hertford Manor Park Jesmond	**MCCA CHAMPIONSHIP** Bedfordshire v Staffordshire Cheshire v Shropshire Cornwall v Berkshire Cumberland v Suffolk Devon v Oxfordshire Dorset v Wales MC Herefordshire v Wiltshire Hertfordshire v Lincolnshire Norfolk v Buckinghamshire Northumberland v Cambridgeshire
Sun 25 August Wormsley	**TWENTY20 COMPETITION** Finals Day
Wed 28 August Wormsley	**KNOCK-OUT TROPHY** FINAL
Sun 1 – Tue 3 September Wargrave Tring Park Saffron Walden Exeter Grantham Thame Longton Bury St Edmunds Abergavenny Marlborough	**MCCA CHAMPIONSHIP** Berkshire v Dorset Buckinghamshire v Cumberland Cambridgeshire v Hertfordshire Devon v Cornwall Lincolnshire v Bedfordshire Oxfordshire v Cheshire Staffordshire v Norfolk Suffolk v Norfolk Wales MC v Herefordshire Wiltshire v Shropshire
Sun 15 – Wed 18 September tbc	**MCCA CHAMPIONSHIP** FINAL

MCCA TWENTY20 COMPETITION GROUPS

Group 1	Group 2	Group 3	Group 4
Cheshire	Berkshire	Bedfordshire	Cornwall
Cumberland	Buckinghamshire	Cambridgeshire	Devon
Lincolnshire	Herefordshire	Hertfordshire	Dorset
Northumberland	Oxfordshire	Norfolk	Wales MC
Staffordshire	Shropshire	Suffolk	Wiltshire

SECOND XI CHAMPIONSHIP FIXTURES 2019

THREE-DAY MATCHES

APRIL
Tue 16	H Wycombe	MCC YC v Kent
Wed 17	Northampton	Northants v Notts
Tue 23	Tunbridge W	Kent v Essex
Wed 24	Harrogate	Yorkshire v Notts
Tue 30	Newclose IoW	Hampshire v Middlesex
	Crosby	Lancashire v Worcs

MAY
Mon 6	Liverpool	Lancashire v Northants
Tue 7	Rockhampton	Glos v Middlesex
	Blackstone	Sussex v Somerset
	Barnt Green	Worcs v Warwicks
Wed 8	Notts SC	Notts v Leics
Mon 13	Derby	Derbyshire v Durham
Tue 14	Billericay	Essex v Glos
	H Wycombe	MCC YC v Sussex
	Kidderminster	Worcs v Yorkshire
Wed 15	Neath	Glamorgan v Surrey
Tue 21	tbc	Durham v Notts
	Kibworth	Leics v Yorkshire
	Radlett	Middlesex v Glamorgan
	Taunton Vale	Somerset v MCC YC
	LSE, N Malden	Surrey v Glos
	Portland Rd, Birm	Warwicks v Northants
Sun 26	Notts SC	Notts v Warwicks
Mon 27	Milton Keynes	Northants v Durham
	Taunton Vale	Somerset v Hampshire
Tue 28	Uxbridge	Middlesex v Sussex
	York	Yorkshire v Derbyshire

JUNE
Tue 4	B Stortford	Essex v Middlesex
	Chester BH	Lancashire v Durham
	Loughborough	Leics v Derbyshire
	Preston Nom	Sussex v Surrey
Mon 10	Derby	Derbyshire v Notts
Tue 11	Burnopfield	Durham v Warwicks
	Neath	Glamorgan v Essex
	Basingstoke	Hampshire v MCC YC
	Polo Farm, Cant	Kent v Surrey
	Northampton	Northants v Worcs
Mon 17	Belper Mead	Derbyshire v Lancashire
	H Wycombe	MCC YC v Surrey
	Harrogate	Yorkshire v Durham
Tue 18	Newport	Glamorgan v Glos

	Southgate	Middlesex v Somerset
	Portland Road, Birm	Warwicks v Leics
Wed 19	Folkestone	Kent v Hampshire
Mon 24	Billericay	Essex v Sussex
	Taunton Vale	Somerset v Kent
Wed 26	Worcester	Worcs v Derbyshire

JULY
Mon 1	Rockhampton	Glos v Somerset
	Southgate	Middlesex v MCC YC
	Stourbridge	Worcs v Leics
Tue 2	LSE, N Malden	Surrey v Hampshire
	Horsham	Sussex v Glamorgan
	Portland Rd, Birm	Warwicks v Lancashire
Mon 8	Billericay	Essex v Surrey
	Radlett	Middlesex v Kent
	Barnt Green	Warwicks v Derbyshire
Tue 9	S N'berland	Durham v Leics
	Bristol CC	Glos v Hampshire
Wed 10	Liverpool	Lancashire v Yorkshire
Mon 15	Beckenham	Kent v Sussex
Tue 16	Coggeshall	Essex v MCC YC
	tbc	Leics v Northants
	Stamford Brg	Yorkshire v Warwicks
Wed 17	Notts SC	Notts v Lancashire
Mon 22	Chester-le-St	Durham v Worcs
	Taunton Vale	Somerset v Essex
Tue 23	Newport	Glamorgan v Kent
Tue 30	Southampton	Hampshire v Glamorgan
	Desborough	Northants v Yorkshire
Wed 31	Rockhampton	Glos v MCC YC
	Notts SC	Notts v Worcs

AUGUST
Mon 5	Hem Heath	Derbyshire v Northants
Tue 6	Southampton	Hampshire v Essex
	H Wycombe	MCC YC v Glamorgan
	Blackstone	Sussex v Glos
Wed 7	LSE, N Malden	Surrey v Middlesex
Mon 12	Southampton	Hampshire v Sussex
	Kibworth	Leics v Lancashire
	LSE, N Malden	Surrey v Somerset
Tue 13	Bath	Glos v Kent
Tue 20	Taunton Vale	Somerset v Glamorgan

SEPTEMBER
Tue 3	tbc	FINAL (Four days)

SECOND XI TROPHY FIXTURES 2019

ONE-DAY MATCHES

APRIL		
Fri 12	Notts SC	Notts v Northants
Mon 15	Shenley	MCC YC v Kent
	Northampton	Northants v Leics
	Moseley	Warwicks v Derbyshire
Tue 16	Billericay	Essex v Middlesex
Wed 17	Southampton	Hampshire v Sussex
	Radlett	Middlesex v Somerset
Thu 18	Moseley	Warwicks v Worcs
	Scarborough	Yorkshire v Lancashire
Mon 22	Preston Nom	Sussex v Kent
Tue 23	Ticknall	Derbyshire v Lancashire
	Taunton Vale	Somerset v Glamorgan
	Preston Nom	Sussex v Glos
	Worcester RGS	Worcs v Leics
	York	Yorkshire v Notts
Wed 24	Sudbrook	Glamorgan v MCC YC
	Southampton	Hampshire v Surrey
	Desborough	Northants v Warwicks
Thu 25	Leicester	Leics v Durham
	Taunton Vale	Somerset v Glos
Fri 26	Bedminster	Glos v Hampshire
	Tunbridge W	Kent v Essex
	LSE, N Malden	Surrey v MCC YC
Mon 29	Bedminster	Glos v Glamorgan
	Newclose IoW	Hampshire v Middlesex
	Southport	Lancashire v Worcs
	Watford	MCC YC v Essex
MAY		
Wed 1	Derby	Derbyshire v Notts
	Billericay	Essex v Somerset

Fri 3	Worksop Coll	Notts v Warwicks
	LSE, N Malden	Surrey v Sussex
Mon 6	Rockhampton	Glos v Kent
	Radlett	Middlesex v Surrey
	Blackstone	Sussex v Somerset
Tue 7	Southampton	Hampshire v MCC YC
	Polo Farm, Cant	Kent v Surrey
Thu 9	Liverpool	Lancashire v Northants
Fri 10	Brandon	Durham v Yorkshire
Mon 13	Billericay	Essex v Glos
	Lutterworth	Leics v Lancashire
	Shenley	MCC YC v Sussex
	Kidderminster	Worcs v Yorkshire
Tue 14	Pontypridd	Glamorgan v Surrey
Thu 16	Denstone Coll	Derbyshire v Durham
	Polo Farm, Cant	Kent v Middlesex
Mon 20	Hartlepool	Durham v Notts
	Lutterworth	Leics v Derbyshire
	Radlett	Middlesex v Glamorgan
	Moseley	Warwicks v Northants
	Worcester	Worcs v Derbyshire
Thu 30	Taunton Vale	Somerset v Hampshire
Fri 31	Barnsley	Yorkshire v Derbyshire
JUNE		
Mon 3	Chester BH	Lancashire v Durham
Mon 10	Jesmond	Durham v Warwicks
	Monmouth S	Glamorgan v Essex
	Finedon	Northants v Worcs
Thu 13	Trent Coll	Notts v Leics
Fri 21	tbc	Semi-finals
Thu 27	tbc	FINAL

SECOND XI TWENTY20 CUP FIXTURES 2019

ONE-DAY MATCHES

MAY		
Thu 30	Milton Keynes	Northants v Durham
JUNE		
Thu 6	Stourport	Worcs v Warwicks
Mon 17	Barnt Green	Warwicks v Leics
Tue 18	Folkestone	Kent v Hampshire
Mon 24	Leicester	Leics v Notts
Thu 27	Billericay	Essex v Sussex
	Shenley	MCC YC v Hampshire
	Taunton Vale	Somerset v Kent
JULY		
Mon 1	Horsham	Sussex v Glamorgan
	Moseley	Warwicks v Lancashire
Thu 4	Finchley	MCC YC v Middlesex
Fri 5	Northampton	Northants v Notts
Mon 8	S N'berland	Durham v Leics
	Newport	Glamorgan v Somerset
	Leeds W'wood	Yorkshire v Worcs
Thu 11	Radlett	Middlesex v Kent
	Taunton Vale	Somerset v MCC YC
	Kidderminster	Worcs v Northants
Fri 12	Derby	Derbyshire v Warwicks
Mon 15	Cardiff, Cath S	Glamorgan v Glos
	Rugby S	Leics v Northants
	Welbeck	Notts v Derbyshire
	Leeds W'wood	Yorkshire v Warwicks
Wed 17	Rockhampton	Glos v Somerset
Thu 18	Beckenham	Kent v Sussex
Fri 19	Coggeshall	Essex v MCC YC
Mon 22	Newport	Glamorgan v Kent
	Westhoughton	Lancashire v Derbyshire

	Taunton Vale	Somerset v Essex
	LSE, N Malden	Surrey v Glos
	Hove	Sussex v Hampshire
Wed 24	Glossop	Derbyshire v Yorkshire
	Bristol CC	Glos v Middlesex
	Westhoughton	Lancashire v Leics
	LSE, N Malden	Surrey v Hampshire
Thu 25	Burnopfield	Durham v Worcs
	Blackpool	Lancashire v Yorkshire
Mon 29	Chelmsford	Essex v Surrey
	Southampton	Hampshire v Glamorgan
	Desborough	Northants v Yorkshire
	Worcester	Worcs v Notts
Tue 30	Rockhampton	Glos v MCC YC
	Radlett	Middlesex v Sussex
Wed 31	LSE, N Malden	Surrey v Somerset
AUGUST		
Thu 1	Rugby S	Leics v Derbyshire
	LSE, N Malden	Surrey v Middlesex
Fri 2	Burnopfield	Durham v Lancashire
	Northwood	Middlesex v Essex
Mon 5	Southampton	Hampshire v Essex
	Finchley	MCC YC v Glamorgan
	Grantham	Notts v Worcs
	Blackstone	Sussex v Surrey
	Marske	Yorkshire v Durham
Wed 7	Grantham	Notts v Lancashire
	Barnt Green	Warwicks v Durham
Thu 8	Hem Heath	Derbyshire v Northants
Fri 9	Polo Farm, Cant	Kent v Glos
Thu 15	Arundel	FINALS DAY

ICC CRICKET WORLD CUP FIXTURES 2019

Thu 30 May	10.30	The Oval	England v South Africa
Fri 31 May	10.30	Nottingham	Pakistan v West Indies
Sat 1 June	10.30	Cardiff	New Zealand v Sri Lanka
	13.30	Bristol	Afghanistan v Australia
Sun 2 June	10.30	The Oval	Bangladesh v South Africa
Mon 3 June	10.30	Nottingham	England v Pakistan
Tue 4 June	10.30	Cardiff	Afghanistan v Sri Lanka
Wed 5 June	10.30	Southampton	India v South Africa
	13.30	The Oval	Bangladesh v New Zealand
Thu 6 June	10.30	Nottingham	Australia v West Indies
Fri 7 June	10.30	Bristol	Pakistan v Sri Lanka
Sat 8 June	10.30	Cardiff	England v Bangladesh
	13.30	Taunton	Afghanistan v New Zealand
Sun 9 June	10.30	The Oval	Australia v India
Mon 10 June	10.30	Southampton	South Africa v West Indies
Tue 11 June	10.30	Bristol	Bangladesh v Sri Lanka
Wed 12 June	10.30	Taunton	Australia v Pakistan
Thu 13 June	10.30	Nottingham	India v New Zealand
Fri 14 June	10.30	Southampton	England v West Indies
Sat 15 June	10.30	The Oval	Australia v Sri Lanka
	13.30	Cardiff	Afghanistan v South Africa
Sun 16 June	10.30	Manchester	India v Pakistan
Mon 17 June	10.30	Taunton	Bangladesh v West Indies
Tue 18 June	10.30	Manchester	Afghanistan v England
Wed 19 June	10.30	Birmingham	New Zealand v South Africa
Thu 20 June	10.30	Nottingham	Australia v Bangladesh
Fri 21 June	10.30	Leeds	England v Sri Lanka
Sat 22 June	10.30	Southampton	Afghanistan v India
	13.30	Manchester	New Zealand v West Indies
Sun 23 June	10.30	Lord's	Pakistan v South Africa
Mon 24 June	10.30	Southampton	Afghanistan v Bangladesh
Tue 25 June	10.30	Lord's	England v Australia
Wed 26 June	10.30	Birmingham	New Zealand v Pakistan
Thu 27 June	10.30	Manchester	India v West Indies
Fri 28 June	10.30	Chester-le-St	South Africa v Sri Lanka
Sat 29 June	10.30	Leeds	Afghanistan v Pakistan
	13.30	Lord's	Australia v New Zealand
Sun 30 June	10.30	Birmingham	England v India
Mon 1 July	10.30	Chester-le-St	Sri Lanka v West Indies
Tue 2 July	10.30	Birmingham	Bangladesh v India
Wed 3 July	10.30	Chester-le-St	England v New Zealand
Thu 4 July	10.30	Leeds	Afghanistan v West Indies
Fri 5 July	13.30	Lord's	Bangladesh v Pakistan
Sat 6 July	10.30	Leeds	India v Sri Lanka
	13.30	Manchester	Australia v South Africa
Tue 9 July	10.30	Manchester	First semi-final
Thu 11 July	10.30	Birmingham	Second semi-final
Sun 14 July	10.30	Lord's	FINAL

PRINCIPAL FIXTURES 2019

CC1	Specsavers County Championship Division 1	
CC2	Specsavers County Championship Division 2	
F	Floodlit	
FCF	First-Class Friendly	
LOI	Royal London Limited-Overs International	

50L	Royal London One-Day Cup
T20	Vitality Blast
IT20	Vitality Twenty20 International
TM	Specsavers Test Match
MCCU	MCC University
Uni	University match

Sun 24 – Wed 27 March
FCF	Dubai	MCC v Surrey

Tue 26 – Thu 28 March
Uni	Cambridge	Cambridge MCCU v Essex
Uni	Derby	Derbyshire v Loughboro MCCU
Uni	Chester-le-St	Durham v Durham MCCU
Uni	Leicester	Leics v Loughboro MCCU
Uni	Northwood	Middlesex v Oxford MCCU
Uni	Taunton	Somerset v Cardiff MCCU

Sun 31 March – Tue 2 April
Uni	Cambridge	Cambridge MCCU v Notts
Uni	Canterbury	Kent v Loughboro MCCU
Uni	Weetwood	Leeds/Brad MCCU v Yorkshire
Uni	Northampton	Northants v Durham MCCU
Uni	Oxford	Oxford MCCU v Hampshire
Uni	Hove	Sussex v Cardiff MCCU

Thu 4 – Sat 6 April
Uni	The Oval	Surrey v Durham MCCU

Fri 5 – Mon 8 April
CC1	Southampton	Hampshire v Essex
CC1	Nottingham	Notts v Yorkshire
CC1	Taunton	Somerset v Kent
CC2	Derby	Derbyshire v Durham
CC2	Northampton	Northants v Middlesex
CC2	Hove	Sussex v Leics

Fri 5 – Sun 7 April
Uni	Cambridge	Cambridge MCCU v Worcs
Uni	Cardiff	Glamorgan v Cardiff MCCU
Uni	Bristol	Glos v Oxford MCCU
Uni	Loughborough	Loughboro MCCU v Lancashire
Uni	Birmingham	Warwicks v Leeds/Brad MCCU

Thu 11 – Sun 14 April
CC1	Southampton	Hampshire v Yorkshire
CC1	Nottingham	Notts v Somerset
CC1	The Oval	Surrey v Essex
CC1	Birmingham	Warwicks v Kent
CC2	Chester-le-St	Durham v Sussex
CC2	Cardiff	Glamorgan v Northants
CC2	Bristol	Glos v Derbyshire
CC2	Leicester	Leics v Worcs

CC2	Lord's	Middlesex v Lancashire

Wed 17 April
50L	Chester-le-St	Durham v Northants
50L	Cardiff	Glamorgan v Essex
50L	Bristol	Glos v Surrey
50L^F	Canterbury	Kent v Hampshire
50L	Manchester	Lancashire v Worcs
50L	Leeds	Yorkshire v Leics

Fri 19 April
50L	Derby	Derbyshire v Northants
50L	Chester-le-St	Durham v Leics
50L	Chelmsford	Essex v Middlesex
50L	Southampton	Hampshire v Glamorgan
50L	Nottingham	Notts v Lancashire
50L	Taunton	Somerset v Kent
50L^F	Hove	Sussex v Surrey
50L	Birmingham	Warwicks v Yorkshire

Sun 21 April
50L	Derby	Derbyshire v Notts
50L	Cardiff	Glamorgan v Somerset
50L	Beckenham	Kent v Sussex
50L	Leicester	Leics v Worcs
50L	Lord's	Middlesex v Glos
50L	Northampton	Northants v Warwicks
50L	Leeds	Yorkshire v Lancashire

Tue 23 April
50L	Bristol	Glos v Kent
50L	Southampton	Hampshire v Middlesex
50L	The Oval	Surrey v Essex
50L	Birmingham	Warwicks v Notts

Wed 24 April
50L	Manchester	Lancashire v Northants
50L	Leicester	Leics v Derbyshire
50L	Hove	Sussex v Somerset
50L	Worcester	Worcs v Durham

Thu 25 April
50L	Cardiff	Glamorgan v Kent
50L	The Oval	Surrey v Middlesex

Fri 26 April

50L	Southampton	Hampshire v Glos
50L	Northampton	Northants v Worcs
50L	Nottingham	Notts v Leics
50L^F	Taunton	Somerset v Essex
50L	Birmingham	Warwicks v Durham
50L	Leeds	Yorkshire v Derbyshire

Sat 27 April

50L	Lord's	Middlesex v Sussex
	Beckenham	Kent v Pakistanis

Sun 28 April

50L	Chester-le-St	Durham v Derbyshire
50L	Chelmsford	Essex v Hampshire
50L	Cardiff	Glamorgan v Surrey
50L	Bristol	Glos v Somerset
50L	Manchester	Lancashire v Leics
50L	Nottingham	Notts v Yorkshire
50L	Worcester	Worcs v Warwicks

Mon 29 April

	Northampton	Northants v Pakistanis

Tue 30 April

50L	Derby	Derbyshire v Warwicks
50L	Gosforth	Durham v Lancashire
50L	Chelmsford	Essex v Sussex
50L	Bristol	Glos v Somerset
50L	The Oval	Surrey v Hampshire

Wed 1 May

50L	Radlett	Middlesex v Somerset
50L^F	Northampton	Northants v Yorkshire
50L	Worcester	Worcs v Notts
F	Leicester	Leics v Pakistanis

Thu 2 May

50L	Southampton	Hampshire v Sussex
50L	Manchester	Lancashire v Derbyshire
50L	The Oval	Surrey v Kent

Fri 3 May

LOI	Dublin	Ireland v England
50L	Grantham	Notts v Durham

Sat 4 May

50L	Leicester	Leics v Northants
50L	Birmingham	Warwicks v Lancashire
50L	Worcester	Worcs v Yorkshire

Sun 5 May

IT20	Cardiff	England v Pakistan
50L	Beckenham	Kent v Essex
50L	Lord's	Middlesex v Glamorgan
50L	Taunton	Somerset v Hampshire
50L	Eastbourne	Sussex v Glos

Mon 6 May

50L	Derby	Derbyshire v Worcs
50L	Leicester	Leics v Warwicks
50L	Northampton	Northants v Notts
50L	Leeds	Yorkshire v Durham

Tue 7 May

50L^F	Chelmsford	Essex v Glos
50L^F	Canterbury	Kent v Middlesex
50L^F	Taunton	Somerset v Surrey
50L^F	Hove	Sussex v Glamorgan

Wed 8 May

LOI	The Oval	**England v Pakistan**

Fri 10 May

50L^F	tbc	Quarter-final 1 & 2

Sat 11 May

LOI	Southampton	**England v Pakistan**

Sun 12 May

50L	tbc	Semi-final 1 & 2

Tue 14 – Fri 17 May

CC1	Chelmsford	Essex v Notts
CC1	Canterbury	Kent v Yorkshire
CC1	Taunton	Somerset v Surrey
CC1	Birmingham	Warwicks v Hampshire
CC2	Newport	Glamorgan v Glos
CC2	Manchester	Lancashire v Northants
CC2	Lord's	Middlesex v Leics
CC2	Worcester	Worcs v Durham

Tue 14 May

LOI^F	Bristol	**England v Pakistan**

Fri 17 May

LOI^F	Nottingham	**England v Pakistan**

Sun 19 – Wed 22 May

CC2	Derby	Derbyshire v Glamorgan

Sun 19 May

LOI	Leeds	**England v Pakistan**

Mon 20 – Thu 23 May

CC1	Newport, IoW	Hampshire v Notts
CC1	Beckenham	Kent v Surrey
CC1	Taunton	Kent v Warwicks
CC2	Chester-le-St	Durham v Glos
CC2	Manchester	Lancashire v Worcs
CC2	Northampton	Northants v Sussex

Sat 25 May

50L	Lord's	FINAL

Mon 27 – Thu 30 May

CC1	Chelmsford	Essex v Kent
CC1	Birmingham	Warwicks v Surrey

CC1	Leeds	Yorkshire v Hampshire
CC2	Cheltenham	Glos v Lancashire
CC2	Leicester	Leics v Derbyshire
CC2	Hove	Sussex v Glamorgan
CC2	Worcester	Worcs v Middlesex

Tue 28 May

	Lord's	Oxford U v Cambridge U

Sun 2 – Wed 5 June

CC2	Lord's	Middlesex v Sussex
CC2	Northampton	Northants v Glamorgan

Mon 3 – Thu 6 June

CC1	Guildford	Surrey v Somerset
CC1	Birmingham	Warwicks v Notts
CC1	Leeds	Yorkshire v Essex
CC2	Chester-le-St	Durham v Derbyshire
CC2	Liverpool	Lancashire v Leics

Sun 9 – Wed 12 June

CC1	Mansfield	Notts v Hampshire

Mon 10 – Thu 13 June

CC1	Canterbury	Kent v Somerset
CC1	Guildford	Surrey v Yorkshire
CC2	Chester-le-St	Durham v Northants
CC2	Leicester	Leics v Middlesex
CC2	Worcester	Worcs v Lancashire

Tue 11 – Fri 14 June

CC2	Swansea	Glamorgan v Derbyshire
CC2	Arundel	Sussex v Glos

Sun 16 – Wed 19 June

CC1	Chelmsford	Essex v Hampshire
CC2	Radlett	Middlesex v Glamorgan

Mon 17 – Thu 20 June

CC1	Tunbridge W	Kent v Notts
CC1	York	Yorkshire v Warwicks
CC2	Derby	Derbyshire v Lancashire
CC2	Leicester	Leics v Glos
CC2	Worcester	Worcs v Sussex

Thu 20 June
F

	Northampton	Northants v Australia A

Sun 23 – Wed 26 June

CC1	Chelmsford	Essex v Somerset
CC1	The Oval	Surrey v Warwicks
CC2	Bristol	Glos v Glamorgan

Sun 23 June

	Derby	Derbyshire v Australia A

Mon 24 – Thu 27 June

CC2	Northampton	Northants v Leics
CC2	Hove	Sussex v Durham

Tue 25 June

	Worcester	Worcs v Australia A

Sun 30 June – Wed 3 July

CC1	Canterbury	Kent v Warwicks
CC1	Nottingham	Notts v Essex
CC1	Taunton	Somerset v Hampshire
CC1	Scarborough	Yorkshire v Surrey
CC2	Derby	Derbyshire v Middlesex
CC2	Cardiff	Glamorgan v Worcs
CC2	Sedburgh S	Lancashire v Durham
CC2	Hove	Sussex v Northants

Sun 30 June

	Bristol	Glos v Australia A

Tue 2 – Fri 5 July

FCF	Cambridge	Cambridge U v Oxford U

Tue 2 July

	Bristol	Glos v Australia A

Sat 6 – Tue 9 July

CC1	Southampton	Hampshire v Warwicks

Sun 7 – Wed 10 July

CC1	Chelmsford	Essex v Yorkshire
CC1	Taunton	Somerset v Notts
CC1	The Oval	Surrey v Kent
CC2	Leicester	Leics v Durham
CC2	Northwood	Middlesex v Glos
CC2	Northampton	Northants v Lancashire
CC2	Worcester	Worcs v Derbyshire
FCF	Arundel	Sussex v Australia A

Sat 13 – Tue 16 July

CC1	Southampton	Hampshire v Kent
CC1	Nottingham	Notts v Surrey
CC1	Worcester	Warwicks v Essex
CC1	Leeds	Yorkshire v Somerset
CC2	Chester-le-St	Durham v Worcs
CC2	Cardiff	Glamorgan v Middlesex
CC2	Manchester	Lancashire v Sussex

Sun 14 – Wed 17 July

CC2	Chesterfield	Derbyshire v Northants
FCF	Canterbury	Eng Lions v Aus/Aus A

Mon 15 – Thu 18 July

CC2	Cheltenham	Glos v Leics

Thu 18 July

T20F	Cardiff	Glamorgan v Somerset
T20F	Lord's	Middlesex v Essex
T20F	Nottingham	Notts v Worcs

Fri 19 July

T20F	Chester-le-St	Durham v Northants
T20F	Chelmsford	Essex v Surrey

T20	Cheltenham	Glos v Glamorgan
T20^F	Southampton	Hampshire v Sussex
T20^F	Leicester	Leics v Lancashire
T20	Worcester	Worcs v Warwicks
T20^F	Leeds	Yorkshire v Notts

Sat 20 July

T20	Chesterfield	Derbyshire v Yorkshire
T20^F	Canterbury	Kent v Somerset

Sun 21 – Wed 24 July

CC2	Cheltenham	Glos v Worcs

Sun 21 July

T20	Southampton	Hampshire v Kent
T20	Manchester	Lancashire v Durham
T20	Birmingham	Warwicks v Leics

Tue 23 – Fri 26 July

FCF	Southampton	Australians v Australia A

Tue 23 July

T20^F	Leicester	Leics v Yorkshire
T20^F	The Oval	Surrey v Middlesex

Wed 24 – Sat 27 July

TM	Lord's	ENGLAND v IRELAND

Wed 24 July

T20^F	Nottingham	Notts v Northants
T20^F	Hove	Sussex v Hampshire
T20^F	Birmingham	Warwicks v Derbyshire

Thu 25 July

T20	Cheltenham	Glos v Middlesex
T20^F	The Oval	Surrey v Glamorgan
T20^F	Leeds	Yorkshire v Lancashire

Fri 26 July

T20^F	Derby	Derbyshire v Notts
T20^F	Cardiff	Glamorgan v Middlesex
T20^F	Canterbury	Kent v Essex
T20^F	Manchester	Lancashire v Worcs
T20^F	Leicester	Leics v Durham
T20^F	Northampton	Northants v Warwicks
T20^F	Taunton	Somerset v Hampshire
T20^F	Hove	Sussex v Surrey

Sat 27 July

T20^F	Chelmsford	Essex v Glos
T20	Nottingham	Notts v Leics

Sun 28 July

T20	Derby	Derbyshire v Lancashire
T20	Northampton	Northants v Yorkshire
T20	Taunton	Somerset v Sussex
T20	Worcester	Worcs v Durham

Tue 30 July

T20^F	The Oval	Surrey v Kent

Wed 31 July

T20^F	Chester-le-St	Durham v Leics
T20	Worcester	Worcs v Derbyshire

Thu 1 – Mon 5 August

TM1	Birmingham	ENGLAND v AUSTRALIA

Thu 1 August

T20^F	Chelmsford	Essex v Hampshire
T20^F	Cardiff	Glamorgan v Glos
T20^F	Lord's	Middlesex v Kent

Fri 2 August

T20^F	Chester-le-St	Durham v Lancashire
T20^F	Bristol	Glos v Essex
T20^F	Southampton	Hampshire v Glamorgan
T20^F	Northampton	Northants v Derbyshire
T20^F	Nottingham	Notts v Warwicks
T20^F	Taunton	Somerset v Surrey
T20^F	Hove	Sussex v Kent
T20^F	Leeds	Yorkshire v Worcs

Sat 3 August

T20^F	Manchester	Lancashire v Notts

Sun 4 August

T20	Bristol	Glos v Sussex
T20	Beckenham	Kent v Hampshire
T20	Richmond	Middlesex v Somerset
T20	Worcester	Worcs v Leics
T20	Leeds	Yorkshire v Warwicks

Tue 6 August

T20^F	Hove	Sussex v Glamorgan

Wed 7 – Fri 9 August

FCF	Worcester	Worcs v Australians

Wed 7 August

T20^F	Chelmsford	Essex v Somerset
T20^F	Bristol	Glos v Kent
T20^F	Leicester	Leics v Warwicks
T20^F	Northampton	Northants v Durham

Thu 8 August

T20^F	Lord's	Middlesex v Surrey

Fri 9 August

T20^F	Derby	Derbyshire v Durham
T20^F	Cardiff	Glamorgan v Essex
T20^F	Southampton	Hampshire v Somerset
T20^F	Manchester	Lancashire v Yorkshire
T20^F	Leicester	Leics v Northants
T20^F	The Oval	Surrey v Glos
T20^F	Hove	Sussex v Middlesex
T20^F	Birmingham	Warwicks v Notts

Sat 10 August

T20^F	Taunton	Somerset v Kent

Sun 11 August

T20	Chester-le-St	Durham v Notts
T20	Cardiff	Glamorgan v Surrey
T20	Radlett	Middlesex v Glos
T20	Birmingham	Warwicks v Lancashire
T20	Worcester	Worcs v Northants
T20	Leeds	Yorkshire v Derbyshire

Tue 13 August

| $T20^F$ | Derby | Derbyshire v Worcs |
| $T20^F$ | Bristol | Glos v Hampshire |

Wed 14 – Sun 18 August

| TM2 | Lord's | ENGLAND v AUSTRALIA |

Wed 14 August

$T20^F$	Chelmsford	Essex v Middlesex
$T20^F$	Canterbury	Kent v Glamorgan
$T20^F$	Northampton	Northants v Lancashire

Thu 15 August

$T20^F$	Derby	Derbyshire v Leics
$T20^F$	Chester-le-St	Durham v Worcs
$T20^F$	The Oval	Surrey v Sussex

Fri 16 August

$T20^F$	Chelmsford	Essex v Glamorgan
$T20^F$	Southampton	Hampshire v Surrey
$T20^F$	Canterbury	Kent v Sussex
$T20^F$	Manchester	Lancashire v Warwicks
$T20^F$	Northampton	Northants v Leics
$T20^F$	Nottingham	Notts v Derbyshire
$T20^F$	Taunton	Somerset v Glos
$T20^F$	Leeds	Yorkshire v Durham

Sun 18 – Wed 21 August

CC1	Canterbury	Kent v Essex
CC1	The Oval	Surrey v Hampshire
CC1	Birmingham	Warwicks v Somerset
CC1	Scarborough	Yorkshire v Notts
CC2	Derby	Derbyshire v Glos
CC2	Chester-le-St	Durham v Leics
CC2	Colwyn Bay	Glamorgan v Lancashire
CC2	Northampton	Northants v Worcs
CC2	Hove	Sussex v Middlesex

Thu 22 – Mon 26 August

| TM3 | Leeds | ENGLAND v AUSTRALIA |

Thu 22 August

| $T20^F$ | Lord's | Middlesex v Hampshire |
| $T20^F$ | Hove | Sussex v Essex |

Fri 23 August

$T20^F$	Derby	Derbyshire v Northants
$T20^F$	Chester-le-St	Durham v Yorkshire
$T20^F$	Bristol	Glos v Somerset
$T20^F$	Canterbury	Kent v Surrey
$T20^F$	Leicester	Leics v Notts

Sat 24 August

| T20 | Uxbridge | Middlesex v Sussex |
| $T20^F$ | Taunton | Somerset v Glamorgan |

Sun 25 August

T20	Southampton	Hampshire v Essex
T20	Leicester	Leics v Derbyshire
T20	Nottingham	Notts v Yorkshire
T20	Birmingham	Warwicks v Northants
T20	Worcester	Worcs v Lancashire

Mon 26 August

| T20 | Cardiff | Glamorgan v Sussex |
| T20 | Manchester | Lancashire v Derbyshire |

Tue 27 August

| $T20^F$ | Chester-le-St | Durham v Warwicks |
| $T20^F$ | The Oval | Surrey v Somerset |

Wed 28 August

| T20 | Worcester | Worcs v Notts |

Thu 29 – Sat 31 August

| FCF | Derby | Derbyshire v Australians |

Thu 29 August

$T20^F$	Southampton	Hampshire v Middlesex
$T20^F$	Canterbury	Kent v Glos
$T20^F$	The Oval	Surrey v Essex
$T20^F$	Leeds	Yorkshire v Northants

Fri 30 August

$T20^F$	Chelmsford	Essex v Kent
$T20^F$	Cardiff	Glamorgan v Hampshire
$T20^F$	Manchester	Lancashire v Leics
$T20^F$	Northampton	Northants v Worcs
$T20^F$	Nottingham	Notts v Durham
$T20^F$	Taunton	Somerset v Middlesex
$T20^F$	Hove	Sussex v Glos
$T20^F$	Birmingham	Warwicks v Yorkshire

Wed 4 – Sun 8 September

| TM4 | Manchester | ENGLAND v AUSTRALIA |

Wed 4 September

| $T20^F$ | tbc | Quarter-final 1 |

Thu 5 September

| $T20^F$ | tbc | Quarter-final 2 |

Fri 6 September

| $T20^F$ | tbc | Quarter-final 3 |

Sat 7 September

| $T20^F$ | tbc | Quarter-final 4 |

Tue 10 – Fri 13 September

| CC1 | Chelmsford | Essex v Warwicks |
| CC1 | Southampton | Hampshire v Surrey |

CC1	Nottingham	Notts v Kent
CC1	Taunton	Somerset v Yorkshire
CC2	Bristol	Glos v Sussex
CC2	Manchester	Lancashire v Derbyshire
CC2	Leicester	Leics v Northants
CC2	Lord's	Middlesex v Durham
CC2	Worcester	Worcs v Glamorgan

Thu 12 – Mon 16 September

| TM5 | The Oval | ENGLAND v AUSTRALIA |

Mon 16 – Thu 19 September

CC1	Chelmsford	Essex v Surrey
CC1	Southampton	Hampshire v Somerset
CC1	Nottingham	Notts v Warwicks
CC1	Leeds	Yorkshire v Kent
CC2	Derby	Derbyshire v Sussex

CC2	Cardiff	Glamorgan v Leics
CC2	Manchester	Lancashire v Middlesex
CC2	Northampton	Northants v Durham
CC2	Worcester	Worcs v Glos

Sat 21 September

| T20F | Birmingham | Semi-finals and FINAL |

Mon 23 – Thu 26 September

CC1	Canterbury	Kent v Hampshire
CC1	Taunton	Somerset v Essex
CC1	The Oval	Surrey v Notts
CC1	Birmingham	Warwicks v Yorkshire
CC2	Chester-le-St	Durham v Glamorgan
CC2	Bristol	Glos v Northants
CC2	Leicester	Leics v Lancashire
CC2	Lord's	Middlesex v Derbyshire
CC2	Hove	Sussex v Worcs

TEST MATCH CHAMPIONSHIP SCHEDULE

Months indicate the start of a series. Number of Tests in brackets. All series are subject to confirmation.

2019	Jul	**England hosts Ireland (1)**
	Jul	West Indies hosts India (2)
	Jul	Sri Lanka hosts New Zealand (2)
	Aug	**England hosts Australia (5)**
	Aug	Zimbabwe hosts Afghanistan (1)
	Oct	India hosts South Africa (3)
	Oct	Pakistan hosts Sri Lanka (2)
	Oct	Bangladesh hosts Afghanistan (1)
	Oct	Zimbabwe hosts West Indies (1)
	Nov	**New Zealand hosts England (2)**
	Nov	Australia hosts Pakistan (2)
	Nov	India hosts Bangladesh (2)
	Nov	Afghanistan hosts West Indies (1)
	Dec	Australia hosts New Zealand (3)
	Dec	**South Africa hosts England (4)**

2020	Jan	Zimbabwe hosts Sri Lanka (2)
	Jan	Pakistan hosts Bangladesh (2)
	Feb	New Zealand hosts India (2)
	Feb	Sri Lanka hosts Ireland (1)
	Feb	Bangladesh hosts Australia (2)
	Mar	Afghanistan hosts Ireland (1)
	Mar	**Sri Lanka hosts England (2)**
	Apr	Zimbabwe hosts Ireland (1)
	May	Ireland hosts Bangladesh (1)
	May	**England hosts West Indies (3)**
	July	**England hosts Pakistan (3)**
	July	Sri Lanka hosts Bangladesh (3)
	July	West Indies hosts South Africa (2)
	Aug	Bangladesh hosts New Zealand (2)
	Oct-Nov	**ICC World T20**

Copyright © 2019 Headline Publishing Group

The right of Ian Marshall to be identified as the Author of
the Work has been asserted by him in accordance with the
Copyright, Designs and Patents Act 1988.

First published in 2019

by HEADLINE PUBLISHING GROUP

Front cover photograph
Jos Buttler (Lancashire and England)
© Alex Davidson/REX/Shutterstock

Back cover photograph
Sam Curran (Surrey and England)
© Alan Martin/Action Plus via Getty Images

1

Apart from any use permitted under UK copyright law, this publication
may only be reproduced, stored, or transmitted, in any form, or by any
means, with prior permission in writing of the publishers or, in the case of
reprographic production, in accordance with the terms
of licences issued by the Copyright Licensing Agency.

Every effort has been made to fulfil requirements with regard to
reproducing copyright material. The author and publisher will
be glad to rectify any omissions at the earliest opportunity.

Cataloguing in Publication Data is available from the British Library

ISBN: 978 1 4722 4981 4

Typeset in Times by
Letterpart Limited, Caterham on the Hill, Surrey

Printed and bound in Great Britain by
Clays Ltd Elcograf S.p.A.

Headline's policy is to use papers that are natural, renewable and
recyclable products and made from wood grown in sustainable forests.
The logging and manufacturing processes are expected to conform
to the environmental regulations of the country of origin.

HEADLINE PUBLISHING GROUP

An Hachette UK Company
Carmelite House
50 Victoria Embankment
London EC4Y 0DZ

www.headline.co.uk
www.hachette.co.uk